Lecture Notes in Business Information Processing 267

Series Editors

More information about this series at http://www.springer.com/series/7911

Jennifer Horkoff · Manfred A. Jeusfeld
Anne Persson (Eds.)

The Practice of Enterprise Modeling

9th IFIP WG 8.1. Working Conference, PoEM 2016
Skövde, Sweden, November 8–10, 2016
Proceedings

Springer

Editors
Jennifer Horkoff
City University London
London
UK

Anne Persson
University of Skövde
Skövde
Sweden

Manfred A. Jeusfeld
University of Skövde
Skövde
Sweden

ISSN 1865-1348 ISSN 1865-1356 (electronic)
Lecture Notes in Business Information Processing
ISBN 978-3-319-48392-4 ISBN 978-3-319-48393-1 (eBook)
DOI 10.1007/978-3-319-48393-1

Library of Congress Control Number: 2016955498

Printed on acid-free paper

This Springer imprint is published by Springer Nature
The registered company is Springer International Publishing AG
The registered company address is: Gewerbestrasse 11, 6330 Cham, Switzerland

Preface

The 9th IFIP Working Conference on the Practice of Enterprise Modeling (PoEM 2016), was held during November 8–10 in Skövde, Sweden, hosted by the University of Skövde.

Enterprise modeling (EM) includes a set of activities by which knowledge about several perspectives of an organization is elicited, documented, analyzed, and communicated, typically through a structured, iterative, stakeholder-centric, and model-based approach. This way, the knowledge of the enterprise is made explicit and further actions can be performed, such as making strategic decisions, undertaking organizational reengineering, standardizing ways of working, developing or acquiring information and communication technology. As a consequence, EM has an impact on large economic markets such as consulting and information system development, making it a relevant field of research and industrial practice.

The PoEM conferences, starting in 2008, have contributed to establishing a dedicated forum where the use of EM in practice is addressed by bringing together researchers, users, and practitioners. The main focus of the PoEM conferences is EM methods, approaches, and tools as well as how they are used in practice. More specifically the goals of the conference are to contribute to a better understanding of the practice of EM, to contribute to improved EM practice, as well as to share knowledge among researchers and practitioners.

PoEM is supported by the IFIP WG8.1 and is a very interesting and dynamic event where new research challenges emerge from success and failure stories related to EM practices, and practitioners take the opportunity to learn about new EM methods and tools.

This year PoEM received 54 paper submissions covering a wide variety of EM topics. Each paper was evaluated by at least three members of our expert Program Committee members, providing constructive feedback. We were able to accept 18 full papers and nine short papers, all published in this volume. The acceptance rate for full papers was thus below 35%.

The conference audience enjoyed an excellent keynote by Prof. Robert Winter, from the Institute of Information Management, University of St. Gallen, Switzerland. Prof. Winter's talk was entitled "Establishing 'Architectural Thinking' in Organizations".

This year, the PoEM conference included two associated events, occurring on the first day. A Doctoral Consortium was organized to highlight upcoming EM doctoral research, providing students with valuable feedback. For the first time, PoEM hosted the OMI (Open Models Initiative) Symposium, a gathering to discuss and promote the result of the Erasmus+ project OMI that focusses on developing a shared repository of tools and meta-models for EM.

We hope that this PoEM conference contributed to further strengthening and integrating the field of EM. PoEM is a working conference. Hence, the focus lies on practical concepts, tools, and methods, as well as on the evaluation of the usefulness of

EM. However, we appreciate the community trend of identifying cross-links to related domains, such as requirements modeling.

To conclude, we would like to express our gratitude to a number of people who spent their time and energy in organizing and successfully running PoEM 2016. We would like to thank the Program Committee members and additional reviewers for their help in selecting the papers for the scientific program of the conference, the authors of the papers for their confidence in PoEM, and the presenters and session chairs for lively presentations and discussions. We are grateful to the PoEM Steering Committee chairs for their continuous assistance and the chairs of the doctoral consortium for creating an exciting event. Finally, we extend our gratitude to the local organizing team at the University of Skövde for their hospitality and for organizing this conference. We would also like to thank our colleagues in the local IT department and administration of the University of Skövde for their strong support and enthusiasm.

September 2016

Jennifer Horkoff
Manfred A. Jeusfeld
Anne Persson

Organization

Steering Committee

Anne Persson	University of Skövde, Sweden
Janis Stirna	Stockholm University, Sweden
Kurt Sandkuhl	University of Rostock, Germany

General Chair

Anne Persson	University of Skövde, Sweden

Program Chairs

Manfred A. Jeusfeld	University of Skövde, Sweden
Jennifer Horkoff	City University London, UK

Doctoral Consortium Chairs

Eva Söderström	University of Skövde, Sweden
Kurt Sandkuhl	University of Rostock, Germany

Local Organizing Committee

Joeri van Laere	University of Skövde, Sweden
Jesper Holgersson	University of Skövde, Sweden
Kristens Gudfinnsson	University of Skövde, Sweden

Program Committee

Raian Ali	Bournemouth University, UK
Marko Bajec	University of Ljubljana, Slovenia
Judith Barrios Albornoz	University of Los Andes, Colombia
Giuseppe Berio	Université de Bretagne Sud and IRISA UMR, France
Robert Andrei Buchmann	Babeş-Bolyai University of Cluj Napoca, Romania
Rimantas Butleris	Kaunas University of Technology, Lithuania
Albertas Caplinskas	Institute of Mathematics and Informatics, Lithuania
Tony Clark	Middlesex University, UK
Wolfgang Deiters	Fraunhofer ISST, Germany
Dulce Domingos	Universidade de Lisboa, Portugal
Ulrich Frank	Universität of Duisburg Essen, Germany
Giovanni Giachetti	Universidad Andres Bello, Chile

Jaap Gordijn	Vrije Universiteit Amsterdam, The Netherlands
Jānis Grabis	Riga Technical University, Latvia
Stijn Hoppenbrouwers	HAN University of Applied Sciences, The Netherlands
Paul Johannesson	Royal Institute of Technology, Sweden
Håvard Jørgensen	Commitment AS, Norway
Monika Kaczmarek	University of Duisburg Essen, Germany
Dimitris Karagiannis	University of Vienna, Austria
Lutz Kirchner	Scape Consulting GmbH, Germany
Marite Kirikova	Riga Technical University, Latvia
John Krogstie	IDI, NTNU, Norway
Robert Lagerström	Royal Institute of Technology, Sweden
Birger Lantow	University of Rostock, Germany
Ulrike Lechner	Universität der Bundeswehr München, Germany
Pericles Loucopoulos	The University of Manchester, UK
Florian Matthes	Technische Universität München, Germany
Raimundas Matulevičius	University of Tartu, Estonia
Graham McLeod	Inspired.org, South Africa
Christer Nellborn	Nellborn Management Consulting AB, Sweden
Selmin Nurcan	Université Paris 1 Panthéon-Sorbonne, France
Andreas L Opdahl	University of Bergen, Norway
Oscar Pastor	Universitat Politecnica de Valencia, Spain
Anne Persson	University of Skövde, Sweden
Michaël Petit	University of Namur, Belgium
Ilias Petrounias	University of Manchester, UK
Henderik Proper	Public Research Centre Henri Tudor, Luxembourg
Jolita Ralyté	University of Geneva, Switzerland
Colette Rolland	Université Paris 1 Panthéon-Sorbonne, France
Kurt Sandkuhl	University of Rostock, Germany
Ulf Seigerroth	Jönköping University, Sweden
Khurram Shahzad	Royal Institute of Technology, Sweden
Nikolay Shilov	SPIIRAS, Russian Federation
Pnina Soffer	University of Haifa, Israel
Janis Stirna	Stockholm University, Sweden
Darijus Strasunskas	POSC Caesar Association, Norway
Eva Söderström	University of Skövde, Sweden
Victoria Torres	Universidad Politécnica de Valencia, Spain
Olegas Vasilecas	Vilnius Gediminas Technical University, Lithuania
Hans Weigand	Tilburg University, The Netherlands
Robert Winter	University of St. Gallen, Switzerland
Eric Yu	University of Toronto, Canada
Jelena Zdravkovic	Stockholm University, Sweden

Additional Reviewers

Aleatrati Khosroshahi, Pouya
Blaschke, Michael
Bock, Alexander
Borchardt, Ulrike
Bork, Dominik
de Kinderen, Sybren
Dännart, Sebastian
Heumüller, Erich
Holgersson, Jesper
Huth, Dominik
Kapocius, Kestutis
Korman, Matus
Marosin, Diana
Normantas, Kestutis
Pant, Vik
Razo-Zapata, Iván S.
Savickas, Titas
Schilling, Raphael
Tantouris, Nikolaos
Uludag, Ömer
Välja, Margus
Walch, Michael

Contents

Keynote

Short Papers

Keynote

Establishing 'Architectural Thinking' in Organizations

Robert Winter(✉)

Institute of Information Management, University of St. Gallen,
Unterer Graben 21, 9000 St. Gallen, Switzerland
Robert.Winter@unisg.ch

Abstract. After having harvested 'low hanging fruits' in early stages of Enterprise Architecture Management (EAM), it becomes increasingly difficult to keep up with large benefit realizations in later stages. The focus on the traditional EAM players (IT unit, architects, enterprise management) should be widened to 'that other 90 % of the enterprise' that are not directly related to the IT function. In order to create impact beyond IT, it appears necessary to complement the enforcement-centric view (i.e., enhancing EAM governance) by an influence-centric view (i.e., improving the EAM influence on local stakeholder decisions). Our research has shown that local stakeholders' acceptance of restricted design freedom depends on certain preconditions: (1) Actors need to be convinced that their social status will be raising if they comply with EAM measures – and vice versa. (2) Actors need to understand that they can be more efficient if they comply with EAM measures – and vice versa. (3) Actors need to perceive EAM as something that is strategically important for the organization. (4) Actors need to perceive EAM deployment as transparent, useful, and professional. In this talk, we will elaborate on the necessity, justificatory foundations, and supporting artifacts to create supportive conditions for 'Architectural Thinking', the influence-based complement of governance-based EAM.

Keywords: Enterprise architecture management · Architectural coordination · Architectural thinking

1 Extended Abstract

Over the past decades, we have witnessed an enormous growth of investments in information systems (IS) in organizations. On the one hand, increasing investments in IS had a significant impact on most organizations' performance. On the other hand, these investments resulted in a significant complexity of the corporate IS architecture (i.e., the organization's fundamental IS components, their inter-relationships, and the principles governing their design and evolution [1]), which mainly results from the allocation of project ownership and IS design decision authority to local (business) units. This practice of managing the IS architecture has brought about a large and ever-growing number of heterogeneous IS, which are costly to maintain, tightly interrelated, and which lack flexibility with regard to business changes and technical innovations. Over the years, many organizations have lost control of their IS

J. Horkoff et al. (Eds.): PoEM 2016, LNBIP 267, pp. 3–8, 2016.
DOI: 10.1007/978-3-319-48393-1_1

architecture complexity, i.e., were unable to steer the evolution of their IS architecture so that it maintains a sufficient flexibility in conforming to constantly changing business requirements and technical innovation.

To address this challenge, scholars and practitioners have broadly propagated the concept of enterprise architecture management (EAM) for systematically aligning locally governed IS investments with enterprise-wide objectives. In its traditional fashion, EAM establishes centralized, top-down driven, enterprise-wide governance mechanisms that aim at maintaining transparency, coherency, and ultimately flexibility of IS architecture. Such governance mechanisms include, but are not limited to developing, maintaining, and enforcing top-down, centralized architecture principles, architecture compliance checks, to-be architectures, and committees or procedures for architectural coordination, to eventually influence local IS development projects. The EAM discipline has matured over the last decades by (i) diversifying its scope from software architecture to application architecture and from process architecture to business architecture, (ii) widening its focus from single solutions to functional/business areas, to enterprise-wide, or even to cross-enterprise architecture management, (iii) expanding its sphere of influence from a single architectural layer (e.g., IT artifacts or business artifacts) to various interdependencies across the entire business-to-IT stack, and by (iv) representing not only as-is or to-be states of architectural entities, but also roadmaps or scenarios to cover the entire architecture life cycle. Following EAM's raise in maturity, it has largely gained momentum so that organizations established various 'architect' roles and functions.

Notwithstanding the abovementioned advances, the EAM discipline still struggles with some formational challenges. First, although many architects tried to position themselves as a linking-pin 'between' corporate management, business/project owners and IT, their backgrounds and competency profiles often kept them close to the corporate IT functions [2]. Second, exercising EAM as a centralized mechanism for coordinated IS development, which aligns local projects with enterprise-wide priorities, is the antagonist of un-coordinated IS development projects in pursuing local goals. From local business stakeholders' perspective (e.g., a particular market, product, function owner), the promoted enterprise-wide coordination by EAM are naturally regarded as a "restriction of design freedom" [3]. The latter hence threatens EAM's acceptance by those local actors that not only own business change problems, but also respective IS development projects.

EAM's traditional way of dealing with "resistance to coordination" is (i) to communicate its local efficiency contributions (e.g., reduced IT operations costs due to less heterogeneity and more re-use) and (ii) to increase its local effectiveness (e.g., by governance measures). For both strategies, however, empirical research demonstrates an S-shaped benefit curve [4]. After harvesting 'low hanging fruits' in early stages of EAM, it becomes increasingly difficult to keep up with large benefit realizations in later stages. At some point, an optimal productivity level of EAM will be reached after which additional EAM efforts cannot justified with the argument of realizable business value [4]. Simultaneously, IS architecture complexity can be expected to remain high or even increasing.

The above mentioned observation cannot be related to immaturity of EAM concepts or deployment, but rather to general acceptance problems of EAM by local stakeholders [5]. Convincing local stakeholders that overall benefits on the enterprise-wide level justify individual sacrifices remains a difficult undertaking. Illustrative examples of such challenge cannot only be found in enterprises (e.g., centralizing procurement processes), but are also common in public policy (e.g., imposing speed limits around schools, imposing smoking bans in public areas, transforming energy production and consumption).

In order to move to the next level of EAM productivity, it appears necessary to shift the focus from an enforcement-centric view (i.e., enhancing EAM governance) towards an influence-centric view (i.e., improving the EAM influence on local stakeholder decisions) [5]. This implies not to focus on the traditional EAM players (IT unit, architects, enterprise management) any more, but instead on "that other 90 % of the enterprise" that are not directly related to the IT function [6]. As these stakeholders (e.g., business market, product, function owners) cannot be controlled by EAM measures with a reasonable effort, EAM needs to focus not only on enforcement, but also (or even more) on influence. As a consequence, control as a central theme of EAM research is complemented by informing, legitimating, and socializing [7].

How can the behavior of independent actors be effectively influenced so that enterprise-wide objectives are sufficiently addressed even if they require individual sacrifices? The "New institutionalism" offers an explanation why and how regulations become institutionalized by actors, i.e., develop "a rule-like status in social thought and action" [8]. Relying on this theoretical lens, when a pressure is exerted with the aim of complying with some 'grand design', individuals' reactions to such pressure can be explained in a range of acquiescence, compromise, avoidance, defiance and manipulation reaction [9, 10]. Weiss et al. [11] employed this theoretical lens to study EAM and show that an individual actor's response towards EAM measures (i.e., pressures) depends on social legitimacy, efficiency, organizational grounding, and trust. Following Social legitimacy, actors gain social fitness inside the organization when they comply with architectural guidelines. Furthermore, actors become more efficient when following architectural guidelines. Organizational grounding that EAM is anchored within the organization's values in terms of strategy definition, top management support or the position in the organizational hierarchy. Finally, trust reflect actors' confidence on the fact that the EAM function does the right things in a right way [11].

Based on these insights, which explain under which conditions individual actors comply with restricted design freedom, appropriate preconditions can be derived to increase the acceptance of EAM:

1. Actors need to be convinced that their social status will be raising if they comply with EAM measures – and vice versa.
2. Actors need to understand that they can be more efficient if they comply with EAM measures – and vice versa.
3. Actors need to perceive EAM as something that is strategically important for the organization.
4. Actors need to perceive EAM deployment as transparent, useful, and professional.

Exemplary measures to create such preconditions can be:

1. Create transparent conditions to business people who of their peers is compliant and who is not. For instance, label applications in a way that users see whether they use a compliant or a non-compliant application (works like energy efficiency labels) – and provide evidence that the user perception of an actor's compliance is impacting his/her social status.
2. Demonstrate the positive impact of EAM measures – as well as the damage of ignored or compromised EAM measures. For instance, seriously calculate the avoidable lifetime ownership costs of a redundant application. For IS portfolios of a business unit, as another example, explain complexity costs and show how EAM measures reduce operations or project costs.
3. Position EAM leaders on high levels of the organizational hierarchy – and not as a specialist team in IT management. Discuss architectural issues in important/powerful corporate committees. Promote successful specialists or line/project managers to architect functions and successful architects back into line/project management.
4. Ensure that architects and architectural artifacts are not only visible in the business, but also are able to credibly position themselves as business- and synergy-oriented. For instance, the use of coherency-oriented, high complexity models should be avoided. Instead, when interacting with local business stakeholders the focus of architects should be on lightweight artifacts and local concerns ("boundary objects" [12, 13]).

The presented measures promise to influence local decision-makers on the business side towards increasing their acceptance of EAM-related design restrictions. This way of thinking and acting by local and individual actors (i.e., not only restricted to architects and IT people) in considering enterprise-wide, long-term concerns as well as fundamental IS design and evolution principles in day-to-day decision making practices (e.g., change requests), has been termed "Architectural Thinking" (AT) by Ross and Quaadgras [4]. AT promises to move EAM to the next productivity level, as additional acceptance (and thus EAM impact) can be achieved without heavily increased (and expensive) EAM governance efforts. However, AT can neither be designed, deployed, nor implemented like traditional EAM governance. As a way of thinking, AT can only be propagated in an organization by creating supportive conditions [5].

While we have yet not witnessed large-scale AT initiatives in practice, many organizations have become aware of the approach and have implemented selected measures in order to explore potentials of EAM evolution (e.g., [14]). A frequently implemented measure is to move the architecture function away from IT and more towards a business unit, and to create architecture spin-offs in business units or project offices of large projects ("Design Authority"). We also note an increasing number of initiatives to broadly demonstrate the value contribution of EAM and/or to explain architectural coordination goals to the business. Likewise, architecture functions have started to develop and track strategy- or business-oriented performance indicators (e.g., resistance to change, solution sustainability, or architectural fit [15]).

In order to design effective and efficient artifacts that raise EAM impact to the next level, further insights into the institutionalization mechanisms are necessary. From a static perspective, explanatory research may identify additional or modified justificatory foundations. Differentiated studies are also needed to better understand contingencies, such as organizational subcultures, industry characteristics (e.g., speed), or management styles, among others.

From a dynamic perspective, one avenue is to analyze the overall performance of EAM (both on the project and the enterprise-wide level) as a result of de-central knowledge acquisition and cooperative learning [16]. Being very much in line with our call for shifting EAM focus on influence rather than enforcement, the autonomous character of knowledge acquisition as well as learning would imply major EAM capability and instrument adaptations.

A second avenue for dynamic analysis is based on archetype theory [17] which understands organizations as configurations of (i) structural arrangements and (ii) interpretative schemes. An interpretative scheme describes an organization's conception on what it should be doing, how it should be doing, and how it should be judged. This conception is shaped by the prevailing set of ideas, beliefs, and values. The structural arrangement implements and reinforces the ideas, beliefs, and values through establishing organizational structures and processes that reflect the respective beliefs and values [18]. In an ideal case, organizations will evolve towards a situation of organizational coherence, where the structural arrangement and the interpretative scheme represent an "appropriate design for adequate performance" [18] Schilling et al. [19] explore this lens from an IS research perspective. Such an analysis could help to better understand how "measures aimed at creating preconditions for EAM acceptance" interact with organizational ideas, beliefs and values so that, ultimately, local actors can be effectively influenced to better comply with enterprise-wide goals.

While the static and the dynamic perspectives help to better understand AT and design appropriate interventions, continuing empirical analyses will be needed on how organizations learn to move from traditional EAM towards AT and how these two approaches complement each other.

Acknowledgement. The author wishes to thank Stephan Aier, Maximilian Brosius and Kazem Haki for their feedback to earlier version of this text.

References

1. IEEE Recommended Practice for Architectural Description of Software Intensive Systems (IEEE Std. 1471-2000), New York, NY (2000)
2. Aier, S., Riege, C., Winter, R.: Unternehmensarchitektur – Literaturüberblick und Stand der Praxis. Wirtschaftsinformatik **50**(4), 292–304 (2008)
3. Dietz, J.L.G.: Architecture. Building Strategy into Design. Academic Service, The Hague (2008)
4. Ross, J.W., Quaadgras, A.: Enterprise Architecture Is Not Just for Architects. Center for Information Systems Research Sloan School of Management Massachusetts Institute of Technology, Cambridge (2012)

5. Winter, R.: Architectural thinking. Bus. Inf. Syst. Eng. **6**(6), 361–364 (2014)
6. Gardner, D., Fehskens, L., Naidu, M., Rouse, W.B., Ross, J.W.: Point-counterpoint: enterprise architecture and enterprise transformation as related but distinct concepts. J. Enterp. Transform. **2**(4), 283–294 (2012)
7. Haki, M.K., Aier, S., Winter, R.: A stakeholder perspective to study enterprise-wide IS initiatives. In: Proceedings of European Conference on Information Systems (ECIS), Istanbul, Turkey (2016)
8. Meyer, J.W., Rowan, B.: Institutionalized organizations: formal structure as myth and ceremony. Am. J. Soc. **83**(2), 340–363 (1977)
9. Oliver, C.: Strategic responses to institutional processes. Acad. Manag. Rev. **16**(1), 145–179 (1991)
10. Pache, A.-C., Santos, F.: Embedded in hybrid contexts: how individuals in organizations respond to competing institutional logics. In: Lounsbury, M., Boxenbaum, E. (eds.) Research in the Sociology of Organizations, pp. 3–35. Emerald Group Publishing Limited, Bingley (2013)
11. Weiss, S., Aier, S., Winter, R.: Institutionalization and the effectiveness of enterprise architecture management. In: Proceedings of 2013 International Conference on Information Systems (ICIS 2013), Milano, Italy. Association for Information Systems (2013)
12. Abraham, R., Aier, S., Winter, R.: Crossing the line: overcoming knowledge boundaries in enterprise transformation. Bus. Inf. Syst. Eng. **57**(1), 3–13 (2015)
13. Star, S.L., Griesemer, J.R.: Institutional ecology, 'translations' and boundary objects: amateurs and professionals in Berkeley's Museum of Vertebrate Zoology, 1907–39. Soc. Stud. Sci. **19**(3), 387–420 (1989)
14. Aier, S., Labusch, N., Pähler, P.: Implementing architectural thinking. In: Persson, A., Stirna, J. (eds.) CAiSE 2015 Workshops. LNBIP, vol. 215, pp. 389–400. Springer, Heidelberg (2015)
15. Stutz, M.: Kennzahlen für Unternehmensarchitekturen - Entwicklung einer Methode zum Aufbau eines Kennzahlensystems für die wertorientierte Steuerung der Veränderung von Unternehmensarchitekturen, Dissertation. University of St, Gallen (2009)
16. Brosius, M., Haki, K., Aier, S., Winter, R.: A Learning Perspective on Enterprise Architecture Management (2016, Forthcoming)
17. Miller, D., Friesen, P.H.: Organizations: A Quantum View. Prentice-Hall, Englewood Cliffs (1984)
18. Greenwood, R., Hinings, C.R.: Organizational design types, tracks and the dynamics of strategic change. Organ. Stud. **9**(3), 293–316 (1988)
19. Schilling, R.D., Haki, M.K., Aier, S.: Introducing archetype theory to information systems research: a literature review and call for future research. Unpublished Working Paper, Institute of Information Management, University of St. Gallen (2016)

Regular Papers

Causes and Consequences of Application Portfolio Complexity – An Exploratory Study

Pouya Aleatrati Khosroshahi[1(✉)], Jannis Beese[2], Florian Matthes[1], and Robert Winter[2]

[1] Chair for Informatics 19 (sebis), Technical University of Munich, Boltzmannstr. 3, 85748 Garching b. Munich, Germany
{p.aleatrati,matthes}@tum.de
[2] Institute for Information Management, University of St. Gallen, Unterer Graben 21, 9000 St. Gallen, Switzerland
{jannis.beese,robert.winter}@unisg.ch

Abstract. Application Portfolio (AP) complexity is an increasingly important and strongly discussed issue by both researchers and practitioners. Application portfolios in large organizations have become more and more difficult to understand, resulting in costly efforts to maintain and operate them. Although this is an urgent topic in large organizations, researchers and industry experts do not yet have a common understanding of this phenomenon and lack appropriate methods to measure and manage the respective complexity. We conduct an exploratory case study with the central enterprise architecture management (EAM) governance team and ten application owners of a large European automotive company to identify and link root causes and consequences of AP complexity. Furthermore, we evaluate possible solutions to decrease or manage this complexity from an application owners perspective. The results are interpreted from a socio-technical systems perspective.

Keywords: Application portfolio complexity · Complexity management · Socio-technical theory

1 Introduction

Technological advances, such as new possibilities for customer interactions enabled by digital platforms, require various industry sectors to fundamentally adapt their business models [1,2]. Furthermore, increasing regulatory pressure also necessitates changes in the enterprise architecture (EA) domain due to a lack of transparency about enterprise information and poor data quality [3,4]. Consequently, todays organizations need to undergo fundamental changes in their EA in general, and in their Application Portfolio (AP) in particular, and face multifarious obstacles in this transformation process [5,6]: poor AP documentations leads to time-consuming and error-prone initiatives. As a result, enterprises are unable to efficiently adapt to changes since they are missing essential information about their AP.

J. Horkoff et al. (Eds.): PoEM 2016, LNBIP 267, pp. 11–25, 2016.
DOI: 10.1007/978-3-319-48393-1_2

Lacking a complete and consistent high-level view, organizations tend to introduce further services and applications to fulfill business needs, which leads to a perceived growth of complexity in the enterprise in the EA domain [7] and a growth of investments in the operation of information systems [8]. This manifests in a large number of heterogeneous information systems, which are costly to maintain and lack flexibility with regard to business changes [9].

Although the challenge of increasing AP complexity was already highlighted in research [10, 11] and by industry experts [12, 13], there is still a lack of research that explicitly addresses how to tackle this issue [14]. This is compounded by the fact that there exist multiple interpretations of the term AP complexity that depend on the specific context in which it is used [11, 15–17]. Based on our conducted literature review and state of the art research (see Sect. 2), we define AP complexity as the compilation of organizational and technical characteristics in an enterprise that lead to avoidable costs and decreased agility of the AP. In order to identify root causes and possible solutions of this phenomenon, we conduct an explorative qualitative case study, as proposed by Yin [18], at a large European automotive company. Our analysis relies on data gathered from ten expert interviews, meetings with the central enterprise architecture management (EAM) team, and data from previously conducted complexity assessments. We employ socio-technical theory, in particular the *Punctuated Socio-Technical Information Systems Change* (PSIC) model [19], for organizing, grouping, and interpreting this data and corresponding results.

First, to gain a better understanding of the phenomenon at hand, we identify *root causes* of AP complexity as perceived by application owners in todays organizations. These root causes are then linked to specific *consequences* that negatively impact the organization. Finally, we evaluate technical and organizational *solutions* for managing AP complexity based on the identified root causes and their consequences. We address the following research questions (RQ):

- *RQ1: What root causes for AP complexity do application owners perceive in their daily activities?*
- *RQ2: What are the consequences of these root causes?*
- *RQ3: What kind of technical or organizational actions can help to control identified AP complexity?*

The rest of this paper is organized as follows: in Sect. 2 related literature on AP complexity is reviewed and socio-technical systems theory is introduced as a lens for organizing and interpreting our findings. We then elaborate our methodology and data collection process in Sect. 3. In Sect. 4 we present our results, comprising root causes of AP complexity (*capacity*, *code quality*, *subjective complexity*, *technical support*, *design of data flows*, *quality of interfaces*, *IT authority of business*, *change management plan*, and *role allocation*), consequences of AP complexity (*lack of time/quality*, *data quality issues*, *performance issues*, *chain reaction to other functions*, *avoidable efforts*), and solutions to control AP complexity (*increased capacities*, *technical support*, *pool of experts*, *stronger IT governance*, *code reviews*, *automated checks*, *stronger data management*, *improved knowledge management*, and *technical renewals*). The interpretation, applicability and consequences of these findings are then discussed in Sect. 5. The paper concludes with a discussion of implications and limitations of this research.

2 State of the Art

There exist diverse and multi-faceted understandings of AP complexity in extant literature, which has been investigated from a number of different perspectives by previous researchers [10,11,14,20–25]. Thus, we review conceptualizations of AP complexity and how these are used in practice, noting that research is still at an early stage regarding the identification of complexity drivers of APs and the development of technical and organizational actions to control this phenomenon.

At the beginning of the 2000s the scope of complexity exploration in the information systems domain was enlarged from single applications to entire APs. The definition of the term AP complexity is, however, still fragmented: Following Schneider et al. [11], the view of AP complexity in the EA domain comprises different categories – such as subjective versus objective complexity or perceived versus objective complexity – each considering this phenomenon from a different perspective. Similarly, Beetz et al. [14] point out the variety of the term complexity, showing that various initiatives have taken place in this context and concluding with a research gap on this topic. Thus, when analyzing the increasing complexity of APs in today's organizations "a number of statements in the academic and consulting literature that include several implicit propositions on causes as well as on impacts" [23] need to be considered, such as the age of applications or a decreasing agility of APs [26].

Notwithstanding the difficulties in conceptualizing and operationalizing AP complexity, several studies find dependencies between drivers of AP complexity, e.g., the age of applications, interdependencies, and redundancies, and related effects such as maintenance and operating costs [23]. An increasing number of components in an AP and an increase in their dependencies to each other negatively affect the flexibility with regard to architectural changes [20]. Proposed measures for AP complexity both in literature (e.g. [21,22,25]) and in practice [24] thus usually include the number of used components, their heterogeneity, and interdependencies between them, such as interfaces or information flows. Research in this area generally aims to identify and uncover hidden structures in APs to guide enterprise transformation [10]. For example, heterogeneity-based metrics can be employed to measure the complexity of employed applications within an portfolio, and the Design Science Matrix proposed by Lagerström et al. [21,22] was found useful for assessing the criticality of IS change projects [24].

3 Research Methodology

Previous studies on AP complexity [3,23] follow a quantitative approach to identify dependencies between business application characteristics (e.g., interfaces,

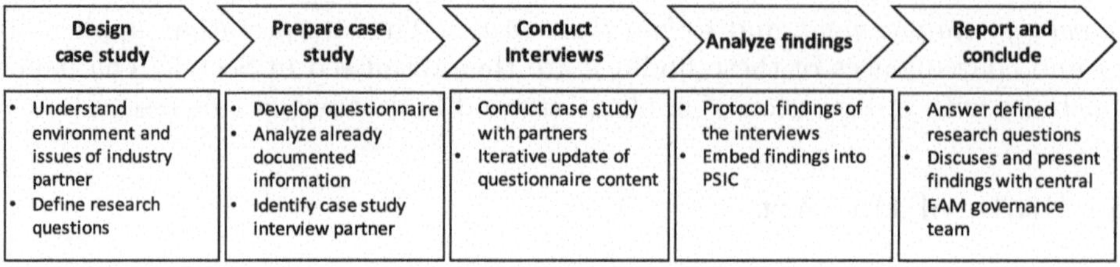

Fig. 1. Case study process

type of application) and dependent variables (e.g., the amount of created incident tickets and operation costs of applications). While the conducted analysis allows to study statistical dependencies between the considered constructs, it turns out that AP complexity is also affected by organizational choices in a more complicated way: interdependencies and interactions may lead to emergent properties that are not easily captured by statistics [27]. Thus the extant quantitative results would benefit from a complementary qualitative investigation. To better understand the complicated ways in which AP complexity manifests and is affected by organizational choices, we employ an exploratory case study research, following the recommendations of Yin [18]. The conducted research approach is divided into five stages and is illustrated in Fig. 1.

3.1 Case Study Approach

Our discussion of related literature (see Sect. 2) shows that current research on AP complexity includes both qualitative and quantitative approaches. After reviewing the mentioned sources, we subsequently defined the research questions and decided on a research partner to conduct a case study in order to investigate the phenomenon of interest.

Case Company Description: The investigated organization is a large automotive company with over 100.000 employees. The headquarter of the company is located in Europe, whereas the plants are distributed in all continents and the dealers operate on an international level. Being one of the largest companies in its industry and currently investing significantly in AP complexity management initiatives, this company provides deep insights into the phenomenon of AP complexity. The first author has been involved with the ongoing efforts of the central EAM governance team since April 2015, allowing us to acquire rich data over a sustained period of time from internal complexity assessments, participation in meetings, and access to relevant interview partners. The IT section of the automotive company is organized in twelve main departments and employs over 3.500 internal employees. The EAM governance team acts as an own department. All information about the deployed applications in the AP is documented in a central EA repository. Previous initiatives of the central EAM governance team on AP complexity revealed organizational and technical issues in the IT section, leading to decreased agility in projects and high operational costs to run the AP. It also turned out that the IT section is characterized by a silo mentality between the main departments, leading to missing transparency about deployed applications.

Design Case Study: We designed the content and structure of the case study in cooperation of the EAM governance team, aiming to identify technical and organizational actions (RQ3) to tackle AP complexity through group discussions with affected stakeholders. Consequently, we decided to interview two types of stakeholders: first, application owners, who are confronted with the consequences of AP complexity in their daily business and projects, and second, the EAM governance team, who has an aggregated view on this topic trough the complete organization. We discussed and finalized our proposed RQs with the EAM governance team, based on the findings of our literature review and experiences of the central EAM governance team.

Prepare Case Study: Based on our defined RQs and the findings of our literature review, we developed a questionnaire in cooperation with the EAM governance team. In developing the questionnaire we aimed to define the questions in a way that elicits concrete root causes of AP complexity as perceived by the application owners, and that allows to identify specific consequences and solutions for AP complexity, rather than strategic advice and general issues. The questionnaire is divided into six parts (general information, technical infrastructure and interfaces, problem/incident management, release management, software quality). The first part ensures the correctness of general information that was gathered before the interview (e.g., the name of the application, the application ID, and data about productive users). The following parts aim to identify current issues of the application on the respective topic. The application owners are asked to name root causes for each issue, its consequences and possible solutions to solve it.

In order to select a subset of applications from the company's AP for a detailed investigation, we started with all applications that were used productively by the company as a basis for further selection, excluding pure infrastructure components. From this set, comprising more than 7.000 applications, only those with significant costs for maintenance and errors were selected. Next, we employed data from internal complexity assessments, including information about application interfaces, monthly changes, incidents, and releases as well as sourcing and vendor information and information about the technical architecture. We include only applications for which this complexity index exceeds a predefined threshold, indicating that these applications are somehow more complex. Finally, we limit our analysis to lead applications, i.e., applications, which the company considers to be fundamentally important for the operation of the enterprise. This set of 105 applications was then discussed with the EAM governance department, and 10 applications, deemed to be the most relevant, critical, and interesting, were selected as a final set for a detailed analysis together with the respective application owners.

Conduct Interviews: We then conducted a series of ten semi-structured interviews with the application owners during November and December 2015. These interviews covered the areas identified in our research questions, namely, (RQ1) perceived root causes of AP complexity, (RQ2) consequences of these root causes, and (RQ3) technical or organizational actions employed to deal with AP complexity. All interviews were conducted face-to-face and followed a semi-structured approach in order to discuss a wide range of aspects [28].

Analyze Findings: We then employed the PSIC model of Lyytinen et al. [19] to group root causes of EA complexity and link these with consequences and applicable actions. The allocation of the findings to the PSIC model were conducted by our research team. To ensure the correctness of the findings, we presented and discuss our allocation with the EAM governance team (see step five *Report and conclude*).

Report and Conclude: The results of the expert interviews and the allocation of the PSIC model were presented to and discussed with the company's EA governance department and the head of application portfolio management. It was considered a useful tool for dealing with problems arising as a consequence of AP complexity. Aside from the company-internal evaluation, the results were also presented by one of the authors and discussed at a two-day focus group on EA, involving senior enterprise architects and IT managers from five large European organizations in February 2016 [29].

3.2 Socio-Technical Systems Theory

This research relies on the PSIC model of Lyytinen et al. [19] for organizing and interpreting results, since an analysis of AP complexity requires a comprehensive framework that also captures the dynamics and interactions between a multitude of different organizational elements [27,30]. Socio-technical systems theory has been a useful perspective for ordering these diverse elements and interactions, thus allowing researchers to make sense of and reason about complex systems, such as enterprise architectures [31]. The PSIC model provides an established framework that also allows to reason about temporal causalities, such as the connection between root causes of AP complexity and related consequences.

Following this model, socio-technical systems comprise a social subsystem, consisting of actors and structure, and a technical subsystems, consisting of technology and tasks (Fig. 2). The overall behavior of the system is then determined by the interactions between all of these components. As a very general example, an enterprise can be considered as humans (*actors*) using IT systems (*technology*) to perform work (*task*), which they have been assigned according to their role and position (*structure*). Transformation processes in large enterprises comprise a series of local changes within the organization, often in reaction to new and evolving external requirements [23,32]. While these local adaptations manage to temporarily fulfill the requirements, a series of such changes across different parts of the organization generally introduces inconsistencies, unnecessary

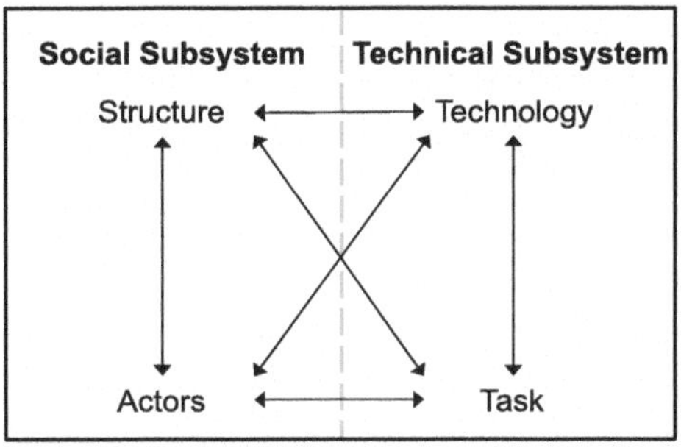

Fig. 2. Socio-technical systems theory [19]

redundancies or dependencies, which are typical drivers of complexity [10,33]. At some point, the misalignment between at least two socio-technical components will be noticeable and large enough to require the EA to undergo fundamental changes, termed *punctuated changes* [19]. For example, people will take action to change the system if the IT applications cannot handle new processes (technology-task misalignment) or if an application is too complicated for people to understand (actor-technology misalignment). Thus, root causes of AP complexity may be interpreted in the context of the related misalignment in the AP, i.e., *technology-people*, *technology-task*, *technology-structure*, *task-structure*, *task-people*, and *people-structure*.

4 Results

We use socio-technical systems theory as a lens to group and interpret our findings. First, identified root causes for AP complexity are discussed, which are considered as misalignments between any two socio-technical system components (see Fig. 2) and are grouped accordingly. Table 1 lists all identified root causes and also links them to related consequences of AP complexity. Finally, we present potential types of technical and organizational actions that are expected to deal with the root causes or to offset the consequences of AP complexity (see Table 2). The identified causes, consequences and actions are the result of aggregating similar elements found in the interviews through group discussions between the authors, also relying on feedback from meetings within the company and data from the complexity assessments. The results were discussed and validated with the EAM governance team to ensure the correctness of our findings.

4.1 Root Causes

In total, we identified 13 root causes of AP complexity (see Table 1). Most of the named root causes relate to technical issues within the EA landscape as a result of either misalignments between the technical system and the people that use and develop this system or misalignments between the technical system and the tasks that this system is supposed to carry out. The identified root causes are based on statements from multiple experts (application owner and employees of the central EAM governance team).

Technology/Actors: Issues with code complexity relate to the inability of people to use and maintain the technical system adequately since they are unable to make sense of too complex software code. Similarly, code quality relates to issues due to poorly written or documented code. Discussions with application owners revealed that one major problem is missing knowledge and documentation about single applications. This makes it difficult to steer the AP in an efficient way. The source code of old and highly customized applications often includes unused lines of code that cannot be deleted due to missing knowledge about the content and possible consequences. This results in complex and costly change activities in respective IT projects and additional maintenance activities. The application owners often mentioned unnecessary transitive interfaces in legacy systems. The quality of these interfaces is usually also lacking in terms of technical design and documentation. These circumstances decrease the transparency about the AP and lead to further workarounds to fix issues within data flows and thus to increased AP complexity. This is compounded by people lacking time and other resources to perform maintenance and development activities.

Technology/Task: Application owners state that applications are frequently missing adequate technical support such as dedicated testing instances for new deployments. One further issue is the quality of the implemented interfaces and the respective data flows. Often, these do not fit the required data formats, lack plausibility checks or include erroneous implementations. As a consequence, the transferred data might include useless information for the recipients and hinder the performance of planned tasks and thus the fulfillment of business requirements. Also, the quality of the source code might deliver wrong results and thus hinder the performance of the planned tasks.

Technology/Structure: Two application owners stated that the IT authority of business stakeholders leads to fundamental issues within the EA and increases the respective complexity. In their cases, business stakeholders have the permission to implement technical scripts within applications. As a consequence, enterprise architects face the challenge of redundant implementations that do not follow defined data dictionary standards and thus lead to missing transparency and a lack of knowledge about the state of the application. This also affects the knowledge about the AP and ends in inefficient decisions in daily projects such as the introduction of redundant applications.

Task/Structure: Application owners named the setup of change management plans as another root cause for AP complexity. The change cycle of several applications in the organization is faster than the planned changes within one fiscal year. As a consequence, IT projects face the challenge of outdated data and have to perform several workarounds to fix these issues. Also the IT authority of business stakeholders was highlighted as a structural issue that hinders the fulfillment of planned tasks.

Task/Actors: The capacity issue, already explained for the misalignment technology/actors, also relates to this misalignment. Projects often lack resources, in particular people and time, what affects the fulfillment of tasks.

People/Structure: Large applications require collaboration between multiple stakeholders such as operations-, maintenance-, and defect-managers. Application owners identified the missing role allocation between these stakeholders as one root cause for AP complexity. Missing communication and the lack of a common language lead to undesirable conditions within the respective application such as missing maintenance activities.

4.2 Consequences

The identified root causes were linked to the following five consequences (see Table 1). The identified root causes are based on the conducted expert interviews (application owner and employees of the central EAM governance team).

Lack of Time/Quality: As a consequence of technical (C8) and organizational issues (C1, C6, C9), the implemented AP does not fit the defined requirements. Consequently, business stakeholders face the challenge of missing information and enterprise architects do not complete projects in time. This often leads to a number of manual and undocumented workarounds, which increase the amount of activities in the operation of the AP and thus lead to missing transparency.

Data Quality Issues: Application owners stated that business stakeholders have extensive permission rights in the investigated applications (C8), leading to the implementation of redundant scripts that lack a comprehensive picture of the application. Moreover, these scripts might include business-related errors, due to missing testing activities and ad-hoc implementations of scripts. There is the risk that the implemented scripts do not match the defined data quality standards within the application - such as the required granularity - ending in data quality issues. In several cases the design of ingoing or outgoing interfaces (C6) does not match the required data format or lacks necessary plausibility checks, which also leads to hidden data quality issues.

Performance Issues: The quality of the source code of the applications often leads to major performance issues: calculations and report preparations exceed available time slots of batch jobs, which then result in automated cancellations of these jobs. As a consequence, the employees have to take further efforts in order to fulfill business requirements.

Table 1. Identified root causes of AP complexity and related consequences

Socio-technical misalignment	Root cause	Consequences				
		Lack of time / quality	Data quality issues	Performance issues	Chain reaction to other functions	Avoidable efforts
Technology/Actors	(C1) Capacity	×				
	(C2) Code quality				×	×
	(C3) Subjective complexity					×
	(C4) Code complexity					×
Technology/Task	(C5) Technical support	×				
	(C6) Design of data flows		×			
	(C2) Code quality		×	×	×	
	(C7) Quality of interfaces					×
Technology/Structure	(C8) IT authority of business	×				
Task/Structure	(C9) Change management plan	×				
	(C8) IT authority of business		×			
Task/Actors	(C1) Capacity	×				
Actors/Structure	(C10) Role allocation					×

Avoidable Efforts: The implementation of manual workarounds, data cleansing activities, and other efforts within IT projects could be avoided if the number of AP complexity root causes were decreased. Missing transparency leads to the implementation of redundant applications and thus to further efforts for maintaining and operating the complete AP. Moreover, the named technical (C2, C4, C3, C7) and organizational issues (C10) require manual efforts that also need a time-consuming coordination between different stakeholders and project teams.

Chain Reaction to Other Functions: Technical and business related issues within applications often also affect other related functions within the organization. Application owners stated that the quality of the source code might hinder the fulfillment of business requirements due to cancelations of batch jobs. This in turn leads to missing information in other departments.

4.3 Solutions

The interviewed experts identified the following technical and organizational actions that are expected to reduce AP complexity or offset respective negative consequences (see Table 2). All listed solutions were named by application owners in interviews and were validated with the EAM governance team.

Table 2. Named solutions for each consequence

Solutions	Lack of time / quality	Data quality issues	Performance issues	Chain reaction to other functions	Avoidable efforts
Increased capacities	×				
Technical support	×				
Pool of experts	×				
Stronger IT governance		×			×
Code reviews					×
Automated data checks		×			×
Stronger data management					×
Improved knowledge management					×
Technical renewals		×	×	×	×

Technical Renewals: Experts suggested selected technical renewals of the source code. While it is not necessary to shut down complete applications within the AP, the renewal of single elements, e.g., lines of source code or outdated interfaces, may increase the quality of applications and reduce the extent of the consequences, leading to an improved steering of the AP. The identification of renewal candidates, however, requires time-consuming analysis activities of the source code and group discussions between application owners and enterprise architects in order to evaluate the added value of such renewals.

Improved Knowledge Management: Missing information about the AP directly leads to inefficient steering of it. It is crucial to define clear knowledge management initiatives in order to ensure a high transparency. As an example, we note that the automotive company uses an EA repository that acts as a single point of truth for technical-, business-, process-, and application-architecture information. The interviewed experts suggested to further increase the documentation of single applications and data flows between them, which is expected to increase transparency about already available technical solutions within the organization.

Stronger IT Governance: The IT governance department needs to clearly define and implement rights and obligations of IT and business stakeholder. The business-side should not implement technical scripts. Upcoming projects should verify AP changes within a blueprint process, e.g., by employing a business capability map, in order to ensure up-to-date information about the operating AP.

Pool of Experts: The operating automotive company runs over 7.000 applications within their AP, including a large stack of used technologies and standards. Enterprise architects are required to make decisions in projects without having a deep understanding of the respective technologies. There is a risk that stakeholders make wrong decisions, e.g. by implementing functionally redundant technologies, leading to an inefficient AP. The interviewed experts recommend to establish a pool of experts for all used technologies within the AP blueprint, which can be consulted for respective decisions in projects.

Further solutions are an increased technical support and capacity when operating the application portfolio. These approaches simply provide additional resources for overcoming extant problems. In a similar manner, detailed code reviews were mentioned, which might help to identify hotspots within the AP. Moreover, a stronger implementation of automated checks at interfaces as well as an improved data management can prevent the origination of data quality problems within the AP.

5 Discussion

In Sect. 1, we defined three RQs, aiming to evaluate root causes (Q1) and consequences (Q2) of AP complexity and to identify solutions (Q3) that decrease AP complexity or offset negative consequences. The identified root causes were embedded in the PSIC model in order to provide a structured and coherent overview of our findings. Each root cause leads to at least one consequence and each consequence is ameliorated by at least one proposed solution (see Table 1) and 2).

Considering Q1, we identified 13 root causes for AP complexity. The identified issues paint a comprehensive yet diverse picture, including technical (e.g., code quality), process-driven (e.g., change management plan), and organizational (e.g., capacity) findings, revealing that the phenomenon of AP complexity is a result of the interplay between different factors within an enterprise. A concluding discussion of our findings with the EAM governance team of our research partner confirms this: the technical reassessment of AP parts is not sufficient to decrease the respective complexity in long term. The controlled reduction of AP complexity also has to consider non-technical enterprise conditions, such as process management issues, e.g., change management plans, and requires sophisticated knowledge management processes.

The second research question revealed consequences of AP complexity in daily projects. We identified five consequences of AP complexity, including technical (data quality, performance) and business (lack of time/quality) related consequences. The interviewed application owners emphasized the importance of AP complexity in IT projects and in their daily business, but also highlighted that critical business processes, i.e. processes that are related to the operation of plants in the automotive company, are not strongly affected by this issue. This may be due to a high amount of attention being allocated to these functions, resulting, for example, in a close monitoring of the application landscape, sharper governance principles and increased capacities for the operation of these business processes. This statement reflects the findings of our third research question: the suggested solutions, illustrated in Table 2, mainly include initiatives that aim to increase supporting capacities for the AP (e.g. pool of experts) and stronger monitoring operations (e.g., automated checks). However, to resolve the historically grown AP complexity application owners also suggest technical improvements in the currently operated applications (e.g. renewals, code reviews).

6 Conclusion

Our research aims to identify root causes, consequences, and possible solutions for AP complexity in large enterprises. We employed a case study approach, including ten expert interviews with application owners and group discussions with the central EAM governance team of a large European automotive company with an application portfolio of over 7.000 applications. Our results reveal the diverse issues related to AP complexity, including technical and organizational root causes, consequences, and solutions of this phenomenon. Our research extends current research on AP [9–11,21–23,25] by analyzing specific instances of real-world problems in connection with proposed solutions that might decrease AP complexity. The research results discover concrete characteristics of AP complexity in large organizations, which might be useful for further research in order to evaluate further solutions that might tackle this issue in practice. This is in line with calls to move research in this area away from abstract speculation towards an analysis of real-world issues [23].

The generalizability of these results requires further verification, in particular from organizations operating in different industries. A first step was made by discussing our findings in a focus-group with seven senior enterprise architects and IT-Managers from four other companies in the banking, logistics and insurance sectors. This discussion indicated that our results are applicable to other companies, as issues with AP complexity and attempted solution approaches are similar across different industries. Further research should specify the outlined solutions and define concrete procedures and methods. The expert interviews and group discussion reveal that the emergence of AP complexity is not observed for all functions of the organization: critical functions, in this case the operation of plants in the automotive sector, seem to be less affected by complexity in achieving their objectives. An evaluation of the technical and organizational factors that lead to the success of such functions seems to be promising.

References

1. Baharadwaj, A., El Sawy, O.A., Pavlou, P.A., Venkatraman, N.: Digital business strategy: toward a next generation of insights. MIS Q. **37**(2), 471–483 (2013)
2. Malhotra, Y.: Knowledge Management and Business Model Innovation. Idea Group Publishing, Hershey (2001)

3. Aleatrati Khosroshahi, P., Beese, J., Aier, S.: What drives application portfolio complexity? An empirical analysis of application portfolio cost drivers at a global automotive company. In: 18th IEEE Conference on Business Informatics (CBI 2016), Paris (2016)
4. Aleatrati Khosroshahi, P., Roth, S., Hauder, M.: Impact of solvency II on the enterprise architecture of insurances: a qualitative study in Germany. In: Multikonferenz Wirtschaftsinformatik, Paderborn (2014)
5. Purchase, V., Parry, P., Valerdi, R., Nightingale, D., Mills, J.: Enterprise transformation: why are we interested, what is it, and what are the challenges? J. Enterp. Transform. **1**(1), 14–33 (2011)
6. Rouse, W.B., Marietta, L.B.: Enterprise transformation. Commun. ACM **49**(7), 66–72 (2006)
7. Ashkenas, R.: Simplicity-minded management. Harv. Bus. Rev. **85**, 202–209 (2007)
8. Zammuto, R.F., Griffith, T.L., Majchrzak, A., Dougherty, D.J., Faraj, S.: Information technology and the changing fabric of organization. Organ. Sci. **18**(5), 749–762 (2007)
9. Schmidt, C., Buxmann, P.: Outcomes and success factors of enterprise IT architecture management: empirical insight from the international financial services industry. Eur. J. Inf. Syst. **20**(2), 168–185 (2011)
10. Beese, J., Aier, S., Winter, R.: On the role of complexity for guiding enterprise transformations. In: 5th Enterprise Engineering Working Conference, Prague, pp. 113–127 (2015)
11. Schneider, A.W., Zec, M., Matthes, F.: Adopting notions of complexity for enterprise architecture management. In: Proceedings of the 20th American Conference on Information Systems, Savannah (2014)
12. Akella, J., Buckow, H., Rey, S.: IT architecture: cutting costs and complexity (2009). http://www.mckinsey.com/insights/business_technology/it_architecture_cutting_costs_and_complexity. Accessed 10 Apr 2016
13. Reiner, J., Schaper, M.: Tackling IT complexity in product design (2010). http://www.mckinsey.com/insights/business_technology/tackling_it_complexity_in_product_design. Accessed 13 Apr 2016
14. Beetz, K.R., Kolbe, L.M.: IT organization and business-IT power sharing for the ability to manage IT complexity: an agenda for action. In: The International Multiconference on Complexity, Informatics and Cybernetics, Orlando (2010)
15. Cookie-Davies, T., Cicimil, S., Crawford, L., Richardson, K.: Were not in Kansas anymore, Toto: mapping the strange landscape of complexity theory, and its relationship to project management. Proj. Manag. J. **38**(2), 50–61 (2007)
16. Dewar, R., Hage, J.: Size, technology, complexity, and structural differentiaton: toward a theoretical synthesis. Adm. Sci. Q. **23**(1), 111–136 (1978)
17. Geraldi, J., Maylor, H., Williams, T.: Not lets make it really complex (complicated), a systematic review of the complexities of projects. Int. J. Oper. Prod. Manag. **31**(9), 996–990 (2011)
18. Yin, R.K.: Case Study Research: Design and Methods. Sage Publications, Thousand Oaks (2013)
19. Lyytinen, K., Newman, M.: Explaining information systems change: a punctuated socio-technical change model. Eur. J. Inf. Syst. **17**(6), 589–613 (2008)
20. Dreyfus, D., Wyner, G.M.: Digital cement: software portfolio architecture, complexity, and flexibility. In: Proceedings of the 17th Americas Conference on Information Systems, Detroit (2011, submission 62)

21. Lagerström, R., Baldwin, C.Y., Maccormack, A.D., Aier, S.: Visualizing and measuring enterprise application architecture: an exploratory telecom case. In: Harvard Business School Working Paper no. 13-103 (2013)
22. Lagerström, R., Baldwin, C.Y., Maccormack, A.D., Dreyfus, D.: Visualizing and measuring enterprise architecture: an exploratory biopharma case. In: Harvard Business School Working Paper no. 13-105 (2013)
23. Mocker, M.: What is complex about 273 applications? Untangling application architecture complexity in a case of European investment banking. In: Hawaii International Conference on System Sciences, Big Island, pp. 1–14 (2009)
24. Schneider, W., Reschenhofer, T., Schtz, A., Matthes, F.: Empirical results for application landscape complexity. In: Hawaii International Conference on System Sciences, Kauai (2015)
25. Schuetz, A., Widjaja, T., Kaiser, J.: Complexity in enterprise architectures - conceptualization and introduction of a measure from a system theoretic perspective. In: 21st European Conference on Information Systems, Utrecht, pp. 1–12 (2013)
26. Ross, J.W., Weill, P., Robertson, D.C.: Enterprise Architecture as Strategy. Harvard Business Scholl Press, Boston (2006)
27. Kulik, B.W., Baker, T.: Putting the organization back into computational organization theory: a complex Perrowian model of organizational action. Comput. Math. Organ. Theory **14**(2), 84–119 (2008)
28. Kvale, S.: Doing Interviews. Sage Publications, London (2008)
29. Tremblay, M.C., Hevner, A.R., Berndt, D.J.: Focus groups to artifact refinement and evaluation in design research. Commun. Assoc. Inf. Syst. **27**(27), 599–618 (2010)
30. Hanseth, O., Lyytinen, K.: Design theory for dynamic complexity in information infrastructures, the case of building internet. J. Inf. Technol. **25**(1), 1–19 (2010)
31. Wu, P.P.-Y., Fookes, C., Pitchforth, J., Mengersen, K.: A framework for model integration and holistic modelling of socio-technical systems. Decis. Support Syst. **71**, 14–27 (2015)
32. Vessey, I., Ward, K.: The dynamics of sustainable IS alignment: the case for IS adaptivity. J. Assoc. Inf. Syst. **14**(6), 283–311 (2013)
33. Dooley, K.J., Van de Ven, A.H.: Explaining complex organizational dynamics. Organ. Sci. **10**(3), 358–372 (1999)

Enterprise 2.0 – Literature Taxonomy and Usage Evaluation

Mayla Alimam[1,2(✉)], Emmanuel Bertin[1,2], and Noël Crespi[2]

[1] Orange Labs, Caen, France
{mayla.alimam, emmanuel.bertin}@orange.com
[2] Telecom SudParis - Institute Mines-Telecom – CNRS 5157, Évry, France
{mayla.alimam, emmanuel.bertin, noel.crespi}@telecom-sudparis.eu

Abstract. In the ten years since the emergence of the Enterprise 2.0 phenomenon, many studies have been realized in this field. This paper surveys today's Enterprise 2.0 literature. Based on the ITIL methodology, it outlines its main research areas and highlights the remaining issues. Also, starting from the lack of empirical evaluation of the real usage of Enterprise 2.0 tools, it proposes to evaluate the use of a social networking platform in a large company based on the relationships created therein. Our findings indicate that social networking tools are not reflecting the employees' actual relations at work.

Keywords: Enterprise 2.0 · ITIL · Enterprise social network · Email · Social graph

1 Introduction

Enterprise 2.0 (E2.0) was the term coined by Andrew McAfee ten years ago to describe "the use of emergent social software platforms within companies, or between companies and their partners or customers" [1]. The promising potentials of E2.0 tools have boosted their adoption in companies. For example, Gartner predicted in 2012 that 50 % of large companies will have a deployed E2.0 solution by the end of 2016 [2].

Along with the rapid and wide spread use of these tools, many scholars have contributed to the understanding of this phenomenon. When they emerged, E2.0 tools were first considered as experimental [3], and studies mainly focused on their functionalities and potentials [4, 5]. However, now that one decade has passed after this emergence, other trends are observed. In their survey of E2.0 literature, Williams et al. [6] reveal a number of remaining issues in the research on these tools. The authors mainly argue that the rising E2.0 phenomenon has reached the point of sustainability and thus scholars must turn their focus to the empirical large-scale examination of their initiatives. In fact, E2.0 tools should be considered in the same way as Enterprise Resource Planning (ERP) systems. Research on these tools needs to be modelled and classified in order to point out whether they are aligned with the business needs. Hence, this paper provides a modelling perspective of E2.0 research that addresses the call of Williams et al. We consider E2.0 tools as standard enterprise IT services and propose to model their research into the processes of ITIL framework for the IT service

J. Horkoff et al. (Eds.): PoEM 2016, LNBIP 267, pp. 26–40, 2016.
DOI: 10.1007/978-3-319-48393-1_3

management at enterprises. This modelling allows summarizing the literature within categories representing the service lifecycle stages while identifying the remaining gaps at each stage. Furthermore, this paper provides an illustrative example of how to contribute to a main gap identified through the ITIL: evaluating the returned value of E2.0 tools. Based on a qualitative case study, we empirically analyze the links created in an enterprise social network and explore the similarity between these links and the employees' daily work flows carried by the enterprise's email tool.

The rest of the paper is organized as follows. Section 2 explains the methodology of our work. Section 3 presents the categories of E2.0 research modelled based on the lifecycle stages of the ITIL framework. Section 4 is devoted to our empirical contribution in an enterprise social network. Finally, Sect. 5 contains conclusions.

2 Research Methodology

This research study provides two main contributions addressing the following research questions. Considering E2.0 research field as a stable field after ten years of its emergence [6], is research within this field completely covering all aspects related to the entire lifecycle of E2.0 tools? How should the remaining gaps be addressed by researchers?

To answer the first question we model and evaluate E2.0 literature by mapping a selection of major contributions onto the five lifecycle stages provided by ITIL framework for delivering valuable IT services to the business. For that purpose, we followed a structured and iterative process built on Webster and Waston's approach [7] to search, identify, and analyze the relevant literature. We considered within our scope the social media used in the workplace for corporate objectives. As this notion emerged in 2006, we deliberately excluded from our scope, scholarships appearing during the three years following this emergence in order to avoid the bias of exploratory and descriptive literature [6]. We therefore performed a keyword-based search[1] for peer-reviewed articles published in major scholarly journals and conferences proceedings since 2010 using the following digital libraries: Wiley Online Library, IEEE Xplore, SpringerLink, and Science Direct. Based on the abstracts of the returned 298 articles, 27 articles were identified as relevant to the defined scope. After a comprehensive analysis, we classified each article to one or more of the ITIL lifecycle stages.

Second, we highlight the need for research to turn its focus to empirical case studies. To address the second research question we observe the service's overall lifecycle. ITIL's guidelines emphasize the importance of continually evaluating the delivered tool once it comes into use. In fact, it's based on empirical usage evaluation that scholars as well as practitioners can better look into improving the tools' design and methods of control. This evaluation should be able to assess the benefits of the implementation and measure its returned value based on tangible indicators. We provide, thus, in Sect. 4, an illustrative example of how to perform such evaluation.

---

[1] In addition to "E2.0", the notion of using social media tools in organizational contexts is also referred to as "Enterprise Social Media". Both terms were thus included in our search.

3 Literature Review Based on ITIL Perspective

3.1 ITIL Framework Overview

Information Technology Infrastructure Library (ITIL) is a globally recognized standard that contains a series of best practices for IT Service Management (ITSM) in organizations. First published in 1989, ITIL has grown to be the most popular and complete ITSM framework that aligns IT services with business needs [8, 9]. It provides in its latest edition of 2011 a revolving flow of five core stages that cover and manage the lifecycle of the IT service. These stages are as follows: service strategy, design, transition (for its deployment management), operation and continual service improvement.

3.2 Distribution of E2.0 Literature on the ITIL Lifecycle Stages

Stage 1: Service Strategy. During the service strategy stage, the enterprise management decides on the strategy to serve its employees starting from their needs aligned by the company's strategic objectives. At this stage of the lifecycle, researchers are interested in defining the concerned tools, describing their behavior and providing their characteristics and specifications. Regarding its scope, E2.0 is still considered as a combination of Web 2.0 technologies integrated into multiple organizational processes for which no specific set of tools has been provided. However, current research seems to have an implied consensus about the key tools that are the most often deployed in enterprises. Table 1 interprets this consensus, providing an overall list of E2.0 tools noted in major contributions in this area [3, 4, 10–13] while comparing them to a primitive list that has been provided at the early stage in [3].

Regarding the specifications of E2.0 tools, scholars are now contributing more deeply to the definition of these tools' characteristics. Several aspects are being discussed, with the objective of assisting companies in deciding on the appropriate tool for adoption [13, 14]. In terms of functionality, researchers tend to explore the tools' capabilities and potentials on two levels: collective and individual. At the collective

Table 1. Common research contributions on listing E2.0 tools

Contributions	E2.0 Tools	Web services	P2P networking	Collective intelligence	**Social networking**	Podcasts	**Blogs**	**Microblogging**	RSS feeds	**Wikis**	Mash-ups	**Social bookmarking**	Virtual worlds	Social customer relationship management
Early stage	Bughin [3]	❍	❍	❍	❍	❍	❍		❍	❍	❍			
Current	Androile [4]			●	●	●	●		●	●	●	●	●	
	McAfee [12]				●		●		●	●		●		
	Schubert&Glitsch [13]				●		●	●		●		●		
	Treem& Leonardi [11]				●		●	●		●		●		
	Burégio et al. [10]				●			●		●		●		●
	Common tools				✓		✓	✓		✓		✓		

level, E2.0 tools are categorized based on their functional features with the aim of highlighting their potential. The following capabilities are offered by these tools according to the literature:

- Information sharing [15–17],
- Communication and social relations [4, 13, 15, 18],
- Collaboration/cooperation and innovation [4, 13, 15, 18],
- Training and learning [4, 15],
- Knowledge management [4, 15], and
- Management activities and coordination [4, 13, 15].

At a more specific level, the degree to which a capability is afforded in each tool is highlighted in [15]. For example, wikis support a high degree of collaboration and innovation but a low degree of management activities and problem solving. Reference [10] also provides a detailed description of each tool's benefits and possible risks. According to its authors, wikis co-create knowledge through shared content but require strong commitment to keep content updated; online social networks support access to expertise, resources, and leaders with the provided social profiles, however, their advantages are only useful when they are accessed by a large number of users; Microblogging encourages interactive discussions and allows an informal information communication, but its unstructured content might cause information overload; social bookmarking promotes a useful information resources assessment, but raises confidentiality concerns when the access to resources is open; and finally, social customer relationship management allows to get closer to customers and derives meaning from social data through analytics, but risks consumers' limited engagement if no tangible value is added to their experience.

At the same individual level, another perspective of exploring the tools' capabilities is provided in [11]. This approach particularly looks into the communicative behavior of E2.0 tools while comparing them to the enterprise's traditional communication tools. The authors identify four capabilities emerging from the use of E2.0 tools. They refer to these capabilities as affordances and identify them as follows: visibility, editability, persistence, and association.

Finally, on the enterprise side, studies are emphasizing the need to correlate between the organizational requirements and the specifications of E2.0 tools. To that end, a framework is proposed in [13]. The framework supports companies in performing their requirement analysis based on an established overview of activities (business processes and use cases). While arguing that business activities that have a non-sequenced ad-hoc structure cannot be modeled, the authors propose describing these types of activities through use cases. These use cases differ from business processes in being flexible and unpredictable in their sequence. Consequently, the framework uses the activities' description to identify candidate areas for collaboration scenarios. These scenarios are then matched with features of the tools. The authors finally propose to establish a generic catalogue of predefined collaboration scenarios that occur frequently occur in companies.

Nevertheless, researchers are neglecting to consider at this stage the variation of companies' size between small and large which influences the company's requirements and financial capacity.

Stage 2: Service Design. The service design includes all actions related to the design of the ESM. The enterprise management decides whether to develop a new private ESM or otherwise to select and customize a market offering. These models of delivery are provided in [19] as follows:

- Making use of public sites such as publicly available microblogs and online social networking sites (e.g. Facebook) to enable employees' interactions with external customers;
- Private solutions exclusively for internal audiences, implemented and hosted either by the company itself or as cloud-based services; and
- In-house developed proprietary solutions, often built as prototypes.

Reference [20] goes beyond the delivery to provide a classification that explores the business models of social networking product providers. It outlines three types of these models: a consumer model which is community driven (e.g. Facebook), a corporate model, tightly integrated with organizational processes and technologies (e.g. Microsoft SharePoint), and finally, an emerging hybrid model, which blends the community driven benefits with the corporately focused models (e.g. Jive).

Further technical specifications are also discussed in [21] and [10]. From a systemic perspective, [21] proposes two possible scenarios for the design of systems containing E2.0 tools: either to have them federated in a single integrated platform, or to maintain their individuality while enabling coordination between their data. In addition, [10] conceptualizes an architecture where the level of control varies based on the process type (i.e. strict for structured data in the business world and loose for unstructured data in the social world).

However, we highlight here the need for the design to cover more technical details related to its consistency and compliance with the company's processes, infrastructure, policies, etc. The analysis of their social interaction patterns in corporate environment is also necessary as these tools are usually designed for smaller numbers of users.

Stage 3: Service Transition. Deploying ESM is achieved at the service transition stage. Various approaches to explore the deployment process of E2.0 tools and assist the organizations in performing this deployment are present in the literature. Some studies propose checklists and guiding frameworks consisting of steps to be engaged by the companies wanting to succeed at this operation [3, 10, 15, 20]. In addition to the technological aspect, these studies also incorporate the organizational as well as the managerial considerations in the tool's deployment process.

A wide perspective of tool deployment frameworks is presented in [15] where authors adopt a fit-viability model to evaluate E2.0 initiatives. Two major considerations are exploited within this framework. For its decision to select a technology to be deployed, the company should consider the right fit between the tasks to be performed, and the selected tool. The adoption decision should also consider the viability of three organizational factors to ensure the readiness of the company before the deployment. These factors concern the financial aspect of the adoption, the existing IT infrastructure for the adoption's feasibility, and finally, the human and organizational factors, including for example managers' and employees' readiness, legal issues, etc. After these factors have been examined, the framework proposes to adopt a well-defined deployment strategy, and to, finally, pursue the deployment process by measuring the performance of the tool to assess the business value of this adoption.

Other studies, however, contribute specifically to the practical deployment of the tool. Regarding the definition of the deployment strategy, its several approaches are explored in [22] while discussing each approach's advantages and challenges. The chosen strategy must be aligned with the organization's mission, work processes, culture and industry. A bottom-up approach is best applicable in growing organizations with a critical mass of younger employees or in flatter organizations where younger employees have better visibility to senior management. A middle-out approach is optimal in larger, globally dispersed organizations where entrepreneurs and middle managers have enough technical knowledge to master these tools and enough influence over the projects and work processes to diffuse this usage. A top-down approach is however optimal in situations where a rapid adoption is needed to meet competitive challenges. Furthermore, a hybrid approach is proposed in [20]. It combines top-down elements with bottom-up elements to provide guidance and managerial support while allowing a degree of autonomy in usage and content creation by the end-users. Particularly in the case of small or medium enterprises, the deployment strategy has to be totally supported by the top management [23].

Researchers are also bringing attention to the organizational challenges and risks related to the deployment of E2.0 tools. These challenges concern factors mainly related to the enterprise culture and strategic thinking which might be against adopting this technology [15, 20, 24], and to the information management (i.e. legality, security and privacy, and intellectual property and copyright) [15]. A governance policy that complies with the company's regulation and strategic objectives should be thus elaborated [15, 25]. Also, the company's financial resources may also be a factor in the case of small and medium-sized enterprises. External expertise can be consulted in this case to ensure avoiding a failed adoption [17]. Furthermore, [26] provides in a systematic approach four main risk categories described in a risk catalog. The catalog is obtained from an evolved conceptual risk model that characterizes the risks based on their properties (i.e. the causes, factors and consequences of the risks). The four outlined categories are as follows: loss of control, loss of reputation, information leakage, and managerial risks.

Nevertheless, challenges and successful deployments are tightly related to the organizational form as argued in [27]. E2.0 tools are a good fit in enterprises characterized as highly fluid and horizontal. Their deployment in rigid enterprises can also assist in achieving an organizational transformation towards more agility if this latter is specifically targeted.

Finally at this stage, we highlight the need for more empirical experiments and case studies to evaluate the theoretical frameworks and provide strategies for risk mitigation.

Stage 4: Service Operation. The service operation stage is responsible for technical, applications and operation management. Research at this stage is focusing on promoting users' participation and defining methods for controlling the tools' operations and generated information. According to scholars, the perception of benefits can vary between users. This perception can be a contextual phenomenon influenced by user types as captured and interpreted in [28]. E2.0 tools are qualified here as technologies-in-practice [29] for which the usage patterns take shape during practice according to users' specific work practices. Three uses are outlined for three levels of users: as a social tool for task coordination in teams, as a social tool for organizing within projects or as a networking and crowd-sourcing space at enterprise-wide levels. This perception can also be related to the user's appropriation of the tool. Reference [18] highlights how the intensity of usage impacts this perception. Only active contributors experience most of the benefits consistently. A moderate level of contribution is, however, sufficient for a user to experience the spirit of belonging and sense-making. Reference [30] also reveals a broader factor impacting the user appropriation and the perceived usefulness of E2.0 tools. This factor is related to the formerly established assumptions of a company's employees about the usage of the tool. The authors outline how the personal advanced experience of a category of employees in public social media is paradoxically limiting these employees' perception of a tool's usefulness. This skeptical category, usually consisting of younger employees, is resisting shifting its technological frame to a corporate context. This resistance is explained by the category's concerns about potential distraction or threats resulting from the use of E2.0 tools. In contrast to older employees, this category finds these tools unsuitable for task-orientated usages.

Regarding the control of the tools, [25] argues that companies should formulate and apply, by means of a decision making authority, a practical technology roadmap. This latter should involve training, communication and promotion program supported by online training content and live workshops and training sessions. It should also involve aspects related to user rights and content diffusion permissions [13, 23]. Reference [20] suggests empowering end-user participation and giving users sufficient autonomy to exploit, contribute and distribute content. Users have to be convinced of the benefits of the selected tool, as the act of using it is often voluntary [13]. This is why, according to [23], considering the employees' mindset is a key factor of a successful implementation, especially in the case of small and medium-sized enterprises. In terms of practice, [31] suggests integrating the social dimension into the development and maintenance of the organizational information system. It creates social networks represented by relations between the process's components. These relations serve solving the resources conflicts and monitoring the performance of the business processes.

Nevertheless, research needs to bring other control aspects into focus. The matter of how controlling and protecting the privacy of the generated knowledge while empowering users' participation and initiatives remains problematic.

Stage 5: Continual Service Improvement. During the continual service improvement, the enterprise focuses on the value returned to its employees and its outcomes while ensuring that the service is continually addressing future needs. Particularly in large-scale organizations, analysis and mining approaches are being applied to datasets derived from enterprise social networking platforms to evaluate users' interactions over the tool and to thus evaluate the impact of these platforms. The relationship between users' interactions on their social network and their attributes derived from the company's hierarchal graph is explored in [32]. Several formal statistical models based on logistic regression are built here to quantify the effects of these attributes on the interaction patterns. Two influencing attributes are revealed as follows. Regarding the geo-location, users are more likely to interact when they are employed in the same country. Regarding the hierarchical level, pairs of peered employees or employee/direct manager pairs seem to have more interactions than pairs that have several hierarchal levels between them.

Also in a global organizational context, the financial aspect is mined in [33], however, through a broader analysis. Data here are gathered not only from the company's social networking platform, but also from other sources including e-mails and instant message communications. These findings reveal that mixing genders in teams produces a better financial performance, and that projects, with too many managers seem, to be less successful financially.

Other approaches to evaluating E2.0 tools based on their performance assessment are proposed in [10, 15]. Scholars contribute to this area by proposing key performance indicators. A set of impact metrics is derived from tools' capabilities and provided in [4]. These metrics remain, however, at a high, general level, as they are not directly related to the technology itself. For example, what the author derives from the functionality of knowledge management are the following metrics: ability to share knowledge, ability to retrieve knowledge, ability to organize knowledge, and ability to leverage knowledge. Clearly such metrics need to be more specific. They should, in fact, be derived from each tool's technical specification, as suggested in [15]. The authors here propose sample criteria for measuring the performance of contributors on an online social networking platform. Their sample contains the following criteria: increased conversion rate, increased employee and/or customer satisfaction, reduced customer service cost, reduced rate of customer attrition, increased stickiness (time spent on vendor's web site), intensity of customer-to-customer communication, increased revenue, number of ideas generated by employees and partners, and online social shopping volume (if available).

Finally here, we highlight the high importance of this stage as it examines the overall lifecycle of the tool. The definition of the returned value of E2.0 and how this value can be measured is yet ambiguous. More focus on its actual usage and on the analysis of its generated data is thus indispensable.

Within this context, we propose in the next section a contribution to this specific stage of the lifecycle.

4 Contribution to the Evaluation of an E2.0 Tool

Our contribution provides an example of how empirical analysis can be performed to evaluate the use of an E2.0 tool. We propose a new approach that evaluates the benefit of a tool by comparing its use to the work patterns at the workplace. The objective is to assess the usage offered by this tool and its influence on/by the employees' practices.

To that end, we select to evaluate one of the most deployed E2.0 tools in the workplace; an enterprise social networking platform [34]. The power of this tool resides in its ability to link between people on a large scale. Its established network of relations offers its users a social base wherein various activities such as communication and collaborating can be performed depending on the platform's enabled features. In fact, since its emergence in knowledge-working corporations, the use of this tool has been often supported by the leading authority aiming to shift its internal communicational activities towards this new wave of tool [35]. We are therefore interested in exploring the social graph underlying the design of this tool.

To obtain our objective, we attempt to determine whether the tool's established social network reflects the real-life relations that exist between employees at work. We argue that, prior to using enterprise social networking platforms in companies, employees already had their own implicit social networks, expressed through their daily communicational activities. To this day, the majority of these activities are performed through email message exchanges. In fact, the electronic messaging system (email) has been the primary enabler of a wide variety of activities due to the plasticity of use it offers [36]. We therefore consider its residing social network as the most representative graph of workers' professional relations we can use for comparison.

Next, we define the questions and the main observations that we are aiming to perform based on the comparison between the two graphs. Is the established social relation network of the enterprise social networking platform reflecting the existing workers' relations expressed in the email social graph? What characterizes the identified relations in the enterprise social networking platform?

Finally, we search to answer the defined question by conducting an experiment on a qualitative sample of participants. We chose the qualitative approach because we needed to obtain a qualitative data set for the base of our comparison [37]. Indeed, workers' professional inboxes are the most appropriate sources for modeling their relations; however, at the same time, these inboxes contain a large portion of clutter. We did not want such unrelated messages to impact the credibility of our results.

Further details about the collected data and the performed analysis are provided in the next sub-sections.

4.1 Experimental Data Collection

To obtain our data sets, we conducted an experiment in a large telecommunication provider where knowledge work is prominent. The company has a social networking platform based on Jive Software. Further in this paper, we will refer to this tool as "Jive". Jive was deployed in the targeted company in 2014. Its use has now become more popular as it is being supported by the hierarchal authority.

As explained earlier, the experiment was conducted on a qualitative sample of representative users. Our sample involved 37 participants. Profiles of the participants were carefully selected to include employees of various ages, types and backgrounds (i.e. project managers, team leaders, research and development engineers, academic researchers). Further, we made sure to select participants who are active workers at the enterprise as well as active to moderate users on Jive.

The purpose of selecting this sample was to build the social participants' sub-graphs at the two environments and compare the resulting two graphs. To that end, we asked each participant to provide us with an accurately selected sample of his/her own messages. Each participant's selected messages had to be representative of his/her daily and recent activities at the workplace (i.e. containing exchanges with the most relevant persons as estimated by the participant himself/herself).

Two data sets were collected to build our graphs using NodeXL [38]. Data set A concerned data from the participants' email messages. The data collecting went was as follows: for each message, collect the sender's name u, the recipient(s) name(s) vi; create an undirected edge between the nodes:

$$e(u, vi);\ i = 1 \text{ to } n \tag{1}$$

Note that we only involved the recipients in the "To" field and considered the "CC" field as less relevant.

Data set B concerned data from Jive, collected as follows: for each participant u, collect his/her list of relations vi; create an undirected edge between the nodes as in (1). Duplicate edges were eliminated from both graphs. Table 2 provides information about the two graphs.

Table 2. Information about the two graphs

Type	Nb of nodes	Nb of edges	Connected components	Diameter	Average distance
Email graph	193	282	16	10	4.4
Jive graph	177	492	3	5	2.69

4.2 Similarity Comparison

We approach the similarity comparison between the two built graphs at two levels. The first level provides an overall comparison between the two graphs whereas the second level looks into the correlation between the two graphs based on their common nodes and corresponding distances. More details are provided below.

Overall Similarity. To make an overall comparison between the email graph A and Jive graph B, we apply a method that measures their similarity and provides a single similarity score [39]. The advantage of this method among the other measures proposed in the literature is that it involves nodes' neighbor matching while performing an iterative calculation of the nodes' similarity.

The concept of the developed algorithm is as follows: two nodes i in A and j in B are considered similar if the neighbor nodes of i can be matched to similar neighbor nodes of j.

$$x_{ij}^{k+1} = \frac{s_{in}^{k+1}(i,j) + s_{out}^{k+1}(i,j)}{2} \tag{2}$$

Equation (2) calculates the similarity of the i th node of graph A and j th node of graph B in (k + 1) th iterations where s(i,j)in is the in degree similarity of node i in A and j in B, and s(i,j)out is the out degree similarity of node i in A and j in B. These degrees are calculated in (3) and (4), respectively, using the summation of the neighbors' similarity in the previous iteration.

$$s_{in}^{k+1}(i,j) = \frac{1}{m_{in}} \sum_{l=1}^{n_{in}} max\left(s_{in}^{k}(l,f)\right);\ f = 1\ to\ m_{in}$$
$$m_{in} = \max(id(i), id(j))$$
$$n_{in} = \min(id(i), id(j)) \tag{3}$$

Note that id(i) stands forth in-degree of node i and od(i) the out-degree of node i.

$$s_{out}^{k+1}(i,j) = \frac{1}{m_{out}} \sum_{l=1}^{n_{out}} max\left(s_{out}^{k}(l,f)\right);\ f = 1\ to\ m_{out}$$
$$m_{out} = \max(od(i), od(j))$$
$$n_{out} = \min(od(i), od(j)) \tag{4}$$

Iteration of node similarity calculation is repeated until convergence. An epsilon value ε is defined to determine that point, based on the difference between node similarities in two iterations.

$$x_{ij}^{k} - x_{ij}^{k+1} < \varepsilon \tag{5}$$

A matrix of similarity scores of the nodes in the two graphs is then calculated. The final similarity value is provided in (6) as the sum of the maximum similarity values of the two graph nodes divided by the size of the smaller graph.

$$s(A,B) = \frac{1}{n} \sum_{l=1}^{n} max\left(s_{lf}^{k}\right);\ f = 1\ to\ m$$
$$m = \max(A,B)$$
$$n = \min(A,B) \tag{6}$$

Correlation Between Corresponding Nodes and Edges. The second level of comparison involves the node's identity in the analysis. It searches for correlation between pairs of nodes based on their corresponding distances. This approach applies the following method:

- Define the Jive distance d as the calculation of the shortest path between a given pair of nodes (i, j) in Jive graph B; and then
- For each pair of nodes in email graph A, calculate its corresponding value d in B.

4.3 Results

Overall Similarity. Applying the first measure indicated a low level of similarity between the two graphs. Details about the results of the algorithm are as follows: the optimal ε value that allowed obtaining the convergence of iterations according to our

Table 3. Similarity calculation for two identical graphs

ε	0.1	0.01	0.001
s(A,B)	93.75 %	99.22 %	99.90 %

tests was 0.1. For a better estimation of this value, we provide the similarity calculation results for two given identical graphs in Table 3.

For our two graphs, the returned similarity percentage was:

$$\mathrm{s(A,B)} = 24.97\,\%$$

Correlation Between Corresponding Nodes and Edges. Regarding the Jive distances of the email graph's pairs, Fig. 1 gives the summary of the Jive distances' calculation for all the email pairs. Recall that a Jive distance d represents the shortest path calculation for a given pair of nodes (i, j).

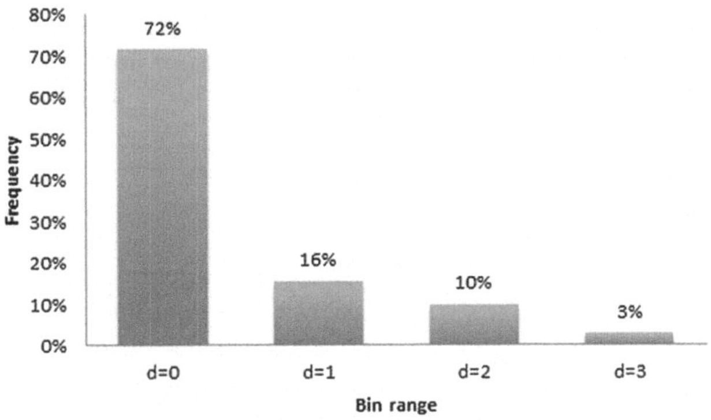

Fig. 1. Histogram of Jive distances

As seen in the Figure, Jive distances range between 0 and 3. The value of 0 indicates that a given email pair does not exist in the Jive graph (i.e. no relation is found between the two people in a Jive graph). On the other hand, a value of 3 indicates that a given email pair is related in the Jive graph, however not directly. The majority of Jive distances (72 %) have a value of 0.

However, the majority of distances found range between the values of 1 and 2. Only a few Jive distances have a value of 3. These results are discussed in the next sub-section.

4.4 Discussion

The low percentage of the measured similarity calculated based on neighbor matching provides a first indication of the lack of overall correlation between the two graphs. The distance calculation also demonstrates this low correlation by the variation of distances between 0 (non-existent relations) and 1 to 3 (existent; however, not always directly). Our results indicate that the majority of email relations located in the email graph could not be located in the Jive graph; the relations in the two graphs are not correlating. Only 16 % of the email relations took place directly in the Jive graph. We infer from these findings that the Jive relations do not reflect the worker's existing activities at the workplace. Reciprocally, identified Jive relations that are not located in the email graph express the new channels of communication that were created with the use of the tool.

These channels demonstrate the potential of a social networking tool, when used in a corporate context, to expand a worker's scope of relations for future collaboration or communication.

Nevertheless, the correlated portion of workers' relations in the two graphs opens the question of how the usage of these two tools is taking place. The dual existence of relations indicates parallel communication channels between the same people.

Finally, the purpose of this usage needs to be characterized in future research to provide some insight into how new tools are impacting the existing working tools. The scope of this analysis can also be expanded to include, in addition to email, other working tools such as instant messaging, conferencing, etc. The same analysis can thus be applied to measure the benefit of other types of E2.0 tool. However, our approach here does not include, within its comparison, the analysis of users' interaction over the platform. We consider this lack as a limitation that can be included in future research.

5 Conclusion

This paper develops the understanding about the current state of Enterprise 2.0 research. It provides a brief review of the recent major contributions to E2.0 literature while modelling it to ITIL processes for IT service management. Our overall observation of the five resulted categories suggests the following: the goal of introducing the tool should be clearly and precisely stated from the beginning and not be a somehow vague objective such as "bringing agility" or "transforming ways of working". All the lifecycle processes should be then oriented toward this goal, which can then be continuously monitored and evaluated (through well-defined KPIs).

Our paper, therefore, contributes to the evaluation stage by providing an empirical example of how the use of an E2.0 tool can be assessed. The example evaluates users' relations on an enterprise social networking platform by comparing them to the natural relations that the same users create while performing activities at the workplace. Analysis of the qualitative data that we collected indicates that workers' relations on their social networking tool are not similar to their actual relations. This outlines how enterprise social networking is providing new scopes for interacting, rather that reflecting the existing work processes of an enterprise.

In conclusion, since empirical results are more reliable, we highlight the need for case studies and experiments such as the one provided in our example to develop further understanding about the remaining issues in E2.0 research. We therefore prompt scholars to consider empirical methods in their future research to provide more insights into the adoption of these tools, especially for practitioners.

References

1. McAfee, A.P.: Enterprise 2.0: the dawn of emergent collaboration. MIT Sloan Manag. Rev. **47**, 21–28 (2006)
2. Mann, J., Austin, T., Drakos, N., Rozwell, C., Walls, A.: Predicts 2013: social and collaboration go deeper and wider. Gartner, Inc. report (2012)
3. Bughin, J.: The rise of Enterprise 2.0. J. Direct Data Digit. Mark. Pract. **9**, 251–259 (2008)
4. Andriole, S.J.: Business impact of Web 2.0 technologies. Commun. ACM **53**, 67–79 (2010)
5. Kuettner, T., Diehl, R., Schubert, P.: Change factors in Enterprise 2.0 initiatives: can we learn from ERP? Electron. Mark. **23**, 329–340 (2013)
6. Williams, S.P., Hausmann, V., Hardy, C.A., Schubert, P.: Enterprise 2.0 research: meeting the challenges of practice. In: BLED 2013 Proceedings (2013)
7. Webster, J., Watson, R.T.: Analyzing the past to prepare for the future: writing a literature review. MIS Q. **26**, xiii–xxiii (2002)
8. Marrone, M., Kolbe, L.M.: Impact of IT service management frameworks on the IT organization. Bus. Inf. Syst. Eng. **3**(1), 5–18 (2011)
9. Arraj, V.: ITIL®: the Basics. Buckinghampshire, UK (2010)
10. Buregio, V., Maamar, Z., Meira, S.: An architecture and guiding framework for the social enterprise. IEEE Internet Comput. **19**, 64–68 (2015)
11. Treem, J.W., Leonardi, P.M.: Social media use in organizations. Commun. Yearb. **36**, 143–189 (2012)
12. McAfee, A.: Enterprise 2.0: How to Manage Social Technologies to Transform Your Organization. Harvard Business Press, Boston (2013)
13. Schubert, P., Glitsch, J.H.: Adding structure to enterprise collaboration systems: identification of use cases and collaboration scenarios. Procedia Comput. Sci. **64**, 161–169 (2015)
14. Williams, S.P., Schubert, P.: An empirical study of Enterprise 2.0 in context. In: Proceedings of the Bled Conference, pp. 42–55 (2011)
15. Turban, E., Bolloju, N., Liang, T.-P.: Enterprise social networking: opportunities, adoption, and risk mitigation. J. Organ. Comput. Electron. Commer. **21**, 202–220 (2011)
16. Fulk, J., Yuan, Y.C.: Location, motivation, and social capitalization via enterprise social networking. J. Comput. Mediat. Commun. **19**, 20–37 (2013)
17. Gibbs, J.L., Rozaidi, N.A., Eisenberg, J.: Overcoming the "Ideology of Openness": probing the affordances of social media for organizational knowledge sharing. J. Comput. Mediat. Commun. **19**, 102–120 (2013)
18. Holtzblatt, L., Drury, J.L., Weiss, D., Damianos, L.E., Cuomo, D.: Evaluating the uses and benefits of an enterprise social media platform. J. Soc. Media Organ. **1**, 1–21 (2013)
19. Leonardi, P.M., Huysman, M., Steinfield, C.: Enterprise social media: definition, history, and prospects for the study of social technologies in organizations. J. Comput. Mediat. Commun. **19**, 1–19 (2013)
20. Mathiesen, P., Fielt, E.: Enterprise social networks: a business model perspective. In: 24th Australasian Conference on Information Systems (ACIS), pp. 1–12. RMIT University (2013)
21. Alimam, M., Bertin, E., Crespi, N.: Enterprise social systems: the what, the why, and the how. In: 2015 IEEE 17th Conference on Business Informatics, pp. 9–17. IEEE (2015)
22. Guinan, P.J., Parise, S., Rollag, K.: Jumpstarting the use of social technologies in your organization. Bus. Horiz. **57**, 337–347 (2014)
23. Meske, C., Stieglitz, S.: Adoption and use of social media in small and medium-sized enterprises. In: Harmsen, F., Proper, H.A. (eds.) PRET 2013. LNBIP, vol. 151, pp. 61–75. Springer, Heidelberg (2013)

24. Haefliger, S., Monteiro, E., Foray, D., von Krogh, G.: Social software and strategy. Long Range Plan. **44**, 297–316 (2011)
25. Louw, R., Mtsweni, J.: The quest towards a winning Enterprise 2.0 collaboration technology adoption strategy. Int. J. Adv. Comput. Sci. Appl. **4**, 34–39 (2013)
26. Braun, R., Esswein, W.: Towards a conceptualization of corporate risks in online social networks: a literature based overview of risks. In: Proceedings - IEEE International Enterprise Distributed Object Computing Workshop, EDOC, pp. 267–274 (2013)
27. Alimam, M., Emmanuel, B., Noel, C.: Social and collaborative services for organizations: back to requirements. In: The Spring Servitization Conference (2015)
28. Richter, A., Riemer, K.: The contextual nature of enterprise social networking: a multi case study comparison. In: ECIS 2013 Proceedings, p. 12 (2013)
29. Orlikowski, W.J., Iacono, C.S.: The truth is not out there: an enacted view of the "digital economy". In: Understanding the Digital Economy: Data, Tools, and Research, pp. 352–380 (2000)
30. Treem, J.W., Dailey, S.L., Pierce, C.S., Leonardi, P.M.: Bringing technological frames to work: how previous experience with social media shapes the technology's meaning in an organization. J. Commun. **65**, 396–422 (2015)
31. Maamar, Z., et al.: Enterprise 2.0: research challenges and opportunities. In: Monfort, V., Krempels, K.-H. (eds.) WEBIST 2014. LNBIP, vol. 226, pp. 16–30. Springer, Heidelberg (2014)
32. Cao, J., Gao, H.Y., Li, L.E., Friedman, B.: Enterprise social network analysis and modeling: a tale of two graphs. In: Proceedings of the IEEE Infocom, pp. 2382–2390 (2013)
33. Lin, C.-Y., Wu, L., Wen, Z., Tong, H., Griffiths-Fisher, V., Shi, L., Lubensky, D.: Social network analysis in enterprise. Proc. IEEE **100**, 2759–2776 (2012)
34. Chui, M., Manyika, J., Bughin, J., Dobbs, R., Roxburgh, C., Sarrazin, H., Sands, G., Westergren, M.: The social economy: unlocking value and productivity through social technologies. McKinsey Global Institute, London (2012)
35. Silic, M., Back, A., Silic, D.: Atos-towards zero email company. In: ECIS 2015 Proceedings (2015)
36. Alimam, M., Bertin, E., Crespi, N.: Improving the capabilities of email for businesses – the case of social tagging. In: ECIS 2016 Proceedings (2016)
37. Miles, M.B., Huberman, A.M.: Qualitative Data Analysis: A Sourcebook of New Methods. SAGE, California (1984)
38. Smith, M., Milic-Frayling, N., Shneiderman, B., Mendes Rodrigues, E., Leskovec, J., Dunne, C.: NodeXL: a free and open network overview, discovery and exploration add-in for Excel 2007/2010 (2010). http://nodexl.codeplex.com/ (from the Social Media Research Foundation). http://www.smrfoundation.org
39. Nikolić, M.: Measuring similarity of graph nodes by neighbor matching. Intell. Data Anal. **16**, 865–878 (2012)

Towards Support for Strategic Decision Processes Using Enterprise Models: A Critical Reconstruction of Strategy Analysis Tools

Alexander Bock[1(✉)], Ulrich Frank[1], Arne Bergmann[2], and Stefan Strecker[2]

[1] Research Group Information Systems and Enterprise Modeling, University of Duisburg-Essen, Essen, Germany
{alexander.bock,ulrich.frank}@uni-due.de

[2] Enterprise Modelling Research Group, University of Hagen, Hagen, Germany
{arne.bergmann,stefan.strecker}@fernuni-hagen.de

Abstract. Strategic decision processes are traditionally thought to affect an organization's long-term success, motivating the development of strategy analysis tools. But ordinary strategy analysis tools have been criticized on several grounds, such as the neglect of organizational context and ill-defined concepts. This paper explores whether enterprise models can provide a richer foundation for strategic analysis, intending to lay the ground for the development of a modeling language. Specifically, the paper analyzes key concepts of traditional strategy analysis tools, reconstructs these concepts in the form of a meta model, and demonstrates integration potentials with enterprise models. The paper closes with implications and lessons learned for future research.

Keywords: Enterprise modeling · Domain-specific modeling languages · Strategic decision processes · Strategy analysis tools

1 Introduction

It is traditionally thought that "to forecast and provide means examining the future and drawing up the plan of action" is a prime responsibility of the manager [1, p. 5]. With the publication of Ansoff's *Corporate Strategy* [2] and Andrews' *The Concept of Corporate Strategy* [3], related processes have come to be placed predominantly under the heading of *strategic planning* and *strategic decision processes.* In the light of an on-going digital transformation, these processes seem more relevant than ever. New, sometimes disruptive technologies may emerge at any time, rapidly replacing established products. But while environmental contingencies motivate strategic planning, they also represent its key challenge. In the face of an uncertain future, the meaningfulness of detailed planning at a top level has long been questioned—to the extent that the 'Fall of Strategic Planning' has been posited two decades ago [4].

J. Horkoff et al. (Eds.): PoEM 2016, LNBIP 267, pp. 41–56, 2016.
DOI: 10.1007/978-3-319-48393-1_4

The complexity, contingency, and ambivalence of strategic problems motivate the use of approaches that facilitate the systematic analysis of a company's situation and the construction and assessment of strategic courses of action—without imposing too rigid constraints on future actions. Starting from this assumption, a variety of strategy analysis tools have been devised in the past decades. Examples include the *Balanced Scorecard* [5], the *Five Forces* framework [6], and *Portfolio Analysis*. However, while remaining popular, these tools exhibit remarkable shortcomings. For instance, important organizational context is neglected. This comes at a price of increased difficulty when interpreting a strategic plan and the danger of divergent interpretations. Furthermore, essential concepts (e.g., 'perspective' or 'activity') remain too ambiguous, underspecified, or even misleading. Finally, extant strategy analysis tools do not account for the peculiarities of information technology (IT), treating it largely as a black box.

Enterprise models provide detailed organizational context relevant to and necessary for strategic planning [7,8]. Specifically, enterprise models allow to identify enablers and inhibitors of strategic change in an organization at a detailed level, in particular concerning the interplay of business patterns and information systems. Thus, they provide a promising foundation to support strategic decision processes in a methodical way. However, even elaborate enterprise modeling methods such as ArchiMate [9], Multi-perspective Enterprise Modeling (MEMO) [8], or For Enterprise Modeling (4EM) [7] do not offer nuanced concepts to describe and (re-)assess corporate strategies, and they lack comprehensive support for the task of strategic planning. Some conceptual modeling methods to analyze strategic issues have been proposed (e.g., [10]). But these are not meant as extensions to comprehensive enterprise modeling methods.

The purpose of this paper is to prepare the design of a DSML in support of strategic planning using enterprise models. Specifically, the contribution of this paper is threefold. First, we analyze traditional strategy analysis tools and critically reconstruct their concepts. This approach is based on the assumption that before reshaping or developing new concepts, it is reasonable to consider and critically review what concepts are well-accepted in practice. Second, we demonstrate how the reconstructed concepts relate to, and can be integrated with, an existing enterprise modeling method. Third, we discuss prospects and limitations of the identified concepts and outline routes for future research.

The paper is structured as follows. In Sect. 2, we consider theoretical groundwork, before analyzing selected strategy analysis tools in Sect. 3. Key concepts of these tools are reconstructed in Sect. 4, in which we also illustrate and discuss integration points with enterprise models. We provide closing remarks in Sect. 5.

2 Theoretical Background: Strategies and Decisions

In order to prepare our analysis and reconstruction of existing strategy analysis tools, this section provides a brief synthesis of theoretical arguments centering around the notions of 'strategy' and 'decision' in the literature.

The Notion of Strategy. One of the first works in management literature explicitly referring to the term 'strategy' was *Strategy and Structure* by Chandler [11]. Since then, a large body of literature on the subject emerged (e.g., [2,4,12,13]), producing a wide range of definitions of the term 'strategy'. Chandler, for instance, defines strategy as "the determination of the basic longterm goals and objectives of an enterprise and the adoption of courses of action and the allocation of resources necessary for carrying out these goals" [11, p. 13]. For Hofer, a strategy is "concerned with the development of a viable match between the opportunities and risks present in the external environment and the organization's capabilities and resources for exploiting these opportunities" [14, p. 3]. In these interpretations, the term strategy is mostly prescriptive in nature, and based on the presumption of a formal, systematic planning process. Further, these definitions indicate a core set of domain-specific terms—including 'goal', 'resource', and 'external environment'—without which it seems hard to communicate about the concept of strategy.

However, the traditional view of strategic planning has been subject to considerable critique (see, e.g., [4, pp. 110–111]). In later work, therefore, varied other research branches emerged in the literature. One branch, although still accepting basic assumptions of traditional planning, pays less attention to a formalized planning process and more strongly focuses on the contents of a strategy (such as competition, resources, and competencies; e.g., [12]). Another branch, for example, is concerned with how strategies actually form. This branch, descriptive in nature, places emphasis on concepts like 'organizational learning' or 'strategic thought' (e.g., [15–17]). In line with the indicated variety, a paradigm change is observable since the 1990s, from the belief in one 'true' definition towards a pluralistic view where strategy is seen as a multi-dimensional construct whose understanding depends on the perspective(s) taken [18].

Strategic Decision Processes. Although there are many views of what a 'strategy' entails in particular, one of the most common ways to frame the processes in which strategies are devised is as strategic *decision processes* (see, e.g., [19]). Just as for the concept of 'strategy', different views on decisions have been advanced. A traditional view, found in major parts of decision research, states that the "one essential element of a decision is the existence of *alternatives* [...], a choice to make" [20, p. 2]. In this view, the "rational" decision maker's task is often seen to consist in choosing among given alternatives so that given goals are attained to the highest degree possible (see, e.g., [21, pp. 79–109]).

However, it follows from the above account of 'strategy' that a purely choice-centric view is incomplete. First, it disregards the observation that often, in considering strategic courses of action, there are no or only few 'alternatives' given at the outset (e.g., [22, pp. 251, 255–256] [2, pp. 15–16]). Instead, there is a need to *search* for, or *construct*, possible alternatives (e.g., [2, pp. 15–16] [23, p. 58]). This is considered in a process view of decision making. In this view, it has been observed that strategic decision processes are typically time-consuming and highly fragmented [19, p. 46] [24, pp. 203–205], "taking years and involving many members of the organization" [23, p. 60]. In particular, the *construction* of alternatives has been recognized as important; "a great deal of effort goes into the development of solutions, especially design activity, since solutions must often be custom made" [23, p. 61]. In this connection, research has also highlighted the close connection between organizational decision making and *problem solving* (e.g., [25, pp. 855–856] [26, p. 321]). A problem solving view emphasizes that decision processes are largely concerned with *analyzing*, constructing, interpreting, and revising representations of the (problem) situation in question [26, p. 321–324]. Specifically, it has been suggested that strategic problems are "ill-structured, nonroutine, and complex" [27, p. 379–380]. Similarly, strategy has also been claimed to be a 'wicked' problem, which "has innumerable causes, is tough to describe, and doesn't have a right answer" [28, p. 100]. In sum, (strategic) decision processes need to incorporate, rather than presuppose, the construction of problem definitions, goals, and alternatives [26, p. 321–324].

3 Strategy Analysis Tools: Overview and Assessment

As strategic decision-making requires to structure and interpret rich and ambiguous (problem) situations, it comes at no surprise that numerous analysis tools have been proposed to support this task (for an overview, see, e. g., [29]). In this section, we conceptually analyze five widely discussed and applied tools to identify their inherent domain-specific concepts. This study is meant to help prepare the design of a future DSML in which refined or extended versions of the identified concepts might appear to support strategic decision processes.

Taking into account studies on the dissemination of analysis tools in practice [30–32], five tools have been selected as a starting point: *SWOT analysis*, *Portfolio Analysis*, the *Balanced Score Card*, Porter's *Value Chain*, and his *Five Forces* framework. The selection is neither exhaustive nor representative, but the selected tools have certainly received widespread recognition and are assumed to indicate concepts that are in common use in the domain of discourse. Following a synoptic overview of each strategy analysis tool that outlines its purpose and key concepts (Sect. 3.1), we assess the suitability of the tools and their concepts with regard to devising a DSML (Sect. 3.2). To improve clarity, identified key concepts will appear *in italics*. Common visualizations for each tool are shown in Fig. 1, alongside semantic nets summarizing the distilled key concepts.

3.1 Synoptic Overview of Selected Strategy Analysis Tools

SWOT Analysis. Although its origin remains unclear, SWOT analysis started to gain traction in the 1960s with its inclusion in textbooks at Harvard Business School [33]. SWOT analysis is based on a simple idea: to start devising basic strategic directions, it is useful to assess the internal and external context of the firm in a contrasting way [34, p. 342]. For this purpose, SWOT analysis builds on a small number of key concepts. *'Strength'* and *'Weakness'* are intended to capture abilities and limitations of a company and are interpreted as *'Internal Factors'*. *'Opportunity'* and *'Threat'* serve to analyze a firm's environment with respect to either new possibilities or obstructions for current ways of doing business. They are interpreted as *'External Factors'*. Implicit in this structure is also the idea of a *'Positive Valence'* or a *'Negative Valence'* ascribed to each factor. SWOT analysis is typically visualized in the form of a 2×2 grid (Fig. 1, pt. 1a).

Portfolio Analysis is used to consider the allocation of resources to different strategic areas [34, pp. 347–349]. At its core, it is even more generic than SWOT analysis. In essence, portfolio analysis advises to place concrete *'Values'* for a *'Strategic Object'* of a *'Portfolio'* along two specific *'Dimensions'* (see Fig. 1, pt. 2a). This general idea can be illustrated by means of one of its more popular variants, the Boston Consulting Group Matrix (BCG Matrix) [34, pp. 353–363]. The *'Strategic Object'* of analysis here is a strategic business unit (SBU) or a product. The first dimension is market growth, supposed to express the attractiveness of a *'Market'*. The second dimension is relative market share, assumed to represent the competitiveness of the *'Strategic Object'*. The BCG approach (as other variants of portfolio analysis) advises to divide the overall portfolio area into different *'Quadrants'*, where each *'Quadrant'* is linked to a different *'Norm Strategy'* (an idealized recommended strategy formulation) [34, pp. 353–363].

The *Balanced Scorecard* (BSC) has been developed by Kaplan and Norton as a "mechanism for strategy implementation" [35, pp. 37–38]. The BSC is based on several assumptions [5,36]. First, corporate strategy and vision are essentially considered in terms of interlinked *'Objectives'*. To assess the attainment of *'Objectives'*, it is suggested to define (quantifiable) *'Measures'* for all objectives [5]. Second, it is assumed that a strategy can (and should) cover objectives assigned to different *'Perspectives'*. An essential contribution of the BSC is the differentiation of financial and non-financial perspectives. The original BSC includes four perspectives: *'Financial'*, *'Customer'*, *'Internal Processes'*, and *'Learning & Growth'*. Third, the BSC assumes 'causal' relationships among objectives in the sense that the attainment of *'Objectives'* from non-financial perspectives is assumed to contribute to achieving *'Objectives'* in the financial perspective, meant to capture organizational performance [34, p. 221]. In a later version [35], two further concepts are added: *'Targets'* describe concrete values to be reached for a given *'Measure'*, while *'Initiatives'* describe courses of action intended to achieve *'Targets'*. Figure 1, pt. 3a, shows a typical visualization of the BSC.

The *Value Chain* (VC) was proposed by Porter [37]. Its main objective is to assist in identifying (possible) competitive advantages of a firm by focusing on its presumed value creation [34, p. 305]. The main concept *'Value Chain'* is decomposed into so-called *'Activities'*. These represent a functional abstraction; temporal aspects are not accounted for. *'Activities'* are distinguished into *'Primary Activities'* (directly contributing to value creation) and *'Support Activities'* (needed to perform primary activities) [34, p. 307]. The prototypical definition of a Value Chain includes a fixed set of five *'Primary Activities'* and four *'Support Activities'*, shown in Fig. 1, pt. 4a. When using a *'Value Chain'*, it is suggested to reflect on how each *'Activity'* is, and could possible be, decomposed in more detail. In line with Porter's general positioning view [37], competitive advantages

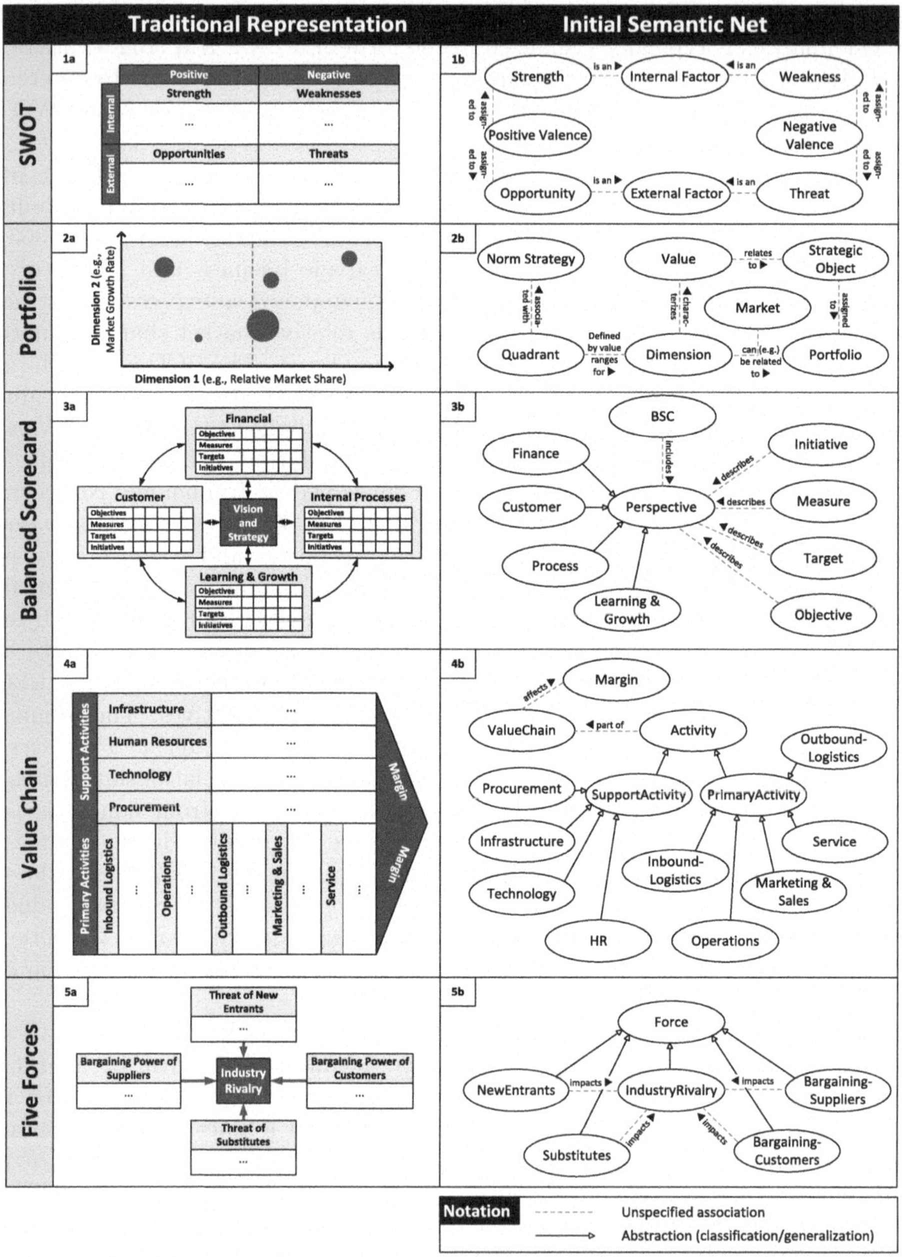

Fig. 1. Strategy analysis tools: traditional representations and initial semantic nets

are hypothesized to result from how the performance of *'Activities'* compares to competitors (or an industry average) in the same market [34, p. 308]. The configuration of all *'Activities'*, finally, is assumed to affect the overall *'Margin'*.

The *Five Forces* framework has also been proposed by Porter [6,38]. In contrast to the Value Chain, this framework more explicitly concentrates on the industry environment. The basic assumption is that an interplay of five forces determines an industry's intensity of competition and, as a result, potentials for generating profits [34, p. 311]. Accordingly, the core concept is *'Force'*. More specifically, Porter posits the existence of five kind of forces [6,38]: (1) The threat of *'New Entrants'* (affected by, e.g., market entry barriers like needed production technologies); (2) the threat of *'Substitutes'* (affected by the availability of alternatives for a firm's products or services, like new technologies); (3) the *'Bargaining Power of Suppliers'* and (4) the *'Bargaining Power of Customers'* (affected by, e.g., the number of possible suppliers or customers, respectively), and (5) *'Industry Rivalry'* (affected by the combined strength of the other forces) [38]. Considering these forces, Porter suggests to position a "company where the forces are the weakest" [6, p. 24]. Porter also provides a list of factors assumed to influence the strength of the different forces, alongside various guidelines on how to react to certain force constellations. When using this tool, it is customary to draw on a representation as shown in Fig. 1, pt. 5a [6].

3.2 Assessment: Conceptual Suitability for Enterprise Modeling

All of the analysis tools portrayed above have been discussed in the literature for long. In these discussions, they have been subject to fundamental criticism. Generally, they have been criticized for simplifying a complex 'strategic problem' (cf. Sect. 2) to an unacceptable degree by fading out important contextual aspects [39,40]. Fundamental criticism also pertains to questionable epistemological assumptions underlying the tools. For instance, it is seen as a misconception to assume cause-and-effect relationships between financial and non-financial measures, as is suggested by [5,35] (for a discussion, see [41]). Beyond such general criticism, devising modeling concepts in the context of enterprise modeling comes with specific requirements concerning conceptual clarity. Below, therefore, we assess the suitability of the analysis tools' specification of key concepts as well as the proposed (or missing) abstractions in respect of the design of a DSML.

It applies to all analysis tools that key concepts are not precisely, i.e., unequivocally, let alone formally, defined. The intended meaning of concepts as well as their intended usage in the context of an analysis tool is typically described in natural language and illustrated by a few examples which leaves room for unintended interpretation. Important concepts such as 'value' or 'strength' are not defined at all, consequently referring to a colloquial understanding. Resolving the resulting ambiguities during conceptual reconstruction is not trivial, not only because of careless concept definitions and the difficulties resulting from reconstructing implicit (potentially intended) meaning from natural language descriptions, but also because of the peculiarities of a contingent subject.

It is characteristic for the studied tools that their core concepts reflect the perspective of top management, that is, a high level of abstraction where most details are faded out on purpose. However, oftentimes it is important to develop a more detailed appreciation of selected aspects. For example, when reflecting about possible (strategic) paths to achieve desired goals, it is necessary to consider actors, resources, IT, and related aspects. Also, to develop a grounded assessment of internal processes, it oftentimes appears mandatory to analyze aspects of the control flow or the resource consumption. However, none of the investigated tools provides concepts for supporting analyses at that level of detail. Moreover, none of the tools provides an elaborate conception of the IT infrastructure which, if it is accounted for at all, is represented as a black box.

A particular challenge for conceptual reconstruction of the studied tools results from a lack of explicit abstraction. For example, it remains unclear whether 'primary activity' and 'support activity' in the Value Chain are meant to be *instances of* a meta concept 'activity' or rather *sub-concepts*. Furthermore, concepts such as 'objective', 'activity', and 'dimension' are introduced without defining a level of classification. For specifying a DSML, however, it is essential to make an informed design decision at which language level to provide a concept (e.g., at type, meta type, or even a higher level). Arriving at such a decision is not trivial for many of the identified concepts (e.g., what is an *instance* of a 'dimension', and how can a *type* of a 'dimension' be meaningfully specified?).

4 A Conceptual Reconstruction in the Context of Enterprise Modeling

The previous analysis has brought to the fore a number of concepts for strategic analyses. The discussion has also indicated a number of shortcomings of the considered tools. To prepare the development of a DSML to support strategic decision processes in future work, we aim to reconstruct and integrate the distilled concepts in a meta model in this section. In doing so, we also intend to place the reconstructed concepts in the context of an existing enterprise modeling method, seeking to outline integration possibilities with concepts already available. This exercise is intended to help clarify two questions. First, we wish to analyze whether embedding concepts of selected strategy analysis tools in traditional enterprise modeling languages can provide a meaningful basis to support strategic decision processes. Second, we would like to examine whether the design of language concepts for strategic analyses is associated with specific challenges.

We will first describe the procedure followed (Sect. 4.1), before presenting the meta model (Sect. 4.2). Following this, we will discuss resulting insights and point out prospects and challenges for a future development of a DSML (Sect. 4.3). To illustrate the integration possibilities with existing enterprise modeling methods, we will draw on a method for multi-perspective enterprise modeling (MEMO) [8]. This enterprise modeling method is selected because it has been found to feature an especially comprehensive set of modeling concepts [42].

4.1 Background and Procedure

In order to arrive at a meta model that couches the identified concepts in the context of enterprise modeling, we conducted several steps. In a first step, we prepared a straightforward representation of identified concepts using semantic nets (Fig. 1, part b). Subsequently, we merged the initial semantic nets into a single coherent semantic net and refined it successively by adding detail, removing conceptual redundancies, and identifying abstractions (e.g., generalizations). The final semantic net served as a foundation for creating a meta model.

To specify the meta model, we used the Flexible Meta-Modeling and Execution Language ($FMML^x$) [43]. This language features a recursive language architecture, enabling an arbitrary number of classification levels. It also includes 'intrinsic features' to define (meta) attributes, operations, and associations on M_n that are to be instantiated at level M_m, where $m < n - 1$. Intrinsic features are visually represented by small black squares attached to model elements. For example, an intrinsic feature reading '0' (e.g., attached to an attribute at M_2) states that the attribute is to be instantiated at level M_0 only.

In the design of the meta model, we were immediately confronted with a number of challenges. First, the design of language concepts generally requires a decision as to whether a concept should be part of the language (usually, at M_2) or rather be specified with the language (usually, at M_1). It does not come as a surprise the level of classification seems contingent for most reconstructed concepts. Furthermore, none of the original concepts was defined with properties that could directly be mapped to attributes. This required us to conceive of possible useful (example) attributes. The next section will present preliminary design solutions, identifying implications for future work (discussed in Sect. 4.3).

4.2 Meta Model

As a result of interpreting and refining the semantics nets, a meta model has been devised that incorporates the concepts extracted from the analysis tools and integrates them with concepts of MEMO. The meta model is shown in Fig. 2. The reconstructed concepts have been assigned to four perspectives, indicated by the gray colored boxes. In addition, blue colored areas are found in which MEMO concepts are placed that constitute possible integration points for the perspective in question (an overview of MEMO concepts is found in [8]). Each perspective encompasses a set of meta types (M_2; elements with a black colored header), reconstructing concepts of one or several analysis tools. To illustrate how concepts could be enriched as part of a future language, we have defined a number of example attributes. Further, for most meta types, example instantiations at type level (M_1; elements with a white colored header) and instance level (M_0; gray colored header) have been added to aid the interpretation of the meta types. This also exemplifies the value of the intrinsic features of the $FMML^x$, enabling to clearly define at which level (meta) model elements are to be instantiated.

The first perspective is *Internal and External Strategic Assessment*, summarizing concepts from SWOT analysis and the Five Forces framework. Central abstractions here include the abstract concept *'StrategicFactor'* (M_2)

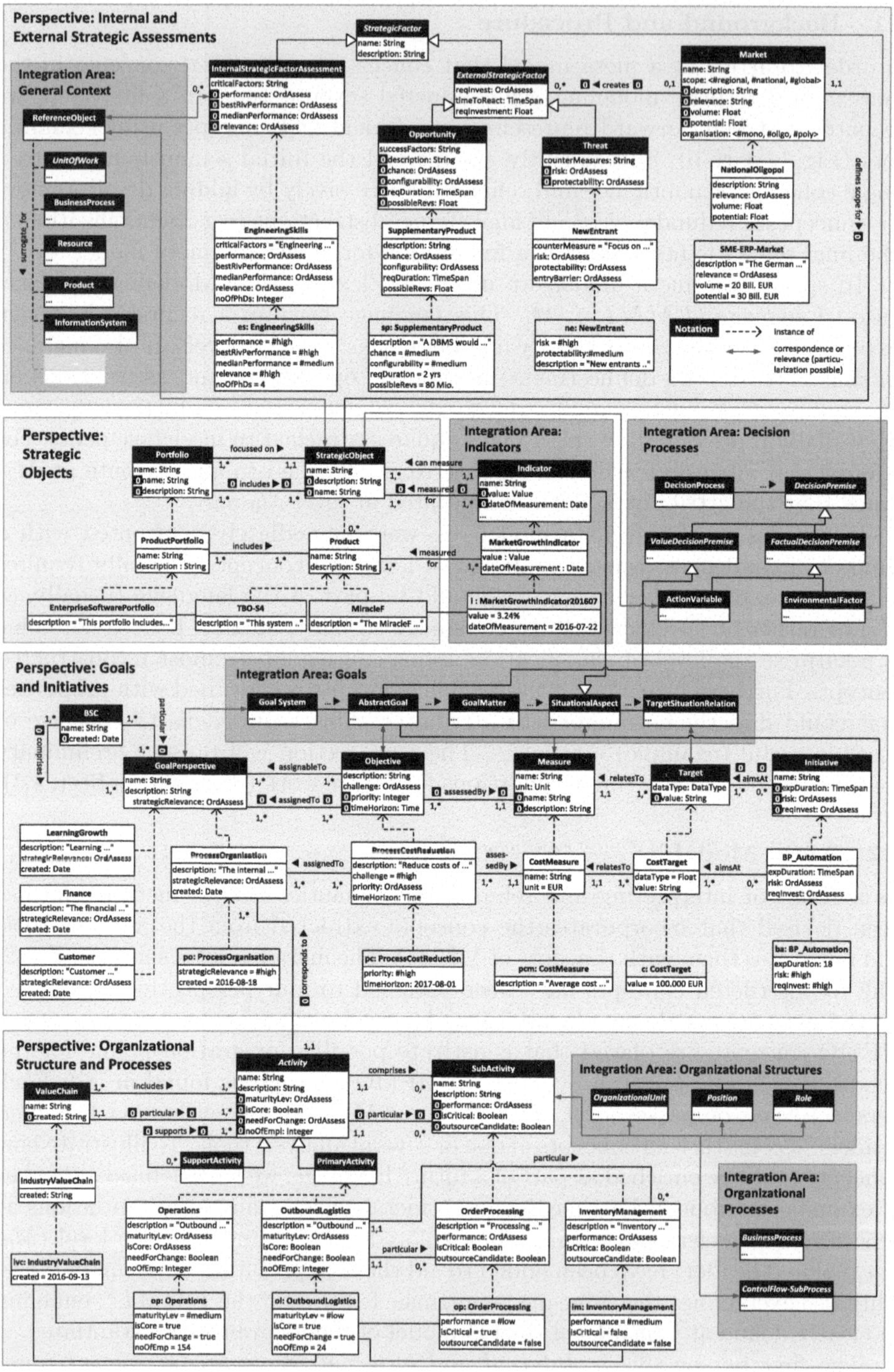

Fig. 2. Meta model including reconstructed strategy concepts (Color figure online)

and its two specializations *'ExternalStrategicFactor'* and *'InternalStrategicFactorAssessment'*. *'Opportunity'* and *'Threat'* are specializations of *'ExternalStrategicFactor'*. Because the Five Forces can be regarded as possible instantiations of *'Threat'* and *'Opportunity'*, they do not appear as dedicated concepts in the meta model. For instance, a *'Threat'* can be instantiated into a *'New Entrant'* on M_1 and a concrete entrant on M_0 (see Fig. 2). The concepts *'Strength'* and *'Weakness'* have been condensed into the concept *'InternalStrategicFactorAssessment'*, located on M_2. This concept is supposed to serve as an unitary way of evaluating whether elements in an enterprise are regarded as a *'Strength'* or a *'Weakness'*. The auxiliary type *'OrdAssess'*, used here and in other concepts, is meant to provide an ordinary assessment for such evaluations (e.g., using values from 'low' to 'high'). The perspective *Strategic Objects* pools concepts drawn from portfolio analysis, most importantly *'Portfolio'* and *'StrategicObject'*. In this conceptualization, a 'Product' or 'SBU' would result as an instantiation at M_1, while a specific product (e.g. 'TBO-S4') would be located on M_0. Rather than relying on a generic concept *'Dimension'*, a domain-specific MEMO concept, *'Indicator'*, is used to arrange *'StrategicObject'* for purposes of comparison. Furthermore, portfolio analysis has prompted us to include the concept *'Market'*, as this concept is often referenced in dimensions to consider *'StrategicObjects'*. However, because a *'Market'* is closely related to external factors, it is placed in the perspective above. The third perspective is called *Goals and Initiatives*. This perspective solely includes concepts that have been reconstructed from the BSC. Similarly, the fourth perspective *Organizational Structure and Processes* contains concepts reconstructed from the Value Chain. Note that *'Activity'* and *'SubActivity'* are not identical with the concept of a *'BusinessProcess'*. They instead represent a functional abstraction, such as *'Outbound Logistics'* (at level M_1; see Fig. 2).

Importantly, for concepts from all perspectives, integration points with existing MEMO concepts have been identified. These appear in the blue colored areas. For example, goals occupy a central role in the meta model, representing the prime integration point for the perspective advocated by the BSC. The corresponding MEMO language GoalML provides various concepts that can be mapped directly to BSC concepts (e.g., a BSC 'Measure' corresponds to a 'SituationalAspect' in GoalML). Of course, the full MEMO language also provides a richer way of describing goals than is enabled by the BSC. Similarly, there are MEMO languages to describe organizational structures and processes (bottom perspective) and decision processes (second perspective). More generally, when intending to assess reference objects of varied nature (top perspective), a comprehensive enterprise modeling method would enable to integrate the assessment concepts with diverse concepts to describe elements in an organization. This could be realized using a placeholder concept such as *'ReferenceObject'* (see Fig. 2, top left). For present purposes, MEMO concepts are linked to the reconstructed concepts only by means of a green colored placeholder association. This association expresses that a correspondence or relevance exists, but it does not specify how it should be specified in more detail as part of a future DSML. For example, it can be found that a *'SubActivity'* (bottom perspective in Fig. 2) is generally related to MEMO concepts describing organizational structures (e.g., *'OrganizationalUnit'*) and dynamic abstractions (e.g., *'BusinessProcess'*). Disentangling these relations would imply considering associations of different nature, such as responsibility and decomposition relations, which further indicates the level of detail an enterprise modeling context would offer for strategic analyses. Finally, this same point is also stressed by the fact that the various MEMO languages are integrated (see the links between the blue colored areas). In consequence, the integration of strategy analysis concepts with enterprise modeling concepts also establishes a closer connection between the original strategy concepts, potentially enabling a richer way of thinking about the problem domain.

4.3 Discussion: Lessons Learned and Implications

The meta model in the previous section has shown that enterprise modeling in fact provides a rich conceptual framework into which strategy analysis concepts can be embedded in meaningful ways. Below, we discuss key insights and implications for future research that have emerged during this conceptual study.

Implicitness of the Strategy Concept. It is an interesting observation that although all considered tools are intended to aid strategic reflections in one way or another, no tool introduces an explicit and clear concept of *'Strategy'*. In consequence, when intending to design a DSML for strategic support, it needs to be clarified whether it makes sense to specify a distinct 'Strategy' modeling concept at all or whether strategy should be regarded as an abstract notion that emerges from a set of other modeling concepts. This is related to the next issue.

Conveyed Perspectives. While no considered tool provides an explicit strategy concept, all of them, by virtue of their tool-specific concepts, convey a specific notion of what is relevant for strategizing. In general, it can be concluded that many of these concepts are *domain-specific* in nature. This contrasts with classical general-purpose decision modeling approaches, which exclusively provide generic concepts like 'alternative' (see [44]). Two more specific points follow. First, in line with the theoretical strategy discourse (cf. Sect. 2), it appears that strategy can in fact be regarded as a multi-perspective construct, irreducible to a single real-world aspect. Using Berger and Luckmann's words, strategy might be understood as "an object of thought" which "becomes progressively clearer with this accumulation of different perspectives on it" [45, p. 22]. Second, when thinking about support for strategic decision processes, it follows that each tool will direct attention at certain real-world aspects and of necessity neglecting others. In fact, this is an important pitfall inherent in model-based decision aids in general (see [46]). The practical implications are significant because, as has been discussed in Sec. 2, problems considered in strategic decision processes are in need of constant (re-)interpretation and (re-)formulation. Overreliance on single tools might thus lead to a neglect of important aspects (for example, a Value Chain will by definition not be able to systematize strategic goals). In consequence, researchers should devote attention to a modeling language design that fosters a reflective account of multiple perspectives on strategy and and strategic problems. At the same time, language concepts for different perspectives should nonetheless be integrated—to be able to analyze dependencies among them.

Significance of 'Qualitative' Aspects. As a further issue, many concepts in strategic planning seem to resist a convincing characterization through attributes. This seems to occur because, from an ontological view, these identified concepts relate to qualitative *judgments* rather than to (real-world) objects whose state can be distinguished. When considering the meta model (Fig. 2), this is reflected in the many attributes with the data type *'OrdAssess'*, which is supposed to enable a judgment on an ordinal scale. With respect to language design, the issue suggests to develop conceptual means that stimulate a critical review of values assigned to evaluative attributes to avoid misleading models.

Need for Theoretical Reconciliation and Clarity. The analysis has shown that any attempt to design a DSML for supporting strategic reflections needs to conduct significant conceptual and theoretical groundwork in advance. First, this relates to the inherent conceptual vagueness of the domain (cf. Sects. 2 and 3.2). Beyond the examples considered in the meta model (Sect. 2), it would be necessary to clarify a number of further key terms in the domain (e.g., 'strategic plan'). A second implications concerns the clarification of theoretical claims. It is important to critically consider to what extent theoretical hypotheses in the strategy literature should be accepted for the desired modeling language.

Tool Support. Finally, the meta model indicates how tools for enterprise modelling could be enhanced with components for strategic planning. For this purpose, the multilevel approach used to specify the meta model seems to be especially promising. Since the underlying architecture allows for a common representation of models and code [43], it can be used to integrate an enterprise modeling environment with enterprise software. Such a 'self-referential enterprise system' [47] could enable the runtime monitoring of strategy execution. This would, however, first require to tackle the above-indicated challenges for the development of a comprehensive DSML to support strategic reflections.

5 Conclusions

Strategic decision processes are thought to significantly affect an organization's long-term success, motivating the development of strategy analysis tools. In this paper, we have conducted a conceptual analysis of popular practical tools, reconstructing their key concepts in the form of a meta model and exploring potentials for the integration with enterprise modeling. The study has yielded several contributions. The presented meta model outlines how enterprise modeling could be enriched with concepts for strategic planning, while conversely showing a way of augmenting strategy analysis tools with relevant context. Furthermore, the analysis has revealed a number of challenges as an orientation for the future design of a DSML to aid strategic decision processes. Our future research agenda covers several aspects. First, we will (re-)investigate and expand the outlined integration potentials between strategy analysis tools and enterprise modeling in-depth. Second, we will conduct a more comprehensive requirements analysis for a DSML to support strategic planning, considering both the body of theoretical work as well as practical use case scenarios for strategic analysts, managers, and consultants. Finally, we will investigate the design of software tools to analyze and simulate possible paths for strategic development using enterprise models.

References

1. Fayol, H.: General and Industrial Management. Pitman, London (1949)
2. Ansoff, H.I.: Corporate Strategy: An Analytic Approach to Business Policy for Growth and Expansion. McGraw-Hill, New York (1965)
3. Andrews, K.R.: Concept of Corporate Strategy. Richard D Irwin, New York (1987)
4. Mintzberg, H.: Rise and Fall of Strategic Planning. Free Press, New York (1994)
5. Kaplan, R.S., Norton, D.P.: The balanced scorecard - measures that drive performance. Harvard Bus. Rev. **70**(1), 71–79 (1992)
6. Porter, M.E.: The five competitive forces that shape strategy. Harvard Bus. Rev. **1**, 23–40 (2008)
7. Sandkuhl, K., Stirna, J., Persson, A., Wißotzki, M.: Enterprise Modeling: Tackling Business Challenges with the 4EM Method. Springer, Heidelberg (2014)
8. Frank, U.: Multi-perspective enterprise modeling: foundational concepts, prospects and future research challenges. Softw. Syst. Model. **13**(3), 941–962 (2013)
9. The Open Group: ArchiMate 2.0 Specification: Open Group Standard. The Open Group Series. Van Haren, Zaltbommel (2012)
10. Horkoff, J., Barone, D., Jiang, L., Yu, E.S., Amyot, D., Borgida, A., Mylopoulos, J.: Strategic business modeling: representation and reasoning. Softw. Syst. Model. **13**(3), 1015–1041 (2014)
11. Chandler, A.D.: Strategy and Structure. MIT Press, Cambridge (1962)
12. Porter, M.E.: Competitive Advantage. Free Press, New York (1985)
13. Kaplan, R.S., Norton, D.P.: Strategy Maps: Converting Intangible Assets into Tangible Outcomes. Harvard Business School Press, Boston (2004)
14. Hofer, C.W.: Some preliminary research on patterns of strategic behavior. In: Academy of Management Proceedings, pp. 46–54 (1973)
15. Huff, A.S.: Mapping Strategic Knowledge. Thousand Oaks (2002)
16. Reger, R.K., Huff, A.S.: Strategic groups: a cognitive perspective. Strateg. Manag. J. **14**(2), 103–123 (1993)
17. Barr, P.S., Stimpert, J.L., Huff, A.S.: Cognitive change, strategic action, and organizational renewal. Strateg. Manag. J. **13**(S1), 15–36 (1992)
18. Cummings, S.: Strategy: past, present, future. In: The Sage Handbook of New Approaches in Management And Organization, pp. 184–194. SAGE, Los Angeles (2008)
19. Harrison, E.F.: A process perspective on strategic decision making. Manag. Decis. **34**(1), 46–53 (1996)
20. Kirkwood, C.W.: Strategic Decision Making: Multiobjective Decision Analysis with Spreadsheets. Wadsworth, Belmont (1997)

21. Simon, H.A.: Administrative Behavior: A Study of Decision-Making Processes in Administrative Organization, 3rd edn. Free Press, New York (1976)
22. Mintzberg, H., Raisinghani, D., Théorêt, A.: The structure of unstructured decision processes. Adm. Sci. Q. **21**(2), 246–275 (1976)
23. Mintzberg, H.: The Structuring of Organizations: A Synthesis of the Research. Prentice-Hall, Englewood Cliffs (1979)
24. Becker, A.: Rationalität strategischer Entscheidungsprozesse: Ein strukturationstheoretisches Konzept. Deutscher Universitätsverlag, Wiesbaden (1996)
25. Lang, J.R., Dittrich, J.E., White, S.E.: Managerial problem solving models: a review and proposal. Acad. Manag. Rev. **3**(4), 854–866 (1978)
26. Dery, D.: Decision-making, problem-solving and organizational learning. Omega **11**(4), 321–328 (1983)
27. Dean Jr., J.W., Sharfman, M.P.: Does decision process matter? A study of strategic decision-making effectiveness. Acad. Manag. J. **39**(2), 368–392 (1996)
28. Camillus, J.C.: Strategy as a wicked problem. Harv. Bus. Rev. **86**(5), 98–106 (2008)
29. Grant, R.M.: Contemporary Strategy Analysis, 9th edn. Wiley, Chichester (2016)
30. Stenfors, S., Tanner, L., Haapalinna, I.: Executive use of strategy tools: building shared understanding through boundary objects. In: Frontiers of E-Business Research 2004 (Proceedings), pp. 635–645 (2004)
31. Clark, D.N.: Strategic management tool usage: a comparative study. Strateg. Chang. **6**(7), 417–427 (1997)
32. Gunn, R., Williams, W.: Strategic tools: an empirical investigation into strategy in practice in the UK. Strateg. Chang. **16**(5), 201–216 (2007)
33. Learned, E.P., Christensen, R.C., Andrews, K.R., Guth, W.D.: Business Policy - Text and Cases, 1st edn. Richard D. Irwin Inc., New York (1969)
34. Macharzina, K., Wolf, J.: Unternehmensführung: Das internationale Managementwissen: Konzepte - Methoden - Praxis, 7th edn. Gabler, Wiesbaden (2010)
35. Kaplan, R.S., Norton, D.P.: The Balanced Scorecard: Translating Strategy into Action. Harvard Business Press, Brighton (1996)
36. Kaplan, R.S., Norton, D.P.: Putting the balanced scorecard to work. Harvard Bus. Rev. **5**, 134–147 (1993)
37. Porter, M.E.: The value chain and competitive advantage. In: Barnes, D. (ed.) Understanding Business. Understanding Business Behaviour, pp. 50–66. Routledge, London (2001)
38. Porter, M.E.: Competitive Strategy: Techniques for Analyzing Industries and Competitors. Free Press, New York (1980)
39. Derkinderen, F.G., Crum, R.L.: Pitfalls in using portfolio techniques? Assessing risk and potential. Long Range Plan. **17**(2), 129–136 (1984)
40. Helms, M.M., Nixon, J.: Exploring swot analysis-where are we now? A review of academic research from the last decade. J. Econ. Manag. **3**(3), 215–251 (2010)
41. Norreklit, H.: The balance on the balanced scorecard a critical analysis of some of its assumptions. Manag. Acc. Res. **11**(1), 65–88 (2000)
42. Bock, A., Kaczmarek, M., Overbeek, S., Heß, M.: A comparative analysis of selected enterprise modeling approaches. In: Frank, U., Loucopoulos, P., Pastor, Ó., Petrounias, I. (eds.) PoEM 2014. LNBIP, vol. 197, pp. 148–163. Springer, Heidelberg (2014). doi:10.1007/978-3-662-45501-2_11
43. Frank, U.: Multilevel modeling: toward a new paradigm of conceptual modeling and information systems design. Bus. Inf. Syst. Eng. **6**(6), 319–337 (2014)

44. Bock, A.: The concepts of decision making: an analysis of classical approaches and avenues for the field of enterprise modeling. In: Ralyté, J., et al. (eds.) PoEM 2015. LNBIP, vol. 235, pp. 306–321. Springer, Heidelberg (2015). doi:10.1007/978-3-319-25897-3_20
45. Berger, P.L., Luckmann, T.: The Social Construction of Reality: A Treatise in the Sociology of Knowledge. Doubleday, Garden City (1966)
46. Bock, A.: How modeling language shapes decisions: problem-theoretical arguments and illustration of an example case. In: Schmidt, R., Guédria, W., Bider, I., Guerreiro, S., Buckley, O. (eds.) BPMDS/EMMSAD 2016. LNBIP, vol. 248, pp. 383–398. Springer, Heidelberg (2016). doi:10.1007/978-3-319-39429-9_24
47. Frank, U., Strecker, S.: Beyond ERP Systems: An Outline of Self-Referential Enterprise Systems. ICB Research Report 31, University of Duisburg-Essen, Essen (2009)

Strategic Enterprise Architectures

Evellin Cardoso[1(✉)], John Mylopoulos[1], Alejandro Mate[1,2], and Juan Trujillo[2]

[1] University of Trento, Trento, Italy
{evellin.souzacardoso,john.mylopoulos}@unitn.it
[2] University of Alicante, Alicante, Spain
{amate,jtrujillo}@dlsi.ua.es

Abstract. Enterprise models are useful managerial tools for decision making and control, supporting the planning and design of enterprise strategic objectives as well as day-to-day operations. Although much research on the topic has been carried out since the 80s, most approaches offer rudimentary support for the representation of goal-related concepts, focusing either on the representation of strategic or operational goals, lacking a comprehensive ontology for goals. In contrast, this paper is interested in: (a) delineating differences between various shades of goals (mission, vision, strategic, tactical and operational goals) and operations, (b) proposing a hierarchical architecture for strategic enterprise models that includes goals and the operations/processes through which they are operationalized and (c) offering methodological guidelines on how to elaborate such models.

1 Introduction

Enterprise models are useful managerial tools for decision making and control. They can support the design of an enterprise given its strategic objectives, its long term planning and evolution, as well as its day-to-day operations. Surprisingly, although much research on the topic has been carried out since the 80s, most approaches offer rudimentary support for the representation of goal-related concepts. For example, ArchiMate [1] ignores the existence of operational goals, while Business Process Management (BPM) proposals [9,10,12,14] link operational goals to processes or connect short-term goals to operations, ignoring the existence of long-term, strategic goals.

We are interested in strategic enterprise models that capture strategic and tactical objectives and the processes through which they are realized. Such models are grounded on ontologies of goals of various shades (missions, visions, strategic, tactical, and operational), as well as ontologies of processes and operations. These models can be used both for strategic analysis and planning, as well as business analytics and monitoring. The research baseline for our work is the Business Intelligence Model (a.k.a BIM) [6] and the Business Motivation Model (BMM), an OMG standard [5]. BMM offers a rich vocabulary of concepts for

J. Horkoff et al. (Eds.): PoEM 2016, LNBIP 267, pp. 57–71, 2016.
DOI: 10.1007/978-3-319-48393-1_5

modeling enterprises but lacks in formal rigor. BIM offers a core ontology of strategic enterprise concepts founded on the notions of **goal** and **situation** to define a formal framework for strategic enterprise models.

The main objective of this paper is to improve on BIM by introducing other strategic concepts. In particular, the contributions of this paper can be stated as follows: we delineate the differences in semantics and usage of different shades of goals found in BMM (distinguishing among strategic, tactical and operational goals, mission and vision) and also offer distinctions between the concepts of operation vs. process. Further, we propose a hierarchical architecture for strategic enterprise models that includes goals and the operations/processes through which they are operationalized and finally, we offer methodological guidelines on how to elaborate such models and when should each be used in enterprise modeling.

Our StrategIc ENterprise Architecture (SIENA) modeling framework consists of two views, namely, a Goal and an Operation View. Within the Goal View, our framework distinguishes among three layers of abstraction Strategic, Tactical and Operational, whereas the Operation View depicts the set of operations and processes, i.e., the enterprise process architecture. Further, given that strategic processes may deal with a number of aspects of strategic nature and may vary according to the type and size of an enterprise, we provide methodological guidelines on how to deal with such variability in the elaboration of an enterprise's strategic models. By proposing a richer ontology of goals/operations, we lay the foundations for future reasoning capabilities, but leave the specifics to future work.

This paper is structured as follows: Sect. 2 provides the research baseline for our work that includes conceptualization extracted from Management Sciences and the BIM and BMM frameworks extracted from Conceptual Modeling. Section 3 describes different types of goals and operations proposed by our modeling framework, whereas Sect. 4 provides methodological guidelines on how to elaborate them. Section 5 contrasts our framework with related work and Sect. 6 summarizes the discussion and outlines future work.

2 Baseline

Organizations distinguish three levels of decision-making, *Strategic*, *Tactical* and *Operational* [17]. Inside each level of abstraction, managers have to specify a number of strategic, tactical and operational goals that focus on different enterprise concerns and must be achieved within distinct time frames.

Mission [2,7,19]**.** A formal expression of an organization's purpose, i.e., the reason why the organization exists. An example of mission is "Manufacture both standard and metal products" [2].

Vision [7,19]**.** Comprises a description of a desired future state of the company, meant to close the gap between the current reality and a potential future. An example of vision could be: "To be the market leader of standard and custom metal products in the machine tool industry" [2].

Strategic Goal [19]**.** Represents concrete outcomes or status to be achieved to measure if mission are being achieved [7,17]. They are directional as they guide the strategy towards achieving the organization's mission [7,19]. Further, strategic goals are statements about external and internal company's conditions that reflects company's strategy to succeed on business [17]. Examples of strategic goals are "Improve market share from 15 % to 20 % over the next three years" and "Increase gross margin on current sales" [2].

Tactical Level. Involves the planning of the actual steps required to implement such strategy [17,18].

Tactical Goals (or Objectives) [2,18]**.** Define the outcomes to be achieved by major divisions and departments in the context of strategic goals. Commonly, Strategic goals can be either segmented into tactical goals that specify responsibilities of functional areas (Finance, Production and Marketing) (e.g., "Manufacture 1200000 products at average cost of $19" from Operations [2]) or can define tactics for its corresponding Strategic Goal. In [19], the Border Inc.'s Tactical Goal "Open 20 new stores by the end of the planning period" specifies a tactics for the "Borders will be the leading retail distribution outlet of books in the US" Strategic Goal.

Operational Level. Concerns the planning and management of daily operations responsible for delivering products and services on behalf of the company [17]. Operations implement the tactical initiatives that are elaborated for supporting organization's strategy. Such tactical initiatives are then scheduled and eventually emerge as the set of organization's operation specifications [15].

Operational Goals [2,17]**.** Consists of quantitative and measurable results expected from departments, work groups and individuals within the organization. Most of approaches [2,17] mention that both tactical and operational goals should be achieved by departments. Further analysis also reveals that both types of goals can be scheduled (e.g. "Resolve employee grievances within 3 working days" and "Respond to employee grievances within 24 h"). As tactical and operational goals in Management literature present similar conceptual characteristics, it is also not clear how the achievement of operational goals entails the achievement of tactical goals. Finally, there is also a lack of clear connection of operational goals with their respective operations and the activities that compose such operations.

2.1 Goal and Operation Modeling in Conceptual Modeling

The *Business Intelligence Model (BIM)* [6] enterprise modeling approach links the business-level representation of an enterprise with the data stemmed from databases and data warehouses. In BIM, a *goal* represents an objective of a business which captures strategic enterprise's concerns, such as "Increase sales". Goals may be related by either *refinement* of *influence relationships.* In a refinement relation, goals are decomposed into a finer-grained structure by means of AND/OR relationships, with an AND decomposition supporting a goal to be decomposed in a series of sub-goals and an OR decomposition allowing analysts to model alternative ways of achieving a goal. Influence relationships among goals specify how the satisfaction/denial of one goal implies the (partial) satisfaction/denial of another goal. Influence strengths are modeled using qualitative values: + (weak positive), ++ (strong positive), - (weak negative) and – (strong negative).

Goal models may be enriched with *domain assumptions*, *processes* and *situations*. *Domain assumptions* indicate properties that are assumed to be true for some goal to be achieved. For example, "High demand" must be true for the "Increase Sales" goal to be satisfied and if such assumption is false, then its associated goal is not satisfied. *Processes* can be associated with a particular goal via an "achieves" relation to denote that this process is intended to achieve the goal. Besides domain assumptions and processes, managers are usually interested in foreseeing other aspects that influence the fulfillment strategic goals during enterprise planning. In that respect, SWOT analysis [19] consists of a useful tool to identify internal and external factors that may impact positively or negatively the achievement of strategic goals. SWOT stands for Strengths (internal and favorable factors), Weaknesses (internal and unfavorable factors), Opportunities (external and favorable factors) and Threats (external and unfavorable factors). BIM proposes to model SWOT factors in terms of the concept of *situation*. A situation characterizes a state of affairs (state of the world) in terms of the entities that exist in that state, their properties and interrelations. Favorable situations are represented via positive influence links on goals, whereas unfavorable situations are represented via negative influence links.

The *Business Motivation Model (BMM)* [5] is a specification adopted by OMG for structuring the development, communication and management of business plans in enterprises. Although the importance of BMM justifies its inclusion here (Table 1), we omit a detailed description of its concepts due to space constraints, directing the interested reader to the specification in [5].

Table 1. Summary of concepts from literature together with concepts from our framework

Manag. Sciences	BIM	BMM	SIENA framework
Mission, vision	-	Mission, vision	Mission, vision
Strategic goal	Goal	Goal	Strategic goal
Tactical goal		Objective, strategy, tactics	Tactical goal
Operational goal		-	Operational goal
-	Goal refinements and influences	-	Goal refinements and influences
Operation	Process	-	Operation
-	-	-	Business process
-	Domain assumption	-	Domain assumption
-	Situation	Influencers	Situation

An interpretation of the semantics of definitions and examples of each concept found on Management and Conceptual modeling literatures allowed us to find overlaps and gaps in the conceptualization provided by the three aforementioned proposals of our Baseline (Sect. 2). Table 1 summarizes this discussion by depicting the three areas and their respective correspondences among concepts. Such overlaps and gaps have been used as input in our framework to promote a consistent integration of all concepts in the fourth column of Table 1.

3 The Strategic Enterprise Architecture (SIENA) Modeling Framework

3.1 Goal View

This section introduces the goal-related concepts of our framework following the same three-layered distinction proposed by Management Sciences (i.e., *Strategic*, *Tactical* and *Operational* Layers). Within our *Strategic Layer*, we use the concepts of *Mission*, *Vision* and *Strategic Goals* as can be seen at Table 1. Strategic Goals present key characteristics in Management that we consolidate as follows:

Strategic Goals. Represent goals that specify concrete outcomes that must be achieved to measure the achievement of mission, reflecting the organization's strategy to achieve success in business. Strategic goals are global to the *overall organization* as the entire organization is responsible for their achievement.

As Strategic Goals are global to the entire organization, they represent the problem space of a given enterprise, defining the space of *all* alternatives goals that can be implemented by enterprise. To precisely characterize such variability and unambiguously characterize Strategic Goals, our framework introduces the distinguishing feature of *refinement dimensions*. *Refinement dimensions* correspond to different properties along which goals can be characterized, for example, location, time or product types properties. To exemplify the use of *refinement dimensions*, consider the "Increase sales by 2 % over 3 years" goal in Fig. 1. This parent goal defines the space of all possible *locations* (countries, in this example) in which the company operates. Therefore, this parent goal can be refined into the following sub-goals: "Increase sales in Italy by 2 % over 3 years", "Increase sales in Germany by 2 % over 3 years" and "Increase sales in NL by 2 % over 3 years". Another refinement of the same parent goal across *time* (within the *year* granularity) is also depicted in Fig. 1, yielding the "Increase sales by 2 % over 1st year", "Increase sales by 2 % over 2nd year" and "Increase sales by 2 % over 3rd year" sub-goals.

As Strategic Goals define the space of all possible alternatives, they can be only AND-decomposed, but not OR-decomposed. Positive and negative contributions among Strategic Goals may be used to depict how they influence each other inside the *Strategic Layer*.

Within the *Tactical Layer*, Management literature (Sect. 2) commonly specifies tactical goals either as responsibilities of functional areas or tactics to achieve strategic goals. We consolidate both views in our definition of *Tactical Goals* as follows:

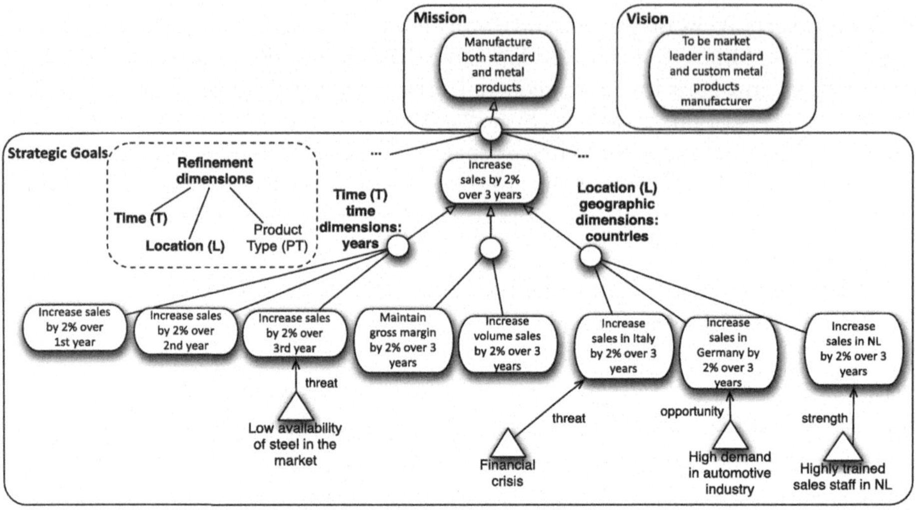

Fig. 1. Strategic goal hierarchy

Tactical Goals. Represent goals that specify particular ways for fulfilling Strategic Goals with the available resources and capabilities of the company. Tactical Goals have no dimensions, but rather depict particular solutions ("tactics") for each point of the refinement dimension in order to fulfill a Strategic Goal. Alternatively, they can also be interpreted as responsibilities to be achieved by specific *functional areas* (marketing, operations, finance and human resources management) to accomplish their specific part of the organization's strategy.

In order to exemplify this discussion, we use the refinement of "Increase sales by 2 % over 3 years" Strategic Goal across the *location* dimension (depicted in Fig. 2). For one of the points of the *location* dimension (Italy) represented by the Strategic sub-goals ("Increase sales in Italy by 2 % over 3 years"), there are two alternative tactics for increasing sales, i.e., promotions ("Increase sales in Italy by 2 % over 3 years through promotions") or create new sales channel ("Increase sales in Italy by 2 % over 3 years by opening new sales channels" Tactical Goal). For other point of the *location* dimension (NL), training sales people corresponds to a tactics for increasing sales ("Increase sales in NL by 2 % over 3 years by training sales staff" Tactical Goal). Concerning the relation of Strategic and Tactical Goals, it said that Tactical goals *implement* Strategic Goals. In the example, it is said that promotions ("Increase sales in Italy by 2 % over 3 years through promotions") is the tactics that *implements* the increase of sales ("Increase sales in Italy by 2 % over 3 years"). Further, Tactical Goals may be structurally refined into sub-goals by means of AND-relationships and several alternative Tactical Goals may be also represented by means of OR-relationships. Finally, they can be also related by positive and negative contributions that depict how Tactical Goals influence each other inside the *Tactical Layer*.

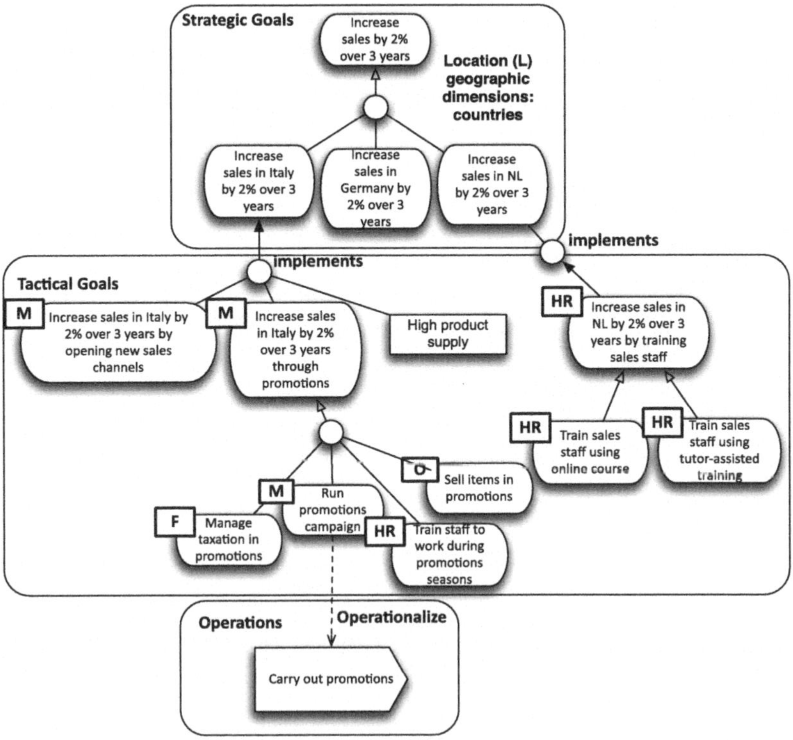

Fig. 2. Tactical goal hierarchy

Once the organization has established its competitive requirements to achieve success in business (Strategic Goals) and subsequently has devised particular ways (Tactical Goals) for implementing such requirements, it has to plan the implementation of such goals with the available company's capabilities by means of the concept of operation. This discussion is reflected in Fig. 2 with the Tactical Goals connected to operations in the *Operations Layer*.

Within the *Operational Layer*, as Management Sciences provides a simplistic treatment for the specification of operational goals, our framework starts with the same definition of this discipline and subsequently refines it:

Operational Goals. Operational goals correspond to the results that must be achieved in the course of performing the organization's operations. Our framework further details their definition by arguing that they represent a description of milestones the operation must reach in order to ensure that they are indeed planning the execution of tactics. Operational goals can be further refined with respect to the entities that are responsible for their achievement as follows:

(Operational) Role Goals. Correspond to goals that specify the results to be achieved by *roles and individuals* in the course of the performing their daily work. In Fig. 3(b), "Choose items for promotion" and "Choose promotions price" consist of operational goals assigned to roles of the company.

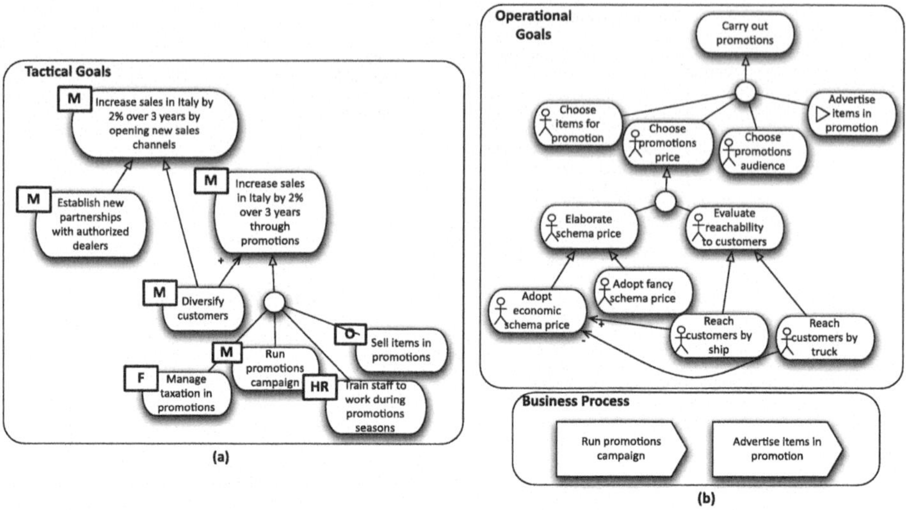

Fig. 3. Operational goals and business processes hierarchy

(Operational) Business Process Goals. Correspond to goals that represent the final state to be achieved by a *business process*. The concept of *Business Process* is explained in Sect. 3.2. In Fig. 3(b), "Advertise items in promotion" is a business process goal as it reflects the final state to be achieved by the "Advertise items in promotion" business process.

Operational Goals may be related by AND/OR-relationships to represent refinements among them as well as Influence relationships (+/− contributions).

As one of the purposes of our modeling framework is to enable managers to adequately plan enterprise's goals and the corresponding operational elements that satisfy them, during the enterprise planning activity is important to foresee the potential future scenarios that facilitate or hinder the achievement of enterprise's goals (i.e., SWOT factors) together with assumptions about the environment. Therefore, our framework inheres the concepts of Situation and Domain Assumption from BIM framework. Situations are represented by triangles attached to goals by means of arrows annotated with the type of influence of situations on goals, whereas Domain Assumptions are represented by means of rectangles attached to goals. Figure 1 admits that a financial crisis may threat the achievement of the "Increase sales in Italy by 2 % over 3 years" Strategic Goal. Further, for both tactics to work for this goal (new sales channel and promotions), analysts assume a high supply of products for Italy (Fig. 2).

3.2 Operations View

While the concept of *Operation* is central within the Management literature as a process that transforms inputs into useful outputs, in our framework, we go further by distinguishing between *Operation* and *Business Process*:

Operation. Consists of a high-level process in charge of planning the execution of a specific tactics. A given operation encompass both *what* has to be achieved (Operational Goals) to concretize the tactics as well as *how* to conduct operational steps to achieve such tactics (business process). As operations plan the implementation of a given strategy, it is said that an operation *operationalize* Strategic or Tactical Goals in our framework, i.e., operations are solutions for Strategic/Tactical goals. Notice also that while operations may run independently, a given tactics is a plan of how to implement a *particular* strategy.

The concept of business process inheres the same definition of *Operation* from Management Sciences as follows:

Business Process. Consists of an activity conducted with the purpose of transforming a set of inputs into useful outputs (products or services) using some sort of transformation process. Differently from Operations, business processes intend to produce products or provide services to final customer.

To exemplify the concepts of *Operation* and *Business Process*, we use Figs. 2 and 3. In Fig. 2, one can see that the organization decided to either use promotions or open new sales channel as tactics for increasing sales in Italy and therefore, "Carry out promotions" is the *Operation* used to plan the execution of the promotion tactics. In its turn, the "Carry out promotions" Operation consists of collections of operational goals and business processes (depicted in Fig. 3(b)). The operational goals specify certain milestones to be achieved during the planning of promotions, such as to choose how many promotions are required and decide what to offer in each promotion ("Choose items for promotion"), choose promotions price and audience ("Choose promotions price" and "Choose promotions audience") and advertise items in a promotion ("Advertise items in promotion'). Finally, "Run promotions campaign" and "Advertise items in promotion" business processes are the entities that are responsible for indeed executing the planning of the promotions and advertising the items in promotion.

4 Methodological Guidelines for Goal-Driven Design of Operations Architecture

This section provides methodological guidelines that prescribe how to elaborate, refine and operationalize goals by means of operations and business processes in our modeling framework. In order to prescribe such guidelines, as goals and operation planning occurs at formalized, step-by-step procedures in companies, we start by describing managers' concerns during goal and operations planning extracted from Strategic Planning literature. Subsequently, we explain how these concerns should be specified in our modeling framework. Although Strategic Planning literature mentions the existence of both a (top-down) deliberate and (bottom-up) emergent strategy formation process [15], we here focus on a traditional, top-down strategic planning for goal definition and implementation, leaving as future work the bottom-up strategy formation.

4.1 Guideline G1: Elaborate Mission and Vision Statements

At the *Strategic Level*, the first managers' step comprehends the articulation of organization's mission and vision as means of providing a general sense of direction for the company.

Mission and Vision Elaboration. The guideline is to elaborate a mission statement that reflects the value the organization intends to deliver to the external world. For *profit* companies, given that organizations can be either manufacturing or service organizations [13,18], value aggregation is performed by enumerating the products or services the company produces. For *non-profit* companies, the mission statement should capture other forms of value that provide social justification and legitimacy of the existence of the organization. For instance, Greenpeace's mission reflects this aggregation of value as "... Greenpeace's goal is to ensure the ability of the earth to nurture life in all its diversity..." [4]. The guideline for the elaboration of vision statements is to enumerate the products and services which are currently not implemented by the organization's, but there is an intention to address them on the company's portfolio.

4.2 Guideline G2: Elaborate Strategic Requirements

Strategic planning within the *Strategic Level* intends to guide the organization to achieve a successful position in a competitive environment, while achieving its goals [17].

Strategic Goals Elaboration. In order to compete, managers first identify external aspects that impact the ability of the organization to surpass its competitors. Following, internal aspects that enable the organization to gain competitive advantage such as capabilities, resources and competences are also evaluated. With such aspects in hands, the organization defines how it intends to compete and then elaborates its Strategic Goals. For instance, the Acer PC manufacturer [2, p. 492] identified that Dell competes on the basis of low manufacturing costs. This could represent an external threat for Acer that may lead Dell to become the market leader in computers. Based on internal evaluation of its assets, Acer decided to gain competitive advantage based on management philosophy of highly motivated employers. Therefore, Acer elaborated the "Increase sales" Strategic Goal. With the elaboration of this Strategic Goal, Acer intended to become the market leader supported by an internal capability.

Strategic Goals Refinement Rules. Strategic Goals can be AND-refined by following structural domain rules or based on dimensional refinement. Refinement based on structural domain rules is applied when there exist a mathematical formula that relates domain variables and enables one to structurally decompose a goal into sub-goals using this formula. For example, once we know the profit stemmed from sales can be described by the formula $salesProfit = numberSoldItems * profitMarginPerItem$ and managers intend to increase this profit ("Increase sales profit by 2 % over 3 years" goal), one can increase volume sales (*numberSoldItems*) and maintain profit margin, yielding the following goals: "Increase volume sales by 2 % over 3 years" and "Maintain gross margin by 2 % over 3 years" (Fig. 1). An alternative decomposition of the same root goal could also consider an increase in the profit margin, yielding "Maintain volume sales by 2 % over 3 years" and "Increase gross margin by 2 % over 3 years" as sub-goals.

Dimensional refinement allows one to AND-decompose a goal with respect to a number of *refinement dimensions* introduced in Sect. 3.1. A dimension is introduced when a Strategic Goal has different operationalizations for different parts of the problem space. For example, there exist different solutions for increasing sales in Italy, Germany and NL ("Increase sales by 2 % over 3 years" goal in Fig. 1) and therefore, the *location* is an eligible *refinement dimension*. The following rules can be applied when using dimensional refinement: (i) **time dimension**: used when seasonal variations of business aspects (e.g., toys sales increase during Christmas season) may impose different operationalizations for the Strategic Goal; (ii) **location dimension**: used when the company presents a distributed organizational structure across distinct locations (e.g., sales departments for different countries) and the way in which the company pursue the Strategic Goal varies according to place under consideration; (iii) **product, service, customer type dimensions**: products, services and customers usually have a number of properties that characterize them (e.g., patients under 20 years old, different metal products, etc.) and operationalizations of the Strategic Goal varies according to the values that such properties may assume.

4.3 Guideline G3: Elaborate Tactical Requirements and Operations

Within the *Tactical Level*, the strategy is put into action by creating "tactics" that are particular ways for implementing the achievement of Strategic Goals with the deployment of organizational assets [17,20].

Tactical Goals Elaboration and Implement-Relationship. For the elaboration of Tactical Goals, "tactics" (particular solutions) must be found to implement each point of the refinement dimensions introduced during the Strategic Goals Refinement. This discussion has been exemplified in Sect. 3.1 with the "Increase sales by 2 % over 3 years" Strategic Goal refined in terms of the *location* refinement dimension and implemented by offering promotions or opening new sales channel (in Italy) or alternatively, by training sales people in NL (depicted in Fig. 2). Observe that Tactical Goals inhere the properties of parent goals that have been refined through dimensional refinement, i.e., the Tactical Goal "Increase sales in Italy by 2 % over 3 years through promotions" inheres the same properties of the refinement across location from the "Increase sales in Italy by 2 % over 3 years" Strategic Goal. Further, each leaf level Strategic Goal has to be *implemented* by one or more Tactical Goal, otherwise strategies will be not effective. Inversely, each Tactical Goal *implements* one and just one Strategic Goal to avoid confusions between tactics that implement different Strategic Goals.

Tactical Goals Refinement Rules. AND-Refinement. After finding solutions for points of refinement dimensions (tactical refinement), managers must AND-refine such solutions across the responsibilities of each functional area of the company. For instance, in order to increase sales in Italy, offering promotions or opening sales channel correspond to two tactics that pertain to the responsibilities of the Marketing area. In its turn, other functional areas of the company have also responsibilities in the context of promotions. This is reflected in Fig. 2 with the "Increase sales in Italy by 2 % over 3 years through promotions" AND-refined into four distinct goals, each of them representing the responsibility of each functional area. Functional areas are represented in our model by attaching squares with their first letter to goals (see Fig. 2). **OR-refinement:** a Tactical goal is OR-refined if there are different alternatives for achieving the same Tactical Goal. In our example, two alternative types of sales channels can be opened, i.e., by finding new partners to distribute the products or by finding new customers. Therefore, the "Increase sales in Italy by 2 % over 3 years by opening new sales channels" is OR-refined into "Establish new partnerships with authorized dealers" or "Diversify customers" (Fig. 3(a)).

Tactical Goal Operationalization and Operations Modeling. The refinement of Tactical Goals finishes when it is possible to plan and schedule the achievement of a Tactical Goal by assigning it an operation. In this case, it is said that an operation *operationalizes* a Tactical Goal which corresponds to the final state to be achieved by its corresponding operation. Tactical operations can be scheduled and executed with a certain frequency in order to achieve the Tactical Goal.

4.4 Guideline G4: Elaborate Operational Requirements and Business Processes

At the *Operational Level*, the execution of tactics is planned by planning the expected results from organization's daily operations [17]. In our framework, expected results are delivered by means of setting the Operational Goals together with the business processes that deliver such results.

Operational Goals Elaboration. As the Tactical Goal corresponds to the final state to be achieved by the operation that *operationalizes* such Tactical Goal, the elaboration of Operational Goals indeed starts by refining this Tactical Goal into intermediate milestones that compose its corresponding operation. These milestones are elaborated by specifying *which* results the operation must accomplish, regardless *how* this is accomplished. For the company's operations to be valuable, milestones must be elaborated considering that they need to add value to the final product. Therefore, these operational milestones are value-adding responsibilities (e.g., "Choose items for promotion" like the ones provided in Sect. 3.2).

Operational Goals Refinement Rules. AND-Refinement. An AND-refinement is used for structurally decompose a Tactical Goal (operationalized by a given operation) into intermediate Operational Goals (milestones) necessary for the execution of some tactics. An example of milestones refinement has been provided in Sect. 3.2. **OR-refinement.** An Operational goal is OR-refined if there are different alternatives for achieving the same Operational Goal.

Operational Goals Operationalization and Business Process Architecture Modeling. As Operational Goals may be achieved by either roles or business processes, the refinement of Operational Goals finishes when it is possible to find a business process whose final state corresponds to the Operational Goal under consideration. When a greater level of granularity should be considered, the refinement may finish when it is possible to assign roles for the satisfaction of Operational Goals (Fig. 3(b)).

Situation Modeling. As SWOT analysis intends to spot the conditions in company's environment that affect the achievement of its goals and the nature of this impact, analysts should spot the internal enterprise's conditions (strengths/weaknesses) and external (opportunities/threats) and represent them as situations and domain assumptions attached to goals. In particular, situations may be suitable for devising SWOT factors that affect the ability of the company to surpass competitors in the *Strategic Layer*. In the *Tactical Layer*, situations may be useful for reasoning about the applicability of certain tactics in certain specific contexts. In Fig. 1, one can see the "high demand in automotive industry" as an opportunity for increasing sales in Germany and the "low availability of steel in the market" as a threat for increasing the sales in the 3rd year.

5 Related Work

Goal and operations modeling have a long trajectory in a number of areas of computer science, such as Enterprise Modeling (EM) and Business Process Management (BPM), among others. Enterprise modeling frameworks inherited the GORE idea that goals can be used as the driving principle for the generation of the enterprise architectures. In this context, the ArchiMate Motivational Extension (AME) extends the core ArchiMate enterprise framework by introducing common GORE concepts like (soft)goals, AND/OR refinements and contribution relations among goals and requirements. Goals are connected to other concepts of ArchiMate by means of a realization relation with services and business processes. In [1], similarly to our approach, authors analyze strategic planning literature to extend AME with finer grained concepts such as mission, vision, precedence among goals, time interval for goal achievement, responsibility and delegation among goals. However, the extension solely focuses on strategic concerns, thus not presenting a layered structure like our approach.

Similarly to our approach, other frameworks in enterprise modeling, such as the EKD [8], ARIS [16] and i* [11,21] also consider the generation of a set of business processes having goals as a starting point. Although the generation of the architecture of process from goals is a similar feature to our approach, proposals either focus on the representation of strategic or operational goals, do not taking an integrated approach to link the whole hierarchy of enterprise goals to the architecture of operations.

A large body of knowledge in BPM has also explored the interconnection between goals and operations (or business processes), by relating goals with the internal logics of the process [9,10,12,14]. We consider our approach to advance the representation features of this group of approaches as we distinguish among distinct types of goals and operations, while such approaches sole focus on the representation of our concept of operational goals.

6 Conclusions and Future Work

In this paper, we have proposed the Strategic Enterprise Process Architecture (SEPA) modeling framework that extends BIM and BMM by including different shades of goals and operations extracted from Management literature. In particular, we provide clear-cut definitions for goals and operations and also include methodological guidelines on how to build enterprise process architecture models. Regarding evaluation of our modeling framework, we are currently working on the evaluation of our proposal by means of a real-world case study in a hospital setting. Further, although we are not able to depict our full hierarchy of strategic enterprise models due to space constraints, we make it available at: https://www.dropbox.com/s/azvehs3eabugpzc/Full.

As a future work, we envision three natural directions for refinement of our modeling framework. The first direction concerns the representation of detailed consumer-producer and triggering relationships among operations and business processes. Second, a reasoning approach that generates alternative set of operations/business processes (enterprise process architecture) on the basis of the goal hierarchy should also be considered. Finally, although the goal structure is richly grounded on key distinctions of Management literature, we refrain from addressing how the execution of operations and processes entails the achievement of strategic goals. This is certainly an important step to be tackled by our methodology.

Acknowledgments. We would like to thank Jennifer Horkoff for her useful comments in the research reported in this paper. This work has been partially funded by the Spanish Ministry of Economy and Competitiveness (MINECO/FEDER) under the Granted Project SEQUOIA-UA (Management requirements and methodology for Big Data analytics) (TIN2015-63502-C3-3-R).

References

1. Azevedo, C., Almeida, J., van Sinderen, M., Ferreira Pires, L.: Towards capturing strategic planning in EA. In: IEEE 19th International Enterprise Distributed Object Computing Conference (EDOC2015), pp. 159–168 (2015)
2. Daft, R., Samson, D.: Fundamentals of Management: Asia Pacific Edition. Cengage Learning, Boston (2014)

3. DuBrin, A.: Essentials of Management. Cengage Learning, Boston (2011)
4. Greenpeace.org: Greenpeace Core Values. http://www.greenpeace.org/international/about/our-core-values/. Accessed 11 July 2016
5. Object Management Group: Business Motivation Model - Version 1.0. Object Management Group (OMG) (2015)
6. Horkoff, J., Barone, D., Jiang, L., Yu, E., Amyot, D., Borgida, A., Mylopoulos, J.: Strategic business modeling: representation and reasoning. Softw. Syst. Model. **13**(3), 1015–1041 (2014)
7. Joyce, P., Woods, A.: Strategic Management: A Fresh Approach to Developing Skills, Knowledge and Creativity. Kogan Page, Philadelphia (2001)
8. Kavakli, V., Loucopoulos, P.: Goal-driven business process analysis application in electricity deregulation. In: Pernici, B., Thanos, C. (eds.) CAiSE 1998. LNCS, vol. 1413, p. 305. Springer, Heidelberg (1998)
9. Koliadis, G., Ghose, A.K.: Relating business process models to goal-oriented requirements models in KAOS. In: Hoffmann, A., Kang, B.-H., Richards, D., Tsumoto, S. (eds.) PKAW 2006. LNCS (LNAI), vol. 4303, pp. 25–39. Springer, Heidelberg (2006)
10. Korherr, B., List, B.: Extending the EPC and the BPMN with business process goals and performance measures. In: 9th International Conference on Enterprise Information Systems (ICEIS2007), pp. 287–294 (2007)
11. Lapouchnian, A., Yu, E., Sturm, A.: Re-designing process architectures towards a framework of design dimensions. In: IEEE 9th International Conference on Research Challenges in Information Science (RCIS2015), pp. 205–210 (2015)
12. Lapouchnian, A., Yu, Y., Mylopoulos, J.: Requirements-driven design and configuration management of business processes. In: Alonso, G., Dadam, P., Rosemann, M. (eds.) BPM 2007. LNCS, vol. 4714, pp. 246–261. Springer, Heidelberg (2007)
13. Mahadevan, B.: Operations Management: Theory and Practice. Pearson, Upper Saddle River (2010)
14. Markovic, I., Kowalkiewicz, M.: Linking business goals to process models in semantic business process modeling. In: IEEE 12th International Enterprise Distributed Object Computing Conference (EDOC 2008), pp. 332–338 (2008)
15. Mintzberg, H., Ahlstrand, B., Lampel, J.: Strategy Safari: A Guided Tour Through the Wilds of Strategic Management. Prentice Hall, Upper Saddle River (2005)
16. Neiger, D., Churilov, L.: Goal-oriented business process modeling with EPCs and value-focused thinking. In: Desel, J., Pernici, B., Weske, M. (eds.) BPM 2004. LNCS, vol. 3080, pp. 98–115. Springer, Heidelberg (2004)
17. Plunkett, W., Attner, R., Allen, G.: Management: Meeting and Exceeding Customer Expectations. Cengage Learning, Boston (2007)
18. Reid, R., Sanders, N.: Operations Management: An Integrated Approach. Wiley, Hoboken (2005)
19. Saloner, G., Shepard, A., Podolny, J.: Strategic Management. Wiley, Hoboken (2001)
20. Srivastava, R., Verma, S.: Strategic Management: Concepts, Skills and Practices. PHI Learning (2012)
21. Yu, E., Mylopoulos, J.: Using goals, rules, and methods to support reasoningin business process reengineering. In: Proceedings of the Twenty-Seventh Hawaii International Conference on System Sciences, vol. 4, pp. 234–243, January 1994

Data Journey Modelling: Predicting Risk for IT Developments

Iliada Eleftheriou(✉), Suzanne M. Embury, and Andrew Brass

School of Computer Science, University of Manchester, Oxford Road, Manchester, UK
iliada.eleftheriou@manchester.ac.uk

Abstract. Information sharing is a vital element of a successful business. However, technological, organisational and human challenges obstruct the effective movement of data. In this paper, we analyse a collection of case studies from healthcare describing failing information systems developments. A set of 32 failing factors were extracted showing that data movement, either between systems, people or organisations, is a key indicator of IT failure. From this examination, we derived anti-patterns for data movement in which some key differences between the source and target location of the movement caused high costs to the developments. Finally, we propose data journey modelling as a lightweight technique that captures the movement of data through complex networks of people and systems, with the aim of improve go/no-go decision making for new IT developments, based on the anti-patterns we have identified.

Keywords: Information sharing · Data movement modelling · Data journey · Socio-technical challenges

1 Introduction

While software has the capability to bring many benefits to organisations, it can be a mixed blessing [5]. New software developments can be unexpectedly costly to develop and run. It may be necessary to employ new personnel or retrain existing staff. New ways of working may need to be devised, to fit with the constraints of the new software and the technical infrastructure on which it runs. One does not need to spend long looking through newspaper headlines or the Risks List digest[1] to know that new software developments can sometimes result in costs that far outweigh the value they propose to create.

Clearly, a lightweight and reliable means is needed of helping us to make good go/no go decisions regarding new software developments. Current approaches to managing risk and estimating the cost of software development are principally focused on creating detailed predictions based on substantial models of

[1] www.risks.org.

J. Horkoff et al. (Eds.): PoEM 2016, LNBIP 267, pp. 72–86, 2016.
DOI: 10.1007/978-3-319-48393-1_6

the planned development [2]. They are aimed at supporting project managers throughout the development process itself, rather than giving a low-cost indicator for use in early-stage decision making. What is needed is a lightweight approach, that can be completed in the course of a small number of days, and that gives reliable predictions of the likely success of a planned IT development. And since the reasons for software failure are rarely technical in nature, the indicator must take account of social and organisational factors, as well as the technologies to be used.

We set out to design an indicator of this kind for use in large complex organisations. As a starting point, we analysed a set of 18 case studies of new software developments in the UK's National Health Service (NHS). The case studies were written by NHS staff as coursework for the "Informatics for Healthcare Systems" course unit run by the University of Manchester, in the 2013 academic session. The study authors came from a variety of roles, and the studies describe new IT developments from a broad range of NHS functions, including cancer care, ambulance service management, in-patient management, heart failure care, diabetes care, bed management and more.

A common feature of the cases where the new software was deemed to have been unsuccessful was the movement of data. Whenever data was moved to new contexts, and used for a purpose other than that for which it was originally designed, the system owners and end-users faced a host of additional challenges, be they organisational, technical, human, governance oriented or political in nature [12]. These challenges lead to unforeseen costs and sometimes dramatic reductions in the benefits expected from the new software. We therefore hypothesised that identifying the need for movement of data in a new development could provide the early warning signal for success or failure that we were looking for.

To test this hypothesis, we developed a way of modelling the movement of data through and across organisations, and of identifying the kinds of data movement that lead to high risk and cost. The technique is lightweight because it abstracts away from the details of the business processes that use the data, and focuses just on the bare movement of data between significant entities. This paper describes the process we used to define it, and the basis for the model in information we extracted from the case studies. We began by extracting from the case studies a list of the root causes of failure (Sect. 3). We further analysed the case studies to extract the data movement patterns involved in each case, and combined this with the failure causes to produce a set of problematic data movement patterns (Sect. 4). From these patterns, we extracted the minimum information that must be captured about a new development in order to identify the presence of the patterns (Sect. 5). We called the resulting model the "data journey" model, since it models the paths data takes through the socio-technical enterprise, from point of entry to point of use.

2 Modelling Data Movement

A plethora of modelling techniques and notations have been proposed for use during information systems design, some of which include elements of the movement of data. In this section, we survey the principal modelling techniques, to see if any meet our requirements and can be used as the basis for modelling data journeys. We need a modelling technique that:

- allows us to model the movement of data within and between organisations,
- gives equal prominence to both social and technical factors affecting the movement of data, and
- is sufficiently lightweight to be used as a decision-making aid in the early stages of a development cycle.

A number of software design techniques allow modelling of data from a technical point of view. Data flow diagrams (DFDs) are the most directly relevant of these [3]. Unfortunately, the focus in DFDs is on fine-grained flows, between low-level processing units, making it hard to capture higher-level aspects of the enterprise that can bring cost and risks, i.e. the social factors. Similarly, the Unified Modelling Language (UML) contains several diagrams detailing movement of data, notably sequence diagrams, collaboration diagrams and use case diagrams [7]. Although the abstraction level at which these diagrams are used is in the control of the modeller, to an extent, they provide no help in singling out just those elements needed to predict costs and risks of a potential development. Also, social factors influencing information portability and introducing cost to the movement aren't part of the focus of those approaches. These models are helpful in designing the low level detailed data flows within a future development, but can't help us decide which flows may introduce costs and risks to the development.

Other techniques are able to model high-level data movement between systems and organisations. Data provenance systems, for example, log the detailed movement of individual data items through a network of systems [8]. While these logs can be a useful input to data journey modelling, they describe only the flows that are currently supported and that have actually taken place. They are not suited to modelling desired flows, and do not directly help us to see what social and organisation factors affect the flow.

Business process modelling (BPM) captures the behaviour of an organisation in terms of a set of events (something happens) and activities (work to be done) [1]. Although BPM can implicitly model flows of data between a network of systems, they typically contain much more detail than is needed for our purposes. Data journey models aim to abstract away from the nitty-gritty of specific business processes, to give the big picture of data movement.

Models that combine technical and social information, such as human, organisational, governance and ethical factors, can be found in the literature [6,10,11]. For example, the i* modelling framework aims to embed social understanding into system engineering models [10]. The framework models social actors (people, systems, processes, and software) and their properties, such as autonomy and intentionality. Although a powerful mechanism to understand actors of an organisation, the i* framework does not give us the information flows happening between the systems, nor any measures to identify costs.

In summary, we found no existing model that met all our requirements. The extant technical modelling methods give us a way to model the detail of a system to be constructed, but provide no guidance to the modeller as to which parts of the system should be captured for early-stage decision making and which can be safely ignored. The socio-technical models allow us to capture some of the elements that are important in predicting cost and risk in IT developments, but need to be extended with elements that can capture the technical movement of data. We therefore set out to define a new modelling approach for data journeys, focused wholly on capturing the data movement anti-patterns we located in the case studies. In the sections that follow, we describe and justify the model we produced.

3 Data Movement and IT Failure

Data movement is crucial to the functioning of most large organisations. While a data item may first be introduced into an organisation for a single purpose, new uses for that data will typically appear over time, requiring it to be moved between systems and actors, to fulfil these new requirements. Enterprises can thus be viewed, at one level of abstraction, as networks of sub-systems that either produce, consume or merely store data, with flows between these sub-systems along which data travels.

When we plan to introduce new functionality into an enterprise, we must make sure that the data needed to support that functionality can reach the sub-system in which it will be consumed, so that value can be created from it. The costs of getting the data to its place of consumption must be worth the amount of value generated by its consumption. Moreover, new risks to the enterprise will be introduced. The enterprise must evaluate the effects on its core functions if the flow of data is prevented by some reason, or if the costs of getting the data to its place of use rise beyond the value that is produced.

We wanted to understand whether this abstraction could provide a light-weight early-warning indicator of the major costs and risks involved in introducing new functionality in an enterprise. We began by examining the collection of case studies from the NHS, first to categorise each one as a successful or a failing development, and second to understand the major root causes of failure in each case. These were relatively straightforward tasks, as the authors of the case studies were asked in each case to diagnose for themselves the causes of failure.

Of the 18 case studies, only 3 were described by their authors as having been successful. The remaining 15 were categorised as having failed to deliver the expected benefits. We extracted and organised the failure factors identified by the authors, and aggregated the results across the full set of case studies. The results are summarised in Fig. 1, which lists the failure factors in order of

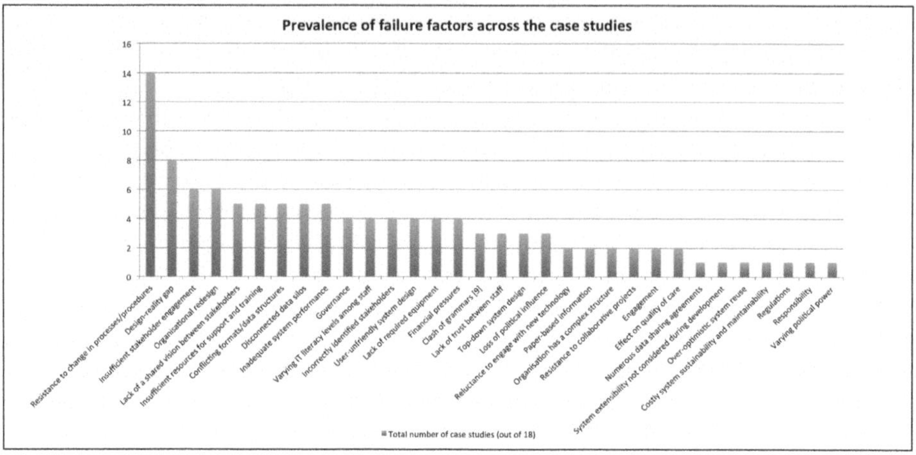

Fig. 1. Prevalence of failure factors across the case studies.

prevalence (with those factors occurring in the most case studies appearing on the left, and those occurring in the least, on the right). A brief explanation of each factor is given in Appendix A.

Clearly, the technical challenges of data movement are implicated in many of these failure factors. Costs introduced by the need to transform data from one format to another have long been recognised, and tools to alleviate the problems have been developed. However, from the chart, we see that the most common causes of IT failure in our case studies are related to people and their interactions. Of the 32 factors identified, less than a quarter are primarily technical in nature. Can an enterprise model focused on data movement take into account these more complex, subjective failure factors, without requiring extensive modelling?

Looking more closely, we can see that data movement is implicated in many of the non-technical failure factors, too. Many of the factors come into play *because* data is moved to allow work to be done in a different way, by different people, with different goals, or to enable entirely new forms of work to be carried out using existing data. Data moves not only through the technical infrastructure of databases and networks, but also through the human infrastructure, with its changing rules, vocabularies and assumptions. All this suggest that data movement could be a proxy for some of the non-technical risks and cost sources the study authors experienced, as well as the technical costs and challenges.

The question therefore arises as to whether we can use the presence of data movement as the backbone for our prediction model of cost and risk. If we can abstract the details of the new IT development into a sequence of new data movements that would be required to realise it, can we quickly and cheaply assess the safety of those new movements, combining both technical and social features to arrive at our assessment of the risk?

To do this, we need to understand the specific features of data movements that can indicate the presence of costs and risks. We returned to our case studies, to look for examples of data movement that were present when the IT development failed, and to generalise these into a set of data movement patterns that could become the basis for our prediction method. The results of this second stage of the analysis are described in the following section.

4 Data Movement Patterns

Having examined the case studies, we found that data movement is a key indicator of most of the IT failing factors. In this section, we propose a catalogue of data movement anti-patterns, each describing movements of data that might introduce some type of cost or risk to the development. We also give the conditions under which a pattern causes a failure, and the type of cost or risk it might impose on the organisation.

To develop the data movement patterns catalogue, we first went through the case studies and extracted any data movement or information sharing example that caused a cost or risk contributing to an IT failure. The case study authors had not been asked to provide this information explicitly in their assignment, and therefore we used our own judgement as to what data movement was involved. We then transformed those examples into a set of generic anti-patterns.

All of the case studies involved some kind of data movement and it was commonly the case that the data movement was at the heart of the part of the development that failed. Although there were many examples of movement of data between computer systems we found a richer variety of movement patterns between people, from people to systems, and vise-versa. We describe below the anti-patterns we identified from the case studies; of course, other potentially problematic data movement patterns may exist. For each pattern we give an identifying name, define the context in which it can happen, and provide the conditions that should hold for the costs to apply. Any examples given are taken directly from the case studies (but with identifying details removed).

4.1 Change of Media

Often, a change of medium is required when data is moved between a producer and a consumer. This is straightforward in the case of electronic data, which can be easily converted into report form, for document generation and printing. But the situation is more complicated when data on paper must be entered into a destination software system. Data entry is a time consuming process typically done by clerical staff, who may not have a strong understanding of the meaning of the data they are entering. Errors can easily be injected that may significantly reduce the quality of the information. We illustrate this pattern in Fig. 2(a), and we define it as:

"When data moves from a source 'S' to a target 'T' of a different media (i.e. physical to electronic), then a transformation cost exists, either before or after the transportation of the data, that can lead to decreased quality at the T side."

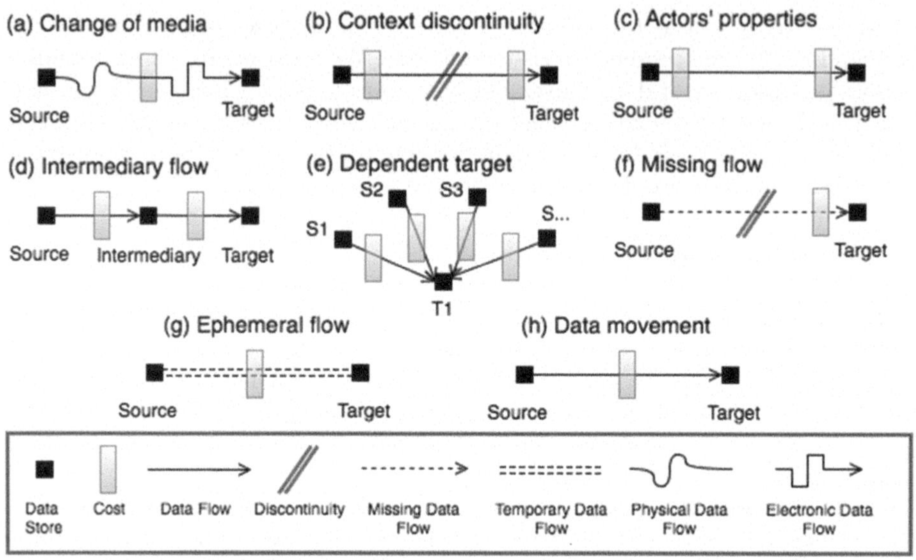

Fig. 2. Data movement anti-patterns retrieved from the case studies.

4.2 Context Discontinuity

Sharing data outside the immediate organisational unit can result in a number of administrative costs, such as reaching and complying with data sharing agreements, as well as complying with wider information governance requirements. Also, a risk of staff reluctance to share ownership of data, may exist on both sides of the movement. Additionally, if the source of data belongs to a different context than the target, then there is the risk of clash of grammars (the meaning of the data moved being altered by the change of context because of a cultural, experience or other type of reason [9]), and a cost of lower data quality at the target side. For example, data entered into a system by secretarial staff can contain errors if the information requires medical knowledge/vocabulary that the staff lack. Also, if the data to be moved are in physical form (e.g. letter, cassette, X-ray film, blood sample etc.), then there are transportation costs. Generally, if there is a discontinuity in the flow of data caused by a change in context, costs will be imposed to the movement. The context discontinuity pattern is showed in Fig. 2(b) and defined as:

"When data moves from a source 'S' to a target 'T' of a different context (i.e. organisation, geographical area, culture, etc.) and a discontinuity exists in the flow, then a bridging cost is imposed to either or both sides of the flow."

4.3 Actors' Properties

Costs can also be introduced by key heterogeneities in the properties of the consumer and producer. Differences in system requirements, business processes, governance, and regulations between producers and consumers of data create transformation costs that must be borne either at the source, or target location (or both). Integrating data from "data island" sources (sources that haven't previously been shared up to this point) can have high costs; such sources typically have limited external connectivity, and are tailored for use by one type of users bringing a risk of data quality problems at the target side.

"When data moves from a consumer 'C' to a producer 'P' (system or human), a difference in a property of either source or target introduces a transformation cost to the movement (Fig. 2-c)".

4.4 Intermediary Flow

Intermediary systems or staff may be introduced with the aim of reducing some up-front cost (such as the use of lower-paid staff to enter data on behalf of higher-paid staff), but can actually create downstream costs in the longer term such as those caused by lower data quality or missing data.

"When data moves from a source 'S' to a target 'T' through an intermediary step, a cost is introduced to either flow (Fig. 2-d)".

4.5 Other Data Movement Patterns

- *Dependent target:* Often, data needed in a target location (T), partly exists in several sources. If the business processes of the T depend on the data of the sources, then the cost of transformation is usually done on the T side. When data moves from multiple sources 'S1', 'S2', etc. to a target 'T', and the T depends on the data in S then a cost of extraction, transformation and integration appears in each of the flows, possibly at the T side (Fig. 2-e).
- *Missing flow:* Often, there is a technical or governance barrier introducing a prohibitive cost that obstructs the implementation of the flow. Data needed by a consumer exists at a S, but are not able to reach the consumer (Fig. 2-f).
- *Ephemeral flow:* is a flow from S to T that exists for a short period of time (i.e. migration purposes) and is planned to be deleted in the future. Ephemeral flows are often created cheaply, with a short-term mindset, but then become part of the system, leading to future costs and complexity (Fig. 2-g).
- *Data movement:* Whenever data moves from its source to a destination there is the accumulative cost of extracting, transforming and loading the data from the source to the target. The cost might include staff training and support, and can be in either side of the flow (Fig. 2-h).

As shown in the patterns, costs and risks are likely to arise when data is moved between two entities that differ in some key way. When data is moved from producer (or holder) to consumer, it typically needs to be transformed from one format to another. Data values that make sense in the producer environment need to be converted into values that will be interpreted equivalently in the consumer environment. However, this conversion process is often difficult to apply correctly and completely, as the knowledge that is required is often stored tacitly in the heads of the data producers and consumers, rather than being explicitly declared in an easily accessible form. Where data is sensitive (as health care data often is) there are also governance issues to be considered. Data often cannot be shared unless it has been appropriately aggregated or otherwise anonymised. Data may need to be filtered before it is moved, or moved through a particular set of systems, purely to be cleared for export to the real data consumer.

The outcome of our analysis of the case studies is a hypothesis regarding the features of a proposed IT development, and the socio-technical environment in which it is to be implemented, that act as early-stage indicators of implementation risk. We have designed a method for modelling just the parts of an organisation's IT infrastructure that is needed to detect these features. In the next section, we present this model, and the method we have designed for constructing and using it to predict the risk of a proposed new IT development.

5 The Data Journey Model

Having characterised the kinds of data movement that can be problematic, the next step is to create a method for identifying the presence of the movement anti-patterns in a new development. In this section, we describe the modelling approach we have designed, aimed at capturing only the information needed to discover the movement patterns.

The core requirement is to identify the points in an information infrastructure where data is moved between two organisational entities which differ in some way significant to the interpretation of the data. These are the places where the portability of the data is put under stress, where errors can occur when the differences are not recognised, and where effort must be put in to resolve the differences. The model must therefore allow us to capture:

- The movement of data across an information infrastructure, including the entities which "hold" data within the system, and the routes by which data moves between them; we call this the model's landscape.
- The points at which key differences in the interpretation of data occur, both social and technological.

5.1 The Model

We model the information infrastructure of an IT development in terms of the existing data containers, actors and links of the data journey model landscape. We use *data containers* to note the places where data rests when is not moving. A data container can be a system's database whenever the data are in electronic form, or even a file cabinet, a pigeon hole, or a desk whenever the data are in a physical form. For example, when a general practitioner (GP) requests blood test results from the lab pathology of a hospital, data needs to travel from the GP secretary's desk (where the request card and the blood sample rests), to the hospital porter's pigeon holes, to the lab's database (where results are input by the lab analyst), and back to the GP's database to discuss with the patient. We model data containers using a rectangular box, as shown in Fig. 3.

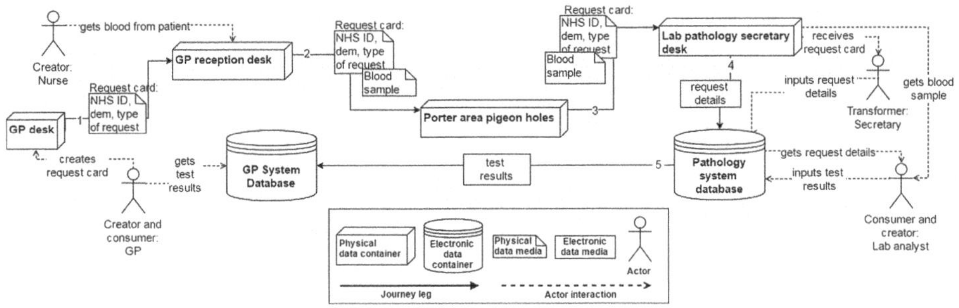

Fig. 3. Data journey diagram of a GP requesting blood test results from a pathology lab.

Actors are the people or systems that interact with the containers to create, consume, or transform the data resting in them. In the example described above, a lab analyst interacts with the lab system database to input the results of the analysis in. He is the creator of the test results data. The GP consumes those data by interacting with the GP system database. Actors are modelled using the actor symbol of the UML notation, and the interaction with the containers with a dotted arrow, as shown in Fig. 3.

While data may be stored in one container, it may be consumed at several places in the landscape. *Links* are the routes that currently exist between two containers along which data can move, and are modelled as straight lines between two containers.

To move along a link, data must be represented in a *medium* of physical or electronic form. For example, the request card resting in the secretary's office is moved to the pathology lab by post. The test results move from the lab's database to the GP's system through an internet connection.

Containers, actors and links are parts of the landscape of the existing infrastructure in which data moves. Often, a new movement must be implemented. A *journey* describes the movement of data that needs to occur for a piece of data that is needed by some consumer to move from its point of entry into the landscape, to its point of use by the new actor. A data journey begins from a container storing the source data, and ends at the container which the end consumer interacts with. In Fig. 3, the initial container of the journey is the GP desk and the final consumer is the GP.

Sometimes a direct link between the source and target container doesn't exist making the data to move through intermediary containers using existing links. Those intermediate links are called *legs*. A data journey is made up of a number of journey legs. Journey legs are modelled with an arrow connecting the containers in which data are moved between. The direction of the arrow shows the direction in which data needs to move. Journey legs can constitute existing links or create a new link between two containers.

Figure 4 shows the meta-model for the data journey model, expressed in UML. A data journey diagram is a set of consecutive journey legs. A journey leg moves a piece of data from a source container to a target container through an electronic or physical medium. An actor interacts with a container to create, consume or transform the data stored in it.

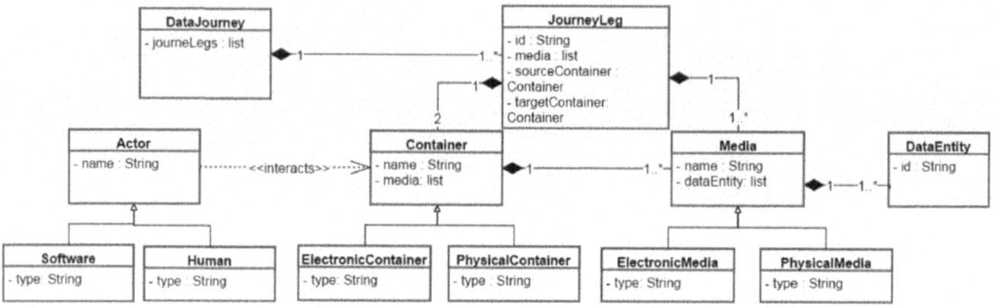

Fig. 4. The meta model of the data journey.

5.2 Identifying Potential Costs

Having created a data journey model, the next step is to add in the information that can help us identify the legs where high cost or risk might be involved. We have seen from the case study analysis that costs and risks arise when data is moved between two entities that differ in some key way. Thus, when a human enters data into a software system, or two humans with very different professional backgrounds share data, or when software systems designed for different user sets communicate with each other, there is the potential need to transform or filter the data, to make it fit for its new context of use. However, to predict those places where costs might appear, we need cheap to apply information, since there is little value in predictions that cost a significant fraction of the actual development costs to create. We therefore focus on obtaining only the bare minimum of information needed, and ideally only on information that is readily available or cheap to acquire.

In the case studies, we found that high cost and risk occurred when data was shared between actors and containers with the following discrepancies:

1. Change of media: Containers using different media. For example, when a legacy X-Ray image on film must be scanned into a PDF for online storage and manipulation.
2. Discontinuity - external organisation: Containers belonging to different organisational units. For example, cancer data captured by a F.T needed for researching purposes by another agency.
3. Change of context, clash of grammars [9]: People speaking different vocabularies. For example, when a secretary is asked to transcribe notes dictated by a consultant.

We need low cost ways of incorporating these factors into the data journey model. In some cases, the information is readily available. For example, it is normally well known to stakeholders when information is stored on paper, in a filing cabinet, or in electronic form. However, other factors, like people's vocabularies, are less obvious. For these factors we use a proxy; some piece of information which is cheap to apply, and approximates the same relationship between the actors and containers as by the original factor. For example, we use salary bands as a proxy indicator for the presence of "clash of grammars", on the grounds that a large difference in salary bands between actors probably indicates a different degree of technical expertise.

We use the following rules and proxies for indicating the presence of a boundary between the source and target of a data journey leg. A boundary indicative of high cost/risk can be predicted to be present when:

- the medium of the source container of a journey leg is different from the medium of the target,
- the source container of a journey leg belongs to a different organisational unit from the target container, or
- the actor creating the data at the source container has a different salary band than the actor consuming it at the target.

To identify the places in which the above factors may impose costs, we group together the elements of the data journey diagram with similar properties. For example, we group together all physical containers, or electronic containers, or clerical staff, clinical staff, elements belonging to the radiology department of a Foundation Trust (F.T.), elements belonging to the GP, and so on. These groupings are overlaid onto the landscape of the data journey model and form boundaries. For example, Fig. 5 shows the containers belonging to the GP organisation with blue colour and the ones belonging to the F.T. with orange colour. The places where a journey leg crosses from one grouping into another are the predicted location of the cost/risk introduced by the external organisational factor. In Fig. 5, the costly journey legs are noted with a red warning sign.

Other boundaries stemming from factors other than those stated above, are also likely to exist. However, we do not include them in this analysis since the amount of work needed to evaluate is another paper of its own. Both the boundaries described above and the data journey model have been evaluated in a retrospective study of a real world case study from the NHS domain. The study describes data moved from a GP organisation to the radiology department of a F.T. The results of the evaluation showed that our model can identify places of high costs and risks. A further description of the results is given in [4].

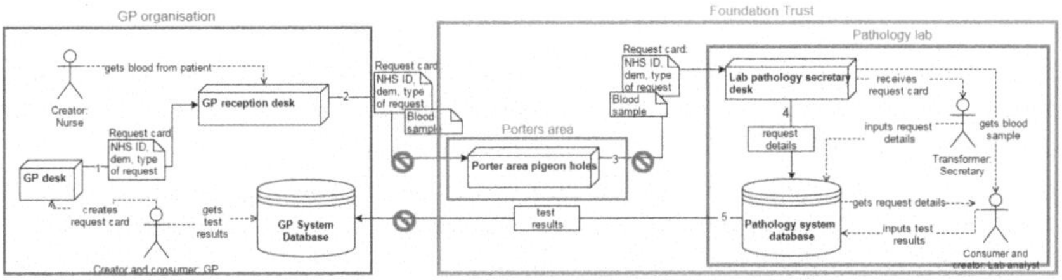

Fig. 5. Organisational boundaries and costs of the data journey diagram.

6 Conclusions

In this paper, we have presented and motivated a new form of enterprise modelling focused on data journeys, which aims to provide a lightweight and reliable means of identifying the social and technical costs/risks of a planned IT development. Our approach is based on lessons learnt from case studies written by experienced NHS staff. The case studies showed how complex data movement can be in large organisations, and the numerous barriers that exist that introduce unexpected costs into seemingly straightforward data movement.

We have evaluated the effectiveness of the data journey approach, through a retrospective study of data movement in a nearby hospital trust. In this study, new software was brought in to reduce the costs of an existing data movement. Our approach was able to predict all the changes made by the development team, as well as proposing further improvements that the domain expert agreed looked promising. The details of the evaluation can be found elsewhere [4].

However, further evaluation of the approach is needed to fully test the hypothesis, and especially to test it in contexts that go beyond the healthcare setting of the case studies from which it was developed. In addition, we wish to explore further modes of use for the technique, since it is potentially capable of highlighting cost saving opportunities in existing systems, and of assessing organisational readiness to comply with new regulations (such as clinical care pathways and guidelines).

A The Failure Factors

People-Oriented Factors
Resistance to change: new IT systems can require staff to follow new processes and procedures, which they may resist. Staff can also fear replacement
Reluctance to engage with new technology: staff may resist a change from familiar to unfamiliar technologies.
Varying IT literacy levels among staff: this can reduce or delay the benefits of the new IT systems, until the necessary skills are acquired.
Clash of grammars[9]: Specialist vocabulary used by, e.g., clinicians may be misunderstood by, e.g., secretaries, leading to delays and data quality problems.
Lack of trust: staff often don't trust the IT implementation team and don't share knowledge, domain expertise and ideas with them.
Incorrectly identified stakeholders: key users might not be identified as stakeholders and then will not be involved in decision making.
Insufficient stakeholder engagement: communication and engagement may vary between stakeholder groups (e.g. secretaries, clinicians, GPs, developers).
Lack of a shared vision between stakeholders.
Insufficient resources for support and training: lack of training and support can cause resistance to use the new system, thus reducing/delaying benefits.

Data-Oriented Factors
Numerous data sharing agreements: records may be subject to many sharing agreements, each controlling a different, narrowly defined subset of clinical data.
Conflicting formats/data structures : data needs to be transformed before it can be used, often requiring substantial manual input.
Disconnected data silos: clinicians may trust their own legacy databases more than shared ones, leading to duplicated, fragmented and inconsistent data.
Paper-based data: Paper-based data transfer is still widespread, and brings many additional costs to a project.

System-Oriented Factors
System extensibility not considered during development: extending an existing system with extra functionality can require significant reconfiguration.
Over-optimistic system reuse: when a system designed for one user group is adopted by another, major reconfiguration/process redesign may be needed.
Inadequate system performance: system performance problems, especially over the long term, can have a de-motivating effect on users.
User-unfriendly system design: new IT systems can be complex and inflexible. Systems may be wholly or partially unused, or workarounds may be needed.
Costly system sustainability and maintainability: systems that cannot change over the long term become decreasingly useful.
Top-down system design: managers may take decisions without consulting the end-users. The needs of specific regions, departments or users may not be met.
Lack of required equipment: if insufficient or inadequate equipment is provided, stakeholders may not receive the expected value from a new development.

Organisation-Oriented Factors
Organisation has a complex structure: large organisations are typically coalitions of sub-groups, each with its own politics, culture, technologies and structures.
Regulations: organisational policies may conflict with the new system, and vice versa, leading to reduced/delayed benefits and need for reconfiguration.
Organisational redesign: IT developments often demand organisational restructuring, which is time consuming and often unwanted by staff.
Resistance to collaborative projects: staff may be reluctant to participate in IT projects, fearing loss of data/process ownership, control and influence.

Governance-Oriented Factors.
Governance: organisations may resist sharing data due to concerns over information and corporate governance, data ownership, privacy and confidentiality.
Responsibility: it may be unclear which organisational unit is responsible for developing/procuring and maintaining new systems, and who owns the data.

Requirements-Oriented Factors.
Design-reality gap: the new system may not work as envisaged, or may contradict processes and practises previously in use. Workarounds must be devised.
Engagement: if the implementation team doesn't engage with clinicians and other key stakeholders, the system functionality may not meet user needs.
Effect on quality of care: the need to input new data cuts in time that would otherwise be spent focusing on the patient, and can reduce the quality of care.

Politically-Oriented Factors.
Loss of political influence: a department may fear loss of influence and power when a new IT system is introduced.
Financial pressures: projects are often expected to deliver with a tight budget/insufficient resources, leading to expensive and risky workarounds.
Varying political power: the functionality that is built may be determined by those with the most influence, rather than the actual end users.

References

1. Aguilar-Saven, R.S.: Business process modelling: review and framework. Int. J. Prod. Econ. **90**(2), 129–149 (2004)
2. Boehm, B., Abts, C., Chulani, S.: Software development cost estimation approaches - a survey. Ann. Softw. Eng. **10**(1–4), 177–205 (2000)
3. Chen, Y.L., Li, Q.: Data flow diagram. In: Chen, Y.L., Li, Q. (eds.) Modeling and Analysis of Enterprise and Information Systems, pp. 85–97. Springer, Heidelberg (2009)
4. Eleftheriou, I., Embury, S., Moden, R., Dobinson, P., Brass, A.: Data journeys: identifying social and technical barriers to data movement in large, complex organisations. Technical report, School of Computer Science, The University of Manchester (2016). www.datajourney.org/publications/tech_rep_data_journey.pdf
5. Marshall, J.P.: The social (dis)organisation of software: failure and disorder in information society. Aust. J. Anthropol. **25**(2), 190–206 (2014)
6. Pardo, T., Cresswell, A.M., Dawes, S.S., Burke, G.B., et al.: Modeling the social & technical processes of interorganizational information integration. In: Proceedings of the 37th Annual Hawaii International Conference on System Sciences, p. 8. IEEE (2004)
7. Rumbaugh, J., Jacobson, I., Booch, G.: Unified Modeling Language Reference Manual. Pearson Higher Education, New York (2004)
8. Simmhan, Y.L., Plale, B., Gannon, D.: A survey of data provenance in e-science. ACM Sigmod Rec. **34**(3), 31–36 (2005)
9. Vann, J.L.: Resistance to change and the language of public organizations: a look at "clashing grammars" in large-scale information technology projects. Public Organ. Rev. **4**(1), 47–73 (2004)
10. Yu, E.S.: Social modeling and i*. In: Borgida, A.T., Chaudhri, V.K., Giorgini, P., Yu, E.S. (eds.) Conceptual Modeling: Foundations and Applications. LNCS, vol. 5600, pp. 99–121. Springer, Heidelberg (2009)
11. Yusof, M.M., Kuljis, J., Papazafeiropoulou, A., Stergioulas, L.K.: An evaluation framework for health information systems: human, organization and technology-fit factors (hot-fit). Int. J. Med. Inf. **77**(6), 386–398 (2008)
12. Zheng, L., Yang, T.-M., Pardo, T., Jiang, Y.: Understanding the "boundary" in information sharing and integration. In: Proceedings of the 42nd Hawaii International Conference on System Sciences (HICSS 2009), pp. 1–10. IEEE (2009)

Data Model Development for Process Modeling Recommender Systems

Michael Fellmann[1(✉)], Dirk Metzger[2], and Oliver Thomas[2]

[1] Institute of Computer Science, Rostock University, Rostock, Germany
michael.fellmann@uni-rostock.de

[2] Information Management and Information Systems, Osnabrück University, Osnabrück, Germany
{dirk.metzger,oliver.thomas}@uni-osnabrueck.de

Abstract. The manual construction of business process models is a time-consuming and error-prone task. To ease the construction of such models, several modeling support techniques have been suggested. However, while recommendation systems are widely used e.g. in e-commerce, such techniques are rarely implemented in process modeling tools. The creation of such systems is a complex task since a large number of requirements and parameters have to be addressed. In order to improve the situation, we develop a data model that can serve as a backbone for the development of process modeling recommender systems (PMRS). We systematically develop the model in a stepwise approach using established requirements and validate it against a data model that has been reverse-engineered from a real-world system. We expect that our contribution will provide a useful starting point for designing the data perspective of process modeling recommendation features.

Keywords: Enterprise process modeling · Recommender systems · Requirements · Data model

1 Motivation and Relevance

Business process modeling and reorganization are still among the top-ten of relevant topics of today's CIOs [1]. However, the construction of semi-formal process models is even today, after two decades of research on business process modeling, a highly manual task involving substantial human effort. Regarding the modeling activity, effort is required to create models conforming to specified rules regarding the naming of model elements and the abstraction level of model elements. Concerning the naming of model elements, terminological problems are amongst the main problems when using conceptual (process) models [2]. Moreover, effort and difficulty arises due to the complexity of today's business processes. It might not be easy to figure out where to start modeling a process and where to stop and on which abstraction level to model [3, 4] since guidance in modeling is largely missing in current tools. These barriers call for process modeling support features, which assist users during process modeling and make suggestions how to complete a currently being edited process model. Such assistance functions are common features in programming environments (in terms of

J. Horkoff et al. (Eds.): PoEM 2016, LNBIP 267, pp. 87–101, 2016.
DOI: 10.1007/978-3-319-48393-1_7

auto-completing e.g., Java code) or e-commerce systems (e.g., amazon.com). Although it has been demonstrated that assistance functions are beneficial in these domains [5, 6], assistance functions are not considered in commercial BPM tools. However, since recommender systems "generate meaningful recommendations to a collection of users" [7], development activities towards such systems should be given a priority in order to offer assistance functions in process modeling tools too.

Up to now, some proposals that lead to prototypical developments have been made in the area of recommendation-based process modeling [8] such as auto-completion approaches [6, 9–11] or auto-suggest features [12, 13] or recommendation methods for improving business process modeling [14]. However, these contributions rarely provide an explicit and detailed data model, so modelling the data perspective when building such tools has to start from scratch. It is not an easy task since a large number of requirements and parameters have to be addressed. To improve the situation and to fill this gap, we systematically develop requirements-based data model for process modelling recommender systems (PMRS) that can serve as a backbone for the development of modeling recommender systems. The development is based on a requirements catalog previously developed [15] from a literature analysis as well as from three different empirical studies that also involve business users.

The remainder is structured as follows. At first, we describe methodological aspects (Sect. 2). We then systematically construct the data model based on requirements before we present the integrated model (Sect. 3). We then critically review our model (Sect. 4) and finally end with a summary and conclusion (Sect. 5).

2 Methodological Considerations

We systematically develop the model in a stepwise approach using established requirements. These have been elicited from literature (for short: *R-Lit*), a survey among practitioners (for short: *R-Prac*), from a case study (for short: *R-Case*) and by demonstrating a prototypical system to real users (for short: *R-Prot*) that used it and commented on their experience. The detailed requirements elicitation is part of our previous work [15]. Since scientific progress is cumulative, we need to re-introduce these requirements throughout this paper in order to be able to construct our data model. The construction of the data model is done in a step-wise procedure. Thereby, requirements stemming from the before mentioned sources are used to derive partial data models. These models are then combined to a single integrated model. After the model has been constructed, we critically review our model by comparing it with a data model being reverse-engineered from a real-world system. This critical review leads to adaptations of the integrated model. Our research process is depicted in Fig. 1. Solid arrows mean "leads to", the dashed arrow means "go back and revise".

3 Requirement-Based Design of the Reference Model

In this section, we systematically derive our data model based on requirements. We use the term *implementation* to denote that a requirement is embodied in the data model, meaning the data model reflects the requirement.

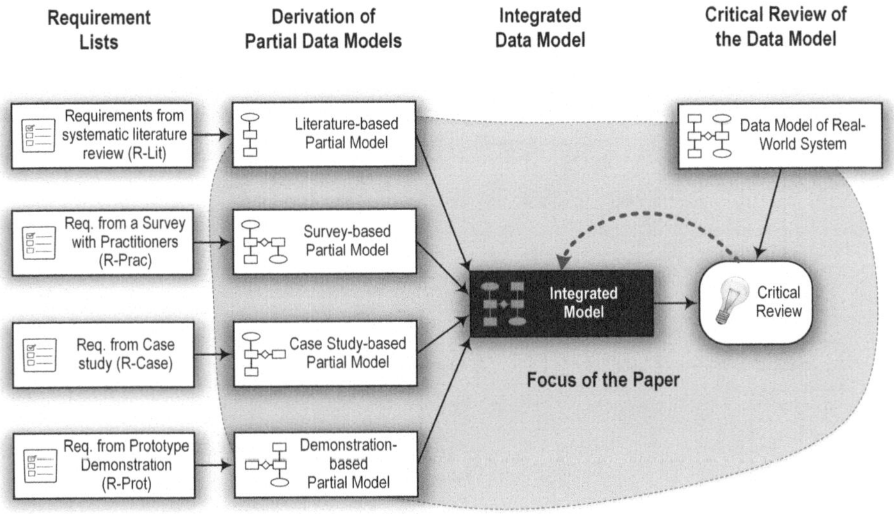

Fig. 1. Overview on research process taken

3.1 Implementation of Requirements from Literature (R-Lit)

Requirements from literature have been elicited by reviewing related works found in the databases Science Direct, ISI Web of Knowledge, Springer and EBSCO that in sum cover approx. 950.000 journals, books and conferences (see [15] for more details). Requirements fall into three broad categories: Requirements in regard to the *content* that is recommended, the *recommendation capabilities* and the *recommendation system*. We introduce each requirement briefly and comment on how these requirements are reflected in the data model. The data model in this section (cf. Fig. 2) and subsequent sections are constructed using the well-established notation of Entity Relationship Diagrams that supports the specification of data structures on a conceptual level.

Content-Related Requirements

R-Lit-1. *Recommendation of basic process model constructs.* The system should be able to recommend constructs such as elements, their structure and labels.

R-Lit-2. *Recommendation of additional process model constructs.* The system should provide recommendations for other constructs such as resources.

R-Lit-3. *Provide descriptive meta-information about the recommendations.* The system should provide relevant meta-information about the suggested elements.

R-Lit-4. *Provide provenance information about the recommendation.* The system should provide information to judge the quality of the recommendation.

We implement R-Lit-1 by introducing the entity *Basic Recommendation Element*, R-Lit-2 by introducing the entity *Additional Recommendation Elements* (cf. Fig. 2). We generalize both by introducing a more abstract *Recommendation Element*-entity. In order to capture descriptive meta-information about elements that may also comprise

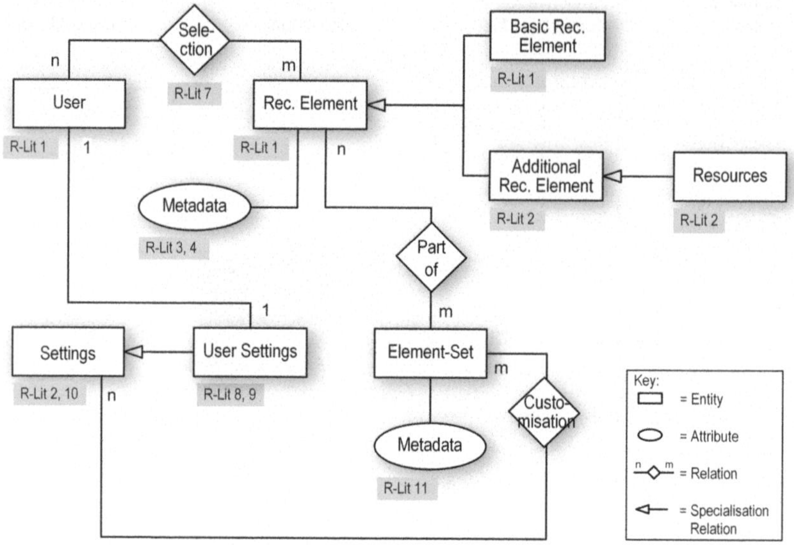

Fig. 2. Literature-based partial model

provenance information (i.e. source of origin) as demanded by R-Lit-3 and R-Lit-4 respectively, we introduce the attribute *Metadata* and associate it to the entity *Recommendation Element*.

Capability-Related Requirements

R-Lit-5. *Ensure recommendations with a high semantic quality.* The system should provide recommendations that are adequate and lead to a high semantic model quality.

R-Lit-6. *Flexible and easy application of recommendations.* The system should make it easy to work with recommendations and may guide the user in the selection of suggestions.

R-Lit-7. *Use personalization mechanisms.* The system should provide personalized recommendations tailored to the needs of the specific user in her specific modeling situation.

R-Lit-8. *Adjustable filtering options for recommendations.* The user should be able to adjust the filtering criteria for recommendations.

R-Lit-9. *Adjustable amount of recommendations.* The user should be able to adjust the amount of recommendations.

R-Lit-10. *Multiple recommendation strategies.* Recommendations should be determined using different calculation strategies in order to fit the user requirements.

The semantic quality of recommendations is mainly dependent on the concrete algorithm used to calculate recommendations as well as on the concrete instance data, so R-Lit-5 is not directly relevant for the data model. Likewise, R-Lit-6 cannot easily be reflected in the data model on account of its non-functional nature (e.g. due to terms such as "flexible" and "easy").

In contrast to that, R-Lit-7 can be embedded in the data model by introducing the relation *Selection* between the entities *Recommendation Element* and *User*. In this way, decisions to include a recommended element in the model that a user has been made are recorded as "selections" and can be leveraged for computing future recommendations.

R-Lit-8 and R-Lit-9 are requirements that permit a user to adapt the system to his or her individual preferences. Hence, an entity *User Settings* has been introduced as a specialized form of a more general *Settings*-entity. Since selecting the best recommendation calculation technique as required by R-Lit-10 may be a matter that requires experience, this is probably best set by an expert user engaged in setting up the system. So R-Lit-10 has been attributed to this more general *Settings*-entity.

System-Related Requirements

R-Lit-11. *Support knowledge base evolution.* The system should provide capabilities such as versioning, change management, importing new content or learning.

R-Lit-12. *Compatibility to existing tools and languages.* The system should work with existing modelling languages and in conjunction with existing tools.

We reflect R-Lit-11 by introducing a separate entity *Element-Set* that represents an arbitrary number of collections of elements (e.g. process activities to be suggested for several business domains). In addition, to provide for versioning and change management capabilities, the attribute *Metadata* is associated to *Element-Set*. R-Lit-12 demanding compatibility to existing tools finally is not eligible for representation in the data model. Figure 2 shows the derived partial model from the requirements along with the requirements that are depicted as graphical annotations.

3.2 Implementation of Requirements from Practitioners (R-Prac)

The following requirements have been derived based on studies that involved 48 participants as described in more detail in [15].

R-Prac-1. *Various sources for recommendations.* The recommendation system should be able to generate recommendations from various sources.

R-Prac-2. *Provenance information.* The recommendation system should provide background information regarding the source and quality of a recommendation.

R-Prac-3. *Display of recommendations on request.* Recommendations should be provided when the user requests the system to do so.

R-Prac-4. *Multiple ways of displaying recommendations.* The recommendation system should provide multiple ways of displaying the recommendations varying in their degree of non-obtrusiveness.

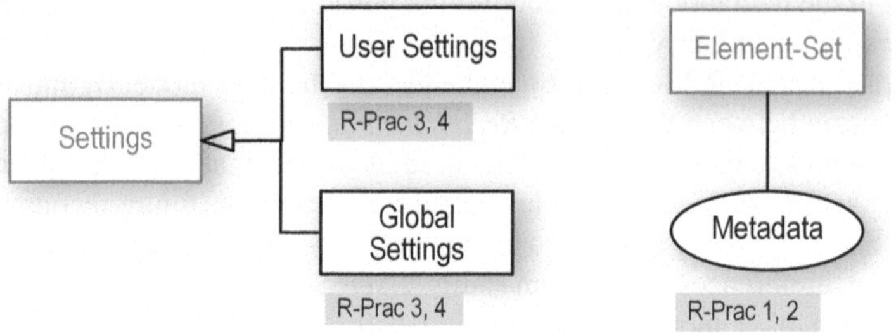

Fig. 3. Practitioner survey-based partial model

We implement R-Prac-1 and R-Prac-2 by introducing an additional attribute *Metadata* and associating it with the entity *Element-Set*. In this way, the source and the origin of a recommendation can be recorded and exploited by the algorithm computing the recommendations. Adjustments to the provision of suggestions that a user or system administrator might want to set according to R-Prac-3 and R-Prac-4 can be stored in the *User Settings* and *Global Settings* respectively. Figure 3 shows the derived partial model from the requirements.

3.3 Implementation of the Requirements from the Case Study (R-Case)

Requirements that have been collected involving 100 participants in a case study as described in more detail in [15].

R-Case-1. *Understandable recommendations.* Since one main positive aspect of using standardized activities has been that their interpretation is less ambiguous, the PMRSs should use such standardized activities.

R-Case-2. *Recommendation of "uncommon", innovative contents.* For example, the system may suggest activities that are executed typically in another industry and in that way inspire the process design.

R-Case-3. *Extension capability of the pre-defined contents.* To provide a remedy for missing activities, the recommendation system should include a feature to extend the internal knowledge base.

R-Case-4. *Benchmarking feature.* The system should facilitate benchmarking e.g. by suggesting Key Performance Indicators (KPI) or by enabling a comparison of KPI values.

R-Case-5. *Advanced model processing features.* The system should offer advanced features for the translation of models in multiple languages (e.g. process taxonomies such as PCF exist in different languages), to compare models or to show which area of enterprise activities they cover based on their semantics.

R-Case-6. *On/off switch and decent presentation of recommendations.* The system should be switched off easily and the recommendations should be presented decently.

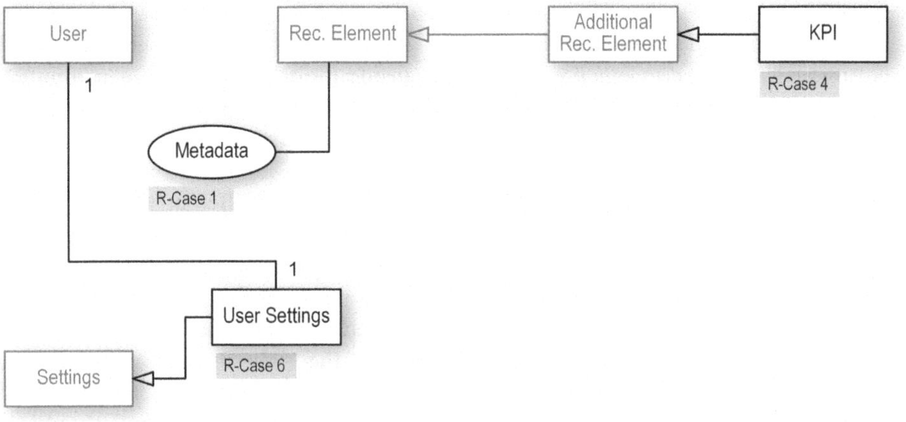

Fig. 4. Case study-based partial model

We reflect R-Case-1 by the attribute *Metadata* associated to the entity *Recommendation Element* since additional information stored as metadata might help to provide understandable recommendations. Their "uncommonness" or innovativeness as requested by R-Case-2 however is an attribute of the data being stored in the *Element-Set* and as such cannot be reflected in terms of structures in the data model. Further, import features for new content as demanded from R-Case-3 as well as advanced model processing features required by R-Case-4 have to be implemented as part of the functionality of a PMRs and thus are not reflected in the data model. In order to provide a benchmarking feature as implied by R-Case-4, Key Performance Indicators are required since they form the basis of any comparisons. These factors can be suggested similar to other *Additional Recommendation Elements* and thus are introduced as a specialization of the latter. An on/off-switch required by R-Case-6 can be realized as part of the *User Settings* data. Figure 4 shows the derived partial model from the requirements.

3.4 Implementation of the Requirements from Assessing a Prototype (R-Prot)

This section describes the implementation of the following requirements that have been collected by assessing a prototype with 66 business users as described in more detail in [15].

R-Norm-1. *Recommendation of organizational units.* The system should recommend additional elements such as organizational units executing the activities.

R-Norm-2. *Recommendation of resources.* The system should recommend resources such as documents, tools or information systems.

R-Norm-3. *Customized specific taxonomies.* To make sure a plethora of potential use cases is covered, the predefined contents in the system should be customizable.

R-Norm-4. *Mobile version of the recommender.* Due to the fact that an increasing amount of work is done on the go, a mobile version should be offered.

R-Norm-5. *Interface to other systems.* Data inside the PMRSs used for recommendations such as taxonomies of pre-defined activities or organizational units should be updated frequently via interfaces to systems containing that data.

R-Norm-6. *Support multiple platforms.* As there are different platforms and architectures used in companies the support of the most important of them is needed to make sure the system gains acceptance.

R-Norm-7. *"Intelligent recommendations".* This requirement is more an overall characteristic of the whole system and demands that recommendations should be made on the right time in the right manner with adequate content.

R-Norm-8. *Show recommendation context.* The user of the system should be informed about the semantic context of a recommendation that is offered.

The requirement of suggesting additional elements as stated in R-Prot-1 and R-Prot-2 can be implemented by introducing the requested elements as specialized *Resource* entities *Documents*, *Tools* and *Information Systems*. The requirement of customizing the element collection used to calculate recommendations stated in R-Prot-3 can be reflected by the *Part-of*-relation between *Recommendation Elements* and *Element-Set*. In this way, the same recommendation elements may be part of different element sets (e.g. an element set for each industry the recommendation tool is used in). The usage of the PMRs in a mobile version (R-Prot-4) and its interfaces to other systems (R-Prot-5) as well as support for multiple platforms (R-Prot-6) are outside the scope of the data model. Also, "intelligent" recommendations (R-Prot-7) are an obligation of the algorithm that operates on top of the data. However, showing the recommendation context as requested by R-Prot-8 may be supported using the information stored in the attribute *Metadata* associated to the *Recommendation Element*-entity. Figure 5 shows the derived partial model from the requirements.

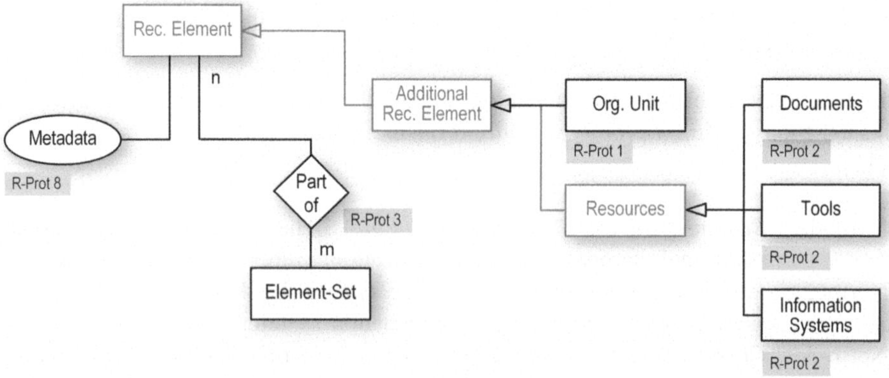

Fig. 5. Demonstration-based partial model

3.5 Integrated Data Model

The partial models that have been developed in the previous sections are integrated into a single model that is depicted by Fig. 6.

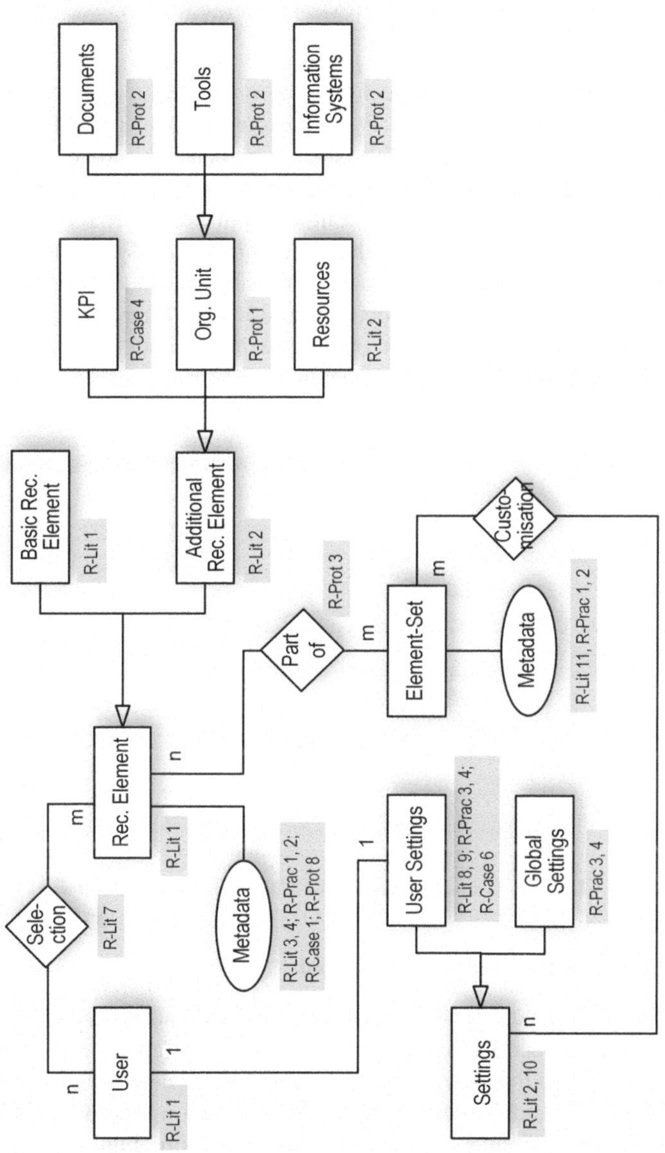

Fig. 6. Integrated model

4 Critical Review and Refinement of the Information Model

In this section, we first introduce a real-world implementation of a PMRS. After this, we present the data model of the implementation in the next section.

4.1 Introduction of a Real-World PRMs Implementation

The prototype has been built with the purpose to design an artifact that is useable, testable and evaluable. We used web technologies on the frontend in conjunction with a server-based backend (PHP, MySQL). With this tool, a modeler is able to create simple linear process models (cf. Fig. 7a) and use the recommending and autocomplete-feature of the system. The auto-completion feature (cf. Fig. 7b) allows completing the labels of model elements based on keywords typed in an input field. The recommendation part of the system is capable of suggesting the next element (cf. Fig. 7c). The system had been populated with process information (the labels and hierarchy of approx. 1000 enterprise functions) from the Process Classification Framework (PCF) in version 6 (see www.apqc.org), although other ontologies in semantic business process modelling [16] might also provide relevant contents.

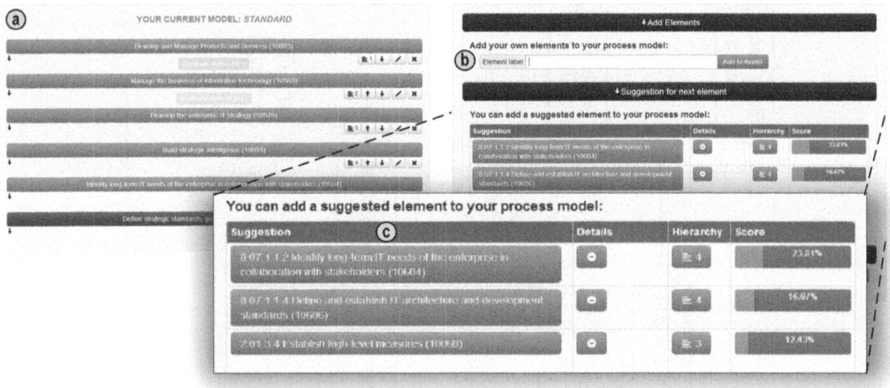

Fig. 7. User interface of the PMRs implementation

4.2 Data Model of the Implemented Tool

The tool was implemented initially to serve as a testbed and evolved over time. Hence the data model that has been derived systematically was not present in the beginning of the tool development. In this way, the data model of the real-world tool provides a good opportunity to review and refine the requirements-based normative data model leveraging the experiences from a real-world implementation. Figure 8 shows the data model which we reverse-engineered for the sake of our data model development. Shaded elements indicate the recommendation-specific parts; non-shaded parts represent data needed for more general modelling functionality.

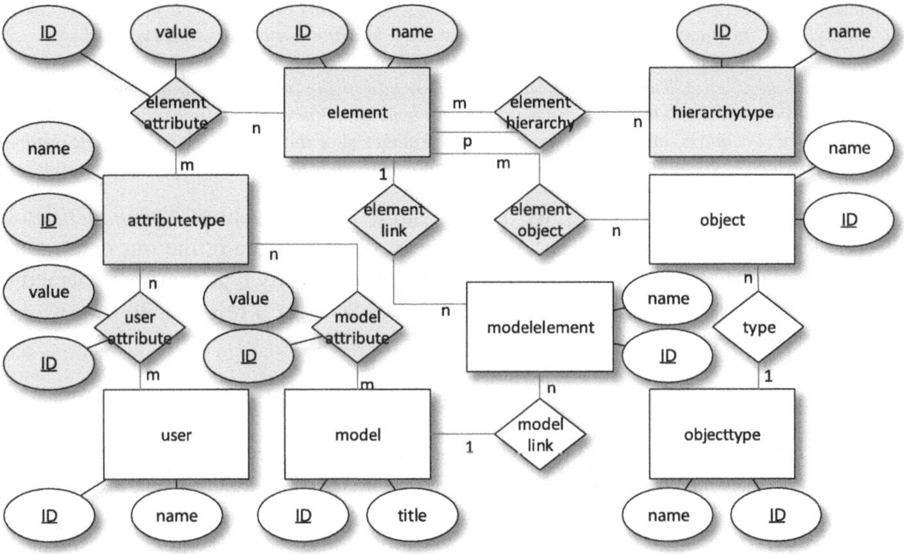

Fig. 8. Data model of the real-world PMRs

The following description (in italics) of the data model was given by the person who was involved in the development and was in charge of managing the data model. References to elements of the implemented PMRS inside the description are made using single quotation marks ‘’. We interrupt the description to comment on missing parts in our data model and begin such comments in a new line and enumerate them. For the sake of brevity, we do *not* comment on equivalences between the two models.

"The central aspect of the conceptual data model is the 'element' entity. It conduces as the central aspect for saving information about potential elements that could be used in a recommender system. As the recommending is mainly based on names the attribute 'name' is important. Furthermore, as in mostly all entities the use of an ID as primary key is compulsory. As one of the requirements has been to allow any kind of hierarchies, the entity 'hierarchytype' became part of the conceptual data model. First the information about what kind of hierarchy can be defined such as superior, inferior, equal, parent or child relations. In combination with the relation 'elementhierarchy' which combines two entities 'element' and an entity 'hierarchytype' the saving of generic hierarchies becomes possible. The design with the generic entity and the ternary relation is necessary to make sure individual terminologies as well as different kinds of relations are possible. Potentially the generic construct could be replaced with individual relations named after the kind of hierarchy (e.g. three relations named 'follower', 'parent' and 'child'). However, in a conceptual data model generalization is preferred."

(1) In our current data model, we cannot represent relations such as hierarchies or follower-successor relations. We therefore have to extend the model with an entity *Relation Type* and a ternary relation *Element Relation*.

"Another essential requirement of a generic conceptual data model is the need to save relevant metadata about an element such as the industry for which the element is specific, the context in the enterprise (e.g. production, HR), etc. To make sure that all potential values for arbitrary

metadata are savable, this has been included in a generic way. Therefore, a new entity 'attributetype' is introduced. This entity represents meta-information about what types of information could be saved. Consequently, this entity will hold the name of the information (e.g. industry, context, etc.). The information itself will reside in the attached relation between the 'attributetype' and the 'element' which is called 'elementattribute'. It includes the value and, untypical for a relation, an ID as primary key. This makes sure that for a defined 'element' and one 'attributetype' more than one 'value' is saveable (e.g. multiple industries for an activity)."

(2) In our current data model, we cannot store metadata about *Recommendation Elements* and *Element-Sets* in a generic way. We therefore refine our data model and switch *Metadata* from an attribute to a separate entity type that is connected to both *Recommendation Elements* and *Element-Sets* via a relation. In this way, a generic mechanism for storing metadata is possible.

"For a modeling environment, the central entity is the model with its very own data such as 'title' and ID and potentially many more. It is connected through the relation 'modellink' to the entity 'modelelement' which saves the elements within the model with their name and with an ID. However, from the central entity 'element' a relation was built which bridges the recommending to the modeling system. To make sure that certain 'modelelements' that got inserted into a 'model' do not lose their link to an element proposed by the recommender this link is saved within the relation 'elementlink'. So, after inserting a recommended element into a model the conceptual data model will be able to record this."

(3) In our current data model, we cannot record the information that a user has accepted a recommendation and inserted an element in his or her model. Therefore, we have to extend our data model with the entities *Model* and *Model-Element*.

"Furthermore, to provide for the possibility that not only following 'modelelements' are suggested but also objects that are annotated to a certain 'element' (such as Organizational units and Resources), the entity 'object' has been inserted. With its 'objecttype', the relation 'type' and the relation 'elementobject' it provides the basis for saving complex objects to the suggestable elements. This provides the option to recommend objects.

Another part of the conceptual data model is a relation called 'modelattribute' between a 'model' and an 'attributetype'. The potential of the relation is to save information for a whole 'model' of the same kind an 'element' can have attributes of (e.g. industry, context, etc.). This guarantees that potential recommendation algorithms can take account of model information and adapt their recommendations."

(4) In our current data model, we can only specify settings with the help of the entities *User Settings* or *Global Settings*. We however cannot specify settings related to a model (e.g. the industry for which a model is constructed). We hence have to extend the data model with an attribute *Model Settings*.

"Equally to the 'modelattribute' the conceptual data model was extended to the relation 'userattribute' which connects the user from the modeling system with the 'attributetype'. For the same reason of saving special informations about a model the system is enabled to save information about the user (e.g. the user is from a special industry, context, etc.). This can also be integrated in the recommending system to make sure the recommendations are adapted accordingly."

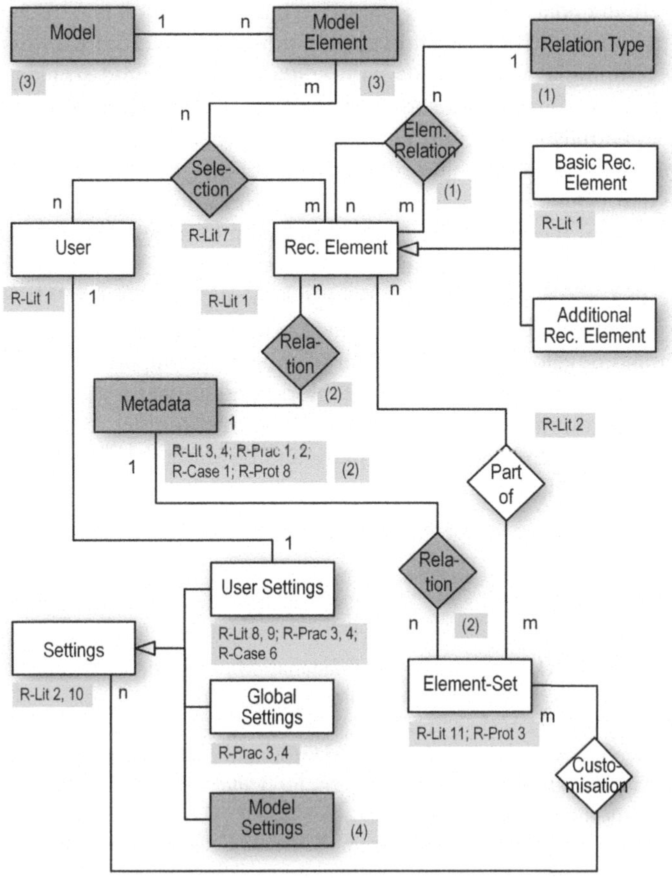

Fig. 9. Overview on research process taken

4.3 Final Refined Data Model

In the following, we present the final refined data model (cf. Fig. 9) that implements the changes identified above. Added/refined elements are depicted with shading and the number of the change identified above is added. Further, simplifications regarding the sub-types of recommendation elements (cf. Fig. 6) have been made.

5 Summary and Outlook

Although sophisticated modeling tools exist, guidance in process modelling in terms of auto-completion and recommendation features is – apart from some few research proposals – largely missing even in today's tools. However, to build such tools is a challenging task since a multitude of data and parameters have to be organized. Unfortunately, existing research works either do not make the data structures underlying recommendation-based systems explicit or the data structures are not developed in a systematic way. In this contribution, we therefore fill this gap in systematically developing a requirements-based data model. We did so using previously elicited requirements from various sources in order to construct partial models. We then combined these partial models into an integrated model. In a last step, we critically reviewed our data model in the light of a data model that was obtained by analyzing a real-world system. This analysis led to interesting insights that in turn caused extensions and revisions of the initial integrated model. These insights would not have been possible without the experiences gained in the implementation of the real-world system. We hope that our model will ease the implementation of new PMRS or informs further development activities around existing systems and that we can help to inspire more research and development in the field of modeling support.

Future research opportunities exist in exploring additional real-world data models of other types of recommendation or assistance systems in order to additionally refine our data model. Moreover, we plan to explore and develop algorithms and parameters working on top of the data model.

References

1. Luftman, J., Zadeh, H.S., Derksen, B., Santana, M., Rigoni, E.H., Huang, Z.D.: Key information technology and management issues 2012–2013: an international study. J. Inf. Technol. **28**, 354–366 (2013)
2. Sarshar, K., Weber, M., Loos, P.: Einsatz der Informationsmodellierung bei der Einführung betrieblicher Standardsoftware : Eine empirische Untersuchung bei Energieversorgerunternehmen. Wirtschaftsinformatik **48**, 120–127 (2006)
3. Nielen, A., Költer, D., Mütze-Niewöhner, S., Karla, J., Schlick, C.M.: An empirical analysis of human performance and error in process model development. In: Jeusfeld, M., Delcambre, L., Ling, T.-W. (eds.) ER 2011. LNCS, vol. 6998, pp. 514–523. Springer, Heidelberg (2011)
4. Wilmont, I., Brinkkemper, S., Weerd, I., Hoppenbrouwers, S.: Exploring intuitive modelling behaviour. In: Bider, I., Halpin, T., Krogstie, J., Nurcan, S., Proper, E., Schmidt, R., Ukor, R. (eds.) Enterprise, Business-Process and Information Systems Modeling. LNBIP, vol. 50, pp. 301–313. Springer, Heidelberg (2010)
5. Sen, S., Baudry, B., Vangheluwe, H.: Towards domain-specific model editors with automatic model completion. Simulation **86**, 109–126 (2010)
6. Kuschke, T., Mäder, P.: Pattern-based auto-completion of UML modeling activities. In: Proceedings of the 29th ACM/IEEE International Conference on Automated Software Engineering, 15–19 September, Vasteras, Sweden, pp. 551–556. ACM, New York (2014)
7. Melville, P., Sindhwani, V.: Recommender systems. In: Sammut, C., Webb, G.I. (eds.) Encyclopedia of Machine Learning, pp. 829–838. Springer, Heidelberg (2010)
8. Hornung, T., Koschmider, A., Lausen, G.: Recommendation based process modeling support: method and user experience. In: Li, Q., Spaccapietra, S., Yu, E., Olivé, A. (eds.) ER 2008. LNCS, vol. 5231, pp. 265–278. Springer, Heidelberg (2008)
9. Wieloch, K., Filipowska, A., Kaczmarek, M.: Autocompletion for business process modelling. In: Abramowicz, W. (ed.) BIS 2015. LNBIP, vol. 228, pp. 30–40. Springer, Heidelberg (2011). doi:10.1007/978-3-642-25370-6_4

10. Born, M., Brelage, C., Markovic, I., Pfeiffer, D., Weber, I.: Auto-completion for executable business process models. In: Reichert, M., Reijers, H.A. (eds.) BPM 2015. LNBIP, vol. 256, pp. 510–515. Springer, Heidelberg (2009). doi:10.1007/978-3-642-00328-8_51
11. Mazanek, S., Maier, S., Minas, M.: Auto-completion for diagram editors based on graph grammars. In: Bottoni, P., Rosson, M.B., Minas, M. (eds.) IEEE Symposium on Visual Languages and Human-Centric Computing (VL/HCC 2008), September 15–19, Herrsching am Ammersee, pp. 242–245. IEEE (2008)
12. Mazanek, S., Minas, M.: Business process models as a showcase for syntax-based assistance in diagram editors. In: France, R.B., Kazmeier, J., Breu, R., Atkinson, C. (eds.) MODELS 2012. LNCS, vol. 7590, pp. 322–336. Springer, Heidelberg (2009). doi:10.1007/978-3-642-04425-0_24
13. Clever, N., Holler, J., Shitkova, M., Becker, J.: Towards auto-suggested process modeling prototypical development of an auto-suggest component for process modeling tools. In: Jung, R., Reichert, M. (eds.) Enterprise Modelling and Information Systems Architectures (EMISA 2013), September 5–6, St. Gallen, Switzerland, pp. 133–145. Köllen, Bonn (2013)
14. Li, Y., Cao, B., Xu, L., Yin, J., Deng, S., Yin, Y., Wu, Z.: An efficient recommendation method for improving business process modeling. IEEE Trans. Ind. Inform. **10**, 502–513 (2014)
15. Fellmann, M., Zarvic, N., Metzger, D., Koschmider, A.: Requirements catalog for business process modeling recommender systems. In: Thomas, O., Teuteberg, F. (eds.) Proceedings of the 12th International Conference on Wirtschaftsinformatik (WI 2015), March 4–6, Osnabrück, Germany, p. 14 (2015)
16. Thomas, O., Fellmann, M.: Semantic process modeling – design and implementation of an ontology-based representation of business processes. Bus. Inf. Syst. Eng. **1**, 438–451 (2009)

Value-Driven Risk Analysis of Coordination Models

Dan Ionita[1(✉)], Jaap Gordijn[2], Ahmed Seid Yesuf[3], and Roel Wieringa[1]

[1] Cybersecurity and Safety Group, University of Twente Services,
Drienerlolaan 5, 7522 NB Enschede, The Netherlands
{d.ionita,r.j.wieringa}@utwente.nl
[2] Vrije Universiteit Amsterdam,
De Boelelaan 1105, 1081 HV Amsterdam, Netherlands
gordijn@cs.vu.nl
[3] D-Telekom Chair of Mobile Business & Multilateral Security,
Goethe University, Frankfurt am Main, Germany
ahmed.yesuf@m-chair.de
http://scs.ewi.utwente.nl/

Abstract. Coordination processes are business processes that involve independent profit-and-loss responsible business actors who collectively provide something of value to a customer. Coordination processes are meant to be profitable for the business actors that execute them. However, because business actors are independent, there is also an increased risk of fraud. To compute profitability as well as quantify the risk of fraud, we need to attach value models to coordination process models. In this paper, we propose guidelines for deriving a value model from any coordination process model. Next, we show how our approach can be used to identify possibilities of fraud offered by a coordination process, as well as quantify the financial impact of known fraudulent processes. Finally, we discuss additional applications, such as identifying commercially superfluous tasks, or missing tasks needed to achieve a financially sustainable process.

Keywords: Risk-aware BPM · Cost-aware BPM · Process analysis and improvement

1 Introduction

Today, *electronic commercial* services, are an important source of revenue for many businesses. For instance, consider companies such as Netflix, Spotify, or in our case study domains, Internet service providers and telecoms. Most e-services share two common attributes: (1) they are paid, usually by a customer and (2) they are provided by a complex network of enterprises. As a result, these services are open to opportunities to commit fraud. For example, a fraudulent actor may use the telephone subscription of someone else to place expensive phone calls.

J. Horkoff et al. (Eds.): PoEM 2016, LNBIP 267, pp. 102–116, 2016.
DOI: 10.1007/978-3-319-48393-1_8

Although fraud is often performed by misusing a business or coordination processes, its impact is actually on the business *value* level. Therefore, we need an instrument to analyze and express its financial effects for all actors involved. In line with previous work on value-based fraud analysis [1,2], we use an e^3*value* model [3] for this purpose. Because a value model represents what actors exchange with each other in terms of *economically valuable* objects (such as products, services or information), it is fundamentally different from a process model. Abstracting away from operational details, e^3*value* models only show *what* is offered, and not *how*.

Unfortunately, for many commercial services, information contained in a value model only exists in the mind of stakeholders, but an explicitly stated model is lacking. Coordination process models, however, often *are* available or can be harvested from existing coordination and orchestration systems [4]. While several approaches can be useful for designing a process model based on given value model [5–10], to the best of the authors' knowledge no previous work exists looks at an inverse technique.

Our contribution is therefore a new set of guidelines by which an available *BPMN* coordination process model can be used to derive a corresponding e^3*value* model (Sect. 3). With the resulting value model, we can use existing tools to identify and prioritize fraud and misuse scenarios (see Sect. 4.1), as well as estimate the impact in terms of lost value, and potential gain in terms of misplaced value for the actors involved (see Sect. 4.2). This assists the decision making process by enabling quantification of risks, but is also useful for rationalizing coordination models (see Sect. 5).

2 Background

2.1 Business Process Modelling

Business process models describe sequences of activities in business units or organizations. There exist a large variety of techniques to document processes, ranging from flowcharts to Gantt charts and from Data Flow Diagrams to UML. For coordination process modelling, two established notations currently stand out: The *Business Process Model and Notation (BPMN)* and the *Business Process Execution language (BPEL)*. The BPMN notation [11], is designed to appeal to technical users while being understandable to business users as well. BPEL [12], on the other hand, is mainly targeted at web service developers and lacks a standard graphical notation. Several approaches for translating between BPMN and BPEL have been proposed [13–15], but they have mainly served to expose fundamental differences between BPMN and BPEL [16,17].

Given the difference between BMNP and BPEL, we decide to use BPMN in this paper because of its standardized notation and because its audience and scope are closer to that of value models.

2.2 Value Modelling

The purpose of value modelling is to aid in business development, namely to explore, develop, and evaluate the value proposition of an enterprise, or a constellation of these. There are three important approaches: (1) the Business Model Ontology/Canvas (BMO/BMC) [18], (2) the Resource/Event/Agent (REA) ontology [19], and (3) the e^3*value* ontology [3].

The BMO approach takes one enterprise as point of departure, and considers its customers, suppliers, and other surrounding actors. However, since for fraud analysis we are mainly interested in *networks* of enterprises rather than just one, the BMO/BMC is less suitable for our purposes. The REA ontology is based on accounting theory, more specifically double entry bookkeeping. For our goal, it adds unnecessary complexity by requiring that each business transaction has four actions, namely increasing the amount of money and decreasing the stock at the seller's side, and decreasing the amount of money and increasing possession (of the delivered good) at the customer's side. Additionally, REA does not explicitly support multi (>2) transfer transactions. Therefore, in this paper, we utilize the e^3*value* approach, which recognizes the importance of the *network* of actors, and the idea of economic reciprocity in multi-transfer transactions.

In e^3*value*, there are a number of modelling constructs available to express a value proposition [3], which we discuss below. Figure 3b shows a very simple e^3*value* model. Enterprises and customers are represented as *actors*, and a set of actors of the same type (e.g. customers) is represented as a *market segment*. These actors are economically independent actors that intend to make a profit (in case of companies), to play break-even (in case of non-for-profit organizations), or to increase economic utility (in case of end users). Actors exchange *objects of value* with others, by *value transfers*. Some value transfers belong to each other, as they are reciprocal. For instance, a good may be transferred in return for the transfer of money. Such transfers have a mutually opposite direction; money is paid to the seller by the customer, and the good is transferred from the seller to the customer. Actors have *value interfaces*, consisting of *value ports*. These interfaces model economic reciprocity, as each interface has at least one *ingoing* port (e.g. a payment), and one *outgoing* port (e.g. delivery of a good). Actors may have a customer *need*, which results in value transfers (e.g. obtaining a product in return for a payment). Similarly, enterprises may express relations between value interfaces, denoting that in order to sell a product, other product(s) must be obtained. The dependencies among transactions needed to sell a product, are represented by a *dependency path*. *Boundary elements* express that we do not consider additional transfers anymore, and as such represent system boundaries.

It is important to understand that the e^3*value* approach is different from what is usually done in process models [20]. The most important differences are: (1) e^3*value* recognizes explicitly the notion of *economic value*, (2) e^3*value* has a modelling construct for the notion of *economic reciprocity*, and (3) e^3*value* only has dependency constructs and therefore can not represent *time-ordering* and control flows as used in process models. this corresponds to the goal of e^3*value*, which is to understand financial effects in a network of enterprises, and to do business development.

2.3 Relating Value Models and Process Models

Value models and coordination models have different goals and thus represent different types of information. At the same time, they are also related because they express different aspects of the same artifact, namely a set of enterprises and customers aiming to make a profit or to increase their economic value.

When designing a new e-business network, the designer starts with the development of a value model, often as a result of a series of business development workshops. The primary goal is to arrive at a shared understanding amongst the participating enterprises about what they offer each other of economic value, *without* considering *how* these value propositions are executed in terms of operational business processes. This allows identification of potentially profitable e-business models from a management point of view. If a profitable e-business network has been designed, the next step is to asses operational feasibility, which includes assessing and mitigating risks of fraud. This requires a coordination process model. Schuster et al. discuss the design of UMM models from e^3*value*/REA models [6,7]. The design of a process model from a value model can be also based on a consideration of trust issues [1,8] or on the distinction between ownership and possession of value objects [9,10].

In this paper we consider the case where businesses are already cooperating, but they want to assess the business value of this cooperation, for example in order to assess if the cooperation is still profitable, to assess the economic necessity of all parts of the coordination process, or to assess the potential for fraud, as we do in this paper. In the real world, many business processes and coordination processes evolve without regular consideration of the underlying value model, and it has been observed earlier that identification of the value proposition of a business process is a key concern of practitioners [21].

In the next section we show how to derive a value model from an existing process model, in Sect. 4 we show how to use the resulting pair of models in fraud analysis and in Sect. 5 we discuss further applications.

3 From Coordination Process Model to Value Model

As the value model represents different information about a value web than a coordination process model does, deriving a value model from a process model cannot be fully automated: information needs to be added to as well as deleted from a process model. Moreover, to add this information, value design decisions need to be made, such as which step in a process actually adds value for which actor, how much value is added, and which dependencies exist among economic transactions. These informal decisions - underlined in Fig. 2 - cannot be automated, and which of these decisions need to be made differs per process model and depends on the intended value model. The rest of this section elaborates on the derivation process proposed in Fig. 2 and gives guidelines for these decisions.

As a *running example* we take the simple process of setting up a new home Internet connection which requires network credentials. This applies to some telephony connections and/or ADSL connections where each user is authenticated to the provider via a username and password that are not linked to the equipment used to enable logical access to the provider's network (e.g. modem).

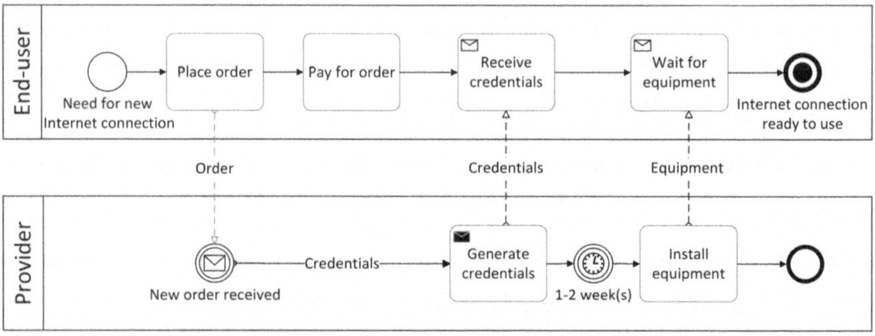

Fig. 1. Ideal coordination model for setting up a new home Internet connection

The normal (i.e. ideal, from the perspective of the provider) process by which a new subscriber requests and receives access to the network is shown in Fig. 1. When a customer places an order for a new Internet connection, it triggers the generation of new access credentials. While the user pays for the first month of service, the credentials are sent to him by mail. A technician is scheduled a week or two later to install the necessary equipment (usually a modem). Once the equipment is installed, the credentials can be used to obtain access to the Internet. Note that, for simplicity and didactical reasons, we assume the provider does not wait for the payment to be received before proceeding with setting up the connection. Since modelling physical objects (such as money) as a message is only necessary if their arrival acts as a message event or is expected as input for some activity [22, Sect. 5.2] we omit modelling the payment as a cross-border message flow.

3.1 Mapping Process Elements to Value Elements

Several BPMN concepts do have corresponding concepts in e^3*value*. Elements such as BPMN pools, swimlanes, start points and flows share semantic similarities e^3*value* actors, sub-actors, needs and value transfers. We propose the following mapping:

Pools to Actors: Instantiate every BPMN pool as an e^3*value* actor and every BPMN swimlane as a e^3*value* sub-actor.

Running Example: BPMN Swimlanes *End-user* and *Provider* are instantiated as e^3*value* Actors with the same name.

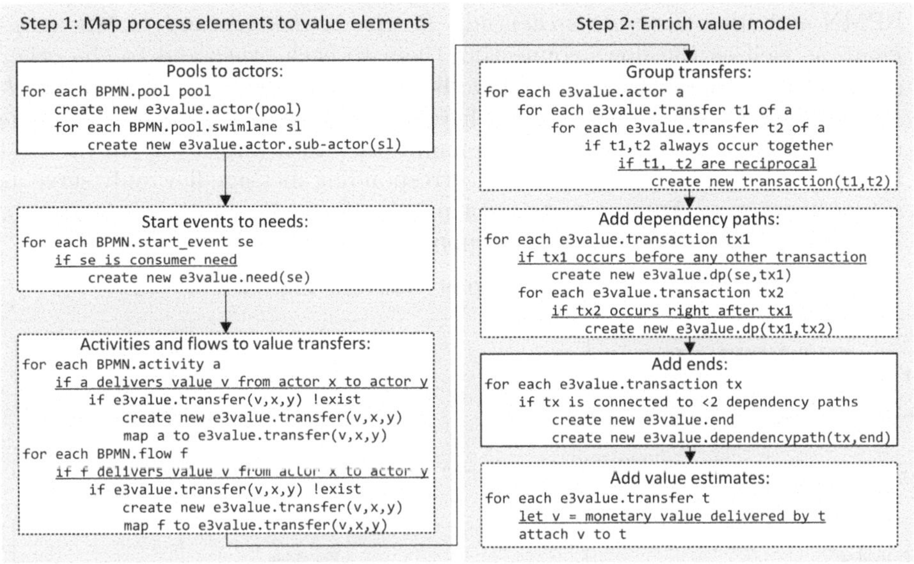

Fig. 2. Proposed derivation approach: solid boxes can be fully automated; dotted boxes require human decisions (underlined).

Start Events to Needs: Select the BPMN Start Event(s) that correspond(s) to consumer need(s). Instantiate as corresponding e^3*value* need(s), located at the same actor as the selected start event.

Running Example: BPMN Start Event *Need for new Internet connection* becomes an e^3*value* Need associated with *End-user*.

Activities and/or Flows to Value Transfers: Per activity and per flow, state if they deliver value and to which actor. Then, create a corresponding transfer in the value model.

Guideline: A BPMN activity maps to an e^3*value* activity if and only if the BPMN activity results in a potential profit. In many situations, this is not the case; many BPMN activities are generating costs. Therefore, the mapping from BPMN activities to e^3*value* activities is non-trivial. To find such a mapping, the modeler should ask himself: which BPMN activities and flows relate logically, such that together, they create a profit.

Running Example

- BPMN activity *Pay for order* provides (monetary) value to the *Provider*. Therefore, it is mapped to an e^3*value* transfer of type *MONEY* which we name *Payment*.

- BPMN activities *Generate credentials*, *Receive credentials* and *Install equipment*, as well as the flows connecting them to each other and to the other components of the process model together provide (service) value to the *End-user*, in the form of Internet access. Therefore, they are grouped into an e^3*value* transfer of type *SERVICE* which we name *Internet access*.
- BPMN activity *Place order* and the corresponding message flow only serve as a coordination mechanism and do not provide any value to any of the actors. Therefore, they do not have a corresponding transfer in the value model.

The value model after this first step is shown in Fig. 3a.

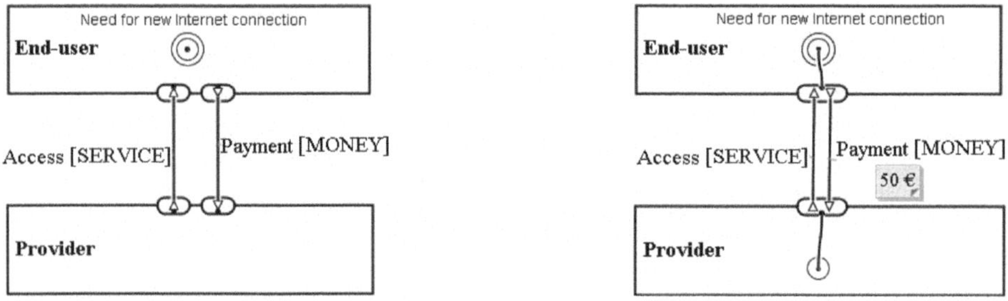

(a) After step 1 (b) After step 2

Fig. 3. Evolution of the derived value model for setting up a new home Internet connection

3.2 Enriching the Value Model

Group Transfers: Per actor, reciprocal transfers which always occur together should be grouped as part of a single e^3*value* interface.

Guideline: For each actor, two transfers he is engaged in are reciprocal (and therefore part of the same interface) if that actor considers that the outgoing transfer provides adequate compensation for what he offers [23]. Note that this does not have to be a on-to-one mapping: an interface may contain any number of incoming and outgoing transfers. While BPMN does not contain sufficient information to decide when two transfers are reciprocal, the execution semantics of BPMN can help ruling out transfers which are not. Specifically, exclusive gateways, event gateways and multiple start events give birth to *alternative paths* [24]. Depending on the conditions of the split or which start event is triggered, activities belonging to one of the alternative paths might not be executed. Conversely, a process model with a single start node and no OR or XOR splits will always terminate, and all activities will be executed [25]. Two e^3*value* transfers between the same two actors, can be grouped if and only if *all* BPMN activities that were mapped to these transfers in the previous step are part of the same path. Conversely, if any two activities required for the realization of any of the two transfers are located on alternative paths, then the two transfers should not be part of the same interface.

Running Example: The two transfers (*Payment* and *Access*) are reciprocal and part of the same path and can therefore grouped.

Add Dependency Paths: Following the sequence and message flow of the original BPMN model from the start, add corresponding dependency paths between the elements of the value model.

Guideline: Since e^3*value* models lack procedural information such as timing, the goal of this step is not to accurately represent the order in which the transactions take place but rather the causal dependencies between these transaction. Therefore, care must be again given to *alternatives paths.* As a guideline, map parallel gateways to AND nodes and exclusive gateways and event-based gateways to OR nodes. e^3*value* OR node are annotated with *fractions.* These fractions should reflect the relative likelihood of the condition-events (in case of event-based gateways) or of the conditions (in case of exclusive gateways).

Running Example: we just need to connect the Need to the only transaction.

Add Ends: Add e^3*value* ends as needed to any transactions without a connection to a dependency path.

Running Example: we are left with one transaction which has no outgoing dependency paths so we add an end point and connect it to this transaction.

Add Value Estimates: Quantify the value being generated or transfered by the activities in the process model and attach these values to the corresponding transfers.

Guideline: e^3*value* provides two ways of attaching monetary values to transfers: if the object being transferred has the same value for both the actors involved, then this value is attached to the transfer itself; otherwise, each individual valuation is attached to the corresponding end of the transfer.

Running Example: We add the value of the payment to the "Payment [MONEY]" transfer. We may also add the valuation by any or both of the actors of the "Access [SERVICE]" to the model.

The final value model is shown in Fig. 3b.

4 Applications to Fraud Analysis

Once we derive a value model from an *ideal* coordination model, we can leverage previous work on value models in order to run various value-based analyses on it, such as fraud assessment using e^3*fraud* [2]. Or, if we started out with a coordination model which includes fraudulent activities, we can do impact estimation using e^3*value* [3].

4.1 Fraud Assessment of an Ideal Coordination Process

In this section, we apply the e^3*fraud* methodology for automated identification and prioritization of business risks in e-service networks [2] to a derived value model and discuss the implications of the results on the initial process model. The associated e^3*fraud* tool[1] can generate possible fraudulent variations, in terms of (1) transactions that might not occur as agreed, (2) transactions that were not expected to occur and (3) collusion, where two or more actors thought to be independent act together against the interests of the provider. It also orders these sub-ideal scenarios based on potential gain for the fraudster, impact for the service provider, or both.

For instance, if we load the derived value model of our simple running example (Fig. 3b) into the e^3*fraud* tool, breaking transactionality by bypassing the only payment is – quite obviously – identified as the most damaging scenarios. Figure 4 shows the corresponding e^3*fraud* model, as generated by the e^3*fraud* tool. The *Payment* transfer is marked as dashed to highlight the fact that it does not occur.

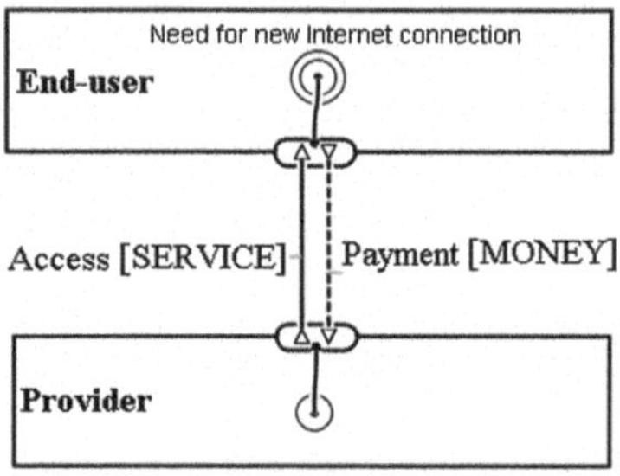

Fig. 4. Highest ranked sub-ideal model generated by the e^3*fraud* tool from the model in Fig. 3b

Leveraging the decisions made during the derivation process, we can now extend the e^3*fraud* analysis by mapping a fraudulent scenario back to the original process model, adding mitigations to this process model, and assessing the impact of those mitigations on the profitability as well as the fraud risks of the value model. This too is a partly automated and partly manual process, and could be a topic for further investigation.

4.2 Impact Estimation of a Sub-ideal Coordination Process

The above approach allows us to find fraud using a process model and a corresponding value model of the ideal, non-fraudulent way of doing business. In many economic sectors, there are however known process models of fraud. For these process models, our approach can help estimating the economic impact of the fraud by constructing the corresponding value model of the fraud.

For instance, a known vulnerability of the process of setting up a new Internet connection – as described in Sect. 3 – involves exploiting the time delay between receiving the credentials and the physical installation of the equipment by a technician. A BPMN model of this fraudulent process is shown in Fig. 5.

By applying the proposed model transformation steps, we end up with a corresponding value model of the fraud, as shown in Fig. 6. We can now evaluate this value model using the established e^3*value* profitability analysis [3] to estimate the profit made by the fraudster as well as the associated costs for

[1] https://github.com/danionita/e3fraud.

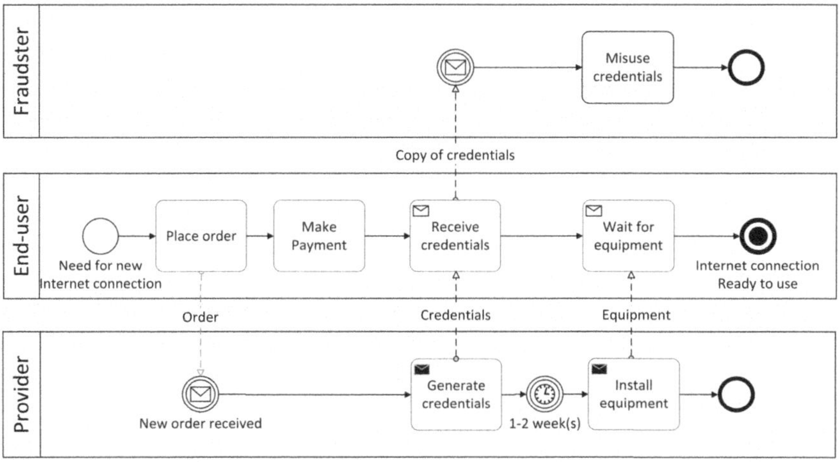

Fig. 5. Manually created sub-ideal process model of setting up a new home Internet connection

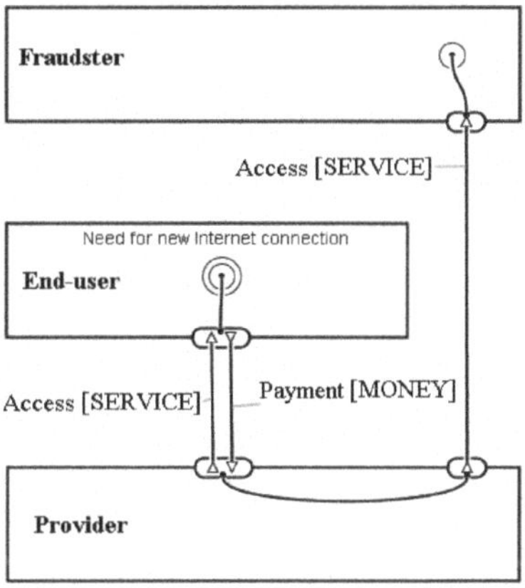

Fig. 6. Value model derived from the model in Fig. 5

the internet provider. Furthermore, we can apply extensions of e^3*value* aimed at analyzing sub-ideal value models – such as e^3*control* [26] – in order to help implement preventive measures.

5 Case Study: The Roaming Service

In the previous sections we used a simple, didactic example to introduce our proposed derivation approach and and demonstrate how it can be used to asses the potential for fraud in an existing non-fraudulent process as well as to estimate the financial impact of a fraudulent process. Next, we test our approach on a realistic business model obtained from a telecom service provider in order to discuss alternative applications which were not visible in the first example. Specifically, we investigate if we can leverage the process-to-value mapping created as part of the derivation process to identify potential risks related to the commercial feasibility of a coordination process. To this end, we obtained and analyzed a coordination model of the process of calling from abroad, also known as roaming. This is a telephony service which involves multiple providers (both the home and the visited provider need to collaborate to provide the service) and several payments (between providers and between providers and the user).

The ideal process by which roaming services are provided and charged is shown in Fig. 7. The process is triggered when the subscriber receives or initiated a call. Calling is a looping activity that triggers a technical sub-process (mobile subscriber identification, network routing, and so on). When a call is ended, a record of that call is saved. At fixed intervals, call records are billed and these bills are sent to the respective home providers. In turn, the home provider performs a corresponding payment and adds these costs to the subscriber's monthly bill.

We derive a value model from the process model shown in Fig. 7 above by applying the transformation steps described in Sect. 3. The resulting value model is shown in Fig. 8. Note that the transfer *Call* has no reciprocal transfer. This unusual result is discussed next.

Non-reciprocal Transfers: In the value model shown in Fig. 8, obtained by applying the proposed derivation method to the process model shown in Fig. 7, there is a transaction consisting of a single, non-reciprocal transfer: the *Call[SERVICE]*.

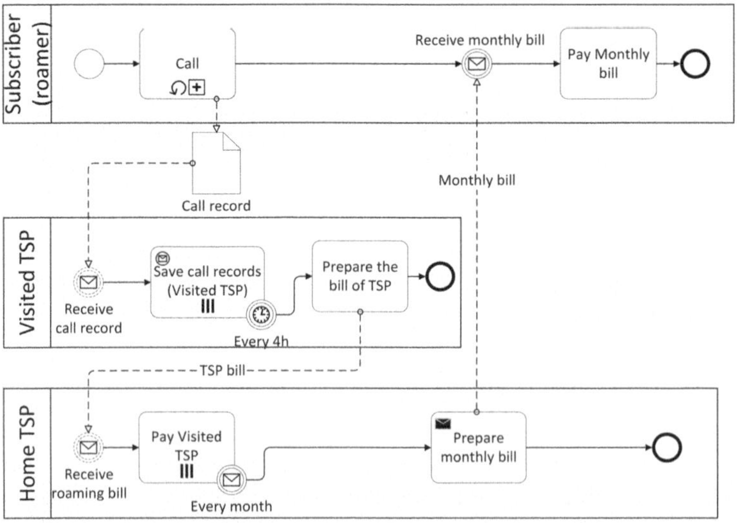

Fig. 7. Ideal process model - roaming service

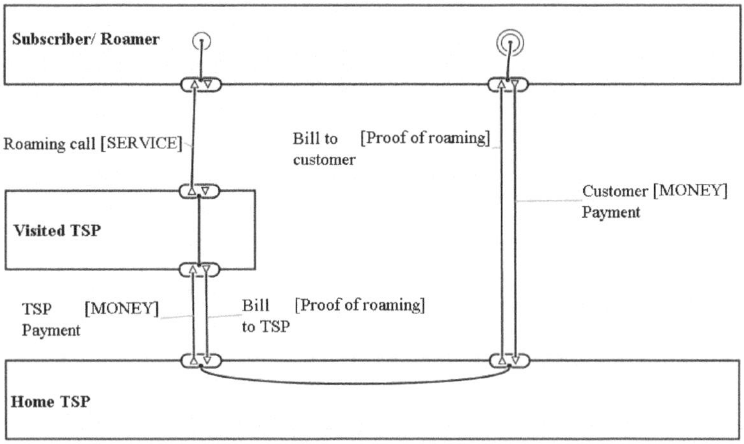

Fig. 8. Ideal value model - roaming service

A non-reciprocal transfer implies that something realizing the reciprocal value transfer, is missing from the initial process model. Such duality problems in value models created with our approach can have one of two causes: either (1) there is a problem in the process or (2) there is a problem in the model of the process. The former is indicative of a financially unfeasible process, which means the process is either altruistic or fraudulent. The latter means that the activities or flows realizing the reciprocal transfer are intentionally left out (i.e. are out of scope of the model) or unintentionally omitted (as a result of improper modelling or poor data quality). Deciding which cause applies in a certain case is important as it might trigger a re-design of the process or an update of the model. Checking the process model against consistency rules, such as realizability [27], local enforceability [28] and desynchronizability [29] might help identify which of the three situations described above we are in and why, but this is subject of further research.

In the example of Fig. 8, the process model is incomplete: it lacks information with regard to what is provided by the customer whenever he wishes to make a call, namely an identifier (commonly referred to as an IMSI[2] in telecom) which acts as proof that the subscriber has the right to perform roaming calls. This right was obtained when the SIM card was first purchased or is included in the monthly subscription fee.

The fact that reciprocal value-producing tasks missing from the process model will result in incomplete or incorrect value models when transformed using our approach suggests that we can also use the approach proposed in this paper to rationalize and validate coordination models and processes in terms of their financial sustainability.

[2] International Mobile Subscriber Identity, used to identify the user of a cellular network and is a unique identification associated with all cellular networks [30].

Superfluous Activities: Another result of the derivation of a value model from the process model in Fig. 7, is that one of the tasks - namely, *Save call records* was not identified as being part of a value transfer. Similarly, in Sect. 3.1 we did not map the *Place order activity* of Fig. 1 to a value transfer. This indicates that these tasks do not have a commercial purpose. Therefore, from a commercial point of view, the process can be streamlined by eliminating the task. But perhaps from another point of view, e.g. auditing, the task may still have to be included. Whichever the case, but observations such as these could provide a starting point for process optimization activities.

6 Conclusions and Future Work

Our derivation approach can be used to construct a value model from a multi-actor BPMN process model, which in turn allows profitability analysis of the original process model, the generation of fraudulent variations of the process model, and the analysis of the financial effects of changes (fraudulent or not) in the process model. By starting with a fraudulent instead of an ideal process model, we can also use it to estimate to impact of fraud and of fraud-mitigating measures.

The derivation approach proposed is feasible: it was applied by two authors independently to two case studies and was found to produce very similar results. Of course, further real-world validation is needed to get a better idea as to how difficult and error-prone the derivation process is.

We envision supporting the process by means of a software tool. Such a tool would implement the algorithmic part of Fig. 2, and guide the user through the non-automatable decisions he/she has to make. Another related topic which merits further investigation is whether a similar tool could use these decisions to maintain dynamic consistency between the two models, thereby supporting a wider range of applications, such as sensitivity analyses.

We believe that associating value models to coordination process models empowers the organization by promoting an understanding of the value creation activities inside the process and allowing usage of value analysis tools, such as income/cost estimations and fraud assessment.

Acknowledgments. The authors would like to thank Manfred Jeusfeld (University of Skovde) for his valuable input. The research leading to these results has received funding from the European Union Seventh Framework Programme (FP7/2007–2013) under grant agreements SEC-261696 (SESAME) and ICT-318003 (TREsPASS). This publication reflects only the authors views and the Union is not liable for any use that may be made of the information contained herein.

References

1. Ionita, D., Wieringa, R.J., Wolos, L., Gordijn, J., Pieters, W.: Using value models for business risk analysis in e-service networks. In: Ralyté, J., et al. (eds.) PoEM 2015. LNBIP, vol. 235, pp. 239–253. Springer, Heidelberg (2015). doi:10.1007/978-3-319-25897-3_16
2. Ionita, D., Wieringa, R.J., Gordijn, J.: Automated identification and prioritization of business risks in e-service networks. In: Borangiu, T., Dragoicea, M., Nóvoa, H. (eds.) IESS 2016. LNBIP, vol. 247, pp. 547–560. Springer, Heidelberg (2016). doi:10.1007/978-3-319-32689-4_42
3. Gordijn, J., Akkermans, H.: Designing and evaluating e-business models. IEEE Intell. Syst. **16**(4), 11–17 (2001)
4. vam der Aalst, W.M.P.: Discovering coordination patterns using process mining. In: Bocchi, L., Ciancarini, P. (eds.) Proceedings of the First International Workshop on Petri Nets and Coordination, PNC 2004, CNR PISA, Italy, STAR (Servizio Tipografico Area della Ricerca), pp. 49–64 (2004)
5. Fatemi, H., van Sinderen, M., Wieringa, R.: E^3value to BPMN model transformation. In: Camarinha-Matos, L.M., Pereira-Klen, A., Afsarmanesh, H. (eds.) PRO-VE 2011. IFIP AICT, vol. 362, pp. 333–340. Springer, Heidelberg (2011)
6. Schuster, R., Motal, T., Huemer, C., Werthner, H.: From economic drivers to B2B process models: a mapping from REA to UMM. In: Abramowicz, W., Tolksdorf, R. (eds.) BIS 2010. LNBIP, vol. 47, pp. 119–131. Springer, Heidelberg (2010)
7. Schuster, R., Motal, T.: From e3-value to REA: modeling multi-party e-business collaborations. In: Proceedings of the 2009 IEEE Conference on Commerce and Enterprise Computing, CEC 2009, pp. 202–208. IEEE Computer Society, Washington, DC (2009)
8. Kartseva, V., Gordijn, J., Tan, Y.-H.: Designing value-based inter-organizational controls using patterns. In: Lyytinen, K., Loucopoulos, P., Mylopoulos, J., Robinson, B. (eds.) Design Requirements Engineering. LNBIP, vol. 14, pp. 276–301. Springer, Heidelberg (2009)
9. Weigand, H., Johannesson, P., Andersson, B., Bergholtz, M., Edirisuriya, A., Ilayperuma, T.: Value modeling and the transformation from value model to process mode. In: Doumeingts, G., Mller, J., Morel, G., Vallespir, B. (eds.) Enterprise Interoperability: New Challenges and Approaches, pp. 1–10. Springer, London (2007)
10. Pijpers, V., Gordijn, J.: Bridging business value models and process models in aviation value webs via possession rights. In: 40th Annual Hawaii International Conference on System Sciences, HICSS 2007, p. 175a. IEEE (2007)
11. Weske, M.: Business Process Management: Concepts, Languages, Architectures. Springer Science & Business Media, Berlin (2012)
12. Juric, M.B.: Business Process Execution Language for Web Services BPEL and BPEL4WS, 2nd edn. Packt Publishing, Birmingham (2006)
13. Ouyang, C., van der Aalst, W.M.P., Dumas, M., Ter Hofstede, A. H.: Translating BPMN to BPEL. Technical report BPM-06-02, BPM Center (2006)
14. White, S.A.: Using BPMN to model a BPEL process (2005)
15. Ouyang, C., Dumas, M., ter Hofstede, A.H., van der Aalst, W.M.: Pattern-based translation of BPMN process models to BPEL web services. Int. J. Web Serv. Res. (JWSR) **5**(1), 42–62 (2007)
16. Weidlich, M., Decker, G., Großkopf, A., Weske, M.: BPEL to BPMN: the myth of a straight-forward mapping. In: Tari, Z., Meersman, R. (eds.) OTM 2008, Part I. LNCS, vol. 5331, pp. 265–282. Springer, Heidelberg (2008)

17. Recker, J.C., Mendling, J.: On the translation between BPMN and BPEL: conceptual mismatch between process modeling languages. In: Latour, T., Petit, M. (eds) 18th International Conference on Advanced Information Systems Engineering, Proceedings of Workshops and Doctoral Consortiums, pp. 521–532. Namur University Press (2006)
18. Osterwalder, A., Pigneur, Y.: An eBusiness model ontology for modeling eBusiness. In: BLED 2002 Proceedings 2 (2002)
19. McCarthy, W.E.: The REA accounting model: a generalized framework for accounting systems in a shared data environment. Account. Rev. **57**(3), 554 (1982)
20. Gordijn, J., Akkermans, H., van Vliet, H.: Business modelling is not process modelling. In: Mayr, H.C., Liddle, S.W., Thalheim, B. (eds.) ER Workshops 2000. LNCS, vol. 1921, p. 40. Springer, Heidelberg (2000)
21. Indulska, M., Recker, J., Rosemann, M., Green, P.: Business process modeling: current issues and future challenges. In: van Eck, P., Gordijn, J., Wieringa, R. (eds.) CAiSE 2009. LNCS, vol. 5565, pp. 501–514. Springer, Heidelberg (2009)
22. Object Management Group (OMG): BPMN 2.0 by example. Technical report dtc/2010-06-02, June 2010
23. Gordijn, J.: E-business value modelling using the e3-value ontology, chap. 5, pp. 98–127. Elseviers, Butterworth-Heinemann, Oxford (2004). Preprint available
24. Onoda, S., Ikkai, Y., Kobayashi, T., Komoda, N.: Definition of deadlock patterns for business processes workflow models. In: HICSS 1999: Proceedings of the Thirty-Second Annual Hawaii International Conference on System Sciencess, Washington, DC, USA, vol. 5, pp. 55–65, January 1999
25. Awad, A., Puhlmann, F.: Structural detection of deadlocks in business process models. In: Abramowicz, W., Fensel, D. (eds.) BIS 2008. LNBIP, pp. 239–250. Springer, Berlin (2008)
26. Kartseva, V., Gordijn, J., Tan, Y.-H.: Designing value-based inter-organizational controls using patterns. In: Lyytinen, K., Loucopoulos, P., Mylopoulos, J., Robinson, B. (eds.) Design Requirements Engineering. LNBIP, vol. 14, pp. 276–301. Springer, Heidelberg (2009)
27. Fu, X., Bultan, T., Su, J.: In: Conversation Protocols: A Formalism for Specification and Verification of Reactive Electronic Services. Springer, Berlin (2003)
28. Decker, G., Weske, M.: Local enforceability in interaction Petri nets. In: Alonso, G., Dadam, P., Rosemann, M. (eds.) BPM 2007. LNCS, vol. 4714, pp. 305–319. Springer, Heidelberg (2007)
29. Decker, G., Barros, A., Kraft, F.M., Lohmann, N.: Non-desynchronizable service choreographies. In: Bouguettaya, A., Krueger, I., Margaria, T. (eds.) ICSOC 2008. LNCS, vol. 5364, pp. 331–346. Springer, Heidelberg (2008)
30. Scourias, J.: Overview of the global system for mobile communications. Technical report (1995)

A Semi-automated Method for Capturing Consumer Preferences for System Requirements

Vu Nguyen, Eric-Oluf Svee(✉), and Jelena Zdravkovic

Department of Computer and Systems Sciences, Stockholm University, Forum 100, 16440 Kista, Sweden
vung9316@student.su.se, {eric-sve,jelenaz}@dsv.su.se

Abstract. There is a pressing need in the modern business environment for business-supporting software products to address countless consumers' desires, where customer orientation is a key success factor. Consumer preference is thus an essential input for the requirements elicitation process of public-facing enterprise systems. Previous studies in this area have proposed a process to capture and translate consumer preferences into system-related goals using the Consumer Preference Meta-Model (CPMM) used to integrate consumer values from the marketing domain into objectives of information systems. However, there exists a knowledge gap between how this process can be automated at a large scale, when massive data sources, such as social media data, are used as inputs for the process. To address this problem, a case in which social media data related to four major US airlines is collected from Twitter, is analyzed by a set of text mining techniques and hosted in a consumer preference model, and is further translated to goal models in the ADOxx modelling platform. The analysis of experimental results revealed that the collection, recognition, model creation, and mapping of consumer preferences can be fully or partly automated. The result of this study is a semi-automated method for capturing and filtering consumer preferences as goals for system development, a method which significantly increases the efficiency of large-scale consumer data processing.

Keywords: Consumer preferences · Social media · Requirements engineering · Term frequency analysis · Occurrence analysis · Sentiment analysis

1 Introduction

Deep insight into various consumer preferences provides a basis for companies to design better, customized services for different customer segments. In the current business environment, where consumers are often bombarded with multiple alternatives for the same product or service, understanding their preferences becomes a competitive advantage for business entities [1]. Accordingly, consumer preferences should be taken into consideration in the development process of customer-facing enterprise systems. A challenge of consumer value-oriented requirements engineering (RE) compared to the traditional RE process is the necessary amount of input

J. Horkoff et al. (Eds.): PoEM 2016, LNBIP 267, pp. 117–132, 2016.
DOI: 10.1007/978-3-319-48393-1_9

information that system analysts must collect and manage: to efficiently address the desire of countless consumers, they must take into account a wide variety of consumer preferences, not only from existing consumers, but also from potential ones.

Conventional methods to gather consumer information such as marketing surveys or interviews possess a critical disadvantage in the development of public systems: they can be difficult to conduct on a large scale without expert assistance. Additionally, interviews—perhaps the most commonly employed consumer preference discovery method—are not economically tractable or practically feasible for more than perhaps a few dozen customers, particularly in the area of requirements elicitation and discovery.

An alternative way for collecting preferences from the public is utilizing social media, which has become increasingly popular within the last decade. Using social media, companies have the ability to treat the market as a "conversation" between businesses and their customers instead of the more traditional "one-way marketing" [2]. Social media data reflects the most updated trends and real-time opinions of the general public, many of which may contain the preference of consumers towards public-facing systems.

The diversity of consumer opinions derived from social media is not only an advantage for enterprises, but also a challenge. Since information systems are generally not able to address the desire of every consumer in the community, it is more feasible to concentrate development efforts on functionalities that are of interest to sufficiently large groups of users. Therefore, the process of capturing preferences from social media needs to be guided by a methodological framework which enables consumer profiling and priority measuring.

In their previous paper [3], the authors proposed such a method to accommodate consumer preferences within the software development process. The main aspect of this method is to link consumer modeling using a predefined Consumer Preference Meta-Model (CPMM) with Goal-Oriented Requirements Engineering (GORE). CPMM bridges consumer opinion analysis and system-related goals by categorizing recognized preferences, as well as prioritizing them based on importance. Issues such as resource allocation, as well as proper slotting for developing different system components, make such categorization and prioritization vital. CPMM functions as a cleaner for massive data, a conceptual model housing key information derived from the processed data, and a resource capable of spawning additional elements for system development. At a high-level, the proposed method involves three major steps: (i) collect input data from consumers, recognize consumer preferences, and determine their importance; (ii) initialize an instance of CPMM; and (iii) derive goals for the development of supporting systems from the consumer values captured and prioritized in the instance of CPMM. While results of related case studies [4] proved the feasible process for capturing consumer preferences, most of the major steps in this method were conducted manually.

The study aims to explore possibilities for automation in the consumer preference capture and categorization process and their mapping to goals for information systems, to address the knowledge gap of how the method can be applied when a high-volume data source from social media is used as input for the process.

The paper is structured as follows. Section 2 briefly describes related concepts, background theories, and previous studies. Section 3 introduces a semi-automated consumer preference capture process with the assistance of context-aware text mining techniques. Section 4 demonstrates the feasibility of the proposed method by applying it to a case study. Section 5 presents the conclusions and future work.

2 Theoretical Foundations and Related Work

2.1 Consumer Preference as a Value

In business modelling, a transaction is an exchange of value objects between actors. In [5], a definition of value object is given as something that carries economic value for at least one actor. A value object can for instance be a physical product such as books, or a service such as internet access [6].

According to [7], customer experience is also recognized as a value. Although this type of value cannot be transferred directly from one actor to another and has no associated ownership and legal rights, it still plays an important role in the value exchange process between a business entity and its customer. For example, when a client feels secure about an online payment service provided by a bank, there is a higher chance that the client would use this service. A client feeling secure, which can be neither valued directly nor transferred, acts as an internal driver that encourages the client to choose that specific service.

The concept of consumer preference can be broken down into two types: attribute-based, where the preference of one brand over another brand is determined by attribute-to-attribute comparison, and attitude-based, involving the general attitude at the time of preference judgment [8]. In marketing science, consumer preference is defined as "the subjective tastes, as measured by utility, of various bundles of goods" [9].

2.2 Holbrook's Typology of Consumer Value

In the context of this study, consumer preferences as a value are refined in Holbrook's Typology [10], a well-known framework from product marketing in which three value dimensions provide a basis to classify the motivations that cause people to consume products and services: Extrinsic/Intrinsic, Self-oriented/Other-oriented, and Active/Reactive. Each intersection of these three dimensions forms an archetype representing a unique type of value in the consumption experience (Table 1):

Table 1. Holbrook's typology of consumer values

Dimensions		Extrinsic	Intrinsic
Self-oriented	Active	Efficiency *(convenience)*	Play *(fun)*
	Reactive	Excellence *(quality)*	Aesthetics *(beauty)*
Other-oriented	Active	Status *(success)*	Ethics *(virtue, justice)*
	Reactive	Esteem *(reputation)*	Spirituality *(faith, sacred)*

Extrinsic values correspond to consumption experiences determined by the functionalities of a service or product which can act as a means to complete some goals or objectives of the consumer. *Intrinsic*, on the other hand, is when the driver behind consumption is the pleasure of using the product or service itself. A traveler may decide to use a particular airline because it provides the fastest flight between two cities (Extrinsic) or because of a desire to experience world-class service (Intrinsic). With the Active dimension, a consumer controls their experience and enjoys the process of consuming a product or service, and such consumption can be either physical or mental. For example, a traveler prefers an airline service since it provides amazing in-flight entertainment and delicious meals. On the contrary, in a Reactive value, the experience when using the good or service controls the consumer. For instance, a traveler can be attracted to an airline when they are impressed by an airplane co-branded to promote a current blockbuster movie. Value is *Self-oriented* when a consumer evaluates some aspects of the consumption for their own sake. For example, an airline service brings value to a client when it enables them to conveniently travel to a desired destination. Conversely, *Other-oriented* value occurs when a consumer uses a service or product for the sake of others. "Others" in this case can be on a micro-level such as friends, family or a macro-level like society or community. For example, a traveler decides to purchase the service of an airline because it promises to donate five percent of each ticket purchased to charitable causes.

2.3 The Consumer Preference Meta-Model

CPMM presented in Fig. 1 is used to house, classify, and categorize consumer preferences for products or services.

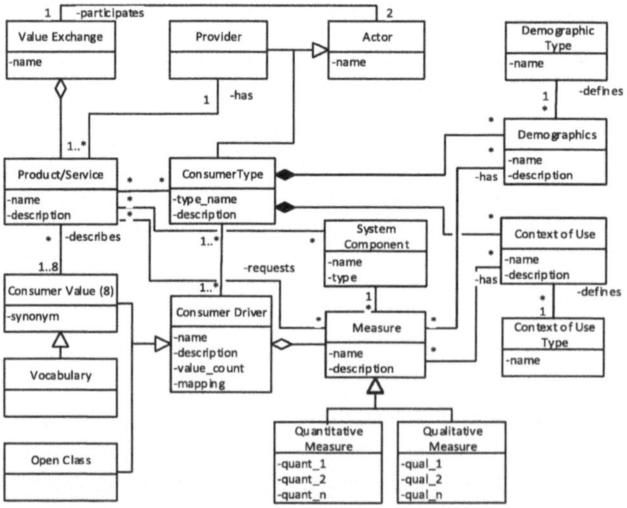

Fig. 1. The consumer preference meta-model (CPMM)

CPMM aims to elicit the preferences from different sources of data, as well as to manage them according to different value frameworks as shown in our previous studies [3, 4, 11].

Class *Actor* contains both *Consumer* and *Provider*, economically independent entities that are the primary participants within the *ValueExchange* of the focus of the *Consumers*' aspirations - *Products* or *Services*.

Consumer Driver is the preference that drives a consumer's evaluative process as they seek fulfillment. It can be taken from different frameworks, such as Holbrook's Typology, and houses the top level of a taxonomy of consumer values. The second level of the taxonomy are the terms which Holbrook designates as the synonyms to his primary typological terms, as seen in Table 1. The final of the three levels is *Vocabulary,* developed by using the Oxford English Dictionary (OED) to provide synonyms for the second level. *Open Class* represents any other considered value framework that is of type *Consumer Driver*. Examples of value frameworks analyzed in our previous work include Schwartz's Basic Values [12], Aaker's Brand Personality [13], and Maslow's Hierarchy of Needs [14]. Holbrook was chosen for this work because of its origins as a consumer preference-specific framework, as opposed to others from psychology and advertising.

Measure is aggregated in *Consumer Driver* by *Qualitative Measure* and *Quantitative Measure*, with the first describing an "unrefined" preference, while the latter quantifies its importance for a *Product/Service* for eventual support by *System Component(s)*. Depending on the source of data, as well as of the domain of interest, both *Qualitative* and *Quantitative Measures* could vary in the number of attributes for consideration.

Context of Use and *Context of Use Type* indicate when the activity that is the focus of the tweet occurs, either the intention behind that activity or at the time/place of writing. *Demographics* and *Demographic Type* classes situate *Consumer* and assist in consumer profiling - including home city, URLs within the profile, descriptive text and keywords from the profile, as well as any geolocation data that might be present.

2.4 Natural Language Processing

Streaming data collected from Twitter is in the form of free text and contains a limitless variety of topics. Unlike mainstream textual datasets such as newspapers, the style of there is no restriction in terms of writing standard for social media. People thus make use of jargon, slang, emoticons, informal abbreviations, and URLs, causing many challenges in processing the tweets on a large scale. For this reason, multiple text mining techniques must necessarily be applied to the collected raw textual data to assist the tasks of preprocessing, context analysis, and recognition of significant information.

Sentiment analysis aims to determine the attitude of a speaker regarding some topic, which is used in this study as one of the *Quantitative Measures* for collected preferences. Sentiment analysis is the process of identifying the polarity of the opinions, emotions, and evaluations captured in the text by classifying via the distinct labels positive, neutral or negative [15].

n-gram Analysis and Term Co-occurrence. To recognize popular preferences in a group of consumers' opinions, a natural approach is to look at words with high frequency of occurrence, because such words may carry useful information about common thoughts among multiple consumers. However, a single word usually cannot reflect the meaning of an entire sentence containing that word due to the diversity of the spoken context. This leads to the need of a context-aware method for term frequency analysis such as n-gram and term co-occurrence.

An n-gram is a slice of n consecutive elements of a longer string [16], in which n is a positive integer indicating the size of word sequence. An n-gram with only one element is usually referred to as "unigram" while larger values of n create "bigram" (n = 2), "trigram" (n = 3), and so on. N-grams carry more context-related information than a unigram. Term co-occurrence is similar to n-gram but is not limited to consecutive words. This type of analysis takes into account the co-occurrence of any combination of words.

Python was used as the main scripting language, and the necessary text mining techniques were provided by the Natural Language Toolkit (NLTK), a leading open source platform supporting the analysis of human language data [17].

3 Semi-automated Process for Capturing Consumer Preferences

In this section, we present the design of a semi-automated process to capture consumer preferences from social media and translate them into system-related goals. The process involves the following steps: *Data collection*, *Data cleaning and pre-processing*, *Qualitative measure recognition*, *Quantitative measure calculation*, *Constructing CPMM instances* and *Mapping CPMM instances to i* goal model.* An overview of the process design is presented in Fig. 2 below.

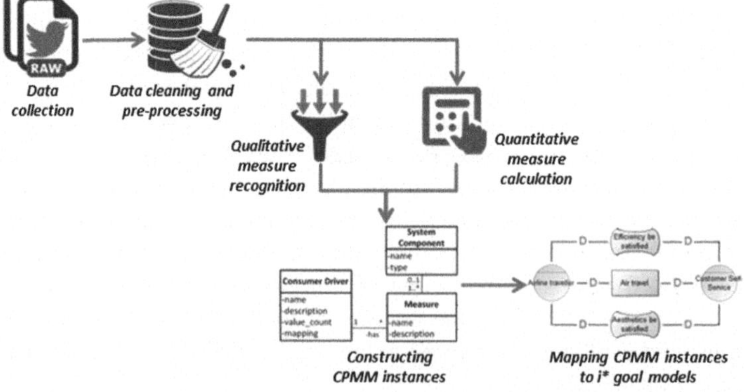

Fig. 2. Design of the semi-automated consumer preference capturing process

3.1 Data Collection

Utilizing the collaborative tools that are the foundation of Web 2.0, over the past decade a wide variety of social networking sites such as Facebook, YouTube and Flickr, have sprung up, creating a vast repository of data. Among the various websites available, two characteristics were used to choose a source for this research: (i) contain detailed personal information from which consumer preferences can be collected; and (ii) the designated content can be processed via existing text mining techniques.

The micro-blogging service Twitter was chosen as the social media data source for several reasons. First, whereas traditional blogs have no real size limit, micro-blogging is defined as having a strict limitation on message size (a tweet can be no more than 140 characters). This restriction provides an important advantage: it forces concision and directness in posts. A tweet is therefore often more expressive and univocal than a normal blog [18]. This is important for the precision of opinion mining techniques such as sentiment analysis as determining the polarity of short pieces of text tends to be more accurate. It is in this first step of the process that tweets are collected automatically using programming interfaces provided by Twitter [19].

3.2 Data Cleaning and Pre-processing

In this phase, data collected from the previous step is preprocessed and stored for further analysis. Twitter uses JSON objects to transfer data between the programming interfaces to the client's machine but JSON objects are structured as a set of multi-level nested dictionaries and lists which are inconvenient for instant access to any attribute under interest. Both redundant data and the complex structure of the JSON text objects hinder effective data queries from being executed for further analysis purposes. To resolve these issues of the raw data source, we developed a solution to parse JSON objects, filter out unnecessary information and store clean data in a well-organized form by using a database which provides an efficient, non-redundant data repository with fast query capability.

3.3 Qualitative Measure Recognition

The next step is to extract the preferences from the scrubbed dataset. Since the tweet content is natural language and has a high level of ambiguity, fully automated recognition of system-related ideas was not feasible in practice. We therefore used a set of computer-aided techniques to simplify the effort of data analysts.

Here, *Qualitative Measures* are extracted from the collected tweets. Text mining techniques designed for context-awareness such as n-gram analysis and term co-occurrence are utilized to help users, such as system analysts and requirements engineers, detect popular system-related preferences from the consumer community. This semi-automated approach is described as a sequence of the following steps:

i. Develop a list of information system-related "seed words" that are relevant to the functionalities of the future system using subject-matter expertise as well as related sources such as domain ontologies and industrial standards. These seed words are also considered as measures: groups of related qualitative measures in CPMM.

ii. Examine the popularity of seed words in the tweet database using term frequency analysis.
iii. Refine term frequency results using context-aware text mining techniques (n-gram and term co-occurrence) to discover potential qualitative measures.
iv. Analyze the set of refined tweets, record qualitative measures, and classify them to an appropriate consumer value category.

The approach employs a keyword filtering method to scan through the dataset and locate potential preferences. Acquiring a complete set of seed words from domain-specific documents and industrial standards is thus a key success factor of this phase.

3.4 Quantitative Measure Calculation

In this step, a set of scripts are developed to calculate and extract priority metrics for features recognized from the dataset. Assuming that certain opinions wield greater influence (for example coming from a public figure or celebrity) these would in turn have greater impact upon the preferences of the general public and thus offer a clearer path to uncover the common preference of a certain community. Therefore, a higher priority should be given to the consumer preferences with:

- *Higher influence* (influence-based Quantitative Measures). Messages tweeted by a high-influence individual disproportionately affect the opinion of a wider group of social network users, and thus better represent the desire of a larger consumer community.
- *Higher number of distinct tweets sharing a preference* (similarity-based Quantitative Measures). If the rebooking function is mentioned in 50 tweets while the seat changing function is mentioned in 15 tweets, rebooking should be prioritized.
- *Higher rate of negative sentiment* (sentiment-based Quantitative Measures). If a function receives too much negative feedback, there should be immediate action taken to improve that function in the future system.

This research employs and extends the social influence metrics for Twitter messages defined in [20] for *Influence-based quantitative measures*. While these metrics aim to assess the influence of single tweets, this research focuses more on groups of tweets that share similar opinions. Additionally, because analysis needs and data sets differ widely. CPMM allows social influence metrics to be flexibly assigned.

This study makes use of the following, differing from [11] which made use of a derived measure called "social weight":

- *Follower measure (FM):* The total number of followers of users who post a group of related tweets. The more followers a group of users has, the more influential this group of users is.

- *Reply measure (RpM):* The total number of replies to all tweets in a group. The more replies a group of tweets receives, the more influential it is.
- *Retweet measure (RtM):* The total number of times all tweets in the group are retweeted. Greater influence is indicated based on the frequency of retweets.

Regarding *similarity-based* and *sentiment-based* quantitative measures, we extend these metrics by introducing two more measurements:

- *Similarity-based quantitative measures (SiM):* The number of tweets sharing the same consumer preference. Distinct tweets mentioning a common consumer preference should receive higher priority.
- *Sentiment-based quantitative measures (SeM):* The dominant (> 50 %) sentiment label among a group of related tweets. For example, an SeM of *Negative* would be given to a group of 20 tweets mentioning a common preference in which 12 tweets are labeled as *Negative*, 5 as *Neutral,* and 3 as *Positive*.

3.5 Building CPMM Instance

Up to this step of the process, a list of measures and Qualitative Measures with corresponding Quantitative Measures has been defined and classified into relevant Consumer Value categories. In other words, the data processing phase is completed and sufficient information has been gathered to construct a consumer preference model. In this step, an automated tool is developed to generate CPMM instances from collected, processed data. A configuration interface is also provided for users to set model generation parameters, allowing users to control the size of generated models and to focus on particular areas depending on their particular analysis needs.

3.6 Mapping CPMM Instances to i* Goal Model

In the final step of the process, an automated tool maps CPMM instances generated in the previous steps to i* goal models. This is an implementation of mapping rules from CPMM to i* defined in [3]. Some adjustments are made to these rules to cope with the automation context. Table 2 below lists the revised mapping rules:

4 Case Study: Consumer Preferences in the Airlines Industry

The selected case study for this research is the requirement development for a *customer self-service system* of four major US-based airlines: American, United, Delta, and JetBlue. Most aspects of the airlines' customer service have been assisted by information systems. For this reason, when a passenger comments or provides feedback about airline services, there is a high likelihood to relate the comment to a respective system function. Also, the high volume of passengers using airline services results in a large customer community. According to [21], the US airline industry transported a total number of 769 million passengers in 2007. Given the popularity of Twitter in the

Table 2. Mapping rules from CPMM to i*

From	To	Mapping description
CPMM class	i* element	
Actor	i* Agent	*Consumer* and Provider specializations from CPMM are represented as distinct agents in i* SDM
Context of use/Demographics	i* Agent	Each consumer's segment in CPMM is mapped to an agent that is, by the relationship *"is part of',*' related to the agent in i* representing Consumer
Feature/ service	i* Agent (System)	*Feature/Service* (future system) in CPMM is mapped to a system-type agent in i*, between consumer and provider agents
Value exchange	i* Resource dependency	*Value Exchange* of the *Feature/Service* in CPMM is mapped to a resource dependency in i*, between the *Consumer* and *Provider* specializations
Consumer value	i* Soft goal	Each *Consumer Value* is expressed as a soft-goal dependency from the i* agent for a consumer's segment to the agent representing the system
Qualitative measure	i* Goal	*Qualitative Measures* from CPMM are represented as the intentions of each i* agent representing Consumers with a specific Context of Use or Demographic (pre-Traveler, Traveler, etc.)
Quantitative measure	i* Note	*Quantitative Measures* from CPMM are represented as the priorities for the corresponding soft goals representing qualitative measures

US, tweets related to these airlines can be considered as a promising source of social media data to capture consumer preferences for an information system.

4.1 Application of the Semi-automated Consumer Preference Process

Step 1: Data Collection. To capture only the relevant tweets, the Python script's listening stream is filtered with Twitter mentions corresponding to the selected airlines: *@AmericanAir*, *@united*, *@Delta* and *@JetBlue*.

To maximize the likelihood that relevant consumer preferences can be captured, we ran the listening script around the time of the winter storm Jonas from 21 to 25 January 2016. This was based on the assumption that an increase in storm-related flight delays would result in more customer tweets about the airlines' services, thus increasing the chance for system-related consumer preferences. Approximately *212* megabytes of plain text data were captured during this period, corresponding to *51,397* single tweets.

Step 2: Data Cleaning and Pre-processing. Textual data collected in the previous step was converted to SQLite tables for further querying purposes. Results of this step involve SQLite tables containing *51,397* tweets posted by *29,784* distinct Twitter users. *48,733* of these tweets are in English and thus useable for further analysis.

Step 3: Qualitative Measure Recognition. Since a keyword-based filtering method is utilized, the first task is to construct a complete and reliable list of seed words related to information systems in the airline industry. To ensure that the seed word list was constructed from both academic and practical perspectives, a set of academic publications [22, 23] and industry reports about IT strategies and ICT trends in the aviation domain [24] were consulted.

Having the list of seed words constructed, the next task was to apply the four-step process designed in Sect. 3.2 to identify useful tweets. Since the application of the process for the entire list is highly detailed, this process is demonstrated by the following example. In the case where the analyst is interested in discovering consumer preferences related to the email notification function of a future system, the corresponding process is as follows:

i. Select *"email"* from the list of seed word list.
ii. Use term frequency analysis to assess how often consumers mention *"email"* in their tweets. From the dataset the word "*email*" appears in 308 of *48,773* tweets, which is sufficient for further analysis.
iii. Use bigram/trigram analysis and co-occurrence analysis techniques to analyze the context in which the word *"email"* is used. In the case study, applying term co-occurrence with the seed word "*email*", it is revealed that the most common words that co-occur with "*email*" are "*cancelled*" (or "*canceled*") and "*flight*" (*65* tweets). This leads to an initial idea that many consumers demand an email notification function when their flights are cancelled.
iv. Finally, filter the tweets containing these three co-occurring words in the database. Part of the result is shown in the following Fig. 3:

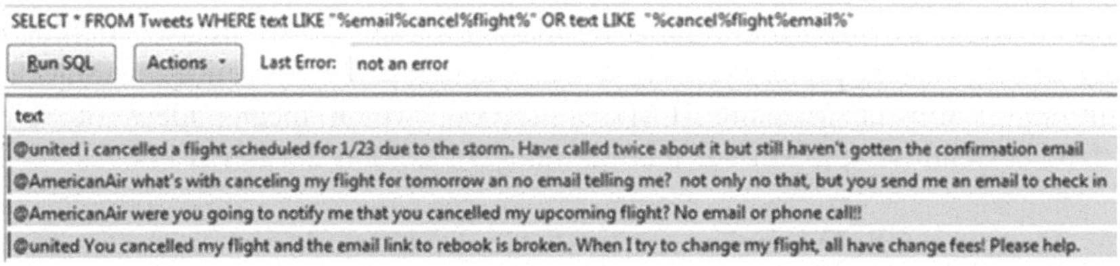

Fig. 3. Qualitative measure recognition from the seed word "email"

From four filtered tweets in this figure, two qualitative measures can be derived:

- *Notification email should be sent to travelers when a flight is cancelled).* This qualitative feature—*Efficiency*—is indicated by the first three tweets.
- *Reliable rebooking functions should be provided via email when a flight is cancelled.* This qualitative feature—*Excellence*—is suggested by the fourth tweet.

Step 4: Quantitative Measure Calculation. In this step, Quantitative Measures are automatically calculated for the captured Qualitative Measures as seen in Fig. 4.

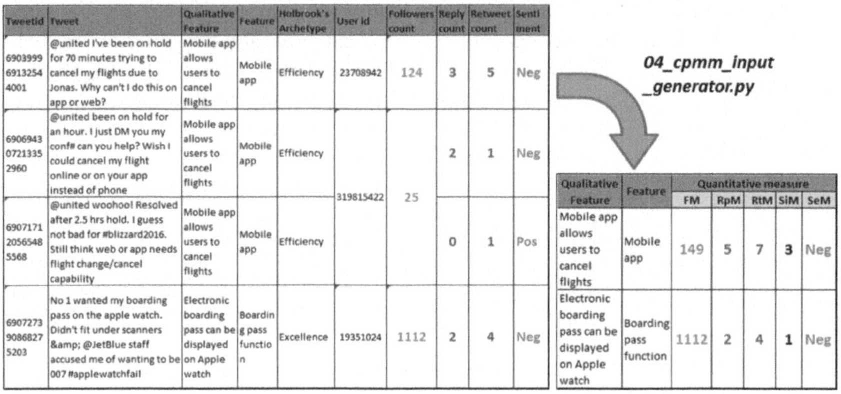

Fig. 4. Illustration of quantitative measure calculation

The result of this step is a list of selected tweets with qualitative features captured and classified into the relevant Holbrook archetype.

Step 5: Constructing CPMM Instances. By this step, input data for CPMM has been completely prepared. Additionally, we developed a tool to read this input data and generate CPMM instances, one that allowed users to configure model generation parameters depending on their analysis demands. These parameters are defined around core elements of CPMM, including Context of Use, Consumer Driver (archetype) and Quantitative Measure. As seen in Fig. 5, only qualitative measures satisfying the following criteria are represented in CPMM instances:

- Only measures belonging to *Efficiency* and *Ethics* categories are considered.
- Only system-related preferences from Delta and JetBlue customers are selected.
- Minimum Follower Measure (FM) of 25,000, which means ideas of selected preferences can be spread over a community of 25,000 Twitter users.

Step 6: Mapping CPMM Instances to i* Goal Model. In the final step, CPMM instances are mapped to SDM and SRM models by an automated tool utilizing ADOxx. Following the same example with the previous step, the SRM model is shown in Fig. 6 below.

4.2 Case Study Summary

Applying the semi-automated consumer preference capturing process to this case study, *1,374* tweets containing possible features for the future customer self-service system

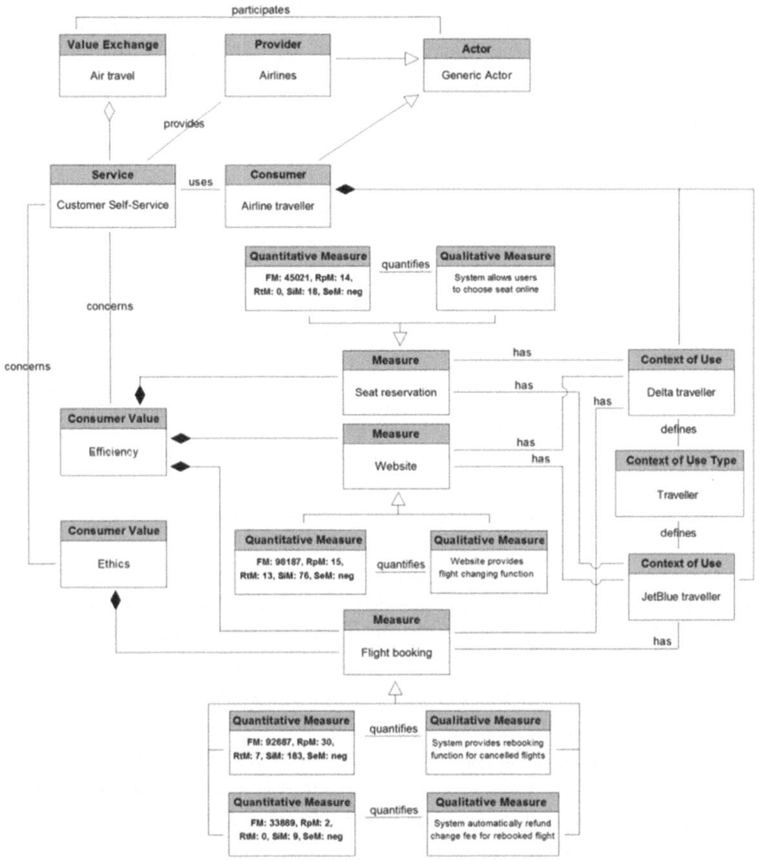

Fig. 5. A CPMM instance for the described example, utilizing Delta and JetBlue

have been recognized from a dataset of *48,733* tweets collected in English. These tweets were posted by a community of *1,183* distinct Twitter users. *207* qualitative features have been derived from the selected tweets into *18* groups of features.

5 Discussion, Conclusions and Future Work

In this research, we have (i) designed a semi-automated method with the assistance of automated techniques based on natural language processing to recognize preferences; (ii) proposed adjustments to the mapping rules from CPMM to i* to utilize social media data collected from Twitter; (iii) defined the revised CPMM meta-model in ADOxx; and (iv) implemented an automated mapping from CPMM instances to i* goal models.

The extent to which the entire process can be automated can be concluded as follows. Five of the six steps of the proposed method (*Data collection*, *Data cleaning and pre-processing*, *Quantitative measure calculation*, *Constructing CPMM instances*

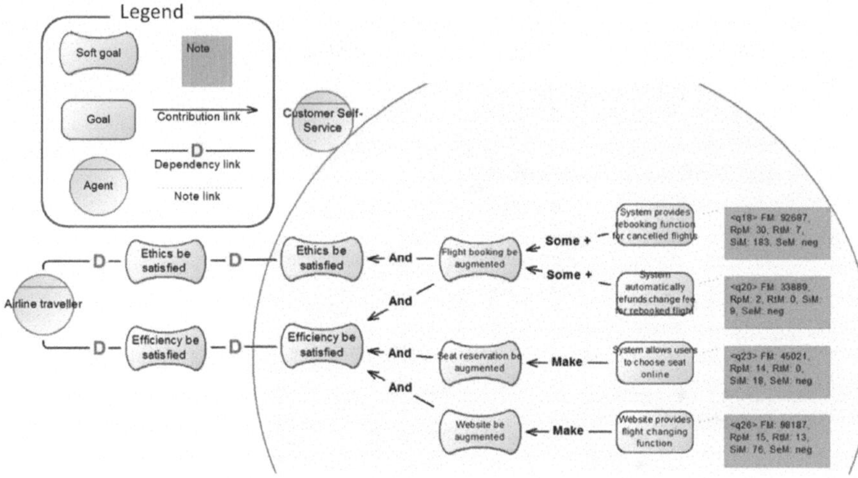

Fig. 6. Generated i* SRM model

and *Mapping CPMM instances to i* goal model)* can be fully automated with the implementation of different Python modules. The remaining step (*Qualitative measure recognition*) is a combination of sub-activities, in which classification of captured preference and feature definition are handled manually. Although preference classification can be automated with text classification techniques, it is not the focus of this study. Feature definition, i.e. writing the system features suggested by selected tweets in requirement engineering terms, is a pure natural language expression task and therefore cannot be supported by automation techniques. The other sub-activities can be partially automated with the term frequency and occurrence analysis tools.

This research extends work presented in [3, 4, 11] as the part of an overall effort to move consumer preferences toward greater model orientation. It considers opportunities for automation related to the development and application of the Consumer Preference Meta-Model to support user preferences according to their value-related content and segmentation, as well as the quantitative thresholds set by decision makers. In the semi-automated method introduced by this research, CPMM functions as the connecting bridge between consumer opinion analysis and system-related goal definition, in addition to facilitating the design of a method which categorizes recognized features into different consumer segments and prioritizes those features by quantitative measures. CPMM is thus equivalent to the role of Business Intelligence (BI) solutions, allowing business analysts to observe enterprise data from various dimensions and, depending on the analysis demand, present only the most significant and appropriate information.

Additionally, this research extends the social influence metrics for Twitter messages defined by Ye [20] by introducing Similarity Measure (SiM) and Sentiment Measure (SeM). These new influence metrics are useful for situations where opinions are extracted from a group of tweets instead of single and isolated tweets.

In terms of practical contributions, this study demonstrates a set of tools implemented in Python to automate different aspects and activities of the consumer preferences capture process. Additionally, CPMM was defined as a class library in ADOxx, thus serving as a machine-processable representation of this meta-model.

For future work, classification techniques from the data mining domain such as Naïve Bayes, Decision Tree or k-Nearest Neighbors can be employed to automate the preference classification task in the method. Different factors affecting the sentiment analysis of collected tweets such as sarcasm and negation should also be considered more carefully in future research. This would ensure the significance of Sentiment Measure when applying the proposed method for consumer preferences capturing.

References

1. Carpenter, G.S., Nakamoto, K.: Competitive strategies for late entry into a market with a dominant brand. Manag. Sci. **36**, 1268–1278 (1990)
2. Lusch, R., Liu, Y., Chen, Y.: The phase transition of markets and organizations: the new intelligence and entrepreneurial frontier. IEEE Intell. Syst. **25**(1), 71–75 (2010)
3. Zdravkovic, J., Svee, E.-O., Giannoulis, C.: Capturing consumer preferences as requirements for software product lines. J. Requirements Eng. **20**(1), 71–90 (2015). doi:10.1007/s00766-013-0187-2. Springer
4. Svee, E.O., Zdravkovic, J.: Case-based development of consumer preferences using brand personality and values co-creation. In: Ralyté, J., España, S., Pastor, O. (eds.) The Practice of Enterprise Modeling. LNBIP, vol. 235, pp. 159–173. Springer, Heidelberg (2015)
5. Weigand, H., Johannesson, P., Andersson, B., Bergholtz, M., Edirisuriya, A., Ilayperuma, T.: On the notion of value object. In: Dubois, E., Pohl, K. (eds.) Advanced Information Systems Engineering. LNCS, vol. 4001, pp. 321–335. Springer, Heidelberg (2006)
6. Schuster, R., Motal, T.: From e3-value to REA: modeling multi-party e-business collaborations. In: 2009 IEEE Conference on Commerce and Enterprise Computing. IEEE (2009)
7. Gordijn, J., Akkermans, H., Van Vliet, H.: Business modelling is not process modelling. In: Liddle, S.W., Mayr, H.C., Thalheim, B. (eds.) Conceptual Modeling for E-Business and the Web. LNCS, vol. 1921, pp. 40–51. Springer, Heidelberg (2000)
8. Mantel, S.P., Kardes, F.R.: The role of direction of comparison, attribute-based processing, and attitude-based processing in consumer preference. J. Consum. Res. **25**(4), 335–352 (1999)
9. Veres, Z., Tarjan, T., Hamornik, B.P.: Product attribute preferences–a multidisciplinary approach. Eur. Sci. J. **1**, 1–10 (2014)
10. Holbrook, M.B.: Introduction to consumer value. In: Consumer Value: A Framework for Analysis and Research, pp. 1–28 (1999)
11. Svee, E.O., Zdravkovic, J.: A model-based approach for capturing consumer preferences from crowdsources: the case of Twitter. In: 10th International Conference on Research Challenges in Information Science (RCIS), pp. 65–76. IEEE Press (2016)
12. Schwartz, S.: Basic human values: their content and structures across countries. In: Tamayo, A., Porto, J.B. (eds.) Values and Behavior in Organizations, Vozes, pp. 21–55 (2005)
13. Aaker, J.L.: Dimensions of brand personality. J. Mark. Res. **34**(3), 347–356 (1997)
14. Maslow, A.: Motivation and Personality. Harper, New York (1954). ISBN 0060419873

15. Wilson, T., Wiebe, J., Hoffmann, P.: Recognizing contextual polarity in phrase-level sentiment analysis. In: Proceedings of the Conference on Human Language Technology and Empirical Methods in Natural Language Processing. Association for Computational Linguistics (2005)
16. Cavnar, W.B., Trenkle, J.M.: N-gram-based text categorization. Ann Arbor MI **48113**(2), 161–175 (1994)
17. Bird, S., Klein, E., Loper, E.: Natural Language Processing with Python—Analyzing Text with the Natural Language Toolkit. O'Reilly Media, Sebastopol (2009)
18. Kontopoulos, E., Berberidis, C., Dergiades, T., Bassiliades, N.: Ontology-based sentiment analysis of twitter posts. Expert Syst. Appl. **40**(10), 4065–4074 (2013)
19. Twitter Streaming APIs. https://dev.twitter.com/streaming/overview
20. Ye, S., Wu, S.: Measuring message propagation and social influence on Twitter.com. In: Bolc, L., Makowski, M., Wierzbicki, A. (eds.) SocInfo 2010. LNCS, vol. 6430, pp. 216–231. Springer, Heidelberg (2010)
21. Belobaba, P., Odoni, A., Barnhart, C.: The Global Airline Industry. Wiley, Hoboken (2015)
22. Buhalis, D.: eAirlines: strategic and tactical use of ICTs in the airline industry. Inf. Manag. **41**(7), 805–825 (2004)
23. Chu, R.: What online Hong Kong travelers look for on airline/travel websites. Int. J. Hospitality Manag. **20**(1), 95–100 (2001)
24. SITA – Airline IT Trends Surveys (2012, 2013, 2014, 2015). https://www.sita.aero/resources/type/surveys-reports

Scaffolding Stakeholder-Centric Enterprise Model Articulation

Stefan Oppl[1(✉)] and Stijn Hoppenbrouwers[1,2]

[1] Department of Software Science, Radboud University, Toernooiveld 212, 6525 EC Nijmegen, Netherlands
stefan.oppl@jku.at, stijn.hoppenbrouwers@han.nl
[2] Model-Based IS Group, HAN University of Applied Sciences, Ruitenberglaan 26, 6802 CE Arnhem, Netherlands

Abstract. Involving stakeholders in enterprise modeling, besides rendering valid models, also helps stakeholders articulate and align their views on their organization. This requires that stakeholders are able to understand and actively perform conceptual modeling for representing their views on enterprise structure and behavior. The specific skills required for this should not be taken for granted and need to be developed explicitly. Scaffolding is an educational concept that allows to embed learning support mechanisms in operative modeling processes. The present article introduces a framework that makes it possible to view scaffolding as an integral part of stakeholder-centric modeling activities. The framework is validated with respect to its descriptive and discriminatory power by an ex-post analysis of the design and application of an existing modeling method.

Keywords: Scaffolding · Stakeholder-centric modeling · Articulation · Alignment

1 Introduction

Enterprise modeling is a form of conceptual modeling that is concerned with representing organizational phenomena and their relationships among each other [1]. The developed conceptual models provide the foundation for describing present or required [2] properties of enterprises as socio-technical systems, to document their operational and structural properties [3] and aid the communication with social and technical stakeholders throughout the design process [4].

The topic of how to facilitate the development of skills in conceptual modeling in organizational research has been addressed as early as in the 1960s, when Morris [5] stated that "if one grants that modeling is and, for greatest effectiveness, probably ought to be, an intuitive process for the experienced, then the interesting question becomes the pedagogical problem of how to develop this intuition." This question has also been picked up in enterprise modeling as the discipline continued to mature [6], and has moved away from being considered an "art" that requires "intuition" to a more scientifically grounded discipline [7].

J. Horkoff et al. (Eds.): PoEM 2016, LNBIP 267, pp. 133–147, 2016.
DOI: 10.1007/978-3-319-48393-1_10

In recent years, literature examining conceptual model processes [8, 9] recognizes a trend towards a strong and active involvement of stakeholders, who are usually not formally trained in modeling [10]. Models are considered to act as boundary objects [11] that enable people to articulate and align their understanding of their work systems [12]. Research in this domain has focused on how to facilitate modeling activities under involvement of such "novice modelers" [8] for generating models appropriate for the respective aims of modeling [13]. In contrast, the question of how to support the development of skills to work with and on the basis of conceptual enterprise models for this group of people, who usually does not have the opportunity to dedicate effort and time to formal modeling education, has hardly been a subject of research. The potential added value of such skills for this group, however, has been recognized repeatedly over the last decades in terms of pursuing a deeper understanding of the domain and phenomenon being subject of modeling [3, 13, 14].

The aim of the present work is to address this issue by making a step towards a framework for embedding *scaffolding* (offering help and guidance for as long as necessary; see Sect. 2.2) in stakeholder-oriented enterprise modeling to enable stakeholders to directly contribute to modeling. Our framework aims at enabling theory-informed method design. We thus methodologically follow Walls et al. [15], and identify meta-design requirements based on our kernel theories, derive a meta-design based on these requirements and give a first validation of our framework by ex-post analysis of a workshop design for stakeholder-oriented enterprise modeling. The contribution of the present work is that it augments current practices for enterprise model elicitation with an explicit skill development perspective that aims at enabling stakeholders to actively participate in modeling.

This paper is structured as follows: In the next section, we elaborate on background and related work to establish the foundation for our framework. The meta-requirements in terms of embedding scaffolding in modeling workshop designs are established in Sect. 3 and are encoded in a framework that serves as the meta-design. Section 4 validates this framework on two levels: we first use it to conduct an ex-post analysis of an existing modeling method and second deploy it as a lens for analyzing concrete workshops from a learning support perspective. We close with a discussion of our findings and derive directions of future research.

2 Background and Related Work

In this section we introduce the background theories and related work our research is based on. This establishes the research framework of the present work and allows to derive design guidelines for scaffolds in the following section.

2.1 Enterprise Modeling as a Form of Stakeholder Articulation

The creation of enterprise models under the involvement of stakeholders not only is a form of model elicitation [6], but – if performed collaboratively in a group of stakeholders – can be considered a form of Articulation Work [16]. Articulation Work refers to all activities concerned with setting up and maintaining cooperative work in organizations (ibid.). Articulation work in most cases happens implicitly and is triggered during the ongoing productive work activities whenever contingencies arise. When aligning views on organizational work with those of others and aligning them to form a coherent, normative model of enterprise structure and behavior [17], articulation work takes a more explicit form that allows to establish work practices or structures beyond the immediate context of the group of involved people [18]. Enterprise modeling as a form of creating external artifacts to represent organizational phenomena in conceptual models is a means to support such activities [19]. The potential added value of enterprise modeling activities in that respect, however, can only be realized if the stakeholders are able to understand and use the respective means of representation [20]. The availability of the necessary skills must not be taken for granted [21] and must be developed explicitly [22]. Based on existing empirical evidence [23], we hypothesize that support for the development of these skills can be embedded in the modeling process by means of scaffolding.

2.2 Scaffolding

Scaffolding is a concept introduced in the field of educational tutoring by Wood et al. [24]. It originally refers to having an experienced person help an unexperienced learner to acquire knowledge about a particular topic. Scaffolding is a metaphor adopted from construction industry and refers to a temporary means of support that is present until the entity supported by scaffolds (here: a subject participating in conceptual modeling) can accomplish a given task herself [25]. It is usually motivated by the aim of keeping subjects in their "zone of proximal development" (ZPD) during a learning process [26], i.e., putting them in a situation, which is challenging, yet attainable to them. In order for scaffolds to be acceptable for subjects and provide added value to them, they need to be appropriated to their current skill level [27].

Scaffolding can take different forms. Based on a meta-study of scaffolding research, Jumaat and Tasir [28] distinguish conceptual scaffolds, procedural scaffolds, metacognitive scaffolds and strategic scaffolds. *Conceptual scaffolds* help learning to decide what to consider to be worth learning. In particular, they can help to prioritize fundamental concepts. *Procedural scaffolds* assist students in using available tools and methods and point them at potentially useful resources. *Strategic scaffolds* suggest alternative ways to tackle problems in learning. Finally, *metacognitive scaffolds* guide students in how to approach a learning problem and what to think about when elaborating on a problem. Orthogonally to these categories, Bulu and Pedersen [29] identify differences in the sources of scaffolding. *Scaffolds provided by teachers* are considered the original form of scaffolding. *Scaffolds provided in interactions among learning peers* refer to the phenomenon that scaffolding can arise from the collective knowledge of a learning group. Scaffolds can also be provided as *textual or graphical representations*, similar to a manual. *Technology-driven scaffolding* uses (information) technology to provide scaffolds. This includes interactive systems that try to intervene appropriately in the learning process based on observing learners' behaviors or static intervention rules.

Independently of which form of scaffolding is pursued, it is always characterized via the presence of three principles that have been identified by van de Pol et al. [25]: The first common principle is *contingency*, which is often referred to as responsiveness or calibrated support. Scaffolds need to be adapted dynamically to the learners' current level of performance. The second principle is *fading*, which refers to the gradual withdrawal of the scaffolding. As learners develop their skills, support becomes less necessary and is decreased over time. This is closely connected to the third principle *transfer of responsibility*. Via fading, responsibility for the performance of a task is gradually transferred to the learner. The responsibility for learning is transferred when a student takes increasing control about the learning process. The implementation of these principles is based on *diagnosis* of a learners' need for support, which is usually done by a teacher [23], but also can be implemented in interactive systems [30].

On an operative level, scaffolding is implemented via different means. Van de Pol et al. [25] list a (non-exhaustive) set of measures such as giving feedback, providing hints, instructing, explaining, modeling (i.e. demonstrating the skill to be acquired) and questioning. They differ in their depth of intervention and the reduction of freedom in students' learning processes. How to appropriately select and implement scaffolding as interventions in the learning process is disputed (ibid.). The described categories and means thus should be considered a framework for observing and designing learning settings, rather than attribute them any normative value.

2.3 Related Work

In the context of conceptual modeling, several authors have examined how scaffolds can be used to facilitate the modeling process.

Fretz et al. [31] propose a software tool that provides conceptual and procedural scaffolds to subjects confronted with a conceptual modeling tasks in the context of science learning. In addition, they examine additional strategic and procedural scaffolds provided by teachers or peers. They use prompting to trigger reflection of modeled structures and allow to validate the model by interactive simulations. As such, the tool uses scaffolds to implement a setting that facilitates argumentative discourse via procedural guidance. The authors do not refer to principles like fading or transfer of responsibilities, but rather focus on examining the effect of the different types of scaffolds in the argumentative design. They found that—although the designed scaffolds achieved their intended effects—the role of teachers and peers in association with designed scaffolds appears to be vital for successful deployment.

Sandkuhl et al. [32] and Carstensen et al. [33] use the term scaffolding in the context of enterprise modeling, but refer to it in an architectural sense. They aim at creating "shared knowledge and understanding" among subjects in a collaborative modeling session before the actual problem-solving process starts. While this is fundamentally different from the understanding of scaffolding put forward above, the means they propose still can inform scaffold design for conceptual modeling. In particular, they use metacognitive scaffolds encoded in graphical modeling templates that indicate which perspectives should be considered relevant for a particular enterprise modeling problem.

Oppl [34] has reviewed the state of the art of conceptual modeling workshop facilitation techniques with a focus on how scaffolding concepts are used to support modeling processes. The results indicate that in particular metacognitive and procedural scaffolds are regularly used for facilitation, usually in an implicit way, without referring to scaffolding as such. They also show that hardly any existing approaches give an explicit account on the fundamental scaffolding principles: contingency, fading, and transfer of responsibility. Related work thus currently does not enable to systematically embed scaffolding measures in modeling workshop design. We thus derive a framework to address this issue from research performed on scaffolding for supporting collaborative articulation in general in the next section.

3 Scaffolds for Stakeholder-Centric Enterprise Modeling

Our review of related work has shown that, while scaffolding has already implicitly and, to some extent, explicitly been deployed in the field of conceptual modeling, a structured approach to describe and design scaffolding in modeling activities is not available. As argued for in the introduction, augmenting the design of stakeholder-centric modeling activities with a scaffolding perspective could help improve the understanding and creation of enterprise models in the target group. In the following, we therefore review scaffolding approaches proposed in other disciplines, which require similar skills as stakeholder-centric conceptual modeling, in particular with respect to articulation of abstract concepts describing real-world phenomena [21] and the support of developing a common understanding about these phenomena [35]. Based on these approaches, we develop a framework for scaffolding in enterprise modeling.

3.1 Scaffolding the Articulation of Models

The process of articulating abstract concepts, being a main activity in conceptual modeling, has been widely examined regarding potential scaffolding support in the field of mathematical and science education.

Ozmantar and Roper [36] consider teacher interventions as the major means of scaffolding (in the context of mathematical abstraction problems). Their study focusses on examining the activities of the person providing scaffolds. They identify three major facets that they could observe. First, they observed that scaffolding strategies were chosen in an ad-hoc manner based on continuous monitoring and analyzing the subjects' performance. Which scaffold is appropriate in which situation needs (and—they pose—cannot) be determined ex-ante. However, continuous monitoring allows to analyze, whether a provided scaffold achieves the intended effect and eventually adapting ones scaffolding strategy. Second, they identify a major means of scaffolding to provide meta-cognitive scaffolds by organizing the main goal of the learning activity into hierarchical sub-goals. Third, they could observe fading and transfer of responsibility to take place when models went beyond their initial construction and had begun to stabilize via consolidation activities.

Land and Zembal-Saul [37] examine how reflection and articulation processes on scientific explanations can be scaffolded. This focus is conceptually close to what other authors refer to as conceptual modeling. They examine means that to scaffold reflection and articulation on a longer-term time scale and focus on means of scaffolding via peers. Their scaffolds are deployed via a software platform, and are mainly meta-cognitive, based on task-specific prompting. They could show that their design was useful to learners and led to sophisticated explanations, indicating the construction of elaborate abstractions. They, however, found that the utility of "static" scaffolds as provided by their platform was dependent on the background knowledge of the learners. They thus suggest to combine their approach with human instruction that provides more explicit scaffolding especially for novices.

Stender and Kaiser [23] discuss the value of scaffolding the process of developing mathematical models of real-world-problems and validate their appropriateness for problem-solving. Rather than describing concrete scaffolds, they focus on diagnosis of student needs and fading support measures to facilitate independent problem-solving by students. Based on existing research on adaptive teacher interventions, they identify the invasiveness of different types of scaffolding in terms of restricting student's freedom of choice on action. Based on their empirical results, they suggest scaffolding interventions in the model articulation process to facilitate problem solving. Their results indicate, among others, the usefulness of decomposition of the modeling task, availability of model simulation tools and referring to existing knowledge via metacognitive scaffolds.

3.2 Scaffolding Argumentative Collaboration

Several authors have also examined how to scaffold collaborative articulation, in particular with focus on peer-facilitation of argumentative processes.

Abdu et al. [38] examine how the process of peer-facilitation can be scaffolded with whole-group interventions in classroom settings. Their focus consequently is on argumentative design that should prevent unguided model creation. They propose to provide strategical scaffolds by means demonstrating solution paths upfront, before peer interaction starts. Furthermore, they establish explicit prompting practices for peer collaboration to establish collective responsibility for the learning process.

Chin and Osborne [39] show how discursive interaction (i.e. argumentation) can be scaffolded in science education. They propose to provide question prompts for enabling peers to ask questions that allow to explore a problem or proposed solution more in depth [40]. They propose to provide conceptual scaffolds in the form of additional resources on the topic of interaction and procedural scaffolds in the form of guiding structures (such as writing stems or diagram templates). They furthermore propose to work with heterogeneous groups, where participants have different views, to facilitate confrontative argumentation [35].

Xun and Land [41] focus on the development of domain-specific question prompts to scaffold problem-solving in peer interaction settings. They establish guidelines for designing such scaffolds that are based on a combination of generic discursive prompting [40] and domain-specific prompts that they claim should be developed in cooperation with domain experts. They also suggest to structure discourse via explicit assignment of roles to learners they should take in their interaction.

Vogel et al. [42] present a meta-study on how collaboration scripts can be used for scaffolding in IT-supported learning environments. Collaborations scripts [43] are strategic scaffolds that specify a sequence of learning activities to be completed to achieve the aim of a particular task. They found that collaboration scripts have positive effects on the acquisition of domain-specific knowledge in relation to the task and collaboration skills in general. They claim that repeated participation and practice in activities scaffolded by collaboration scripts leads to an internalization of the required performative knowledge and gradually allows to withdraw the script guidance while still maintaining the developed problem-solving strategies not only in terms of collaboration, but also regarding domain-specific skills.

3.3 A Framework for Scaffolding Model Articulation

Based on the empirical results presented in [23, 37, 42] and informed by the methodological considerations outlined in [36, 38, 39, 41], we hypothesize that scaffolds can be developed for the purpose of skill development in stakeholder-centric modeling settings. The modeling process in this context is considered a process of articulation. It is indivisibly embedded in its social context that requires to view conceptual modeling as a process of co-construction ultimately leading to a shared understanding about the topic of modeling among the participating subjects. Consequently, a conceptual model always only can represent the agreed upon abstractions of the perceived real world phenomena considered relevant by the participants. Its value is further determined by the chosen representational system, that needs to be selected based on the intended purpose, i.e. goal of modeling.

Informed by the prior research discussed above, modeling approaches from a scaffolding perspective need to address the following meta-requirements [15]: (A1) provide scaffolds for the level of model representation (i.e. encoding abstractions in an external representation) [23, 37], (A2) provide scaffolds for the level of model articulation (i.e. developing an understanding about the real world phenomenon that is the topic of modeling) [23, 41], and (A3) provide scaffolds for the level of collaborative model alignment (i.e. the process of mutually supporting the development of a shared understanding about the topic of modeling and the modeling process itself) [38, 39, 42]. The identified meta-requirements A1-A3 link issues discussed in the field of stakeholder-centric model articulation [18–20] with potential support measures provided by scaffolding practices.

Furthermore, in order to account for the aim of supporting modeling skill development [21, 22] and allow for contingency, fading and transfer of responsibility, (A4) scaffolds need to be provided with different degrees of invasiveness to allow to adapt modeling support to the current needs of the modelers [36, 42].

Based on these requirements, we draw from the results of our literature review in the following and propose a meta-design [15] in the form of a scaffolding framework which should support the process of enterprise modeling on all three levels identified above. The framework is visualized in Fig. 1.

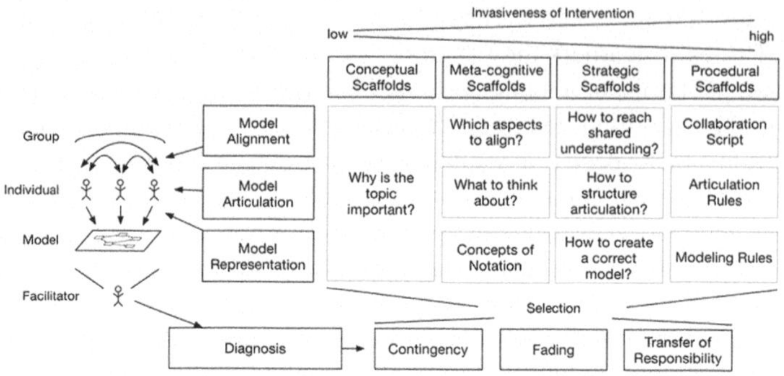

Fig. 1. Dimensions of scaffolding during enterprise modeling

The fundamental constituents of the framework are visualized on the top, bottom and left margin of Fig. 1. Its starting point can be found on the left, where our conceptualization of enterprise modeling being activities of a group of individuals (stakeholders) to create a common conceptual model is shown. As identified above, this requires to perform model representation, model articulation and model alignment activities, and is usually supported by a facilitator.

The top margin of Fig. 1 structures different types of scaffolds [25] according to their invasiveness of intervention [23] (cf. A4). Depending on the diagnosis of current needs of the group of stakeholders engaged in modeling, the facilitator is deploying different types of scaffolds following the principles of scaffolding visualized at the bottom margin of Fig. 1. The more responsibility is transferred to the modelers, the more support measures are faded out, and scaffolds are deployed (if any) that are less invasive. In case of contingency, the facilitator is free to temporarily fade in stronger support to keep the modelers oriented towards the aim of modeling.

The center area of Fig. 1 shows the aspects of modeling that should be addressed by different types of scaffolds for model representation (cf. A1), articulation (cf. A2) and alignment (cf. A3). In general, conceptual scaffolds independently of the addressed level motivate the topic of modeling, show its relevance and allow to validate the model with respect to their appropriateness in real-world use. Metacognitive scaffolds support to understand the structure of the modeling task and indicate how conceptualize the real-world phenomenon. On the level of model alignment, metacognitive scaffolds indicate which aspects of a model are subject to alignment (i.e. interfaces between model parts, in contrast to those aspects that remain in the responsibility of individual modelers). Strategic and procedural scaffolds aim at supporting the modeling process itself, either by showing potential behavioral strategies in the first case or providing stricter guidance in the second case. On the level of model representation, such scaffolds focus on syntactic aspects of modeling, whereas articulation and alignment focus on semantic aspects.

Scaffolds of either form and on either level can be delivered via different channels. They can be provided by procedural guidance or by artifacts (static or interactive media) designed to mediate the modeling process. Procedural guidance can be provided by a human facilitator or an IT-based system, if the latter is capable of monitoring the

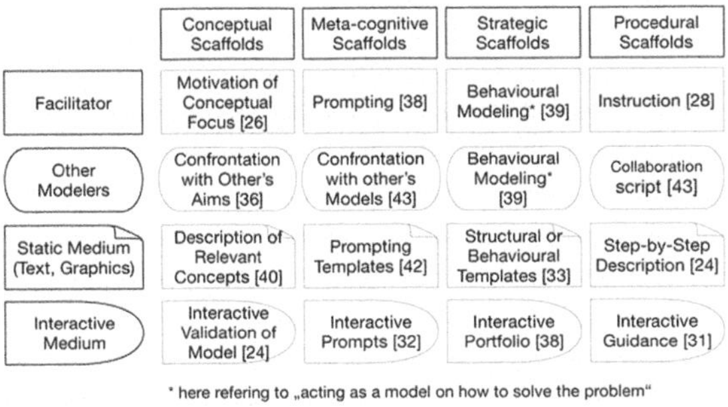

Fig. 2. Examples of different forms of scaffolds for enterprise modeling as described in related work.

modeling progress and analyze the challenges participants currently face on their individual skill level. Procedural guidance by humans can be provided by expert facilitators or peers, if the latter are provided with further scaffolds, that guide the facilitation process itself. Designed artifacts can be provided for domain-specific support and for collaboration support, whereas in both cases their value is determined by an anticipated fit between the skill level of the addressed subjects and the support provided by the artifact. As this fit usually cannot be taken for granted, pre-designed scaffolds are usually combined with a form of procedural guidance.

Figure 2 gives examples for these different types of scaffolds, distinguishing between different sources of scaffolding as described in Sect. 2.2. The examples are taken from related work (references provided for each example in the figure).

The examples should be considered a non-tentative overview about how the different forms of scaffolding can be provided via different delivery channels. They are deliberately not assigned to the different levels of support indicated in Fig. 1 (model representation, model articulation, model alignment), as existing literature does not distinguish between these levels. For validation, we combine the delivery channels with the forms of scaffolding and levels of support for an actual method (cf. Fig. 3).

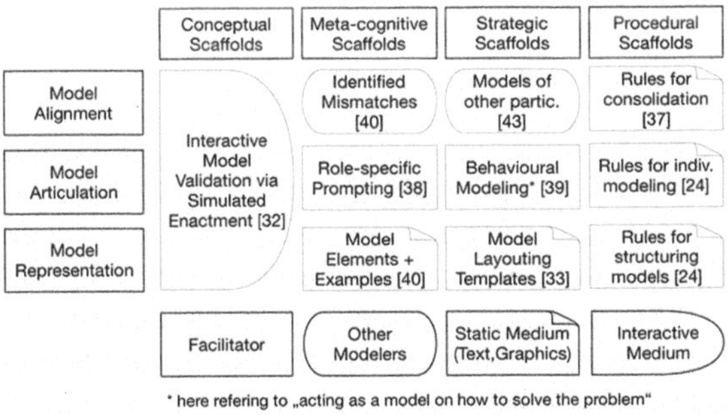

Fig. 3. Scaffolds deployed in CoMPArE/WP (references indicate the foundation for design)

4 Validation

We validate the framework developed above by using it for analysis of modeling method designs. This analysis examines the framework's descriptive and discriminatory value and its usefulness for assessing observed modeling processes with a scaffolding lens. We hypothesize that the framework enables a structured review of support measures embedded in modeling method designs and provides an analytical lens for observed modeling processes that allows to analyze potential reasons for the success (or lack thereof) of stakeholder-centric modeling workshops.

Based on the meta-requirements A1–A4 formulated in Sect. 3.3, we formulate testable hypotheses (designated with Hx.y in the following) for assessing the appropriateness of the proposed framework [15]. In ex-post analysis of modeling method designs, we hypothesize that (H1.1) the support measures embedded in the method are classifiable with respect to whether they target model alignment, model articulation, or model representation. Furthermore, (H1.2) the support measures are classifiable with respect to the form of scaffolding and the proposed delivery channel (facilitator, peer, static media, interactive media). In analysis of observed modeling processes, we hypothesize that (H2.1) the observed support measures are classifiable with respect to whether they target model alignment, model articulation, or model representation. Furthermore, (H2.2) they are classifiable with respect to form and delivery channel of scaffolding. Finally, (H2.3) the observed behavior of the facilitator is classifiable with respect to properties of scaffolding implemented during modeling (contingency, fading, transfer of responsibility).

If any of the hypotheses could not be validated in the study, i.e., any method design property (for H1.x) or observed behavior (for H2.x) cannot be classified in the framework, this would indicate a conceptual deficiency in the framework that would need to be addressed in future refinements of the framework. If the hypotheses could be confirmed, this would indicate appropriate discriminatory power of the framework. If the results of workshop analysis (H2.x) furthermore allowed the linking to the deployed scaffolding measures of outcomes of the model representation, articulation and alignment (according to the respective aims of modeling), this would indicate appropriate descriptive power of the framework.

4.1 Sample Instantiation in CoMPArE/WP

H1.1 and H1.2 have been validated by ex-post analysis of the CoMPArE/WP method [44], which explicitly aims at supporting articulation and alignment of stakeholders' views on their contributions to enterprise processes and the collaboration necessary to implement them. The method follows a multi-step modeling approach, in which participants first collaboratively create a concept map to agree on the notions used to refer to the relevant aspects of their work, then individually model their views on their own contributions and interfaces with others, and finally consolidate these models in a discursive way to create an agreed-upon representation of the overall work process. If modeling rules are adhered to, the resulting models are technically interpretable by a workflow engine and in this way can be validated through simulated execution [44].

Although not designed with a scaffolding background, CoMPArE/WP offers support measures to enable modeling by stakeholders, who do not have any prior knowledge in conceptual modeling. These support measures are briefly described in the following and then classified using the proposed framework (cf. Fig. 3). The *global multi-step modeling procedure* is introduced by a facilitator, who is expected to be trained in the implementation of the method. The participants are also provided with a *one-page written/graphical summary of the global procedure*. The used modeling notations are pre-specified and are provided via *cardboard model elements* that follow a coloring scheme encoding the semantics the used modeling language. The same coloring scheme is used in *poster-sized printed templates* that indicate the expected model layout that needs to be adhered to in order for the results to be unambiguously interpretable via technical means. Printed *model examples* are provided for reference in case of uncertainty on how to use the model elements or their semantics. The participants have access to *written descriptions of the modeling rules* for each step. During workshop implementation, the facilitator provides *role-specific prompts* to aid model development. If necessary, the facilitator *demonstrates model development using an example*. During consolidation, the participants are expected to contribute their individual models and support the *identification of model parts that indicate divergent views* on how to collaborate. The identification process is supported via the *contributed models of all participants* that should contain semantically identical model elements in case of agreement on how to collaborate. The resulting model is *interactively validated via simulated enactment*, during which participants can identify inadequacies of the developed model.

Figure 3 shows a classification of the available support measures using the proposed scaffolding framework. With respect to the hypotheses formulated above, H1.1 can be confirmed with two exceptions: *validation via simulated enactment* cannot be classified to any particular level of support, as it potentially contributes to all three levels (showing the relevance of syntactic model correctness for representation, the impact of individual contributions to the model on articulation level, and the need for a commonly agreed model on alignment level). As this particular measure acts as a conceptual scaffold in the present method, classification in one specific level, however, is not mandatory in the framework. The *global multi-step modeling procedure* cannot be classified in the framework due to its more generic, level-independent scope. This indicates a shortcoming of the current framework.

H1.2 is not violated for the methodology, as each support measure could be classified with respect to its form of scaffolding and delivery channel. The *global multi-step modeling procedure* is not contained in Fig. 3 due to the problems described for H1.1, but would pose a procedural scaffold delivered by the facilitator.

Using the framework to analyze CoMPArE/WP allows to identify the following potential shortcomings of the method: (1) the scaffolds for model alignment are largely based on peer delivery. However, no meta-scaffolds on how to provide scaffolds to peers are available and thus rely on prior existing knowledge on modeling, and (2) a conceptual scaffold is only available after initial modeling activities, as virtual enactment requires an initial model version.

4.2 Sample Workshops

H2.1, H2.2, and H2.3 have been validated by ex-post analysis of three workshops that were implemented following the CoMPArE/WP method. The workshops were selected to differ in the amount of scaffolds deployed and the behavior of the facilitator to comprehensively assess the framework's elements. Any scaffold that had been deployed was implemented in the way envisaged by the method. Consequently, as the method has already satisfied H1.1 and H1.2, the observable scaffolds in the method's implementation also satisfy H2.1 and H2.2. Differences here could only be anticipated, if the workshop implementation deviated from its design.

H2.3 is discussed in the following by example of the observable effects caused by how the facilitators guided model representation and alignment. Figure 4 shows a *model layout template* which is used as a strategic scaffold for model representation during consolidation. The three photos in Fig. 4 illustrate the different results of consolidation. On representation level, the aim is to resemble the layout indicated in the template (blue elements on top, red elements aligned below in lanes, yellow elements placed between lanes). On alignment level, participants themselves should discover problems in the depicted process (e.g., non-matching communication expectations) and resolve them.

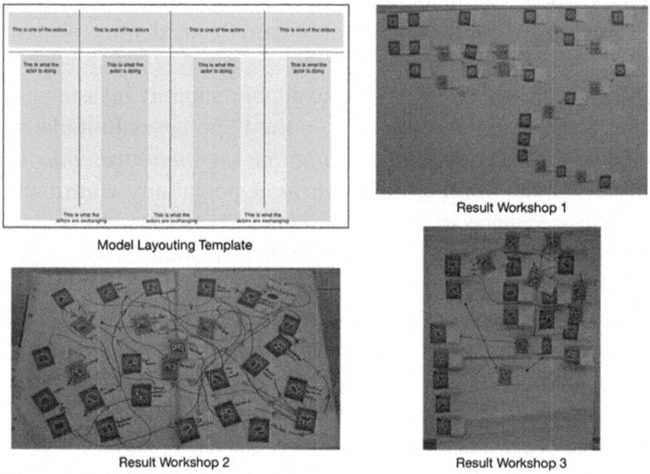

Fig. 4. Top left: model layout template, top right & bottom: modeling results of workshops (Color figure online)

The facilitator in *workshop 1* deployed model representation scaffolds on a strategic and procedural level. Scaffolds for model articulation and alignment were not used. *Fading*, *transfer of responsibility* or *contingency* could not be observed. This resulted in a syntactically correct model, but led to little involvement of the stakeholders in modeling and articulation and no observable alignment activities. The facilitator in *workshop 2* introduced the global multi-step modeling procedure as a high-level procedural scaffold and provided the participants with meta-cognitive scaffolds on representation, articulation and alignment. *Contingency* could not be observed, although participants showed signs of being overwhelmed with the task. He rather *shifted full responsibility* to them after an initial deployment of the metacognitive scaffolds. While high involvement of all participants in articulation could be observed, participation was declining during alignment, and led to a syntactically incorrect modeling result with semantic deviations from the proposed modeling language. The facilitator in *workshop 3* actively implemented *contingency* and *fading*. She started with strategic scaffolds for model representation and articulation, briefly provided procedural scaffolds at the start of the consolidation step and provided metacognitive scaffolds in case of contingency. The observed modeling process continuously showed high involvement in articulation and alignment, with deviations from the proposed modeling notation in the final modeling result.

H2.3 is backed by these results, as classification of the observed behavior of the facilitators was possible with respect to properties of scaffolding implemented during modeling (contingency, fading, transfer of responsibility). Furthermore, their behavior could be described using the addressed levels of support, forms of scaffolding and their delivery channels. This indicates adequacy of the hypotheses H2.1 and H2.2.

5 Discussion and Conclusion

The results of evaluation in Sect. 4 show that the hypotheses formulated based on the identified meta-requirements could be confirmed. Shortcomings in the current version of the framework could be identified with respect to scaffolds that span different levels of support or support the modeling process on a generic level. The findings with respect to the hypotheses H1.x provide evidence that the framework could potentially guide modeling method design from a scaffolding perspective. The findings on hypotheses H2.x indicate that further examination of the framework's potential for training facilitators to provide situation-specific support to stakeholders [13] appears to be worthwhile. The present article has thus introduced a framework on anchoring scaffolding in stakeholder-centric enterprise modeling. It indicates relevant dimensions of design when augmenting modeling activities with scaffolding.

The current state of development of the framework suffers from several limitations that need to be addressed in future research. First, the framework currently lacks instantiation guidelines [15] to apply it in modeling method design. This will be addressed in the next revision of the framework. Second, the validation study currently provides only limited internal validity, as only one method has been examined in this article. Our current research, however, indicates that the framework can be also applied to other methods and exhibits similar shortcomings there.

These limitations will be addressed in our future research by establishing a more comprehensive empirical basis for the next iteration of our framework. Our next steps will go beyond analytical deployment of the framework and will examine whether it can be used to guide method design in practice.

References

1. Sandkuhl, K., Stirna, J., Persson, A., Wißotzki, M.: Enterprise Modeling. Tackling Business Challenges with the 4EM Method. Springer, Heidelberg (2014)
2. Insfrán, E., Pastor, Ó., Wieringa, R.: Requirements engineering-based conceptual modelling. Requir. Eng. **7**, 61–72 (2002)
3. Davies, I., Green, P., Rosemann, M., Indulska, M., Gallo, S.: How do practitioners use conceptual modeling in practice? Data Knowl. Eng. **58**, 358–380 (2006)
4. Heemskerk, M., Wilson, K., Pavao-Zuckerman, M.: Conceptual models as tools for communication across disciplines. Conserv. Ecol. **7**, 8 (2003)
5. Morris, W.T.: On the art of modeling. Manag. Sci. **13**, B–707–B–717 (1967)
6. Sandkuhl, K., Stirna, J., Persson, A., Wißotzki, M.: Elicitation approaches in enterprise modeling. In: Sandkuhl, K., Stirna, J., Persson, A., Wißotzki, M. (eds.) Enterprise Modeling. The Enterprise Engineering Series, pp. 39–51. Springer, Heidelberg (2014)
7. Willemain, T.R.: Model formulation: what experts think about and when. Oper. Res. **43**, 916–932 (1995)
8. Tavella, E., Papadopoulos, T.: Expert and novice facilitated modelling: a case of a viable system model workshop in a local food network. J. Oper. Res. Soc. **66**, 247–264 (2014)
9. Recker, J.C., Safrudin, N., Rosemann, M.: How novices design business processes. Inf. Syst. **37**, 557–573 (2012)
10. Powell, S.G., Willemain, T.R.: How novices formulate models. Part I: qualitative insights and implications for teaching. J. Oper. Res. Soc. **58**(8), 983–995 (2007)
11. Franco, L.A.: Rethinking soft OR interventions: models as boundary objects. Eur. J. Oper. Res. **231**, 720–733 (2013)
12. Briggs, R.O., Kolfschoten, G.L., De Vreede, G.J., Lukosch, S., Albrecht, C.C.: Facilitator-in-a-box: process support applications to help practitioners realize the potential of collaboration technology. J. Manage. Inform. Syst. **29**, 159–194 (2013)
13. Hjalmarsson, A., Recker, J.C., Rosemann, M., Lind, M.: Understanding the behavior of workshop facilitators in systems analysis and design projects. CAIS **36**, 421–447 (2015)
14. Mayer, R.E.: Models for understanding. Rev. Educ. Res. **59**(1), 43–64 (1989)
15. Walls, J.G., Widmeyer, G.R., El Sawy, O.A.: Building an information system design theory for vigilant EIS. Inf. Syst. Res. **3**, 36–59 (1992)
16. Strauss, A.: Continual Permutations of Action. Aldine de Gruyter, New York (1993)
17. Feldman, M.S., Pentland, B.T.: Reconceptualizing organizational routines as a source of flexibility and change. Adm. Sci. Q. **48**, 94–118 (2003)
18. Herrmann, T., Hoffmann, M., Kunau, G., Loser, K.U.: Modelling cooperative work: chances and risks of structuring. In: Proceedings of COOP 2002, pp. 53–70 (2002)
19. Dix, A., Gongora, L.: Externalisation and design. In: Presented at the Proceedings of the Second Conference on Creativity and Innovation in Design (2011)
20. Weick, K.E., Sutcliffe, K.M., Obstfeld, D.: Organizing and the process of sensemaking. Organ. Sci. **16**, 409–421 (2005)
21. Frederiks, P.J.M., van der Weide, T.P.: Information modeling: the process and the required competencies of its participants. Data Knowl. Eng. **58**, 4–20 (2006)
22. Bider, I., Henkel, M., Kowalski, S., Perjons, E.: Technology enhanced learning of modeling skills in the field of information systems. In: Proceedings of 8th IADIS IS (2015)
23. Stender, P., Kaiser, G.: Scaffolding in complex modelling situations. ZDM Math. Educ. **47**, 1255–1267 (2015)
24. Wood, D., Bruner, J.S., Ross, G.: The role of tutoring in problem solving. J. Child Psychol. Psychiatr. **17**, 89–100 (1976)
25. Van de Pol, J., Volman, M., Beishuizen, J.: Scaffolding in teacher-student interaction: a decade of research. Educ. Psychol. Rev. **22**, 271–296 (2010)

26. Vygotsky, L.S.: Mind in Society. Harvard University Press, Massachusetts (1978)
27. Dennen, V.P.: Cognitive apprenticeship in educational practice: research on scaffolding, modeling, mentoring, and coaching as instructional strategies. Handbook Res. Educ. Commun. Technol. **2**, 813–828 (2004)
28. Jumaat, N.F., Tasir, Z.: Instructional scaffolding in online learning environment: a meta-analysis. In: Proceedings of Teaching and Learning in Computing and Engineering (LaTiCE) (2014)
29. Bulu, S.T., Pedersen, S.: Scaffolding middle school students' content knowledge and ill-structured problem solving in a problem-based hypermedia learning environment. Educ. Technol. Res. Dev. **58**, 507–529 (2010)
30. Su, J.-M.: A self-regulated learning tutor to adaptively scaffold the personalized learning: a study on learning outcome for grade 8 Mathematics. In: Proceedings of UMEDIA 2015 8th (2015)
31. Fretz, E.B., Wu, H.-K., Zhang, B., Davis, E.A., Krajcik, J.S., Soloway, E.: An investigation of software scaffolds supporting modeling practices. Res. Sci. Educ. **32**, 567–589 (2002)
32. Sandkuhl, K., Lillehagen, F.: The early phases of enterprise knowledge modelling: practices and experiences from scaffolding and scoping. In: Stirna, J., Persson, A. (eds.) The Practice of Enterprise Modeling. LNBIP, vol. 15, pp. 1–14. Springer, Heidelberg (2008)
33. Carstensen, A., Holmberg, L., Sandkuhl, K., Stirna, J.: Integrated requirements and solution modeling: an approach based on enterprise models. In: Innovations in Information Systems Modeling: Methods and Best Practices (2008)
34. Oppl, S.: Towards scaffolding collaborative articulation and alignment of mental models. In: Proceedings of ICKM 2016 (2016)
35. Prusak, N., Hershkowitz, R., Schwarz, B.B.: From visual reasoning to logical necessity through argumentative design. Educ. Stud. Math. **79**, 19–40 (2012)
36. Ozmantar, M.F., Roper, T.: Mathematical abstraction through scaffolding. In: Proceedings of the 28th Conference of the International Group for the Psychology of Mathematics Education (2004)
37. Land, S.M., Zembal-Saul, C.: Scaffolding reflection and articulation of scientific explanations in a data-rich, project-based learning environment: an investigation of progress portfolio. Educ. Technol. Res. Dev. **51**, 65–84 (2003)
38. Abdu, R., Schwarz, B., Mavrikis, M.: Whole-class scaffolding for learning to solve mathematics problems together in a computer-supported environment. ZDM Math. Educ. **47**, 1163–1178 (2015)
39. Chin, C., Osborne, J.: Students' questions and discursive interaction: their impact on argumentation during collaborative group discussions in science. J. Res. Sci. Teach. **47**, 883–908 (2010)
40. King, A., Rosenshine, B.: Effects of guided cooperative questioning on children's knowledge construction. J. Exp. Educ. **61**, 127–148 (1993)
41. Xun, G.E., Land, S.M.: A conceptual framework for scaffolding III-structured problem-solving processes using question prompts and peer interactions. Educ. Technol. Res. Dev. **52**, 5–22 (2004)
42. Vogel, F., Wecker, C., Kollar, I., Fischer, F.: Socio-cognitive scaffolding with computer-supported collaboration scripts: a meta-analysis. Educ. Psychol. Rev. 1–35 (2016). doi:10.1007/s10648-016-9361-7
43. Kobbe, L., Weinberger, A., Dillenbourg, P., Harrer, A., Hämäläinen, R., Häkkinen, P., Fischer, F.: Specifying computer-supported collaboration scripts. Int. J. Comput.-Support. Collaborative Learn. **2**, 211–224 (2007)
44. Oppl, S., Alexopoulou, N.: Linking natural modeling to techno-centric modeling for the active involvement of process participants in business process design. Int. J. Inf. Syst. Model. Des. (IJISMD) **7**(2), 1–30 (2016)

An Artifact-Based Framework for Business-IT Misalignment Symptom Detection

Dóra Őri(✉)

Department of Information Systems,
Corvinus University of Budapest, Budapest, Hungary
DOri@informatika.uni-corvinus.hu

Abstract. Enterprise architecture-based approaches give an in-depth analytic potential for alignment and misalignment assessment. The ability to incorporate these analytic potentials is an ongoing concern in the state-of-the-art strategic alignment literature. This paper proposes a framework for EA artifact-based misalignment symptom detection. The framework aims to perform a systematic, EA-based analysis of mismatches between the business and IT dimensions of the traditional Strategic Alignment Model (SAM). By operating the framework, containing EA-artifacts and suitable EA analysis types are connected to typical misalignment symptoms along the traditional alignment perspectives. The operation of the framework is illustrated with a case study about a fleet management project at a road management authority.

Keywords: Strategic alignment perspectives · Misalignment symptoms · EA artifacts · Enterprise architecture analysis

1 Introduction

Business-IT alignment is regarded as one of the most important issues on information systems (IS) research, since information systems foster the successful execution of business strategies. While organizations are continually trying to achieve or sustain alignment, they are suffering from difficulties which encumber the achievement of alignment. These difficulties, inabilities and unpleasant circumstances lead us to the phenomenon of misalignment, which is referred to as the inverse state of strategic alignment. In this undesired state organizations fail to achieve or sustain alignment, i.e. information systems and information technology (IT) are not used consistently with the business strategy. In addition, strategies, structures, processes and technology considerations are not perfectly harmonized between business and IT domains in an organization. There are several traditional alignment studies on evaluating alignment performance. On the contrary, misalignment issues are insufficiently emphasized in the alignment literature. Since organizations operate in the state of misalignment most of the times, considerable attention should be paid to the concept of misalignment. Misalignment assessment techniques help to understand the nature and the constraints of alignment. Furthermore, after assessing the state of misalignment, more precise re-alignment initiatives can be recommended. Beside the low attention on misalignment issues, (mis)alignment literature suffers from another severe shortage. Existing

J. Horkoff et al. (Eds.): PoEM 2016, LNBIP 267, pp. 148–163, 2016.
DOI: 10.1007/978-3-319-48393-1_11

misalignment assessment frameworks incorporate different concepts from related research areas (such as [6, 20]). However, the innate ability of the enterprise architecture (EA) concept to support (mis)alignment analysis is also insufficiently addressed in the literature (for exceptions see e.g. [7, 16, 19]).

The aim of the paper is to contribute to the above mentioned concerns by introducing a framework that addresses these issues. The proposed framework performs misalignment analysis by taking a symptom-based approach. It uses an EA-based technique to detect the typical symptoms of misalignment in an organization. The framework builds on the traditional SAM model, in particular on the concept of alignment perspectives [12]. Misalignment symptoms are connected to the four traditional alignment perspectives (Strategy Execution, Technology Transformation, Competitive Potential and Service Level). The framework identifies typical misalignment symptoms within the traditional alignment perspectives. Relevant EA artifacts and EA analysis types are recommended to every detected symptom along the perspectives. The justification of recommended artifacts and EA analysis types lies in the following: EA artifacts may contain the misalignment symptom in question, while EA analysis types are – by functionality – able to detect the symptom in the artifacts. The contribution of the paper is that it connects typical misalignment symptoms with relevant EA artifacts and suitable EA analysis types along the traditional alignment perspectives.

The rest of the paper is organized as follows: Sect. 2 summarizes the theoretical context. Section 3 presents the proposed framework by introducing its construction and its constituent parts. Section 4 shows the operation of the framework. Section 5 discusses a case study including EA model structure and some symptom detection results. Section 6 introduces related work regarding EA-based (mis)alignment assessment. At the end of the paper conclusions are drawn and future research directions are determined.

2 Theoretical Foundation

The theoretical foundation of the paper is based on three parts. The first subsection deals with the concept of strategic alignment, especially the role of alignment perspectives. It is followed by a succinct introduction on misalignment assessment. Subsequently, the concept of enterprise architecture artifacts is deduced from EA basics.

Strategic Alignment Perspectives. Strategic alignment is an ideal organizational state/position in which IT is used consistently with the business strategy. Alignment models or approaches prescriptively define the method of achieving and sustaining alignment. There are several influential and well-recognized alignment models, such as the MIT model [18], the Baets model [2] or Henderson and Venkatraman's Strategic Alignment Model (SAM) [12]. The SAM model has four key domains of strategic choice (a.k.a. alignment domains): (1) Business Strategy, (2) Business Structure, (3) IT Strategy and (4) IT Structure [12]. There are four dominant alignment perspectives in the SAM: (1) Strategy Execution perspective highlights the supporting role of IT in business strategy-based business structure. (2) Technology Transformation perspective deals with the business value of IT. (3) Competitive Potential perspective emphasizes emerging information technologies which are able to provide competitive potential to the business. (4) Service Level perspective indicates different ways to IT-based business service improvement. Alignment perspectives cover 3 alignment domains in order to define directions for alignment domain analysis. Every alignment perspective consists of 2 alignment domain matches, a.k.a. perspective components. The SAM model detailed only four perspectives out of the 8 possible alignment perspectives. Additional perspectives are analysed by [10].

Misalignment Assessment. The common way of evaluating the state of business-IT alignment is alignment evaluation, which analyses the presence of this phenomenon. In case of analysing its absence or deficiencies, misalignment assessment is conducted. The need for misalignment assessment has already been mentioned in the high-profile literature review on business-IT alignment, presented by [8]. Misalignment is an undesired state in which organizations fail to achieve or sustain alignment. The set of detection, correction and prevention is the general process of handling misalignment [6]. There are different ways of categorizing misalignment assessment methods [6], e.g. the sign-based, the syndrome-based or the symptom-based approach. Misalignment symptoms are regarded as inefficiencies, difficulties or inabilities which encumber alignment achievement. The identification (detection) of these symptoms indicates the state of misalignment in an organization. [6, 16, 19] introduce misalignment symptom collections, showing typical mismatches in the operation of an organization. Misalignment symptoms can be classified via misfit categorizations. The categorization of Strong and Volkoff [20] builds on the misfit types of (1) Functionality, (2) Data, (3) Usability, (4) Role, (5) Control and (6) Organizational Culture.

Enterprise Architecture Artifacts. An architecture defines the fundamental structure of a system, including its components and their relationships [21]. Enterprise architecture is the fundamental setup of an enterprise, described by its components and their relationships [21]. An EA framework is a collection of descriptions and methods to create and manage EA. There are several influential EA frameworks, such as the Zachman Framework [25], the TOGAF framework [21] or the DODAF framework [11]. TOGAF (The Open Group Architecture Framework) is a holistic EA framework. It describes a metamodel for EA and proposes methods for building and maintaining enterprise architectures. Architecture domains are considered as different conceptualizations of an enterprise. TOGAF provides 4 architecture domains: (1) Business Architecture, (2) Data Architecture, (3) Application Architecture and (4) Technology Architecture. The core of the TOGAF approach is the Architecture Development Method (ADM), which proposes an iterative method for developing and managing enterprise architecture. It consists of 10 phases. Phase B-D cover the four architecture domains. TOGAF provides a minimum set of necessary EA models, called artifacts. These artifacts are attached to certain ADM phases. Enterprise architecture analysis types are methods that are capable of assessing EA models, e.g. evaluating dependencies, isolated objects, complexity, or heterogeneity.

3 Towards an Artifact-Based Misalignment Detection Framework

This section provides an overview on the components and the construction of the proposed framework. The framework described in the subsequent parts of this section is a well-structured, easy-to-use tool to support misalignment symptom detection. The structure of the framework is based on 5 parts:

(1) To provide a systematic way of constructing the framework, an adaptation of Noran's Meta-methodology [15] was used.
(2) Alignment perspectives are used to structure the approach of misalignment symptom detection. Alignment perspectives are decomposed into the constituent SAM domain matches.
(3–5) Misalignment symptom catalogue, artifact catalogue and EA analysis catalogue describe the potential elements of the misalignment detection framework.

The proposed framework uses an alignment perspective-driven approach. In the first step traditional alignment perspectives are provided with typical misalignment symptoms. In the second step relevant artifacts are connected to the misalignment symptoms, which may contain the symptom in question. In the third step suitable EA analysis types are recommended to the misalignment symptoms. These EA analysis types are able to detect the symptoms in the recommended containing artifacts. Figure 1 introduces the constituent parts and the structure of the proposed framework. In the next subsections the construction of the framework will be described. The operation of the framework will be introduced in Sect. 4.

To support the construction as well as the coherence of the proposed framework, Meta-methodology concept [15], an EA-based supportive method was used.

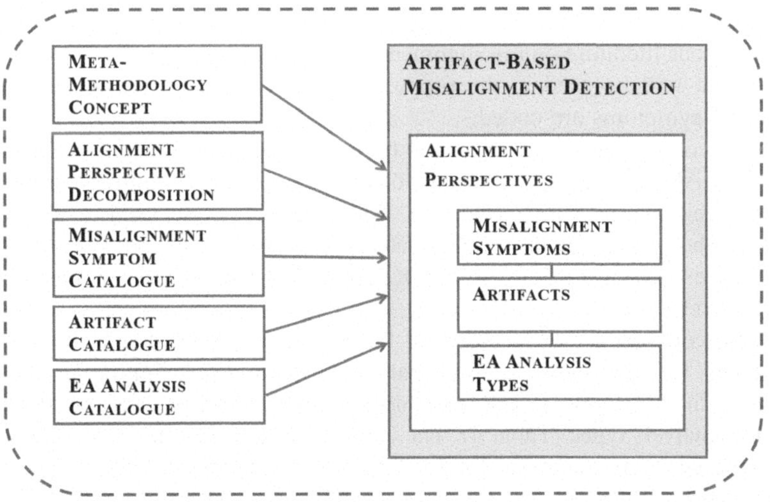

Fig. 1. The construction of artifact-based misalignment detection framework

Table 1. Decomposition of alignment perspectives (based on [12])

Alignment Perspective / Perspective Component	P.01 strategy execution	P.02 technology transformation	P.03 competitive potential	P.04 service level
C.01 matching of business strategy and business structure domains	●		●	
C.02 matching of business structure and IT structure domains	●			●
C.03 matching of business strategy and IT strategy domains		●	●	
C.04 matching of IT strategy and IT structure domains		●		●

Meta-methodology provides a systematic method to set up research frameworks. The concept builds on transformation logic, i.e. to produce new knowledge from input knowledge by means of operating the constructed research framework. The methodology was used to connect research concepts, related models and empirical data collections (misalignment symptom catalogues, artifact catalogues, EA analysis catalogues) in the proposed framework.

Traditional alignment perspectives were used to structure the approach of misalignment symptom detection. In the first step alignment perspectives were decomposed into the corresponding SAM domain matches. Table 1 introduces the constituent parts (the necessary SAM domain matches) of each traditional alignment perspective. To ease further reference, alignment perspectives and perspective components are coded.

Alignment domain matches may contain the signs of misalignment. In this approach the state of misalignment were identified by its symptoms. This framework uses specific symptoms to be detected along the alignment perspectives. The misalignment symptom catalogue (Table 2) is a collection of smaller symptom lists found in previous literature on misalignment [6, 16, 19]. The table shows misalignment symptoms that will be used in the proposed framework. To ease further reference, misalignment symptoms are coded.

The next component of the proposed framework is the collection of possible EA artifacts. TOGAF-based artifacts are able to contain certain misalignment symptoms. In Table 3 possible artifacts are introduced. These artifacts were used in the proposed framework. The content of the artifact catalogue derives from the TOGAF standard [21]. It is an excerpt from the whole TOGAF artifact list. To ease further reference, artifacts are coded.

The final component of the proposed framework is the catalogue of suitable EA analysis types. EA analysis types are capable of revealing misalignment symptoms in the artifacts. In this framework 8 possible EA analysis types were used as recommended EA analysis types (Table 4). The content of the catalogue was collected from related literature on EA analysis [3, 14, 23]. To ease further reference, EA analysis types are coded.

Table 2. Misalignment symptom catalogue (based on [6], [16] and [19])

CODE	MISALIGNMENT SYMPTOM
S.01	Undefined organizational mission, strategy and goals
S.02	Undefined business process goals, business process owners
S.03	Lack of relation between process goals and organizational goals
S.04	Undefined business roles or responsibilities
S.05	Undefined or multiple hierarchy or lines of reporting
S.06	Application functionality does not support at least one business process task
S.07	Business process task supported by more than one application
S.08	Critical business process does not depend on scalable and available applications
S.09	Inappropriate application functionality
S.10	Insufficient IT resources
S.11	Lack of IT skills and competencies
S.12	Lack of skills to develop or innovate certain types of products
S.13	Poor IT planning and portfolio management
S.14	Under capacity infrastructure
S.15	Lack or poor systems performance monitoring
S.16	Out of date technological infrastructure
S.17	Technological heterogeneity
S.18	Incompatible platforms or technologies
S.19	Frequent periods while applications are unavailable
S.20	Information consistency or integrity problems
S.21	Undefined business service levels

Table 3. Artifact catalogue (based on [21])

CODE	ARTIFACT	BRIEF CONTENT	TOGAF ADM PHASE
AF.01	Driver/goal/objective catalogue	A breakdown of drivers, goals, and objectives to provide a cross-organizational reference of driver fulfilment	Phase B
AF.02	Role catalogue	A list of all authorization levels of an organization	Phase B
AF.03	Business service/function catalogue	A functional decomposition to identify capabilities of an organization	Phase B
AF.04	Contract/measure catalogue	The master list of all agreed service contracts (and contract measures) within an organization	Phase B
AF.05	Actor/role matrix	A matrix to show which actors perform which roles	Phase B
AF.06	Business footprint diagram	A mapping of business goals, organizational units, business functions, business services, and delivering technical components	Phase B

(*Continued*)

Table 3. (*Continued*)

CODE	ARTIFACT	BRIEF CONTENT	TOGAF ADM PHASE
AF.07	Functional decomposition diagram	A list of relevant capabilities within an organization	Phase B
AF.08	Goal/objective/service diagram	A mapping to show how a service contributes to the achievement of a business strategy	Phase B
AF.09	Business use-case diagram	A diagram to show the relationships between consumers and providers of business services	Phase B
AF.10	Organizational decomposition diagram	A list of links between actors, roles, and locations within an organization tree	Phase B
AF.11	Process flow diagram	A model to show sequential flow of tasks within a business process	Phase B
AF.12	Data entity/data component catalogue	A list of all the data used across the enterprise, incl. data entities & components	Phase C
AF.13	Data entity/business function matrix	A list that links data entities and business functions within an organization	Phase C
AF.14	Data migration diagram	A diagram that displays the flow of data from the source to the target applications	Phase C
AF.15	Application portfolio catalogue	A catalogue to identify and maintain all the applications in the organization	Phase C
AF.16	Application/function matrix	It links applications and business functions within an organization	Phase C
AF.17	Application interaction matrix	A mapping that describes communications relationships between applications	Phase C
AF.18	Application and user location diagram	A diagram to show the geographical distribution of applications	Phase C
AF.19	Application use-case diagram	A diagram to link consumers and providers of application services	Phase C
AF.20	Process/application realization diagram	A diagram to depict the sequence of events when multiple applications are involved in executing a business process	Phase C
AF.21	Software distribution diagram	A diagram to show how physical applications are distributed across physical technology and the location of that technology	Phase C
AF.22	Technology portfolio catalogue	A catalogue to identify and maintain all the technology across the organization	Phase D
AF.23	Application/technology matrix	A mapping of applications to technology platform	Phase D
AF.24	Platform decomposition diagram	A diagram to cover all aspects of the infrastructure and technology platform	Phase D
AF.25	Processing diagram	A diagram to show deployable units of code/configuration and how these are deployed onto the technology platform	Phase D

Table 4. EA analysis catalogue (based on [3, 14, 23])

Code	EA Analysis Type	Brief Content
A.01	Dependency analysis	Analysis of directly or indirectly linked EA entities, relationship analysis and impact analysis
A.02	Network analysis	Analysis of EA domain network and elements
A.03	Coverage analysis	Analysis of business structure coverage (by supportive application systems)
A.04	Interface analysis	Analysis of interfaces between application systems
A.05	Complexity analysis	Analysis of architecture complexity by architecture components and relationships
A.06	Enterprise interoperability assessment	Analysis of interoperability between architecture entities and architecture domains
A.07	Enterprise coherence assessment	Analysis of coherence between architecture entities
A.08	Heterogeneity analysis	Analysis of IT assets heterogeneity

4 Operation of the Framework

Section 4 introduces the operation of the proposed framework. It is built on the above introduced framework components. Four traditional alignment perspectives (P.01 Strategy Execution, P.02 Technology Transformation, P.03 Competitive Potential and P.04 Service Level) are analysed according to the approach of the framework. The main steps are presented in Fig. 2.

Traditional alignment perspectives are analysed according to the following steps: Firstly, alignment perspectives are decomposed into corresponding perspective components, a.k.a. alignment matches (C.§§). Secondly, the most typical misalignment symptoms are connected to the perspective components – using the misalignment symptom catalogue (S.§§) as reference. Thirdly, relevant containing artifacts are attached to the misalignment symptoms in question. The artifact catalogue (AF.§§) is

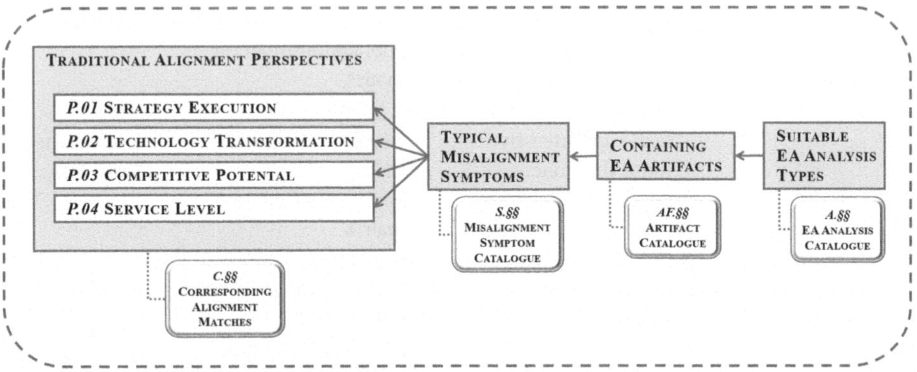

Fig. 2. The operation of artifact-based misalignment detection framework

used as reference. Finally, suitable EA analysis types are collected to the containing artifacts, using the EA analysis catalogue (A.§§) as reference. Results of this matching are presented in the following structure:

- Results of Strategy Execution perspective are shown in Table 5. Investigated perspective components include: C.01 and C.02.
- Results of Technology Transformation perspective are introduced in Table 6. C.03 and C.04 perspective components were analysed in this part.
- Results of Competitive Potential perspective are displayed in Table 7. Inspected perspective components include: C.01 and C.03.
- Results of Service Level perspective are collected in Table 8. This perspective was analysed by C.02 and C.04 perspective components.

The results of this matching are presented in the following parts of the section. This contribution is part of an ongoing research. In this paper an excerpt is given from these matching results. In this digest the most typical misalignment symptoms are identified and analysed along the four traditional alignment perspectives.

Table 5. Results of strategy execution perspective (P.01)

Perspective Component	Misalignment Symptom	Artifact	EA Analysis
C.01 matching of business strategy and business structure domains	S.01 undefined organizational mission, strategy and goals	AF.01 driver/goal/objective catalogue AF.06 business footprint diagram	A.03 coverage analysis
	S.03 lack of relation between process goals and organizational goals	AF.06 business footprint diagram AF.08 goal/objective/service diagram	A.01 dependency analysis
C.02 matching of business structure and IT structure domains	S.06 application functionality does not support at least one business process task	AF.15 application portfolio catalogue AF.16 application/function matrix	A.01 dependency analysis
	S.07 business process task supported by more than one application	AF.15 application portfolio catalogue AF.16 application/function matrix	A.01 dependency analysis
	S.09 inappropriate application functionality	AF.19 application use-case diagram AF.20 process/application realization diagram	A.03 coverage analysis

Table 6. Results of Technology transformation perspective (P.02)

Perspective Component	Misalignment Symptom	Artifact	EA Analysis
C.03 matching of business strategy and IT strategy domains	S.11 lack of IT skills and competencies	AF.02 role catalogue AF.10 organizational decomposition diagram	A.03 coverage analysis
	S.13 poor IT planning and portfolio management	AF.07 functional decomposition diagram AF.15 application portfolio catalogue	A.03 coverage analysis
C.04 matching of IT strategy and IT structure domains	S.10 insufficient IT resources	AF.21 software distribution diagram AF.24 platform decomposition diagram	A.05 complexity analysis
	S.15 lack or poor systems performance monitoring	AF.25 processing diagram	A.07 enterprise coherence assessment

Table 7. Results of competitive potential perspective (P.03)

Perspective Component	Misalignment Symptom	Artifact	EA Analysis
C.03 matching of business strategy and IT strategy domains	S.11 lack of IT skills and competencies	AF.02 role catalogue	A.03 coverage analysis
	S.12 lack of skills to develop or innovate certain types of products	AF.03 business service/function catalogue AF.07 functional decomposition diagram	A.03 coverage analysis
	S.13 poor IT planning and portfolio management	AF.07 functional decomposition diagram AF.15 application portfolio catalogue	A.03 coverage analysis
C.01 matching of business strategy and business structure domains	S.03 lack of relation between process goals and organizational goals	AF.06 business footprint diagram AF.08 goal/objective/service diagram	A.01 dependency analysis
	S.05 undefined or multiple hierarchy or lines of reporting	AF.02 role catalogue AF.09 business use-case diagram AF.10 organisational decomposition diagram	A.06 enterprise interoperability assessment

Table 8. Results of service level perspective (P.04)

Perspective Component	Misalignment Symptom	Artifact	EA Analysis
C.04 matching of IT strategy and IT structure domains	S.17 technological heterogeneity	AF.22 technology portfolio catalogue AF.23 application/ technology matrix AF.24 platform decomposition diagram	A.08 heterogeneity analysis
	S.14 under capacity infrastructure	AF.24 platform decomposition diagram	A.02 network analysis
C.02 matching of business structure and IT structure domains	S.19 frequent periods while applications are unavailable	AF.18 application and user location diagram AF.25 processing diagram	A.07 enterprise coherence assessment
	S.20 Information consistency or integrity problems	AF.12 Data Entity/Data Component Catalogue AF.13 Data Entity/Business Function Matrix	A.07 Enterprise coherence assessment
	S.21 Undefined business service levels	AF.04 Contract/Measure Catalogue	A.03 Coverage analysis

5 Case Study

To demonstrate the applicability of the proposed framework, as well as to better understand how the proposed framework works in practice, a case study has been conducted. The case study clarifies the operation of the framework by applying it in the context of a real EA model structure. The empirical investigation focuses on a *road management authority*. The study was carried out in fragment of the road management authority's EA model structure. It describes a *fleet management initiative*, showing the relevant EA models and artifacts to be modified during the progression of the project. Figure 3 shows EA model contents investigated in this project. The model structure consists of 4 EA domains: Business Architecture, Data Architecture, Application Architecture and Technology Architecture. These domains are connected to the corresponding TOGAF ADM phases [21]. EA domains contain several artifacts, indicated as rectangles in the figure. Artifacts are connected with each other according to the possible relationships in content between EA models/artifacts.

To highlight the feasibility of the proposed framework, Table 9 shows an excerpt from the results of dependency analysis between business process tasks and applications. In this illustrative example the business processes of *Road Control* and *Dispatcher Service* are matched with application components that play essential role in business process realization. The result of the dependency analysis appears in a matrix form. Rows represent business process tasks, while applications are illustrated in columns. Dependency relations are displayed in cells: business process task depends on an application during the sequence flow of the business process.

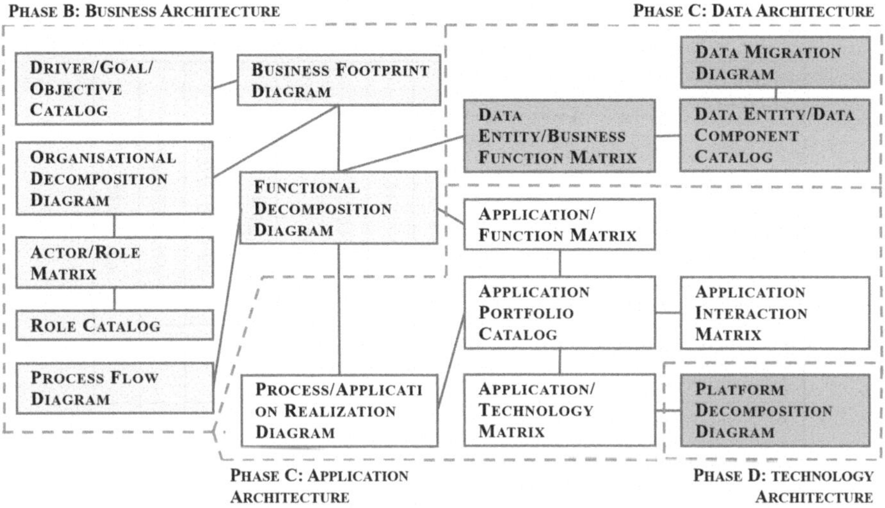

Fig. 3. EA model structure at the road management authority

The example illustrates misalignment symptom *S.07 Business process task supported by more than one application*, which is a typical symptom of *P.01 Strategy Execution perspective*, *C.02 Matching of Business Structure and IT Structure domains* perspective component. The artifact that may contain this symptom is *AF.16 Application/Function Matrix*. Suitable analysis that is able to detect the symptom in the artifact is *A.01 Dependency analysis*. As we can see from the figure, three business process tasks fulfil the requirements of this misalignment symptom: *Administrating road control tasks*, *Forwarding information* and *Road control plan preparation*.

Another symptom that can be verified by matching business process tasks and applications is *S.06 Application functionality does not support at least one business process task*. It is also a typical symptom of *P.01 Strategy Execution perspective*, *C.02 Matching of Business Structure and IT Structure domains* perspective component. The artifact that may contain this symptom is also *AF.16 Application/Function Matrix*. Finally, suitable analysis that is able to detect the symptom in the artifact is also *A.01 Dependency analysis*. Contrary to the similarities in misalignment symptom set up, the above introduced excerpt does not show the realization of this symptom. As we can see from this fragment of dependency analysis, each application plays role in the realization of the illustrated business process tasks.

6 Related Work

There have been many attempts to investigate reciprocal contributions between strategic (mis)alignment assessment and EA analysis. Recently, there has been an increased interest in EA-based alignment assessment, especially in matching EA domains to evaluate the state of alignment in an organization. The following section

Table 9. Excerpt from a dependency analysis between business process tasks and applications

APPLICATION / BUSINESS PROCESS TASK	*EASYWAY*	*INFOPULT*	*ERP*	*KOMVIR*	*SPREADSHEET*	*SHAREPOINT*	*OKA2000*
Administrating road control tasks			•		•		
Forwarding information	•	•					
Information recording and consolidation				•			
Receiving notification						•	
Road control plan preparation					•	•	•
Road control plan verification					•		

provides an insight into the components of this concept: (1) EA analysis (2) misalignment assessment and (3) enterprise architecture alignment.

A number of research efforts have focused on proposing models for EA analysis – EA-based analysis types that are capable of assessing EA models. [5, 22] introduce general process models for EA analysis. [5, 13, 14] propose potential EA analysis categorizations according to e.g. (1) quantitative/qualitative, or (2) static/dynamic groupings. [3, 14, 23] propose EA analysis collections. Tools for supporting the process of EA analysis are expounded by [4, 5]. Several works have addressed the problem of EA analysis. All these works explore the applicability of EA analysis for EA evaluation, however, they do not specialize EA analysis for (mis)alignment assessment.

In the literature, different misalignment assessment techniques have been put forward to succeed in dealing with alignment evaluation from misalignment perspective. Most of them are symptom-based [6, 19], while other works such as [16] focused on proposing a process for misalignment assessment. Several approaches have been developed, but they do not provide any support for EA-based implementation.

The problem of enterprise architecture alignment has been extensively studied in the literature. [1] focuses on the integration of business and IT architecture domains. It collects requirements for architecture alignment and propose artifacts for alignment architecture. [7] deals with semi-automatic business process and data architecture alignment. It detects alignment patterns in the EA domains. [9] proposes an approach which supports architecture alignment. [17] introduces an EA metamodel for different business-IT alignment situations. [24] provides a description about an ideal alignment situation. EA alignment methods try to integrate alignment evaluation frameworks, misalignment assessment frameworks and EA analysis techniques to propose EA-based tools for (mis)alignment assessment. However, for the most part, existing approaches have no explicit potential for misalignment *symptom* detection. None of the proposed techniques can be directly applied to this problem.

The contribution of this study extends results on approaching *EA-based* misalignment symptom detection. The framework proposed in this paper can be considered as a precursory step for integrating the concepts and potentials of EA analysis, (mis)alignment assessment and EA alignment. In this framework typical misalignment symptoms are connected with relevant EA artifacts and suitable EA analysis types along the traditional alignment perspectives.

7 Conclusion and Future Work

In this paper a new way of misalignment symptom detection have been presented, which is able to reveal typical symptoms along the four traditional alignment perspectives by assessing the underlying EA models. The proposed artifact-based misalignment detection framework is built on matching the symptoms of misalignment with possible containing artifacts and suitable EA analysis types along alignment perspectives. The proposed framework has the potential to extend our understanding on assessing the state of misalignment in a complex EA model structure. The framework allowed us to identify and detect malfunctioning procedures along the alignment perspectives. It highlighted the importance of and a need for both an artifact-based and an EA analysis-based approach. The main contribution of the paper was that it connected typical misalignment symptoms to relevant containing artifacts and suitable EA analysis types along the perspectives of the SAM model.

The construction and operation of the framework have been discussed and explained in detail in the previous sections. To illustrate the feasibility of the proposed framework in practice as well as to provide guidance on applicability, a case study was performed. Examples of mismatches have been provided in the investigated EA models by using the proposed artifact-based and EA analysis-based approach. With this case study considerable progress has been made with regard to the practical application of the proposed framework. However, this study also encounters some challenges and questions in need of further investigations. Topics reserved for further examinations include (1) the automatization of EA analysis types and (2) decoupling the framework from built-in EA tool features. The next research step will be to focus on a tool-independent, automated implementation of the artifact-based misalignment symptom detection framework. In the meantime, a general assessment framework will be developed on alignment performance to be able to give feedback after detecting misalignment symptoms in the investigated companies. Feedback will include both alignment performance evaluation and possible misalignment correction and re-alignment activities. Apart from automating the framework, there are also some less radical development initiatives. As part of future work, the approach will be evaluated against some set of testable criteria. Future work will also concentrate on further refinements on the proposed framework: to enhance the accuracy and quality of misalignment symptom detection. Additionally, even more discussion is planned to provide on its practical applicability. Finally, since results are promising, the framework should be validated on some more complex EA model environments within other organizations.

References

1. Aier, S., Winter, R.: Virtual decoupling for IT/Business alignment – conceptual foundations, architecture design and implementation example. Bus. Inf. Syst. Eng. **2009**(2), 150–163 (2009)
2. Baets, W.: Aligning information systems with business strategy. J. Strateg. Inf. Syst. **1**(4), 205–213 (1992)
3. Buckl, S., Matthes, F., Schweda, C.M.: Classifying Enterprise Architecture Analysis Approaches. In: Sinderen, M., Chapurlat, V. (eds.) IWEI 2015. LNBIP, vol. 213, pp. 66–79. Springer, Heidelberg (2009). doi:10.1007/978-3-642-04750-3_6
4. Buckl, S., Buschle, M., Johnson, P., Matthes, F., Schweda, C.M.: A meta-language for enterprise architecture analysis. In: Schmidt, R., Guédria, W., Bider, I., Guerreiro, S. (eds.) BPMDS/EMMSAD 2016. LNBIP, vol. 248, pp. 511–525. Springer, Heidelberg (2011). doi:10.1007/978-3-642-21759-3_37
5. Buschle, M., Ullberg, J., Franke, U., Lagerström, R., Sommestad, T.: A tool for enterprise architecture analysis using the PRM formalism. In: Soffer, P., Proper, E. (eds.) CAiSE Forum 2010. LNBIP, vol. 72, pp. 108–121. Springer, Heidelberg (2011). doi:10.1007/978-3-642-17722-4_8
6. Carvalho, G., Sousa, P.: Business and information systems MisAlignment model (BISMAM): an holistic model leveraged on misalignment and medical sciences approaches. In: Johannesson, P., Gordijn, J. (eds.) Proceedings of the Third International Workshop on Business/IT Alignment and Interoperability (BUSITAL 2008). CEUR, vol. 336, pp. 104–119. CEUR-WS, Aachen (2008)
7. Castellanos, C., Correal, D.: KALCAS: a framework for semi-automatic alignment of data and business processes architectures. In: Pokorný, J., Ivanović, M., Thalheim, B., Šaloun, P. (eds.) ADBIS 2016. LNCS, vol. 9809, pp. 111–124. Springer, Heidelberg (2012). doi:10.1007/978-3-642-33074-2_9
8. Chan, Y.E., Reich, B.H.: IT alignment: what have we learned? J. Inf. Technol. **22**(2007), 297–315 (2007)
9. Clark, T., Barn, B.S., Oussena, S.: A method for enterprise architecture alignment. In: Harmsen, F., Proper, H.A. (eds.) PRET 2013. LNBIP, vol. 151, pp. 48–76. Springer, Heidelberg (2012). doi:10.1007/978-3-642-31134-5_3
10. Coleman, P., Papp, R.: Strategic alignment: analysis of perspectives. In: Murray, M., Weistroffer, H.R. (eds.) Proceedings of the 2006 Southern Association for Information Systems Conference, pp. 242–250. MPublishing, Michigan (2006)
11. DoDAF Architecture Framework. http://dodcio.defense.gov/Portals/0/Documents/DODAF/DoDAF_v2-02_web.pdf
12. Henderson, J.C., Venkatraman, N.: Strategic alignment: leveraging information technology for transforming organizations. IBM Syst. J. **32**(1), 4–16 (1993)
13. Lankhorst, M.: Enterprise Architecture at Work. Modelling, Communication and Analysis. Springer, Heidelberg (2013)
14. Niemann, K.D.: From Enterprise Architecture to IT Governance. Elements of Effective IT Management. Friedr. Vieweg & Sohn Verlag, Wiesbaden (2006)
15. Noran, O.: A decision support framework for collaborative networks. Int. J. Prod. Res. **47** (17), 4813–4832 (2009)
16. Pereira, C.M., Sousa, P.: Enterprise architecture: business and IT alignment. In: ACM Symposium on Applied Computing, pp. 1344–1345. ACM, New York (2005)

17. Saat, J., Franke, U., Lagerström, R., Ekstedt, M.: Enterprise architecture meta models for IT/Business alignment situations. In: 14th IEEE International Enterprise Distributed Object Computing Conference, pp. 14–23. IEEE Press, New York (2010)
18. Scott Morton, M.S.: The Corporation of the 1990s: Information Technology and Organizational Transformation. Oxford Press, London (1991)
19. Sousa, P., Pereira, C.M., Marques, J.A.: Enterprise architecture alignment heuristics. Microsoft Architects J. **4**, 34–39 (2005)
20. Strong, D.M., Volkoff, O.: Understanding organization-enterprise system fit: a path to theorizing the information technology artifact. MIS Q. **34**(4), 731–756 (2010)
21. The Open Group Architecture Framework (TOGAF). http://theopengroup.org/
22. Ullberg, J., Franke, U., Buschle, M., Johnson, P.: A tool for interoperability analysis of enterprise architecture models using Pi-OCL. In: Popplewell, K., Harding, J., Poler, R., Chalmeta, R. (eds.) Enterprise Interoperability IV. Making the Internet of the Future for the Future of Enterprises, pp. 81–90. Springer, London (2010)
23. Wagter, R., Proper, H.A., Witte, D.: A practice-based framework for enterprise coherence. In: Harmsen, F., Proper, H.A. (eds.) PRET 2013. LNBIP, vol. 151, pp. 77–95. Springer, Heidelberg (2012). doi:10.1007/978-3-642-31134-5_4
24. Wegmann, A., Regev, G., Rychkova, I., Lam-Son Le, de la Cruz, J.D., Julia, P.: Business and IT alignment with SEAM for enterprise architecture. In: 11th IEEE International Enterprise Distributed Object Computing Conference, pp. 111–121. IEEE Press, New York (2007)
25. Zachman, J.A.: A framework for information systems architecture. IBM Syst. J. **26**(3), 276–292 (1987)

Coopetition with Frenemies: Towards Modeling of Simultaneous Cooperation and Competition Among Enterprises

Vik Pant[1(✉)] and Eric Yu[1,2]

[1] Faculty of Information, University of Toronto, Toronto, Canada
vik.pant@mail.utoronto.ca, eric.yu@utoronto.ca
[2] Department of Computer Science, University of Toronto, Toronto, Canada

Abstract. Enterprise modeling frameworks are concerned with the representation of social phenomena and researchers have proposed a number of notations and techniques for depicting social behaviors. However, coopetition, which is a specific type of social interaction, has not been explored in the enterprise modeling literature. Coopetition, which refers to simultaneous cooperation and competition, has been studied extensively in the social sciences where conceptual theorizing and empirical fieldwork have established it as a prominent field of research. It is regularly observed in dealings between many kinds of enterprises, such as businesses and governments, where it has been analyzed at both inter- as well as intra-organizational levels. Coopetition is especially relevant for enterprise modeling because goal alignment/convergence can yield cooperation among actors while goal conflict/divergence can lead to competition among actors. In this paper we (a) present an overview of academic research into coopetition, (b) discuss the requirements for representing coopetition, and (c) propose future work that will be relevant for the modeling and analysis of cooperation, competition, and coopetition between enterprises.

Keywords: Enterprise modeling · Coopetition · Strategy · Design · Review

1 Introduction

A number of researchers have proposed modeling notations and techniques for expressing and evaluating organizational strategy [1, 2] and a variety of modeling approaches have been developed to describe different aspects of enterprises (e.g., goal, actor, value, process, etc.) [3]. Additionally, requirements engineering (RE) researchers have applied many goal- and actor-oriented approaches to model and analyze business strategy [4, 5]. However, none of these approaches have focused directly on this phenomenon of simultaneous cooperation and competition. This is a gap in the RE literature because strategic coopetition impacts many entities (such as actors, goals, tasks, resources, boundaries, value, etc.) that are relevant for these approaches.

Coopetition, which refers to simultaneous cooperation and competition, has become "increasingly popular in recent years" [6] and is "an integral part of many companies' daily agenda" [7]. While some research papers in the RE literature have discussed competition and cooperation between enterprises [8, 9]—there are many

J. Horkoff et al. (Eds.): PoEM 2016, LNBIP 267, pp. 164–178, 2016.
DOI: 10.1007/978-3-319-48393-1_12

characteristics of these strategic behaviors that are unexplored in the Enterprise Modeling (EM) literature. It can be argued that these gaps "make it difficult for requirements engineers to validate low-level requirements against the more abstract high-level requirements representing the business strategy" [10]. Therefore, the ability to articulate cooperation, competition, and coopetition represents advancement in the state-of-the-art in EM.

In the introductory section of this paper, we discussed the relevance of coopetition for EM. In the next section, we describe the development of coopetition research within the field of Strategic Management. In the third section, we discuss key characteristics of coopetition that are relevant for EM. In the final section, we summarize our current research into coopetition modeling and propose next steps for future research.

2 Enterprise Cooperation, Competition, and Coopetition

Strategic Management (SM), which is a branch of Organizational Theory (OT), is an academic discipline that is concerned with the structure, behavior, and performance of organizations [11]. It emerged in the 1950s as an explanation of the strategic dynamics between firms in competitive industries [12]. It was closely related to Bain's SCP (structure, conduct, performance) paradigm according to which the performance of a firm was determined by its conduct, which, in turn, was impacted by various industry factors [13]. Starting in the late 1970s, Porter popularized this view through his advancement of economic theories of "competitive advantage" [14, 15]. A number of economists, including Porter, helped to establish this competitive view of strategy as the dominant paradigm during the first three decades of SM research.

This "militaristic" view in SM was challenged throughout the 1980s and 1990s by researchers who argued in favor of "cooperative advantage" and "collaborative advantage" [16, 17]. This stream of research posited that firms could improve their performance and increase their profits by partnering with other firms. Dyer and Singh promoted the notion of "relational rents" as profits that were generated through relationship-specific idiosyncratic assets and resources [18]. Many rationales and justifications were offered for inter-firm relationships such as strategic alliances. These included the ability for partner firms to acquire knowledge [19], share risks [20], access markets [21], spread costs [22], pool resources [23], and achieve strategic objectives [24].

By the mid-1990s, the field of SM was divided into two camps that offered incompatible and divergent explanations of inter-firm behaviors. The competitive camp argued that cooperation among rivals led to collusion/cartelization while the cooperative/collaborative camp asserted that competition between allies led to mutually destructive outcomes. An esemplastic theory was needed to resolve this creative tension.

Coopetition theory was proposed as a syncretistic means for reconciling the competitive and cooperative perspectives [25]. It was introduced in 1995 by two economists who adopted a game-theoretic lens for interpreting inter-firm behaviors [26]. In the two decades since its introduction, coopetition theory has become a prominent field of scholarly inquiry. A number of literature reviews have noted the increase in research interest in this field [27–29] and eminent scholarly publications have devoted special issues to this topic [30, 31]. Empirical fieldwork has also been used to explore "coopetition along the antecedents-process-outcomes trail" [17, 28]. Additionally, coopetition research has progressed beyond SM into other disciplines including political science [32], diplomacy [33], and civics [34].

3 Emerging Requirements for Modeling Enterprise Coopetition

OT researchers have identified various characteristics that define coopetitive relationships [6, 35]. These include, but are not limited to, complementarity [36], interdependence [37], trustworthiness [38], and reciprocity [39]. It should be noted that cooperation and competition are germane to coopetition because coopetition represents the coaction of these phenomena. Therefore, a RE framework for coopetition ought to support the depiction of cooperation and competition separately as well as simultaneously (i.e., coopetition). This section discusses the key characteristics of coopetition between enterprises that are essential for modeling it.

3.1 Key Features of Coopetitive Relationships

Table 1 presents a partial list of requirements that are relevant for modeling coopetition phenomenon. Table 2 presents a preliminary assessment of various techniques in terms of requirements for representing coopetition. We acknowledge that each of these entries merit debate and critique and are offering them to stimulate discussion and more in-depth analysis. Please note that this assessment does not consider the syntax and semantics of extensions, derivatives, or combinations of the reviewed techniques. The column titled 'Key' from Table 1 should be used to interpret the coded column headings in Table 2.

Table. 1. Partial list of requirements for modeling enterprise coopetition.

Characteristics	Features	Key	Description for modeling support
Actor	2 Actors or Dyad	A1	Two actors with links between them
	>2 Actors or network	A2	More than two actors with links between them
	Actor intention	A3	Internal intentional structure of actor(s)
Complementarity	Resource/asset/object	C1	Entity associated with some value, benefit, or utility
	Value added	C2	Incremental addition of some value, benefit, or utility
	Added value	C3	Worth of an actor in terms of value, benefit, or utility
Interdependence	Positive dependency	I1	Existence of dependency(ies) between actors.
	Negative dependency	I2	Non-existence of any dependency between actors
	Strength of dependency	I3	Magnitude of dependency (however measured)
Trustworthiness	Goal convergence	T1	Agreements between goals within and across actors
	Goal divergence	T2	Conflict between goals within and across actors
	Compliance	T3	Evaluation of abidance with terms and conditions
Reciprocity	Activity or task	R1	Individual (step) or collection (process) of actions
	Sequence	R2	Transition from predecessor to successor action
	Condition	R3	Constraints or restrictions on actions

Table. 2. Preliminary assessment of modeling support for requirements from Table 1.

Technique	A1	A2	A3	C1	C2	C3	I1	I2	I3	T1	T2	T3	R1	R2	R3
NFR Framework	✗	✗	✗	✗	✗	✗	✗	✗	✗	✓	✓	✗	✓	✗	✗
i* Strategic Rationale	✓	✓	✓	✓	✗	✗	✓	✗	✗	✓	✓	✗	✓	✗	✗
KAOS	✓	✓	✗	✓	✗	✗	✗	✗	✗	✗	✓	✗	✓	✓	✓
e3Value	✓	✓	✗	✓	✓	✗	✗	✗	✗	✗	✗	✗	✓	✓	✗
Business Model Canvas	✗	✗	✗	✓	✓	✗	✗	✗	✗	✗	✗	✗	✓	✗	✗
Value Network Analysis	✓	✓	✗	✓	✗	✗	✗	✗	✗	✗	✗	✗	✗	✗	✗
Game Tree	✓	✗	✗	✗	✓	✗	✗	✗	✗	✗	✗	✗	✓	✓	✗
Payoff Table	✓	✗	✗	✗	✓	✗	✗	✗	✗	✗	✗	✗	✓	✗	✗
Change Matrix	✓	✗	✗	✗	✓	✗	✗	✗	✗	✗	✗	✗	✓	✗	✗

Prominent goal- and/or actor-modeling approaches such as NFR framework, KAOS, and i* are able to support the representation of some, but not all, of these requirements. Similarly, practitioner tools such as Business Model Canvas and Value Network Analysis are also deficient with respect to some of these requirements. Nonetheless, these approaches can be extended and combined in creative ways to overcome their respective limitations for modeling coopetition. This is appropriate because according to [40], "depending on the needs, several languages can also be used together in a complementary way".

3.2 Strategic Competition Between Enterprises

A number of theories have been proposed to explain the nature and characteristics of strategic competition between enterprises. These include Industrial Organization, Chamberlinian, and Schumpeterian explanations that refer to different core concepts and units of analysis [41]. For example, [42] claims that "there is no reason to think of business competitive systems as different in any fundamental way from other biological competition". This view posits that much like biological competition (between organisms) economic competition (between enterprises) occurs due to resource conflicts [43]. Indeed, this view is in line with a functional definition of economics as the "study of the allocation of 'scarce' resources among competing ends" [44]. This means that actors (enterprises), goals (ends), and resources (means) are pertinent for the modeling of strategic competition between enterprises.

Figure 1 presents an i* SR (Strategic Rationale) diagram of competition between enterprises caused by typical resource conflicts. Two firms, A and B, are in the same industry such that their products/services are substitutes which serve similar customer needs. These firms require similar resources (capital and employees) and consume similar raw materials (ingredients and supplies). They interact in two arenas which are factor and output markets wherein a factor market is comprised of investors, suppliers, and job agencies while an output market is comprised of customers, and an intellectual property office (i.e., patent issuer). We have chosen i* SR modeling because it supports the depiction of resource dependencies across actors as well as means-ends decomposition and softgoal contributions within actors.

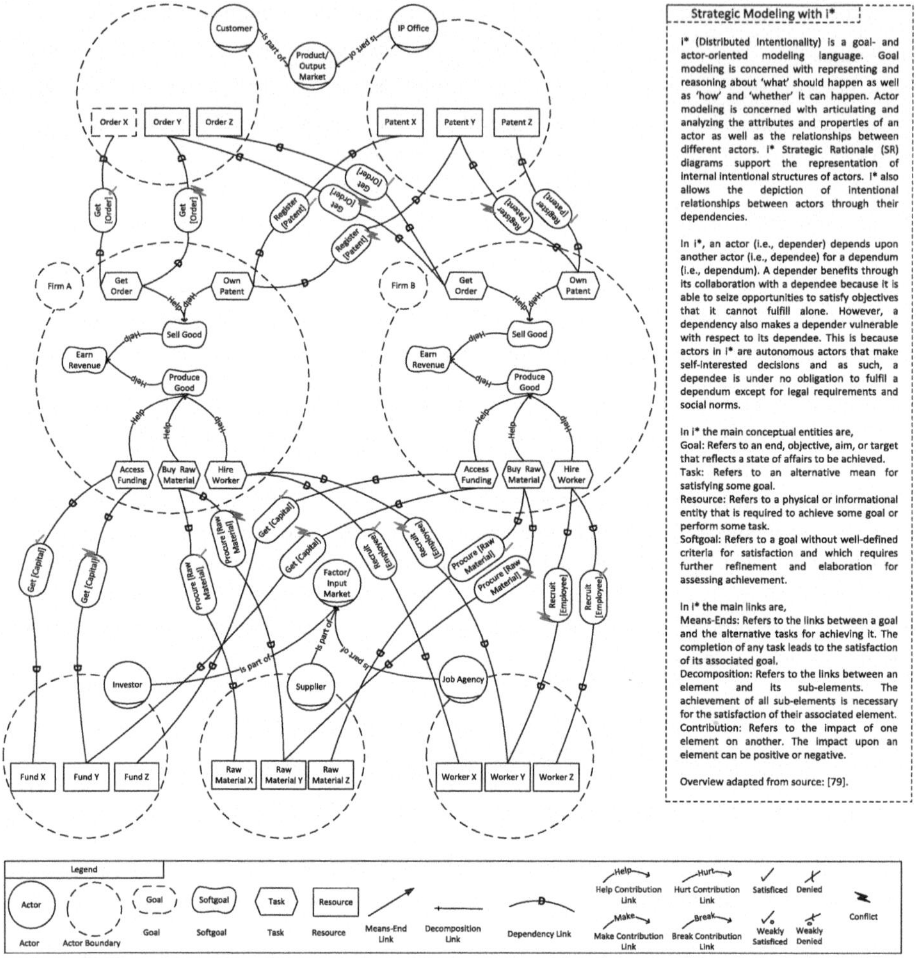

Fig. 1. i* SR diagram of competition from typical resource conflicts among enterprises.

Each firm depends on these stakeholders for different reasons. An investor offers funds to firms (shown) in return for principal + interest and/or profits (not shown). A supplier sells raw materials to firms (shown) in return for principal + interest and/or profits (not shown). A job agency helps a firm to recruit employees (shown) in return for a charge (not shown). The Intellectual Property Office issues patents (not shown) after a firm attempt to register its design (shown). A customer offers its business to firms via orders (shown) and in return pays the firm for its products (not shown). We have excluded certain details from the Fig. 1 in order to simplify the diagram.

There are two main types of interactions that can take place between two enterprises such as firms A and B. These are depicted in Fig. 2 which is an i* SR diagram of abstract resource conflicts between enterprises (i.e., it represents a strategic pattern). In the first type of interaction, an enterprise (e.g., Firm A) depends on a resource (i.e., Resource X)

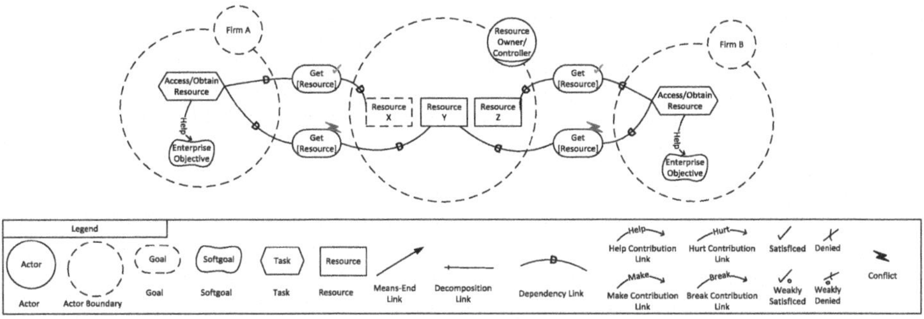

Fig. 2. i* SR diagram of competition depicting abstract resource conflict among enterprises.

while another enterprise (e.g., Firm B) depends on a different resource (i.e., Resource Z). In this case, there is no conflict between these enterprises as they depend on, and are interested in, different resources. In the second type of interaction, two enterprises (e.g., Firm A and Firm B) depend on the same resource (i.e., Resource Y). In this case, there is a conflict between these enterprises as they depend on, and are interested in, the same resource. This scenario is likely to lead to strategic competition if only one of these firms is able to satisfy its resource dependency (means) that is necessary for achieving its goal (ends).

The ability to represent the heterogeneous facets of resources are also relevant for the modeling of strategic competition between enterprises. This is because [45] argues that a resource that is valuable, rare, inimitable, and non-substitutable serves as a source of competitive advantage for its owner/controller. A resource is considered to be valuable if rivals cannot: obtain/access it, mimic/copy it, or generate comparable value from alternative/replacement resources [46].

3.3 Tensions in Paradoxical Relationships

Competition and cooperation are diametric social behaviors that are undergirded by opposite logics and assumptions [47]. Their co-occurrence in any relationship represents a paradox that creates tensions between the coopeting actors [48]. Different degrees of cooperation and competition can co-exist [47] within vertical (i.e., buyer-supplier) as well as horizontal (i.e., firm-to-firm) relationships [49]. Moreover, coopetition can occur within a dyad (i.e., between two actors) or in a network. Dyadic coopetition necessitates direct coopetition between two actors but network coopetition enables direct as well as indirect coopetition (i.e., via an intermediary). Dyadic coopetition can be regarded as procedural coopetition [50] where activity is an appropriate unit of analysis while network coopetition can be regarded as contextual coopetition [51] where actor is a suitable unit of analysis. Coopetition is also a multilevel phenomenon wherein an actor may exhibit different behaviors at different levels (i.e., within a dyad or network) [52].

3.4 Complementarity, Interdependence, Trustworthiness, and Reciprocity

Complementarity. According to [53],"complementarity refers to the combined returns from the combination of two or more assets, with some combinations resulting in higher value creation than other combinations." It is informally referred to as synergy wherein: 'the whole is greater than the sum of its parts'. Complementarity motivates cooperation within competitive relationships and competition within cooperative relationships. Researchers have identified various ways through which firms can develop complementarities with their partners. These include overlap avoidance, knowledge protection, and development of common objectives. [54] note that multifaceted dealings between Sony and Samsung illustrate a coopetitive relationship that is based on complementary R&D and manufacturing skills.

Interdependence. According to [55], "strategic interdependence is concerned with the extent to which work processes that have strategic implications are interrelated." Firms are typically incentivized to become mutually reliant when they have "partially congruent interest structures" [56]. Interdependence fosters coopetition because it ensures that "each competitor will have a specific individual interest in carrying out an agreement" [57]. Researchers have identified various ways through which firms can become more interdependent with each other. These include investing in relationship-specific assets, interconnecting resources, and knowledge sharing. [47] observed such coopetitive interactions between a number of European firms in the rack and pinion as well as lining industries.

Trustworthiness. According to [58], "trust refers to the expectation that another business can be relied on to fulfill its obligations." It "is expected to reduce the level of potential and actual opportunism" [59] through "(a) impartiality in negotiations, (b) trustworthiness, and (c) keeping of promises" [38]. Moreover, "while trust is an attribute of a relationship between exchange partners, trustworthiness is an attribute of individual exchange partners" [60]. Trustworthiness is an important consideration in coopetition because trust and contracts serve as governance mechanisms in cooperative relationships. Researchers have identified various techniques through which firms can grow their trustworthiness. These include increasing communication, avoiding coercion, and increasing linkages. [61] identified trust as a "key factor for success of co-opetitive strategies" through an empirical study of the telecommunications satellite industry in Europe.

Reciprocity. According to [62], "reciprocity is defined as rewarding kindness with kindness and punishing unkindness with unkindness." [63] note that a social actor should "expect this behavior from others" because "reciprocity is a rather stable behavioral response by a nonnegligible fraction of the people" [64]. [65] point out "reciprocity has been studied in depth in economics and game theory as a means to enforce cooperative behavior". This is why it is commonly used in game theory to explain social behavior in sequential move games such as ultimatum game and gift-exchange game [66]. In fact, such behavior is not limited to games and has been observed in the industry by [67].

3.5 Example: Inter-partner Learning and Knowledge-Sharing Among Enterprises

An important justification for strategic alliances is the transfer and exchange of organizational knowledge between partners [19, 22]. However, knowledge sharing can also expose partners to risks and vulnerabilities. This is because partners can engage in 'learning races' [68, 69] where each firm tries to 'learn faster' than its partners [70, 71]. This might be motivated by opportunism such as a firm's desire for 'knowledge expropriation' [72–74]. Such strategic interactions between enterprises can be described using models that depict factors such as complementarity, interdependence, trustworthiness, and reciprocity.

Figure 3 shows the strategic dynamics between two enterprises (i.e., Firm A and Firm B) that possess complementary knowledge. This means that each possesses a stock of information that is of use to the other and hence these firms are interdependent on each other. Information stock is a resource that allows each firm to make decisions regarding a number of business activities. These decisions include, but are not limited to, those about entering new markets, designing new products, developing new business processes, building new organizational structures, and creating new business relationships.

In such inter-partner learning arrangements, each firm must disclose its information stock to its partner in order to access the information stock of its partner in return. Each firm identifies learning opportunities from its partner by evaluating the usefulness of the information stock of its partner for its own business requirements. After identifying learning opportunities, a firm tries to access information from the information stock of its partner so as to add it to its own information stock. However, in order to access information from its partner a firm also has to disclose information from its own information stock. This is necessary because for information exchange to be mutually beneficial both firms must act on reciprocal learning opportunities.

A firm can exchange information with its partner through two main methods which are accessing and disclosing information. Accessing and disclosing information are two components of the same process because accessing information depends on the ability of a firm to get information from a dependee (i.e., someone that is depended upon) as well as the ability of the dependee to give information to the depender (i.e., someone that depends). Likewise, disclosing information depends on the ability of a firm to give information to a depender as well as the ability of the depender to get information from the dependee.

Learning ability is a socio-technical resource that enables activities related to the acquisition, assimilation, absorption, and application of organizational knowledge. This resource allows a firm to learn from its partners and also makes it possible for a firm to learn faster than its partner (i.e., allows it to get more information than it gives). The ability to learn faster than a partner is advantageous for a firm because it allows that firm to achieve a higher return from the sharing of its knowledge. Indeed, [75] argues that superior organizational learning leads to improved organizational performance and that "the only source of sustainable competitive advantage for a company may lie in its ability to learn faster than its competitors" [76].

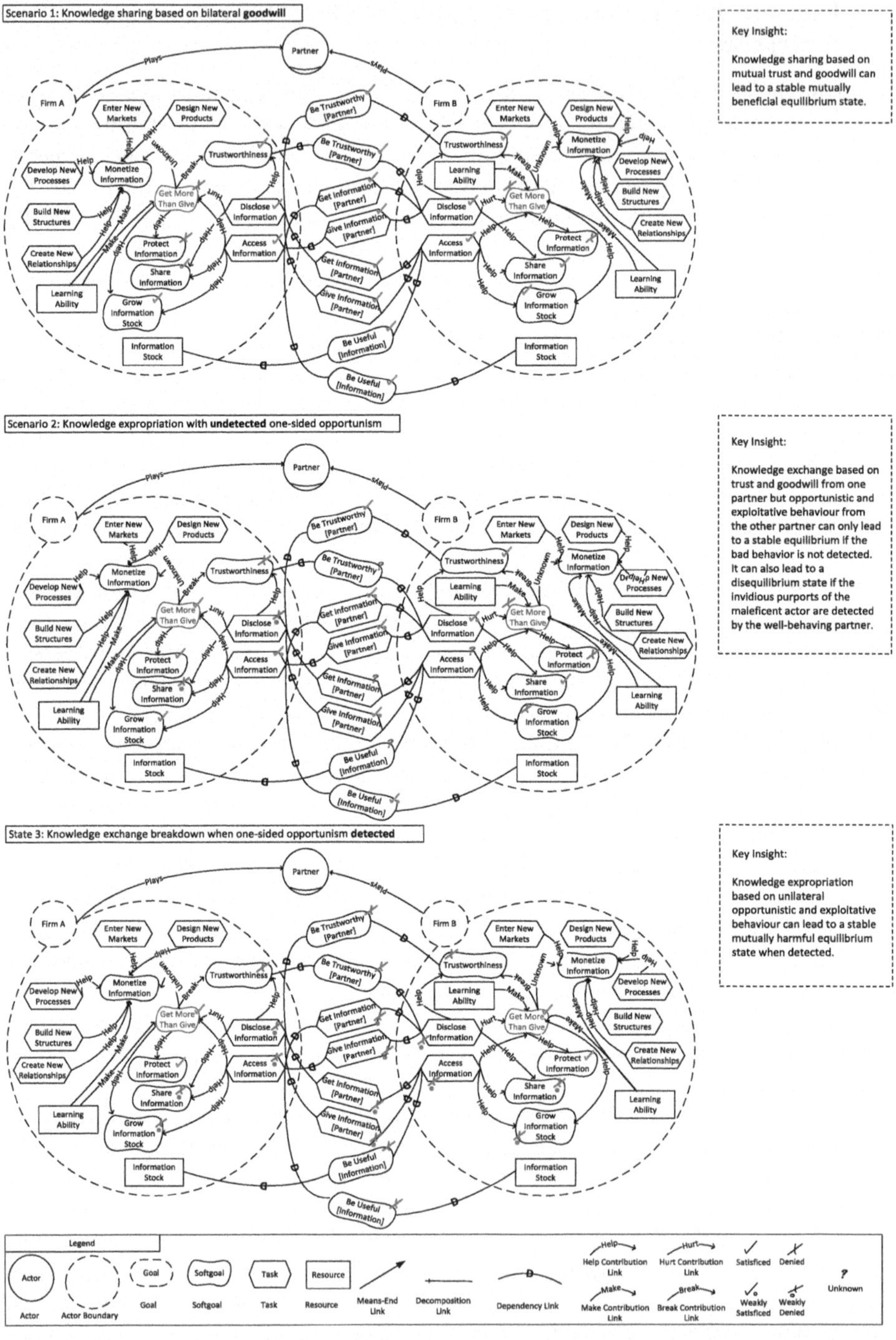

Fig. 3. i* Strategic Rationale diagrams of inter-partner learning and knowledge sharing between enterprises.

A superior learning ability also functions as de facto insurance policy because it precludes a firm from being shut out from the information stock of its partner before it has had a chance to access all the information that it is seeking from that partner. Conversely, a firm that can learn faster than its partner can access all of the relevant information from the information stock of its partner first and then terminate the knowledge sharing arrangement before that partner has had an opportunity to learn all of the relevant information from its information stock. This is why firms evaluate the trustworthiness of partners in order to minimize the risk of exploitation through opportunism (e.g., knowledge expropriation) in knowledge-sharing scenarios.

There are three main types of interactions that can take place between two enterprises (such as firms A and B) in inter-partner learning arrangements. The top diagram in Fig. 3 depicts a situation in which both firms perceive the knowledge exchange to be equitable as well as fair and therefore they will continue to cooperate by sharing knowledge. This might happen if both partners have foregone opportunism in their dealings and have built up a reservoir of goodwill and understanding. In contrast, the bottom diagram in Fig. 3 depicts a situation in which any/all firm(s) perceive the knowledge exchange to be harmful as well as malicious and therefore they will conflict and compete with each other. For example, this might happen if any firm detects its partner(s) of engaging in opportunistic behavior because such behavior will create distrust/mistrust in the partnership.

The middle diagram in Fig. 3 depicts a situation in which one firm is cooperating fully (i.e., Firm B) while the other firm (i.e., Firm A) is cooperating partially. This is because while Firm A is sharing its information with Firm B it is also attempting to learn faster than Firm B (i.e., it is competing). In such a situation the stability of the partnership depends on whether or not Firm B detects the opportunistic behavior of Firm A. If Firm B does not detect the opportunistic behavior of Firm A then Firm B will continue to grant unrestricted access to its information stock to Firm A while Firm A will only grant partial access to its information stock to Firm B. However, if Firm B detects the opportunistic behaviour of Firm A, as shown in the bottom diagram in Fig. 3, then the knowledge sharing will break down on account of Firm B feeling exploited by Firm A. This example shows simultaneous competition and cooperation between the actors because competitive behaviour is present within a cooperative relationship.

4 Conclusions and Future Work

This paper provided an overview of the phenomenon of coopetition as well as some of its key facets and characteristics that are relevant for EM. In addition to being an eminent research area, coopetition is also widely observed in practice. [77] claim that "coopetition is common in several industries" and [78] note that roughly 50 % of strategic alliances are between competitors. Nonetheless, in spite of its prominence, coopetition has not been explored in the EM literature. We intend to address this shortcoming by developing a modeling framework that is suitable for representing cooperation, competition, and coopetition.

The next logical step in our research is to identify and catalog the requirements for modeling these phenomena. Table 1 presents a partial list of these requirements however it needs further elaboration and refinement. After identifying the requirements for modeling coopetition, our next step will be to assess the adequacy of extant modeling languages for satisfying those requirements. Table 2 presents preliminary findings however they merit improvement through more rigorous and detailed assay. Moreover, any revisions to Table 1 will necessarily require Tables 2 to be revised as well. We are also interested in exploring alternate approaches for representing the information that is depicted in Fig. 3.

After evaluating individual modeling languages for satisfying the requirements from our catalog, our next step will be to address their shortcomings. We will do this by developing a conceptual modeling framework that extends and combines extant notations and techniques. To verify this framework, our goal will be to share it with management practitioners and industry specialists. Additionally, our intention is to validate this framework in the field by collaborating with industry partners. This framework will allow the modeling of opportunities and alternatives for strategic coopetition in a structured and systematic manner. As a result, it is our expectation that, this framework will advance the state-of-the-art for the practice of EM.

References

1. Giannoulis, C., Petit, M., Zdravkovic, J.: Modeling business strategy: a meta-model of strategy maps and balanced scorecards. In: Fifth International Conference on Research Challenges in Information Science (RCIS), pp. 1–6. IEEE, May 2011
2. Weigand, H., Johannesson, P., Andersson, B., Bergholtz, M., Edirisuriya, A., Ilayperuma, T.: Strategic analysis using value modeling–the c3-value approach. In: Hawaii International Conference on System Sciences, 40(6). IEEE, January 2007
3. Johannesson, P.: The role of business models in enterprise modelling. In: Krogstie, J., Opdahl, A.L., Brinkkemper, S. (eds.) Conceptual Modelling in Information Systems Engineering, pp. 123–140. Springer, Heidelberg (2007)
4. López, L.C., Franch, X.G.: Applying business strategy models in organizations. In: Proceedings of the 7th International i* Workshop 2014, Thessaloniki, Greece, 16–17 June 2014, pp. paper-6 (2014)
5. Paja, E., Maté, A., Woo, C., Mylopoulos, J.: Can goal reasoning techniques be used for strategic decision-making? In: Proceedings of the 35th International Conference on Conceptual Modeling, Gifu, Japan, 14–17 November 2016
6. Gnyawali, D.R., Park, B.: Co-opetition and technological innovation in small and medium-sized enterprises: a multilevel conceptual model. J. Small Bus. Manage. **47**(3), 308–330 (2009)
7. Bengtsson, M., Kock, S.: Coopetition—Quo vadis? Past accomplishments and future challenges. Ind. Mark. Manage. **43**(2), 180–188 (2014)
8. Giannoulis, C., Petit, M., Zdravkovic, J.: Modeling competition-driven business strategy for business IT alignment. In: Salinesi, C., Pastor, O. (eds.) Advanced Information Systems Engineering. LNBIP, pp. 16–28. Springer, Heidelberg (2011)

9. Liu, X., Peyton, L., Kuziemsky, C.: A requirement engineering framework for electronic data sharing of health care data between organizations. In: Babin, G., Kropf, P., Weiss, M. (eds.) MCETECH 2009. LNBIP, pp. 279–289. Springer, Heidelberg (2009)
10. Bleistein, S.J., Cox, K., Verner, J.: Modeling business strategy in E-business systems requirements engineering. In: Wang, S., et al. (eds.) ER Workshops 2004. LNCS, vol. 3289, pp. 617–628. Springer, Heidelberg (2004)
11. Scott, W.R., Davis, G.F.: Organizations and Organizing: Rational, Natural and Open Systems Perspectives. Routledge, Abingdon-on-Thames (2015)
12. Linstead, S., Maréchal, G., Chanlat, J.F.: Towards Euranglo research? A critical comparison of thirty years of Anglo-Saxon and French organizational analysis. Revue Sciences De Gestion **65**(30th Anniversary Issue), 357–376 (2008)
13. Bain, J.S.: Barriers to New Competition: Their Character and Consequences in Manufacturing Industries. Harvard University Press, Cambridge (1956)
14. Porter, M.E.: How competitive forces shape strategy. Harvard Bus. Rev. **57**(2), 137–145 (1979)
15. Porter, M.E.: Towards a dynamic theory of strategy. Strateg. Manag. J. **12**(S2), 95–117 (1991)
16. Ketelhöhn, W.: What do we mean by cooperative advantage? Eur. Manag. J. **11**(1), 30–37 (1993)
17. Lado, A.A., Boyd, N.G., Hanlon, S.C.: Competition, cooperation, and the search for economic rents: a syncretic model. Acad. Manag. Rev. **22**(1), 110–141 (1997)
18. Dyer, J.H., Singh, H.: The relational view: cooperative strategy and sources of interorganizational competitive advantage. Acad. Manag. Rev. **23**(4), 660–679 (1998)
19. Jiang, X., Li, Y.: An empirical investigation of knowledge management and innovative performance: the case of alliances. Res. Policy **38**(2), 358–368 (2009)
20. Das, T.K., Teng, B.S.: Risk types and inter-firm alliance structures. J. Manag. Stud. **33**(6), 827–843 (1996)
21. Gebrekidan, D.A., Awuah, G.B.: Interorganizational cooperation: a new view of strategic alliances: the case of Swedish firms in the international market. Ind. Mark. Manag. **31**(8), 679–693 (2002)
22. Todeva, E., Knoke, D.: Strategic alliances and models of collaboration. Manag. Decis. **43**(1), 123–148 (2005)
23. Koza, M., Lewin, A.: Managing partnerships and strategic alliances: raising the odds of success. Eur. Manag. J. **18**(2), 146–151 (2000)
24. Inkpen, A.C., Ross, J.: Why do some strategic alliances persist beyond their useful life? Calif. Manag. Rev. **44**(1), 132–148 (2001)
25. Padula, G., Dagnino, G.B.: Untangling the rise of coopetition: the intrusion of competition in a cooperative game structure. Int. Stud. Manag. Organ. **37**(2), 32–52 (2007)
26. Brandenburger, A.M., Nalebuff, B.J.: Co-opetition. Doubleday, New York (1996)
27. Walley, K.: Coopetition: an introduction to the subject and an agenda for research. Int. Stud. Manag. Organ. **37**(2), 11–31 (2007)
28. Czakon, W., Mucha-Kus, K., Rogalski, M.: Coopetition research landscape - a systematic literature review 1997-2010. J. Econ. Manag. **17**, 121–150 (2014)
29. Bouncken, R.B., Gast, J., Kraus, S., Bogers, M.: Coopetition: a systematic review, synthesis, and future research directions. Rev. Manag. Sci. **9**(3), 577–601 (2015)
30. Roy, F.L. Czakon, W. (eds.): Managing coopetition: transcending a paradox [special issue]. Ind. Mark. Manag. 53 (2016)
31. Dagnino, G.B. (ed.): Coopetition strategy: toward a new kind of interfirm dynamics [special issue]. Int. Stud. Manag. Organ. 37(2), 3–10 (2007)

32. Fleisher, C.S.: Managing business political activities in the USA: bridging between theory and practice—another look. J. Public Aff. **1**(4), 376–381 (2001)
33. Alber, A., de Boisgrollier, N., Kourkoumelis, D., Micallef, R.: Does Europe have something to offer the world. Fletcher Forum World Aff. **30**(2), 179–190 (2006)
34. Racine, D.: Dissolving dualities: the case for commonsense replication. Nonprofit Voluntary Sect. Q. **32**(2), 307–314 (2003)
35. Zineldin, M.: Co-opetition: the organisation of the future. Mark. Intell. Plan. **22**(7), 780–790 (2004)
36. Tee, R., Gawer, A.: Industry architecture as a determinant of successful platform strategies: a case study of the i-mode mobile internet service. Eur. Manag. Rev. **6**(4), 217–232 (2009)
37. Luo, Y.: Toward coopetition within a multinational enterprise: a perspective from foreign subsidiaries. J. World Bus. **40**(1), 71–90 (2005)
38. Bouncken, R.B., Fredrich, V.: Coopetition: performance implications and management antecedents. Int. J. Innov. Manag. **16**(05), 1–28 (2012)
39. Rossi, A., Warglien, M.: An experimental investigation of fairness and reciprocity as determinants of intraorganizational coopetition. In: Dagnino, G.B., Rocco, E. (eds.) Coopetition Strategy: Theory, Experiments and Cases, pp. 74–100. Routledge, New York (2000)
40. Giannoulis, C., Zikra, I., Bergholtz, M., Zdravkovic, J., Stirna, J., Johannesson, P.: A comparative analysis of enterprise modeling approaches for modeling business strategy. In: 6th IFIP WG 8.1 Working Conference on the Practice of Enterprise Modeling (PoEM 2013), Riga, Latvia, 6–7 November 2013, pp. 193–204 (2013)
41. Barney, J.B.: Types of competition and the theory of strategy: toward an integrative framework. Acad. Manag. Rev. **11**(4), 791–800 (1986)
42. Henderson, B.D.: The anatomy of competition. J. Mark. **47**(2), 7–11 (1983)
43. Henderson, B.: Understanding the forces of strategic and natural competition. J. Bus. Strateg. **1**(3), 11–15 (1981)
44. Chiswick, B.: The economics of language for immigrants: an introduction and overview. In: Wiley, T.G., Lee, J.S., Rumberger, R.W. (eds.) The Education of Language Minority Immigrants in the United States, pp. 72–91. Multilingual Matters, Bristol (2009)
45. Barney, J.: Firm resources and sustained competitive advantage. J. Manag. **17**(1), 99–120 (1991)
46. Barney, J.B.: Is the resource-based "view" a useful perspective for strategic management research? Yes. Acad. Manag. Rev. **26**(1), 41–56 (2001)
47. Bengtsson, M., Kock, S.: "Coopetition" in business networks—to cooperate and compete simultaneously. Ind. Mark. Manag. **29**(5), 411–426 (2000)
48. Raza-Ullah, T., Bengtsson, M., Kock, S.: The coopetition paradox and tension in coopetition at multiple levels. Ind. Mark. Manag. **43**(2), 189–198 (2014)
49. Dowling, M., Roering, W., Carlin, B., Wisnieski, J.: Multifaceted relationships under coopetition. J. Manag. Inq. **5**(2), 155–167 (1996)
50. Rusko, R.: Perspectives on value creation and coopetition. Probl. Perspect. Manag. **10**(2), 60–72 (2012)
51. Rusko, R.: Mapping the perspectives of coopetition and technology-based strategic networks: a case of smartphones. Ind. Mark. Manag. **43**(5), 801–812 (2014)
52. Chiambaretto, P., Dumez, H.: Toward a typology of coopetition: a multilevel approach. Int. Stud. Manag. Organ. **46**(2,3), 110–129 (2016)
53. Tee, R., Gawer, A.: Industry architecture as a determinant of successful platform strategies: a case study of the i-mode mobile Internet service. Eur. Manag. Rev. **6**(4), 217–232 (2009)
54. Gnyawali, D.R., Park, B.: Co-opetition between giants: Collaboration with competitors for technological innovation. Res. Policy **40**(5), 650–663 (2011)

55. Luo, Y.: Toward coopetition within a multinational enterprise: a perspective from foreign subsidiaries. J. World Bus. **40**(1), 71–90 (2005)
56. Castaldo, S., Dagnino, G.B.: Trust and coopetition: the strategic role of trust in interfirm coopetitive dynamics. In: Dagnino, G.B., Rocco, E. (eds.) Coopetition Strategy: Theory, Experiments and Cases, pp. 74–100. Routledge, New York (2009)
57. Garraffo, F., Rocco, E.: Competitor analysis and interfirm coopetition. In: Dagnino, G.B., Rocco, E. (eds.) Coopetition Strategy: Theory, Experiments and Cases, pp. 44–63. Routledge, New York (2009)
58. Hutchinson, D., Singh, J., Svensson, G., Mysen, T.: Inter-relationships among focal dimensions in relationship quality: a quantitative and exploratory approach. Int. J. Procurement Manag. **5**(2), 229–252 (2012)
59. Judge, W.Q., Dooley, R.: Strategic alliance outcomes: a transaction-cost economics perspective. Br. J. Manag. **17**(1), 23–37 (2006)
60. Barney, J.B., Hansen, M.H.: Trustworthiness as a source of competitive advantage. Strateg. Manag. J. **15**, 175–190 (1994)
61. Fernandez, A.S., Le Roy, F., Gnyawali, D.R.: Sources and management of tension in co-opetition case evidence from telecommunications satellites manufacturing in Europe. Ind. Mark. Manag. **43**(2), 222–235 (2014)
62. Ashraf, N., Bohnet, I., Piankov, N.: Decomposing trust and trustworthiness. Exp. Econ. **9**(3), 193–208 (2006)
63. Sobel, J.: Interdependent preferences and reciprocity. J. Econ. Lit. **43**(2), 392–436 (2005)
64. Fehr, E., Gächter, S.: Fairness and retaliation: the economics of reciprocity. J. Econ. Perspect. **14**(3), 159–181 (2000)
65. Lee, J. G., Antoniadis, P., Salamatian, K.: Faving reciprocity in content sharing communities a comparative analysis of Flickr and Twitter. In: Proceeding of International Conference on Advances in Social Networks Analysis and Mining (ASONAM) (2010)
66. Falk, A., Fischbacher, U.: A theory of reciprocity. Games Econ. Behav. **54**(2), 293–315 (2006)
67. Krämer, A., Jung, M., Burgartz, T.: A small step from price competition to price war: understanding causes, effects and possible countermeasures. Int. Bus. Res. **9**(3), 1 (2016)
68. Kale, P., Singh, H., Perlmutter, H.: Learning and protection of proprietary assets in strategic alliances: building relational capital. Strateg. Manag. J. **21**(3), 217–237 (2000)
69. Khanna, T., Gulati, R., Nohria, N.: The dynamics of learning alliances: competition, cooperation, and relative scope. Strateg. Manag. J. **19**(3), 193–210 (1998)
70. Petts, N.: Building growth on core competences—a practical approach. Long Range Plan. **30** (4), 551–561 (1997)
71. Carayannis, E.G., Alexander, J., Ioannidis, A.: Leveraging knowledge, learning, and innovation in forming strategic government–university–industry (GUI) R&D partnerships in the US, Germany, and France. Technovation **20**(9), 477–488 (2000)
72. Heiman, B.A., Nickerson, J.A.: Empirical evidence regarding the tension between knowledge sharing and knowledge expropriation in collaborations. Manag. Decis. Econ. **25**(6–7), 401–420 (2004)
73. Ritala, P., Olander, H., Michailova, S., Husted, K.: Knowledge sharing, knowledge leaking and relative innovation performance: an empirical study. Technovation **35**, 22–31 (2015)
74. Trkman, P., Desouza, K.C.: Knowledge risks in organizational net-works: an exploratory framework. J. Strateg. Inf. Syst. **21**(1), 1–17 (2012)
75. Jashapara, A.: Cognition, culture and competition: an empirical test of the learning organization. Learn. Organ. **10**(1), 31–50 (2003)
76. Jashapara, A.: The competitive learning organization: a quest for the Holy Grail. Manag. Decis. **31**(8), 52–62 (1993)

77. Baglieri, D., Carfì, D., Dagnino, G.B.: Asymmetric R&D alliances and coopetitive games. In: Greco, S., Bouchon-Meunier, B., Coletti, G., Fedrizzi, M., Matarazzo, B., Yager, R.R. (eds.) IPMU 2012. CCIS, pp. 607–621. Springer, Heidelberg (2012)
78. Harbison, J.R., Pekar, P.P.: Smart Alliances: A Practical Guide to Repeatable Success. Jossey-Bass, San Francisco (1998)
79. Yu, E.S.: Towards modelling and reasoning support for early-phase requirements engineering. In: Proceedings of the Third IEEE International Symposium Requirements Engineering, pp. 226–235. IEEE, January 1997

Defining the Responsibility Space for the Information Systems Evolution Steering

Jolita Ralyté[1(✉)], Wanda Opprecht[2], and Michel Léonard[1]

[1] Institute of Information Service Science,
University of Geneva, Carouge, Switzerland
{jolita.ralyte,michel.leonard}@unige.ch
[2] Ensemble Hospitalier de la Côte, Morges, Switzerland
wanda.opprecht@ehc.vd.ch

Abstract. Information System (IS) evolution is today a continuous preoccupation of every modern organization that aims to have a perfect support for its constantly changing business ecosystem. However, the task of IS evolution is not anodyne, it presents several risks towards IS sustainability as well as towards enterprise activity. Taking a decision related to any IS change can be a troublesome responsibility because of the amount of information that has to be processed and the uncertainty of the impact of the change on the enterprise and its IS. To reduce this uncertainty, we have developed a conceptual framework for IS evolution steering. This framework allows to capture the information on how enterprise IS supports its activities and regulations, and then to extract the information relevant for realizing IS evolution activities, simulating their impact, and taking appropriate decisions. This second part of the framework is called the responsibility space of IS evolution steering and is the main subject of this paper.

Keywords: Information system evolution · IS evolution steering · IS steering model · Responsibility space of IS evolution steering

1 Introduction

The constantly changing business and technology environment of modern organizations implies the necessity for continuous evolution of their Information Systems (IS) that are expected to fit it perfectly. However, the task of IS evolution is not anodyne, it presents several risks towards IS sustainability as well as towards enterprise structure and activity [1]. Taking a decision related to any IS change can be a troublesome responsibility. First, because of the amount of information that has to be processed while this information is not always available or easy to find, which creates the feeling of uncertainty. Second, because of the uncertainty of the impact of the change on the enterprise and its IS. Some of the problems that could appear are: the undetected inconsistency between the organization's activity and the IS functionality, the loss of regulatory compliance, conflicting IS evolutions, the impossibility to undo IS/Organizational changes, the loss of information, and the need to change the whole system when only part of it is impacted. Therefore, a tool supporting IS evolution

J. Horkoff et al. (Eds.): PoEM 2016, LNBIP 267, pp. 179–193, 2016.
DOI: 10.1007/978-3-319-48393-1_13

steering is indispensable to guide and to reassure the officers responsible for this task. In our previous work [2] we have introduced a conceptual framework for IS evolution steering. This framework includes several conceptual models each of them taking into account a particular perspective of IS evolution steering:

- the information on how enterprise IS supports its activities and regulations is captured in the *IS Steering Model* (IS-SM);
- the notion of IS evolution including its structure, lifecycle and impact assessment is represented in the corresponding *Evolution Models*;
- the responsibility of IS evolution steering actors on (1) the consistency of enterprise information (data) and on (2) the enterprise compliance with regulations governing its activities is formalized in *Ispace* and *Rspace* models respectively; and
- the guidance to use the aforementioned models, and so to help the actors in charge of IS evolution steering, is formalized in the *Evolution Steering Method.*

The framework constitutes the foundation for developing an Informational Steering Information System (ISIS). Up to now we only presented the general overview of the framework and its IS-SM model [2], and partially discussed the IS evolution models [3]. In this paper we focus our attention on the third part of our framework that deals with the notion of responsibility in IS evolution steering. In particular, we explain how to extract the information that is necessary to understand the scope of a particular IS evolution, to asses its impact, and finally to take appropriate decisions. We call this type of information the *Responsibility space*. As mentioned above, we distinguish two types of responsibility: the one over the enterprise information space that we call *Ispace*, and the other over the regulation space that we call *Rspace*.

The rest of this paper is organized as follows: in Sect. 2 we discuss the responsibility issues in the domain of IS evolution. Section 3 provides an overview of the fundamental model of our framework – the IS-SM. Section 4 presents the main contribution of this paper – the models for defining the responsibility space of IS actors. In Sect. 5 we briefly discuss the related works and we conclude in Sect. 6.

2 Responsibility Issues in IS Evolution Steering

Information systems evolution is closely related to the changes undertaken in the organization itself and in its environment. A decision to move the organization from a current situation (ASIS-Org) to a new one (TOBE-Org) generally implies a more or less important change in its information system – the move from a current IS (ASIS-IS) to the new one (TOBE-IS). At each increment of ASIS-IS evolution towards TOBE-IS, the IS evolution steering officers have to take important decisions that could have more or less important impact on the TOBE-IS and therefore on the TOBE-Org. Indeed, they are directly responsible for the quality and sustainability of the TOBE-IS as well as its fitness to the TOBE-Org business. Besides, they are indirectly responsible for the future sustainability of the organization and its business, which depend on the result of the IS change. Therefore, the task of IS evolution steering is not so simple and is characterized by a high level of uncertainty, and the main reasons of that are as follows:

- Besides its operational importance, an information system has also a strategic significance for the organization. Indeed, it holds key information for the organization, and represents a strategic resource which underpins its key functions and decision-making processes.
- IS evolution may be triggered by business needs, legislation and/or strategic technological decisions. An organization, its business activities and its information systems are interwoven, so changes to one of them are likely to affect the others [4].
- The decisions on how to change the organization and how to change its IS are not taken at the same level and not by the same people.
- The decisions at organization's strategic level are generally made in situations distinguished by their uniqueness and uncertainty (e.g. business innovation). That makes the decisions at IS level even more risky. These decisions may have serious consequences and could jeopardize the sustainability of the organization [5].
- IS evolution requires knowledge [4] about IS structure, about dependencies between IS components and applications and how they support business activities, about how people work with the IS, and what are their rights and responsibilities. Having this knowledge is of prime importance in the IS evolution steering as it provides the basis for the action [6]. Knowledge deficiency, in the contrary, creates the situation of uncertainty.
- The complexity of IS evolution is due to the fact that several IS dimensions have to be taken into consideration [7, 8]: the *information dimension* responsible for the availability and integrity of data, the *regulatory dimension* ensuring IS compliance with the enterprise regulatory framework (standards, laws, regulation policies), the *activity dimension* supporting enterprise business activities, and the *technology dimension* dealing with the implementation and integration solutions.
- Finally, there are many different ways to realize an IS evolution, each of them having a different impact on the current and future condition of the organization's IS, and therefore, of the organization itself.

To reduce the uncertainty level that IS evolution steering actors have to face we need to guarantee that they possess all the required knowledge allowing to observe IS changes, to understand their impact, and to identify potential risks on the TOBE-IS and TOBE-Org. We agree with [4] that models are means to record this knowledge and make it accessible. Hence, to capture this knowledge, we have developed an Information System Steering Model (IS-SM) that allows to define how exactly enterprise activities and regulations are implemented in its information system. Actually, IS-SM is the underpinning model for the development of a meta-IS (IS upon IS in [9]) that we call ISIS – Informational Steering Information System. Enterprise IS and ISIS are not at the same level. IS is at the operational level, where actors (IS users) can query/create/delete/modify objects of IS classes, and trigger/control/stop operations on these objects according to their access rights. ISIS is at the IS steering level, where actors (IS steering officers) can query/create/delete/modify the design of classes, operations on these classes, integrity rules, processes, and access rights of the IS.

When a particular IS evolution is at stake, only a part of the information available in ISIS is needed – the ISIS entities that are directly or indirectly concerned by the evolution. They represent the *responsibility space* of this IS evolution steering.

Identifying this space contributes to reduce the risk of information overload [10], which could lead the IS steering actors to confusing estimations and inappropriate decisions. The main role of the responsibility space is to assist the evolution impact analysis.

Inspired by [11, 12], we define the responsibility space as a set of ISIS instances that represent accountabilities and capabilities of an actor to perform a task. We distinguish two perspectives of responsibility:

1. *Ispace* representing the responsibility over information elements (i.e. objects, operations, and integrity rules implemented in the enterprise IS), and
2. *Rspace* representing the responsibility over regulatory elements (i.e. laws and regulation policies governing enterprise activities supported by its IS).

Formally, the Ispace/Rspace model is defined as a part of IS-SM. With Ispace/Rspace, we create sub-sets of information, extracted from ISIS, that inform the IS steering actors about the changes caused by an evolution affecting the responsibility of IS users. They allow to simulate IS evolutions and to identify potential risks. In the next section we overview IS-SM, and then in Sect. 4 we define mechanisms to extract the Ispace and Rspace from IS-SM.

3 Overview of the Information System Steering Model

The role of the Information System Steering Model (IS-SM) consists in defining the information that can be obtained from the enterprise IS in a generic way. In particular, it allows representing the information related to the enterprise structure (organizational units and their composition), positions in an organizational unit, persons' assignments to one or several positions, their responsibility over different information elements, etc. Figure 1 depicts a simplified version of IS-SM. More details about IS-SM can be found in [1], and its complete version is available online [13]. IS-SM contains three main

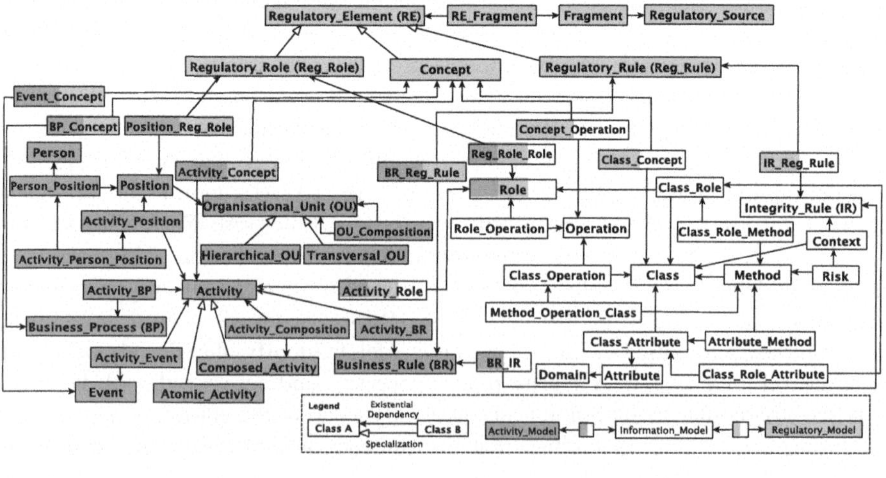

Fig. 1. Simplified version of IS-SM, see [13] for details

parts: activity, information, and regulatory. In this section we provide a short summary of each of them.

The *activity part* of IS-SM (the left side in Fig. 1) describes the organization of the enterprise activity. In particular, it allows to capture the information on how different *persons* are related to the *organizational units* trough *positions* they hold, which *activities* they can perform in these positions, how activities are combined in larger *business processes* and what are the *business rules* that control the execution of activities and business processes.

The *information part* of IS-SM (the right side in Fig. 1) reflects the usual definition of IS concepts such as *class*, *operation*, *integrity rule*, and their interrelations. In addition, this part takes into account the fact that usually an enterprise has several more or less interdependent information systems and many services can be built upon an IS. Therefore, IS-SM also includes the concept of *IS* and the concept of *service*, and relates all the elements of its information part with the IS and services where they are present. For readability purposes, these two concepts are not shown in Fig. 1; the complete model can be found in [13].

The main interrelations between the activity and information parts are established trough the concept of *role*, which is a pivotal concept of IS-SM. It allows to connect activities and, consequently, persons who may perform these activities, to the IS classes and operations by defining the appropriate access rights. Other interrelations concern business rules from the activity part and integrity rules from the information one. A business rule is related to an integrity rule if the later was created from the former.

The *regulatory part* of IS-SM (the top part in Fig. 1) expresses knowledge about science, techniques, standards, skills, laws, policies and regulations that are independent of the enterprise but govern enterprise activities. As a consequence, enterprise IS, supporting these activities, has to comply with them. This knowledge is formalized in terms of *regulatory elements* that can be *concept*, *regulatory role* and *regulatory rule*.

The interrelations between the activity and information part elements on one hand and the regulatory part elements on the other hand are established if the former are founded on the later. Indeed, laws or other regulatory instruments can impose the creation of particular classes, operations, business rules, or positions. Generally, this information is not made explicit in the traditional IS. However, it is very important for the IS evolution steering to trace regulatory elements inside the IS [8]. In case they change (e.g. a change of a law), a conforming IS evolution must be triggered.

To conclude, we claim that an ISIS based on the IS-SM allows to capture all the information necessary to deal with IS evolution steering. However, this information is still too large when considering a particular ASIS-IS transformation into TOBE-IS. In the following sections we define mechanisms to extract the information that is really at stake for a particular IS change – the responsibility space of the change.

4 Defining the Responsibility Space from IS-SM

We study the notion of responsibility from the enterprise activity point of view, i.e. how any change in the organization (e.g. a hospital) affects the responsibility of a particular role in this organization (e.g. prescribing drugs to patients), an activity where this role has to be played (e.g. visit patients), a position to which this activity is allocated (e.g. doctor) and finally a person that is allocated to this position (e.g. Dr Laennec). In the following sub-sections we formally define how the Ispace/Rspace can be calculated for different IS-SM activity part elements. We illustrate these definitions with a simple example from the hospital domain.

4.1 Responsibility on the Information Space

The information space of a particular IS-SM activity part element x (i.e. role, person, position, or activity), retrieved from IS-SM and denoted *Ispace(x)*, represents the space of information accountability and capability of x. For example, if the Ispace of a person p, *Ispace (p)*, includes a class *cl*, then p has accountability over the objects of *cl*, and p is expected to have capabilities thereof (e.g. create, update, delete the objects of *cl*).

The formalization of Ispace(x) and Rspace(x) is inspired by the relational algebra in the following way:

$$Ispace/Rspace\ (x) = (Cl_A * Cl_B * Cl_C)[Cl_A = x][Cl_B]$$

where * expresses the join between IS-SM classes, $[Cl_A = x]$ represents the selection of the object x from the class Cl_A, and $[Cl_B]$ expresses the projection on the class Cl_B.

Formally, Ispace of an element x is defined as a powerset Ispace(x) = <Cl(x), Op(x), IR(x)> that includes a set of classes *Cl(x)*, a set of operations Op(x) and a set of integrity rules *IR(x)* accessible from x and defined in IS-SM.

For example, the Ispace of a role r is defined as *Ispace(r) = <Cl(r), Op(r), IR(r)>*. The part of IS-SM allowing to retrieve *Ispace(r)* is shown in Fig. 2. Here, *Cl(r)* represents the set of classes that r can access, and, therefore, for which r carries accountability (probably shared with other roles) and holds capability to execute methods on these classes. This set of classes can be accessed through the operation:

$$Cl(r) = (Role * Class\_Role * Class)\ [Role = r][Class]$$

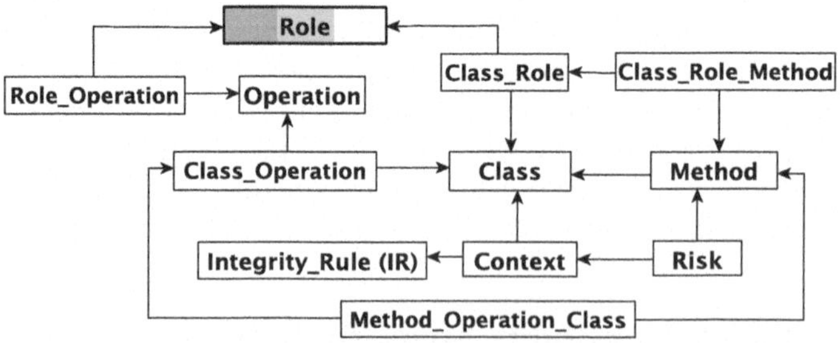

Fig. 2. The part of IS-SM allowing to retrieve the Ispace of a role.

Op(r) represents the set of operations that can be executed by the role *r*, and for which *r* carries accountability and holds the necessary capability. This set of operations can be accessed through the operation:

*Op(r) = (Role * Role_Operation * Operation) [Role = r] [Operation]*

Finally, *IR(r)* includes the set of integrity rules that can be accessed by the role *r* via the methods and operation of the classes that are in *Cl(r)* of its Ispace. Therefore, *r* carries accountability to validate these rules when this validation is not completely automatized and holds capability for that. The set of integrity rules of a role can be accessed through the operation:

*IR(r) = (Role * Class_Role * Class_Role_Method * Method * Risk * Context * Integrity_Rule) [Role = r] [Integrity_Rule] ∪ (Role * Role_Operation * Operation * Class_Operation * Method_Operation_Class * Method * Risk * Context * Integrity_Rule) [Role = r] [Integrity_Rule].*

The Ispace of a person *p*, *Ispace(p)*, represents the information elements (classes, operations and integrity rules defined in the organization's IS) that *p* needs to access in order to perform the activities related to her position(s) in the organization. Figure 3 shows the part of IS-SM allowing to retrieve the *Ispace(p)*. In the course of evolution, if a person leaves the organization, her information space should be identified and transferred to another person to ensure the continuity of the business activities. On the opposite, if a new person enters the organization, she should be trained to use her information space. Because a person may have several roles, each of them related to the activities for which she has the duty in her position(s), *Ispace(p)* is defined by the union of the *Ispace(r)* of each of its roles:

$Ispace(p) = \cup_{r \in Role(p)} Ispace(r)$, where
*Role(p) = (Person * Person_Position * Activity_Person_Position * Activity_Position * Activity * Activity_Role * Role) [Person = p] [Role]*

In a similar way, Ispace is defined for positions and activities.

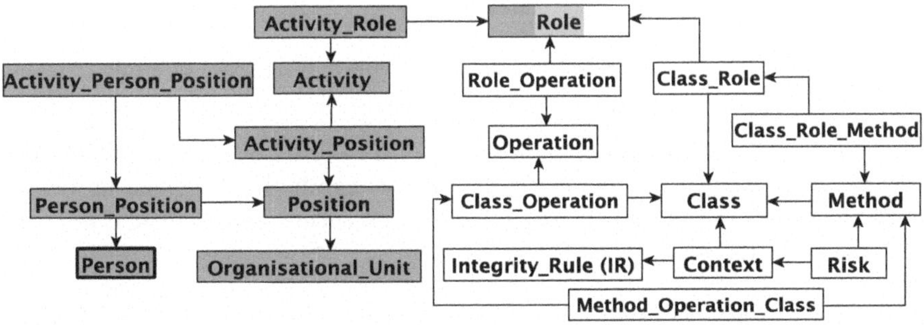

Fig. 3. The part of IS-SM allowing to retrieve the Ispace of a person.

4.2 Responsibility on the Regulatory Space

The regulatory space of a particular IS-SM activity part element *x* (i.e. role, person, position, and activity), denoted *Rspace(x)*, is also retrieved from IS-SM. It represents a space of regulatory accountability and capability of *x*, i.e. how *x* is related to the regulatory elements (i.e. concepts, regulatory rules and regulatory roles) of the regulatory part of IS-SM. For example, if the Rspace of a person *p*, *Rspace(p)*, includes a concept *c*, then *p* has compliance responsibility over the objects of *c*, and possesses the capability thereof, i.e. the required knowledge.

Rspace of an element *x* is defined as a powerset *Rspace(x)* = *<Co(x), RRole(x), RRule(x)>* including a set of concepts *Co(x)*, set of regulatory roles *RRole(x)*, and a set of regulatory rules *RRule(x)* accessible from *x* and defined in IS-SM. An IS-SM activity part element *x* may access a regulatory element in three different ways (see Fig. 1):

- Via a direct relation, e.g. *Activity* has a direct link to *Concept* via *Activity_Concept.*
- Indirectly via intermediate activity part elements, e.g. *Activity* can be related to *Regulatory_Role* through *Position* and *Position_Reg_Role*, or it can be related to *Concept* via *Event* and *Event_Concept*.
- Indirectly via intermediate information part elements, e.g. *Role* can be related to *Concept* via *Class*, and to *Regulatory_Rule* via *Class* and *Integrity-Rule*, where *Class* and *Regulatory_Rule* are elements of the information part of IS-SM.

The total Rspace of *x* will take into consideration all possible ways *x* can access the regulatory elements.

Figure 4 shows the Rspace model for a role. The Rspace of a role *r* is defined as:

Rspace(r) = *<Co(r), RRole(r), RRule(r)>.*

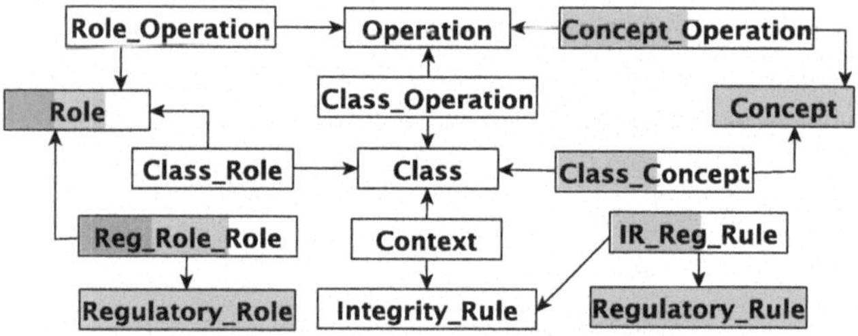

Fig. 4. The part of IS-SM that allows to retrieve the Rspace of a role.

Co(r) includes a set of concepts (instances of the class *Concept*) that represent the regulatory foundation of the role *r*. These concepts can be implemented in the enterprise IS as classes or operations to which the role has access. To calculate *Co(r)* we use the following operation:

*Co(r) = (Role * Class_Role * Class * Class_Concept * Concept) [Role=r][Concept])*
*∪ (Role * Role_Operation * Operation * Concept_Operation * Concept) [Role=r] [Concept]*

RRole(r) represents the set of regulatory roles that are the "raison d'être" of a role *r*. In the course of IS evolution, if it happens that a regulatory role has no more corresponding role, we can deduce that either the IS is not compliant with the regulatory framework of the organization, or this regulatory role is now out of the IS scope. The set of regulatory roles of a role *r* can be accessed through the operation:

*RRole(r) = (Role * Reg_Role_Role * Regulatory_Role) [Role = r][Regulatory_Role]*

Finally, *RRule(r)* represents a set of regulatory rules that the role *r* has to be compliant with. This compliance is implemented through the integrity rules over the classes to which this role has access. The operation to calculate *RRule(r)* is:

*RRule(r) = (Role * Class_Role * Class * Context * Integrity_Rule * IR_Reg_Rule * Regulatory_Rule) [Role = r][Regulatory_Rule]*

In a similar way we define the Rspace for activities, positions and persons.

4.3 Illustrating Example

To illustrate the Ispace and Rspace definitions proposed above we use an example of the hospital ROL. Figure 5 depicts a small part of the kernel of its information system schema.

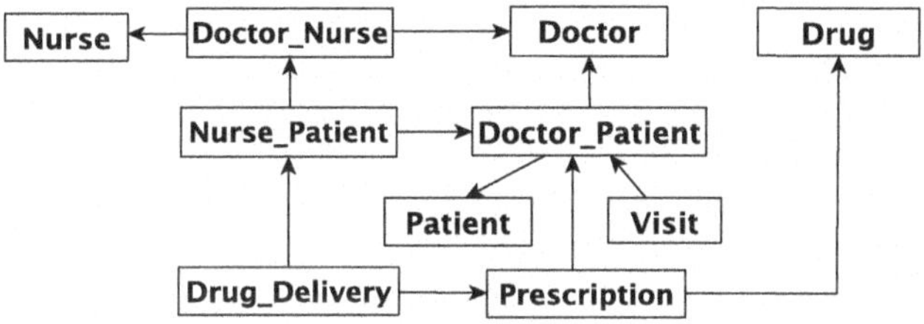

Fig. 5. A small part of the IS schema of the hospital ROL.

In this example we will consider:

- one organizational unit: the general medicine department,
- two positions: the doctor and the nurse,
- two activities of a doctor: a_1 concerning the care of patients (visit, diagnostic, prescription) and a_2 concerning the management of the nurses working in her team.

The activity a_1 is associated with two roles: r_{11} for the visit of patients, and r_{12} for the prescription of drugs to patients. To calculate the Ispace of the role r_{11} we apply the formulas provided above.

$Ispace(r_{11}) = <Cl(r_{11}), Op(r_{11}), IR(r_{11})>$:
$Cl(r_{11})$ = *{Doctor, Patient_Doctor, Patient, Visit, Prescription, Drug_Delivery, Nurse_Patient}* is the list of classes that the role r_{11} should access;
$Op(r_{11}) = \{(\forall cl \in Cl(r_{11}), read(cl)), create(visit)\}$: r_{11} can read the objects of any class of $Cl(r_{11})$ and can create an object of the class *Visit*;
$IR(r_{11})$ is empty.

Therefore, the ISpace of the doctor Laennec related to the role r_{11} is:

$Ispace\ (Laennec\ /\ r_{11}) = (Cl(r_{11}), Op(r_{11}), ø)\ [Doctor = \text{'Laennec'}]$.

This selection, as in the relational model, means that any object accessible by Laennec must be reachable by join operation with the object of the class *Doctor* identified by Laennec. So, for instance, Laennec can create an object of *Visit* only for his patients and can access to the objects of *Patient* only for his patients.

Similarly, we calculate the Ispace of the role r_{12}:

$Ispace\ (r_{12}) = <Cl(r_{12}), Op(r_{12}), IR(r_{12})>$:
$Cl(r_{12}) = Cl(r_{11})$;
$Op(r_{12}) = \{(\forall cl \in Cl(r_{12}), read(cl)), create(prescription)\}$; $IR(r_{12}) = ø$.

The activity a_2 is associated with two roles: r_{21} and r_{22} – the arrival and the departure of a nurse in/from the team of a doctor. Indeed, in the ROL hospital, a doctor has the responsibility to accept/refuse/fire a nurse in her team. The Ispace of the roles r_{21}/r_{22} is as follows:

$Ispace\ (r_{21}) = <Cl(r_{21}), Op(r_{21}), IR(r_{21})>$:
$Cl(r_{21})$ = *{Doctor, Docor_Nurse, Nurse)*;
$Op(r_{21}) = \{(\forall cl \in Cl(r_{21}), read(cl)), create(doctor\_nurse)\}$; $IR(r_{21}) = ø$.

$Ispace\ (r_{22}) = <Cl(r_{22}), Op(r_{22}), IR(r_{22})>$.
$Cl(r_{22})$ = *{Doctor, Docor_Nurse, Nurse)*;
$Op(r_{22}) = \{(\forall cl \in Cl(r_{22}), read(cl)), delete(doctor\_nurse)\}$; $IR(r_{22}) = ø$.

To illustrate an evolution case, let's suppose that now the ROL hospital wants to get into improving patients safety. To this end, it proposes to introduce the concept of skill. Following international standards, some particular skills will be required for the delivery of drugs to patients. The doctor will be in charge to guarantee that nurses of her team have sufficient competences for administrating all the drugs she can prescribe. So, the IS of ROL must evolve, especially by introducing new classes such as *Skill*, *Nurse-Skill* associating a nurse to her skills, *Required-Skill* associating a drug to the skills required to administrate it, and the class *Doctor_Drug* associating a doctor to any drug she can prescribe. The new IS schema is shown in Fig. 6.

After this evolution, the position "doctor" has still the same activities a_1 and a_2, and the activity a_1 has the same roles r_{11} and r_{12}. But, for the activity a_2, the roles r_{21} and r_{22}, must be extended into r_{211} and r_{221}. Furthermore, this activity has additional roles r_{23} and r_{24} related to the skills and the drugs. Here are the definitions of the Ispace of r_{211}, r_{221}, r_{23} and r_{24}:

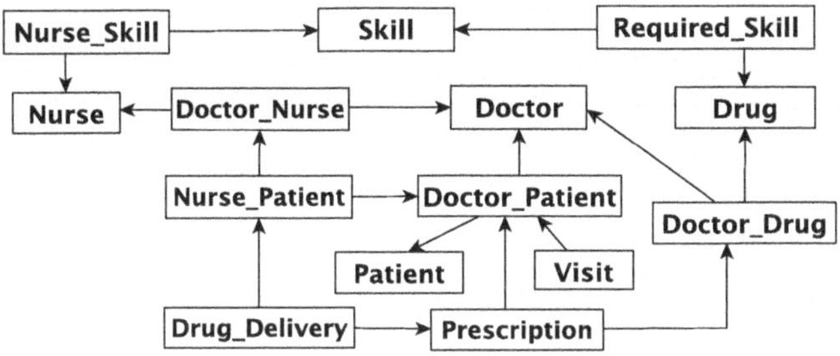

Fig. 6. The IS schema of the hospital ROL after the evolution.

r_{211}: when dealing with the arrival of a new nurse, the doctor can check if the nurse has sufficient skills given the skills of the other team nurses.

Ispace $(r_{211}) = <Cl(r_{211}), Op(r_{211}), IR(r_{211})>$:
$Cl(r_{211})$ = *{Doctor, Doctor_Nurse, Nurse, Nurse_Skill, Skill, Doctor_Drug, Drug, Required_Skill);*
$Op(r_{211}) = \{(\forall cl \in Cl(r_{211}), read(cl)), create(doctor\_nurse)\}$;
$IR(r211) = \emptyset$.

r_{221}: the doctor can check if the departure of the nurse has serious consequences given the skills of the other team nurses.

Ispace $(r_{221}) = <Cl(r_{221}), Op(r_{221}), IR(r_{221})>$:
$Cl(r_{221})$ = *{Doctor, Doctor_Nurse, Nurse, Nurse_Skill, Skill, Doctor_Drug, Drug, Required_Skill);*
$Op(r_{221}) = \{(\forall cl \in Cl(r_{221}), read(cl)), delete(doctor\_nurse)\}$; $IR(r_{221}) = \emptyset$.

r_{23}: the doctor can add or remove skills to a nurse.

Ispace $(r_{23}) = <Cl(r_{23}), Op(r_{23}), IR(r_{23})>$:
$Cl(r_{23})$ = *{Doctor, Doctor_Nurse, Nurse, Nurse_Skill, Skill, Doctor_Drug Drug, Required_Skill);*
$Op(r_{23}) = \{(\forall cl \in Cl(r_{23}), read(cl)), delete(nurse\_skill), create(nurse\text{-}skill)\}$;
$IR(r_{23}) = \emptyset$.

r_{24}: the doctor can add/remove a drug to/from her list of drugs.

Ispace $(r_{24}) = <Cl(r_{24}), Op(r_{24}), IR(r_{24})>$:
$Cl(r_{24})$ = *{Doctor, Doctor_Drug, Drug);*
$Op(r_{24}) = \{(\forall cl \in Cl(r_{24}), read(cl)), create(doctor\_drug), delete(doctor\_drug)\}$;
$IR(r_{24}) = \emptyset$.

With this example we can also briefly show the relevance of the Rspace. The class *Skill* can be considered as a concept of the regulatory space because its origin can come from an international standard, which is independent of the hospital. Thanks to this concept, a nurse can position herself in her work domain. For example, if she wishes to move to another team, she should compare her present skills with the required skills of this team. To make the transfer possible, she needs to know the list of the skills required by this team. Consequently, she must be allowed not only to access all the skills of her team (through the required skills of the drugs of her doctor) but also all the skills of the other teams. This situation emerges only because of the regulatory space, not at all because of the operational activities of the hospital. Hence, this situation shows how the knowledge of the enterprise IS and its different dimensions can be useful not only for operational purposes but also to support IS evolution.

5 Related Works

The subject of IS evolution was largely discussed in the literature taking into account various perspectives and positions. Most of the works consider a particular aspect of evolution (e.g. changes in data schema, requirements, technology, and architecture, business reengineering and enterprise reorganization) without trying to provide a holistic approach and tool support for its steering. Though, IS evolution steering is at the crossroads of several research areas such as: evolution models, Business/IT alignment, Enterprise Architecture (EA) and Enterprise Modelling (EM), IS governance and risk management. Here, because of the space limit, we will mention only a few works, mainly with the aim to demonstrate the position of our contribution.

Comyn-Wattiau et al. [14] emphasize that IS evolution and the mechanisms for supporting it highly depend on its different facets or dimensions, like the nature of change, the time frame and the importance. Similarly, various IS change dimensions and taxonomies are proposed in the domains of data management [15] and business process management [16] taking into consideration various aspects of change like its subject, cause, type, extent, effect, swiftness, temporal and spatial issues. We agree with the idea that IS evolution is multifaceted. Our framework for IS evolution steering includes three interrelated dimensions (i.e. activity, information and regulation) each of them being a potential trigger and a subject of the change. Besides, we cope with different IS evolution perspectives: its structure, lifecycle, impact and responsibility.

Let's look now how our framework could be situated with regards to the EA/EM contributions. Based on the literature review, Niemi and Pekkola [17] define EA as 'an approach to managing the complexity of an organization's structures, information technology (IT) and business environment, and facilitating the integration of strategy, personnel, business and IT towards a common goal through the production and use of structural models providing a holistic view of the organization'. They also claim that 'because of this scope, EA can be approached from a number of viewpoints'. Indeed, most of the EA frameworks (e.g. Zachman Framework [18], TOGAF [19], CIMOSA [20]) and EM languages (e.g. EKD-CMM [21], DEMO [22], ArchiMate [23]) acknowledge the need for multiple views and abstraction levels. They are necessary to cope with IS/enterprise architecture complexity and separation of concerns, and to address the different life spans of the architecture elements [24, 25]. These approaches expose best practices and generic principles that support the creation of 'blueprints for shared vision' [24] of the current (ASIS-Org and ASIS-IS) and desired (TOBE-Org and TOBE-IS) situations. However, they fail to offer a formal evolution steering method and tool supporting continuous IS changes. We acknowledge that they provide a detailed EA picture and propose approaches for EA evolution [26]. Though, they do not offer means to measure the impact of the changes on the IS instances and on the organisation activities, and the regulation dimension is clearly missing.

Another perspective we would like to address is the notion of risk related to the IS evolution. IS evolution is the entanglement of organizational, information, regulatory and technology issues and hence, the nature of IS evolution risk is as complex as the setting they stem from. In their study of IS risks Alter and Sherer [10, 27] review a large amount of dedicated literature from which they identify risk components (e.g. financial, functionality, organisational, technology, security, people, information, political, etc.), organize risk factors and propose a general and adaptable model of IS risk. From this and other related studies [28, 29] we retain that risk is related to uncertainty. We argue that a way to cope with uncertainty in IS evolution steering is by providing the precise information about the IS elements that are at stake. This is the main role of our framework.

To conclude, we propose to discuss the notion of responsibility, which is, to our best knowledge, the less considered topic in the domain of IS evolution. In [11, 12] Feltus et al. propose a metamodel formalizing the notion of responsibility of IS actors. In this model the responsibility of an actor is related to a business role she plays in the organization, and represents her accountabilities on a business task and the required capabilities and rights to perform those accountabilities. Our framework for IS evolution steering is compliant with this responsibility definition. Furthermore, with the Ispace and Rspace definition mechanisms, we provide a powerful tool for assessing and managing the responsibility of IS actors, and hence, the responsibility of IS evolution steering officers.

6 Conclusion

Every modern organization understands that its prosperity largely depends on the quality and fitness of its information systems. Because of the constant changes in the organization and its environment, IS evolution is permanently at stake. Actors, responsible for IS evolution steering, are challenged to take decisions having impact on the enterprise business. To be able to take these decisions, they must have a thorough knowledge of the situation allowing to assess the impact of changes. The aim of our work is to support IS evolution steering with conceptual tools allowing to reduce the uncertainty inherent to IS evolution and the complexity pertaining to the multiple IS dimensions. The main model of our conceptual framework, named IS-SM, represents a foundation for developing an information system for IS evolution steering, that we call ISIS. After a brief review of IS-SM, we present the main contribution of this paper, which deals with identifying the responsibility space of IS actors. This responsibility is considered from two complementary points of view: information (Ispace) and regulation (Rspace). The Ispace and Rspace defined systematically on the current IS (ASIS-IS) and future IS (TOBE-IS) allow to measure the delta of the IS evolution from information and regulatory points of view respectively. They offer a view on how the responsibility space will change for each actor of the organization. A person can be granted with new responsibilities (e.g. creating, deleting, modifying objects) over an existing or newly created information space. Is she ready to assume them? Does she have capabilities? Such changes at IS level require decisions at organization's steering level, while the information necessary to support the decision taking can be obtained at the IS level. We are convinced that the implementation of ISIS would be helpful not only for IS evolution steering abut also when dealing with enterprise reorganization.

References

1. Mukherji, A.: The evolution of information systems: their impact on organizations and structures. Manag. Decis. **40**(5), 497–507 (2002)
2. Opprecht, W., Ralyté, J., Léonard, M.: Towards a framework for enterprise information system evolution steering. In: Ralyté, J., España, S., Pastor, Ó. (eds.) PoEM 2015. LNBIP, vol. 235, pp. 118–132. Springer, Heidelberg (2014). doi:10.1007/978-3-662-45501-2_9
3. Ralyté, J., Opprecht, W., Léonard, M.: Reorganizing an enterprise thanks to its information system. In: Proceedings of ICEIS 2016, vol. 2, pp. 567–574. SCITEPRESS (2016). ISBN: 978-989-758-187-8
4. Hofer, S.: Modeling the transformation of application landscapes. In: Ralyté, J., España, S., Pastor, Ó. (eds.) PoEM 2015. LNBIP, vol. 235, pp. 101–113. Springer, Heidelberg (2013). doi:10.1007/978-3-642-41641-5_8
5. Lesca, H., Lesca, N.: Strategic Decisions and Weak Signals: Anticipation for Decision-Making, p. 144. Wiley, Hoboken (2014)
6. Davis, G.B.: Information systems conceptual foundations: looking backward and forward. In: Baskerville, R., Stage, J., DeGross, J.I. (eds.) Organizational and Social Perspectives on Information Technology. ITIFIP, vol. 41, pp. 61–82. Springer, Heidelberg (2000). doi:10.1007/978-0-387-35505-4_5
7. Estier T., Falquet G., Guyot J., Léonard, M.: Six spaces for global information systems design. In: TC8 (Ed.) Proceedings of IFIP Working Conference on The Object Oriented Approach in Information Systems (1991)
8. Léonard, M., Khadraoui, A., Ralyté J.: Regulation in information systems at the level of tunement. In: Proceeding of Workshop on Regulations Modelling and their Validation and Verification (REMO2 V), at CAiSE 2006, CEUR-WS, vol. 241 (2006)
9. Le Dinh, T.: Towards a new infrastructure supporting interoperability of information systems in development: the information system upon information systems. In: Konstantas, D., et al. (eds.) Interoperability of Enterprise Software and Applications, pp. 385–396. Springer, Heidelberg (2006)
10. Sherer, S.A., Alter, S.: Information system risks and risk factors: are they mostly about information systems. Commun. AIS **14**(2), 29–64 (2004)
11. Feltus, C., Petit, M., Dubois, E.: ReMoLa: responsibility model language to align access rights with business process requirements. In: Proceedings of RCIS 2011, pp. 1–6 (2011)
12. Khadraoui, A., Feltus, C.: Service specification and service compliance: how to consider the responsibility dimension? J. Serv. Sci. Res. **4**(1), 123–142 (2012)
13. IS-SM. http://cui.unige.ch/~ralyte/ISIS/IS-SM.html
14. Comyn-Wattiau, I., Akoka, J., Lammari, N.: A framework for database evolution management. In: Workshop on Unanticipated Software Evolution (USE 2003), in Conjunction with ETAPS'03, Warsaw, Poland (2003)
15. Roddick, J.F., Al-Jadir, L., Bertossi, L., et al.: Evolution and change in data management: issues and directions. SIGMOD Rec. **29**(1), 21–25 (2000)

16. Regev, G., Soffer, P., Schmidt, R.: Taxonomy of flexibility in business processes. In: Proceedings of the CAISE 2006 Workshop on Business Process Modelling, Development, and Support (BPMDS 2006), CEUR-WS, vol. 236 (2006)
17. Niemi, E., Pekkola, S.: Enterprise architecture quality attributes: a case study. In: Proceding of the 46th Hawaii International Conference on System Sciences (HICSS), pp. 3878–3887 (2013)
18. Zachman, J.A.: A framework for information systems architecture. IBM Syst. J. **26**(3), 276–292 (1987)
19. The Open Group: TOGAF version 9.1, An Open Group Standard (2012). http://pubs.opengroup.org/architecture/togaf9-doc/arch/. Accessed Apr 2016
20. ESPRIT Consortium AMICE (Ed): Open Systems Architecture for CIM, 2nd. Revised and Extended Version. Springer, Berlin (1993)
21. Barrios, J., Nurcan, S.: Model driven architectures for enterprise information systems. In: Persson, A., Soffer, P., Stirna, J. (eds.) CAiSE 2016. LNCS, vol. 3084, pp. 3–19. Springer, Heidelberg (2004). doi:10.1007/978-3-540-25975-6_3
22. Dietz, J.L.G.: DEMO: towards a discipline of organisation engineering. Eur. J. Oper. Res. **128**, 351–363 (2001)
23. ArchiMate. http://www.archimate.nl/
24. Armour, F.J., Kaisler, S.H., Liu, S.Y.: A big-picture look at enterprise architectures. IT Prof. **1**(1), 35–42 (1999)
25. Greefhorst, D., Proper, E.: Architecture Principles - The Cornerstones of Enterprise Architecture. The Enterprise Engineering Series 4. Springer, Heidelberg (2011)
26. Gaaloul K., Guerreiro, S.: A decision-oriented approach supporting enterprise architecture evolution. In: Proceedings of the 24th IEEE International Conference WETICE 2015, pp. 116–121. IEEE (2015)
27. Alter, S., Sherer, S.: A general, but readily adaptable model of information system risk. Commun. AIS **14**(1), 1–28 (2004)
28. Barki, H., Rivard, S., Talbot, J.: Toward an assessment of software development risk. J. Manag. Inf. Syst. **10**(2), 203–225 (1993)
29. Copas, J.: Statistical modelling for risk assessment. Risk Manag. **1**(1), 35–49 (1999)

A Textual Description Based Approach to Process Matching

Maria Rana[1], Khurram Shahzad[1(✉)], Rao Muhammad Adeel Nawab[3], Henrik Leopold[2], and Umair Babar[1]

[1] University of the Punjab, Lahore, Pakistan
{maria.rana, khurram, umair.babar}@pucit.edu.pk
[2] Vrije Universiteit Amsterdam, Amsterdam, The Netherlands
h.leopold@vu.nl
[3] COMSATS Institute of Information Technology, Lahore, Pakistan
adeelnawab@ciitlahore.edu.pk

Abstract. The increasing number of process models in an organization has led to the development of process model repositories, which allow to efficiently and effectively manage these large number of models. Searching process models is an inherent feature of such process repositories. However, the effectiveness of searching depends upon the accuracy of the underlying matching technique that is used to compute the degree of similarity between query-source process model pairs. Most of the existing matching techniques rely on the use of labels, structure or execution behavior of process models. The effectiveness of these techniques is, however, quiet low and far from being usable in practice. In this paper, we address this problem and propose the use of a combination of textual descriptions of process models and text matching techniques for process matching. The proposed approach is evaluated using the established metrics, precision, recall and F_1 score. The results show that the use of textual descriptions is slightly more effective than activity labels.

1 Introduction

Business process models (hereafter process models) are widely used to formally document the business operations of an enterprise. That is because process models are proven to be an effective means for visualizing and improving their complex operations [1]. Due to the increasing number of models, enterprises have to maintain process model repositories which may contain up to hundreds or thousands of process models [2, 3]. The effective use of these collections requires searching relevant source process models against a given query process model [4]. This makes searching an integral feature of process model repositories [5–7]. The effectiveness of searching depends upon the efficiency of the underlying matching techniques that determines the degree of similarity between a pair of process models [8]. Existing matching techniques [9–13] take into account the three established feature classes of process models: label features, structural features, and behavioral features. However, the effectiveness of these techniques, is not sufficient [9] and far from being usable in practice [13]. Therefore, several efforts are being made to develop new techniques or to combine existing

J. Horkoff et al. (Eds.): PoEM 2016, LNBIP 267, pp. 194–208, 2016.
DOI: 10.1007/978-3-319-48393-1_14

techniques for process matching. Another limitation is that most of the techniques require a process *model* as input, which limits the number of users who can search process models.

As a contribution towards addressing these problems, in this paper, we propose to exploit the presence of textual descriptions of process models in a process repository and the availability of established text matching techniques for process matching. Specifically, we investigate, whether the use of textual descriptions performs better than using label features of process models. The reason for the choice of label features over structural and behavioral features is rooted in the fact that label features serve as a primary source for generating textual descriptions, whereas the other two features mainly contribute to the flow of the text. We contend, once the superiority of the use of textual descriptions over label features is established, it can be used in combination with structural and behavioral features for process matching.

In this paper, we first generate textual descriptions of 669 process models using a well-established textual description generation technique [18]. Second, we parse the same set of models to extract their activity labels. Subsequently, we apply four established text matching techniques, n-gram overlap [14], edit distance similarity [15], Longest Common Subsequence (LCS) [16], and Vector Space Model (VSM) [17] to evaluate the effectiveness of textual descriptions over activity labels.

The rest of the paper is organized as follows: Sect. 2 provides the background on process models and related work. Section 3 provides an overview of the proposed approach for process matching. Section 4 describes the corpus used for our experiments. Section 5 describes the experimental setup (similarity estimation models), and the analysis of the results. Finally, Sect. 6 concludes the paper.

2 Background

This section introduces the background to this work by first providing an example process model and its equivalent textual description. Then, we reflect on the related work with the help of the example process model.

2.1 Motivating Example

In order to illustrate the correspondences between a process model and its textual description, consider the example of a university's admission process shown in Fig. 1. The example process model is depicted using the Business Process Modeling and Notation (BPMN) – the de facto standard process modeling language. The model contains one start event, seven activities, two XOR gateways, and one end event. The start event is represented by circle, activities are represented by rectangles with round edges, XOR gateways are represented by a diamond shape containing a cross, and the end event is represented by a solid circle.

The corresponding textual description of the example process model generated by using the Natural Language Generated System (NLGS) from [18] is shown in Fig. 2. A careful look at the two specifications reveals the correspondences between the nodes

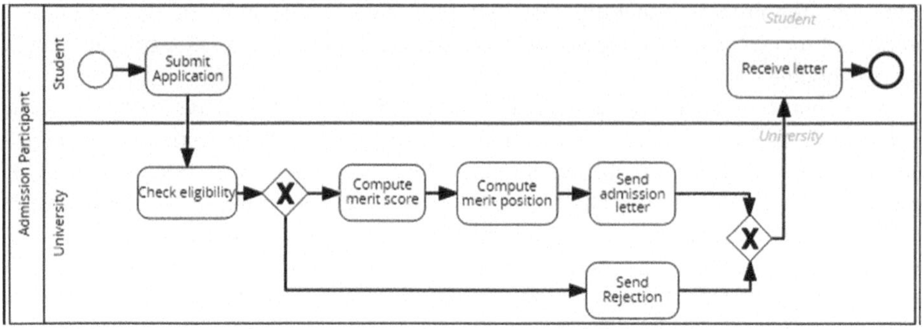

Fig. 1. University admission process model

The process begins when the student submits an application. Then, the university checks the eligibility. Afterwards, one of the following branches is executed:

- The University computes the merit score. Subsequently, the University computes the merit position. Then, the University sends the admission letter.
- The University sends the rejection.

Once one of the following branches was executed the student receives the letter.
Afterwards, the process is finished.

Fig. 2. Textual description of the example process model

(events, activities, and gateways) of the process model and the sentences of the textual description. For instance, both the model and the textual description specify that the process starts when a candidate submits an admission application. Also, it is clear from both specifications that after submitting the application, the eligibility of the candidate is checked.

2.2 Related Work

In line with the three feature classes (label, structural, and behavioral) of process models, the related work to this research is classified into three main categories: label based approaches, structure based approaches, and behavior based approaches.

Label based approaches extract the activity labels of process models and apply matching approaches to evaluate the similarity between query-source process model pairs. The underlying techniques include the edit distance [15], the bag of words model [10] or contextual similarity [9]. Given two labels, approaches based on the edit distance compute the minimum number of atomic string operations (insertion, deletion, substitution of words) required to transform the sequence of query labels into the sequence of source labels and divides it by the maximum length of the two labels. Approaches based on the bag of words model divide labels into individual words and compute the ratio of the number of common words by the number of words in one or both labels [10]. In contrast to latter two techniques, context similarity takes into account the preceding and succeeding label of activities to detect the equivalence of activities [9]. However, a key limitation is that these approaches consider two process models as similar by comparing the labels only. Thus, differences in the structure are not taken into account. For the process model from Fig. 1 this means that any model with identical activity labels is considered as similar, even if the gateways, actors, or the control flow between the activities are entirely different.

Structure based approaches generally disregard the labels of process models and rely on the topology of models to evaluate the similarity between query-source process model pairs. Among others, such approaches [9, 19] rely on the use of the graph-edit distance to compute similarity between models. Given two models, these approaches compute the number of graph edit operations (insertion, deletion or substitution of process elements) required to transform one model into another one. A typical limitation of these approaches is that they assume that semantically identical activities have identical or similar labels. [20] combines label matching and graph edit distance based approaches to compare the models. For the example model given in Fig. 1, these approaches would focus structural aspects such as the decision after the second activity and disregard the specific meaning of the activities.

Behavior based approaches rely on the use of dependency graphs or causal footprints to evaluate the similarly between query-source process model pairs. However, these approaches, such as [12], typically do not distinguish between certain connector types. For the example model from in Fig. 1, such approaches may determine a query-source process model pair as equivalent even if contains OR gateways instead of XOR gateways.

The most relevant work to this paper is a recent contribution from [29], which promotes the use of textual descriptions on top of the process model. Matching the example model from Fig. 1 with a query model requires the consideration of a document for checking the eligibility of student (as additional textual description for the activity *check eligibility*) and the document that explains the process of computing the merit score or the merit position (as additional textual descriptions for the activities *compute merit score* and *compute merit position*). In contrast to that approach, the approach we propose in this paper relies on the use of textual descriptions as an alternative to combining process models with additional textual descriptions of its activities.

3 The Proposed Approach

A brief overview of our proposed approach to process matching is presented in Fig. 3. From the figure it can be seen that our process matching approach consists of a collection of source process models and their corresponding textual descriptions. While keeping textual descriptions alongside process models increases the comprehension of business processes among users, we propose to use the textual description for process matching.

Our approach relies on the use of an automatic approach to generate textual descriptions of a process model if needed. As far as we are aware, the Natural

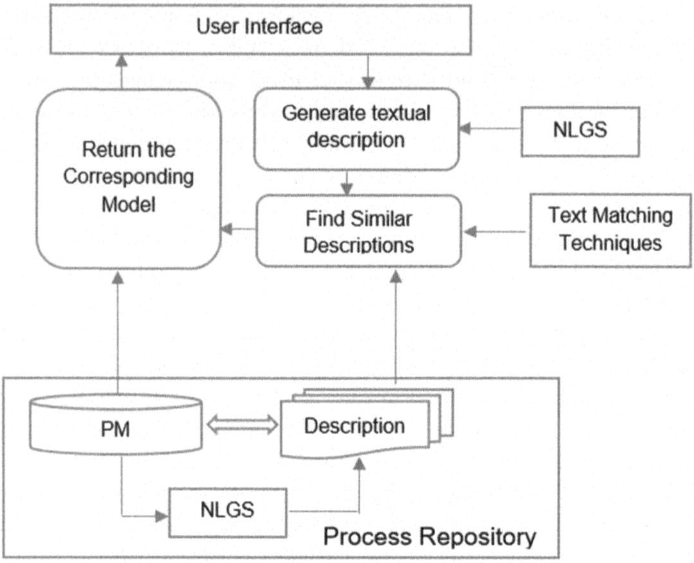

Fig. 3. Overview of the Proposed Approach

Language Generation System[1] (NLGS) is the only available tool that can automatically generate textual descriptions of a process model. It uses a well-established technique[2] that takes a process model in the JSON format as input and generates its textual description. For that reason, this system is used in our approach to automatically generate textual descriptions of all process models in the repository.

The input to our proposed approach is a query process model or its textual description. The task is thus to identify all the process models in the repository which are similar/relevant to the query in two/three major steps: (i) generate textual description, (ii) find similar process descriptions, and (iii) identify the corresponding process models.

In the first step, if the input is a query process model, a textual description of the query process model is generated using the NLGS. Then, the (generated) textual description of the query process is compared to the textual descriptions of all the source process models in the repository. A ranked list of source process models is subsequently generated based on their similarity scores. In the third step, the top K source process models in the ranked list are marked as potential relevant process models against the query and returned to the user.

[1] Available for download at http://www.henrikleopold.com/downloads/.

[2] Runner-up McKinsey BT Award 2013, and winner TARGION Award 2014.

3.1 The Baseline Approach

As a baseline for comparison, we use the *label-based N-gram overlap* approach. That is because, among the three features classes (label, structural, and behavioral), label features serves as a primary source for generating textual descriptions, whereas, the other two features mainly guide the structure and the flow of the textual description. Another reason is that the label contain all the important keywords of the process model, which makes a label based approach a logical baseline. Using this approach, the degree of similarity between the query-source process model pair is computed by counting the number of common words (extracted from the activity labels of the process models) between the query-source process models pair. Subsequently, it is divided by the length of one or both textual descriptions to get a normalized score between 0 and 1. The similarity score of 0 indicates that the query and source process models are entirely different and the similarity score of 1 indicates that they are exactly the same.

3.2 The Similarity Estimation Models

The following paragraphs give a brief overview of the estimation models used in this paper.

3.2.1 N-gram Overlap

The similarity between a query-source textual description pair is computed using a simple and well-known similarity estimation model, the n-gram overlap [14]. Note that we propose to use textual descriptions of process models instead of collections of labels that are used in the baseline approach. Using the similarity estimation model, both the query and the source textual descriptions are divided into chunks of length n (or sets of n-grams with length n). The degree of similarity between the query-source textual description pair is calculated by taking the intersection of the sets of n-grams of the query and the source textual descriptions and dividing it by the length of one or both textual descriptions to get a normalized score between 0 and 1. This similarity estimation model has been used in plagiarism detection [21], duplicate/near-duplicate document detection [22], and measuring text reuse in journalism [23]. For this paper, the similarity between the query-source textual description pair is computed using the overlap similarity coefficient. If S(Q, n) and S(S, n) represent the sets of unique n-grams of length n in a query textual description Q and a source textual description S respectively, then the similarity between them using the overlap similarity co-efficient is calculated using the following equation.

$$\mathrm{S}_{\mathrm{overlap}}(Q,S) = \frac{|S(Q,n) \cap S(S,n)|}{\min(|S(Q,n)|, |S(S,n)|)}$$

The range of the similarity score is between 0 to 1, where 1 means the two textual descriptions are exactly same and 0 means they don't have any common n-gram. In this paper, we have computed the similarity between the query-source textual description pairs for n = 1, i.e. unigrams. Before computing the similarity, all punctuation marks and stop words were removed and remaining words were stemmed using Porter's Stemmer.

3.2.2 Edit Distance Similarity

Edit distance is a distance-based model [15]. Using this model, the query-source textual description pair is first represented as a sequence of words or characters. Then, the number of atomic string edit operations (insert, delete, and substitute) required to transform the query textual description into the source textual description are counted. Subsequently, the edit distance is the minimum number of operations needed to transform the query textual description into the source textual description. For instance, if A = "abcd" and B = "abcdef", then the number of operations required to convert A to B is 2 (i.e. 2 insertions + 0 deletions + 0 substitutions). Similarly, the number of operations required to convert B to A is also 2 (i.e. 0 insertions + 2 deletions + 0 substitutions). The minimum number of operations is also 2. Thereafter, the similarity score between the query textual description (Q) and the source textual description (S) is computed using the following equation.

$$E_s(Q,S) = 1 - \left\{ \frac{ed(Q,S)}{max(|Q|,|S|)} \right\}$$

where ed(Q, S) is the edit distance between query-source textual description pair.

3.2.3 Longest Common Subsequence Approach

The Longest Common Subsequence (LCS) [16] is another similarity estimation model used to compute the similarity between query-source textual description pairs. Using this similarity estimation model, the query-source textual description pair to be compared is represented as a sequence of characters or words. The number of edit operations (deletions and insertions) used to transform the query textual description into the source textual description are thereafter counted to compute the similarity between the textual descriptions. For instance, if A = "abcdef" and B = "abgdef", then abdef is the LCS between A and B.

In this paper, we used LCS to compute a normalized similarity score (called LCSnorm) between the query-source textual descriptions by dividing the length of LCS by the length of the shorter textual description. Since the LCS similarity estimation model is order-preserving, the alterations in the text caused by different edit operations (word substitutions, word re-ordering etc.) are reflected by the length of LCSnorm.

$$LCS_{norm} = \frac{|LCS|}{\min(|Q|,|S|)}$$

where |Q| and |S| are the lengths of the query and the source textual description respectively.

3.2.4 Vector Space Model

The VSM [17] is another similarity estimation model used to compute similarity between query-source textual description pairs. It computes the degree of similarity between manual-automatic description pairs by first representing the texts in a high dimensional vector space. The number of dimensions in the vector space is equal to the number of unique words (or vocabulary) in the document collection. Then, the degree of similarity between a manual textual description (q) and a system textual description (d) is computed using the cosine similarity measure (see the equation below).

$$sim(q,d) = \frac{\hat{q}, \hat{d}}{(|\hat{q}|, |\hat{d}|)}$$

$$sim(q,d) = \frac{\sum_{i=1}^{n} q_i \times d_i}{\sqrt{\sum_{i=1}^{n} (q_i)^2 \times \sum_{i=1}^{n} (d_i)^2}}$$

4 The Corpus

This section provides details about the process model collection, query models, and the human annotations used in the experiment.

4.1 Source Process Models

We generated a collection of 669 BPMN process models and compared it to the widely used SAP Reference Model consisting of 604 process models. The goal was to illustrate the superiority of our developed collection with respect to the diversity in label and structure-related features [27]. For generating the collection, we employed a systematic protocol in order to handcraft the necessary diversity that we deem necessary for a benchmark collection. According to the protocol, at first 150 process models of different sizes, diameters, densities, network connectivity, sequentiality, separability and token split etc., were collected. For the interested reader we kindly refer to [24] for more details about the metrics. To generate diverse label and structural features we reproduced three other variants of these 150 process models, formally called, Near Copy (NC), Light Revision (LR), and Heavy Revision (HR). The NC variant is generated by 'slightly' changing the formulation of each label of a model in such a way that the semantic meanings of the labels are not changed. For instance, a possible NC of the label 'customer inquiry processing' could be 'client inquiry processing'. The LR variant is generated by 'substantially' changing the formulation of each label in such a way that the meanings of the labels are not changed. A possible LR of 'prepare replacement order' could be 'fulfill alteration request'. The HR variant is generated by making two types of changes to process models: (a) changing the formulation of each label without changing the semantic meaning of the labels, and (b) changing the structure (control flow) between activities of a process model in such a way that the semantics of the control flow remains intact.

In order to reduce the human bias, a team of three researchers was formed. To develop a common understanding of the variants, five example process models and their three variants were given to the researchers along with ample time to comprehend these models. This was followed by a discussion and an informal question answering session. The session was led by a three member advisory board with expertise in business process modeling, natural language processing, and corpus generation. Subsequently, the 150 process models were divided into two subsets, 1–75 and 76–150, and each participant was asked to perform two revisions on a subset i.e. one researcher was asked to generate the NC and the HR variant on the first and the second subset respectively. The second participant was asked to generate the LR and the HR variant on the first and the second subset respectively. Similarly, the third participant was asked to generate the NC and the LR on the first and the second subset, respectively.

The smallest model in the collection contains 11 activities and largest model contains 54 activities. In terms of structural features, the average size of our collection of 669 process models is 20.75 with a standard deviation of 7.09, a diameter of 16.78 with a standard deviation of 5.46, a sequentiality ratio of 0.41 with standard a deviation of 0.17, and an average degree of connectors of 2.94 with a standard deviation of 0.52. Another key feature is that the process models in our collection are free of structural errors. For instance, the connector mismatch in our collection is 0. This indicates that there are no process models in our collection with a split connector (AND/OR/XOR) without a corresponding join connector (as requested by prominent process modeling guidelines [24, 25]). It is to be noted that the generation of process models with diverse label features required the participants to perform 24,092 operations (insertion, deletion synonyms replacement, and reordering or words). Similarly, to generate diversity with respect to structural features, 1,764 operations (adding/removing activities, adding/removing/changing gateways, adding/removing/renaming lanes etc.) were performed by the participants.

Mendling et al. [26] highlighted that model understanding strongly depends upon accurate interpretation of the labels. Their study presented four semantic challenges about labels, including, the use of ambiguous grammar, label terms, compound words, and vocabulary with possibly different semantics. We generated another 69 process models for our collection by explicitly inducing semantic challenges to labels. Note that at least 17 models were added for each of the four semantic challenges. Accordingly, the generated collection has 669 process models. In addition to the 669 models, we generated textual description for each process model. The size of the descriptions ranges from 48 words to 394 words with an average of 13.7 words per label.

4.2 Query Process Models

From the collection of 669 models we selected 56 process models as query models. These numbers should be seen in the context of existing studies, such as [9], which *randomly* selected 10 query models and 100 source models to evaluate the effectiveness of their proposed approaches. In contrast to that, the choice of 56 query models in our case is not arbitrary. We rather employed a systematic procedure to choose the necessary and sufficient set of query models. The necessary and sufficient set is required because the chosen set of queries will afterwards be used to manually determine the relevance of the query process model against the set of 669 source process models. In case, the query models include models that are irrelevant, it will unnecessarily increase the human effort for manually determining the relevance between models. Similarly, if relevant models are not included, the approach is not sufficiently useful.

Our set of 56 query models includes models with diverse structural and label features. For choosing the necessary and sufficient set of query models with respect to the *structural* features, we first computed the values of 15 widely used structural metrics (M) of 150 original process models. The structural metrics include size, diameter, density, coefficient of connectivity, average degree of connectors, maximum degree of connectors, separability ratio, sequentiality ratio, and token split. Subsequently, the correlation was calculated between all possible combinations of these metrics, i.e. $|m_i|^2 \mid \forall\ m_i \in M$. The pair of structural features ($m_1 - m_2$) with a correlation value of 0.95 indicates that if we choose a process model with a higher score of the structural feature m_1, it is likely that the process model with a higher value m_2 is also chosen and vice versa. This part of the procedure ensures the choice of a sufficient set of query models. For the necessary set of structural features we chose query models with minimum and maximum value of each structural metric $\{m_i \mid \forall\ corr(m_i, m_j) <= 0.95\ \&\ m_i, m_j \in M\}$. Accordingly, 14 query models were chosen from the collection of 150 original models (recall Sect. 4.1 the collection of 669 models contains 150 original models).

For choosing the necessary and sufficient set of query models with respect to the *label* features, 14 query models from each process model variant (NC and LR) were chosen by using the procedure described in the preceding paragraph. Note that the diversity in the label features comes from the fact that the near copy variant was generated by 'slightly' changing the formulation of each label of the model and the light revision variant was generated by 'substantially' changing the formulation of each label of the model. Thus, the choice of queries from each variant ensures sufficient diversity in query models with respect to the *label* features.

The chosen set of 42 query models (14 query models from each, original, NC and LR) were analyzed once again to identify the necessary set of query models. The analysis revealed that the identified set of query models includes variants of the same query model, i.e. if P1 query model is included for the reason that it has the maximum value of the structural metric m_1, P1NC (its near copy variant) was also included. This is unnecessary because the query model P1 will be matched with all source models, including P1NC, to challenge the ability of the text matching technique to detect the label variant of P1. Nonetheless, the inclusion of P1NC also does not have a different value of the structural metric m_1, i.e. the inclusion of P1NC as query model simply add another model with exactly the same structural feature. To ensure a sufficient set of query models, the duplicate models (P1NC in the example case) were replaced by another near copy variant process model with the next maximum value of m_1. This ensures that another near copy variant of process model with next maximum value of metric m_1 is also included. The process was repeated until a unique set of query models were identified.

These 42 query models do include the structural and label variants. However, they do not include the process models where labels as well as the structure was changed. To overcome this limitation, 14 query models from the heavy revision process models are also chosen by using the same procedure described earlier. Heavy revision variants are generated by making two types of changes to the process models: re-writing labels and changing the structure (control flow) between activities. Thus, the inclusion of heavy revision variants will challenge the ability of the text matching techniques to detect the process models where label and structure was changed as well. Accordingly, 56 queries models were generated for the experiment.

4.3 Human Annotations

To evaluate the retrieval performance of our proposed automatic methods (see Sect. 3), we need manual annotations of relevant source process model(s) against each query process model. This would require a comparison of 37,464 query-source model pairs. Given that, declaring the two process models to be equivalent requires comparing all activities, the amount of human effort is even more substantial. This is also the reason why existing studies, such as [9], used a small sample of 10 query models and 100 source models. In contrast to that approach, we created a sharply defined relevance screening criteria. Subsequently, two researchers were asked to independently compare 56 query models with 150 original models only to significantly reduce the human effort. At first glance, one may question the manual benchmark because not all pairs were compared. However, this is far from being true, since the remaining 519 models in the collection are handcrafted variants of these models with the same meaning. Hence, such a comparison is not necessary. We subsequently calculated the inter-rater agreement using Kappa statistics [28], which was 0.906. The inter-rater agreement score is very good which demonstrates that the human judgement was consistent across the researchers, and that the relevance screening criteria was sharp enough to be used in practice.

5 Experimental Setup

The proposed approach presented in Sect. 3 is implemented as a Java Prototype. For the experiments the complete collection of 669 process models and the 56 query models serve as input to the prototype. For each query the prototype returned a text file which contains the names of the source models and their similarity score with the query model, i.e. each file contains 669 source models and their similarity scores in descending order. The top *K* process models were subsequently separated. Afterwards, we used the manual annotations for computing average precision, recall, and F measure across different values of *K*.

Note that the experiments were repeated by using the collection of labels of all elements of the process models and by applying the four similarity estimation models explained in Sect. 3.2. We call it label-based approach. Similarly, the experiments were repeated after preprocessing, i.e. before applying the similarity estimation models for computing similarity between the query-source pairs. Each textual description/labels was pre-processed by removing stop words and remaining words were stemmed using the Snowball stemmer.

5.1 Evaluation Measures

The main goal of this experiment is to measure the effectiveness of the proposed approaches in retrieving relevant source process models (from the repository) against a given query process model. To evaluate the retrieval performance of our proposed approaches we have used the metrics precision, recall, and F_1. The reason for selecting these measures is that they are standard evaluation measures for evaluating the performance of information retrieval approaches. In this context, precision represents the percentage of source process models that are retrieved and are relevant. Its value varies from 0 to 1, where 0 means that all the process models retrieved by the matching technique are irrelevant and 1 means that all the process model(s) retrieved by the matching technique are relevant, i.e. no irrelevant process model is retrieved. The precision score is computed by using the following equation.

$$Precision = \frac{|retrieved \cap relevant|}{|retrieved|}$$

Recall represents the percentage of source process models that are relevant and retrieved. The value of recall also varies from 0 to 1, where 0 means that none of the source process models that are relevant to the query model are retrieved by the process matching technique and 1 means all the source process models that are relevant to the query model are retrieved by the process matching technique, i.e. no relevant process model is missed by the matching technique. The recall score is computed by using the following equation.

$$Recall = \frac{|retrieved \cap relevant|}{|relevant|}$$

There is a trade-off between precision and recall. To give equal weight to both, F_1 measure is used, which is the harmonic mean of precision and recall. Formally, the F_1 score is computed by using the following equation.

$$F_1 = 2 * \frac{Precision * Recall}{Precision + Recall}$$

6 Results and Analysis

Table 1 shows macro-averaged precision, recall and F_1 scores for 56 queries for the four similarity estimation approaches n-gram overlap, edit distance, Longest Common Subsequence (LCS), and Vector Space Model (VSM). In the table, the results are reported for the top 3, 6, 9, 12, 15 source process models returned by a process matching technique against a query process model. The reason for keeping the gap to three is to evaluate whether the three variants (NC, LR, HR) of the process models are matched or not. Note that we also evaluated the effect of stop word removal and stemming on our proposed process matching techniques. The best results were obtained by using stop word removal.

Overall it can be noted that our proposed textual description based approach outperforms the label based approach in all cases and for all values of top K process models. This gives a clear indication that, compared to the label based approach, the process models returned by the textual description based approach is more effective for process retrieval. This is likely to happen because textual descriptions contain

Table 1. Results using baseline and proposed approaches

			Top K process models				
			3	6	9	12	15
Unigram	Label based (baseline)	P	0.51	0.38	0.29	0.25	0.21
		R	0.27	0.37	0.42	0.47	0.49
		F_1	0.35	0.37	0.34	0.33	0.30
	Text based	P	0.66	0.48	0.36	0.30	0.26
		R	0.37	0.50	0.54	0.58	0.61
		F_1	0.47	0.49	0.43	0.39	0.36
Edit distance	Label based	P	0.57	0.40	0.30	0.24	0.21
		R	0.30	0.39	0.42	0.47	0.50
		F_1	0.39	0.40	0.35	0.32	0.29
	Text based	P	0.71	0.46	0.35	0.28	0.24
		R	0.42	0.52	0.57	0.59	0.63
		F_1	0.53	0.49	0.43	0.38	0.35
LCS	Label based	P	0.52	0.38	0.31	0.26	0.23
		R	0.28	0.37	0.44	0.49	0.52
		F_1	0.37	0.38	0.36	0.34	0.32
	Text based	P	0.66	0.47	0.37	0.30	0.26
		R	0.38	0.49	0.55	0.60	0.63
		F_1	0.48	0.48	0.44	0.40	0.36
VSM	Label based	P	0.61	0.46	0.39	0.32	0.27
		R	0.33	0.46	0.57	0.61	0.64
		F_1	0.43	0.46	0.46	0.42	0.38
	Text based	P	0.73	0.53	0.42	0.35	0.30
		R	0.42	0.56	0.63	0.69	0.73
		F_1	0.53	0.54	0.50	0.46	0.42

additional information about the process models in comparison to the labels of activities and events. It, for instance, includes, the actors associated with each activity as well as the flow between activities.

As expected, the precision score decreases as the value of K increases. These decreasing values indicate that the more models we consider, the more irrelevant models are returned by all techniques. On the other hand, as expected, the recall score increases as the value of K increases. These increasing trends indicate the strength of the proposed method in detecting relevant process models. However, overall the F_1 score decreases as the value of K increases. This indicates that as we increase the value of K, the decrease in precision drops more sharply than the increase in recall, i.e. the proportion of irrelevant models returned are more than the numbers of relevant models returned.

Overall, the highest precision (P = 0.73 for top 3 process models) recall (R = 0.73 for top 15 process models) and F_1 (F_1 = 0.54 for top 6 process models) are obtained using the VSM approach. These scores are significantly higher than the baseline approach (P = 0.21, R = 0.49 and F1 = 0.30). This also reflects that among all the proposed approaches, VSM is the most effective in retrieving relevant process models from the corpus used in this study.

7 Discussion and Conclusions

In this paper, we presented a novel process model matching approach that relies on the use of textual descriptions of processes. The approach exploits the fact that process model repositories often include textual descriptions of processes. For the evaluation we implemented the proposed approach in Java and used it for a set of experiments. The prototype takes textual description or a process model as input and generates its textual description using a NLGS. Subsequently, various similarity estimation models used in text matching are applied to compute the similarity between the query-source process descriptions. We evaluated the proposed approach in terms of precision, recall, and F_1 metrics. The results show that the use of textual descriptions for process matching is slightly more effective for retrieval than the collection of labels.

Note that we are aware that the textual descriptions generated by the NLGS may not perfectly match the textual descriptions produced by a human. However, we content that it represents a separate research problem to investigate the similarity and differences between human and system generated textual descriptions and their use. For instance, what would be the impact of using a text crafted by human for process matching? How to correct the auto-generated textual description? Is the auto-generated and human generated textual description equally useful for process comprehension? All these questions represent promising directions for future work. Also, the comparison of textual descriptions using structure and behavior based approaches needs to be investigated.

References

1. Dumas, M., La Rosa, M., Mendling, J., Reijers, H.A.: Fundamentals of Business Process Management. Springer, Heidelberg (2013)
2. van der Aa, H., Leopold, H., Reijers, H.A.: Detecting inconsistencies between process models and textual descriptions. In: Motahari-Nezhad, H.R., Recker, J., Weidlich, M. (eds.) BPM 2015. LNCS, vol. 9253, pp. 90–105. Springer, Heidelberg (2015)
3. Zha, H., Wang, J., Wen, L., Wang, C., Sun, J.: A workflow net similarity based on transition adjacency relations. Comput. Ind. **61**, 463–471 (2010)
4. Kunze, M., Weidlich, M., Weske, M.: Querying process models by behavior inclusion. Softw. Syst. Model. **4**, 1105–1125 (2015)
5. La Rosa, M., Reijers, H.A., Aalst, W.M.P., Dijkman, R., Mendling, J., Dumas, M., Banuelos, L.: APROMORE: an advanced process model repository. Expert Syst. Appl. **38**, 7029–7040 (2011)
6. Shahzad, K., Elias, M., Johannesson, P.: Requirements for a business process model repository: a stakeholders' perspective. In: Abramowicz, W., Tolksdorf, R. (eds.) BIS 2010. LNBIP, vol. 47, pp. 158–170. Springer, Heidelberg (2010)
7. Elias, M.: Design of business process model repositories requirements, semantic annotation model and relationship metamodel. Ph.D. thesis, Department of Computer and Systems Sciences, Stockholm University, Sweden (2015)
8. Becker, M., Laue, R.: A comparative survey of business process similarity measures. Comput. Ind. **63**, 148–167 (2012)
9. Dijkman, R., Dumas, M., Dongen, B., Kaarik, R., Mendling, J.: Similarity of business process models: metrics and evaluation. Inf. Syst. **36**, 498–516 (2011)

10. Klinkmüller, C., Weber, I., Mendling, J., Leopold, H., Ludwig, A.: Increasing recall of process model matching by improved activity label matching. In: Daniel, F., Wang, J., Weber, B. (eds.) BPM 2013. LNCS, vol. 8094, pp. 211–218. Springer, Heidelberg (2013)
11. Grigori, D., Corrales, J., Bouzeghoub, M., Gater, A.: Ranking BPEL processes for service discovery. IEEE Trans. Serv. Comput. **3**, 178–192 (2010)
12. Weidlich, M., Mendling, J., Weske, M.: Efficient consistency measurement based on behavioral profiles of process models. IEEE Trans. Softw. Eng. **37**, 410–429 (2011)
13. Cervantes, A.A.: Diagnosing behavioral differences between business process models. Ph.D. thesis, University of Tartu (2016)
14. Barrón-Cedeño, A., Rosso, P., Benedí, J.-M.: Reducing the plagiarism detection search space on the basis of the Kullback-Leibler distance. In: Gelbukh, A. (ed.) CICLing 2009. LNCS, vol. 5449, pp. 523–534. Springer, Heidelberg (2009)
15. Sankoff, D., Kruskal, J.: Time Warps, String Edits and Macromolecules: The Theory and Practice of Sequence Comparison. Addison-Wesley Publications, Boston (1983)
16. Nawab, R.: Monolingual paraphrased text reuse and plagiarism detection. Ph.D. thesis, University of Sheffield, UK (2012)
17. Salton, G., Wong, A., Yang, C.: A vector space model for automatic indexing. Commun. ACM **18**, 613–620 (1975)
18. Leopold, H., Mendling, J., Polyvyanyy, A.: Supporting process model validation through natural language generation. IEEE Trans. Softw. Eng. **40**, 818–840 (2014)
19. Dijkman, R., Dumas, M., García-Bañuelos, L.: Graph matching algorithms for business process model similarity search. In: Dayal, U., Eder, J., Koehler, J., Reijers, H.A. (eds.) BPM 2009. LNCS, vol. 5701, pp. 48–63. Springer, Heidelberg (2009)
20. La Rosa, M., Dumas, M., Uba, R., Dijkman, R.: Business process model merging: an approach to business process consolidation. ACM Trans. Softw. Eng. Methodol. **22**, 1–46 (2013)
21. Lane, C., Lyon, C., Malcom, J.: Demonstration of the Ferret plagiarism detector. In: Proceedings of 2nd International Plagiarism Conference, UK (2006)
22. Shivakumar, N., Molina, H.: SCAM: a copy detection mechanism for digital documents. In: Proceedings of 2nd International Conference on Theory and Practice of Digital Libraries, USA (1995)
23. Clough, P., Gaizauskas, R., Piao, S., Wilks, Y.: Measuring text reuse. In: Proceedings of 40th Annual Meeting on Association for Computational Linguistics, Stroudsburg, pp. 152–159 (2002)
24. Mendling, J.: Metrics for Process Models: Empirical Foundations of Verification, Error Prediction, and Guidelines for Correctness. Springer, Heidelberg (2008)
25. Mendling, J., Reijers, H.A., Aalst, W.M.P.: Seven process modeling guidelines (7PMG). Inf. Softw. Technol. **52**, 127–136 (2010)
26. Mendling, J., Leopold, H., Pittke, F.: 25 challenges of semantic process modeling. Int. J. Inf. Syst. Softw. Eng. Big Co. **1**, 78–94 (2015)
27. Shahzad. K., Shareef., K., Ali, R.F., Nawab, R.M.A., Abid, A.: Generating process model collection with diverse label and structural features. In: Proceedings 6th International Conference on Innovative Computing Technology (IEEE-INTECH 2016) (to appear)
28. Fink, A.: Conducting Research Literature Reviews: From the Internet to Paper, 3rd edn. Sage, London (2010)
29. Leopold, H., van der Aa, H., Pittke, F., Raffel, M., Mendling, J., Reijers, H.A.: Integrating textual and model-based process descriptions for comprehensive process search. In: Schmidt, R., Guédria, W., Bider, I., Guerreiro, S., Buckley, O. (eds.) BPMDS/EMMSAD 2016. LNBIP, vol. 248, pp. 51–65. Springer, Heidelberg (2016). doi:10.1007/978-3-319-39429-9_4

Securing Airline-Turnaround Processes Using Security Risk-Oriented Patterns

Silver Samarütel[1], Raimundas Matulevičius[1(✉)], Alex Norta[2], and Rein Nõukas[2]

[1] University of Tartu, Tartu, Estonia
silver.samarytel@gmail.com, rma@ut.ee
[2] Tallinn University of Technology, Tallinn, Estonia
alex.norta.phd@ieee.org, rein.noukas@gmail.com

Abstract. Security risk management is an important part of system development. Given that a majority of modern organisations rely heavily on information systems, security plays a big part in ensuring smooth operations of business processes. For example, many people rely on e-services offered by banks and medical establishments. Inadequate security measures in information systems have unwanted effects on an organisation's reputation and on people's lives. In this case study research paper, we target the secure system development problem by suggesting the application of security risk oriented patterns. These patterns help find security risk occurrences in business processes and present mitigations for these risks. They provide business analysts with means to elicit and introduce security requirements to business processes. At the same time, they reduce the efforts needed for risk analysis. These security risk oriented patterns are applied on business processes from an aviation-turnaround system. In this paper, we report our experience to derive security requirements to mitigate security risks in distributed systems.

1 Introduction

Security is a very important software quality for the ability to protect information and information systems from unauthorized access, use, disclosure, disruption, modification, or destruction [3]. Modern organisations rely heavily on information systems and security is essential for ensuring smooth operations of business processes. For example, the socio-technically rich case of airline industry experiences a quick and holistic penetration with information technology [5]. A socio-technical system is a complex organizational work design in which people solve problems at their workplaces with the means of rather sophisticated technology. This trend leads to many new risks and security issues that are associated with civil aviation resulting in worst cases of catastrophic airline crashes. Communication is another critical security issue, e.g., a deliberate

J. Horkoff et al. (Eds.): PoEM 2016, LNBIP 267, pp. 209–224, 2016.
DOI: 10.1007/978-3-319-48393-1_15

jamming of automatic dependent surveillance-broadcast (ADS-B) systems [9], a surveillance technology to determine an aircraft position. Furthermore, the recognition arises that the aviation industry turns rapidly into a cyber-physical system (CPS) [18] that poses additional novel risks and security issues. Briefly, a CPS [4] is a system composed of physical entities that are controlled or monitored by computer-based algorithms. The initial approach to studying airport-related security is rather technical while recent work recognises this is a socio-technical system [10].

In [11], the authors recognize the socio-technical nature of airports by employing use cases and storyboards to discover stakeholder requirements such as security for the development of an airport operating system. Furthermore, in [12] the authors investigate requirements evolution in the context of the SecureChange[1] EU-project with an industry case from the Air Traffic Management (ATM) domain. Safety- and security experts are part of the focus groups while the case study results do not explicitly address security specifics. Parameter measurability and social aspects of security policies in [20], investigate the costs versus benefit trade-offs in alternative airport security policy constellations pertaining to, e.g., passengers, items such as baggage, and so on.

Literature shows security-focused research for airline management is a topical area of interest. But the topics under investigation are very specific and do not acknowledge modern technology enables ad-hoc and process-aware collaborations [8,15,16] that benefit significantly the reduction of time and costs of airline management while yielding simultaneously improvements in service quality. Such novel ways of airline management systems also lead to unusual security risk issues for which the mitigation strategies are unclear.

In this case study research paper we target the secure system development problem by suggesting an application of security risk oriented patterns [1,2]. These patterns help find security risk occurrences in business processes and present mitigations for these security risks. They provide business analysts with means to elicit and introduce security requirements to business processes. More specifically, we consider how security risk oriented patterns could be used in distributed systems, such as an aviation-turnaround system [14]. Consequently, we pursue the research objective to understand *the applicability of specific security risk oriented patterns (SRPs) that have the purpose of securing business processes in distributed systems*. More explicitly, in this paper we report our experience in applying the security risk oriented patterns in aviation-turnaround business processes.

The rest of the paper is structured as follows. Section 3 comprises related work for this paper and Sect. 4 presents the case under investigation about a cross-organisational airline turnaround process. Section 5 gives the results of the investigation that is followed by a discussion in Sect. 6. Finally, Sect. 7 concludes the paper and provides directions for future work.

[1] http://www.securechange.eu/.

2 Related Work

"A security pattern describes a particular recurring security problem that arises in a specific security context and presents a well-proven generic scheme for a security solution" [19]. Software projects tend to run into similar problems. Often these problems do not require new tailor-made solutions, but can be solved with solutions that have already been successfully applied in previous situations. This is where patterns come in handy. Instead of spending time and resources on working out new solutions, software developers can opt to implement already proven solutions by applying the appropriate patterns. Patterns are not independent islands. They are part of a hierarchy where larger patterns contain smaller patterns that solve sub-problems of the main problem. Patterns can be combined together with other patterns and form a larger design. Because of this combinability, patterns can effectively be applied in complex and large scale distributed systems.

There exist numerous classification systems for categorising security patterns. For instance, in [19] Schumacher *et al.* presents a taxonomy comprising enterprise security and risk management, identification and authentication, access control, accounting, firewall, crypto-key management and other security pattern classes. We are also aware of numerous resources available for threat patterns (e.g., CAPEC[2], STRIDE [21], and a security threat taxonomy for distributed systems [22]. In this paper, we focus on the SRPs [1,2] that help determining security requirements from the business processes.

3 Security Risk-Oriented Patterns

A set of security risk oriented patterns (SRPs) is suggested in [1,2]. They are developed using a domain model [6,13] for information system security risk management (ISSRM). This domain model differentiates between three major concept groups – *asset-related concepts*, *risk-related concepts* and *risk treatment-related concepts*. Thus, based on this structure, each SRP comprises a specific security context expressed with asset-related concepts, recurring security problem (analysed in terms of security risk related concepts) and suggests security countermeasures that are presented with security risk treatment concepts.

3.1 Patterns Used in This Study

Below, we shortly characterise each SPR used in this study:

- SRP1: *secures data from unauthorised access.* The security criteria is confidentiality of the data used in a business server. A user might request sensitive data from the server with the intention of misusing it. To reduce the risk, the pattern proposes checking access rights. Sensitivity levels must be assigned to data- and trust levels – to people or devices accessing these data.

[2] https://capec.mitre.org.

- SRP2: *ensures secure data transmission between business entities.* Data confidentiality and integrity are two important security criteria. However, data transmitted through a transmission medium could be intercepted by an attacker. Thus, the data could be stolen, read, changed, and transmitted to the party. In order to reduce these risks, the pattern recommends to make data unreadable and to verify data once they are received at the party.
- SRP3: *ensures secure business activity after data submission.* The security criteria for this pattern are availability and integrity of the business activity. Malicious scripts (e.g. SQL or xPath injections) submitted through an input interface could lead to a disruption of the business activity, making the business activity unavailable and lose its integrity. Furthermore, the pattern proposes a filtering of incoming data, e.g., in the form of input validation, sanitation, filtration and/or canonicalisation.
- SRP4: *secures business services against distributed denial of service (DDoS) attacks.* The security criterion is the availability of a business service. The risk is that there exists a threat agent who creates bots of computers and runs simultaneous requests (e.g., DNS flooding, HTTP spidering, etc.) at the target server. To reduce the risk, the pattern proposes a security requirement checking (i.e., filtering, classifying and detecting) for abnormal requests.
- SRP5: *secures storage of data and data retrieval from storage.* The security criterion for this pattern is confidentiality of data at the storage. The data might leak horizontally across the organisation's departments. A threat agent is a malicious insider with access to data in a storage. Risk could be reduced by making data invisible or using storage monitoring and controlling.

In Sect. 3.2 we discuss the SRP2 pattern, since it is used to illustrate the analysis of the airline-turnaround processes.

3.2 SRP2: Ensuring Data Transmission Between Business Entities

This pattern addresses the electronic transmission of *data* between two entities, as illustrated in Fig. 1. The scenario indicates how the client fills in a form and submits data through the Input interface to the Server for data employment. Here, the *confidentiality* and *integrity* of data are two important security criteria.

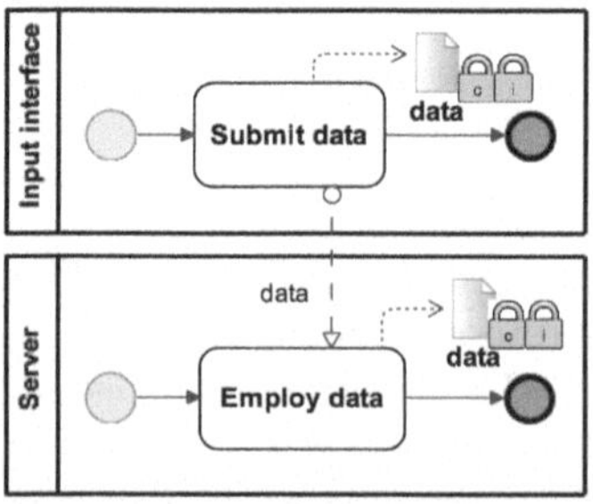

Fig. 1. SRP2: asset modeling.

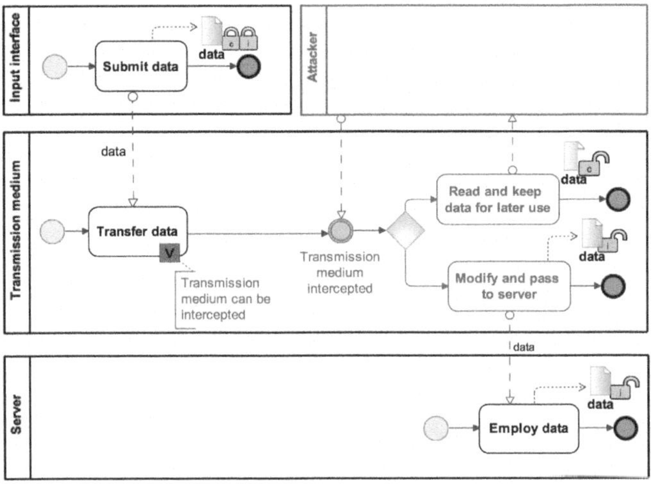

Fig. 2. SRP2: risk modeling.

The assumption is made that the data are transmitted using Transmission medium (see Fig. 2). However, this situation faces (at least) two vulnerabilities. Firstly, such a transmission medium could be intercepted by an Attacker who acts as a proxy. Secondly, since data are not encrypted, they could be misused, e.g., modified and passed to the Server. This event harms the data, leads to the loss of transmission medium reliability, and negates data integrity (if data are transmitted to the server) and confidentiality (if they are kept by the attacker).

Potential risk treatment includes risk reduction by making data unreadable and verifying the received data (see, Fig. 3). The implementation includes the introduction and application of a crypto- and a checksum algorithms.

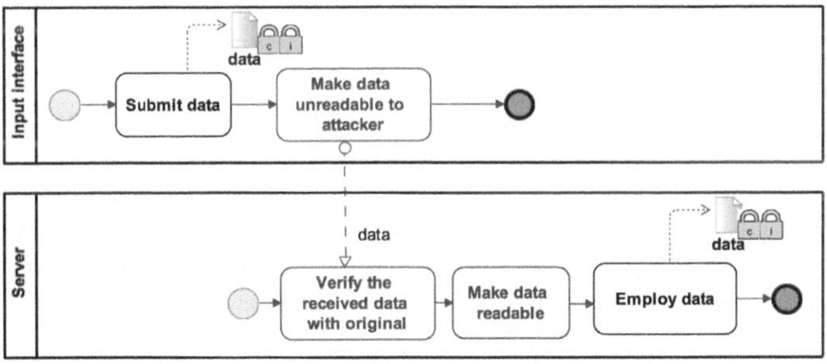

Fig. 3. SRP2: risk treatment modeling.

4 Study Design

As discussed in [7], while developing secure systems, the security engineering focus is placed on system implementation and maintenance. However, since security risk mitigation yields changes to a specification, security analysis is important at an early phase (i.e., business process and requirement analysis). The benefit is the prevention of expensive design changes later in the development. In this paper, we shift the focus to the early stage of security analysis where first the business processes are captured in a conceptual and technology independent way. Consequently, we pose the main research question of *how to apply SRPs for early stage security analysis in the airline turnaround domain.* To establish a separation of concerns and manageable complexity, we deduce the sub-questions. What is the appropriate case study design for exploring the suitability of the security risk oriented patterns? What analysis approach finds risks in the airline-turnaround case? What validity does the case study analysis have?

We apply the five SRPs to the airline turnaround processes, reported in [14]. The analysis scope includes five processes: (*i*) passenger check-in, (*ii*) baggage check-in, (*iii*) fuel service form issuing, (*iv*) fuel service form requesting, and (*v*) loading instruction form requesting. The investigation comprises four steps:

1. *Introducing system support:* The original turnaround processes, described by Nõukas in [14], include rather limited details on how the processes themselves are carried out and how they are supported by information technology systems. The first step is to introduce and model system support by illustrating the major data exchange and usage. The result of this step is a set of models pertaining to the turnaround processes supported by the system.
2. *Validating models with the system expert:* We have invited an expert who is knowledgeable in airline-turnaround processes to validate the developed system support process models. The outcome of this step is expert-validated models of the turnaround processes with corresponding system support.
3. *Deriving security requirements using patterns:* In this step we apply the SRPs to understand the security risks, to derive requirements and to introduce these security requirements to the analyzed processes. The outcome of this step is the turnaround-process models enhanced with security requirements.
4. *Validating the turnaround models enhanced with security requirements:* The received process models are validated by the expert knowledgeable both in the turnaround processes and in security. The outcome of this step is the validated turnaround-process models enhanced with security requirements.

For an extensive report about the above steps, we refer the reader to [17]. In next section, we report on the results of the above steps.

5 Analyzing Airline-Turnaround Processes

First, we present the passenger check-in process, followed by an illustration of how the SPR2 pattern is applied. Next, we summarise the derived security requirements. Finally, we discuss output of other pattern applications.

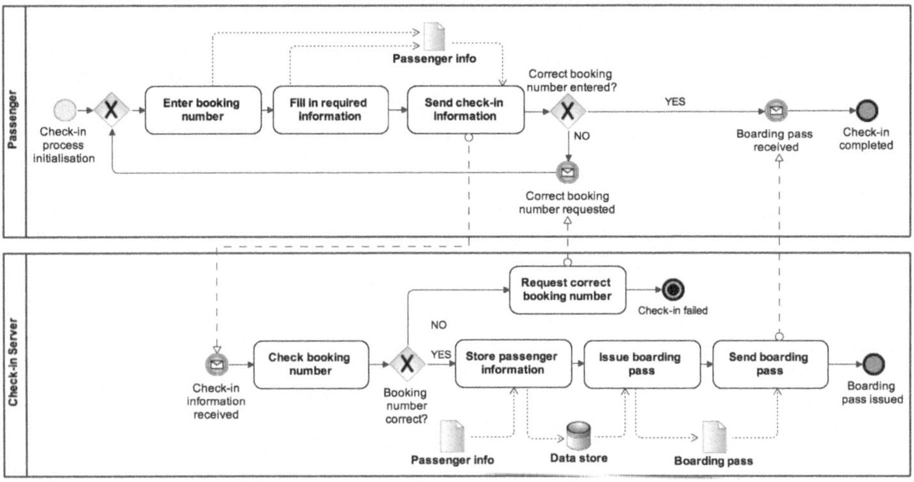

Fig. 4. Passenger check-in process.

5.1 Passenger Check-in Process

Figure 4 represents process for passenger check-in[3]. Once the Passenger initialises the process, he enters the booking number and fills in the required information (see Fill in required information), e.g., preferred seat, meal options, etc. Then the Passenger info is sent to the Check-in Server. At the Check-in Server the booking number is checked (see Check booking number). If it is not correct, the Passenger is requested to correct the check-in details (see Request correct booking number). Otherwise, the Passenger info is stored in the Data store. Next, the Boarding pass is issued (see Issue boarding pass) and sent (see Send boarding pass) to the Passenger. Once the Passenger receives the Boarding pass, the check-in process is completed.

5.2 Application of the SRP2 Pattern

We illustrate how SRP2 is applied to derive security requirements from the *check-in process* and we also introduce measures for securing the process. In the given case, we identify three pattern occurrences: (*i*) when Passenger info is sent from Passenger to Check-in Server; (*ii*) when Check-in Server requests Passenger for the correct booking number; and (*iii*) when Boarding pass is sent from Check-in Server to Passenger. In the given example, we specifically will focus on the first and third occurrences.

In Fig. 5 we consider *integrity* of the Passenger info assuming that the Passenger info is sent using a Transmission channel. However, there exists an Attacker who is able to intercept this Transmission channel (see, *vulnerability* [V] – Transmission can be intercepted), thus resulting in the *man in the middle* attack. The

[3] Captured using check-in process description, such as: https://www.airbaltic.com/en/online check in conditions.

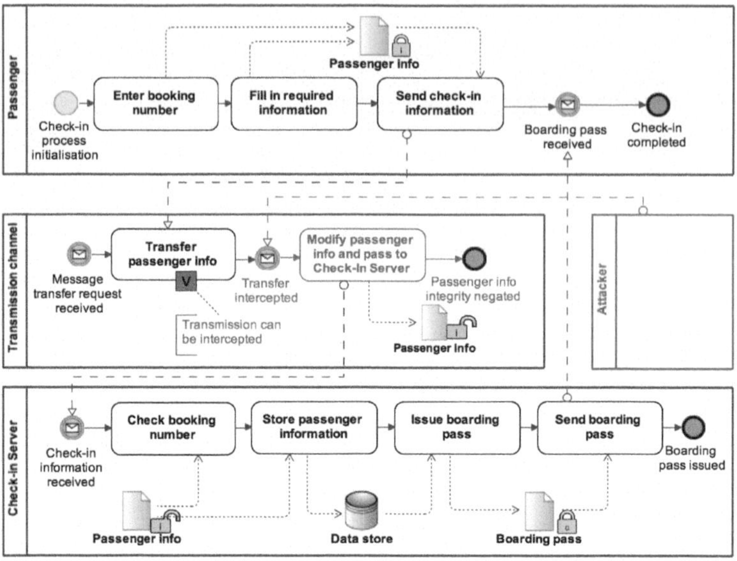

Fig. 5. Capturing potential security risks to the *Passenger info* asset.

Attacker is able to modify passenger information and pass to Check-in Server. This attack results in a negation of integrity of the Passenger info (see the *open lock*). At the Check-in Server, the integrity of the receive passenger info is not checked, which results in storing the changed Passenger info to the Data store.

In Fig. 6, SRP2 is applied regarding the Boarding pass confidentiality. Again, the Transmission channel can be intercepted due to the same vulnerability. But this time, the Attacker reads and keeps the boarding pass (see, Read and keep

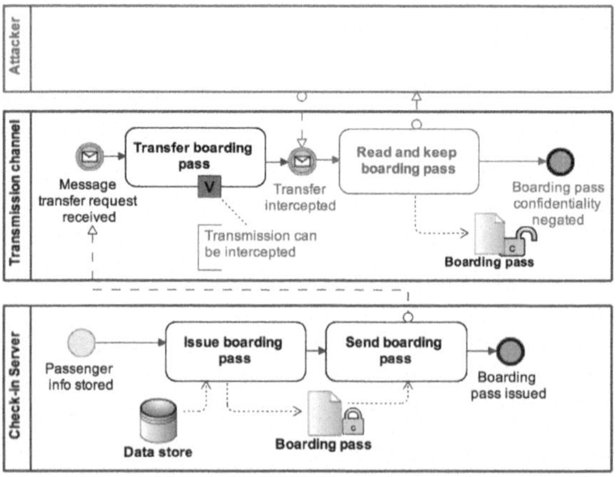

Fig. 6. Capturing potential security risk to the *Boarding pass* asset.

boarding pass). This results in the negation of the boarding pass integrity. By acting as the *man in the middle*, the Attacker is able to change the Passenger info, e.g., by inserting his own name, and steal the Boarding pass in order to access the plane.

5.3 Risk Treatment

To mitigate the first risk, Fig. 7 shows the following security requirements are derived using the SRP2 pattern:

- M1.SRP2a.1: A Passenger should make passenger info unreadable to the attacker before sending it to the Communication channel.
- M1.SRP2a.2: The Check-in Server must make passenger info readable once it is received from the Communication channel.
- M1.SRP2b.1: A Passenger should calculate a checksum of the passenger info.
- M1.SRP2b.2: The Check-in Server must verify the integrity of the *passenger info* once received from the Communication channel.

Similar security requirements must be derived regarding the Boarding pass, as Fig. 8 shows in detail:

- M1.SRP2a.3: The Check-in Server should make the boarding pass unreadable to an attacker before sending it to the Communication channel.
- M1.SRP2a.4: The Passenger must make the boarding pass readable once received from the Communication channel.
- M1.SRP2b.3: A Check-in Server should calculate a checksum of the boarding pass.
- M1.SRP2b.4: The Passenger must verify the integrity of the *boarding pass* once received from the Communication channel.

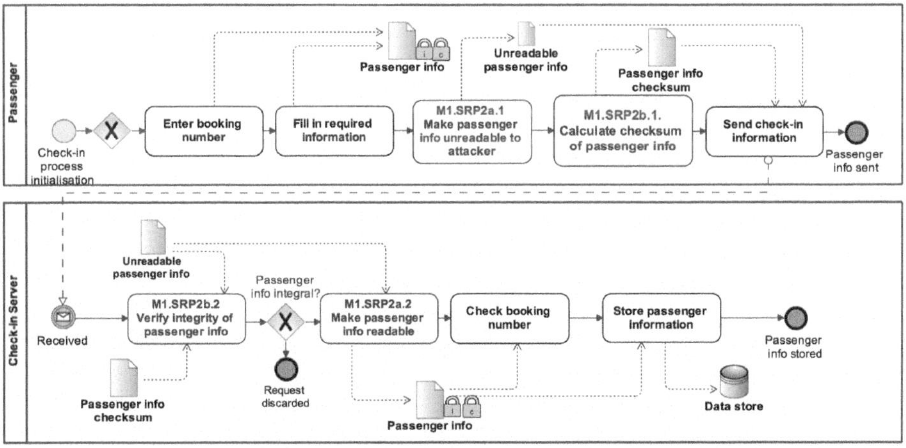

Fig. 7. Derivation of security requirements using SPR2.

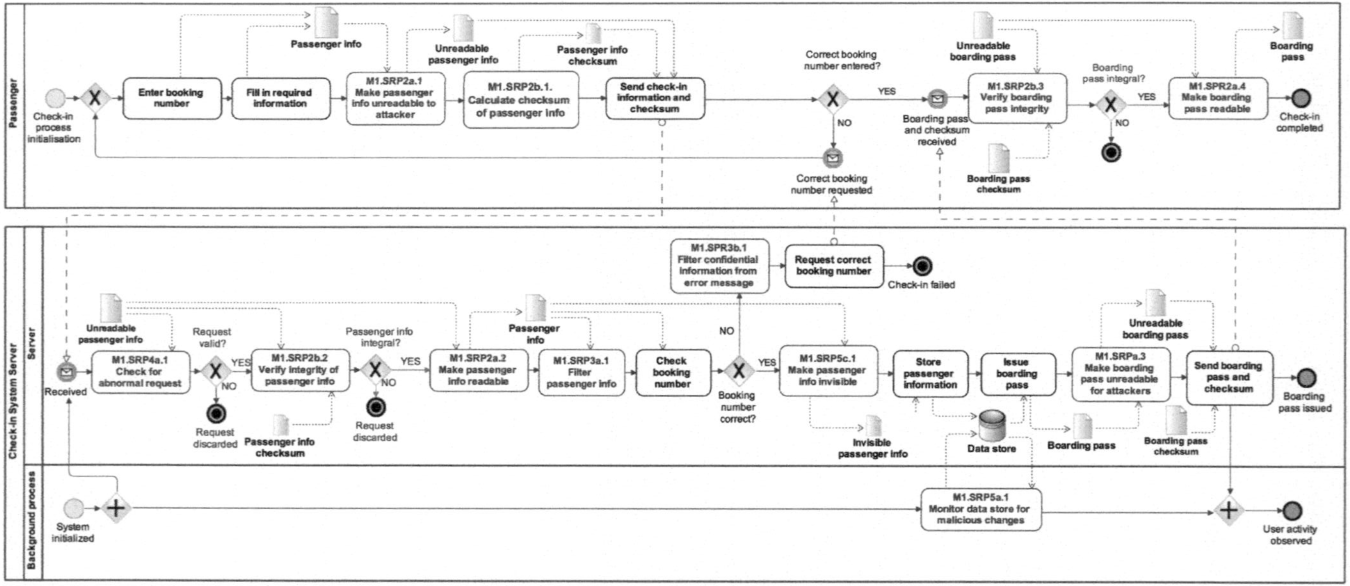

Fig. 8. Security requirements for *Passenger check-in process* derived using the security risk-oriented patterns.

Security requirements M1.SRP2a.1-4 are implemented using the *cryptography algorithms*; for example, see *cryptographic key management* pattern in [19]. Requirements M1.SRP2b.1 and M1.SRP2b.2 are implemented using the *checksum algorithms.*

5.4 Other Patterns

Application of patterns SRP3, SRP4, and SRP5 to the *Passenger Check-in Process* results in at least the following security risks:

- An Attacker capable of writing malicious scripts (e.g., SQL injection, xPath injection, etc.) submits malicious scripts due to the lack of the input filtering at the Check-in Server, thus resulting in the loss of the integrity of the *Passenger info* and potentially integrity of the *Issue board pass* service. The risk results from applying SRP3.
- An Attacker performs many simultaneous requests to the Check-in Server making it not available to the Passenger, thus resulting in a loss of availability of the Issue board pass service. The risk results from applying SRP4.
- A (malicious) insider modifies Passenger info by using the access control rights due to the poor data integrity checks, thus leading to the loss of Passenger info integrity and possibly loss of integrity and/or availability of the Issue board pass. The risk results from applying SRP5.

To mitigate these risks security requirements are introduced in Fig. 8. These security requirements are derived using security-risk-oriented patterns. Their potential implementations, i.e., security controls, are listed in Table 1.

5.5 Application of SRPs to Other Turnaround Processes

The security risk oriented patterns we apply to derive security requirements from other turnaround processed – *baggage check-in* (secured assets - Baggage info and Bag tags), *fuel service form issuing* (secured assets – Fuel quantity info and Fuel service form), *Fuel service form requesting* (secured assets – Fuel service form request and Fuel service form), and *loading instruction form requesting.*

Table 2 (secured assets – Loading instruction form request and Loading instruction form) summarises the number of requirements elicited using the SRPs. The largest number of requirements we derive from the *Fuel service form requesting* process. Other analysis of the processes results in the same number of requirements. We elicit 34 security requirements using the SRP2 pattern and only 2 requirements we derive using the SRP1 pattern.

5.6 Study Limitation

Our analysis comprises a certain degree of subjectivity. Throughout the validation process, we only consult one expert. Although we trust the feedback

Table 1. Security requirements and controls for the *Passenger check-in* process.

Req.ID	Security requirements	Controls
M1.SRP2a.1	Passsenger must make passenger info unreadable to attacker before sending it to the Communication channel	Encryption algorithm
M1.SRP2a.2	Check-in Server must make passenger info readable once received from the Communication channel	Encryption algorithm
M1.SRP2a.3	Check-in Server must make boarding pass unreadable to attacker before sending it to the Communication channel	Encryption algorithm
M1.SRP2a.4	Passenger must make boarding pass readable once received from the Communication channel	Encryption algorithm
M1.SRP2b.1	Passenger must calculate checksum of *passenger info*	Checksum algorithm
M1.SRP2b.2	Check-in Server must verify integrity of *passenger info* once received from the Communication channel	Checksum algorithm
M1.SRP2b.3	Check-in Server must calculate checksum of *boarding pass*	Checksum algorithm
M1.SRP2b.4	Passenger must verify integrity of *boarding pass* once received from the Communication channel	Checksum algorithm
M1.Req3a.1	Check-in Server must filter passenger input once received from the Communication channel	Filter input for special characters and keywords, use whitelist of acceptable inputs
M1.Req3b.1	Check-in Server must filter confidential information from error messages and standard responses	Disable debug messages, use default error messages or error pages
M1.Req4a.1	Check-in Server must filter for abnormal requests	Firewall, DoS Defence System
M1.Req5a.1	Monitor the Data store at Check-in Server for malicious changes	Control database signature changes
M1.Req5c.1	Check-in Server should make passenger info invisible before storing in the Data store	Encryption algorithm, monitor data access

Table 2. Number of security requirements elicited from the turnaround processes using SRPs.

Processes	SRP1	SRP2	SRP3	SRP4	SRP5	Total
Passenger check-in process	–	6	2	1	2	11
Baggage check-in process	–	6	2	1	2	11
Fuel service form issuing	–	10	1	1	3	15
Fuel service form requesting	1	6	1	1	2	11
Loading instruction form requesting	1	6	1	1	2	11
Total	2	34	7	5	11	**59**

we received, opinions by nature are subjective and preferable is a collection of opinions from other experts too.

Another limitation is that we apply the security patterns only to five business processes. Although the processes are based on real life scenarios, we require a larger number of process models. An interesting direction of research is to apply the security patterns to business processes from other industries besides aviation to investigate how well they conform in a different domains.

What should also be considered is that the security patterns are applied to the example business processes by the author of the patterns. Other researchers may have different observations of the security patterns' applicability. We request feedback from practitioners and laymen who are unfamiliar with the SRPs and apply them to business processes.

6 Discusssion

In this paper, we employ a case study to understand security issues resulting from the collaboration between airlines and service providers. We identify relevant assets by modelling the business processes of an airline-turnaround process. We find these assets in the passenger management process and ground operations. The research result is a security requirement and control framework. The risk analysis is supported theoretical methods from the domain of security risk management.

The following observations result from the application of security risk oriented patterns:

- *The expert's feedback to the secured business processes is approving.* Revised airline turnaround models (see step *2* in Sect. 4) and security requirements (see step *4*) are approved as relevant and important by the expert. This also indicates that the applied SRPs are a foundation for the future development of a security catalog pertaining to distributed systems.
- *The SRP application extent is different for various patterns.* This observation results from the number of derived requirements. As discussed in Sect. 5, only two security requirements are derived using SRP1, i.e., access to data within

the system. Additionally, 34 requirements out of 59 result in total from using SRP2, i.e., data transmission. This we explain with the nature of the domain, i.e., a distributed system where communication plays an important role.

- *Not every SRP is applicable for the distributed systems.* For instance, in [17], few other SRPs are suggested. For example, the SRP for protecting against deadlock attacks, the SRP for securing against brute force attacks, the SRP for securing against account lockout attacks, and few other. Although these SRPs are relevant in the business process models where these security risks are possible to capture, this is not the case in the airline-turnaround processes. This again indicates that SRP application very much depends on the modeling domain and the level of model granularity.
- *The sequence of security requirements in a business process does not limit the choice between security controls.* The sequence of security requirements may vary in real-life business process models. When arranging the sequence of the security requirements in the business process models, we rely on a logical viewpoint. For example, in the *fuel service form issuing process*, we introduce that the server *verifies the integrity of fuel quantity information* before *readability access*. In reality, the implementation chosen to satisfy these requirements performs message encryption and an authentication in a reverse order. Thus, it is necessary to assure that implementers depict these business process, security requirements, and their sequence in the business process not necessarily as the end result.

7 Conclusions and Future Work

We examine the applicability of the security-risk oriented patterns in five business-process models originating from airline-turnaround processes. The business processes we enhance with security requirements derived from the security patterns using the security risk aware BPMN modelling language. We submit the secured business processes for review to an expert who has experience with business processes used in the airline industry.

As relations to existing evidence, the case study confirms the application feasibility of the chosen patterns. The study shows that there are many security issues that exist in the airline industry. Specifically problematic is that this industry segment is affected by ICT innovation at a speed where decision makers do not understand the evolving virtual enterprises that match their processes cross-organizationally are suddenly confronted with potentially catastrophic socio-technical security issues.

The implication of our results is that companies that operate in the airline industry must rapidly develop business process awareness as a prerequisite for automation. The subsequent challenge for achieving progress in terms of operational effectiveness and efficiency is to cross-organizationally match in-house processes. While the dominant explored perspective in this case is control flow, security issues also arise from the perspectives of data flow, resource management, exception and compensation management, and so on.

The limitation of this paper is that we only can report on a very limited pattern application for one case due to page limitation. Consequently, in future work we aim to expand on the study by exploring the applicability of other patterns. More specifically, we aim to study patterns that did not apply in this airline-turnaround case study.

References

1. Ahmed, N., Matulevičius, R.: Securing business process using security risk-oriented patterns. Comput. Stand. Interfaces **36**, 723–733 (2014)
2. Ahmed, N., Matulevičius, R.: Presentation and validation of method for security requirements elicitation from business processes. In: Nurcan, S., Pimenidis, E. (eds.) CAiSE Forum 2014. LNBIP, vol. 204, pp. 20–35. Springer, Heidelberg (2015)
3. Anderson, R.: Security Engineering: A Guide to Building Dependable Distributed Systems, 2nd edn. Wiley, Hoboken (2008)
4. Bartelt, C., Rausch, A., Rehfeldt, K.: Quo vadis cyber-physical systems: research areas of cyber-physical ecosystems: a position paper. In: Proceedings of 1st International Workshop on Control Theory for Software Engineering, CTSE 2015, pp. 22–25. ACM, New York (2015)
5. Belobaba, P., Odoni, A., Barnhart, C.: The Global Airline Industry. Wiley, Hoboken (2015)
6. Dubois, E., Heymans, P., Mayer, N., Matulevičius, R.: A systematic approach to define the domain of information system security risk management. In: Nurcan, S., Salinesi, C., Souveyet, C., Ralyté, J. (eds.) Intentional Perspectives on Information Systems Engineering, pp. 289–306. Springer, Heidelberg (2010)
7. Jürjens, J.: Secure System Development with UML. Springer, Heidelberg (2005)
8. Kutvonen, L., Norta, A., Ruohomaa, S.: Inter-enterprise business transaction management in open service ecosystems. In: 2012 IEEE 16th International Enterprise Distributed Object Computing Conference (EDOC), pp. 31–40. IEEE (2012)
9. Leonardi, M., Piracci, E., Galati, G.: ADS-B vulnerability to low cost jammers: risk assessment and possible solutions. In: 2014 Tyrrhenian International Workshop on Digital Communications-Enhanced Surveillance of Aircraft and Vehicles (TIWDC/ESAV), pp. 41–46. IEEE (2014)
10. Long, S.: Socioanalytic Methods: Discovering the Hidden in Organisations and Social Systems. Karnac Books, London (2013)
11. Maiden, N.A.M.D., Ncube, C., Lockerbie, J.: Inventing requirements: experiences with an airport operations system. In: Rolland, C. (ed.) REFSQ 2008. LNCS, vol. 5025, pp. 58–72. Springer, Heidelberg (2008)
12. Massacci, F., Paci, F., Tedeschi, A.: Assessing a requirements evolution approach: empirical studies in the air traffic management domain. J. Syst. Softw. **95**, 70–88 (2014)
13. Mayer, N.: Model-based management of information system security risk. Ph.D. thesis, University of Namur (2009)
14. Nõukas, R.: Service brokering environment for an airline. Master's thesis, Tallinn University of Technology (2015)
15. Norta, A., Grefen, P., Narendra, N.: A reference architecture for managing dynamic inter-organizational business processes. Data Knowl. Eng. **91**, 52–89 (2014)
16. Norta, A., Ma, L., Duan, Y., Rull, A., Kõlvart, M., Taveter, K.: eContractual choreography-language properties towards cross-organizational business collaboration. J. Internet Serv. Appl. **6**(1), 1–23 (2015)

17. Samarütel, S.: Revision of security risk-oriented patterns for distributed systems. Master's thesis, University of Tartu (2016)
18. Sampigethaya, K., Poovendran, R.: Aviation cyber-physical systems: foundations for future aircraft and air transport. Proc. IEEE **101**(8), 1834–1855 (2013)
19. Schumacher, M., Fernandez, E., Hybertson, D., Buschmann, F.: Security Patterns: Integrating Security and Systems Engineering. Wiley, Hoboken (2005)
20. Shim, W., Massacci, F., Tedeschi, A., Pollini, A.: A relative cost-benefit approach for evaluating alternative airport security policies. In: 2014 9th International Conference on Availability, Reliability and Security (ARES), pp. 514–522. IEEE (2014)
21. Shostack, A.: Threat Modeling: Designing for Security. Wiley, Hoboken (2014)
22. Uzunov, A.V., Fernandez, E.B.: An extensible pattern-based library and taxonomy of security threats for distributed systems. Comput. Stand. Interfaces **36**(4), 734–747 (2013)

Enterprise Modelling for the Masses – From Elitist Discipline to Common Practice

Kurt Sandkuhl[1(✉)], Hans-Georg Fill[2], Stijn Hoppenbrouwers[3], John Krogstie[4], Andreas Leue[5], Florian Matthes[6], Andreas L. Opdahl[7], Gerhard Schwabe[8], Ömer Uludag[6], and Robert Winter[9]

[1] University of Rostock, Rostock, Germany
kurt.sandkuhl@uni-rostock.de
[2] University of Vienna, Vienna, Austria
hans-georg.fill@univie.ac.at
[3] HAN University of Applied Sciences, Arnhem, The Netherlands
stijn.hoppenbrouwers@han.nl
[4] Norwegian University of Science and Technology, Trondheim, Norway
john.krogstie@idi.ntnu.no
[5] Sphenon GmbH, Hamburg, Germany
a@leue.net
[6] Technical University of Munich, Munich, Germany
{matthes,uludag}@tum.de
[7] University of Bergen, Bergen, Norway
Andreas.Opdahl@uib.no
[8] University of Zurich, Zurich, Switzerland
schwabe@ifi.uzh.ch
[9] University of St. Gallen, St. Gallen, Switzerland
robert.winter@unisg.ch

Abstract. Enterprise modelling (EM) as a discipline has been around for several decades with a huge body of knowledge on EM in academic literature. The benefits of modelling and its contributions to organizational tasks are largely undisputed. Thus, from an inside-out perspective, EM appears to be a mature and established discipline. However, for initiating serious innovations this view is not sufficient. This position paper takes an outside-in perspective on enterprise modelling and argues that EM is far away from reaching its maximum potential. EM is typically done by a limited number of people in organizations inclined to methods and modelling. What is captured in models is only a fragment of what ought to be captured. Many people actually develop some kind of model in their local practice without thinking about it consciously. Exploiting the potential of this "grass roots modelling" could lead to groundbreaking innovations in EM. The aim is to investigate integration of the established, often systematic and formalized practices of modelling in enterprises with local practices of creating, using and communicating model-like artifacts or objects of relevance for the overall organization.

Keywords: Enterprise modelling · Grass roots modelling · Research roadmap

J. Horkoff et al. (Eds.): PoEM 2016, LNBIP 267, pp. 225–240, 2016.
DOI: 10.1007/978-3-319-48393-1_16

1 Introduction

Enterprise modelling as a discipline in academic research and as a practice in organizations has been around for several decades. The body of knowledge represented by academic publications is huge and includes modelling methods, meta-models, notations, experiences, practice recommendations, organization aspects, value considerations and much more (cf. Sect. 4). The benefits of modelling and its contribution to organizational tasks, like business model development, visualization of the current situation, strategy development or business and IT alignment, and enterprise architecture management are largely undisputed in IT-related research. New challenges for the discipline are addressed by ongoing research work [1] and will eventually be taken up by industrial practice. This inside-out view of enterprise modelling as an established and quite mature discipline might be somewhat idealistic, but is shared by many people in the discipline [2]. However, for initiating serious innovations this view is not very helpful because it fails to address some very serious hindrances to actual, large-scale adoption of modelling in practice, e.g., people refuse to spend time creating and maintaining enterprise models, find modelling and modelling methods complex and cumbersome, or do not immediately see its use for their particular perspective or set of concerns.

The authors of this position paper prefer an outside-in perspective on enterprise modelling and argue that EM is far away from reaching its maximum potential, has yet to prove its benefits for the majority of business stakeholders and is not mission-critical for an enterprise (cf. Sect. 2). Enterprise modelling is typically done by only a few people in the organization who are inclined to methods and modelling/cf. Sect. 4.1). What is captured in models by this small group and made available for organizational purposes is only a fragment of what ought to be captured, discussed and communicated. Many people actually develop some kind of model without thinking upon it as modeling [3, 4]. Examples are spreadsheets[1] used to capture essential features of products and their dependencies, presentation slides with architecture sketches and process descriptions, mindmaps or sketches in drawing tools defining the information flow in a business service. The content of such documents often is highly valuable to the stakeholders in the enterprise but difficult or even impossible to retrieve [5]. It is content which often meets all characteristics of a model (e.g., abstraction, reduction for a purpose at hand, pragmatic use for a defined stakeholder) but the model content is buried in a document format, or is even totally unstructured. The content is created by a domain expert who is doing her/his job and who is probably not explicitly interested in enterprise modelling in the traditional sense. Exploiting the potential of this "grass roots modelling" instead of expert modelling and usage of the unexplored content in existing, non-modelling documents and conversations could lead to groundbreaking innovations in EM as a discipline and a severe upgrade in EM's importance for practice. The aim is to investigate integration of the established, often systematic and formalized practices of modelling in enterprises with local practices of creating, using and communicating model-like artifacts or objects of relevance for at least parts of the overall organization.

[1] Much data relevant for engineers and other business professionals is developed and resides in office automation tools like Excel [5].

This position paper elaborates on the vision of "modelling for the masses" by discussing the problem (Sect. 2), defining the vision (Sect. 3), describing the state of practice in enterprise modelling and beyond (Sect. 4), identifying the dimensions of the challenge and proposing topics for future work (Sect. 5). The main contribution of the paper is an analysis of the situation of EM use in organizations and potential ways of increasing its potential by "grass roots modelling". Both contributions need discussion in the enterprise modelling community. To kick off this discussion is the primary objective of the position paper.

2 The Problem

Starting from the hypothesis that there is a lot of unexploited potential of EM which would require a wider integration of local practices, this section explores causes for the current "problem" in EM from the perspectives of driving stakeholder concerns and sustained model utilization. Stakeholder groups that have a holistic, long-term perspective (like, e.g., IT or corporate management stakeholders), believe or at least should believe that architecture is no emergent feature of a complex system, but needs to be explicitly planned, implemented, controlled and adjusted [6]. Their concerns require models to cover multiple aspects, to cover a large number of artifacts, to ideally cover complete artifact life cycles, and to be coherent - the traditional motivation for EM and its use in enterprise architecture management. The EM discipline matured over the last decades by [7]:

1. diversifying its modelling object from IT infrastructure and software over IT applications, business processes and organizational structures to strategic positioning,
2. widening its modelling scope from single solutions over functional/business areas to enterprise-wide or even cross-enterprise models,
3. extending its scope from single object layer (IT artifacts or business artifacts) to the entire business-to-IT stack (Enterprise Architecture), and
4. representing not only as-is or to-be systems states, but also roadmaps or scenarios in order to cover the entire life cycle [8].

In contrast to the above mentioned 'enterprise-wide' concerns of certain stakeholder groups, most other stakeholder groups in organizations have interests that are more focused or short-term. They mostly prefer an opportunistic systems development process with architecture being an 'emergent' feature. Their concerns require models that cover selected aspects, comprise only artifacts that are 'locally' relevant, focus on their current design problem, and do not necessarily have to be fully coherent with other focus models. As a consequence, a plethora of 'local' models [9] can be found in organizations that are used by only one stakeholder group for 'local' analysis and design, or that serve as boundary objects [10] between two stakeholder groups. The co-existence of different concerns in organizations leads to a co-existence of enterprise and local models at various levels of scope, rigor, and (potential) impact that are not necessarily coherent.

As the benefits of EM were increasingly appreciated by large, complex organizations, the EM discipline matured, and various 'architect' role models were established in such organizations. Although many architects aimed at positioning themselves 'between' corporate management, business/project owners and IT, their backgrounds and competency profiles often kept them close to the corporate IT function [11]. Recently, an MIT CISR study revealed that "more mature architectures do not necessarily lead to business value" [12, p. 1]. In contrast to the historical value perception and impact increase of EM, a turning point might have been reached where additional EM effort is not justified by appropriate impact gains any more [7].

The MIT researchers believe that the capped impact results from the fact that EM is driven primarily by architects and is valued primarily by IT people, so that its effects in an organization are often limited to these stakeholder groups. EM can be thus considered an elitist discipline. It may be possible to reach other stakeholder groups with EM, e.g., by implementing tight governance mechanisms that enforce local model coherence and certain completeness requirements for local models, but such measures would not only require too much governance effort, they would also not gain acceptance with the "90 % of an organization" [13] that have primarily local, focused concerns.

One important aspect of the "problem" in EM is therefore to conceptualize lightweight EM approaches that do not necessarily focus on traditional EM qualities like completeness and coherence, but instead on usefulness and impact not only for architects and corporate IT, but also for the majority of organizational stakeholders that might benefit from more professional modelling to support their decentral, focused analysis and design problems. Another aspect of the "problem" in EM results from the fact that models are used for many different purposes. In [14], the following usage areas are included: model mapping, human [15], communication between different stakeholders, model analysis, quality assurance, model deployment and activation, systems development, model implementation and standardization. Many traditional applications of modelling are limited to one usage area, and thus provide limited value. On the other hand, the fuller long-term effects of modelling in and across organizations can be observed when one uses models over a longer time but also across areas of use [16]. For this to work, though, one has to have the long-term use in mind from the start and prepare for this, and have ways to mature models when beneficial to spread knowledge across the organization [17]. When trying to build upon models meant originally for sense-making in a limited group and turning them into organizational memory, one will often experience limitations in the original modelling approaches and modelling tools used [18]. Few people retain ownership over these models over a long time span so that models gradually decay, unless appropriate mechanisms are put into place to keep them alive and up-to-date as organizational practice.

Both aspects of the "problem" in EM point into a similar direction: The traditional understanding of enterprise models as an instrument of architects and certain roles in project teams to ensure qualities like coherence or alignment, have to be extended to better include many stakeholder groups with their decentral concerns and to cover a longer sustained life span (and thus enhanced value) of enterprise models.

3 The Vision

It can be argued that the main reason that humans have excelled, is their ability to represent and transfer knowledge across time and space, developing new knowledge on the way. Whereas in most areas of human conduct, one-dimensional (textual) languages, either informal (natural language) or formal (as in mathematics) have traditionally been used for this purpose, we see that the use of two and multi-dimensional representational forms is on the rise. Enterprise modelling is one such technique. For modelling to have a larger effect, we propose a move of technologies and approaches to also enable 'normal' knowledge workers to be active modelers, both by adapting the applications they are using to support their daily work tasks and by providing support for specific non-routine situations.

Our vision for the future of EM in an organizational co

Ten years from now, the majority of organizational stakeholders uses enterprise modelling (often without noticing it) to capture, store, distribute, integrate and retrieve essential knowledge of their local practices in a way that supports long-term, cross-concern organizational objectives.

This vision includes many aspects that need further elaboration and refinement, some of which are the following:

- Modelling is embedded in everyday work, not only a distinctive practice: Non-experts in modelling do modelling, sometimes even without knowing it;
- Different kinds of model content, formats and purposes can be extracted (or mined), combined, integrated and federated on demand, either through primarily human intervention or driven by a symbiosis of humans and intelligent agents;
- Local practices in capturing knowledge can be specific yet integrative with other local practices;
- Modelling by non-experts (a.k.a. grass-root modelling) and professional modelling co-exist in synergetic use;
- Models are not primarily developed for one specific purpose, but can be more flexibly used for several purposes, e.g. by using viewing mechanisms to tailor the model for different usages;
- Completeness, coherence and rigor requirements to models and modelling languages in some contexts are softened towards possibilities for incomplete, partly formalized and contradictory model parts, and issue and approach being discussed in work of interactive models [19];
- Modelling is not an end, i.e. a purpose on its own, but a means to an end, e.g., for business model development, visualization of the current situation, strategy development, business and IT alignment, model mapping, human sense-making, communication, model analysis, quality assurance, model deployment and activation, model implementation and standardization.

4 State of Practice in Enterprise Modelling and Beyond

For attaining the vision outlined in the previous section, approaches, methods and technologies from various areas in computer science, business information systems and social sciences will have to be involved, some of them already existing but many others to be adapted or even newly developed. This section identifies and briefly summarizes potentially relevant areas and sources of inspiration from enterprise modelling, knowledge management, model-based collaboration environments, gamification, semantic web, legal visualization, practice theory, CSCW and architectural thinking. This list of areas probably is not exhaustive. For each area, the relevance for the vision is briefly outlined. We structured the above areas into methodical and formal approaches (Sect. 4.1), practice oriented approaches (Sect. 4.2) and approaches relevant to tools support (Sect. 4.3) to improve readability of the section.

4.1 Methodical and Formal Approaches

Enterprise Modelling. In general terms, EM addresses the systematic analysis and modelling of processes, organization structures, products structures, IT-systems or any other perspective relevant for the modelling purpose [20]. A detailed account of EM approaches is provided in [21]. Participative modelling and involving different stakeholder groups in EM has a long tradition (see, e.g., [22]). Domain-specific modelling languages (DSML) [23] are supposed to support these various stakeholders in model creation and use. The scientific literature on EM offers several aspects as its constituents (see, e.g., [21, 24, 25]), like the modelling procedure or *modelling method*, the result of modelling (i.e. the *model*), the *tool support,* and the *organizational structures* establishing modelling within an organization. However, not all scholars in the field agree on all of the above EM constituents. Some researchers consider constructional and functional structures as part of modelling methods and argue that this cannot be separated [26]. Others emphasize the importance of meta-models and modelling languages for capturing different perspectives [27]. Tool support is often seen as inseparable manifestation of modelling approaches and notations [28], but in other research work as aid to support modelling [21]. Organizational structures and role descriptions are often neglected in EM approaches.

Due to this plethora of topics and concepts, a recent study among EM experts suggests that one of the most important topics of future research is EM simplification: "To a great extent, this can be explained in that the variety of different components […] exhibit a high degree of complexity of the subject area, which needs to be reduced in future research efforts" [29].

Knowledge Management. Knowledge engineering [30] and enterprise knowledge modelling [31] contribute to systematic development and reuse of knowledge by offering methods, tools and approaches for capturing knowledge in defined representations in order to support the entire lifecycle of organizational knowledge management [32]. Inspiration for implementing the vision of "modelling for the masses" comes from (organizational and technical) knowledge management. Knowledge management from an organizational perspective addresses how to establish systematic knowledge management in an organization in terms of activities and organizational structures required. Well-known approaches in this area are the "building block" model [33] and the SECI model [34]. IT-based knowledge management systems are support for organizational knowledge management. In this area, Maier et al.'s architecture proposal [35] for such systems and the differentiation between various knowledge services as components of this architecture are often applied. Knowledge reuse in general addresses techniques and approaches for preparing knowledge for reuse in different contexts. Existing work is categorized and structured in [36]. Organizational situations for knowledge reuse were identified by Markus [37]. Knowledge about these situations supports the design of tools and organizational practices.

Semantic Web. The concept of a "semantic web", which originated from the vision that machines are enabled to conduct automated reasoning and can thus infer information from resources on the world-wide-web [38], led to a number of research efforts in regard to EM. In contrast to semi-formal approaches in the area of conceptual modeling that primarily build on a formal syntax with semantic expressed in natural language [39], approaches based on semantic web technologies typically strive for logic-based models that enable automated processing [40]. The spectrum of using semantic web technologies in EM thereby stretches from the use of distinct ontology languages for describing enterprise models, e.g., [41], to the transformation of enterprise models to formal ontologies, e.g., [42], up to the lightweight approaches of using semantic annotations for processing enterprise model content, e.g., [43]. New standards and vocabularies for open data exchange mean that open semantic data may in the future increasingly overlap with EM. They offer new uses of enterprise models for new types of users. For example, open semantic data sets can be used both for enriching and mining enterprise models, and enterprise models can be used to help users by making sense of, providing context for and offering access to semantically annotated information relevant to an enterprise. The research challenge is to connect the implicit, but often tacit, semantic assumptions made in enterprise models and EM languages to link them to the bottom-up web of semantically annotated data where anyone can contribute anything about any topic using their preferred vocabulary [44]. Research on these aspects has to combine approaches from traditional conceptual enterprise modeling with techniques primarily found in areas such as artificial intelligence, semantic web, and linked data.

Legal Visualization. From the field of legal visualization and legal modelling, insights can be gained on the representation of legal information in the form of models and how this can serve for enhancing the expert-lay communication [45]. Examples include the model-based representation of legal options in hereditary law [46] or the use of UML for depicting legal language relationships [47]. From these examples it can be inferred also for other areas of EM how non-experts may be addressed, thus opening the potential user base of such models.

4.2 Practice Oriented Approaches

Practice Theory and Computer Supported Cooperative Work. Organizational research [48, 49] and workplace studies [50] have taken a "practice turn" in recent years. While there is no coherent "practice theory", researchers can learn from philosophers (Heidegger, Marx, Wittgenstein) and sociologists (Bourdieu, Giddens) that human actual practices are fundamental to a human identity and cognition and are an essential building block in understanding higher level concepts like organizations, power and knowledge [51]. Studying practices leads to an understanding what human actors really do, how they make sense of what they do and how they communicate this knowledge to others. This perspective has appealed to researchers of Computer Supported Cooperative Work who wanted to understand frequent failures and unexpected obstacles in adopting collaborative technologies in the field (see e.g., [52, 53]). Typically, those workplace studies have a focus on how artefacts (traditional or digital) are embedded in human activities, e.g., as a tool, as material, as knowledge repository or as symbol. We see a great potential in applying the tool set of practice theory to enterprise modelling. The study of *Enterprise Modelling Practices* enhances our understanding what both modelling laymen and expert really do, when they model, what the role of modelling artifacts really is, how several actors collaborate in modelling or using models, how Enterprise Modelling Practices blend into their other work practices, and how structures like power and information flows are shaped by EM Practices. For example, this approach can help to understand why PowerPoint has been so widely adopted for modelling purposes [54].

Architectural Thinking. As an alternative approach to top-down, governance-based EM, the concept of architectural thinking (AT) has been proposed [3, 6]. AT is understood as *the way of thinking and acting throughout an organization*, i.e. not restricted to architects and system developers, *that considers holistic, long-term system aspects as well as fundamental system design and evolution principles in day-to-day decision making* (e.g., change requests). A traditional approach to implement AT is to 'bring architecture to the business', i.e. to build up modeling and model-based analysis competences and responsibilities in business lines (and not in a central architecture unit or in the IT unit), thereby enabling many additional people in the organization to 'architecturally think and act'. As many organizations however failed to motivate business lines to 'architecturally think and act', research has been addressing the creation of enabling conditions for AT. Weiss et al. [55] adopted institutional theory as a lens to analyze the obvious reluctance of many organizational actors to comply with enterprise-wide norms and guidelines. They show that social legitimacy, efficiency, organizational grounding and trust have significant influence on the actor's response towards "restriction of design freedom" [56] and propose that, as a consequence, supportive conditions need to be created in the form that

- actors gain social fitness inside the organization when complying with architectural guidelines (social legitimacy),
- actors become more efficient when following guidelines (efficiency),

- architecture management is anchored within the organization's values in terms of strategy definition, top management support or the position in the organizational hierarchy (organizational grounding), and
- actors are confident that the architecture does the right things right (trust).

While governance-based architecture management cannot directly 'create' AT, it can create conditions under which AT is more likely to develop and sustain.

4.3 Approaches with Relevance to Tool Support

Gamification. One direction of modelling research has been concerned with the process of modelling: understanding it, but most of all making models and modelling easier, more accessible for stakeholders more 'usable' [57], even more engaging. Inquiries into the process or act of modelling indicate that workflow-based approaches cannot adequately and usefully capture or guide the iterative and unpredictable process of modelling in its operational detail. Alternatively, modelling processes can be framed as games [58–60]. Essential 'modelling game elements' and 'game mechanics' constitute *dialogue games*. The core of such games (typically collaborative in nature) are conversational moves in which modelers propose, discuss, accept or reject model elements, while rapidly switching the specific focus of the dialogue in a goal-driven fashion [4, 60].

Visual Languages. The research area of visual languages is closely related to the field of EM. The focus here is the interaction of humans and machines through visual representations on computer screens [61]. Although the technical realization of visual languages in the context of EM is today often accomplished using meta modelling platforms such as Eclipse-EMF, MetaEdit, or ADOxx, the theories and innovative approaches developed in visual language research can be very valuable. Examples include the technique of visual semantic zooming recently proposed by Yoon and Myers for better understanding and interacting with changes in program code [62] or approaches for recording, processing, and visualizing changes in diagrams [63].

Collaborative Working Environments. From enterprise architecture management (EAM), experiences and practices of model-based collaboration environments supporting collaborative bottom-up modelling can contribute to the vision presented in Sect. 3. EAM addresses the immanent need for mutual alignment of business and IT in enterprises to react upon frequently changing market conditions [64]. It seeks to capture and manage a holistic view of the enterprise to strategically plan enterprise transformations with respect to both, business and IT concerns [56]. [65] describes the underlying approach of the model-based working environment how it empowers information carriers and enterprise architects to collaboratively and incrementally develop and manage a model in a bottom-up fashion by using wiki pages enriched with types and attributes. In practicing EAM, multiple stakeholders have to collaborate to achieve different predefined enterprise-related goals [64]. Additionally, they struggle with inflexible models not meeting the information demand of stakeholders or with heavy-weight tools to manage architectural information [66, 67]. In order to tackle the aforementioned challenges, the lightweight approach Hybrid Wikis was developed. This approach enables the emergent enrichment of unstructured content (e.g., free text or documents) with structure (types, attributes, and relationships) achieving a collaborative model-based collaboration environment that supports the evolution of both the user-model and its data [68, 69]. The Hybrid Wiki approach combines both modelling approaches, namely top-down modelling (model-first) and bottom-up modelling (data-first). Its goal is to empower non-expert users to collaboratively gather and consolidate information in a flexible meta-model-based information system (SocioCortex), which acts as a model-based collaboration environment for members of the organization [69].

5 A Perspective on Challenges for Research and Practice

In order to analyze the challenges in the context of our vision, several dimensions should be considered which also are expected to help structuring future work. Along these dimensions, a roadmap for future research in the field can be developed:

- Stakeholder dimension: Who is creating and using models? At least four stakeholder categories have to be distinguished: Grass-root (i.e. everybody in an enterprise without any particular modelling competence create/use models on their own or in collaboration with peers), participative (participation of domain experts in modelling process led by modelling experts), expert (modelling experts create/use models), and computer (machine-generated or interpreted models, e.g., from enterprise information sources or by integration of existing models). A better understanding is required about how models or model-like content is created and used by non-traditional enterprise model users, e.g., the grass root modelers, and in local practices. This better understanding has to be used for improving model content integration into conventional modelling tools and methods. Additionally, stakeholder perceptions of 'restriction of design freedom' [70] need to be better understood in order to systematically create conditions that are favorable for decentralized EM approaches like "Architectural Thinking" [7, 12].
- Concern dimension: What role do models have for which stakeholder concerns? In order to exploit the full application potential of models, it needs to be better understood which types of concerns of which stakeholder groups can typically be supported by which types of models and which type of content. While certain classifications like strategic, tactical and operational concerns or short-term or long-term concerns were investigated, they need to be linked to stakeholder groups, use situations, and model type/content.
- Model understandability dimension: How easy to understand is the model for different stakeholders and how much is the model formalized? There are representations comparably easy to understand for certain stakeholders (e.g., visual models or tailored model views for experts) or difficult to understand (e.g., formal ontology representations for grass-root), and many levels in between these extremes. What is the meaning of the modelling constructs, the model elements and their relations? The formality of the representation is often linked to the understandability.

- Model scope dimension: In what scope is the model relevant? Categories could be that a model is relevant for individuals only, for an organization unit, a group of people with the enterprise, the enterprise as a whole, or an ecosystem of organizations.
- Model processing dimension: What tasks have to be supported across different model representations, scopes, purposes and local practices? Examples for such tasks are alignment, visualization, ambiguity detection, approximation (find similar models), annotating or linking. How can different models be semantically integrated and processed? To what extent do semantics need to be integrated or, otherwise posted, what extent of ambiguity can be accepted by an organization? How can the semantics of models be gradually evolved?
- Value and quality dimension: Which factors affect quality, success, failure, utility of modelling? How is it related to semantic vocabularies and other semantic standards? How are other information sources linked to models?
- Model lifecycle dimension: What phases of model lifecycles have to be distinguished? Are these lifecycle phases different for different model kinds and do they show different paces? What formal constraints are there on the information?

We propose to use the above dimensions for structuring the challenges to be addressed for achieving the vision. In Table 1, the dimensions are put in relation to the vision's aspects identified in Sect. 3. This allows for systematic identification of topics for future research. As an initial step, the areas discussed in Sect. 4 were analyzed for relevant topics. The identified topics were positioned in Table 1 according to the aspect of the vision and the dimension they address.

6 Summary and Future Work

Starting from a brief analysis of problems in EM this paper proposed a vision for the future of the field which can be summarized as "modelling for and by the masses" and aims at better exploiting the potential of EM from an enterprise perspective. Furthermore, we identified research topics to be investigated on mid-term and long-term which form the basis for a research roadmap. Future work will have to focus on elaborating a research roadmap and on initiating research work required for attaining the vision. An important precondition is discussion of the vision and its consequences in the enterprise modeling community.

Many of the raised issues and open concerns are related to better understanding how people use models, what concerns they have, with whom they need to communicate, etc. Better understanding is often not sufficiently achievable only by eliciting (model engineering) requirements, but needs to connect to behavioral research that provides insights on motivations, perceptions, concerns, and emergence. This calls not necessarily for a methodological evolution of the EM discipline, but for a better integration with other (IS) research communities that could provide such insights. With such foundations, new innovative approaches to modeling, human-model interaction and the processing of information contained in models can be ultimately developed and shared across communities.

Table 1. Research topics relevant for attaining the vision

Vision's aspect	Dimension						
	Stake-holders	Model representation	Model scope	Purpose	Processing	Value and quality	Life-cycle
Modelling is embedded in everyday work	Under-standing grass root model use and creation, improve social legitimacy	Model-generated workspace, model visualization	Model views, simplification of EM methods	Interactive model support	Integrate modelling tools and plat-forms in enterprise environments	Comprehension of 'just sufficient' models	Model at run-time, from ad-hoc model to elaborated model
Model combination, integration, federation on demand	Semantic enrichment when maturing models	Semantic aspects of model representation	Going from local to global scope	Model integration, support of reuse situations	Understanding model semantics by intelligent agents	Manual and automatic quality assurance of models	Model federation and integration life-cycle, value of models
Specific but integrative local practices	Light-weight practices for local workers. Simplification of EM tool	Local representations, semantic annotations, DSML	Local practice, models as boundary objects	Sense-making and local communication	Visualization, sematic integration of models + documents	Model comprehension and stake-holder agreement	Projects and work tasks, knowledge services for EM
Grass-root and professional modelling in synergy	Practices for expert modelers and local workers	Transition between light- and heavy-weight modelling approach	Organizational practice	Alignment of local practices	Semantic enrichment, model merging	Model availability using agreed syntax	Organizational memory
Softened requirements to completeness, rigor	Local workers, modeling games	Local representations, multiple stakeholder environments	Local practice, hybrid models/methods/tools	Sense-making and local comm., limited degree of enterprise wide integration	Process unstructured model content, e.g. NLP, document and EM mining	Model comprehension and stakeholder agreement	Short-term projects and local work tasks

Acknowledgements. This paper is a result of the Dagstuhl seminar no. 16192 on "Supporting Organizational Efficiency and Agility: Models, Languages and Software Systems" (see http://www.dagstuhl.de/de/programm/kalender/semhp/?semnr=16192).

References

1. Zdravkovic, J., Stirna, J., Kirikova, M., Karagiannis, D., Winter, R.: Advanced enterprise modeling. BISE **57**(6), 1–2 (2015). Springer
2. Frank, U., Strecker, S., Fettke, P., Vom Brocke, J., Becker, J., Sinz, E.: The research field "modeling business information systems" – current challenges and elements of a future research agenda. BISE **6**(1), 39–43 (2014). Springer
3. Hoppenbrouwers, S.J.B.A., Schotten, B., Lucas, P.J.F.: Towards games for knowledge acquisition and modeling. Int. J. Gaming Comput.-Mediat. Simul. Special Issue on AI and Games **2**(4), 48 66 (2010). IGI Global
4. Hoppenbrouwers, S., Wilmont, I.: Focused conceptualisation: framing questioning and answering in model-oriented dialogue games. In: van Bommel, P., Hoppenbrouwers, S., Overbeek, S., Proper, E., Barjis, J. (eds.) PoEM 2010. LNBIP, vol. 68, pp. 190–204. Springer, Heidelberg (2010)
5. Hermans, F.F.J.: Analyzing and visualizing spreadsheets. Ph.D. thesis, Software Engineering Research Group, Delft University of Technology, The Netherlands (2012)
6. Winter, R.: Architektur braucht Management. Wirtschaftsinformatik **46**(4), 317–319 (2004)
7. Winter, R.: Architectural thinking. Bus. Inf. Syst. Eng. **6**(6), 361–364 (2014)
8. Fossland, S., Krogstie, J.: Modeling as-is, ought-to-be and to-be – experiences from a case study in the health sector. In: PoEM 2015, Valencia, Spain
9. Theunissen, T., van Heesch, U.: The disappearance of technical specifications in web and mobile applications. In: Proceedings of 10th European Conference on Software Architecture (ECSA), September 2016, Copenhagen, Denmark (2016, to appear)
10. Star, S., Griesemer, J.: Institutional ecology, 'translations' and boundary objects: amateurs and professionals in Berkeley's museum of vertebrate zoology, 1907-39. Soc. Stud. Sci. **19**(3), 387–420 (1989)
11. Aier, S., Riege, C., Winter, R.: Unternehmensarchitektur – Literaturüberblick und Stand der Praxis. Wirtschaftsinformatik **50**(4), 292–304 (2008)
12. Ross, J.W., Quaadgras, A.: Enterprise Architecture is Not Just for Architects. Center for Information Systems Research Sloan School of Management Massachusetts Institute of Technology, Cambridge (2012)
13. Gardner, D., Fehskens, L., Naidu, M., Rouse, W.B., Ross, J.W.: Point-counterpoint: enterprise architecture and enterprise transformation as related but distinct concepts. J. Enterp. Transform. **2**(4), 283–294 (2012)
14. Krogstie, J.: Quality in Business Process Modeling. Springer, Berlin (2016)
15. Weick, K.: Sensemaking in Organisations. Sage, London (1995)
16. Heggset, M., Krogstie, J., Wesenberg, H.: Understanding model quality concerns when using process models in an industrial company. In: Gaaloul, K., Schmidt, R., Nurcan, S., Guerreiro, S., Ma, Q. (eds.) BPMDS 2015 and EMMSAD 2015. LNBIP, vol. 214, pp. 395–409. Springer, Heidelberg (2015)
17. Krogstie, B.R,, Schmidt, A.P., Kunzmann, C., Krogstie, J., Mora, S.: Linking reflective learning and knowledge maturing in organizations. In: Proceedings of ARTEL 2013 (2013)

18. Krogstie, J., Dalberg, V., Jensen, S.M.: Process modeling value framework. In: Manolopoulos, Y., Filipe, J., Constantopoulos, P., Cordeiro, J. (eds.) ICEIS 2006. LNBIP, vol. 3, pp. 309–321. Springer, Heidelberg (2008)
19. Krogstie, J., Jørgensen, H.: Quality of interactive models. In: 1st International Workshop on Conceptual Modelling Quality (IWCMQ 2002), Tampere, Finland (2002)
20. Vernadat, F.B.: Enterprise Modelling and Integration. Chapman & Hall, London (1996)
21. Sandkuhl, K., Stirna, J., Persson, A., Wißotzki, M.: Enterprise Modeling: Tackling Business Challenges with the 4EM Method (The Enterprise Engineering Series). Springer, Berlin (2014). ISBN 978-3662437247
22. Stirna, J., Persson, A., Sandkuhl, K.: Participative enterprise modeling: experiences and recommendations. In: Krogstie, J., Opdahl, A.L., Sindre, G. (eds.) CAiSE 2007 and WES 2007. LNCS, vol. 4495, pp. 546–560. Springer, Heidelberg (2007)
23. Van Deursen, A., Klint, P., Visser, J.: Domain-specific languages: an annotated bibliography. Sigplan Not. **35**(6), 26–36 (2000)
24. Henderson-Sellers, B., Ralyté, J., Ågerfalk, P.J., Rossi, M.: Situational Method Engineering, pp. 1–274. Springer, Heidelberg (2014)
25. Frank, U.: Multilevel modeling - toward a new paradigm of conceptual modeling and information systems design. Bus. Inf. Syst. Eng. **6**(6), 319–337 (2014)
26. Dietz, J.L.G.: Enterprise Ontology—Theory and Methodology. Springer, Heidelberg (2006)
27. Frank, U.: Multi-perspective enterprise modeling: foundational concepts, prospects and future research challenges. Softw. Syst. Model. **13**(3), 941–962 (2014). doi:10.1007/s10270-012-0273-9
28. ISO/IEC 24744: Software Engineering – Metamodel for Development Methodologies (2014). http://www.iso.org/iso/home/store/catalogue_ics/catalogue_detail_ics.htm?csnumber=62644
29. Wirtz, B.W., Pistoia, A., Ullrich, S., Göttel, V.: Business models: origin, development and future research. Long Range Plan. **49**, 36–54 (2016)
30. Studer, R., Benjamins, V.R., Fensel, D.: Knowledge engineering: principles and methods. Data Knowl. Eng. **25**(1), 161–197 (1998)
31. Lillehagen, F., Krogstie, J.: Active Knowledge Modelling of Enterprises. Springer, Heidelberg (2009). ISBN 978-3-540-79415-8
32. Dalkir, K.: Knowledge Management in Theory and Practice. Routledge, Oxford (2013)
33. Probst, G., Raub, S., Romhardt, K.: Managing Knowledge – Building Blocks for Success. Wiley, Chichester (2000)
34. Nonaka, I.: A dynamic theory of organizational knowledge creation. Organ. Sci. **5**(1), 14–37 (1994)
35. Maier, R., Hädrich, T., Peinl, R.: Enterprise Knowledge Infrastructures, 2nd edn. Springer, Heidelberg (2010)
36. Sandkuhl, K.: Knowledge reuse: survey of existing techniques and classification approach. In: Zimányi, E., Kutsche, R.-D. (eds.) eBISS 2014. LNBIP, vol. 205, pp. 126–148. Springer, Heidelberg (2015). doi:10.1007/978-3-319-17551-5
37. Markus, M.L.: Toward a theory of knowledge reuse: types of knowledge reuse situations and factors in reuse success. J. Manag. Inf. Syst. **18**(1), 57–93 (2001). (Summer)
38. Berners-Lee, T., Hendler, J., et al.: The Semantic Web - A New Form of Web Content That is Meaningful to Computers Will Unleash a Revolution of New Possibilities. Scientific American, New York (2001)
39. Fraser, M.D., Kumar, K., et al.: Strategies for incorporating formal specifications in software development. Commun. ACM **37**(10), 74–86 (1994)

40. Obrst, L.: Ontologies for semantically interoperable systems. In: Proceedings of 12th International Conference on Information and Knowledge Management. ACM Press, New Orleans (2003)
41. Tarassov, V., Sandkuhl, K., et al.: Using ontologies for representation of individual and enterprise competence models. In: International Conference on Research, Innovation and Vision for the Future IEEE (2006)
42. Thomas, O., Fellmann, M.: Semantic business process management: ontology-based process modeling using event-driven process chains. IBIS **2**(1), 29–44 (2007)
43. Fill, H.-G.: On the conceptualization of a modeling language for semantic model annotations. In: Salinesi, C., Pastor, O. (eds.) CAiSE Workshops 2011. LNBIP, vol. 83, pp. 134–148. Springer, Heidelberg (2011)
44. Allemang, D., Hendler, J.: Semantic Web for the Working Ontologist: Effective Modeling in RDFS and OWL. Elsevier, Amsterdam (2011)
45. Brunschwig, C.: Multisensory law and therapeutic jurisprudence: how family mediators can better communicate with their clients. Phoenix Law Rev. **5**(4), 705–746 (2012)
46. Fill, H.-G., Haiden, K.: Visuelle Modellierung für rechtsberatende Berufe am Beispiel der gesetzlichen Erbfolge, Jusletter IT, 25. February 2016, Weblaw (2016)
47. Engesser, M.: UML und Sprache – Wirklichkeit und Technik, Jusletter IT, September 2014, Weblaw (2014)
48. Corradi, G., Gherardi, S., Verzelloni, L.: Through the practice lens: where is the bandwagon of practice-based studies heading? Manag. Learn. **41**(3), 265–283 (2010)
49. Schatzki, T.R.: Practice minded orders. In: The Practice Turn in Contemporary Theory, vol. 11 (2001)
50. Luff, P., Hindmarsh, J., Heath, C.: Workplace Studies: Recovering Work Practice and Informing System Design. Cambridge University Press, Cambridge (2000)
51. Nicolini, D.: Practice Theory, Work, and Organization: An Introduction. Oxford University Press, Oxford (2012)
52. Heath, C., Luff, P.: Collaboration and controlCrisis management and multimedia technology in London Underground Line Control Rooms. Comput. Support. Coop. Work (CSCW) **1**(1–2), 69–94 (1992)
53. Luff, P., Heath, C.: Mobility in collaboration. In: Proceedings of 1998 ACM Conference on Computer Supported Cooperative Work. ACM (1998)
54. Ciriello, R.F., Richter, A., Schwabe, G.: PowerPoint use and misuse in digital innovation. In: ECIS 2015 Proceedings (2015)
55. Weiss, S., Aier, S., Winter, R.: Institutionalization and the effectiveness of enterprise architecture management. In: 2013 International Conference on Information Systems (ICIS 2013). Association for Information Systems, Milano (2013)
56. Roth, S., Hauder, M., Matthes, F.: Collaborative evolution of enterprise architecture models. In: 8th International Workshop on Models at Runtime (Models@run.time 2013), Miami, USA (2013)
57. Oppl, S.: Towards scaffolding collaborative articulation and alignment of mental models. In: Proceedings of ICKM 2016. Elsevier Procedia Computer Science (2016)
58. Hoppenbrouwers, S.J.B.A., van Bommel, P., Järvinen, A.: Method engineering as game design: an emerging HCI perspective on methods and CASE tools. In: Proceedings of EMMSAD 2008 at CAiSE 2008. Montpellier, France, June 2008
59. Ssebuggwawo, D., Hoppenbrouwers, S., Proper, E.: Interactions, goals and rules in a collaborative modelling session. In: Persson, A., Stirna, J. (eds.) PoEM 2009. LNBIP, vol. 39, pp. 54–68. Springer, Heidelberg (2009)
60. Hoppenbrouwers, S.J.B.A., Rouwette, E.A.J.A.: A dialogue game for analysing group model building: framing collaborative modelling and its facilitation. Int. J. Organ. Des. Eng.

(IJODE) **2**(1), 19–40 (2012). Ed. by R. Magalhaes, special issue on collaborative modeling. Inderscience, New York, USA
61. Narayanan, N.H., Hübscher, R.: Visual language theory: towards a human-computer interaction perspective. In: Marriott, K. (ed.) Visual language theory. Springer, New York (1998)
62. Yoon, Y., Myers, B.: Semantic zooming of code change history. In: IEEE Symposium on Visual Languages and Human-Centric Computing. IEEE (2015)
63. Maier, S., Minas, M.: Recording, processing, and visualizing changes in diagrams. In: IEEE Symposium on Visual Languages and Human-Centric Computing. IEEE (2015)
64. Ross, J., Weill, P., Robertson, D.: Enterprise Architecture as Strategy: Creating a Foundation for Business Execution. Harvard Business Press, Brighton (2006)
65. Matthes, F., Neubert, C., Schneider, A.W.: Fostering collaborative and integrated enterprise architecture modeling. J. Enterp. Model. Inf. Syst. Architect. **8**(1), 26–39 (2013)
66. Reschenhofer, T., Monahov, I., Matthes, F.: Application of a domain-specific language to support the user-oriented definition of visualizations in the context of collaborative product development. In: Enterprise Interoperability: I-ESA 2014, France (2014)
67. Matthes F., Neubert C.: Wiki4EAM: using hybrid wikis for enterprise architecture management. In: 2011 7th International Symposium on Wikis and Open Collaboration (WikiSym), Mountain View California (2014)
68. Monahov, I.: Integrated software support for quantitative models in the domain of enterprise architecture management. Ph.D. thesis, Technische Universität München (2014)
69. Reschenhofer, T., Bhat, M., Hernandez-Mendez, A., Matthes, F.: Lessons learned in aligning data and model evolution in collaborative information systems. In: Proceedings of International Conference on Software Engineering (ICSE), Austin, Texas USA (2016)
70. Dietz, J.L.G.: Architecture. Building Strategy into Design. Academic Service, The Hague (2008)

Exploring and Conceptualising Software-Based Motivation Within Enterprise

Alimohammad Shahri(✉), Mahmood Hosseini, Keith Phalp, Jaqui Taylor, and Raian Ali

Bournemouth University, Poole, UK
{ashahri,mhosseini,kphalp,jtaylor,rali}@bournemouth.ac.uk

Abstract. Staff motivation leads to more efficiency, quality and enjoyment while performing tasks and fulfilling business requirements. Software-based motivation is the use of technology, such as gamification, persuasive technology and entertainment computing to facilitate and boost such behaviour and attitude. Despite its importance and unique peculiarities, motivation is not yet seen as a first class concept in enterprise modelling and requirements engineering literature. An ad-hoc design and deployment of software-based motivation might be detrimental and menace significantly other functional and non-functional requirements of the business, e.g., giving certain requirements more priority, increasing pressure to complete tasks, increasing competition to win the reward, etc. In this research, we follow a mixed method approach to conceptualise software-based motivation within enterprises taking the perspective of managers and employees and, also, experts from a wide range of domains including psychology, HCI, human factors in computing and software engineering. Our findings suggest the need for a personalised and human-centred engineering method of software-based motivation within enterprises which treats their profiles and preferences as equally important to their business roles. A blueprint of such method is introduced.

Keywords: Requirements engineering · Human centred design · Human factors in computing · Conceptual modelling · Gamificaiton

1 Introduction

Motivation as a research topic has been in the interest of various disciplines, e.g., psychology [1], business management [2], education [3], and healthcare [4]. Several definitions of motivation are available in the literature [5]. However, a widely accepted definition is the "psychological processes that cause the arousal, direction, and persistence of behaviour" [6]. It aims to encourage and increase people's act in a certain manner. The substance that enables motivation to achieve this goal is known as "motive" [7].

J. Horkoff et al. (Eds.): PoEM 2016, LNBIP 267, pp. 241–256, 2016.
DOI: 10.1007/978-3-319-48393-1_17

With the popularity of new advances in computing, motivation has become subject to automation and software support. Examples include gamification and persuasive technology. These techniques, also known as software-based motivation (SbM) [8,9], aim to change users' behaviour towards a desired one through persuasion, social influence, and rewarding, but not *coercion* [10].

Enterprises endeavour to help employees achieve their goals and facilitate tasks. Motivation aims to encourage social actors such as employees to do their tasks and interact efficiently to achieve business goals and quality requirements of the enterprise such as productivity. It is also meant to achieve social requirements such as sense of membership, loyalty and mental well-being within workplace [11]. Hence, motivation is not a standalone requirement but a supplementary one which is meant to improve the fulfilment of other requirements.

Although there are several instances of successful implementations of SbMs available in the literature [12], we argue that ad-hoc introduction of such technique to an enterprise may be detrimental and lead to adverse and undesirable impacts [11,13]. There are various situations where the use of SbM may leave negative effect on the enterprise, e.g., if SbM is not designed carefully, it may put employees in situations that can persuade them to sabotage the performance of others where possible, in order to gain more points for their faction. This can happen especially when two or more groups are competing on gaining points, and one member of a group is delegated a task which ultimately is in benefit of a group, other than the group of the person the task is delegated to.

Therefore, we advocate the need for a systematic introduction of SbM to an enterprise. This requires consideration of various characteristics of the motives and their compatibility with goals and tasks they are meant to support. Furthermore, there is a need for considering the social actors who are subject to the desired behaviour change and their roles and inter-relations. Considering the preferences of all enterprise staff on SbM is challenging and to some extent impossible if the staff are high in number. As a solution to tackle this problem, the use of personas is proposed in [9] which advocates the clustering and grouping of employees with similar preferences and requirements with regards to SbM and furthermore, provides the constituents necessary to create personas with references to SbM. Clustering employees into a set of personas helps designers to focus on a limited number of preferences and requirements about SbM. In case the personas are created carefully and a representative sample of employees were involved in the requirements elicitation phase, every employee in the enterprise should be able to feel related to at least on of the personas in the set.

In this paper, we build on top of our initial statement in [8,9] and conduct a three-phase empirical study to explore the facets that need to be catered for when introducing SbM to an enterprise. We provide a thematic mapping to support a systematic integration of the concept within its organisational ecosystem at the early stages of software engineering, i.e., requirements engineering. Our results are meant to aid software engineers in the analysis and design of SbM that is effective, sustainable and compatible with the rest of the enterprise.

We also propose a requirements-driven conceptual architecture for an integrated and holistic engineering framework.

2 Background and Research Motivation

In this section, we discuss persuasive technology as a representative technique for SbM. We will also highlight various concerns and design issues to be addressed when introducing the concept to an enterprise and, hence, motivate this research.

According to [10, 14], persuasive technology is mostly referred to as a technology which aims at changing human behaviour through persuasion and social influence, not through force and threat. Fogg introduced a model for persuasive design, the Fogg Behaviour Model (FBM) [10]. This model considers three main drivers necessary for human persuasion: *motivation*, *ability*, and *triggers*. FBM sets the target behaviour and suggests that the three mentioned drivers define how the behaviour can change towards achieving a desired target.

Both ability and motivation have direct impacts on the likeliness of achieving target behaviours, for instance, if the ability to perform a task is high, but the motivation is low, e.g., visiting a website regularly, then it is unlikely for the person to perform the desired behaviour. Moreover, if the motivation is high, but the ability is low, e.g., buying an expensive phone, it is still unlikely for the person to perform the desired behaviour. However, when both the ability and the motivation are high, e.g., a reasonable offer on the phone, the likelihood of achieving the desired behaviour increases accordingly. The third factor in the model is trigger and timing. In addition to motivation and ability, the presence of a trigger at the right time is essential for the desired behaviour to occur.

It is assumed that within an enterprise, employees are already assessed to have the ability to perform the tasks assigned to them. This means that ability, as a driver for persuasion, already exists in employees. Besides, employees are always informed of the tasks they need to perform and the time-line needed for the task to be accomplished. Therefore, trigger and timing is also already present for employees in the enterprise. However, according to Fogg's model, the lack of motivation as the third driver in employees can be the main cause that they are not persuaded to perform a desired behaviour. Therefore, there is a need for thoroughly investigating methods that can increase motivation in employees, its potential complications, and possible solutions to these complications.

According to [10], persuasive technology tools aim at easing behavioural change by means of interactive products. FBM consists of seven types of persuasive tools: tunnelling, tailoring, reduction, suggestion, surveillance, self-monitoring, and conditioning.

Tunnelling refers to leading the users through pre-defined structures of events that has to be performed step-by-step. Tailoring tries to provide users with personally relevant information regarding their work performance. It tries to attract employees attention by customising information related to themselves, as it is believed that people pay more attention to the information if they believe it is customised for them [15]. Reduction aims at changing the behaviour of its users by simplifying a complex task to smaller task. This can be achieved by removing some of the steps necessary to perform the task, usually via technology, e.g., automating repetitive tasks. Suggestion tries to persuade users to perform certain behaviours by providing reminders on certain times. In case the suggestion seems rational to the user and is on the right time, it can motivate users to perform desired behaviours, e.g., a break reminder after a certain amount of continuous use of the computer. Self-monitoring tries to persuade users by creating the possibility of monitoring self-progress for self-motivated users. Surveillance aims at using social and peer pressure by capturing performance information from users and making decisions based on the collected information.

Surveillance in enterprise seems to be more acceptable when employees involved in it have work-related interactions with each other [16,17]. However, their usage within enterprise is argued to cause conflict amongst peers [18], or reduce quality of work despite increasing productivity [19]. It can also create ethical issues related to privacy of the users [10,11], or put pressure on employees and menacing their social and mental well-being within the workplace [11]. Finally, conditioning uses the information collected via surveillance to provide tangible or intangible rewards for users. However, in addition to a positive reinforcement, such as rewarding, a negative reinforcement could be introduced, conveying there could be a punishment for not achieving certain behaviours.

There is a trend in enterprises towards using SbM to increase motivation in employees. Authors in [20] developed an SbM to help novice users learn *AutoCad* through motives, such as gaining rewards, time pressure, and levelling up. This was perceived positively by users and increased their engagement, enjoyment, and performance. Despite several successful examples of SbM in the literature [12,21], there is still lack of systematic approaches for designing and implementing SbM in enterprises. The literature also has scarcely addressed potential adverse side effects of ad-hoc implementation of SbM in an enterprise [11,13].

3 Methodology

This research has followed a mixed method approach in order to explore and understand SbM in depth. A three-stage empirical study was conducted: firstly, a qualitative interview with six experts in the field of SbM as the exploration stage, secondly, a quantitative questionnaire with comment boxes to allow for further explanations with 40 expert participating as the confirmation and enhancement, and lastly for confirmation purposes, a qualitative interview with 22 participants from users' and managers' point of view.

3.1 Exploration

This research used interviews to elaborate on initial observations about the diversity of views on SbM, its design principles, its advantages and disadvantages, ethical concerns, evaluation metrics, and also to obtain insights and clarifications from experts in this field. The results of this stage were used to design the questionnaire for the next stage. The interviews followed a semi-structured approach in order to communicate thoughts with experts and allow them to add additional insights that were not thought of prior to the interview. The interviews were recorded and further questions were asked when elaboration was needed.

Six experts participated in the interview. Four of the interviewees were academics, and two came from industry. Three of them were involved in developing theoretical frameworks and three others have developed and applied SbM in practice. All the interviews were recorded and transcribed. The text was then content-analysed to extract important issues related to SbM. These issues were then grouped together to form a number of themes. Two researchers worked on the analysis, and in case of a disagreement, a third researcher was consulted to make a final decision. The questionnaire items, discussed in the next section, were formed based on the agreed themes.

3.2 Confirmation and Enhancement

In this stage, an expert survey with open ended questions was performed to confirm and enhance the views, perspectives, and opinions obtained via the literature review and interviews with experts in the first qualitative stage. The survey comprised a total of 13 sections. Five questions were about the expert profile and general choices, e.g. whether they wish to be sent the results. The other eight questions focused on diverse aspects of SbM in general and Gamification in particular. A total of 71 sub-questions were embedded in these eight questions. These questions were designed as multiple choice questions, provided with an open text box at the end of each general question for participants to put any additional comments. The questionnaire was pilot tested on two participants and refined to ensure ambiguity is removed. No data were collected from these tests. The qualitative responds were statistically analysed and expert comments at the end of questions were content analysed by two researchers and a third researcher was involved when a disagreement occurred.

To ensure that all participants had solid expertise in the field, the survey was completed by invitation only. Authors of peer-reviewed and published papers were invited via email to take part in the survey. Our selection criteria of experts in this stage were similar to those that were followed in the qualitative stage. Experts from different affiliations, e.g., industry and academia, and various backgrounds, e.g., psychology, game design and social sciences, were invited to ensure a diversity of opinions.

3.3 Clarification

The clarification stage was designed to clarify the findings of the first two phases from the perspective of users. Diversity in users' roles in the enterprise was the focus and 22 people were interviewed. The selected participants were familiar with SbM and used computers as a main medium for their jobs. Diversity in age, gender and work domain was also ensured, including 16 males and six females, and their age ranged from 25 to 58 years old.

4 Results

In this section, we report and reflect on the results of our literature review and empirical studies. We provide the constituents that shape SbM and its users' requirements and preferences.

4.1 Software-Based Motivation: Elements and Properties

Various elements, properties, and aspects of enterprises can influence the development of SbM to increase productivity and keep the social and mental well-being of the actors at a desired level. A thematic analysis of our findings following the six stages as recommended in [22], helps us to form three thematic areas that could help identify constituents that influence the perception of SbM amongst its actors. There are three aspects in enterprises with SbM implemented in them that can influence the perception of employees about SbM. Identifying attributes related to these aspects can help achieving a more preferred design of SbM by employees. These attributes relate to the tasks that SbM is being applied to, the rewards that are being introduced, and the information it is capturing. An initial thematic analysis of these findings is depicted in Table 1.

Table 1. Initial thematic map for conceptualising software-based motivation

Motivation	Reward	Policy		
		Nature		
		Strategy		
	Tasks	Uniformity		
		Measurability		
		Subjectivity		
		Standard		
		Nature		
		Values		
	Captured information	Visibility	Everyone	
			Relevant colleagues	
			Managers	
			Self-only	
		What is stored	Personal information	
			Work related information	Detailed information
				General information
		Element	Competition	
			Collaboration	

This study enhances the thematic mapping illustrated in Table 1, forming two distinct thematic areas that can have influence on the preferences and perception of SbM amongst employees in an enterprise. The two main themes derived from the findings are the *environment* and *motives.*

Environment: This refers to the intended enterprise in which SbM is introduced. This theme area consists of five sub-themes that can affect the success of SbM. These sub-themes are *roles*, *values personas*, *tasks*, and *relations*. The full thematic map related to the environment is provided in Table 2.

Roles: One of the very important aspects of any enterprise that can influence the success of a design for any SbM is the roles that are available in that environment. It is important know what roles exist in the environment, and who are the employees responsible for these roles. Roles and employees responsible for them carry information that can lead to detection of potential design problems in SbM. These information will be discussed further in this sub-section.

Table 2. Thematic mapping for conceptualising the environment

Environment	Roles		
	Values		
	Tasks	Uniformity	
		Measurability	
		Quality-oriented	
	Relations	Role role task	
		Task task	
		Task role	
		Role role	
	Persona	Incentives	Quality based
			Availability
			Value
			Chance of winning
		Performance and feedback	Frequency
			Generation type
		Privacy	Self-only
			Acquiaintance
			Managers
			Everyone
		Goal setting	Control over setting
			Opt-out possibility
		Collaboration nature	Collaborative
			Competitive

Value: This is a very important aspect of the enterprise that should be known to the designers of an SbM at early stages of the design. This defines the values of an enterprise that SbM should comply with. The values should be clearly defined before starting the design of any SbM as failure in eliciting correct values of the enterprise may hinder the ultimate goal of introducing SbM.

Tasks: Each task has three attributes that define which motives are suitable to be assigned to them through SbM. *Uniformity, measurability* and *subjectivity* are these attributes. Uniformity seeks to identify whether all employees go through a similar process for performing the task, or intellectual effort and creativity of employees are required. This concerned many employees as they were worried about the SbM being able to identify their additional intellectual effort and creativity. Next attribute is the possibility of measuring the outcome of the tasks. A number of employees stated not only their tasks are not uniform, but the outcome of their job is not measurable and trying to measure their efforts through numbers is either not possible or will diminish their actual effort. The last attribute for the tasks is whether the task is quality oriented or quantity oriented. Many employees stated that if they are performing quality-oriented tasks, they will not like being compared with other employees that perform quantity-oriented tasks, as "it is much easier to gain points if quantity is needed."

Relations: Relations defines possible interactions of elements in the enterprise that can influence the outcome of SbM when introduced to an enterprise. Relations could be between *Roles*, between *tasks*, between *roles* and *tasks*, and between various *roles* and *tasks*. In the following we describe these relations.

Our analysis showed two relations between roles could exist. One is a *supervision* relation. This relation gives privilege to the supervisor to monitor the performance and work-flow of the *supervisee*. Identifying this relation can aid the design of SbM to decide who should be given access to whose work information. In case a visibility to work information of a role is given to another when there is a lack of supervision relation between these two roles, some participants stated that this may lead to such stress that not only will this affect their productivity, but also they may decide to stop working within that enterprise under. The other relation between two roles could be a *promotion* relation. This means one role has the potential of being promoted to some other roles in the enterprise. This relation makes it possible to identify a possible conflict of interest in the enterprise and propose an SbM design that prevents it. To delve more into this, a situation can be assumed where a role is responsible for training new recruits that are supposed to join the same team that this trainer is a member of. Promoting competition in this particular team may persuade the trainer to put less required effort in training new recruits to avoid emergence of potential competitors in the team.

Moreover, our analysis suggests there exists one relation between two or more tasks that may influence the design of SbM and that relation is a *dependency* relation. This relation means the commencement of a task may rely on the outcome of another. This relation becomes important in various situations, e.g., it can create stress and tension if an employee in the enterprise is not able to start the task and gain the designated points merely as a result of relying on another task which has not been delivered on-time.

Beside the clear relation of *performing* a task between a task and a role, it is important to know if there is a *genuine interest* in performing the tasks by responsible roles. There are ways of detecting if roles are interested in performing tasks, e.g., the use of group dynamics, which are out of the scope of this investigation. However, having the information regarding the interest of the role towards specific tasks can help designers to introduce motives that can make tasks more interesting to perform through a rewarding mechanism, or avoid a rewarding mechanism when there is already a genuine interest towards the task available, in order to prevent interference with the present intrinsic motivation.

Personas: Eliciting the preferences, needs, and requirements of SbM users is a necessity. By virtue of various circumstances, it may not be always feasible to elicit all users' requirements, or have a coherent collective decision available due to the diversity of opinions. Therefore, personas can be used in order to create clusters of users with similar SbM preferences [9]. This can help software designers to focus on the requirements, needs, and preferences of a set of personas. Although this solution may not lead to an SbM that satisfies all needs and preferences of all individuals, however, it will enable software designers to develop an SbM which can satisfy a considerable portion of requirements and preferences of a substantial number of users. For the sake of evolution, individuals may provide feedback to enhance or customise personas to become more representative of the actual employees.

Motives. Another new main theme is the motives introduced to the workplace. Various aspects of motives should be known in the development of SbM, also available in Table 3.

Reward: This is one of the main drivers that increases motivation in employees. If the reward is appealing for the employees, they may be persuaded to perform as desired. However, it is necessary for an SbM design to align the rewards with the environment it is being introduced to. Our results show that the policy of rewarding has three attributes, *competition, collaboration*, and *performance.* A reward can try to increase employees' motivation through competition and/or collaboration, based on their performance. However, there is a set of combinations of these policies that can influence how employees may react to the rewarding policy. As an instance, when the reward is promoting group competition based on the performance of each group, it may persuade some employees to rely on others and not perform at their best, whereas adding an individual performance monitoring could possibly prevent this problem.

The element of persuasion that a rewarding mechanism adopts is another important aspect. There are several scenarios that this could impact the success of SbMs, e.g., using social recognition may seem an effective element to increase motivation in employees. However, some employees stated they do not like the idea of being socially recognised as the best employees and if they are working in such environment, they will keep their performance at a lower level that they do

Table 3. Thematic mapping for conceptualising the motives

Motive	Reward	Policy	Competition	Individual
				Group
				None
			Collaboration	Individual
				Group
				None
			Performance	Individual
				Group
				None
		Element	Collaboration	
			Social recognition	
			Communication	
			Accomplishment	
		Nature	Intangible	
			Tangible	
			Combined	
		Strategy	Transparency	True
				False
			Value	High
				Low
				Balanced
			Chance of winning	High
				Low
			Points	Pre-defined
				Calculated
			Reinforcement	Positive
				Negative
				Combined
	Captured information	Visibility	Everyone	
			Acquaintance	
			Managers	
			Self-only	
		What is stored	Personal information	
			Work information	Detailed
				General
			Frequency	Low
				Medium
				High
				Real-time
	Techniques	Conditioning		
		Self-monitoring		
		Surveillance		
		Tunnelling		
		Reduction		
		Tailoring		
		Suggestion		

not gain this provided social recognition through SbM. In addition, the nature of the reward is crucial as some of the employees not only did not find intangible rewards persuasive, but also very useless and a waste of resources.

In addition to all mentioned rewarding aspects, there is the rewarding strategy that the motive is employing. There are several attributes that employees may find appealing or demotivating, depending on each individual. One attribute is the *transparency* of rewarding, as many employees stated, it is necessary to be informed about the exact processes of receiving the rewards to avoid bias. *Value* and the *chance of winning* the reward seem to be effective attributes, some employees eager to have high value rewards even if it means lower chance of winning, and on the contrast, some others preferred lower value prizes with a higher chance of winning. Another important attribute is the way *points* are given. A proportion of the employees believed that a pre-defined set of points will remove bias, on the contrary, some believed that a "human touch" in the calculation of points can understand their work better and provide them with fairer points and detect if they did "exceptionally good". Finally, it is important to know if the enterprise wants to use positive reinforcement, negative reinforcement, or a combination of both. This is a very important attribute as the presence of a negative reinforcement may persuade employees to behave in a manner that they would not do otherwise, e.g., cheating in order to gain more points.

Captured Information: In addition to rewarding, it is important to decide what attributes the *captured information* by means of SbM will have. Employees may care about the captured information by means of SbM from two perspective. *Visibility* of the captured information to others in the enterprise, and *what is stored* as the information. Depending on the preferences of employees, they may agree for *everyone* in the environment to have access to their information, especially if they are seeking social recognition. However, this is not true for all employees, as some may even totally disagree with their *managers* having access to their information for personal reasons, despite their tremendous positive performance. It is also important for employees to know *what is stored* about them by means of SbM. Employees were concerned about the ability of SbM in collecting personal information about them, e.g., detecting their mood throughout the working hours by the use of cameras and face detection technologies. However, mainly they found it acceptable for their general working information to be collected, yet a detailed collection of information was not deemed acceptable. The main concern was about managers being able to detect employees work patterns by looking at the collected information.

Another attribute of the captured information is the *frequency* of collecting the information. Employees showed various preferences, from lower frequencies as they wanted to "enjoy the feeling of accomplishment" without knowing how well they did the task in numbers and have an element of "surprise at the end of the week", to real-time collection of the information to know exactly how they are performing and decide to put more efforts where necessary.

Techniques: Motives can employ *conditioning*, *self-monitoring*, *surveillance*, *tunnelling*, *reduction*, *tailoring* and *suggestion*, described in Sect. 2, as tools to increase motivation via SbM. It is important to know how motives use these techniques as these persuasive techniques rely heavily on the perception and preferences of its users, which may be in some cases conflicting.

Conditioning: This technique may be well perceived by some users and increase their motivation, and in some others, it may create problems. As an example, when the introduced motive is using the conditioning tool, some actors may find virtual badges motivating, some others may find it useless or even stressing when it is difficult to achieve.

Self-monitoring and Surveillance: These two persuasive techniques can be perceived differently by individuals. For example, some participants stated that they really like to have their information available to their managers. They argued that this will enable them to enhance their image in their managers' mind as hard-working employees. However, other participants raised the issue that SbM can capture and store information that is not possible to capture otherwise, e.g., the exact time an employee was either working or idle. This was the concern of some employees, mentioning this would create a very high level of pressure on them as they would think the "big brother is watching them".

Tunnelling: Tunnelling can also be perceived differently. A number of participants mentioned that they would really appreciate having their tasks broken down to smaller chunks and finding it helpful in increasing their productivity. Some others stated that this will limit them and take away their freedom on how to perform their job. Hence, they found it not motivating.

Tailoring: As mentioned in Sect. 2, tailoring tries to provide employees with customised information, such as periodic feedback. Employees may find it very helpful in order to track their performance and identify areas that need more focus to be enhanced. However, the way the feedback is generated and the frequency of updating it is where employees may differ in their preferences. Failure in aligning this with the employees preferences may lead to an increase in their level of stress and mental pressure in the enterprise.

Reduction: This technique tries to make complex tasks simpler, such as automating several tasks by just one click. However, some users may argue that the use of reduction minimises the control over how they can perform the tasks, stating this will make them to "work like a robot".

Suggestion: This tries to alert the employees about performing certain behaviours on specific times. The challenge here is to detect the current activity of employees and react accordingly, as some of the tasks that employees are performing may not be measurable or even detectable by the use of software.

5 Requirements-Driven Architecture for Motivation

Motivation is highly reliant on personal preferences of the staff it is being applied to. Therefore, it is beneficial to employ a user-centred design process for SbM

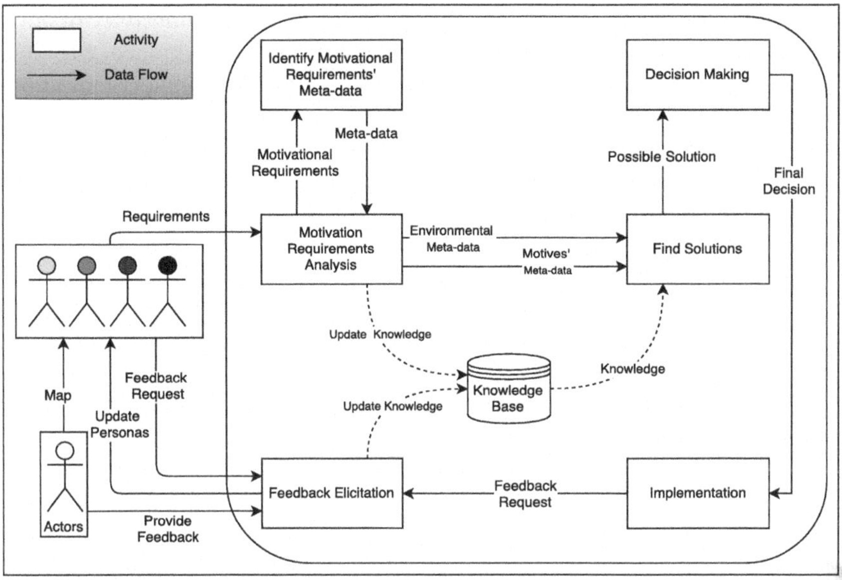

Fig. 1. Conceptual architecture for developing Software-based Motivation

in order to elicit users' requirements and preferences on SbM to ensure a more acceptable design from the perspective of users. Various aspects, e.g., contextual changes or a motive becoming boring over the course of time, may lead to a change in what employees find motivating. The dynamic nature of motivation demands an evolvable approach in order to empower detecting the need for evolution and alter the system according to the new needs and preferences. In the light of our findings, we sketch a blueprint for a conceptual architecture that facilitates a systematic evolvable user-centred design of SbM, depicted in Fig. 1.

Initially, we advocate the creation of personas, based on necessary persona constituents [9]. The identified personas can inform the design with the requirements and preferences of each persona. The provided requirements need to be further analysed by requirements engineers during the motivation requirements analysis. The thematic mapping provided in Tables 2, and 3 can be utilised to identify the motivational requirements' meta-data related to the environment, and the motives. Furthermore, the knowledge-base may be updated at this stage.

Knowledge-base stores information related to personas' preferences and requirements, motivational properties, and possible outcomes of their combinations. Its content originates from new requirements and preferences, plus feedback elicited from actors or employees during later stages of software evolution.

The meta-data, in conjunction with the knowledge taken from the knowledge-base, will be used to find solutions for achieving motivational goals of the enterprise. A recommender system can be utilised at this stage to assess the given meta-data and the content of the knowledge-base to find possible solutions.

Possible solutions, each with their possible effects on the productivity of employees and also their social and mental well-being within the workplace, will be used in the decision making process of the enterprise. Decision makers can choose a final decision based on their policies, business goals, and values.

In the implementation phase, the final decision is used to deploy the SbM in the enterprise. Besides, in order to sustain motivation and ensure the compatibility of the personas with the actual users and also to detect any changes over time, feedback elicitation will be initiated. Feedback elicitation phase tries to elicit any changes that can have an impact on the effectiveness of the design of SbM. The feedback stems from technological advances and changes in employees' preferences or the emergence of new employees in the enterprise, which yields the need for software evolution.

Software engineering can use control theory [23] to evolve and adapt the software system with the required changes through feedback loops. It sets a goal, monitors the output via sensors and measures the output with the reference point value. If the delta results in a need for a change in the software, the controller will introduce relevant changes to achieve desired outputs. However, SbM is highly reliant on users' perception. It is not a viable decision to rely on technological sensors to capture users' feelings and perceptions. The concept of social sensing [24] harnesses the cognitive power of users as monitors. This includes the value of the relevant contextual attributes and quality attributes which have not been thought of by requirements engineers or simply have emerged over time.

We advocate the use of control theory and social sensing, in developing SbM. This will enable a socially adaptive SbM solution. The concept of social adaptation [25], in the context of this study, could be seen as the ability of the system to gather people's perception on the quality of motives and their related concerns, and form a collective judgement and then decide and enact, or recommend, the best alternative to reach a motivational requirement or the best way to reach a business requirement with higher possibility of an increase in motivation.

6 Conclusion

In this paper, we argued the need for a systematic development of SbM in an enterprise. The lack of rigorous engineering principles for the development of SbM may inflict harm on the enterprise, such as creating tension and menacing social and mental well-being of employees within the workplace. Adding SbM introduces new concerns to the enterprise which need to be analysed. Various concerns are to be considered, which current methods and models do not take into account as a first-class problem. We provided a thematic mapping which paves the way for the modelling of SbM in enterprises and proposed a conceptual architecture that can utilise the thematic map for developing SbM. A further investigation is needed to study the use of this conceptual architecture in other enterprise modelling languages, e.g., goal models or process models, or the need for a new domain specific modelling language that can facilitate this conceptual architecture and comply the design of the SbM with the enterprise.

Acknowledgement. This research has been funded by Bournemouth University and a European FP7 Marie Curie CIG grant (SOCIAD Project).

References

1. Webb, E.N.: Gamification: when it works, when it doesn't. In: Marcus, A. (ed.) DUXU 2013, Part II. LNCS, vol. 8013, pp. 608–614. Springer, Heidelberg (2013)
2. Herzig, P., Ameling, M., Schill, A.: A generic platform for enterprise gamification. In: 2012 Joint Working IEEE/IFIP Conference on Software Architecture and European Conference on Software Architecture, pp. 219–223 (2012)
3. Simões, J., Redondo, R.D., Vilas, A.F.: A social gamification framework for a K-6 learning platform. Comput. Hum. Behav. **29**(2), 345–353 (2013)
4. King, D., Greaves, F., Exeter, C., Darzi, A.: Gamification: influencing health behaviours with games. J. Roy. Soc. Med. **106**(3), 76–78 (2013)
5. Kleinginna Jr., P.R., Kleinginna, A.M.: A categorized list of emotion definitions, with suggestions for a consensual definition. Motiv. Emot. **5**(4), 345–379 (1981)
6. Mitchell, T.R.: Motivation: new directions for theory, research, and practice. Acad. Manag. Rev. **7**(1), 80–88 (1982)
7. Kast, F.E., Rosenzweig, J.E.: Organization and management: a systems and contingency approach (1985)
8. Shahri, A., Hosseini, M., Phalp, K.T., Ali, R.: Motivation as a supplementary requirement. In: Proceedings of the 21st International Working Conference on REFSQ, Poster and Demo Track (2015)
9. Shahri, A., Hosseini, M., Almaliki, M., Phalp, K.T., Taylor, J., Ali, R.: Engineering software-based motivation: a persona-based approach. In: IEEE 10th International Conference on Research Challenges in Information Science (RCIS). IEEE (2016)
10. Fogg, B.J.: Persuasive technology: using computers to change what we think and do. Ubiquity (2002)
11. Shahri, A., Hosseini, M., Phalp, K., Taylor, J., Ali, R.: Towards a code of ethics for gamification at enterprise. In: Frank, U., Loucopoulos, P., Pastor, Ó., Petrounias, I. (eds.) PoEM 2014. LNBIP, vol. 197, pp. 235–245. Springer, Heidelberg (2014)
12. Hamari, J., Koivisto, J., Sarsa, H.: Does gamification work?A literature review of empirical studies on gamification. In: 47th Hawaii International Conference on System Sciences (HICSS), pp. 3025–3034 (2014)
13. Nicholson, S.: A user-centered theoretical framework for meaningful gamification. In: Games+ Learning+ Society (2012)
14. Adams, A.T., Costa, J., Jung, M.F., Choudhury, T.: Mindless computing: designing technologies to subtly influence behavior. In: ACM International Joint Conference on Pervasive and Ubiquitous Computing, pp. 719–730 (2015)
15. Khaled, R., Noble, J., Biddle, R.: An analysis of persuasive technology tool strategies. In: Proceedings of the 7th IWIPS Designing for Global Markets 7, Bridging Cultural Differences, 7–9 July 2005, Amsterdam, The Netherlands, pp. 167–173 (2005)
16. O'Donnell, A.T., Jetten, J., Ryan, M.K.: Watching over your own. Eur. J. Soc. Psychol. **40**(6), 1046–1061 (2010)
17. O'Donnell, A.T., Jetten, J., Ryan, M.K.: Who is watching over you? Eur. J. Soc. Psychol. **40**(1), 135–147 (2010)
18. Zeynep, A., Cramer, H., Holmquist, L.E., Rost, M.: Gamification and location-sharing: some emerging social conflicts (2011)

19. O'Donnell, A.T., Ryan, M.K., Jetten, J.: The hidden costs of surveillance for performance and helping behaviour. Group Process. Intergroup Relat. **16**, 246–256 (2013)
20. Li, W., Grossman, T., Fitzmaurice, G.: GamiCAD: a gamified tutorial system for first time autocad users. In: Proceedings of the 25th Annual ACM Symposium on User Interface Software and Technology, pp. 103–112. ACM (2012)
21. Seaborn, K., Fels, D.I.: Gamification in theory and action: a survey. Int. J. Hum.-Comput. Stud. **74**, 14–31 (2015)
22. Braun, V., Clarke, V.: Using thematic analysis in psychology. Qual. Res. Psychol. **3**(2), 77–101 (2006)
23. Carver, C.S., Scheier, M.F.: Control theory: a useful conceptual framework for personality-social, clinical, and health psychology. Psychol. Bull. **92**, 111 (1982)
24. Ali, R., Solis, C., Salehie, M., Omoronyia, I., Nuseibeh, B., Maalej, W.: Social sensing: when users become monitors. In: Proceedings of the 19th ACM SIGSOFT Symposium and the 13th European Conference on Foundations of Software Engineering, pp. 476–479 (2011)
25. Ali, R., Solis, C., Omoronyia, I., Salehie, M., Nuseibeh, B.: Social adaptation: when software gives users a voice. In: The 7th Inernational Conference on Evaluation of Novel Approaches to Software Engineering (ENASE 2012) (2012)

Modeling Organizational Capabilities on a Strategic Level

Janis Stirna[1(✉)], Jelena Zdravkovic[1], Martin Henkel[1], Pericles Loucopoulos[2], and Christina Stratigaki[2]

[1] Department of Computer and Systems Sciences, Stockholm University, Forum 100, 16440 Kista, Sweden
{js, jelenaz, martinh}@dsv.su.se
[2] CLMS Ltd, London, UK
periloucopoulos@icloud.com, xristinastrathgakh@gmail.com

Abstract. The notion of capability has emerged in Information System engineering as the means to support development of context dependent organizational solutions and supporting IT applications. To this end the Capability Driven Development (CDD) approach has been proposed. CDD currently focuses on designing and running applications that need to be adjusted according to changes in context, which can be seen as capability support on an operational level. This paper proposes a method component of CDD for strategic capability modeling in order to support business planning. The proposed component is to be used to analyze the organization's capabilities on a strategic level, including aspects of collaboration with other enterprises. Its application in four companies is outlined and one application of capability design for the industrial symbiosis platform presented in detail.

Keywords: Enterprise modeling · Capability modeling · Strategic planning

1 Introduction

Strategic planning is the process of defining/formulating such a general plan for an organization encapsulating its intentions and actions, encompassing a certain period of time, to achieve its vision. Traditionally, the planning process assumes that the business environment in which the organization will execute the strategic plan will remain reasonably stable for the duration of the foreseen time period. In modern world this however becomes less of a norm because new and unexpected business opportunities and threats arise, demands change, as well as environmental and security risks increase.

To respond to the need of continuous adaptation an EU-FP7 project "Capability as a Service in digital enterprises" (CaaS) has been initiated [1]. Its aim is to develop a support for the capture and analysis of changing business context in the design of information systems (IS) using the capability notion. Capability is seen as a fundamental abstraction to describe what a core business does [2]. Capability is defined "*as an ability and capacity for an enterprise to deliver value, either to customers or shareholders, right beneath the business strategy*" [3], or *"the ability of one or more*

J. Horkoff et al. (Eds.): PoEM 2016, LNBIP 267, pp. 257–271, 2016.
DOI: 10.1007/978-3-319-48393-1_18

resources to deliver a specified type of effect or a specified course of action" [4]. The CaaS project strives towards developing an integrated methodology for context-aware business and IT solutions, under the name Capability Driven Development (CDD).

The CDD methodology is based on *Enterprise Modeling* (EM), *context modeling*, *variability modeling*, *adjustment algorithms*, and *patterns* for capturing best practices. The current thrust of the capability driven approach to IS development is to make IS designs more accessible to business stakeholders by enabling them to use the capability notion to explicate their business needs especially concerning context dependent variability. This can be seen as capability support on an operational level. It is however insufficient for business planners because they need to assess the organization's capabilities on a strategic level. To this end the objective of this paper is *to extend the CDD approach with a strategic planning phase*.

In essence CDD follows the principles of the Model Driven Development (MDD) paradigm, which implies a built-in drawback because it mostly relies on models defined on a relatively low abstraction level. In contrast, EM captures organizational knowledge and provides the necessary motivation and input for designing IS. Hence there is a need to connect the development of CDD with more strategic way of working. We envision that EM has a potentially important role to play in this process because it has been used for strategy development and in particular in the context of IS development [5, 6].

The rest of the paper is organized as follows. Section 2 outlines the research approach. Section 3 summarizes the current use of the capability concept and the CDD methodology. Section 4 presents the method component for Strategic Capability Modeling. Section 5 presents one of the application cases and briefly summarizes the current experiences of capability modeling relevant to the proposed method component. Section 6 provides concluding remarks and issues of future work.

2 Research Approach

The work in this paper is motivated by the industrial use cases that are a part of the CaaS following the principles of Design Science Research (DSR) [7].

By adopting DSR as a paradigm, IS engineering aims to resolve problems by creating innovative scientific artifacts through development- and evaluation cycles within a real life context. The creation of artifacts is iterative and incremental leading to a practical solution. The essential activities of DSR concern the explication of the problem, an outline of the artifact with the related requirements, an artifact's design and development, as well as its application, evaluation, and communication.

The CDD methodology is the main design artifact of the CaaS project. Its purpose is enabling development of IS able to adhere to changes in business context through variability at run-time. CDD methodology as design artifact should be seen as a composite. Its parts, such as the meta-model and the various method components (e.g. capability design and context modeling) are also design artifacts in their own right. This paper presents one such CDD method component, one that addresses strategic capability modeling.

During the DSR process, knowledge was attained through iterative and incremental cycles of constructing the design artifact according to the needs of multiple stakeholders including researchers, technology developers, and practitioners using capability designs for their business purposes. More specifically, participatory modeling workshops, focus-group sessions, interviews with experienced practitioners, and on-line questionnaires were the main techniques used for problem explication and requirements elicitation. The results of this work are reported in [8]. The artifact presented in this paper was developed and validated during a number of design cycles, based on the use cases at SIV (Germany) and CLMS (UK).

3 Background to Capability Driven Development

3.1 Capability as a Concept

The notion of capability has a growing presence in the current business and IT alignment and IS development frameworks starting from more business-oriented such as Business Architecture and Business Modeling, towards the alignment-oriented represented by Enterprise Architecture (EA), and EM. In brief, the emergence of the use of the capability notion seems to have three key motivations: (a) in the context of business planning, it is becoming recognized as a fundamental component to describe what a core business does and, in particular, its ability of delivering value that is relevant to the business strategy; (b) in IS development, it makes IS designs more accessible to business stakeholders by enabling them to use the capability notion to describe their requirements; and (c) it supports the configurability of operations on a higher level than services, business process, resources, and technology solutions.

Capability is used in a wide variety of approaches and frameworks and while there are clearly identifiable similarities, there are also substantial differences in its use. For example, OMG's proposal for Business Architecture (BA) [9] uses business capability for describing what a business does - specifically, it is an ability or capacity that the business may possess or exchange to achieve certain outcome. The resulting capability map encompasses the whole view of what a business does. The Value Delivery Modeling Language (VDML) [10] defines a modeling language for analysis and design of the operations of an enterprise with a focus on the creation and exchange of value. Its aim is to provide an abstraction of the operations appropriate for business planners. VDML links strategy and business models to the activities, roles, and capabilities that run the enterprise. VDML defines capability as the ability of an organization to perform a particular type of work and may involve people with particular skills and knowledge, intellectual property, defined practices, operating facilities, tools and equipment.

Capability is also a key concept of EA frameworks. E.g., Department of Defense Architecture Framework (DOFAF) [11] defines capability as "the ability to achieve a desired effect under specified (performance) standards and conditions through combinations of ways and means (activities and resources) to perform a set of activities". Condition means the state of an environment or situation in which a performer performs; desired effect means desired state of a resource; resource means data, information, performers, materiel, or personnel types that are produced or consumed.

The NATO Architecture Framework (NAF) [4] defines capability as "the ability of one or more resources to deliver a specified type of effect or a specified course of action". The NAF meta-model defines the following key relationships of capability:

- Capabilities may be specialized into more specific capabilities, composed of several capabilities, as well as dependent on other capabilities.
- Capability when applied is associated with measurable categories.
- Capability elaborated into Capability configuration package, which is used to configure resources for capability implementation.
- Enterprise phase exhibits a capability. The connection between capabilities and goals is realized through enduring phase of the enterprise.
- Capability support an enduring task by defining capability for task.

In summary, the current use of capability is concerned with organization's ability for delivering a business function. The "integrational" nature of capability is used to bind the strategic/intentional part of the organizational design with the operational or technical parts. Hence, capability should be seen as a key concept relevant to both strategic planners as well as operational planners. In some of the approaches capability has its own view, for instance, the EA frameworks used in military (e.g. DODAF, NAF), including several sub-views. The capability-centric views are then linked to other views - for services, processes, infrastructure, etc. The majority of the frameworks is so far not providing a methodological guidance for capability elicitation and development.

3.2 Overview of the CDD Methodology

The CDD methodology consists of method components [12]. To structure the methodology, the components have been divided into upper-level method components and method extensions. Each upper-level component describes a certain application area and may also contain sub-components. The upper-level method components are currently the following:

- *Capability Design Process* guiding how to design, evaluate and develop capabilities by using process models, goal models and other types of models.
- *Enterprise Modeling guiding* the creation of enterprise models that are used as input for capability design.
- *Context Modeling* analyzing the capability context, and the variations needed to deal with variations.
- *Reuse of capability design* guiding the elicitation and documentation of patterns for capability design.
- *Run-time Delivery Adjustment* adjusting capability at runtime.

The overall CDD process includes three cycles (1) capability design; (2) capability delivery; and (3) capability refinement/updating. The capability design cycle often starts with *Enterprise Modeling*, i.e. by a business request for a new capability - the request might be initiated by strategic business planning, changes in context, or discovery of new business opportunities requiring reconfiguration of existing or the creation of new goals, business processes or services, and other EM elements. This is followed with a formalized definition of requested capabilities and definition of the relevant contexts according, linking with relevant capability delivery patterns as well as supporting IT applications *(design).*

In addition, several method extensions addressing specific business challenges to which the CDD methodology have been developed by the CaaS consortium:

- The *Capability Ready Business Services* method extension covers the transition step from textual instructions and activity descriptions to business process models ready capability modeling. With this extension many business services in Business Process Outsourcing can be subject to capability based redesign.
- The *Prepare Local and Global Optimization* method extension for the optimization of service delivery and balancing local optimization of services provided to a client and global optimization from a service provider perspective.
- The *Evolutionary Development of Business Information Exchange Capability* method extension for developing capabilities in the case when pre-existing capability delivery solution must be tailored to the needs of a new client.
- The *Integration of CDD and MDD* method extension is analyzing the potential of integrating MDD and CDD concepts in situations when a new capability delivery application needs to be developed, which can be done by an MDD tool.
- The *Analysis of Capability Relationships* method extension is proposing an analysis of capability relationships and mapping of capabilities to delivered services. Through the business case analysis of the CaaS project, it was noticed that during the process of identifying business capabilities it was useful to describe them in relation to other capabilities.
- The *Predictive analysis* method component describes capability delivery adjustment using predicted context values to attain proactive behavior.
- The *Capacity evaluation* method component evaluates capability delivery capacity requirements to determine capability's suitability to context ranges.

3.3 Capability Meta-Model

The theoretical and methodological foundation for pattern use in capability-oriented software applications is provided by the core capability meta-model (CMM) in Fig. 1, and in details presented in [13]. CMM is developed on the basis of requirements from the industrial project partners, and related research on capabilities. Within CDD, patterns are envisioned as reusable solutions for reaching business goals under specific situational context. Individually, they are intended to describe best practices for businesses, and in a collection to form a repository of capability delivery patterns.

In brief, the meta-model has three main sections:

(a) *Enterprise model,* representing organizational designs with Goals, KPIs, Processes (with concretizations as Process Variants), and Resources;
(b) *Context*, represented with Context Set for which a Capability is designed and Context Situation at runtime that is monitored and according to which the deployed solutions should be adjusted. Context Indicators are used for measuring the context properties (Measuring Property); and

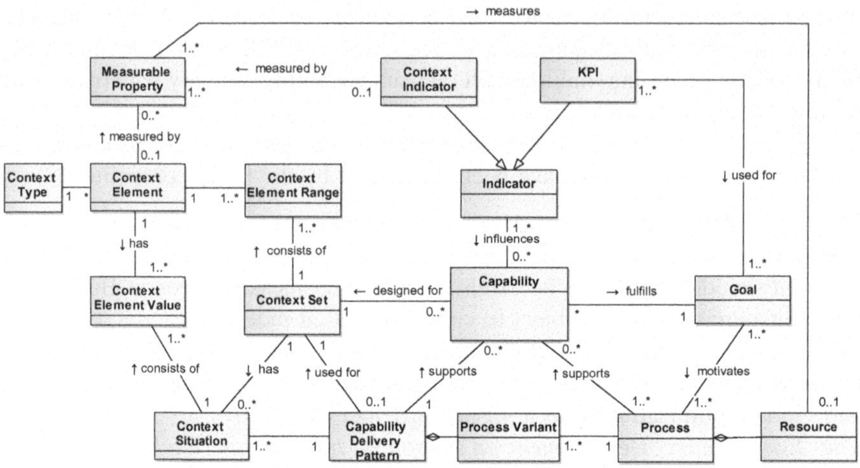

Fig. 1. A core meta-model for supporting Capability Driven Development.

(c) *Patterns,* for delivering Capability by reusable solutions for reaching Goals under different Context Situations. Each pattern describes how a certain Capability is to be delivered within a certain Context Situation and what Processes Variants and Resources are needed to support a Context Set.

Figure 1 is a simplified version of CMM showing only the key components of CDD and omitting, for instance, constructs for representation of goal decomposition relationships and process variants. Complete version including definitions of components is available in [1, 12].

3.4 The Process of Capability Design

The process of capability design considers existing Enterprise Models and other organizational design as well as patterns in order to elaborate a capability design. The process is essentially comprised of three phases as shown in Fig. 2.

Step 1: Capability Design. There are three alternative pathways of proceeding with capability design, shown in Fig. 3.
Step 2: Capability Evaluation. This step checks capability development feasibility from the business and technical perspective before committing to capability implementation.
Step 3: Development of Capability Delivery Application. The design specifications serve as a basis for modifying/implementing capability delivery applications, which are created using methods and technology of preference by the capability stakeholders. The indicators for monitoring and the adjustment algorithms are packaged and passed over to a Capability Navigation Application (CNA) for monitoring capability delivery.

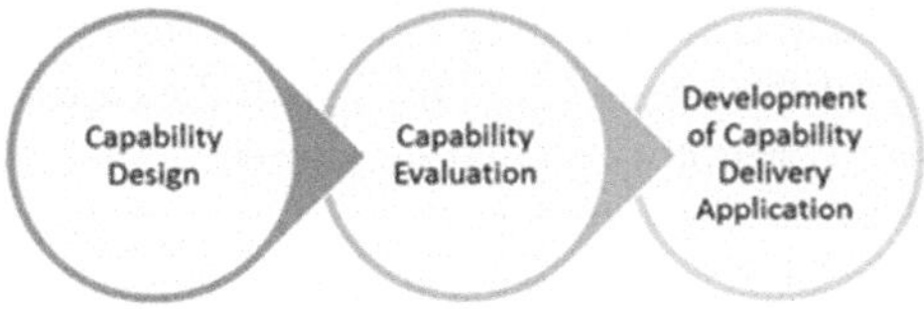

Fig. 2. Capability flow.

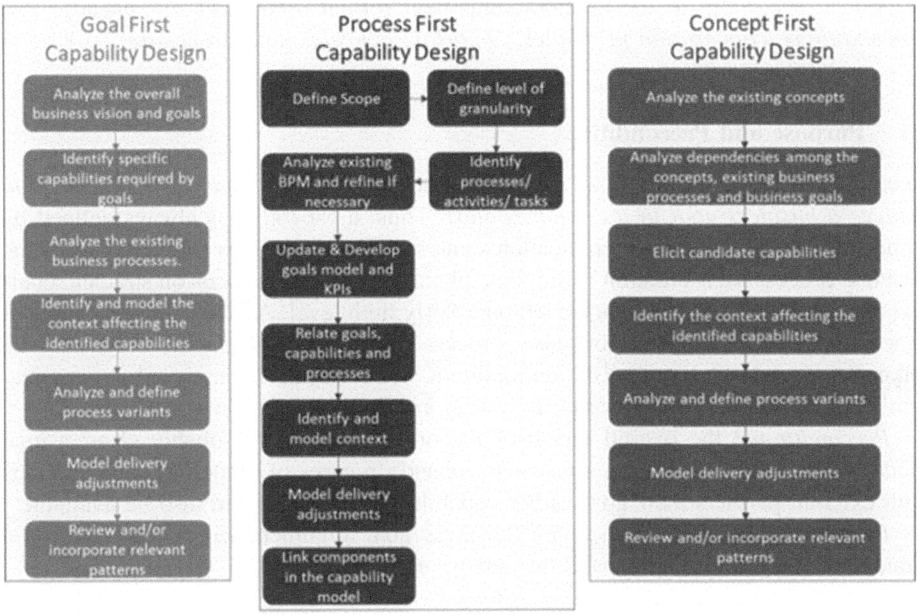

Fig. 3. Alternative approaches for capability design.

4 Strategic Capability Modeling

A business capability is related to the business goals and the context within which it exists. A business analyst, especially in the situations where one organization collaborates with others to deliver value, i.e. an analyst working with partners, needs to have a conceptually clear view of what might constitute a capability so that a revealing dialogue with partners may take place in order to ensure that the capabilities are identified, information about them is recorded, and finally an initial model is built and validated by the partners. This motivates the need for a capability collaboration concept in order to be able to express the possible relations among the different business capabilities within a company. In the context of collaboration there is a need to distinguish between *internal capabilities* and *external capabilities*. The details of external capabilities owned by some other enterprise may not be important to know, or indeed as will probably be the most common case - may never be known, since such capabilities are considered as competitive advantage to the owner's enterprise. What matters however, is that such an external capability is required in order to deliver an internal capability, i.e. capability of the organization for which the capability design is created. Hence, the ownership of a capability should be shown.

Organizations need to be supported in their efforts of analyzing their capability portfolio in terms of what capabilities it currently possesses, i.e. is able to deliver, what capabilities it wants to deliver in the future, and it is able to achieve that. Hence a concept of capability status needs to be considered. To this end a method component for strategic capability analysis is proposed. In the reminder of this section we will describe it according to the method-component format used in [12] – *purpose and preconditions, cooperation principles, important concepts,* and *procedure*.

4.1 Purpose and Preconditions

According to [12] a *capability is the ability and capacity that enable an enterprise to achieve a business goal in a certain context*. Thus, a capability is always defined by some business goal and an application context, as well as it is delivered by some business process. In a situation of strategic planning we need to focus on strategic goals and analyze how they can be achieved on a fairly high level. At this level the details of exactly which patterns and business process variations will be involved may be unknown as well as they may be unimportant. What should be analyzed is organization's ability and capacity to reach its vision in general.

Preconditions: the overall vision of the organization is reasonably clear; a goal model describing organization's vision is created. In cases of modeling collaborations with external partners their goal and/or capability structure should also be available.

Purpose: to create and document business goal alignment with capabilities on a strategic level and to map capabilities among each other.

4.2 Cooperation Principles

The roles and stakeholders identified in the CDD methodology [12] also apply for this method component. The following stakeholders are to be involved:

- *Business service manager*: Responsible for management strategies for changes in business and to identify opportunities for capitalizing on these changes.
- *Business analyst:* a person who analyses the business models and proposes and guides changes in the business models.
- *Capability analyst:* Analyses information about capabilities and operating context, to predict evolution of the context and to take advantage of these predictions by providing new services or improving existing services.
- *Capability provider:* responsible of providing capabilities to the customer.
- *Customer (client):* The end user who benefits from the capabilities.

The way of working should be based on participatory stakeholder involvement with the main focus on capturing the knowledge, i.e. creating the model. Hence, simple tools for documenting might be useful and the team does not necessarily need to use the

Capability Design Tool. It is also possible that while using this method component the developers may also switch to method component Capability Design in order to focus on detailed design of a selected capability.

4.3 Important Concepts

The following concepts are used in this method component:

- *Capability*. Capability is the ability and capacity that enable an enterprise to achieve a business goal in a certain context. Capabilities may be considered as *internal capabilities* and *external capabilities*. The details of external capabilities owned by some other enterprises. They have relationships with business goals of external partners.
- *Goal*. Goal is a desired state of affairs that needs to be attained. Goals can be refined into sub-goals and should typically be expressed in measurable terms such as KPIs. Other modeling components such as problems, opportunities, and causes may also be included in goal modeling. In case of modeling collaboration with external partners it is recommended that the goal hierarchies of the capability delivery organization and partners be clearly identified.
- *Process*. *Process* is series of actions that are performed in order to achieve particular result. A Process supports Goals and has input and produces output in terms of information and/or material.
- *Context Set*. Context Set describes the set of Context Elements including their permitted ranges that are relevant for design and delivery of a specific Capability. While using this method component the links to Context Elements may be omitted, because they might be unknown at the time of strategic capability modeling.

4.4 Procedure

The procedure considers organization's vision and its business partner goals as input. In case this information is unavailable, outdated, or likely conflicts are identified, method component *Enterprise Modeling* should be used for modeling of the strategy or the organization.

Step1: Identify goals in the goal hierarchy that would be appropriate for motivating capabilities. Goal hierarchy typically has strategic goals on the top and operational goals on the bottom. Many of the top goals are visionary statements and are refined into sub-goals. Those sub-goals that are formulated reasonably concretely and have specified KPIs should be considered for motivating capabilities.

Step 2: Analyze goal sub-hierarchies. Typically goals and sub-goals are further refined into more sub-goals in such a way that the overall goal hierarchy consists of sub-hierarchies each of them dealing with a particular aspect of the organization. Many sub-goals in principle are similar to the goals immediately above them in the goal hierarchy, i.e. they are expressed reasonably precisely, have sub-goals on their own, and are linked to KPIs. These kinds of goals should be considered for motivating capabilities.

Step 3: Define capabilities for the selected sub-goals. There can be several capabilities for reaching one goal. Hence, naming of capabilities should reflect the difference, e.g. for what context it is suitable.
Step 4: Define context sets for each capability. At this stage the context sets can be expressed without explicit definition of ranges of context elements. This is permitted because identifying context elements can be done later by using *Capability Design* method component that requires analyzing what measurable properties are available and can be monitored at run-time.
Step 5: Identify external capabilities by analyzing collaborations with external partners. Consider partner goal hierarchies and analyze how their goals relate to capability delivery organization's goals. For the related goals repeat steps 1 to 4 to identify capabilities involved in business collaborations. If partner goal models are unavailable, analyze the overall business model and the collaboration mode.
Step 6: Develop capability relationships. This can be done by following the method component *Analysis of Capability Relationships* described in [14]. At this stage both internal and external capabilities are analyzed. Relationships among capabilities are specified in terms of: capability ownership if capabilities are delivered by external partners; capability collaboration if several capabilities are used to achieve a goal; and capability composition if a capability consists of smaller capabilities.

5 Experiences of Capability Modeling

The CDD methodology components have been developed in the CaaS project and applied in the four industrial use cases, namely at

1. SIV AG (Germany) for standard business processes outsourcing and execution capability,
2. Fresh T Limited (UK) for maritime compliance capability,
3. CLMS Ltd (UK) for collaborative software development using the MDD technology and industrial symbiosis application in particular, and
4. Everis (Spain) for service promotion capability, marriage registration capability, SOA platform capability.

For the purpose of illustrating the proposed method component we have chosen to present the use case of CLMS. Its core business is model driven software development with the zAppDev tool[1]. This use case is based on development and running a website for industrial symbiosis (i-symbiosis) to facilitate the exchange of waste materials among organizations; more in depth presentation of the case and the corresponding capability designs is available in [14]. Considering the core business of CLMS, the following capabilities have been identified: Domain analysis, Architecture design, Business intelligence, Cloud migration, IT change management, Application development, Continuous engineering, Integration APIs connectivity infrastructure, and Software development as a service. They all contribute to the overall core capability of

[1] http://www.zappdev.com.

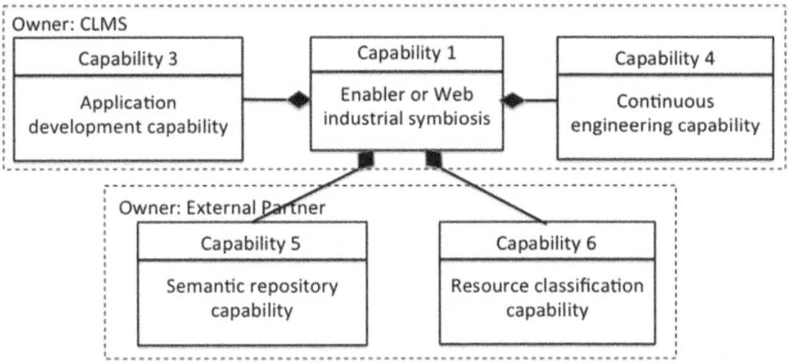

Fig. 4. Capability map of CLMS, adapted from [14].

CLMS, namely, Adaptive and extensible software development. In principle they reflect what a software development company of this kind normally does to reach its business goals. For the case of i-symbiosis, some of these capabilities of CLMS need to be combined with external partner capabilities to deliver capability "*Enabler of web industrial symbiosis*". This capability encompasses the CLMS capabilities and two supporting capacities of an external partner, namely, Semantic repository capability and Resource classification capability. The map of capabilities relevant to development and running the i-Symbiosis is shown in Fig. 4. This is however not sufficient, because there are specific cases of context changes that require sub-capabilities of capability 1, shown in Fig. 5. Due to space limitations this model omits the process variants needed for delivery of sub-capabilities.

Based on the three contextual factors that can affect the industrial symbiosis (*location*, *resources*, *legislation*), three sub-capabilities where designed for situations when the monitoring and adjustment of the existing capabilities was deemed necessary. In each situation three different levels of adjustments are possible: automated adjustments, semi-automated adjustments, and manual adjustments.

The 'Determine Relevance Rating' sub-capability (Capability 1.1 in Fig. 5) makes it possible to calculate a relevance rating based on the type of resources and organizations offering these resources. Matches with high relevance rating are used for proposing synergies. The i-Symbiosis platform shows the possible matches for synergies after calculating a rate of relevance of the two organizations. If this rate is lower than 60 % then the platform rejects the remaining weak matches.

The 'Resource Description and Classification' sub-capability (Capability 1.2) enables the detailed description of resources in order to enable a better match between organizations. The Capability Navigation Application monitoring the performance of i-Symbiosis is checking the compatibility of resources during the match making procedure. The successful resource compatibility is essential for every possible synergy between two organizations. The descriptions of resources to exchange can impact the number of possible synergies (matches). If their quality is low, there will be difficulty to perform matching and hence create synergies. Hence, monitoring this sub-capability would be the early detection of loss in matching power.

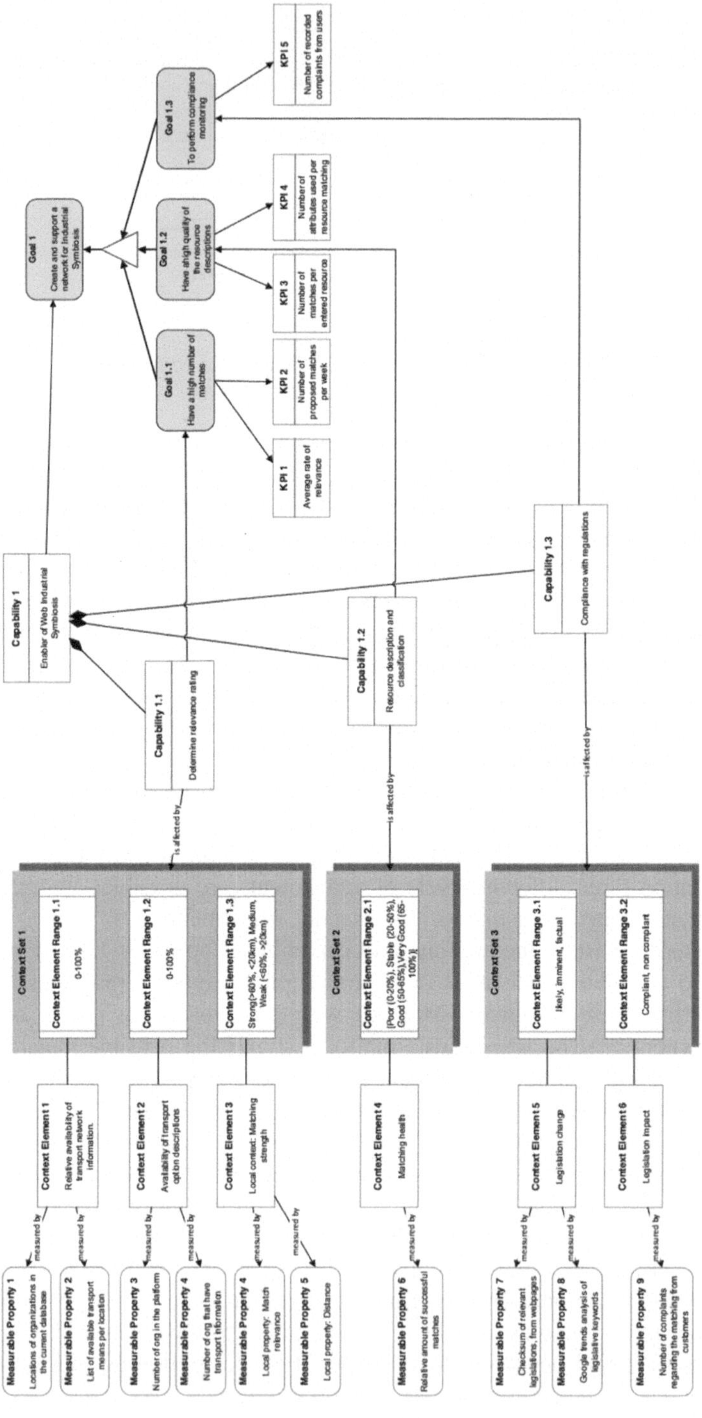

Fig. 5. Capability design for capability enable web industrial symbiosis [14].

Table 1. Overview of strategic capability modeling in CaaS use cases.

Step	SIV	FreshTL	CLMS	Everis
Step1: Identify goals in the goal hierarchy	Yes Goal hierarchies for SIV and for its customers created	Yes Elaborated goal model created for FreshTL's customer	Yes Elaborated goal model created for CLMS	Yes Elaborated goal hierarchy for Everis
Step 2: Analyze goal sub-hierarchies	Yes Goal hierarchy analyzed	Yes Several goal sub-hierarchies	Yes Several goal sub-hierarchies	Yes Several goal sub-hierarchies
Step 3: Define capabilities	Yes Linked to sub-goals	Yes Linked to sub-goals	Yes Linked to sub-goals	Yes Linked to sub-goals
Step 4: Define context sets	Yes, together with context ranges and elements	Partially, defined only for key capabilities	Yes, together with context ranges and elements	Yes, together with context ranges and elements
Step 5: Identify external capabilities	No	Yes, based on the overall business model	Yes based on external partner offers	No
Step 6: Develop capability relationships.	No	Yes Ownership, collaboration, composition	Yes Ownership, collaboration, composition.	No

The 'Compliant with Regulations' capability (Capability 1.3) ensures that the proposed synergies are correct according to the legislative context because it affects the way goods and materials can be handled. E.g. what is being considered as hazardous can differ between countries and change over time. The current capability is designed for a certain legislative context, in this case Greece. If the context changes, the capability may vanish or become useless, hence changes in the legislation need to be monitored and if they are detected their impact should be assessed with respect to possible capability redesign. This should normally be done manually.

Considering other use cases of the project, the method component presented in this paper has not been applied in its entirety at this point. Its parts (the different steps and modeling components) however have been applied and hence we can argue for a partial validation of this method component. In this regard, Table 1 summarizes the steps of the procedure and how they have been carried out in the use cases.

6 Concluding Remarks

The CDD methodology currently focuses on IS development and supports designing and running business applications that need to be adjusted according to changes in the application context, which can be seen as capability support on an operational level. This paper proposes a CDD methodology component for strategic capability modeling in order to support business planners. The proposed component is to be used for analyzing the organization's capabilities on a strategic level. In essence, it aims to bridge the gap between the outcomes that the contemporary approaches for strategic planning produce with the kinds of inputs that are typically needed for application design and adjustment according to situational contingencies. CDD encompasses application design and monitoring in an integral way. The possibility of designing organization's own capabilities together with capabilities offered by external partners help solving the difficulties of assessing what parts of the capability are delivered by outside companies including raising awareness about what aspects of the capability delivery cannot be immediately influenced once changes are needed. Once the capability is running, the proposed method component allows organizations to monitor capability delivery from a more strategic perspective e.g. by providing an overview of performance vs targets. The use of models for capability designs reduces some of the complexity of this task, which would essentially contribute to *capability driven management* of organizations.

Concerning issues for future work, the key area of work is adoption of the CDD methodology in practice. According to the investigation of what aspects of EM approaches stimulate their productization and hence their adoption [15] the following factors should be considered: (1) EM maturity gap particularly focusing on industrial relevance of the method, (2) method and tool development process, (3) application context, (4) marketing and sales aspects, as well as (5) product aspects. The process of CDD methodology development has been primarily focused on the first three factors targeting inbound productization [16] by ensuring industrial relevance by user driven and systematic methodology development resulting in a methodology that is easily extendable according to situational needs. The later two factors directly targeting outbound productization [16] can be seen as issues for future work even if marketing aspects are well addressed by having a methodology that address real business problems and provides value to its users. Development of the product aspects such as alignment with standards, packaging the methodology and tool as well as focusing on the needs of a specific market are being elaborated currently and are also issues for future work.

References

1. EU FP7 CaaS Project. Capability as a Service for digital enterprises, proj. no. 611351. http://caas-project.eu/
2. Ulrich, W., Rosen, M.: The business capability map: building a foundation for business/it alignment. Cutter Consortium for Business and Enterprise Architecture (2012)
3. OPENGROUP TOGAF - enterprise architecture methodology, version 9.1 (2012). http://www.opengroup.org/togaf/
4. UK Ministry of Defence: NATO Architecture Framework v4.0 Documentation (2013). http://nafdocs.org/modem
5. Giannoulis, C., Zikra, I., Bergholtz, M., Zdravkovic, J., Stirna, J., Johannesson, P.: A comparative analysis of enterprise modeling approaches for modeling business strategy. In: PoEM Short Papers 2013, pp. 193–204 (2013). http://ceur-ws.org/Vol-1023/paper19.pdf
6. Niehaves, B., Stirna, J.: Participative enterprise modelling for balanced scorecard implementation. In: ECIS 2006, pp. 286–298 (2006)

7. Hevner, A.R., March, S.T., Park, J., Ram, S.: Design science in information systems research. MIS Q. **28**(1), 75–105 (2004)
8. Bērziša, S., Bravos, G., Gonzalez, T., Czubayko, U., España, S., Grabis, J., Henkel, M., Jokste, L., Kampars, J., Koc, H., Kuhr, J., Llorca, C., Loucopoulos, P., Juanes Pascual, R., Sandkuhl, K., Simic, H., Stirna, J., Zdravkovic, J.: Deliverable D1.4: REQUIREMENTS specification for CDD, CaaS – Capability as a Service for Digital Enterprises, FP7 proj. 611351. Riga Technical University (2014). http://caas-project.eu/deliverables/
9. OMG Business Architecture Special Interest Group&Guild. "What Is Business Architecture?". http://bawg.omg.org/, http://www.businessarchitectureguild.org/
10. OMG: Value Delivery Metamodel, v. 1.0 (2013). http://www.omg.org/spec/VDML/1.0/
11. Department of Defense: DoD Architecture Framework Version 2.0, 28 May 2009. http://dodcio.defense.gov/Portals/0/Documents/DODAF/DoDAF_v2-02_web.pdf
12. Bērziša, S., España, S., Grabis, J., Henkel, M., Jokste, L., Kampars, J., Koç, H., Sandkuhl, K., Stirna, J., Valverde, F., Zdravkovic, J.: Deliverable 5.2: The Initial Version of Capability Driven Development Methodology, FP7 proj. 611351 CaaS – Capability as a Service in digital enterprises. Stockholm University (2015). DOI:10.13140/RG.2.1.2399.4965
13. Bērziša, S., Bravos, G., Gonzalez, T., Czubayko, U., España, S., Grabis, J., Henkel, M., Jokste, L., Kampars, J., Koç, H., Kuhr, J., Llorca, C., Loucopoulos, P., Juanes, R., Pastor, O., Sandkuhl, K., Simic, H., Stirna, J., Valverde, F., Zdravkovic, J.: Capability driven development: an approach to designing digital enterprises. Bus. Inf. Syst. Eng. **57**(1), 15–25 (2015)
14. Loucopoulos, P., Stratigaki, C., Henkel, M., Stirna, J., Zorgios, Y., Migiakis, A.: Deliverable 3.2: CaaS method extension: Capability Modelling for Collaborative Development of Capability Delivery Applications, FP7 proj. 611351 CaaS – Capability as a Service in digital enterprises. CLMS Ltd., UK ((2015)
15. Yilmaz, N., Stirna, J.: Factors influencing productization of enterprise modeling: a qualitative inquiry into the scandinavian strand of methods and tools. In: Ralyté, J., España, S., Pastor, Ó. (eds.) PoEM 2015. LNBIP, vol. 235, pp. 193–208. Springer, Heidelberg (2015). doi:10.1007/978-3-319-25897-3_13
16. Simula, H., Lethtimäki, T., Salo, J.: Re-thinking the product: from innovative technology to productized offering. In: Proceedings of the 19th International Society for Professional Innovation Management Conference, Tours, France (2008)

Explorative Survey into Goals, Focus, Experiences and Extent of Enterprise-Wide Process Modelling in Practice

Frank Wolff(✉)

DHBW-Mannheim, Information Science,
Coblitzallee 1-9, 68163 Mannheim, Germany
frank.wolff@dhbw-mannheim.de

Abstract. Enterprise modelling promises many potential returns to companies but also entails some challenges for those institutions who engage in enterprise-wide modelling activities. To improve understanding in this area, an explorative survey has been devised with a number of companies from diverse industries. The focus is on business process modelling but also IT models are addressed. Most companies align their enterprise process modelling to one leading goal. While the extent of the model portfolios is very impressive, modelling often still does not cover all of the company. Further in many instances reported issues were the motivation of experts to cooperate with modelers, the integration of organizational and IT-models, and modelling tool related topics.

Keywords: Modelling goals · Modelling practice · Enterprise modelling · Business process modelling · Experiences

1 Introduction

Enterprise modelling comprises many facets, notably strategy, organization, and resources, particularly IT-systems. In practice and research diverse modelling methods have been devised (e.g., MEMO [1], ArchiMate [2], BEN [3], or ARIS [4]). In this but also other respects, research in enterprise modelling is predominantly constructive or technically oriented. Only a smaller part of research is concerned with the creation and usage of models in an extensive organizational context.

To provide some more insights in this field, the research documented in this paper is set up to gather (a) experiences on major issues in enterprise modelling and (b) evidence on the extent and the complexity of practical modelling in companies.

Communication with practitioners in enterprise modelling often indicates that enterprise-wide modelling is not executed as intended by management and specialists in charge of modelling methodologies. Therefore, also unresolved questions, dependencies between different areas and frictions in organizational practice are searched for, as they are important for management of enterprise-wide modelling and can well direct new research.

J. Horkoff et al. (Eds.): PoEM 2016, LNBIP 267, pp. 272–285, 2016.
DOI: 10.1007/978-3-319-48393-1_19

1.1 Explorative Research in Enterprise Modelling Practice

Enterprise modelling is in many ways crucial to company interests. Information presented in the models is oriented towards future plans of the company, or it can uncover problems which would otherwise remain unnoticed. For these reasons, it is rather subtle to gather and compile findings on practical usage of enterprise modelling in companies. In Sects. 1.3 and 2 the related problems will be discussed in more detail.

This paper is a first step in research to collect practical experiences in enterprises on the usage of modelling, its extent and main issues to manage enterprise-wide modelling activities. It is connected to endeavours to better understand the underlying mechanisms and dependencies in large concerted modelling activities to support its management and sustainability [5, 6].

It complements other research like (a) related research in theoretical areas with validation by company examples, e.g.: [7, 8], (b) reports from industrial practice cases, e.g.: [9, 10] or (c) surveys on influential factors for success of enterprise modelling in industry [11, 12].

1.2 Issues in Enterprise-Wide Modelling

Enterprise modelling comprises a plethora of aspects which influence the results an organization can reap from its modelling effort [13]. Therefore, in an exploratory study to get more insight into influential factors for management, only a few prominent aspects can be investigated. Hence, the survey centres on: (a) the organizations and their goals which direct the modelling, (b) basic methodological aspects, like, the modelling language, the organization of model development and integration between different kinds of models, (c) crucial elements are captured in two categories, (c1) the modelling tool and (c2) further emphasized experiences. (d) Finally some results from enterprise-wide modelling are reported, the extent of modelling, success stories and economic issues. Figure 1 depicts an overview on the topics.

1.3 Consideration of Potential Research Methods on Enterprise Modelling Practice

Research in enterprise-wide modelling practice is challenging in various respects. The company models often contain vital information of and for an organization. Therefore, also their creation and other aspects are handled confidential. Another aspect is comparability and precision of data. In many contexts of business research one is accustomed to a high degree of precision, especially, if information can be gathered by measurements. But the field of modelling is quite diverse and highly specialized. Also measurements are rarely used. Hence, a study in the practice of enterprise modelling usually relies on information provided by experts. This and the differentiation of organizations advise to consider the effect of varying perspectives and potentially resulting differences in interpretations.

Before considering the demands of adequate interpretation of collected data, the method to gather information must be determined. Generally, there are a number of

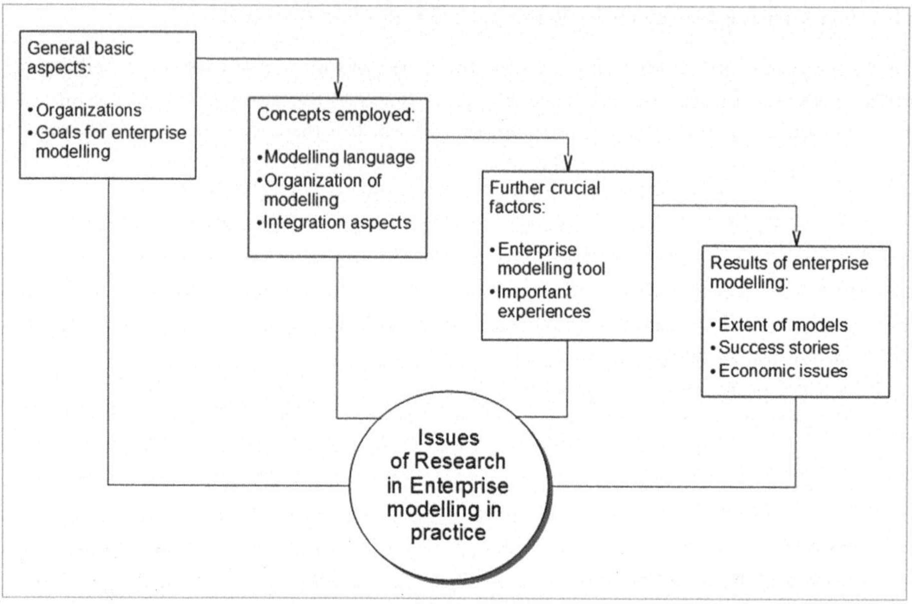

Fig. 1. Issues for research in practice of enterprise-wide modelling activities.

different methods available to collect evidence from a number of organizations. Most prominent are questionnaires and interviews [14].

A questionnaire can be well adapted to standardized or properly understood objects of investigation. As the practice of enterprise modelling as a wider organizational effort has seldom been described in a homogenous frame, an investigation with a questionnaire is not advisable. Also the response rate, in this kind of surveys, is quite low and would probably distort the results [15].

For these reasons and because of the exploratory character, it was decided to base the survey on semi-structured interviews with practitioners. The discussions were directly documented in notes and compiled afterwards. Unclear information was validated after the interviews in a number of cases. Criteria for the selection of partners were: (a) the organization practiced a concerted modelling covering most or crucial parts of its business; (b) it employed a central repository for integrating different results; and (c) the organizations should vary in respect of size or industry or another major characteristic to provide for a more realistic account of enterprise modelling in practice.

In the beginning, it was intended to investigate different perspectives in enterprise models, like business process models, IT models, and strategic models. However in the early stages, most contacts were established with practitioners in the field of business process modelling. This provided a common basis and had positive effects for the documentation of the findings. While not looking at enterprise architecture models directly, nevertheless, the IT perspective was very prominent as for numerous companies the processes are fundamental for IT-system development. Another topic, which was regularly addressed, was supplementing the business processes with relevant information on supporting IT resources.

There are some limits inherent in this kind of approach and research. They are rooted in the subjective judgements and interpretations of the participants, and further connected with the impossibility to reach statistically satisfying samples. Nevertheless, the research is based on input from very experienced practitioners with in depth knowledge on the topic. Also often different hierarchical levels of the organization were involved like senior manager and modelling specialist. So information from different perspectives had been collected. Sometimes a person was only able to provide information from one perspective or specific information was not available. This is a limitation in this survey. It is due to the sophisticated topic and the exploratory character of the talks. Anyway, very illuminative, although not all desirable, information could be obtained. To account for this, the specific number of entries has been documented in most findings of this survey. For the reasons stated, it is in a number of cases lower than the total of the surveyed organizations.

The general method used was the interview. But as the interview part was complemented with information provided by the researcher, the term *talk* is used frequently in this paper. The organizations represented in the survey stem from diverse industries and also have different sizes. However, there are some industries represented with a higher proportion as in industry in general.

Another challenge was to interpret the individual elements of information in an appropriate way. In this respect the interpreter had to work carefully, as the statements from the practitioners in many cases were bound in their experiences and background [16]. It was an advantage that the researcher had worked in this field for many years. So it was usually possible to specify the specific terms used and information given by inquiring their context and meaning.

2 Results of the Survey on Selected Organizations

The talks with the organizations presented in this study started in the middle of 2015 and the last was in spring 2016. When this research was initiated, it was intended to focus on qualitative issues but also collect some quantitative data. This quantitative data was meant to complement the qualitative information. When the interviews were analysed and prepared for communication, another challenge emerged. As the information originated from confidential contexts, it could not be straightforwardly presented. This potentially would have revealed specific organizations described. When considering this, the author remembered research findings of a survey on numerous modelling methods in morphological boxes. This kind of box can represent the distribution of characteristics giving an overview on the findings.[1] This quality makes it particularly suitable for communicating a rich, but nevertheless realistic picture of the current state of enterprise-wide modelling with focus on business processes.

The organizations examined represent a wide variety of typical users of business process modelling as shown in Table 1. The financial industry seems to be over

[1] The research on modelling methods using the morphological box was [17]. In general, the morphological box has been mainly utilised to foster creativity but it is also employed in business analysis [18].

Table 1. Overview on the organizations presented in the study.

Organizations	Overall: 11 - (Major interviews: 10; partial interviews: 1)			
Industry	Financial: 6	Production: 3	Logistics: 1	Public: 2
Employees	Max. 120,000	Aver. 31,000	Min. 400	Entries 7
International organization	Encompassing approach 5	Separate modelling 1	Local organization 5	Entries 11

weighted. This may be due to the available contacts but it also reflects the more widespread use of process modelling in this sector because of legal requirements. The size of the organizations varies widely between medium sized organizations with 400 employees (minimum of stated values) and large organization with 130,000 employees (maximum of stated values). The average number of employees was 31,000. The distribution of sizes of the organisations is mixed in relation to industry, so there are smaller and bigger organizations in most of the industries. Six of the organizations are international. Most of them use an integrated approach with common process patterns shared in all countries and only adapted for specific regional requirements.

2.1 Goals of Enterprise-Wide Business Process Modelling

The goals of a modelling activity are pivotal for many aspects, how modelling is set up and performed in an organization [19]. As modelling can support multiple goals of an organization, this aspect is separately presented in (a) the main goal of business process modelling (Table 2), and (b) further goals the organizations are striving to reach with its modelling activities (Table 3).

Table 2. Main goals of organizations questioned.

Main goal	Number of organizations	Remarks
Fulfillment of legal obligations for documentation	6	Increased focus on international governance standards like COBIT or Sarbanes-Oxley Act
Specifying IT-systems	4	Main focus development projects and integration
Standardization of procedures	1	One focus is to easily establish new sites

The fulfillment of legal obligations is the main goal to model business processes for most companies. Organizations have to comply with standards from regulatory agencies, e.g., in the finance sector or in health care, but also with other governance standards like Sarbanes-Oxley Act or COBIT. Fewer organizations, but still one third, stated that their main focus was on IT and other development projects. One international organization used its models to standardize procedures in different locations, and to swiftly establish new sites.

Table 3. Further goals for business process modelling of organizations questioned.

Additional goal	Number of organizations	Remarks
Business reorganization and improvement	6	
IT-Projects and business changes	4	
Knowledge management	4	
Process controlling	2	
Provision of documentation for data privacy protection	1	
Risk management	1	Often contained in main goal of obligatory documentation

Most, but not all, organizations mentioned further goals, they pursued with business process modelling. Some mentioned more than one additional goal. Perhaps not surprisingly, most organizations (6) regard their models as source to find options for improving their business. Four organizations use their business process models in projects and as knowledge base. Two organizations employ their process models for process controlling. Also mentioned was the provisioning of information for data protection laws and an additional use in risk management. Anyway, the emphasis in the reported experiences was always placed on the main goals.

2.2 Methods and Structures Used for Enterprise Business Process Modelling

The organizations represented in the survey are using different modelling languages and furthermore their methodological rules for model structure vary. In Table 4 the characteristics of the distribution of values are described.

Table 4. Methodological characteristics in process modelling of organizations in the study.

Process modelling methods	EPC: 9 (decreasing)	BPMN: 2 (rising)	ISO Flowchart oriented languages: 4[a]	Entries: 11[b]
Levels of modelling	Max. 6	Aver. 5	Min. 4	Entries 4
Types of base processes	Max. 26	24[c]	Min. 7	Entries 3

[a]Two of the methods used standard symbols from the business modelling tool employed and two other organizations had custom designed symbols and elements. However, they were semantically close to the ISO Standard for Flowcharts which has been noted in the Table.

[b]The overall number of modelling languages used is bigger than the entries (organizations represented in this aspect of the study). The reason for this is that two organizations are temporarily using two languages in parallel.

[c]As for this aspect only three values were available, the value 24 was the middle value stated. It was annotated by the responsible for modelling that the top management had mentioned the extreme values of their competitors having 10 or 32 types of processes which were both reckoned as inacceptable. The result with 24 types was well situated in the middle.

Most organizations used EPC (Event driven Process Chains) as their modelling language. Some tendency was noted to switch to BPMN (Business Process Modelling Notation). Sometimes BPMN was used in parallel with other languages. But in other cases, depending on the overall integration of processes and the repository, a more sophisticated transition was deemed indispensable. Anyway, also disadvantages were noted in respect of BPMN and the compactness of its representation of roles in separate lanes. Besides EPC and BPMN also Process modelling based on ISO (International Standards Organization) Flowchart notation was employed by 4 companies. They noted a good acceptance by readers of the models of business departments.

Concerning the levels of modelling (from process overviews to detailed steps of work), the organizations had similar structures with the number of levels ranging from 4 up to 6 and an average of 5 levels. The number of types of base process areas in the company process map varies to a greater extent, in this study between 7 and 26. As Footnote 4 indicates, this number is depending on diverse organizational conditions and may be dominated by the domain or political valuations of its management.

2.3 Organization of Modelling

The organization of modelling reflects the distribution of work between the central modelling department and the specialists in the field who know how actual work is done and by that the fundamentals of the business processes.

For reasons of the different required know-how[2] and the motivation to share it in models, some advocate a central modelling approach and others a decentralized approach. This was reflected in the approaches chosen by the examined organizations. Five of them followed the strategy of central modelling and the same number used decentralized modellers. All persons responsible for modelling were aware of the limitations of both approaches. One organization reported to use a combined or mixed strategy depending on the know-how of the department. Others mentioned internal discussions to switch from one mode to the other (Table 5).

Table 5. Characteristics of division of labor in modelling activities in organizations of the study.

Kind of division of work	Central modelling: 5	Decentralized modelling: 5	Mixture of both: 1	Entries 11
Central modellers	Max. 10	Aver. 7	Min. 5	Entries 4
Decentralized modellers	Max. 500	Aver. 130	Min. 30	Entries 6

[2] This refers, on one hand, to the knowledge of the domain and, on the other hand, to the knowledge of process modelling and the integration of processes into comprehensive repositories. If modelling is performed only by modelling specialists, the motivation for the domain specialists is lower to support the creation of models than if they are self-constructed. But high demand on quality and integrity seldom can be realized by decentral modellers [13].

A main influential factor in both scenarios is the number of active modellers. The number of central modellers ranged between 5 and 10, and the minimum number of decentralized modellers was 30 and its maximum 500. While the number of central modellers is more likely to be criticised for the associated cost, the higher numbers of decentralized modellers require more support and effort to create high quality models.

2.4 Integration of IT-Modelling and Business Process Modelling

Enterprise modelling is based on an integration of different perspectives. In practice of business process modelling which became the focus of this survey, this is reflected by the high importance of the integration of IT-systems in process models. All partners of the dialogues were aware of the relevance. One organization is using a single repository for IT-system and process models. Two large organizations are replicating their IT-Systems from the EA models or CMDB to the process model repository and three organizations plan to implement a replication. Only two organizations stated that they will not combine the information of the IT and the process sphere. Although there are convincing arguments for full integration (compare [1, 4]), the vast majority of organizations decide for a separated approach. This may originate in its correspondence with the internal department structures (Table 6).

Table 6. Integration between process models and information on IT-Systems used.

Integration of IT-system- and Process models	Single repository: 1	Replication of IT-Systems: 2	Replication of IT-Systems planned: 3	None 2

2.5 Some Important Aspects of Enterprise Modelling Tool in Practice

The modelling tool is an indispensable prerequisite for effective modelling in a long-term and wider organizational context [1]. In many organizations the tool is synonymous for modelling activities. This may entail issues, if a tool gets a bad reputation. In these cases the organizations introduced new labels for the access of the process models. For several organizations a major update of the modelling tool version was mentioned as an important challenge and change. Some organizations reported that they had completed a corresponding update or were considering it. This was independent of the type of tool employed. Some had completed this update, including e.g., new symbols in their models. They reported a considerable effort with 5 or more people working 2 to 4 months to transfer and adapt the models to the new version. This may be a reason, why the other 4 organizations stated, they did not want do this kind of change in the near future, although it would be possible (Table 7).

Table 7. Effect of major version changes of the modelling tool.

Big tool version change with change of modelling elements	Change accomplished: 3	Change planned: 1	Keeping version as long as possible: 4	No version change required until now: 2

Some other aspects concerning the modelling tool were indicated more briefly by a number of the organizations. Two organizations referred to a change of their modelling tool. All others were steady and consistent concerning the tool. Anyhow, some participants mentioned internal discussions about other options to the current modelling tool. More than half of the questioned organizations reported that besides the standard modelling tool, also other tools were used by some departments or for different objectives.

Four organizations used dedicated views for different stakeholders. Additionally, some important supplementary functions were mentioned by the practitioners. These were (a) the provision of workflows for the quality assurance and (b) a publishing portal for an easy access to the models for all employees (Table 8).

Table 8. Further aspects of modelling tools.

Aspect	Number of organizations	Remarks
Change of process modelling tool	2	One after 20 years of usage, the other due to problems in the beginning stages of its utilization
Different tools in the organization besides the central tool explicitly noted	7	
Dedicated views for special stakeholder groups required	4	

2.6 Further Important Experiences

A few more crucial factors for successful enterprise wide modelling were addressed by the practitioners. Three organizations emphasized the relevance of having a sponsor with a high senior management position in the organization. Similarly important to that, others deemed the existence and practical realization of having (a) common reference or contact points for process interfaces and (b) role models employed in a consistent way. For one organization, this was a clear success factor while another organization reported problems due to low realized standards in this respect. Further, two organizations stressed the significance of the training of users and modellers for creating good models and achieving the desired results with them (Table 9).

2.7 Extent of Enterprise-Wide Business Process Modelling

One motive for this survey was to investigate the actual realization of extensive integrated models in practice. So it also inquired on this aspect. The answers were split in two categories. Many, but not all, practitioners declared to have models that were integrated for major parts of the organization. But they also reported of other repositories (or parts of it) that were only fragmentarily integrated.

Table 9. Emphasized experiences of crucial factors for their enterprise-wide process modelling.

Emphasized experiences by the practitioners	Number of organizations	Remarks
Support or direct linkage of process responsibilities to top management	3	E.g., having a CPO in top management or executive manager fostering process governance
Process interfaces and common role models	3	One participant reported good experiences with well-defined interfaces, while another referred to interface problems due to cultural differences
Training of users and modelers	2	A start with E-learning was not sufficient, only when classroom courses started modelling activities were taken up by departments

The maximum number of process models in a systematic framework was 4000. The average was 1850 models and the minimum value stated was 400 process models. These numbers may be criticised because they have not been standardized by weight factors, to account for the fact that the models vary usually in size. Anyway, they convey a notion on the substantial effort the organizations accomplished. The size of an integrated model also accounts for a main influence on the complexity of the models. The overall coverage of the processes of the organization by the available models was asserted only in a few cases. The respective statements supported the impression that the coverage varied by a considerable degree. While some claimed to have an almost full coverage others had just increased the coverage to 50 %.

The number of the systematic models is complemented with the number of models in all repositories of some of the organizations. It is much higher. This was mostly attributed to the fact that these models also contain older versions. Additionally, they also comprise more detailed or specialized models not included in the central core. Overall, the sample represents very experienced organizations and practice. A number of the participants reported systematic process modelling for 20 years and the average was 12 years. Only very few organizations only had a short experience (min 2 years) in enterprise-wide process modelling (Table 10).

Table 10. Number of process models in organizations presented in the study.

Systematic (parts of) overall model	Max. 4.000	Aver. 1.850	Min. 400	Entries 8
Number of actual models in the repository	Max. 55.000[a]	Aver. 22.600	Min. 3000	Entries 4
Active number of years in process modelling	Max. 20	Aver. 12	Min. 2	Entries 10

[a]One administrator of a very large organization indicated to have 900.000 models in about 200 repositories of the company's divisions. They practiced process modelling for more than 20 years. Anyway, this value was not included in the main study, as only few other characteristics of the organization were available.

2.8 Success Stories of Enterprise Business Process Modelling

An important boost for an extensive modelling endeavour may be provided by a very successful application of the process models in an organization which is communicated widely. In this respect, four success stories were reported explicitly. They were based on vital projects of the organizations and ranged from extensive reorganizations for new business requirements over the accomplishment of regulations to providing plans and analytical information for improvement of organizational designs and IT systems (Table 11).

Table 11. Success stories reported.

Reported success story of the presented organizations	
1	Reorganization of one division including a subsequent quality certification
2	Fast accomplishment of regulatory requirements The solution was taken up as blueprint by the modelling tool provider
3	Reorganization of the SEPA-Payments of a company, with continual improvement activities based on the processes
4	Design of a new logistics center based on optimized processes

2.9 Economic Issues for Enterprise Modelling Organizations

A complete and monetary economic evaluation of enterprise modelling activities would be desirable but, from a practical point of view, it would be extremely challenging. In the first place, this is due to inherent problems in the valuation of the benefits [20]. The benefits of models are often connected with a long-term usage and most of the benefits have quite subtle effects on other activities, so a valuation would have to rely on many assumptions. In the second place, in practice, the cost for modelling is not attributed to dedicated cost centres [13].

In the survey, this was reflected by answers of all participants that no direct capitalization of modelling costs is practiced.[3] Hence from a financial perspective, they are not regarded as assets. Anyway, if one considers the typical effort for average models, the number of models and then calculates the value, this easily results in values of several million Euros for the large organizations.[4]

Six organizations explicitly mentioned their current concern to minimize cost for modelling. This is quite reasonable for organizations which are forced by legislation to conform to standards but do not directly reap other substantial benefits from the models (Table 12).

---

[3] The number of organizations is lower than the complete survey as public organizations in Germany do not use typical commercial accounting schemes with the activation of costs for long-term assets.

[4] Although this practice may be justified by the relatively low amounts for these companies in relation to other assets, nevertheless, they represent a distortion of information with relevant motivational effects that impede modelling in many cases. (For the effects of distorted cost information, compare [21]).

Table 12. Economic issues in enterprise-wide business process modelling

Important economic issues of enterprise modelling	Number of organizations	Remarks
No capitalization of modelling costs	8	Modelling costs are sometimes capitalized as costs in larger IT- or change projects
Low cost of modelling	6	One organization is considering to switch from central to decentralized modelling to minimize visible costs
Modelling effort for average business process model = 2 working days	2	To include also the cost for domain specialists, this value has to be multiplied by a factor between 2 and 4

In respect of the typical effort to create a process model, two organizations stated similar experiences for the average effort to model a process. It was 2 days for the modeller and this effort had to be multiplied by 2 up to 4 for the work of other participants in the modelling process. At first glance, this factor may seem somehow too high, but it becomes more reasonable, if one considers the diverse additional effort connected with more people getting informed a few times and involved in quality assurance. This increases the effort for a design activity in enterprise modelling by much more than is obvious and straightforwardly noticed.

3 Critical Remarks, Conclusion and Further Research

The information gathered in this survey represents genuine findings from modelling practice of a considerable number of organizations. But the study has drawbacks in some aspects. They are rooted in (a) the not overall representative sample and (b) a necessity to interpret the statements of the participants. These pitfalls have been addressed in the methodological section.[5] Both have impacted the findings. Nevertheless, the interpretation has been carried out cautiously. This has been documented in the paper by numerous additional notes. The concentration of the survey on enterprise-wide process modelling helped to reach more consistency than if process and IT modelling would have been covered simultaneously.

The findings illustrate a multifaceted picture of process modelling practice. While it is normally emphasized that models easily support a number of goals, most organizations clearly focus on one main goal. This may indicate further potential for higher

[5] One further condition, which was not explicitly addressed, is that the study has been performed in one country, in Germany. Nevertheless, it comprises directly a small number of companies from other countries. Furthermore, the author attended several international conferences of business process modelling practitioners. In these conferences much evidence has also been given on the respective topics of this survey. This evidence corresponds in its general tendency quite well to the findings in the survey. For some respects e.g., the modelling language used other distributions may be found, as EPC have roots in Germany. Nevertheless, EPCs are also in widespread use by many non-German international organizations.

gains from models. On the other hand, organizations do not systematically care for the economics of their modelling activities. Partly they are concerned with the cost aspects, but from a management accountant perspective, it is performed merely superficially. A complete long-term evaluation of benefits and costs is not established in any of the surveyed organizations. It will not be easy to improve on this, while there is only a limited awareness of the economic potential of enterprise models in organizations. This may be connected with the relatively small number of success stories reported in the study.

In respect of IT modelling, there has been high evidence on the demands for a high level of integration in its models. Nevertheless, this is not achieved easily. The challenges only partially appear to originate from the technical domain. However, they are predominantly rooted in the social interaction between the different participants of modelling. The impressive number of process models in the repositories of large organizations demonstrates the relevance of practical modelling in organizations. Combined with the identified challenges, this also indicates some potential for improvements which hopefully may be facilitated by further research.

Generally the findings of this survey advocate research with focus on issues of long-term commitment in enterprise modelling associated with specifically adapted approaches to observe and steer effort and benefits of modelling, in other words, the performance of the crucial interdependent factors involved in the modelling activities.

Further research directly connected to this survey may take a number of directions. This includes the following alternatives: (a) to directly build on this survey and enlarge the sample, (b) to change the perspective and investigate the practice of enterprise architecture modelling (concentrating on IT artefacts), (c) to explore the reasons why most organizations are not able to employ the models for more than one purpose or (d) to investigate the practical obstacles to integration of models. The last questions (c) and (d) seem to be most interesting because they are crucial to improve the options for organizations to obtain substantially higher benefits.

References

1. Frank, U.: Multi-perspective enterprise modeling: foundational concepts, prospects and future research challenges. Softw. Syst. Model. **13**, 941–962 (2014)
2. Lankhorst, M., et al.: Enterprise Architecture at Work - Modelling, Communication and Analysis, 3rd edn. Springer, Berlin (2013)
3. Braun, C., Winter, R.: A comprehensive enterprise architecture metamodel. In: Desel, J., Frank, U. (eds.): Enterprise Modelling and Information Systems Architectures, Proceedings of the Workshop in Klagenfurt 2005. LNI, vol. P-75, pp. 64–79, GI, Bonn (2005)
4. Scheer, A.: ARIS: Business Process Modelling, 3rd edn. Springer, Berlin (2000)
5. Wolff, F.: An Evaluation Framework for Enterprise Architecture Modelling. Enterp. Model. Inf. Syst. Architect. **3**(1), 48–61 (2008)
6. Franz, P., Kirchmer, M.: Value-Driven Business Process Management - The Value Switch for Lasting Competitive Advantage. McGraw-Hill, Maidenherd (2012)
7. Persson, A.: Enterprise modelling in practice: situational factors and their influence on adopting a participative approach. Dissertation, University of Stockholm (2001)

8. Löhe, J., Legner, C.: Overcoming implementation challenges in enterprise architecture management: a design theory for architecture-driven IT Management (ADRIMA). Inf. Syst. e-Bus. Manag. **XII**(1), 101–137 (2014)
9. Kopetzky, M., Reich, G.: When giants learn how to dance – the introduction of process management to a health insurance fund. In: Scheer, A., Kruppke, H., Jost, W., Kindermann, H. (eds.) Agility by ARIS Business Process Management, pp. 27–37. Springer, Heidelberg (2006)
10. Kogelschatz, D., Wyss, P., Bucher, M., Seifert, S.: Closed control cycle for business process management on the credit suisse securities platform. In: Scheer, A., Kruppke, H., Jost, W., Kindermann, H. (eds.) Agility by ARIS Business Process Management, pp. 251–268. Springer, Heidelberg (2006)
11. Yilmaz, N., Stirna, J.: Factors influencing productization of enterprise modeling: a qualitative inquiry into the scandinavian strand of methods and tools. In: Ralyté, J., España, S., Pastor, O. (eds.) The Practice of Enterprise Modeling, pp. 193–208. Springer, London (2015)
12. Eikebrokk, T., Iden, J., Olsen, D., Opdahl, A.L.: Towards a model of process-modelling practice: quantitative validation and results. In: ECIS 2008 Proceedings, Paper 52 (2008)
13. Wolff, F.: Ökonomie multiperspektivischer Unternehmensmodellierung. Gabler, Wiesbaden (2008)
14. Babbie, E.: The Basics of Social Research. Cengage, Boston (2014)
15. Dillman, D., Smyth, J., Christian, L.: Internet, Mail and Mixed Mode Surveys. Wiley, New Jersey (2009)
16. Bonsack, R.: Rekonstruktive Sozialforschung. Budrich, Opladen (2010)
17. Kühn, H.: Methodenintegration im business engineering. Dissertation, University of Vienna (2004)
18. Ritchey, T.: Wicked Problems - Social Messes. Springer, London (2011)
19. Wolff, F.: Better segmentation of enterprise modelling governance through usage perspectives. In: Ralyté, J., España, S., Pastor, Ó. (eds.) PoEM 2014. LNBIP, vol. 235, pp. 224–234. Springer, Heidelberg (2014). doi:10.1007/978-3-662-45501-2_16
20. Wolff, F., Frank, U.: A multiperspective framework for evaluating conceptual models in organisational change. In: Bartmann, D., et. al. (eds.) ECIS 2005 - 13th European Conference on Information Systems, pp. 1–12. Association for Information Systems, Regensburg (2005)
21. Johnson, H., Kaplan, R.S.: Relevance Lost: The Rise and Fall of Management Accounting. Harvard Business School Press, Boston (MA) (1987)

Short Papers

Enterprise Modeling as a Decision Making Aid: A Systematic Mapping Study

Souvik Barat[1(✉)], Vinay Kulkarni[1], Tony Clark[2], and Balbir Barn[3]

[1] Tata Consultancy Services Research, Pune, India
{souvik.barat,vinay.vkulkarni}@tcs.com
[2] Sheffield Hallam University, London, UK
t.clark@shu.ac.uk
[3] Middlesex University, London, UK
b.barn@mdx.ac.uk

Abstract. This paper reviews the state-of-the-art enterprise modelling (EM) techniques with an objective to support decision-making. It describes a Systematic Mapping Study based on 173 publications chosen from 7622 EM related publications collated using five digital libraries: Scopus, ACM Digital Library, IEEE Xplore, ScienceDirect and Web of Science. The study identifies 29 EM techniques and critically analyses them for suitability as an effective aid to complex dynamic decision-making vis-a-vis a set of characteristics. The paper also reports EM publications trends and the challenges aimed at providing effective aids to complex dynamic decision making.

Keywords: Enterprise modelling · Decision making · Systematic mapping study

1 Introduction

One of the key challenges modern organisations face is how to make effective decisions within a dynamic environment [1]. Precise understanding of various aspects of the organisation such as goals, organisation structure, operational processes, historic data and the stakeholders of the organisation is necessary to arrive at effective decisions [2]. Current industry practice of decision making relies heavily on human experts using tools such as spreadsheets, word processors, and diagram editors. Though providing computational and visualization support, these tools are rather primitive as regards analysis capabilities. This leads to excessive cognitive burden on human experts thus adversely affecting the quality and precision of decision making [3].

In recent years, the use of enterprise modelling (EM) is widely discussed in the context of complex enterprise wide missions [4] such as Business-IT alignment, enterprise transformation, etc. A wide range of sophisticated support for

J. Horkoff et al. (Eds.): PoEM 2016, LNBIP 267, pp. 289–298, 2016.
DOI: 10.1007/978-3-319-48393-1_20

comprehending various aspects of enterprises make the EM techniques credible choice for such adoptions. For example, the Zachman framework [5] is capable of representing enterprises in a structured form by visualising them along six interrogative aspects namely *what, where, when, why, who* and *how*; the ArchiMate [6] and tool Archi[1] enable comprehensive specification and visualisation support along *structural, behavioural* and *information* aspects of the organisation. As regards the analysis capabilities, the specification such as BPMN [7], i* [8] and stock-n-flow (SnF) [9] are amenable to sophisticated analysis. For example, the process aspect can be analysed and simulated using BPMN, the high level goals and objectives can be evaluated using i*, and high level system dynamics can be simulated using Stock-and-Flow (SnF) tools such as iThink[2]. These specification and analyses abilities of EM techniques motivated us to explore suitability of EM techniques for complex dynamic decision making (CDDM).

In this paper, we present a critical evaluation of enterprise modelling techniques as an aid for CDDM. We discuss the rigorous analysis carried out using *Systematic Mapping Study* methodology. In particular, we evaluated 173 publications that are rigorously selected from 7622 EM related publications collated from 5 popular digital libraries namely *Scopus, ACM Digital Library, IEEE Xplore, ScienceDirect* and *Web of Science.* The systematic study identified 29 enterprise modelling techniques which were then evaluated for suitability to CDDM. The key contributions of this paper are: (i) A detailed investigation of modelling and analysis needs for addressing CDDM problem leading to enumeration of a set of requirements, (ii) A report on systematic mapping study evaluating EM techniques as aid to CDDM in the context these requirements, and (iii) A report describing the suitability of EM state-of-the-art and industry expectations vis-a-vis CDDM in enterprises.

2 Complex Dynamic Decision Making

The efficacy of decision making primarily depends on two key factors: (i) the ability to capture relevant information, and (ii) the ability to perform *what-if* and *if-what* analyses on available information.

We argue that an enterprise can be understood well by analyzing *what* an enterprise is, *how* it operates, *why* it is so and *who* are the stakeholders [10]. Complex dynamic decision making (CDDM) deals with organisations that typically consist of many autonomous units, organized into dynamically changing hierarchical structures, and managing goals that affect their behaviour over time. They also deal with non-linear causality, several interdependent and localized feedback loops, and indefinite time-delay between action and responses [11]. Essentially, these socio-technical characteristics [2,11] of complex dynamic organisation puts some special demands [12] on specification in terms of desirable characteristics. Table 1 enumerates specification and analysis requirements for CDDM. We conducted a comprehensive systematic mapping study to evaluate the specification

[1] www.archimatetool.com/.

[2] www.iseesystems.com/store/products/ithink.aspx.

Table 1. Specification and analysis requirements for CDDM

	Requirements	Description
Aspects	Why	Intentional specification
	What	Structural specification
	How	Behavioural specification
	Who	Specification on stakeholders and responsible human actors
Socio-technical characteristics	Modularity	Unit must encapsulate internal goal, structure and behaviour
	Composability	Unit can be an assembly of multiple units
	Reactive	Unit must respond appropriately to its environment
	Autonomous	A unit is responsible for its own behavior and it can produce output without an external stimulus
	Intentional	Unit must have intent and it behaves accordingly to achieve its intent
	Adaptable	Unit can adapt itself based on context and situation
	Uncertain	Knowing the unknown - it is not necessary that a unit knows its intention and behaviour a-priori
	Temporal	Indefinite time-delay between an action and its response
Analysis	Visualisation	Support for visualization
	Machine Interpretable	Models that are interpretable by machine (i.e., support for simulation/execution)
	Quantitative	Simulation based quantitative analysis
	Qualitative	Simulation based qualitative analysis

and analysis characteristics of EM techniques described in Table 1. The next section describes the detailed report of the conducted study.

3 Systematic Mapping Study

We adopted systematic mapping study (SMS) methodology proposed by Petersen et al. [13] to conduct this review. Primarily the review process steps conform to three standard phases of SMS methodology namely planning, execution and reporting. The planning phase defines the review protocol that includes *research questions*, *search criteria* (i.e., *inclusion criteria*, *exclusion criteria* and *quality criteria*), selection of *digital libraries*, and the *study template* for conducting review. The execution phase executes the plan through two logical steps namely *exploration of digital libraries* and *conduct studies*. The exploration of digital libraries logical step iteratively explores identified digital libraries using the search criteria described in the planning phase and identifies the relevant publications. The conduct studies logical step studies all identified publications and documents the study outcome as prescribed by the study template of review protocol. Finally, the report review phase summarizes all studies and their outcomes in a precise form. We now describe the activities and outcomes of all the three phases of EM literature review.

3.1 Planning Phase

The planning phase formalize the protocol for conducting review as described in Table 2. The protocol defines two research questions RQ1 and RQ2. The research question RQ1- *What are the papers on Enterprise Modelling (EM) and Enterprise Architecture (EA) that focus on enterprise modelling?* identifies EM related publications. The sub-question RQ1.1 is designed to consolidate cited EM techniques. Research question RQ2 also ascertains suitability and gap of EM techniques to support CDDM.

The inclusion criterion of this review is very broad as it is designed to find all Enterprise Modeling (EM) and Enterprise Architecture (EA) related literature. The exclusion criterion is designed to eliminate EM publications that are irrelevant for this study. We consider publications that solely focus on workflow, process mining, security, and infrastructure related topics as not much relevant to CDDM. Two constraints are defined as part of quality criteria, they are: (i) paper should be aligned with the problem statement and (ii) paper should be

Table 2. Review Protocol for conducting review on EM publications

Artefact name	Artefact description
Research Question	RQ1: What are the papers on Enterprise Modeling (EM) and Enterprise Architecture (EA) that focus on organisation modelling? RQ1.1: What are the EM techniques cited by identified papers? RQ2: What are the modelling and analysis characteristics reported in EM? How these characteristics match with the characteristics described in Table 1?
Inclusion criteria	Keywords: "Enterprise Architecture" OR "Enterprise Model" OR "Enterprise Modelling" OR "Enterprise Modeling" Subject Area: Computer Science Document Type: Conference and Journal Paper Language: English
Exclusion criteria	"workflow" OR "BPR" OR "governance" OR "government" OR security OR "mining" OR "re-engineering" OR "Six Sigma" OR "SOA" OR "mashups" OR "Web Service" OR "Cloud" OR "data warehouse" OR "ERP" OR "SAP" OR "Digital Media" OR "MIS" OR OR "RFID" OR "sensor network" OR "network management" OR "LAN" OR "database" OR "network infrastructure" OR "NAS"
Quality Criteria	(a) Paper is aligned with research problem, and (b) Paper is cited by at least 1 paper if publication date is prior to 2014
Digital libraries	Scopus, ACM Digital Library, IEEE Xplore, ScienceDirect and Web of Science
Study Template	Template to capture Title, Authors information, Citation Count, EM techniques referred, and Key Findings

cited by at least one refereed paper (excluding self-citation) if it is published before 2014. The former quality criterion checks the relevance and the latter validates minimum acknowledgment from research community.

The review protocol of this study chooses five digital libraries namely Scopus, ACM Digital Library, IEEE Xplore, ScienceDirect and Web of Science for identifying EM related publications. This step also specifies all digital library specific search strings for both inclusion criteria and exclusion criteria. The search strings of other digital libraries are available in appendices section[3]. The study template described in Table 2 is an extension of the standard attributes defined by EBSE Research Group in [14]. Additional attribute EM technique referred (see *Study Template* row of Table 2) captures the list of cited EM techniques, and the attribute *Key Findings* captures the high-level description of the publication using free text form.

3.2 Execution Phase

The *exploration of digital libraries* logical step of execution phase explores the five digital libraries using the search criteria described in Table 2 to find relevant publications. The count of identified publications for each process step is depicted in Fig. 1. The inclusion criterion of review protocol collectively selected 7622 publications (with multiple duplicate entries); total 1855 publications were short-listed by exclusion criteria; and finally 173 publications were selected after evaluating quality criteria. The second logical step *conduct study* is performed on 173 publications.

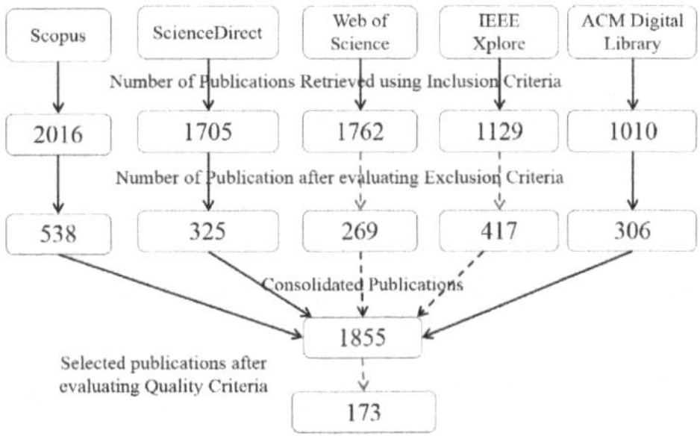

Fig. 1. Overview of execution phase

3.3 Synthesis Phase

The synthesis phase analyzes all studies captured using the study template and reports the answers of two research questions formulated in the study protocol. The final outcome of the review synthesis answering two research questions is described below:

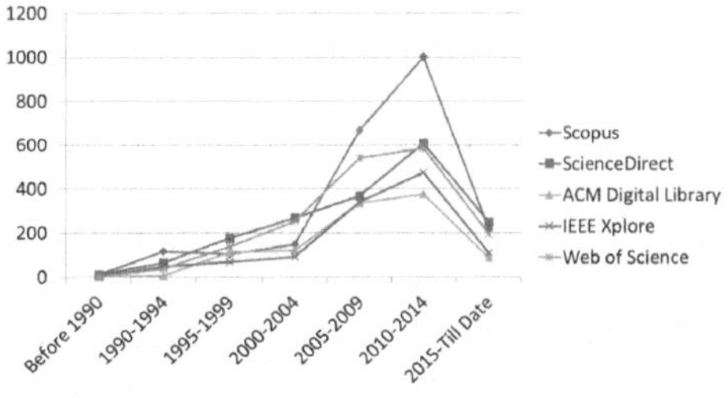

Fig. 2. Publication trends of EM literature

[3] https://www.researchgate.net/publication/305481180_Appendices_of_Paper__Enterprise_Modeling_as_an_Aid_to_Complex_Dynamic_Decision_Making_A_Systematic_Mapping_Study.

Answers to RQ 1 - What are the papers on Enterprise Modeling (EM) and Enterprise Architecture (EA) that focus on organisation modelling?

As shown in Fig. 1, 7622 publications on a range of EM and EA related topics were initially identified. The trend of publications since 1990 with 5 year time-span as a time unit is depicted in Fig. 2. It indicates an increasing trend of EM publications with a significant increase in the last 5-year slot. This trend is consistent over all 5 digital libraries. We also conducted trend analysis on final selection of 173 publications. These publications are contributed from 35 countries involving 161 institutions/organisations in time span of 1987 to 2016. The complete list of publications is presented in appendices section. The consolidation of *EM techniques referred* attribute of 173 publication studies collectively report 29 EM techniques as an answer to sub-question - *What are the EM techniques cited by those publications?* Table 3 describes identified EM techniques. The useful references associated with identified EM techniques are listed in appendices section.

Table 3. Identified EM techniques

Zachman Framework, ArchiMate, Department of Defense Architecture Framework (DoDAF), The British Ministry of Defence Architecture Framework (MoDAF), The Open Group Architecture Framework (TOGAF), ARIS, Extended Enterprise Modeling Language (EEML), Enterprise Knowledge Development (EKD), MoKI, Knowledge Acquisition in automated specification (KAOS), i, Business Motivation Model (BMM), Business Process Model and Notation (BPMN), Integrated enterprise modeling (IEM), Unified Modeling Language (UML), Perdue Enterprise Reference Framework (PERA), GRAI Integrated Methodology (GIM), Computer Integrated Manufacturing Open Systems Architecture Framework (CIMOSA), Generalized Enterprise Reference Architecture and Methodology (GERAM), Design and Engineering Methodology for Organizations (DEMO), Multi-Perspective Enterprise Modelling (MEMO), Integration DEFinition (IDEF), European Interoperability Framework (EIF), Semantics of Business Vocabulary and Rules (SBVR), System Dynamics, Unifed Enterprise Modeling Language (UEML), Systemic Enterprise Architecture Methodology (SEAM), Event-driven process chain (EPC), and Reference Model of Open Distributed Processing (RM-ODP)*

Answers to RQ 2: What are the modelling and analysis characteristics reported in EM? We conducted a series of detailed studies to understand the EM techniques identified by RQ 1.1. Table 4 summarizes the studies wherein each row is a representation of the suitability and gap analysis of a specific EM technique. We omitted TOGAF, EIF, SEAM and MoKI in the below list as TOGAF and SEAM primarily focus only on the method aspects whereas EIF is a set of guidance to European public administrations about the design of European public services and MoKI is an wiki site for enterprise modelling.

The synthesis of Table 4 asserts some characteristics of identified EM techniques. The appearance count of EM techniques in large collections selected

Table 4. Consolidated study report

Enterprise Modeling Technique	Domain	Aspects				Socio-technical Characteristics								Visualisation and Analysis				Selected using Inclusion Criteria	Selected in final consideration
		Why	What	How	Who	Modularity	Composability	Reactive	Autonomous	Intentional	Adaptable	Uncertainty	Temporal	Visualisation	Machine Interpretable	Quantative	Qualitative		
Zachman	IS	S	S	S	S	S	N	N	N	S	N	N	N	N	N	N	N	493	23
ArchiMate	IS	S	S	S	S	S	I	S	N	S	N	N	N	S	N	N	N	190	19
DoDAF	D	S	S	S	S	S	S	S	N	S	N	N	N	I	N	N	N	83	7
MoDAF	D	S	S	S	S	S	S	I	N	S	N	N	N	I	N	N	N	49	3
ARIS	IS	I	S	S	S	S	S	S	S	I	N	N	N	S	S_{How}	N	S_{How}	167	19
EEML	IS	I	S	S	S	N	N	N	N	I	N	N	N	S	N	N	N	9	2
EKD	IS	S	I	S	S	S	N	N	N	S	N	N	N	S	N	N	N	33	2
KAOS	IS	S	N	N	I	S	N	N	N	S	N	N	N	S	N	N	N	13	1
i*	IS	S	N	N	I	S	S	N	N	S	N	N	N	S	S_{Why}	S_{Why}	S_{Why}	71	4
BMM	IS	S	N	I	I	I	N	N	N	S	N	N	N	I	N	N	N	38	5
BPMN	IS	N	I	I	S	S_{How}	S_{How}	S	I	N	N	N	N	S	S_{How}	S_{How}	S_{How}	190	17
UML	IS	I	S	S	S	S	S	N	N	N	N	N	N	S	N	N	N	306	14
IEM	IS	N	S	S	S	N	N	N	N	N	N	N	N	I	N	N	N	8	3
CIMOSA	M	I	S	S	S	I	N	N	N	I	N	N	N	S	N	N	N	126	25
PERA	M	I	I	S	S	I	N	N	N	I	N	N	N	S	N	N	N	32	5
GRAI	M	N	I	S	S	I	N	N	N	N	N	N	N	S	N	N	N	71	17
GERAM	M	S	S	S	S	I	N	N	N	S	N	N	N	S	N	N	N	92	13
DEMO	IS	N	I	S	I	I	I	S	S	N	N	N	N	S	S_{How}	S_{How}	S_{How}	28	2
MEMO	IS	S	I	S	S	S	S	S	I	S	N	N	N	S	S_{How}	S_{How}	S_{How}	61	10
IDEF	D	I	S	S	I	S	I	N	N	I	N	N	N	S	N	N	N	51	6
SBVR	IS	N	I	S	I	I	I	N	N	N	N	N	N	I	S_{what}	I	I	17	2
SD	IS	N	S	I	I	I	N	S	S	N	N	N	N	S	S_{What}	N	S_{What}	11	3
UEML	IS	S	S	S	S	I	I	N	N	S	N	N	N	S	N	N	N	43	6
EPC	IS	N	I	S	N	S_{How}	S_{How}	S	N	N	N	N	N	S	S_{How}	S_{How}	S_{How}	18	2
RM-ODP	IS	S	S	S	N	I	N	N	N	S	N	N	N	N	N	N	N	49	2

S = Suitable, Sx = Suitable for Aspect X, I = Inadequate, N = Not Suitable
Domains : IS = Information System, M = Manufacturing, D= Defence

uning inclusion criteria in Table 4 depicts the popularity of EM techniques. The Zachman Framework, Archimate, ARIS, UML are referred very frequently in EM literature whereas EEML, IEM, KAOS are not referred extensively. The column describing the appearance counts within selected in final consolidation ensure the coverage of this study. We further analyse the capabilities of EM techniques along three dimensions namely specification, visualization and analysis.

Specification: Table 4 shows a consensus among EM techniques that an enterprise should be specified using multiple views or aspects. It is visible throughout the table as all EM techniques support more than one aspect. However, we found only 6 EM techniques (i.e., Zachman Framework, ArchiMate, DoDAF, MoDAF, GERAM and UEML) out of 25 to be capable of specifying all the four aspects. We also see a major inadequacy in supporting specification of adaptability, uncertainty and temporal characteristics. No EM technique is capable of specifying adaptation and uncertainty whereas only the system dynamic model is capable of specifying the temporal property. This leads us to infer that the state-of-the-art of enterprise modeling and specification are purposive and they cover limited aspects.

Visualization: We find adequate visualization aids for most of the EM techniques. 18 EM techniques are supported by advanced visualization aids and 5 other EM techniques also supported with primitive visualization aids.

Analysis: We find considerable lacunae in machine interpretable specification, qualitative analysis and quantitative analysis. In particular, 8 EM techniques partly support machine interpretable specification, 8 EM techniques support partial quantitative analysis and 7 of the 25 identified EM techniques support partial qualitative analysis.

The above analysis shows that the state-of-the-art EM techniques fare better on documentation and visualization than quantitative and qualitative analysis. Also, there is inadequate support for socio-technical characteristics such as adaptability, uncertainty, and temporal properties.

3.4 Threats to Validity

Four kinds of validity threats namely construct validity, conclusion validity, internal validity and external validity are considered while conducting this study. The construct validity is ensured through appropriate measures. Firstly, the search-string for inclusion criteria is formulated using three sufficiently stable terminologies of EM literature namely *Enterprise Model*, *Enterprise Modelling* and *Enterprise Architecture*. Secondly, the search string for exclusion criteria is constructed using an iterative method considering one phrase at a time. The construct validity related to coverage assurance is addressed by considering five digital libraries namely Scopus, ScienceDirect, ACM Digital Library, IEEE Xplore and Web of Science. Finally, the construct validity is ensured through rigorous review process. In particular, three researchers from review team (i.e., authors of this paper) independently validated the review protocol specified by other researcher. The conclusion validity or reliability focuses on whether the data are collected and the analysis is conducted in a repeatable form. We defined search terms based on stable phrases, used a well-defined procedure and emphasized on standard digital libraries to make the study repeatable. The automated search capabilities of proposed digital libraries are used to a large extent for improving the repeatability. All these measures contributed to address conclusion validity.

Internal validity is concerned with the analysis of the data. The analysis primarily based on the descriptive statistics, thus the threats are minimal. Finally, external validity is about generalization from this study. Since we do not draw any conclusion outside of our primary focus on evaluating EM techniques for CDDM, the external validity threats are not applicable.

4 Conclusion

We presented the necessary characteristics of enterprise specification to effectively support CDDM. A systematic mapping study was carried out to evaluate existing EM techniques for supporting CDDM in enterprises. The study concluded with key observations: (i) the majority of the existing EM techniques meet the most basic requirement of specifying relavant aspects of organisation for CDDM, (ii) existing EM techniques display a range of automated analysis also, (iii) however, none of the existing EM techniques is capable of meeting all necessary requirements of enterprise specification for CDDM, and (iv) the key concern is to specify and analyse socio-technical characteristics of complex dynamic organisation. A cursory study of Actor Model of Computation [15] reveals that it can be a good candidate for specifying socio-technical characteristics of enterprises. As a next step, we intent to conduct similar study to explore suitability of Actor languages and frameworks for CDDM in enterprises.

References

1. Shapira, Z.: Organizational Decision Making. Cambridge University Press, Cambridge (2002)
2. Daft, R.: Organization Theory and Design. Cengage Learning, Boston (2012)
3. Sipp, C.M., Elias, C.: Real Options and Strategic Technology Venturing: A New Paradigm in Decision Making, vol. 31. Springer Science & Business Media, Berlin (2012)
4. Loucopoulos, P., Stratigaki, C., Danesh, M.H., Bravos, G., Anagnostopoulos, D., Dimitrakopoulos, G.: Enterprise capability modeling: concepts, method, and application. In: 2015 International Conference on Enterprise Systems (ES), pp. 66–77. IEEE (2015)
5. Zachman, J., et al.: A framework for information systems architecture. IBM Syst. J. **26**(3), 276–292 (1987)
6. Lacob, M., Jonkers, D.H., Lankhorst, M., Proper, E., Quartel, D.D.: Archimate 2.0 Specification: The Open Group. Van Haren Publishing, Zaltbommel (2012)
7. OMG: Business Process Model and Notation (BPMN), Version 2.0, January 2011
8. Yu, E., Strohmaier, M., Deng, X.: Exploring intentional modeling and analysis for enterprise architecture. In: 10th IEEE International Enterprise Distributed Object Computing Conference Workshops (2006)
9. Meadows, D.H., Wright, D.: Thinking in Systems: A Primer. Chelsea Green Publishing, White River Junction (2008)
10. Kulkarni, V., Barat, S., Clark, T., Barn, B.: Toward overcoming accidental complexity in organisational decision-making. In: 17th International Conference on Model Driven Engineering Languages and Systems (MoDELS 2015). IEEE (2015)

11. McDermott, T., Rouse, W., Goodman, S., Loper, M.: Multi-level modeling of complex socio-technical systems. Proc. Comput. Sci. **16**, 1132–1141 (2013)
12. Kulkarni, V., Barat, S., Clark, T., Barn, B.: Using simulation to address intrinsic complexity in multi-modelling of enterprises for decision making. In: Proceedings of the Conference on Summer Computer Simulation, pp. 1–11 (2015)
13. Petersen, K., Feldt, R., Mujtaba, S., Mattsson, M.: Systematic mapping studies in software engineering. In: 12th International Conference on Evaluation and Assessment in Software Engineering, vol. 17, no. sn, pp. 1–10 (2008)
14. Keele, S.: Guidelines for performing systematic literature reviews in software engineering. Technical report, Ver. 2.3 EBSE technical report, EBSE (2007)
15. Hewitt, C.: Actor model of computation: scalable robust information systems (2010). arXiv preprint arXiv:1008.1459

The Value of Enterprise Modelling: Towards a Service-centric Perspective

Martin Benkenstein[1], Michael Fellmann[2], Michael Leyer[1(✉)], and Kurt Sandkuhl[2]

[1] Institute for Business Administration, University of Rostock, Ulmenstr. 69, 18057 Rostock, Germany
{martin.benkenstein,michael.leyer}@uni-rostock.de
[2] Institute of Computer Science, University of Rostock, Albert-Einstein-Str. 22, 18059 Rostock, Germany
{michael.fellmann,kurt.sandkuhl}@uni-rostock.de

Abstract. Enterprise modeling is an important and widespread activity in managing enterprises. A well-founded conceptualization of its value is however missing so far which can be traced back to different understandings of constituents of enterprise modelling. Addressing these different understandings, we propose to take a service-centric perspective to determine the value of enterprise modelling. We describe the benefits of this perspective and justify our positioning regarding a service-centric perspective.

Keywords: Value of enterprise modeling · Economic analysis · S-D logic · Service-centric perspective

1 Introduction

In computer science and information systems development, modelling is an important activity which is used for different purposes, like capturing requirements, visualizing established work processes, specifying system design, expressing information structures, defining variables and their dynamics for simulation purposes, specifying interaction sequences, and many more. In general, the need for modelling is acknowledged and models as a result of the modelling process are established artefacts in systems engineering and development of organizational improvements. In this context, enterprise modelling is used to understand the current situation of an organization, prepare organizational improvements and information systems development or to plan for strategic decision making, to name just a few examples. In general, an enterprise model consists of different perspectives required for the modelling purpose at hand, each focusing on a particular aspect of the enterprise, e.g. processes, business rules, concepts/information, vision/goals, and actors.

Despite this large spectrum of modelling purposes and use cases, the value of enterprise modelling in particular has not yet been subject of extensive research (see Sect. 2). In this position paper we argue that a new perspective on the value of enterprise modelling is required. Enterprise modelling shows characteristics of the service-dominant (S-D) interpretation of services. An example is that S-D logic

J. Horkoff et al. (Eds.): PoEM 2016, LNBIP 267, pp. 299–306, 2016.
DOI: 10.1007/978-3-319-48393-1_21

proposes value creation together with the customer which is the case in enterprise modelling as creation of a model in many cases happens in cooperation between modeller and the enterprise under consideration (cf. Sect. 3).

The main contributions are (a) a summary of existing research work on the value of enterprise modelling and why this motivates additional work, (b) an outline of a service-oriented perspective and of work required to address this perspective. The remainder of the paper is structured as follows: Sect. 2 motivates the need for a value discussion in enterprise modelling, which includes a brief summary of existing work in the field. Section 3 presents initial thought on a service-centric perspective on the value of enterprise modelling. Section 4 gives an outlook on future work.

2 The Need for a Value Discussion

2.1 The Deficit of Works on "Value" and the Lacking Consensus on the Constituents of Enterprise Modeling

The value of modelling in general and of enterprise modelling in particular has not yet been subject of extensive research. A few research activities lead to work on the perceived value of modelling [6], the return on modelling [7], organizational change aspects on modelling [8] and specific economic aspects of modelling (e.g. [5, 23]). The potential benefits of enterprise modelling in various situations in enterprises are a topic in decision sciences, information systems and accounting information systems research (see, e.g., the recent review of [9]). The idea is that the provision of an external model facilitates the evolvement of mental models among decision makers that are necessary to understand the broader picture of decisions and thus make better decisions [10]. However, a comprehensive and generally accepted framework for defining and determining the value of modelling so far has not been proposed.

Among the reasons for this deficit are the different perspectives on "value" and the different perspectives of what is considered as part of "modelling". The scientific literature on enterprise modelling offers several aspects as constituents of enterprise modelling (see, e.g., [2–4]), like

- the modelling procedure, sometimes referred to as the *modelling method*, concerns the way to perform the modelling and the creation of models,
- the result of modelling, i.e. the *model*, and the value of the model for the organization and the individual,
- the *tool support* and infrastructure for supporting the use of modelling method or the use of models, and
- the *organizational structures* and processes establishing modelling within an organization as an organizational task.

However, not all scholars in the field agree on all of the above constituents of enterprise modelling. Some researchers consider constructional and functional structures as part of modelling methods and argue that this cannot be separated [11]. Other scholars emphasize the importance of meta-models and modelling languages for capturing different perspectives [12]. Tool support is often seen as inseparable manifestation of modelling approaches and notations [13], but in other research work as aid to support modelling [2]. Organisational structures and role descriptions often are neglected in enterprise modelling approaches.

Due to this plethora of topics and concepts, a recent study among enterprise modelling experts suggests that one of the most important topics of future research has to be research on components of enterprise modelling. "To a great extent, this can be explained in that the variety of different components [...] exhibit a high degree of complexity of the subject area, which needs to be reduced in future research efforts" [14, p. 49]. Therefore, research should focus on the different *types of models, modelling methods and modelling tools*.

2.2 The Need for a New Perspective in the Enterprise Modelling Value Discussion

The research challenge gets even more complex when taking the definition and measurement of "value" into account. "Value" is considered as "one of the most overused and misused concepts [...] in management literature" [24] that is still subject of scientific debate (e.g., at the VMBO workshop series [25]). Business administration research uses various meanings of the term "value". For instance, accountancy calculates the value of a good based on the costs that incur by its production [15, 16], or at times the value of the good is put on the same level with the market price [17, 18]. Cost theory identifies the value of a good by analysing opportunity costs [19]. In contrast, business studies that are more oriented towards behavioural sciences regard the value as the value of benefit from the customer point of view. This in turn is differentiated in *value in transaction*, *value in use* and *value in context* [20]. The value in transaction is – from a simplified perspective – identical to the market price. Though, this perspective disregards that customers' willingness to pay is not always identical with the actual price paid. By now, value in transaction is therefore rather defined by the willingness to pay. The value of a good ultimately equals the benefit that arises in the utilization phase of the good, whereas the willingness to pay corresponds to the expectation of benefit that customers assume in the utilization phase. Hence, the willingness to pay does not equal the value in use which cannot be identified until the use of the good has progressed. Further it has to be noted that when identifying the value of the good, the value in use is highly dependent on the context. An enterprise model will likely generate a different value in use for a major corporation than for a small enterprise.

These considerations illustrate that different perspectives are needed for the identification of the value of enterprise models and likewise diverse methods of measurement need to be implemented. While costs and accountancy-driven measurements can easily be done on the basis of cost or market price analyses [16, 17], measurements of the *value in transaction*, the *value in use* and the *value in context* may require social-psychological methods (surveys, interviews, experiments) [21, 22]. Since such methods measure the value that an individual ascribes to modelling (models, methods or tools), attention needs to be paid to transform such individual valuations to a person-independent organizational or even social level.

The above situation in research on value of enterprise modelling calls for a change in perspective and a different way of thinking in order to achieve substantial progress in the field. We propose to take a service-centric perspective originating from Service Science, which can be considered as a promising source of inspiration due to its interdisciplinary nature [26].

3 Conceptualizing the Value of Enterprise Modelling from a Service-centric and Stakeholder-Based Perspective

3.1 Enterprise Modelling Value from a Service-centric Perspective

Considering enterprise modelling and its value from a service-centric perspective has substantial innovation potential since it inherently introduces a multi-disciplinary approach due to the multidisciplinary nature of Service Science [26]. This novel thinking disrupts the current situation of disparate, conceptually not aligned and largely incompatible research activities and has the potential to lead to a breakthrough that would not be possible from a mono-disciplinary viewpoint.

The analysis of existing research work showed that so far a service-centric perspective has not been taken when considering the value of enterprise modelling. Vargo and Lusch [1] define services as the application of specialized competences (knowledge and skills) through deeds, processes, and performances for the benefit of another entity or the entity itself. Value considerations in the context of Service Science and the Service Dominant Logic (S-D logic) usually include the *potential*, *process* and *result* perspective on value.

Enterprise modelling shows significant characteristics of the S-D-interpretation of services. S-D logic proposes value creation together with the customer which is the case as the purpose of the enterprise model is to be used by someone and creation of a model in many cases happens in cooperation between modeller and client, e.g. representatives from the enterprise under consideration. From an economics perspective, modelling is information processing as information is gathered, created, transformed and combined. The value and benefits of modelling can be considered from *potential* (existence of the model, method or tool), *process* (usage of the model, method, or tool) and *result* (outcome of the use of a model, method or tool) perspective.

3.2 Enterprise Modelling Value from a Stakeholder-Based Perspective

The service-centric perspective as introduced in the previous section alone will probably not be sufficient for a holistic view on the value of enterprise modelling since the mutual dependencies and effects of potential, execution and results as well as the organizational management and individual stakeholder perspectives are not sufficiently covered. We have to take into account that different stakeholders value not only the finished enterprise model but also the process of enterprise modelling. The reason is that often are members of the modelling team and therefore get insights into the modelling process. We suppose that these insights are also valuable for the enterprise. Thus, the value of enterprise models arises from the model itself but also from the modelling process.

3.3 Integration of the Two Perspectives

Combining the propositions of the two sections before, we create an integrated view on enterprise modelling value depicted by Fig. 1. It illustrates our proposition to differentiate between various service-centric and stakeholder-based perspectives on enterprise modelling value.

The *service-centric perspectives* are implemented in the horizontal dimension of Fig. 1. Columns have been structured in two dichotomous areas of *model development* and *continuous model use*. Already in the *model development*-area, it is important to conceptualize the different values according to the service-centric perspectives. In more detail, the *potential*-perspective covers values at the point in time where a model not (yet) exists, the *process*-perspective covers values arising during model construction and the *result*-perspective covers values at the point in time where the model creation has been completed. In contrast to that, in the *continuous model use*-area, the service-centric perspectives occur in a highly interlinked manner. This is depicted by three arrows forming a cycle in the rightmost column of Fig. 1. It means that each time a model is used, values in all perspectives may occur. In this way, the *potential*-perspective covers values before a model is used, the *process*-perspective covers values arising while the model is in use and the *result*-perspective covers values that can be determined after a model has been used.

The *stakeholder-based perspectives* are implemented in the vertical dimension of Fig. 1 using one row per stakeholder. Among the stakeholders whose perception of

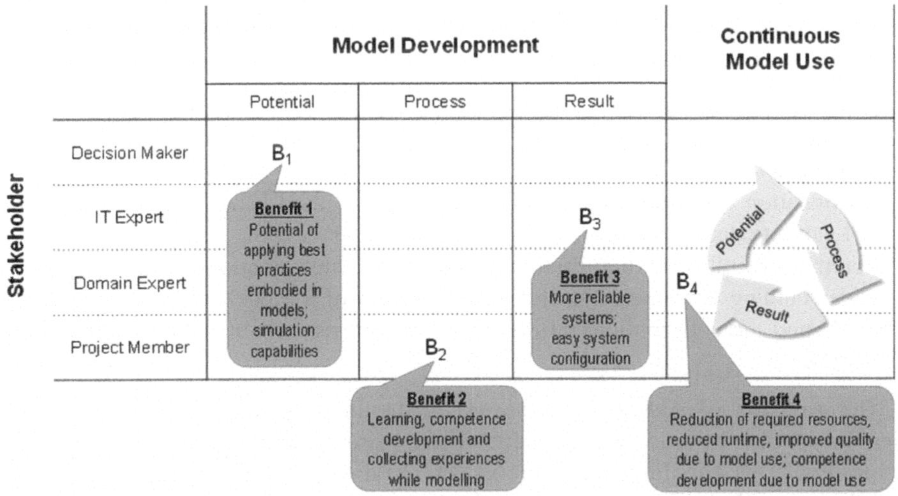

Fig. 1. Enterprise modelling value from a service-centric and stakeholder-based perspective

value has to be understood are, to take some examples, decision makers in enterprises, IT experts with a focus on enterprise modelling methods and models, domain experts for modelling problems under consideration and members of modelling projects.

3.4 Examples for Describing Values

Using our integrated view, different detailed benefits can be described in the cells of the resulting table. Examples for this are shown as B_1–B_4 (cf. Fig. 1). In addition, more coarse-grained questions can be raised involving the constituents of enterprise modelling identified in Sect. 2.1 as a whole, such as:

- *Models*: How do existing models create value covering the potential value of models, the value in use by employees and the value added as outcome of using models?
- *Methods*: How is the value of modelling methods composed by the contributions of different method components and what would be approaches for determining the value of a method from a service-centric perspective?
- *Tools*: How do modelling tools create value covering the potential value of tools, the perceived value in use and the long-term value added as outcome of tool usage?

Moreover, a huge potential for research lies in exploring the value of the whole process of enterprise modelling taking into account the interdependencies between model, method, and tool value and furthermore the moderating and mediating effects of enterprise modelling contexts.

4 Outlook

This paper calls for a service-centric and stakeholder-based perspective in determining the value of enterprise modelling. As such, we propose a first high-level proposal how such a value discussion should be structured. Using the proposed integrated view, the following research topics should be addressed:

- Understanding of the determinants of how enterprise models, methods and tools should be designed to provide a maximum of value for decision makers in companies.
- Identification of interdependencies between method-value, model-value and tool-value (value-in-use).
- Identification of contextual drivers of integrated value creation.
- Understanding of value offer and value creation of a model, method or tool as a whole and the contributions of different constituents to their value (method value model).

The direction of addressing these topics should be to change the view of the scientific community regarding the value of enterprise modelling from a service-centric perspective. This should include a conceptualization what the value of enterprise modelling actually is and this conceptualization has to cover the method or modelling process, the model as an artefact, the tools and organizational context.

The overall aim should be to develop an empirically validated and accepted framework for determining the value of enterprise modelling and its constituents that supports enterprises and method developers. Such a framework can change the way of decision making in what contexts modelling is advisable and contribute to improvement of methods and notations. It would have to come with subsequent methods for determining the actual value and improvement potential of a given enterprise model, method and tool as well as management methods to create and enhance the value of enterprise modelling (concepts for value creation).

References

1. Vargo, S.L., Lusch, R.F.: Evolving to a new dominant logic for marketing. J. Mark. **68**, 1–17 (2004)
2. Sandkuhl, K., Stirna, J., Persson, A., Wißotzki, M.: Enterprise Modeling. Springer, Heidelberg (2014)
3. Henderson-Sellers, B., Ralyté, J., Ågerfalk, P.J., Rossi, M.: Situational Method Engineering. Springer, Heidelberg (2014)
4. Frank, U.: Multilevel modeling: toward a new paradigm of conceptual modeling and information systems design. Bus. Inf. Syst. Eng. **6**, 319–337 (2014)
5. Fettke, P.: Ansätze der Informationsmodellierung und ihre betriebswirtschaftliche Bedeutung: Eine Untersuchung der Modellierungspraxis in Deutschland. Schmalenbachs Zeitschrift für Betriebswirtschaftliche Forschung **61**, 550–580 (2008)
6. Indulska, M., Green, P., Recker, J., Rosemann, M.: Business process modeling: perceived benefits. In: Laender, A.H., Castano, S., Dayal, U., Casati, F., Oliveira, J.P.M. (eds.) ER 2009. LNCS, vol. 5829, pp. 458–471. Springer, Heidelberg (2009)
7. Op 't Land, M., Dietz, J.L.: Benefits of enterprise ontology in governing complex enterprise transformations. In: Albani, A., Aveiro, D., Barjis, J. (eds.) EEWC 2012. LNBIP, vol. 110, pp. 77–92. Springer, Heidelberg (2012)
8. Liberatore, M.J., Hatchuel, A., Weil, B., Stylianou, A.C.: An organizational change perspective on the value of modeling. Eur. J. Oper. Res. **125**, 184–194 (2000)
9. Kelton, A.S., Pennington, R.R., Tuttle, B.M.: The effects of information presentation format on judgment and decision making: a review of the information systems research. J. Inf. Syst. **24**, 79–105 (2010)
10. Sterman, J.D.: Business Dynamics: Systems Thinking and Modeling for a Complex World. Irwin/McGraw-Hill, Boston (2000)
11. Dietz, J.L.G.: Enterprise Ontology: Theory and Methodology. Springer, Heidelberg (2006)
12. Frank, U.: Multi-perspective enterprise modelling: foundational concepts, prospects and future research challenges. Softw. Syst. Model. **13**, 941–962 (2014)
13. ISO/IEC 24744
14. Wirtz, B.W., Pistoia, A., Ullrich, S., Göttel, V.: Business models: origin, development and future research. Long Range Plan. **49**, 36–54 (2016)
15. Weber, J.: Gestaltung der Kostenrechnung. Gabler, Wiesbaden (2005)
16. Plinke, W., Utzig, P., Rese, M.: Industrielle Kostenrechnung: Eine Einführung. Gabler, Wiesbaden (2015)
17. Baetge, J., Kirsch, H.-J., Thiele, S.: Bilanzen. IDW, Düsseldorf (2014)
18. Coenenberg, A., Haller, A., Schultze, W.: Jahresabschluss und Jahresabschlussanalyse. Schäffer-Poeschl, Stuttgart (2016)

19. Adam, D.: Planung und Entscheidung. Modelle – Ziele – Methoden. Gabler, Wiesbaden (1992)
20. Benkenstein, M., Waldschmidt, V.: Wertkettenanalyse und Service Value. Eine Diskussion im Lichte der Service-Dominant Logic. In: Forum Dienstleistungsmanagement: Service Value als Werttreiber. Konzepte, Messung und Steuerung, pp. 205–221. Gabler, Wiesbaden (2014)
21. Voeth, M.: Nutzenmessung in der Kaufverhaltensforschung. Die Hierarchische Individualisierte Limit Conjoint-Analyse (HILCA). Gabler, Wiesbaden (2000)
22. Kim, J.-Y., Brünner, T., Skiera, B., Natter, M.: A comparison of different pay-per-bid auction formats. Int. J. Res. Mark. **31**, 368–379 (2014)
23. Wolff, F.: Ökonomie multiperspektivischer Unternehmensmodellierung. Gabler, Wiesbaden (2008)
24. Khalifa, A.S.: Customer value: a review of recent literature and an integrative configuration. Manag. Decis. **42**, 645–666 (2004)
25. VMBO2016 - 10th International Workshop on Value Modeling and Business Ontologies. http://www.loa.istc.cnr.it/vmbo2016/#
26. Spohrer, J., Maglio, P.P.: The emergence of service science: toward systematic service innovations to accelerate co-creation of value. Prod. Oper. Manag. **17**, 238–246 (2008)

The Goal-Based Selection of the Business Process Modeling Language

Ligita Businska(✉) and Marite Kirikova

Institute of Applied Computer Systems, Riga Technical University, Kalku 1, Riga LV-1658, Latvia
{ligita.businska,marite.kirikova}@rtu.lv

Abstract. Business process models are an essential issue of enterprise modeling because business process modeling is the means for performing a wide range of tasks, such as documentation, communication, business improvement, and capturing requirements for software design up to creation of executable process descriptions. Nowadays a wide range of general purpose business process modeling languages are used for handling these tasks. Constantly also a number of the general purpose modeling language extensions and domain specific modeling languages (DSL) are being developed. Thus, obviously, the universal business process modeling language that would be suitable for all the modeling purposes does not (yet) exist. In such a situation the modeler is faced with the problem of choosing a business process modeling language suitable for a certain modeling purpose. This paper proposes to base the choice of the language on a formalized business process modeling goal and a three dimensional business process modeling framework. The paper also describes how to use the proposed framework to measure the modeling language conformity to a certain modeling goal using a general business process element taxonomy and metrics.

Keywords: Business process modeling goal · Business process modeling framework · Business process element taxonomy · Business process modeling language metrics

1 Introduction

The scope of the business process modeling is wide and is continuously increasing. Business process models are used for business process reengineering and management, business process aware system development, e-commerce solutions, enterprise regulation modeling, business process orchestration and choreography modeling, knowledge management, requirement specification, and other purposes.

Such wide applicability of business process models could be explained by the facts that business process modeling is used as the means for handling a wide range of tasks; and that it is supported by the business process modeling tools with constantly evolving functionality. However, the wide applicability of the business process modeling leads to certain problems. Almost in each area of use a number of appropriate business process modeling languages are available (e.g., formal modeling languages). Constantly also

J. Horkoff et al. (Eds.): PoEM 2016, LNBIP 267, pp. 307–316, 2016.
DOI: 10.1007/978-3-319-48393-1_22

extensions of general purpose modeling languages are being developed. For instance, BPMN is already acknowledged as a *de facto* standard for business process modeling and has been recognized as an inter-organizational standard [1] that covers all necessary business process aspects and is suitable for a wide range of users, from business analysts and developers to managers and external partners and clients. However, the applications of this notation have many subsets of elements and a multitude of extensions, and it still coincides with many other modeling languages, forming a large set of available options for business process modeling languages and dialects [2]. Thus, we can conclude that there is no universal business process modeling language that would be suitable for all modeling goals.

Enterprises are faced with situations where the same business processes are modeled for different purposes [3]. On the other hand, particular business process modeling languages are appropriate for certain business process modeling goals. The question arises, how to find a modeling language that is suitable for a certain modeling goal. While, in general, the goal of modeling is a central notion in the choice of modeling languages, in the most of researches, which propose guidelines, techniques, and methods for business process modeling language evaluation or/and selection, the business process modeling goal is not formalized and respectively not transparently taken into account. To overcome this gap, and to explicate and help to handle the business process modeling complexity, the approach to formalize the business process modeling goal and the supporting three dimensional business process modeling framework were proposed [4].

The way how to formalize the business process modeling goal was discussed in detail in [4], specifying what parameters the desirable business process abstraction should have. On the basis of the formalized modeling goal, business process modeling languages can be evaluated according to the values of the modeling goal parameters. In order to identify the values of the modeling goal parameters this paper describes appropriate metrics and algorithms for evaluating modeling language conformance to selected values of modeling goal parameters.

The remainder of the paper is organized as follows. In Sect. 2 the approach for formalization of business process modeling goal and the supporting Business Process Modeling Framework are described. Section 3 illustrates how the Business Process Modeling Framework can be used for evaluation of business process modeling languages. In Sect. 4 the related work is outlined. Brief conclusions are presented in Sect. 5.

2 Formalization of the Business Process Modeling Goal

A natural way to learn about the world around us is its modeling. When we create models, the object under the research is replaced by another mental or physical object, which is more convenient, safer, or cheaper to use than the original. According to such general explanation of the model, any kind of modeling requires the creation of the abstraction of the research object. In a general sense, abstraction is understood as highlighting of the important properties of the research object and ignoring unimportant properties; or creating the general concepts or ideas from the set of objects or facts [5].

By analyzing the business process modeling language specifications (BPMN, DFD, IDEF0, EPC, UML AD, etc.) and business process modeling framework documentations [6–10], we have found that, in order to create the business process model for a particular goal, the following three types of abstractions are to be used:

- Filtration of the business process elements according to the certain modeling perspective
- Generalization from the details about the business process execution according to the selected level of the uncertainty
- Reducing the complexity by "hiding" the part of the business process in the lower level of the decomposition.

In order to identify the values of a modeling goal parameters we propose the Business Process Modeling Framework that is shown in Fig. 1. This framework is developed by amalgamating business process modeling knowledge available in resources of IEEE, ACM, Elsevier, Springer, and other sources. The framework has three dimensions that are defined according to the modeling goal's parameters. Each framework dimension has appropriate "scale" of "values" shown with the abbreviation GL_i – for generalization, DL_i – for decomposition, and P_i – for perspectives. The detailed description of each dimension with appropriate values of the scale is available from [4].

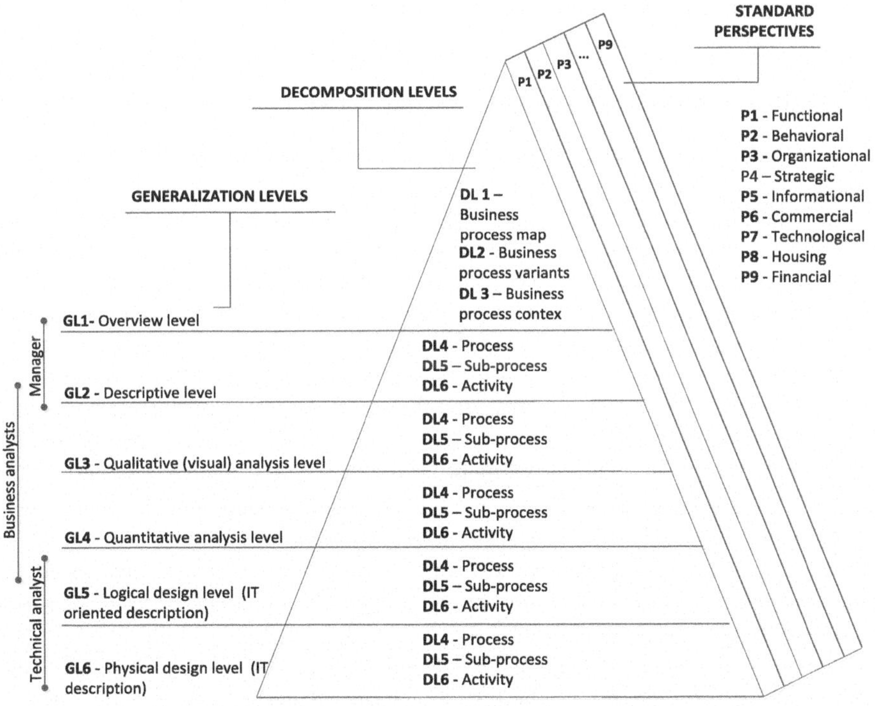

Fig. 1. Business process modeling framework

By modeling the business process at certain generalization and decomposition levels and from a certain perspective, the modeling language that meets the requirements of the modeling goal should be selected. For instance, when creating the business process models at the description level, the attention should be focused at the understanding of the reality, and it is not desirable to spend the time to understand how to use the modeling language. Thus, the modeling language should be intuitively understandable and easy to use. In contrast, when creating a business process models at the logical and physical design levels, there is no need to spend time to create readable and easy understandable for business executive models, i.e., the modeling language should be formal and executable.

3 Goal-Based Selection of the Business Process Modeling Language

This section describes how to use the Business Process Modeling Framework to evaluate the business process modeling language appropriateness to the modeling goal. First, according to the Business Process Modeling Framework, a modeler chooses the perspective and generalization and decomposition levels. Next, it is necessary to evaluate the modeling language with the quantitative metrics, by identifying those languages that are most relevant to the modeling goal parameters. In order to formalize the modeling language notation we propose the General Business Process Modeling Language Taxonomy and the General Business Process Taxonomy.

3.1 The Business Process Modeling Language Taxonomy

The business process modeling language, as any artificial language, could be characterized by semantics and syntax. Some sources, such as [11, 12] separately distinguish a concrete syntax and abstract syntax. For evaluating modeling language appropriateness for a certain modeling goal, we propose to consider only the concrete syntax. For this purpose concrete syntax taxonomy is created for each language that is the set of the language elements arranged in accordance with the General Taxonomy (described in the next section). The modeling language symbols may conform to the General Taxonomy in the following way: the modeling language element corresponds to the appropriate *class of the General Taxonomy* or the modeling language element corresponds to the appropriate *attribute of the General Taxonomy class*. In addition each business process taxonomy element is described using such indicators: *G* – graphical or *T* – textual, *Vr* – vertex, *L* – link or *Gp* – Group, *Vs* – visible or $\overline{Vs}$ – invisible. *Vr*, *L* and *Gp* are defined only for graphical elements.

In this paper only graphical business process modeling languages are considered. Further studies are required to incorporate the textual modeling languages (e.g., formal and executable modeling languages).

To illustrate the Business Process Modeling Language Taxonomy, we demonstrate the part of the BPMN taxonomy that reflects the organizational perspective (Table 1).

Table 1. A part of the BPMN taxonomy (organizational perspective)

General taxonomy element	BPMN element name	BPMN element	Indicators
Active Resource	Pool		*Gp, G, Vs*
Active Resource:: Hierarchy:: Group	Pool		*Gp, G, Vs*
Active Resource:: Hierarchy: Subgroup	Lane	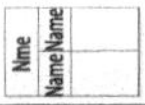	*Gp, G, Vs*
Active Resource:: Dimension:: Horizontal	Horizontal pool		*Gp, G, Vs*
Active Resource:: Dimension:: Vertical	Vertical pool		*Gp, G, Vs*
Active Resource:: Number:: Indefinite	Multiple pool	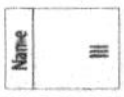	*Gp, G, Vs*
Active Resource:: Transparency:: Closed	Closed pool		*Gp, G, Vs*
Active Resource:: Transparency:: Extended	Extended pool		*Gp r, G, Vs*
Active Resource	Choreography task performer		*V, G, Vs*

3.2 The General Business Process Taxonomy

The General Business Process Taxonomy (or simply the General Taxonomy) is a hierarchical classification structure that allows classifying the normalized set of the business process elements taking into account the degree of the business process elements similarity. The General Taxonomy is obtained by generalizing and normalizing the developed business process modeling language taxonomies. For this research several modeling languages, which have gained wide recognition among both practitioners and scientists, were selected, i.e., BPMN, EPC, UML AD, IDEF0, IDEF3, and KMDL. The General Taxonomy is divided into several levels according to the generalization levels in the Business Process Modeling Framework. The third level of the taxonomy is shown in Fig. 2.

In the next subsection it is described how the General Taxonomy can be used to evaluate the modeling language appropriateness to the modeling goal.

3.3 Metrics for Business Process Modeling Language Evaluation

In order to evaluate compliance with the modeling goal parameters we propose to adopt ideas from approaches based on *Bunge–Wand–Weber* (BWW) ontology [13–16]. However, we have introduced some essential differences. First, the modeling language constructs should be compared with the constructs of the General Taxonomy instead of BWW representation model. Second, it is not always necessary to evaluate the whole

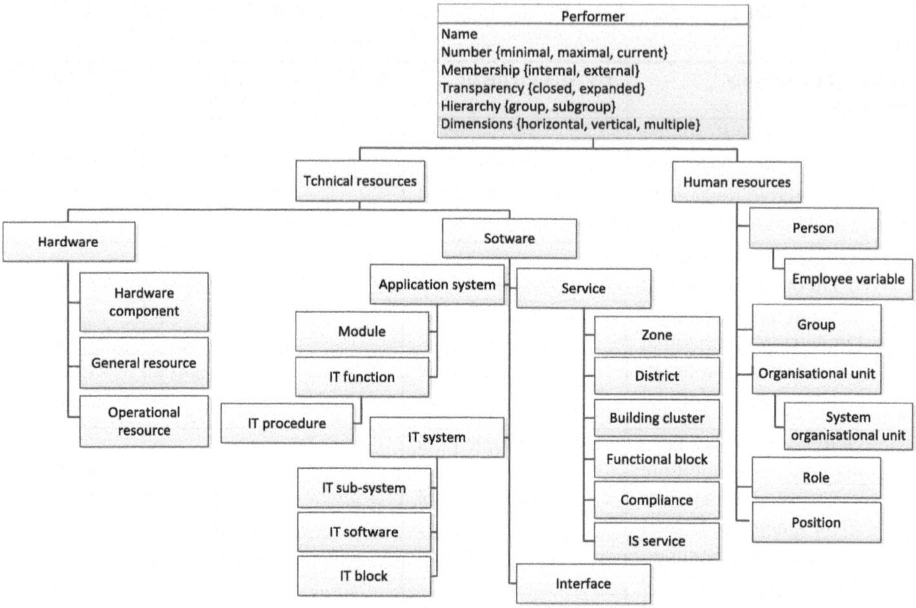

Fig. 2. The third level of the General Taxonomy

General Taxonomy. For instance, when determining compliance with the required perspective, the subset of the General Taxonomy should be built that includes only those elements that are relevant to this perspective. When determining compliance with the generalization level, full General Taxonomy should be estimated. Finally, to estimate the modeling language conformity to the generalization level, the obtained results should be correctly interpreted, i.e., in the highest generalization levels the redundancy (or degree of the construct multiplicity) should be minimized, but overload (or degree of the construct flexibility) should be maximized (see also Fig. 3). On the other hand, in the lowest generalization levels the results should be interpreted inversely, i.e., in the highest generalization levels the redundancy should be maximized, but overload should be minimized.

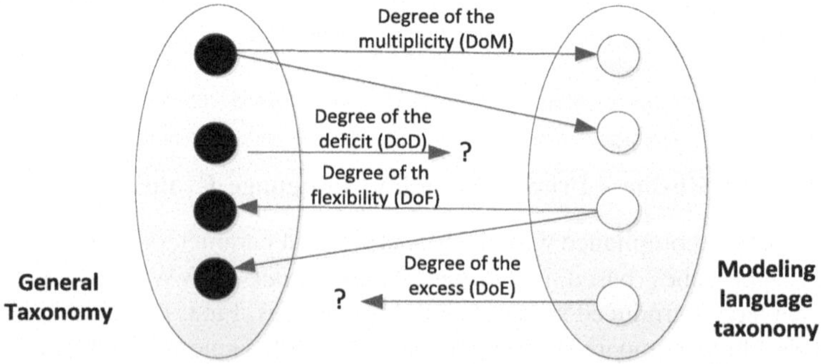

Fig. 3. Metrics for evaluation of the modeling languages

Thus, the following metrics are proposed for business process modeling language evaluation (Fig. 3):

- Degree of the construct deficit (DoD) – is the ratio between the number of constructs (in the subset of the General Taxonomy that reflects certain perspective) found to have a mapping to language constructs divided by the total number of constructs defined in the subset of the General Taxonomy that reflects certain perspective.
- Degree of the construct multiplicity (DoM) – is the ratio between the number of language constructs found to have a mapping to the same General Taxonomy construct divided by the total number of constructs in the modeling language.
- Degree of the construct flexibility (DoF) – is the ratio between the number of language constructs found to have a mapping to the more than one General Taxonomy construct divided by the total number of constructs in the modeling language.
- Degree of the construct (DoE) – is the ratio between the number of language constructs found not to have a mapping to any General Taxonomy construct divided by the total number of constructs in the modeling language.

Thus, the modeling language evaluation consists of the following steps:

1. The modeler selects the desired generalization and decomposition levels and perspective. There are two ways how to specify the perspective: (a) choose one of the standard perspectives; (b) create user perspective, selecting required business process elements from the list of the General Taxonomy elements.
2. According to the selected perspective and generalization level a subset of the General Taxonomy is built (see example in Table 1).
3. Then each of selected modeling language taxonomies is evaluated indicating the degree of the deficit (DoD), the degree of the flexibility (DoF) and degree of multiplicity (DoM).
4. Modeling languages are ranked according to the degree of suitability for the abstraction level, the granularity level, and the perspective. If none of the languages provide complete coverage of the chosen perspective, a modeling language combination is offered. When creating such combinations, the priority is given to modeling languages that have a minimum coverage. In the case when the conflicting assessments are obtained, e.g., when one modeling language provides a better coverage of the perspective and is less appropriate for the chosen generalization level, and another modeling language has the opposite evaluation results; then the priority is given to the modeling language, which has already been used for other modeling goals. If no one of the modeling languages yet have been used, then the modeler makes the decision by himself.

4 Outline of Some Related Works

Analyzing different researches that propose guidelines, techniques, and methods for business process modeling language evaluation and/or selection, it is possible to classify proposed solutions into several groups. One group of solutions, such as [13–16], offers to estimate business process modeling language characteristics. However, it is not explained what are the characteristics the modeling language should have in order to be suitable for a particular modeling purpose. Others researches offer to use particular business process modeling languages for certain modeling purposes (e.g., [17, 18]), but the choice of the modeling language is mostly based on the author's subjective opinion. Another category of solutions (e.g., [19–21]) offers to adapt business process model content to new modeling purpose, using various techniques such as changing the level of granularity, reducing unnecessary details, or generalizing the content of the model. Finally, there are solutions that provide transformations between different abstraction levels [22–24], for instance, the conceptual models are transformed to realization models according to Model Driven Approach (MDA) approach [25]. Each abstraction level is realized by certain modeling language, and the choice of this language is not clarified. Thus, we can conclude that the large part of the solutions do not support the selection of the modeling language according to the modeling goal. The modeler should decide which modeling language is more suitable for a particular goal or to use the offered modeling language without justification and estimation of the alternatives.

5 Conclusions

The paper suggests using the abstraction types (generalization, decomposition and modeling from a particular perspective) for formalizing the business process modeling goal. For better usage of the modeling goal's parameters the Business Process Modeling Framework is proposed. Using this framework, a modeler can choose the perspective and the levels of the generalization and decomposition. In addition, the paper offers appropriate metrics and algorithms for evaluating how modeling languages conform to the selected values of the modeling goal parameters. For instance, in order to evaluate to which extent the business process modeling language conforms to the desired perspective, it is measured whether the modeling language offers syntactical constructions for all necessary business process elements. But in order to evaluate the conformity to the required generalization level, the flexibility and multiplicity of the modeling language is evaluated. That is, for modeling at the highest generalization level, the modeling language should be the simplest and the most flexible and provide only one syntactical construction for each business process element. When modeling at the lower generalization levels, these features are not so relevant, but formality and executability of the language matters.

The proposed solution is the step forward to handling business process modeling complexity semi-automatically and is the first step towards development of a support system for evaluating conformity of the business process modeling languages to particular modeling goals.

Acknowledgment. This work has been supported in part by the European Social Fund within the project «Support for the implementation of doctoral studies at Riga Technical University», and in part by the Latvian Council of Science grant for project No. 342/2012, and in part by the Latvian National research program SOPHIS under grant agreement No. 10-4/VPP-4/11.

References

1. Shapiro, R., White, S.A., Bock, G., Palmer, N., Muehlen, M., Brambilla, M., Gagne, D., et al.: BPMN 2.0 Handbook Second Edition: Methods, Concepts, Case Studies and Standards in Business Process Modeling Notation. Future Strategies, USA (2012)
2. Braun, R., Esswein, W.: Classification of domain-specific BPMN extensions. In: Frank, U., Loucopoulos, P., Pastor, O., Petrounias, I. (eds.) The Practice of Enterprise Modeling. LNCS, vol. 197, pp. 42–57. Springer, Heidelberg (2014)
3. Garcia, H.D.D.: Evaluation of data-centric process modeling approaches. Master thesis. Eindhoven: Eindhoven University of Technology (2011)
4. Businska, L., Kirikova, M.: The formalization of the business process modeling goal: extended abstract. In: Joint Proceedings of the BIR 2016 Workshops and Doctoral Consortium Co-located with 14th International- Conference on Perspectives in Business Informatics Research (2016, in print)
5. Free Dictionary. http://www.thefreedictionary.com/
6. Weske, M.: Business Process Management: Concepts, Languages, Architectures. Springer, Heidelberg (2012)
7. Eid-Sabbagh, R.-H., Dijkman, R., Weske, M.: Business process architecture: use and correctness. In: Gal, A., Kindler, E., Barros, A. (eds.) BPM 2012. LNCS, vol. 7481, pp. 65–81. Springer, Heidelberg (2012)
8. Swenson, K.: The Difference Between Workflow and BPR. http://www.e-workflow.org/downloads/workflow-bpr_kswenson.pdf
9. McLeod, G.: The Difference between Process Architecture and Process Modeling/Design (and why you should care). http://grahammcleod.typepad.com/files/ processarchitecturevsprocessmodelingmcleod.pdf
10. van Nuffel, D., de Backer, M.: Multi-abstraction layered business process modeling. Comput. Ind. **63**(2), 131–147 (2012)
11. Baar, T.: Correctly defined concrete syntax for visual modeling languages. In: Wang, J., Whittle, J., Harel, D., Reggio, G. (eds.) MoDELS 2006. LNCS, vol. 4199, pp. 111–125. Springer, Heidelberg (2006)
12. Brambilla, M., Cabot, J., Wimmer, M.: Model-Driven Software Engineering in Practice. Morgan & Claypool Publishers, USA (2012)
13. Recker, J., Rosemann, M., Indulska, M., Green, P.: Business Process Modeling: A Maturing Discipline? http://www.bpmi.org
14. Green, P., Rosemann, M., Indulska, M.: Ontological evaluation of enterprise systems interoperability using ebXML. IEEE Trans. Knowl. Data Eng. **17**(5), 713–725 (2005)
15. Green, P., Rosemann, M.: Integrated process modeling: an ontological evaluation. Inf. Syst. **25**(2), 73–87 (2000)
16. zur Muehlen, M., Recker J., Indulska M.: Sometimes less is more: are process modeling languages overly complex? In: EDOC Conference Workshop, pp. 197–204. IEEE Press (2007)
17. Lodhi, A., Koppen, V., Saake, G.: Business process modeling. In: Active Research Areas and Challenges: Technical report, 34 p. (2011)
18. Burlton, R.: Perspectives on Process Modeling. http://www.bptrends.com/point-of-view-perspectives-on-process-modeling/
19. Polyvyanyy, A., Smirnov, S., Weske, M.: Process model abstraction: a slider approach. In: Enterprise Distributed Object Computing Conference, pp. 325–331. IEEE Press (2008)
20. Smirnov, S., Reijers, H.A., Weske, M., Nugteren, T.: Business process model abstraction: a definition, catalog, and survey. Distrib. Parallel Databases **30**(1), 63–99 (2012)

21. Rosa, M.L., Dumas, M., ter Hofstede, A.H.M., Mendling, J.: Configurable multi-perspective business process models. Inf. Syst. **36**(2), 313–340 (2011)
22. Dehnert, J., van der Aalst, W.M.P.: Bridging the gap between business models and workflow specifications international. J. Coop. Inf. Syst. **13**(3), 51–69 (2004)
23. Mendling, J., Ziemann, J.: Transformation of BPEL Processes to EPCs. http://citeseerx.ist.psu.edu/viewdoc/summary?doi=10.1.1.90.2429
24. Dreiling, A., Rosemann, M., van der Aalst, W.M.P.: From Conceptual Process Models to Running Workflows: A Holistic Approach for the Configuration of Enterprise Systems. http://aisel.aisnet.org/pacis2005/30/
25. MDA - The Architecture of Choice for a Changing World. http://www.omg.org/mda/

A Toolbox Supporting Agile Modelling Method Engineering: ADOxx.org Modelling Method Conceptualization Environment

Nesat Efendioglu(✉), Robert Woitsch, and Wilfrid Utz

BOC Asset Management GmbH, Operngasse 20B, 1040 Vienna, Austria
{nesat.efendioglu, robert.woitsch, wilfrid.utz}@boc-eu.com

Abstract. The importance of Modelling Method Engineering is equally rising with the importance of domain specific modelling methods and individual modelling approaches. In order to capture the most relevant semantic primitives that address domain specifics needs, it is necessary to involve both, method engineers as well as domain experts. Due to complexity of conceptualization of a modelling method and development of regarding modelling tool, there is a need of a guideline and corresponding tools supporting actors with different background along this complex process. Based on practical experience in business, more than twenty EU projects and other research initiatives, this paper introduces a toolbox to support the conceptualization of a modelling method. The realized toolbox is introduced and evaluated by two EU-funded research projects in the domain of e-learning and cloud computing as well as additionally by an in-house development project in the area of decision modelling extensions. The paper discusses the evaluation results and derived outlooks.

Keywords: Meta-modelling · Modelling method design · Agile modelling method engineering · Conceptualization

1 Introduction

The importance of Modelling Method Engineering is equally rising with the importance of Domain Specific Conceptual Modelling Methods and individual modelling approaches. In addition to existing standards (e.g. BPMN, DMN, CMMN), a growing number of groups around the world design their individual modelling-methods (in accordance with the definition of such a method by [1, 2]) for a variety of application domains. The engineering of such applicable modelling tools as a result of the conceptualization process of modelling methods, is complex, especially when considering the mapping of the entire spectrum from language artefacts and corresponding functionality to concrete implementable and deployable modelling tool capabilities. Besides that, there are branching knowledge domains into more refined and specialized subdomains, where each domain needs to be characterized by its own abstraction and refinement of concepts from reality. Hence, in order to capture the most relevant semantic primitives that address domain specific needs, it is necessary to involve both the method engineers as well as domain experts. Today, there are different approaches,

J. Horkoff et al. (Eds.): PoEM 2016, LNBIP 267, pp. 317–325, 2016.
DOI: 10.1007/978-3-319-48393-1_23

guidelines and practices for the development of modelling tools available that do not consider the full spectrum of the design and collaborative development of a modelling method, which unavoidably leads to limitations in the conceptualization of it [3]. There is a need of a guideline and corresponding tools supporting method engineers along the complex conceptualization process taking all phases into consideration and ensuring collaboration among stakeholders involved in the process. Karagiannis proposes in [2] the Agile Modelling Method Engineering (AMME) framework. Authors of [4] propose the Modelling Method Conceptualization Process that based on AMME, guides the method engineers during conceptualization. The work at hand proposes a toolbox that supports this process, evaluates it in two European Research projects, and one additional in the context of an in-house research project, and discusses evaluation results.

The remainder of the paper is structured as follows: Sect. 2 briefly revisits AMME, the Modelling Method Conceptualization Process and outlines each tool in the toolbox. Section 3 presents evaluation cases and discusses the evaluation results, while Sect. 4 concludes the paper and gives an outlook on future work.

2 Modelling Method Conceptualization Environment

AMME is proposed in [2] to support modelling method engineering during propagation and evolution of modelling requirements. The OMiLab Lifecycle [5] instantiates AMME and defines the internal cycle of a modelling method conceptualization with five phases; (1) "Create" as a mix of goal definition, knowledge acquisition and requirements elicitation activities that capture and represent the modelling requirements; (2) "Design" specifies the meta-model, language grammar, notation and functionality as model processing mechanisms and algorithms; (3) "Formalize" aims to describe the outcome of the previous phase in non-ambiguous, formal representations with the purpose of sharing results within a scientific community; (4) "Develop" produces concrete modelling prototypes and finally (5) "Deploy/Validate" involves the stakeholders in hands-on experience and the evaluation process as input for upcoming iterations.

Due to the involvement of several stakeholders with varying knowledge backgrounds, perspectives and different objectives, in the conceptualization of a modelling method, the authors of [4] propose so-called Modelling Method Conceptualization Process (as depicted in Fig. 1) by adding additional feedback channels into the

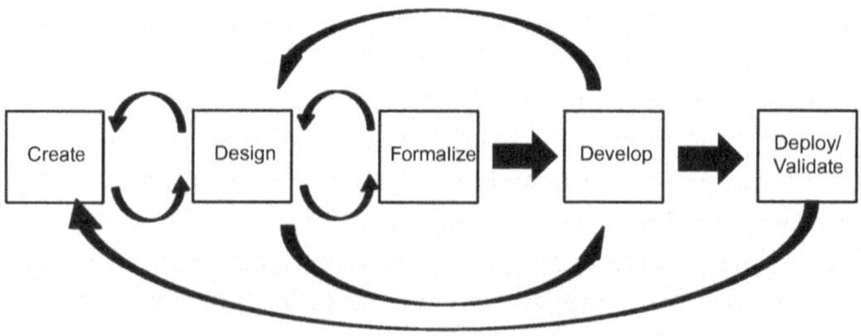

Fig. 1. Modelling method conceptualization process

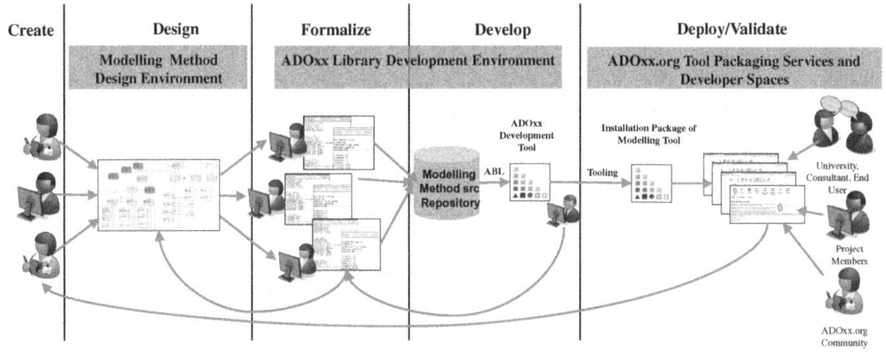

Fig. 2. The toolbox: modelling method conceptualization environment

OMiLab Lifecycle between: (1) Create and Design, to prove, if the designed modelling language covers the identified application scenarios and considers the identified requirements; (2) Design and Formalize to ensure formal approval of modelling language, as well as (3) Design and Develop - to improve modelling language in earlier stages before it is released and deployed.

The work at hand introduces a toolbox called "Modelling Method Conceptualization Environment" (as depicted in Fig. 2) that instantiates the above process and supports method engineers during each phases. The only exception is that of the "Create" phase, as this part is regarded as the most creative phase and standard tools and methods (also in some cases pen and paper can be the most appropriate tools) to can be freely selected. Modelling Method Conceptualization Environment proposes a combination of tools, such as the Modelling Method Design Environment (MMDE, available at [6]) for the Design, the ADOxx Library Development Environment (ALDE) and ADOxx, for Formalize and Develop, ADOxx.org Tool Packing Services and Developer Spaces for Deploy/Validate Phases.

It is worth to mention that one of the objectives is to provide loosely coupled tools, so method engineers have the flexibility to decide to use one, a combination of tools from the toolbox or even use other appropriate tools of their choice, (e.g. method engineer uses MMDE during the Design Phase, but formalize the modelling method design with mathematical models or use another development tool during the Develop Phase and deploys them at the Developer Spaces and enable validation).

In the following sub-sections current abilities of the tools from the environment are shortly presented.

2.1 Modelling Method Design Environment

The Modelling Method Design Environment (MMDE) is itself a modelling tool to design other modelling methods. MMDE has been implemented based on lessons learned and the experience of the authors, who have been involved in modelling method/tool development activities in more than 20 EU research projects for varying domains. Based on these lessons learned, UML [7] has been identified as a fitting starting point. Hence, the MMDE takes a subset of UML and extends it with required concepts and functionalities in order to overcome the following challenges **(Ch)**, which are introduced by [4] after a state of the art analysis about specification of conceptual modelling methods: **Ch1-**Definition of functional and non-functional requirements and their relation between the concepts in modelling methods; **Ch2-**Fragmenting the whole meta-model into individual meta-models composing concepts for different sub-domains and still be able to define links between concepts in different individual meta-models; **Ch3-**Having another abstraction layer to represent modules and layers of modelling language as well as relation among them without representing the complexity of abstract and concrete syntax; **Ch4-**Assigning different concrete syntax to the concepts in modelling language; **Ch5-**Possibility to design modelling procedure and mechanisms & algorithms of a domain specific modelling language.

To overcome **Ch1,** "Requirements" model type is implemented that allows the elicitation of requirements, specifying their status as well as dependencies among them. The described requirements in this model type can be referenced to (a) all the modelling classes modelled in the related model type "Meta-Model" classes, (b) graphical notation (concrete syntax) definitions modelled in the "Graphical Notation" model type, (c) the "Modelling Stack" definition and (d) to the functionalities modelled in "Mechanisms & Algorithms" models. For **Ch2** and **Ch3,** we extend the class diagram from UML with concepts, so method engineers can differentiate between class and relation class as well as relate different meta-models (-fragments) with each other using "Weaving" techniques as they are introduced in [8, 9]. The modularization and layering of modelling language is essential to avoid complexities during the design of domain specific modelling methods [10, 11]. Hence, we propose representation of the modelling stack as the "Meta-models Stack model type allowing method engineers to differentiate meta-models in sense of different model types that target different fragments of the system. In order to target **Ch4** and specify a proper graphical representation (concrete syntax) of each concept in a meta-model, we introduce another model type called "Graphical Notation" model type (allows definition of concrete syntax of model types with specifying graphical representations for each constructs in meta-models. This model type allows the description of graphical representations either assignment of vector graphics code written in GraphRep Language [31] or with the assignment of concrete images in PNG, JPG or Bitmap format including a description of the functionalities in the notation (e.g. attribute-value dependent visualization, context related views) In order to target **Ch5** to define the applicable modelling technique as steps and corresponding results we propose a model type called "Modelling Procedure" model type". The Modelling Procedure Model Type allows method engineers to define the steps with their required inputs and produced outputs, as well as the sequence of steps based on input – output relationships, in order to introduce case specific proper usage of their modelling method. Based on this procedural view, concrete Mechanisms and Algorithms can be derived and depicted as Sequence and Component Diagrams from UML (therefore these diagram types has been implemented as model types in MMDE). Further details about MMDE can be found in [4].

2.2 ADOxx Library Development Environment

The ADOxx Library Development Environment (ALDE) aims to enable formalization and parallel development of modelling tools libraries based on the designs deriving from Design Phase, merging different libraries and ensuring maintainability. As an experimental prototype ALDE uses the Resource Description Framework (RDF) as a format for data interchange [12].

ALDE is a development environment based on the Eclipse IDE [13] and includes a meta^{2}model defined in RDFS, the ALDE vocabulary. Having the vocabulary and utilizing Apache Ant® as a build mechanism [14], the environment enables the definition of the transformation processes from ADOxx Library Languages to RDF and vice versa. Moreover ALDE serializes libraries in an arbitrary RDF format; for the prototypical realization RDF Turtle [15] has been used and includes the RDF XTurtle Editor developed by [16]. Having libraries in RDF Turtle format and a RDF Turtle Editor available, method engineers can adapt declaratively and script libraries collaboratively using standard functionalities of source-code management systems. Merging several libraries or integration of parts of libraries in each other becomes possible.

2.3 ADOxx.org Tool Packaging Services and Developer Spaces

The ADOxx.org Tool Packaging Service [17] is a web-based service that allows method engineers of the ADOxx community to build verified, professional and installable distribution packages that can be distribute to interested stakeholders. The service combines and validates all available inputs, integrates all elements, compiles the necessary artifacts and signs the outcomes and creates the actual installer as a download archive.

As a collaboration space for the development and deployment phases, the concept of "Developer Spaces" has been introduced in ADOxx.org [18]. These spaces enable sharing of intermediate/release results, discussing development resources from all pre/past phases in the form of source code, snippet, examples and distribution packages with the community.

3 Evaluation

The toolbox introduced above has been applied in three different cases for evaluation: two EU-funded research projects in the domain of eLearning and cloud computing and additionally in an in-house development project, in the area of decision modelling extensions. These cases have been selected since the involved partners have varying profiles and expertise in development and in modelling tool engineering. In the following subsection we introduce the cases and their requirements in method engineering manner. Afterwards the evaluation results are discussed.

Case 1: Conceptualization of a Modelling Method for E-Learning: The FP7 project Learn PAd [19] proposes a process-driven-knowledge management approach based on conceptual and semantic models for transformation of public administration organizations into learning organizations. Learn PAd proposes a model-driven collaborative learning environment. In this case, 4 domain experts and method engineers have been involved. In addition, two developer teams, each consisting of 4 developers worked on the implementation of the tool. The results of the conceptualization process of this modelling method can be found at Learn PAd Developer Space [20], as well as the developed prototypes [21] can be downloaded and feedback can be given.

Case 2: Conceptualization of Modelling Method for Cloud Computing: The H2020 project CloudSocket [22] introduces the idea of Business Processes as a Service (BPaaS), where conceptual models and semantics are applied to align business processes with Cloud-deployed workflows [23]. In this case, 6 domain experts and method engineers have been involved, as well as two developer teams, one with 5 developers, the other one with 2 members The results of the conceptualization process of this modelling method can be found at CloudSocket Developer Space [24], as well as developed prototypes [25] can be downloaded and feedback can be given.

Case 3: Integration of Exiting BPMN and DMN Modelling Methods: The in-house project requires integration of an already implemented DMN [26] Modelling Method into existing BPMN 2.0 [27] realization as part of the a commercial product. In this case, 3 domain experts and method engineers, and a team of two developers have been involved.

3.1 Evaluation Results

The evaluation process was enacted in the following steps: (1) Provisioning: the tools - of the toolbox have been provided to the stakeholders in the involved cases. (2) Team Formation: representatives, -of the stakeholders in the project created development teams consisting of domain experts and method engineers following the conceptualization process and developing tools individually. (3) Feedback Phase: individual results have been consolidated periodically through video conferences and workshops, constituting the evaluation results. In all cases each tool from the toolbox except ALDE has been utilized, ALDE has been utilized just in Case 3.

Feedback on MMDE

Pro: It is possible to specify requirements and dependencies among them as well as tracing them; (2) to define modelling language fragments and modules, (3) layering the modelling language with navigational constructs; (4) definition of syntax, semantic and assignment of notation (concrete syntax); (5) definition of weaving among construct in different meta-models; (6) assignment of (multiple-) graphical notation (concrete syntax); (7) explicit definition of modelling procedure;

Contra: It is not possible to define application scenarios and use cases, and design results can be exchanged solely using ADOxx specific formats or as static content (image, PDF or HTML).

Feedback on ALDE

Pro: It is possible to transform libraries in a machine as well as human interpretable format, ability to use reasoning algorithms, due to standard semantic formats; reduces complexity to edit, merge and maintain libraries.

Contra: To take over results from Design Phase require manual steps. Without knowledge of RDF and Turtle syntax, it is difficult for software engineers that using well-known programing languages (e.g. Java, C++), to get used familiar with; it requires different transformation scripts for different meta-modelling technologies (such as ADOxx, EMF).

Feedback on ADOxx.org Tool Packing Services and Developer Spaces

Pro: It is possible to have an installation package to distribute to interested stakeholders, building your own community around the modelling method, and get feedback from them.

Contra: Setting up and handling issues of a certain Developer Space involves certain manual steps, such, as the interested stakeholder has to send an e-mail to the administrator with a request of an own Developer Space.

4 Conclusion and Outlook

In this paper we introduce a toolbox instantiating the Modelling Method Conceptualization Process, which supports agile modelling method engineering. The toolbox has been evaluated through an analysis of three different cases: two EU research projects and one in-house project. The evaluation results put forward that having an approach and a corresponding toolbox following the idea of model-driven engineering approach is effective in terms of transferring knowledge from the analysis of requirements up to the development of solutions. Being two main tools, MMDE and ALDE, experimental prototypes that are at very early stage of development, lack of full integration or automatic data exchange ability, and the need of manual steps building Developer Spaces came out as major limitations of the toolbox. As an outlook the following items derived from the evaluation: (1) currently we are evaluating development alternatives of MM-DSLs with using Java, Xtend [28] or RDF; building on existing work [29] in the field, (2) enabling graphical modelling method design to transform into machine understandable format, (3) formalization of modelling method design using mathematical models such as FDMM [30], (4) automatization of tooling services and deployment onto developer spaces, (5) full integration of tools around new MM-DSL.

Acknowledgment. This work has been partly supported by the European Commission co-funded projects Learn PAd (www.learnpad.eu) under contract FP7- 619583 and CloudSocket (www.cloudsocket.eu), under contract H2020-ICT 644690.

References

1. Karagiannis, D., Kühn, H.: Metamodelling platforms. In: Stuckenschmidt, H., Jannach, D. (eds.) EC-Web 2015. LNCS, vol. 239, p. 182. Springer, Heidelberg (2002). doi:10.1007/3-540-45705-4_19
2. Karagiannis, D.: Agile modeling method engineering. In: Proceedings of the 19th Panhellenic Conference on Informatics, Athens, Greece, pp. 5–10. ACM (2015)
3. Hrgovcic, V., Karagiannis, D., Woitsch, R.: Conceptual modeling of the organisational aspects for distributed applications: the semantic lifting approach. In: IEEE COMPSACW (2013)
4. Efendioglu, N., Woitsch, R., Karagiannis, D.: Modelling method design: a model-drive approach. In: IIWAS 2015: Proceedings of the 17th International Conference on Information Integration and Web-based Applications, Brussels, Belgium. ACM (2015)
5. Open Models Laboratory (OMILab): Idea and Objectives (2015). http://austria.omilab.org/psm/about. Accessed 15 July 2016
6. ADOxx.org: LearnPAd Developer Space (2015). https://www.adoxx.org/live/web/learnpad-developer-space/design-environment. Accessed 07 July 2016
7. Object Management Group (OMG): Documents Associated with UML Version 2.0 (2005). http://www.omg.org/spec/UML/2.0/. Accessed 12 July 2015
8. Kühn, H.: Method integration in business engineering, Ph.D. thesis (in German), University of Vienna (2004)
9. Woitsch, R.: Hybrid modeling: an instrument for conceptual interoperability. In: Revolutionizing Enterprise Interoperability Through Scientific Foundations, Hershey, pp. 97–118 (2014)
10. Selic, B.: The theory and practice of modeling language design for model-based software engineering—a personal perspective. In: Fernandes, J.M., Lämmel, R., Visser, J., Saraiva, J. (eds.) Generative and Transformational Techniques in Software Engineering III. LNCS, vol. 6491, pp. 290–321. Springer, Heidelberg (2011)
11. Karagiannis, D., Hrgovcic, V., Woitsch, R.: Model driven design for e-applications: the meta model approach. In: Proceedings of the 13th International Conference on Information Integration and Web-based Applications and Services, iiWAS11, Ho Chi Minh City, Vietnam, pp. 451–454. ACM (2011)
12. W3C: RDF-Resource Description Framework (2014). https://www.w3.org/RDF/. Accessed 14 July 2016
13. Eclipse Foundation: Eclipse IDE for Java EE Developers (2016). http://www.eclipse.org/downloads/packages/. Accessed 14 July 2016
14. The Apache Software Foundation: Apache Ant Download (2016). https://www.apache.org/dist/ant/binaries/. Accessed 14 July 2016
15. W3C: RDF 1.1 Turtle Terse RDF Triple Language (2014). https://www.w3.org/TR/2014/REC-turtle-20140225/. Accessed 14 July 2016
16. The Research Group Agile Knowledge Engineering and Semantic Web (AKSW), University of Leipzig, "Xturtle" (2015). http://aksw.org/Projects/Xturtle.html. Accessed 15 July 2016
17. ADOxx.org: AutoPDP Tool Packaging Service (2016). https://www.adoxx.org/live/autopdp-packaging-service. Accessed 14 July 2016
18. ADOxx.org: ADOxx.org Developer Spaces (2016). https://www.adoxx.org/live/development-spaces. Accessed 14 July 2016
19. Learn PAd Consortium: The EU Project Learn PAd (2014). http://www.learnpad.eu/. Accessed 15 July 2016

20. LearnPAd Consortium: LearnPAd Developer Space (2015). https://www.adoxx.org/live/web/learnpad-developer-space. Accessed 15 July 2016
21. LearnPAd Consortium: LearnPAd Developer Space - Downloads (2015). https://www.adoxx.org/live/web/learnpad-developer-space/downloads. Accessed 15 July 2016
22. CloudSocket Consortium: CloudSocket Project (2016). https://www.cloudsocket.eu/. Accessed 14 July 2016
23. Woitsch, R., Utz, W.: Business process as a service, model based business and IT cloud alignment as a cloud offering. In: ES 2015, Third International Conference on Enterprise Systems, Basel, Switzerland (2015)
24. CloudSocket Consortium: CloudSocket Developer Space (2015). https://www.adoxx.org/live/web/cloudsocket-developer-space/. Accessed 15 July 2016
25. CloudSocket Consortium: CloudSocket Developer Space - Downloads (2015). https://www.adoxx.org/live/web/cloudsocket-developer-space/downloads. Accessed 15 July 2016
26. Object Management Group (OMG): Decision Model and Notation, Version 1.0 (2015). http://www.omg.org/spec/DMN/1.0/. Accessed 15 July 2016
27. Object Management Group (OMG): Business Model and Notation Version 2.0 (2011). http://www.omg.org/spec/BPMN/2.0/. Accessed 15 July 2016
28. Eclipse Foundation: Xtend (2015). https://eclipse.org/xtend. Accessed 15 July 2016
29. Visic, N., Karagiannis, D.: Developing conceptual modeling tools using a DSL. In: Buchmann, R., Kifor, C.V., Yu, J. (eds.) KSEM 2014. LNCS, vol. 8793, pp. 162–173. Springer, Heidelberg (2014)
30. Fill, H.-G., Redmond, T., Karagiannis, D.: FDMM: a formalism for describing ADOxx meta models and models. In: Proceedings of ICEIS 2012, Wroclaw, Poland, vol. 3, pp. 133–144 (2012)
31. ADOxx.org "GraphRep" (2016). https://www.adoxx.org/live/graphrep. Accessed 31 Aug 2016

Using Attack-Defense Trees to Analyze Threats and Countermeasures in an ATM: A Case Study

Marlon Fraile[1(✉)], Margaret Ford[2(✉)], Olga Gadyatskaya[3(✉)], Rajesh Kumar[4(✉)], Mariëlle Stoelinga[4(✉)], and Rolando Trujillo-Rasua[3(✉)]

[1] GMV, Madrid, Spain
[2] Consult Hyperion, Guildford, UK
[3] University of Luxembourg, SnT, Esch-sur-Alzette, Luxembourg
rolando.trujillo@uni.lu
[4] University of Twente, Enschede, Netherlands

Abstract. Securing automated teller machines (ATMs), as critical and complex infrastructure, requires a precise understanding of the associated threats. This paper reports on the application of attack-defense trees to model and analyze the security of ATMs. We capture the most dangerous multi-stage attack scenarios applicable to ATM structures, and establish a practical experience report, where we reflect on the process of modeling ATM threats via attack-defense trees. In particular, we share our insights into the benefits and drawbacks of attack-defense tree modeling, as well as best practices and lessons learned.

Keywords: Attack-defense trees · Security modeling · ATM security

1 Introduction

Worldwide, the compromise of automated teller machines (ATMs) is a very lucrative criminal business. One of the prime reasons is the monetary incentive, allowing successful attackers to take money instantly. Moreover, their geographical spread, dependence on human interactions, and integration of local and external networks make ATMs a very accessible target for exploitation, vulnerable to a large variety of attack scenarios. Thus, criminals constantly invent new ways to circumvent protections and compromise the machines. The European ATM Crime Report (EAST)[1] evaluates the loss in 2015 due to ATM Related Fraud Attacks in Europe was around 300 millions Euro.

The security of individual ATMs concerns both banks and the organizations hosting the machines. In this context, security risk management, being a critical activity for any enterprise, becomes essential. To support risk analysts, many methodologies have been developed. These include security methods, such

The research leading to the results presented in this work received funding from the European Commission's Seventh Framework Programme (FP7/2007-2013) under grant agreement number 318003 (TREsPASS).

[1] https://www.european-atm-security.eu/tag/european-atm-crime-report/.

J. Horkoff et al. (Eds.): PoEM 2016, LNBIP 267, pp. 326–334, 2016.
DOI: 10.1007/978-3-319-48393-1_24

as NIST SP800-30, standards for the risk management process (e.g. ISO/IEC 27005), and modeling techniques and formalisms (for example, misuse cases [13], anti-goal refinement [10], and attack trees [18]). These methodologies aim at providing structure to the risk assessment process, facilitating interactions among stakeholders, and cataloguing the identified threats. Furthermore, some of these techniques enable advanced quantitative risk analysis with security metrics, e.g. expected time of attack or worst case impact.

In this paper, we report on the application of *attack-defense trees* to security risk assessment of ATMs. Attack-defense trees (ADTrees, [7]) extend the popular attack trees formalism with defenses (also called countermeasures). Similarly to attack trees, ADTrees enjoy an appealing and intuitive visual representation, a structured way to brainstorm about attack scenarios [8] and formal frameworks to analyze the trees qualitatively or quantitatively [7,11]. Additionally, ADTrees support reasoning about potential defenses, enabling highly effective decision-making processes for countermeasure selection. Since defenses are crucial in the case of ATMs, the ADTrees formalism provided valuable support for our case.

Our paper presents a practical experience report, where we reflect on the process of modeling ATM security threats, and potential countermeasures via ADTrees. The paper outlines the case study, and describes our process for designing a large, comprehensive ADTree. We also share techniques that we found useful when working with ADTrees and report caveats that the practitioners need to become aware of.

2 Background and Preliminaries

Attack Trees. Attack trees (ATrees, [11,18]) are a graphical formalism to structure, model and analyze the potential attacks on an asset. An attack tree starts with a security threat, modelled as the root of the tree, representing the attacker's top level goal. This root is recursively refined into the attacker's subgoals through *logical gates*, modelling how successful attack steps propagate through the system. AND-gates model that, to succeed in this step, the attacker must succeed in all of its child nodes; OR-gates model that, to succeed in this step, the attacker must succeed in at least one of its child nodes. When further refinement is not possible or not required, one arrives at the *basic attack steps (BASs)*, sitting at the leaves of the ATree. Leaves can further be decorated with quantitative attributes, such as cost or success probability of the BASs [9,11].

Attack-Defense Trees. Attack-defense trees extend attack trees with defensive measures, also called *countermeasures*, yielding a graphical mathematical model of multi-stage attacks along with safeguards [7]. Defense nodes can appear at any level of the tree, and can be further refined with AND- and OR-gates. Moreover, countermeasures can themselves be attacked. Thus, each node belongs either to the attacker (represented as red ellipses in our figures) or defender (green squares in our figures). Countermeasures prevent an adversary from reaching the goal, thus an ADTree represents an interplay between an attacker, whose goal is to attack the system, and a defender who tries to protect it [7].

Related Work. Several papers report on the applicability of attack trees in practical scenarios. Opdahl and Sindre have empirically compared ATrees with misuse cases and reported that participants were able to identify more threats with ATrees [13]. Saini et al. evaluated security of the MyProxy system with ATrees [17], Byres et al. used attack trees to evaluate the SCADA communication systems security [2], and Ray and Poolsapassit applied the ATree methodology to identify insider threats [15]. Security of vehicular ad-hoc networks was evaluated with ATrees in [3]. In [4], Edge et al. modeled an online banking scenario via deriving protection trees from ATrees. Following the approach of [6], a methodology to construct ATrees based on the system architecture, risk assessment study outcomes and a security knowledge base is proposed in [14]. This methodology follows a layered approach to generate skeletons of attack trees. Morais et al. [12] follow a similar methodology but in a top-down manner, when first high-level attacks are collated, and then these are refined into concrete attack steps. None of these approaches, however, included defenses.

To the best of our knowledge, the ADTree formal language has been empirically validated only once; through a case study on a warehouse goods management system developed by Bagnato et al. [1]. That work focused mainly on the quantitative aspects of the ADTree methodology. In this article, instead, we focus on modeling aspects of the ADTree methodology.

3 The ATM Case Study

Establishing the Context. This case study considers an ATM located inside a gas station, which is split in two main zones: the **store zone**, enabled with a security glass door class RC3 and two security glass windows class RC2[2], and the **internal office**, where the technological components related to the gas station management (workstation, printer, router and local Internet connection used to share information with the headquarters) are located. Customers can transit the store zone to buy or request services, including ATM services, during the business hours of the store. The gas station is open from 6:00 AM to midnight and provides several services including: fuel, car-wash, food, cash, etc.

Identification of Interested Parties. The gas station involves different interested parties that may perform several roles. Physical security is outsourced to a *Security Provider* who has physical countermeasures implemented in the gas station. These include a fire alarm, video surveillance enabled with external cameras, and burglar alarm enabled with several kinds of sensors (window/door vibration and movement detectors) and anti-jamming features. *Insurance provider* lets ATM owners insure their assets in case of any incident based on several scenarios and configurations. The ATM per se is an asset and the investment in each unit can vary widely depending on the brand, model, configuration, etc. *Bank* is an

[2] http://www.din.de/en/getting-involved/standards-committees/nabau/projects/wdc-proj:din21:208343022.

organisation that manages a range of financial services, including ATM transactions from its own ATMs or from other ATMs as issuer/acquirer. *Customers* are users who use the gas station's services, including the ATM. *Attacker* is an interested party responsible for exploiting a vulnerability with the objective of achieving an illegal goal. Finally, *Insider* is an employee who could potentially provide information or physical access (voluntarily or not) to attackers.

4 The Attack-Defense Tree Model

Developing ATree models for complex systems has been traditionally a cumbersome task requiring a team of experts. The first step towards modeling is to understand the system and the context by identifying stakeholders, system components, and attackers. Another important aspect is to grasp the semantics of the ADTree modelling language. We covered both aspects by building a team of four security experts, two from industry and two from academia. One industry expert from our team has experience in security and financial services; he played the domain expert role. The second industry expert has expertise in security assessment, financial services, and has prior experience with ATrees. She played the role of validator and was responsible for quality evaluation. The other team members have extensive knowledge of semantics and analysis techniques for ADTrees. They were responsible for structuring the tree. In the rest of this section we explain the process followed by our team to design a comprehensive ADTree model for the ATM scenario. We used the open source ADTool software for designing the tree [5].

Overcoming the Lack of Attack Intelligence. The task of mapping a security scenario into an ADtree greatly depends on the security expertise of the team developing the tree. However, security expertise needs to be complemented with data about previous attacks. Such data can come in the form of an attack pattern library[3], i.e. a structure containing precondition and postcondition of attacks, attack profiles, and a glossary of defined terms and phrases. Yet, businesses and governments are usually reluctant to disclose attack data, as it may harm their reputation and could help attackers to exploit similar vulnerabilities.

For this case study, the financial services specialist overcame the lack of attack data by using different sources of information on ATM security, such as *PCI-DSS ATM Security Guidelines*[4] to understand how secure channels for payment systems based on smartcards are implemented, *ATM Industry Association*[5] to collect best practices in ATM security, *EU law enforcement agency*[6] to get recent trends in cybercrime, *National Crime Agency*[7] and *ATM Marketplace*[8] to gather recent reports on financial fraud and potential countermeasures.

3 www.sei.cmu.edu/reports/01tn001.pdf.
4 https://www.pcisecuritystandards.org/pci_security/.
5 https://www.atmia.com/.
6 https://www.europol.europa.eu/.
7 http://www.nationalcrimeagency.gov.uk/.
8 http://www.atmmarketplace.com/.

Because it is convenient to structure the tree similarly to standard reports and documentation already familiar to stakeholders, lawyers, and analysts in general, we split the list of attacks and countermeasures resulting from the previously mentioned study in categories that can be found in well-known incident reports (e.g. the EAST report 2015[9] and the ATMIA Global Fraud Survey 2015[10]). This led to the taxonomy of attacks and countermeasures shown in Fig. 1.

Figure 1 shows two main types of ATM fraud: those requiring highly sophisticated software (e.g. malware or blackbox devices) and those which use conventional electronic devices (e.g. card skimmers) and/or require the participation of the victim (e.g. card trapping). The first category led to the notion of *logical* attacks, which require installing malicious software on the ATM or acquiring system credentials through cyber attacks. Malware could be deployed in the ATM PC or a blackbox device connected with the ATM computer system in order to gain access to cash or sensitive data. The second category includes *physical* attacks, where a legitimate user's account is involved, which we call *fraud*, and also physical attacks jeopardizing the physical integrity of the ATM.

Figure 1 also depicts potential countermeasures. For example, card skimming and cash trapping can be prevented by anti-skimming solutions such as stress sensors, or by making compulsory the use of EMV technology (Chip&PIN) and contactless cards. A general countermeasure against this type of fraud is to make customers and employees aware of the fraud in order to perform quick physical inspections themselves. Brute force attacks in contrast, cannot be actually prevented, but detected. Detection mechanisms are GPS-enabled devices to localize the ATM, tilt, vibration, and gas sensors, etc.

Capturing Attack Vectors in a Semantically Meaningful Way. The ADTree we produced, an excerpt of which is shown in Fig. 1, is a useful classification of

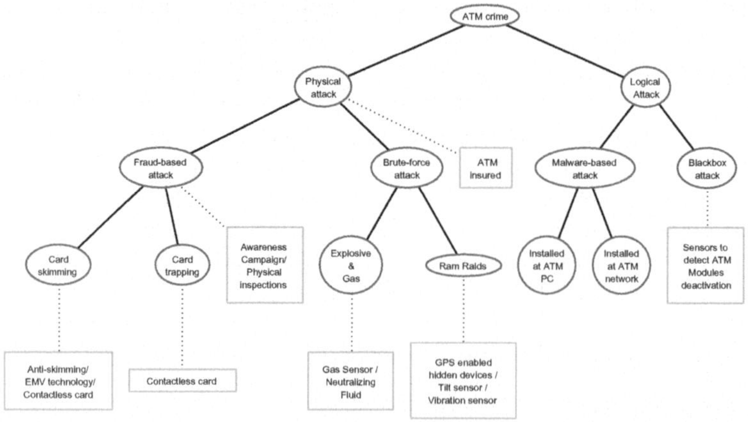

Fig. 1. An excerpt of an ADTree on ATM crime: a taxonomy. (Color figure online)

[9] https://www.european-atm-security.eu/tag/european-atm-crime-report/.
[10] https://www.atmia.com/whitepapers/global-fraud-survey-2015/1104/.

attacks to ATMs, and applicable countermeasures and mitigation strategies. However, it does not benefit from the main feature of ADTrees as a mathematical language, that is, the ability to encode several attack vectors in a compact tree structure. An *attack vector* is a path or a set of attack steps an adversary can follow in order to successfully attack a system. In ADTrees, attack vectors are expressed by using the conjunctive operator AND, which expresses that all subgoals of a given goal ought to be achieved.

The main challenge when modeling many attack vectors in an ADTree is to guarantee that it is semantically meaningful, while keeping its communication potential. The team addressed this challenge by frequently executing two different verification processes. The first one consisted in checking that the taxonomy depicted in Fig. 1 is preserved as much as possible. The second one consisted in keeping track of those attack vectors we expected to model, and verifying that the multiset semantics of ADTrees [7] matches this set of attack vectors. The whole process took 6 days of work, involving all four team members. Each modification to the tree was cross-checked by at least two team members, taking into account the two verification processes explained before. Next we detail one sub-branch of the full ADTree (see Fig. 2); the latter can be downloaded at the ADTool official website: http://satoss.uni.lu/members/piotr/adtool/.

Blackbox Attack. An interesting logical attack to ATMs consists in embedding a blackbox device into the ATM and connecting it to the ATM's computer system (see Fig. 2). This can only be done by accessing the ATM's internal infrastructure without being detected, implying that the adversary needs to get into the facility where the ATM is located. A classical way to enter into a facility is by breaking in, e.g. through a window or a door, but the adversary could also try to social engineer an employee. As contemplated in the ADTree, a burglar alarm can deter or prevent a break in. Consequently, the adversary ought to disable the burglar alarm by, for example, using a radio network inhibitor against the used communication signal or protocol, e.g. Radio Frequency (RF) and General Packet Radio Service (GPRS), respectively. In this particular case, the defender can use anti-jamming techniques or a security guard to counteract the adversary's goal of disabling the alarm.

The use of video surveillance and burglar alarms for gas stations, required by law in many countries, can dissuade the attacker from approaching the ATM in order to install the blackbox device. However, there exist several techniques to disable a burglar alarm, e.g. RF/GPRS inhibitors, and video surveillance system, e.g. infrared light, laser, or video looping. From the defender point of view, making the camera less visible and accessible, or performing regular physical inspections, improve robustness of the video surveillance system.

Remark that owning a functional blackbox device means that the ATM drivers have been disclosed or stolen. Moreover, even if the adversary manages to approach the ATM, he/she still needs to insert the blackbox device into the ATM. That is to say, the adversary must open the ATM and connect the blackbox to either the dispenser or the ATM's internal communication system. Opening the ATM in our case requires getting the cabinet physical key, or social

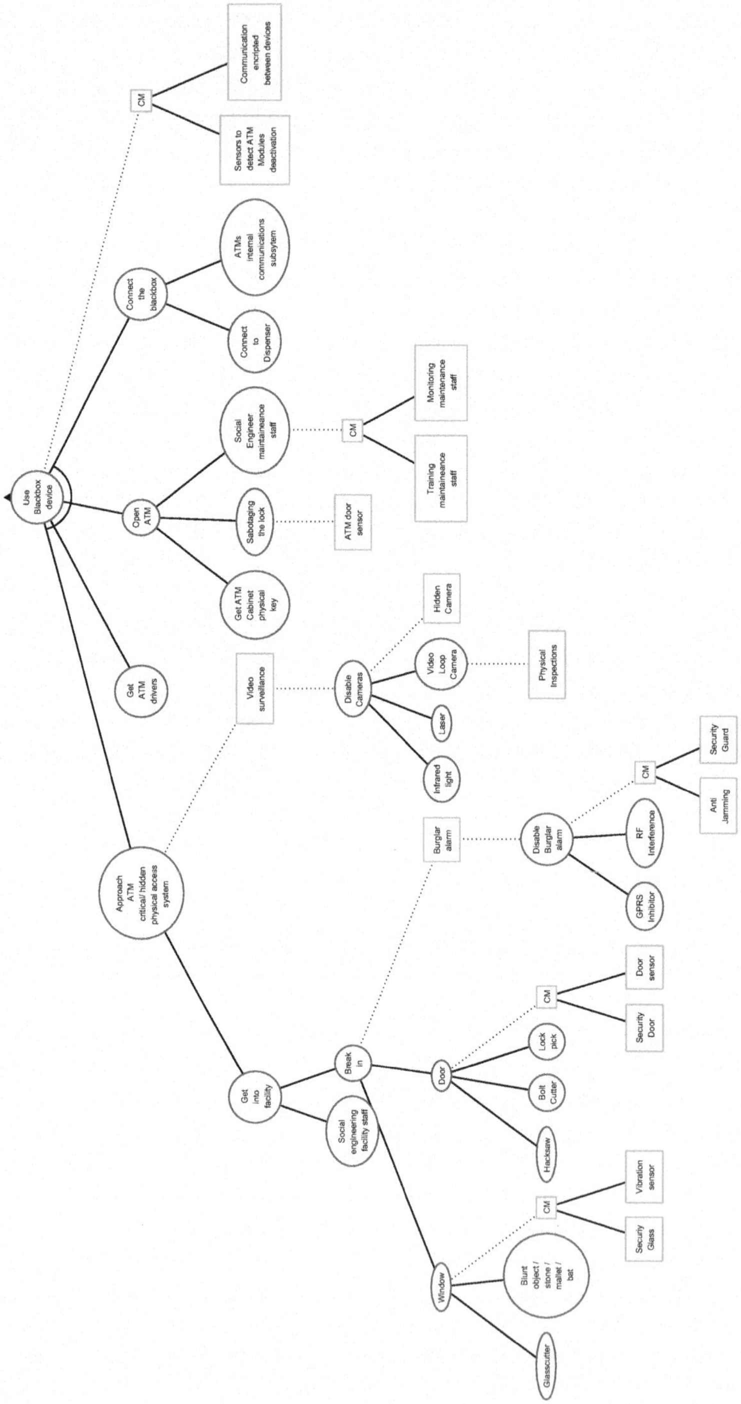

Fig. 2. A sub-branch of the ADTree modelling the use of blackbox devices. (Color figure online)

engineering the maintenance staff, or simply sabotaging the lock. As usual, the success of social engineering attacks diminishes with regular training and monitoring, while the lock sabotage can be prevented with an ATM door sensor. To finalize the description of the ADTree depicted in Fig. 2, we remark that potential countermeasures against blackbox devices are: encrypting the messages exchanged between different components and devices, and a dedicated sensor that detects when a data cable has been disconnected.

It is worth mentioning that the ADTree in Fig. 2 covers 900 attack vectors, called bundles in the multiset semantics in [7]. This emphasizes the modelling power of ADTrees.

5 Discussion and Conclusions

The ATM case study has enabled us to explore the application of ADTrees in a challenging environment, with multiple stakeholders and a diverse range of threats. Through this process, we have evaluated positive and negative aspects of working with ADTrees, identified some best practices that improved the process, and learned a number of lessons regarding the application of the formalism. We share our findings in this section.

The intuitive graphical nature of ADTrees enables them to bridge the gap between stakeholders from diverse backgrounds, providing an environment to brainstorm, amend, document and analyze a wide range of threats. In particular, ADTrees provide a succinct and meaningful structure for a huge number of potential attack vectors. This strength was already prominent when Schneier introduced the attack tree back in 1999 [18], and our own experience reinforces this observation. However, attack trees are constructed from the attacker's perspective. Organizations are more focused on the overall risk (in terms of worst case impact) and the inventory of effective treatment options to be implemented to mitigate those risks. This is where ADTrees are more useful than attack trees.

We started to create the ADTree from a taxonomy of attacks on an ATM, which proved to be very helpful. This established attack taxonomy allowed us to structure the reasoning and compare the attacks we identified with the globally known attacks, thus serving as a reference to check the tree for completeness.

In general, we found several countermeasures that did not really prevent the attack, but triggered actions that could mitigate the impact of the attack. Handling these countermeasures required lengthy team discussions. We suspect that these challenges in handling treatment options arise from the fact that they are not clearly addressed in the ADTree methodology itself (e.g. any of the established semantics). One possibility is to extend the ADTree methodology by explicitly typing defense nodes, following the example of attack-countermeasure trees that support detective and reactive countermeasures [16]. However, this change will also increase the cognitive load on the analysts.

References

1. Bagnato, A., Kordy, B., Meland, P.H., Schweitzer, P.: Attribute decoration of attack-defense trees. Int. J. Secure Softw. Eng. **3**(2), 1–35 (2012)
2. Byres, E.J., Franz, M., Miller, D.: The use of attack trees in assessing vulnerabilities in SCADA systems. In: Proceedings of the International Infrastructure Survivability Workshop (2004)
3. Du, S., Zhu, H.: Security assessment via attack tree model. In: Du, S., Zhu, H. (eds.) Security Assessment in Vehicular Networks. SpringerBriefs in Computer Science, pp. 9–16. Springer, Heidelberg (2013)
4. Edge, K., Raines, R., Grimaila, M., Baldwin, R., Bennington, R., Reuter, C.: The use of attack and protection trees to analyze security for an online banking system. In: Proceedings of HICSS. IEEE Computer Society (2007)
5. Gadyatskaya, O., Jhawar, R., Kordy, P., Lounis, K., Mauw, S., Trujillo-Rasua, R.: Attack trees for practical security assessment: ranking of attack scenarios with ADTool 2.0. In: Agha, G., Van Houdt, B. (eds.) QEST 2016. LNCS, vol. 9826, pp. 159–162. Springer, Heidelberg (2016). doi:10.1007/978-3-319-43425-4_10
6. Kewley, D.L., Bouchard, J.F.: DARPA information assurance program dynamic defense experiment summary. IEEE Trans. Syst. Man Cybern. Part A **31**(4), 331–336 (2001)
7. Kordy, B., Mauw, S., Radomirović, S., Schweitzer, P.: Attack-defense trees. J. Logic Comput. **24**(1), 55–87 (2014)
8. Kordy, B., Piètre-Cambacédès, L., Schweitzer, P.: DAG-based attack and defense modeling: don't miss the forest for the attack trees. Comput. Sci. Rev. **13**, 1–38 (2014)
9. Kumar, R., Ruijters, E., Stoelinga, M.: Quantitative attack tree analysis via priced timed automata. In: Sankaranarayanan, S., Vicario, E. (eds.) FORMATS 2015. LNCS, vol. 9268, pp. 156–171. Springer, Heidelberg (2015)
10. Li, T., Horkoff, J., Paja, E., Beckers, K., Mylopoulos, J.: Analyzing attack strategies through anti-goal refinement. In: Ralyté, J., España, S., Pastor, Ó. (eds.) The Practice of Enterprise Modeling. LNBIP, vol. 235, pp. 75–90. Springer, Heidelberg (2015)
11. Mauw, S., Oostdijk, M.: Foundations of attack trees. In: Won, D.H., Kim, S. (eds.) ICISC 2005. LNCS, vol. 3935, pp. 186–198. Springer, Heidelberg (2006)
12. Morais, A., Hwang, I., Cavalli, A., Martins, E.: Generating attack scenarios for the system security validation. Netw. Sci. **2**(3–4), 69–80 (2013)
13. Opdahl, A., Sindre, G.: Experimental comparison of attack trees and misuse cases for security threat identification. Inf. Softw. Technol. **51**(5), 916–932 (2009)
14. Paul, S.: Towards automating the construction & maintenance of attack trees: a feasibility study. In: Proceedings of GraMSec, vol. 148 of EPTCS, pp. 31–46 (2014)
15. Ray, I., Poolsapassit, N.: Using attack trees to identify malicious attacks from authorized insiders. In: di Vimercati, S.C., Syverson, P.F., Gollmann, D. (eds.) ESORICS 2005. LNCS, vol. 3679, pp. 231–246. Springer, Heidelberg (2005)
16. Roy, A., Kim, D.S., Trivedi, K.S.: Attack countermeasure trees (ACT): towards unifying the constructs of attack and defense trees. Secur. Commun. Netw. **5**(8), 929–943 (2012)
17. Saini, V., Duan, Q., Paruchuri, V.: Threat modeling using attack trees. J. Comput. Sci. Coll. **23**(4), 124–131 (2008)
18. Schneier, B.: Attack trees. Dr. Dobb's J. Softw. Tools **24**(12), 21–29 (1999)

Towards a Classification Framework for Approaches to Enterprise Architecture Analysis

Birger Lantow[1(✉)], Dierk Jugel[1,2], Matthias Wißotzki[1], Benjamin Lehmann[1], Ole Zimmermann[1], and Kurt Sandkuhl[1]

[1] Chair of Business Information Systems, University of Rostock, Rostock, Germany
{birger.lantow,matthias.wissotzki,benjamin.lehmann, ole.zimmermann,kurt.sandkuhl}@uni-rostock.de, dierk.jugel@reutlingen-university.de
[2] Faculty of Informatics, Reutlingen University, Reutlingen, Germany

Abstract. Analysis is an important part of the Enterprise Architecture Management Process. Prior to decisions regarding transformation of the Enterprise Architecture, the current situation and the outcomes of alternative action plans have to be analysed. Many analysis approaches have been proposed by researchers and current Enterprise Architecture Management tools implement analysis functionalities. However, few work has been done structuring and classifying Enterprise Architecture Analysis approaches. This paper collects and extends existing classification schemes, presenting a framework for Enterprise Architecture Analysis classification. For evaluation, a collection of Enterprise Architecture Analysis approaches has been classified based on this framework. As a result, the description of these approaches has been assessed, a common set of important categories for Enterprise Architecture Analysis classification has been derived and suggestions for further development are drawn.

Keywords: Enterprise Architecture Management · Enterprise Architecture Analysis · EAM · EAA · Classification

1 Introduction

Analysis is an important part of the Enterprise Architecture Management (EAM) Process. Many analysis approaches have been proposed by researchers and current Enterprise Architecture Management tools implement analysis functionalities.

In practice, Enterprise Architectures (EA) are often analysed by using visualizations and are typically created using EAM tools. However, several studies show a lack in EAM tools' visualization capabilities [20, 24, 31]. Visualizations generated by EAM tools are often report-like and static in respect to the displayed information. Modern analysis approaches like [21, 24, 25] should combine interactive visualizations with automated analysis techniques. In this regard enterprise architect's responsibilities are changing [30]. By using automated analysis techniques, enterprise architects can focus on more advanced analyses for which no algorithm exists. We investigate related work

J. Horkoff et al. (Eds.): PoEM 2016, LNBIP 267, pp. 335–343, 2016.
DOI: 10.1007/978-3-319-48393-1_25

of classifying EA analysis approaches. Based on the results, we propose a classification framework. Therefore, the remainder of this paper is organized as follows. Section 2 discusses existing approaches to EAA classification and derives a common classification framework based on these approaches and a discussion of general attributes that are important for analysis methods and tools independently of the EAA domain. Section 3 classifies EAA tools and methods that have been described in literature based on the developed EAA classification framework. The last Sect. 4 then summarizes the findings and draws an outlook on further investigations of the topic.

2 EAA Classification Framework

In this section we develop a framework for enterprise analysis classification. It is based on previous work by Buckl et al. [7], Hanschke [14, 15], Niemann [28], and Lankhorst et al. [23] in connection with Ramos et al. [29, 30, 33, 34] which is presented in Sect. 2.1 "Related Work". These major approaches on the field are used to derive dimensions (D) for classification, labelled with roman numbers I to VIII. Additional sources are included were appropriate in order to emphasize on possible additions and alternatives for classification. Section 2.2 then describes the developed classification framework which tries to provide a common view on the topic.

2.1 Related Work

Buckl et al. define in [7] a classification schema that uses five dimensions: (I) *Body of Analysis* (II) *Time Reference* (III) *Analysis Technique* (IV) *Analysis Concern* and (V) *Self-Referentiality*.

Regarding (I) *Body of analysis:* Buckl et al. make a distinction between (1) structure, (2) behaviour statistics and (3) dynamic behaviour. While structure analysis assesses the architecture as it is defined, behaviour statistics include operational data like server availability and dynamic behaviour considers the consequences of changes in the system status on instance level. (II) *Time Reference:* Differentiates between the analysis of current (ex-post) and planned (ex-ante) architectures. (III) *Analysis Technique*: (1) Expert-based means that the analysis is performed manually by experts that may provide concrete action plans or just general strategy recommendations. (2) Rule-based analysis defines constraints to the enterprise architecture that must be fulfilled in the form of rules. (3) Indicator-based analysis describes also automated analysis techniques with results of quantitative nature. (IV) *Analysis Concerns* differentiates between (1) functional and (2) non-functional approaches. Functional approaches check the function of the EA. Non-functional approaches in contrast consider quantitative measures regarding system performance. There is a correlation for analysis approaches between being non-functional and being indicator-based. (V) *Self-referentiality*: aims at the identification of approaches that analyze the Enterprise Architecture Management itself. While EA analysis does not consider EAM parts of the EA in special (self-referentiality: none) also EAM processes might be analysed (self-referentiality: single level). If additional cross-layer aspects of EAM are considered, Buckl et al. speak of multi-level Self-referentiality.

Hanschke provides an operationalization of EA analysis and planning via so-called "patterns" and defines two dimensions for the classification of analysis approaches [14]: (VI) *Analysis function* and (VII) *Architecture Sub-model*. Thus, a particular analysis goal can be intended for a particular layer of the EA. Hanschke identifies Business, Information Systems, Technical, and Infrastructure Layer. Regarding the analysis functions, the following distinctions are made: (1) Discovery of potential redundancies (2) Discovery of potential inconsistencies (3) Needs for organizational changes (4) Implementation of business goals (5) Optimization and required changes on technical and infrastructure layer.

Niemann [28] classifies by analysis function (VI) only and does not consider Architecture Sub-models. He names the following analysis functions: (1) Dependencies (2) Redundancies (3) Interfaces (4) Heterogeneity (5) Complexity (6) Compliance (7) Costs and (8) Benefits. This distinction has also for example been used by [3]. The problem of this classification is the mixture of rather general functionality like assessment of complexity and costs and rather concrete one like the assessment of application interfaces.

Lankhorst et al. [23] use two dimensions in order to classify enterprise architecture analysis approaches. In the first dimension they make a distinction between *functional* and *quantitative* approaches. This is similar to the dimension (IV) *Analysis Concerns* by Buckl et al. [7], considering *non-functional* approaches as *quantitative*. The second dimension by Lankhorst et al. differentiates between *analytical* and *simulation* approaches. These match dimension (III) Analysis Technique by Buckl et al. However, different classes are defined.

Ramos et al. [29, 30, 33, 34] made additions to the classification approach by Lankhorst et al. in order to provide a more detailed classification schema. They assign analysis functions to either quantitative or functional analysis. Thus dimension (IV) Analysis Concern is connected with dimension (VI) Analysis Function. The values are for quantitative approaches: (1) Performance (2) Optimization (3) Cost (4) Availability (5) Capacity Planning (6) Quality Trade-off. Functional analysis functions are: (1) Alignment (2) Coherence (3) Correctness (4) Gap analysis (5) Counting/Complexity (6) Process (7) Human Resources (8) Conformance (9) Graph Structure (10) Impact of Change. Ramos et al. [29, 30] also divide analysis approaches by dimension (VII) Architecture Sub-model. In contrast to Hanschke they base their layering in the ArchiMate standard. An additional dimension for the classification of EAA approaches is provided by Ramos et al. with (VIII) the Status (used in their EAA functions repository [33]). Here the status of implementation is considered. Thus, whether an analysis approach is (1) described in general (2) fully specified or (3) implemented.

Naranjo et al. [26] made a survey regarding enterprise analysis techniques (dimension (III)). The result was a collection of analysis techniques which are more concrete regarding implementation than those provided by Buckl et al. and analysis functions (dimension (VI)) that are implemented by these techniques. In the context of the paper by Naranjo et al. what we consider analysis functions is called analysis concern.

2.2 Framework Construction

Based on the discussion in the previous section, the dimensions for the classification of EAA approaches are derived which and shown in Table 1. The proposed dimensions are assigned to four main EAA questions to be answered.

Most of the dimensions considered so far are dealing with (*question-A*). *(D-I)* basically deals with the origin of data used for analysis. Thus, is only the enterprise architecture model considered (structure) or also the operational data (behaviour)? We do not make the distinction between behaviour statistics and dynamic behaviour as in the original source by Buckl et al. Even there, only one approach has been identified that specifically considers dynamic behaviour. We also decided to omit *(D-II) Time Reference* [7], because in general all analysis approaches can be applied to current and planned enterprise architecture models as well. The distinction between functional and quantitative approaches (*D-IV*) is used by several authors and thus also adopted for our classification framework. *(D-V) Self-referentiality* is not considered because it is only proposed by Buckl et al. They provide only one example for an analysis approach that is explicitly designed to be applied to the EA-function within an enterprise. Furthermore, EA specific analysis can be considered as an analysis function that is specific to a certain architecture sub-model (*D-VII*). Regarding *(D-VII) Architecture Sub-model* we suggest to use the ArchiMate modelling standard – its layers and extensions – as a framework to identify sub-models because of the general acceptance of ArchiMate [3]. Moreover, there is a lot of flexibility in the ArchiMate standard to address very specific EA sub-models.

Table 1. Enterprise architecture classification framework

A) What is being analysed? (D-I, D-IV, D-VII)					
Body of Analysis [7]	Structure		Behaviour		
Analysis Concern [7] [23] [29]	Functional		Quantitative		
Architecture Sub-Model [15] [29]	Business	Application	Technology	…	General
B) How is the analysis performed (D-IX, D-III)					
Coverage	Expert-based	Automated	Integrated		
Analysis Technique [7] [23] [29] [26]	Rule validation	Quantitative Analysis	…	Semantic Technologies	
C) What is the analysis function? (D-X, D-VI)					
Analysis Type	Descriptive	Predictive	Prescriptive		
Analysis Function [15] [28] [29] [26]	Coherence	Process	Alignment	…	General
D) What is the practical relevance of the analysis approach? (D-VIII)					
Validation	Proposed	Prototype	Case Study		

Additionally, there is a class "General" for EAA techniques that are described on an abstraction level that allows their application to all possible EA sub-models.

Although *(question-B)* is only connected to *(D-III) Analysis Technique*, there are different approaches at different abstraction levels to this topic. On the most general level we distinguish expert-based (manual) approaches (cf. Buckl et al.), automated approaches, and integrated approaches. Since, EAA is part of a decision making process, experts' decision and interpretation comes into place at a certain point and expert analysis of EA models must be supported by tools in order to handle the model complexity [21]. However, we consider a method only as integrated when the interplay between expert and automated analysis is explicitly described. We introduce a new *(D-IX) Coverage* to depict this. Regarding automated analysis there is a broad variety of available analysis techniques. Describing them on the level of being rule-based/indicator based [7] or analytical/simulation based [23] is too coarse. As shown for example by [25] there are families of techniques that can be used to implement a variety of analysis functions (e.g. Quantitative Performance Analysis, Probabilistic Relational Models, Rule Validation). Furthermore, techniques for expert based analysis may be described. Typically, expert-based analysis techniques are used to analyse complex or new situations for that no rules or algorithms exists. Another reason why expert-based analyses are used is a lack in the underlying EA model. In this case, relevant characteristics are missing in the model and therefore only exist in human brains. Jugel et al. describe in [19] interactive functions of a cockpit. The interactive function "graphical highlighting and filtering" is an example of an expert-based analysis. Using this interactive functions, e.g. stakeholders are able to enrich elements of the EA model by using annotations. In addition, annotations can be used as criteria to highlight elements of the architecture. Thus, we populated this dimension with values from Naranjo et al. and our literature review that is described in the next section.

Also regarding *(question-C)*, different sets have been proposed for possible answers *(D-VI)* by the respective authors. The most comprehensive set based on the number functions of has been defined by Ramos et al. [33, 34]. Still, there are EAA functions that are not covered by this set and the field is developing. Thus, values should be based on an analysis of EAA approaches in the field. Furthermore, some approaches describe general techniques that are not bound to a certain analysis function. Thus, we introduce a class "General" here. From the general analysis perspective we add *(D-X)*, analysis type based on the analysis taxonomy provided by Delen et al. [11]. Analysis can be either descriptive, predictive, or prescriptive. While the last type - prescriptive analysis - covers the complete decision making process. There are clear criteria necessary in order to make a distinction between descriptive and predictive analysis. Generally, an analysis based on models that describe the current state is descriptive and an analysis that bases on models that describe a future state is predictive. Thus, each technique that analyzes a model is descriptive and predictive as well. We attribute "predictiveness" to all EAA approaches that do not rely on current operational data and that are able to describe future EA states.

(Question-D) aims at the validation EAA approaches. While Ramos et al. [33, 34] only consider the status of implementation in their EAA framework, a broader view is necessary. Thus we differentiate between (1) proposed (2) prototype and (3) case study here.

3 Assessment of EAA Approaches from Literature

While there are many applications for the developed EAA classification framework like providing a catalogue of EAA approaches or assessing the descriptions of EAA approaches, in a first step we investigate, how the classes defined by the framework are filled by current EAA approaches from literature. This is on the same hand a first validation of the framework by validating its applicability and coverage. We performed a Systematic Literature Review (SLR) according to Kitchenham [17, 22]. The literature review process generally consists of 4 steps. The first three steps are described in Sect. 3.1. Table 2 describes the result of data analysis which includes the application of our EAA classification framework.

3.1 Paper Selection and Data Extraction

The goal of the literature search was to systematically identify EAA approaches that are present in scientific publications while being replicable and thorough. Finally, 16 relevant publications have been identified (AIS Electronic Library: 3, IEEE Xplore: 6, Science Direct: 1, Springer Link: 6) listed in the reference section [1, 2, 4–6, 8–10, 12, 13, 16, 18, 25, 27, 31, 35].

We conducted the data extraction with a focus on EAA techniques. Thus, first we clustered the approaches by used techniques/technologies and then we made a classification according to our framework. For reasons of brevity not all dimensions are covered. Most Publications (5) used *Probabilistic Relational Models (PRM)* for EAA. Based on literature, their main area of application is the predictive, quantitative analysis of technical and of application components. The mentioned analysis functions were Availability, Maintainability, and Security or in general system performance. The second cluster of approaches uses *semantic technologies*. Out of the 5 publications [1, 2, 4–6], three refer to the same approach [1, 2, 4]. Generally, semantic technologies are fit for structural, functional analysis. An advantage is the good integration of different domains. Thus, the technology is applicable to generally all possible architecture sub-models/sub-domains. A common analysis function of all described semantic approaches is *Impact Analysis*. Graph-based approaches have been presented by two authors [5, 25]. These approaches assess graph characteristics of the EA-model in order to analyze the EA. The remaining three EAA techniques have been presented by just one paper each. The paper regarding AHP [31] on its very general level also considers the use of operational data (Body of Analysis – Behaviour) and is the only approach performing a prescriptive analysis. The Wiki-based approach [9] remains on a very general level. The Extended Influence Diagram (EID) approach [18, 27] is very close to PRM in its classification.

Looking at the framework dimensions and the classes defined in this dimensions regarding their coverage (Table 2), it reveals that there are approaches missing that consider operational data (Body of Analysis – Behaviour), that describe solely interaction of experts (Coverage – Expert-based), and that provide prescriptive analysis. On the other hand, most of the approaches have been validated in form of a prototype or a case study.

Table 2. Class instances based on the performed SLR (number of instances in braces ())

A) What is being analysed? (I, IV, VII)					
Body of Analysis	Structure (11)		Behaviour (1)		
Analysis Concern	Functional (4)		Quantitative (8)		
Architecture Sub-Model	Business (9)	Application (11)	Technology (10)	…	General (3)
B) How is the analysis performed (IX, III)					
Coverage	Expert-based (0)	Automated (8)	Integrated (3)		
Analysis Technique	…				
C) What is the analysis function? (X, VI)					
Analysis Type	Descriptive (6)	Predictive (9)	Prescriptive (1)		
Analysis Function	…				
D) What is the practical relevance of the analysis approach? (VIII)					
Validation	Proposed (2)	Prototype (4)	Case Study (5)		

4 Summary and Outlook

The developed framework for EAA classification uses established dimensions for classification by deriving a common view based on existing EAA classification approaches from literature. This comes with omitting dimensions that did not seem to have established and with suggestion of new ones. Within the dimensions, a possible class structure has been presented. Section 3 proved the general applicability of the framework based on a SLR. It also showed its usefulness for the assessment of EAA techniques. Furthermore, possible directions for future research can be derived, which is one of the goals of an SLR and in this case supported by the framework (see Table 2). For example, prescriptive analysis approaches are underrepresented, as well as approaches explicitly including operational data and methodological support for experts performing EAA.

However, more insight should be provided by extending the number of assessed EAA approaches. The SLR base may be extended. Furthermore, the authors of EAA classification approaches provide examples themselves, that be applied to our framework. Ramos et al. present a variety of EAA techniques on their project site (see [33, 34]). Even more insight can be gained from the assessment of EAA in practice: Which of the techniques are actually used in enterprises? How is EAA done in practice? Results may be an assessment of the practical relevance of certain EAA classes but also additional dimensions for classification. Possible points for an extension of the framework may be the analysis effort that is of course relevant for practice and a deeper investigation of the role of EAA in the EAM process.

In addition to the assessment of EAA techniques and the identification of research gaps, the framework may also be used to improve the description of EAA approaches by providing a template and also to create an EAA catalogue that allows the selection of appropriate EAA approaches depending on the situation at hand.

References

1. Antunes, G., Caetano, A., Borbinha, J.: Enterprise architecture model analysis using description logics. In: IEEE 18th International Enterprise Distributed Object Computing Conference Workshops and Demonstrations (2014)
2. Antunes, G., Bakhshandeh, M., Mayer, R., Borbinha, J., Caetano, A.: Using ontologies for enterprise architecture analysis. In: 17th IEEE EDOCW (2013)
3. Sandkuhl, K., et al.: Enterprise Modeling - Tackling Business Challenges with the 4EM Method. Springer, Heidelberg (2014)
4. Caetano, A.: An application of semantic techniques to the analysis of enterprise architecture models. In: 49th Hawaii International Conference on System Sciences (2016)
5. Osenberg, M., Langermeier, M., Bauer, B.: Using semantic web technologies for enterprise architecture analysis. In: Sack, H., Blomqvist, E., d'Aquin, M., Ghidini, C., Ponzetto, S.P., Lange, C. (eds.) ESWC 2016. LNCS, vol. 9678, pp. 668–682. Springer, Heidelberg (2015). doi:10.1007/978-3-319-18818-8_41
6. de Boer, F.S., et al.: Enterprise architecture analysis with XML. In: 38th Annual Hawaii International Conference on System Sciences (2005)
7. Buckl, S., Matthes, F., Schweda, C.M.: Classifying enterprise architecture analysis approaches. In: Poler, R., Sinderen, M., Sanchis, R. (eds.) IWEI 2009. LNBIP, vol. 38, pp. 66–79. Springer, Heidelberg (2009)
8. Buckl, S., et al.: A pattern-based approach to quantitative enterprise architecture analysis. In: AMCIS 2009 Proceedings (2009)
9. Buckl, S., Matthes, F., Neubert, C., Schweda, C.M.: A wiki-based approach to enterprise architecture documentation and analysis. In: ECIS, pp. 1476–1487 (2009)
10. Buschle, M., et al.: The enterprise architecture analysis tool–support for the predictive, probabilistic architecture modeling framework. In: AMCIS (2013)
11. Delen, D., Haluk, D.: Data, information and analytics as services. Decis. Support Syst. **55**(1), 359–363 (2013)
12. Ekstedt, M., et al.: A tool for enterprise architecture analysis of maintainability. In: CSMR (2009)
13. Närman, P., et al.: Using enterprise architecture analysis and interview data to estimate service response time. J. Strateg. Inf. Syst. **22**(1), 70–85 (2013)
14. Hanschke, I.: Strategisches Management der IT-Landschaft: Ein praktischer Leitfaden für das Enterprise Architecture Management. Carl Hanser Verlag GmbH Co KG, Munich (2013)
15. Hanschke, I.: Strategisches Management der IT-Landschaft: Ein praktischer Leitfaden für das Enterprise Architecture Management (Download-Anhang A). Carl Hanser Verlag GmbH Co KG, Munich (2013)
16. Buschle, M., Ullberg, J., Franke, U., Lagerström, R., Sommestad, T.: A tool for enterprise architecture analysis using the PRM formalism. In: Proper, E., Soffer, P. (eds.) CAiSE Forum 2010. LNBIP, vol. 72, pp. 108–121. Springer, Heidelberg (2011)
17. Ivarsson, M., Gorschek, T.: Technology transfer decision support in requirements engineering research: a systematic review of REj. Requirements Eng. **14**(3), 155–175 (2009)

18. Johnson, P., Lagerström, R., Norman, P., Simonsson, M.: Extended influence diagrams for enterprise architecture analysis. In: 10th IEEE EDOC (2006)
19. Jugel, D., Schweda, C.M.: Interactive functions of a cockpit for enterprise architecture planning. In: 18th IEEE EDOCW, pp. 33–40 (2014)
20. Jugel, D., Schweda, C.M., Zimmermann, A., Läufer, S.: Tool capability in visual EAM analytics. Complex Syst. Inform. Model. Q. (CSIMQ) **2**, 46–55 (2015)
21. Jugel, D., Kehrer, S., Schweda, C.M., Zimmermann, A.: A decision-making case for collaborative enterprise architecture engineering. In: INFORMATIK 2015. LNI-Lecture Notes in Informatics. GI-Gesellschaft für Informatik (2015)
22. Kitchenham, B.: Procedures for performing systematic reviews, vol. 33. Keele University, Keele (2004)
23. Lankhorst, M., et al.: Enterprise Architecture at Work: Modelling, Communication and Analysis, 3rd edn. Springer, Berlin (2013)
24. Matthes, F., et al.: Enterprise architecture management tool survey 2008. Technical University, München (2008)
25. Naranjo, D., Sánchez, M., Villalobos, J.: PRIMROSe: a graph-based approach for enterprise architecture analysis. In: Cordeiro, J., Hammoudi, S., Maciaszek, L., Camp, O., Filipe, J. (eds.) ICEIS 2014. LNBIP, vol. 227, pp. 434–452. Springer, Heidelberg (2015)
26. Naranjo, D., Sánchez, M., Villalobos, J.: Towards a unified and modular approach for visual analysis of enterprise models. In: IEEE 18th EDOCW (2014)
27. Johnson, P., Lagerström, R., Närman, P., Simonsson, M.: Enterprise architecture analysis with extended influence diagrams. Inf. Syst. Front. **9**(2–3), 163–180 (2007)
28. Niemann, K.D.: Von der Unternehmensarchitektur zur IT-Governance. Vieweg+Teubner Verlag, Berlin (2005)
29. Ramos, A., Gomez, P., Sánchez, M., Villalobos, J.: Automated enterprise-level analysis of archimate models. In: Bider, I., Gaaloul, K., Krogstie, J., Nurcan, S., Proper, H.A., Schmidt, R., Soffer, P. (eds.) BPMDS 2014 and EMMSAD 2014. LNBIP, vol. 175, pp. 439–453. Springer, Heidelberg (2014)
30. Ramos, A., Sáenz, J.P., Sánchez, M., Villalobos, J.: On the support of automated analysis chains on enterprise models. In: Gaaloul, K., Schmidt, R., Nurcan, S., Guerreiro, S., Ma, Q. (eds.) BPMDS 2015 and EMMSAD 2015. LNBIP, vol. 214, pp. 345–359. Springer, Heidelberg (2015)
31. Razavi, M., Aliee, F.S., Badie, K.: An AHP-based approach toward enterprise architecture analysis based on enterprise architecture quality attributes. Knowl. Inf. Syst. **28**(2), 449–472 (2011)
32. Roth, S., Zec, M., Matthes, F.: Enterprise Architecture Visualization Tool Survey 2014, München (2014)
33. Universidad de los Andes: Analysis function catalog (2015). http://backus1.uniandes.edu.co/enar/dokuwiki/doku.php?id=archianalysis#dokuwiki__top. Accessed 27 Feb 2016
34. Universidad de los Andes: QPR001 - Infrastructure services workload (2014). http://backus1.uniandes.edu.co/enar/dokuwiki/doku.php?id=qpr001. Accessed 27 Feb 2016
35. Singh, P.M., van Sinderen, M.J.: Lightweight metrics for enterprise architecture analysis. In: Abramowicz, W., et al. (eds.) BIS 2015 Workshops. LNBIP, vol. 228, pp. 113–125. Springer, Heidelberg (2015). doi:10.1007/978-3-319-26762-3

Measuring and Visualising Projects' Collective Method Rationale

Fredrik Linander[1,2(✉)], Kai Wistrand[1], and Fredrik Karlsson[1]

[1] Department of Informatics, CERIS, Örebro University School of Business, Örebro, Sweden
{fredrik.linander, kai.wistrand, fredrik.karlsson}@oru.se
[2] Saab Dynamics AB, Karlskoga, Sweden
fredrik.linander@saabgroup.com

Abstract. Existing research provide frameworks for analysing the rationale behind engineering methods and how this rationale matches the rationale of individual project members. As methods are used in groups, this raises questions about how to study method rationale on an aggregated project level. We propose an elaboration of method rationale theory to enable this type of analysis. We introduce the concept of collective method rationale together with metrics to capture this aggregated rationale. The conceptual work is implemented in a computerized tool, which enables analyses of collective method rationale in product development projects. These are the results of an action research project and we present a pilot test of the computerized tool to demonstrate the concept.

Keywords: Method rationale · Collective method rationale · Modelling rationale

1 Introduction

Organisations choose to apply engineering methods for many reasons. These methods provide guidance through complex scenarios and tasks. Methods can be regarded as theories about actions to perform in order to reach given goals. This implies that they have an inherent conception of a desired target state. Subsequently, there are relations between this target state and the proposed actions [1]. Ultimately, methods can be viewed as reason based statements regarding target states, and as such they represent rationality [2]. The concept of method rationale has been suggested as a way of describing the underlying arguments for a method's appearance [e.g. 3, 4].

The concept intends to capture the relations between a method, or parts thereof, and the goal that this method (part) aims to fulfil. A potential method user has goals and chooses between method parts that can help reach his/hers own goals. A wise choice of method parts would of course be parts that have goals overlapping those of the method user, i.e. to achieve rationality resonance [5].

As methods usually are put to use in groups, this raises the question about how to study the phenomenon of method rationale on an aggregated project team level. Most of the studies on method rationale have focused how the concept can be used as a

J. Horkoff et al. (Eds.): PoEM 2016, LNBIP 267, pp. 344–352, 2016.
DOI: 10.1007/978-3-319-48393-1_26

facilitator for planning a project based on individual rationality resonance [e.g. 6–8]. An exception is Wistrand [9] and Karlsson [10], they have aggregated individual rationality resonance into a collective concept. Still, both of them build on the individual preferences towards the selection of certain method parts. Moreover, there are few studies that have focused on method rationale in retrospection, i.e. studying what kind of method rationale a project has emphasized when it was carried out.

Therefore in this paper we pose the following research question: *how can we measure and visualise method rationale on a project level?* For this purpose we introduce the concept of "collective method rationale", complemented with newly developed metrics operationalizing this concept, and a computerized tool where the metrics are implemented as part of a process modelling approach.

2 Existing Research on Method Rationale

Several scholars [e.g. 11–13] have concluded that methods are based on the rationale of the method engineer, which has provided guidance through the method design. Hence, each engineering method is founded in a goal and value system [1]. Fitzgerald et al. [14] have suggested that methods are adapted when applied, which is in line with Argyris' and Schön's [15] theory on organizational learning. Argyris and Schön [15] have highlighted that organisations' explicit action strategies, such as prescribed engineering methods, are enacted and realised through the actions taken by the individual practitioners. In other words, it has been shown that action strategies are adapted to the current situation based on the situational and local character of knowing, where the project member's rationale come into play. Argyris and Schön [15] have distinguished between "espoused theory" – an ideal established by the organisation "to explain or justify a given pattern of activity" – and "theory-in-use", representing "the performance of that pattern of activity".

In the quest for situational methods, both Ågerfalk [16] and Wistrand [9] have stressed the importance that the rationale of project members and the prescribed method need to match. Both scholars draw on the concept of rationality resonance [5]; rationality resonance occurs when the (private) rationale of the project member and the (public) rationale of the method match and the method is perceived as support.

Most of the above-mentioned research takes an individual approach to 'theory-in-use', i.e. situational methods, and method rationale. They either focus on rationality resonance between the individual project member and the chosen method [e.g. 5, 16], or how the private rationale of a project member can be used to transform a prescribed method into a situational one [e.g. 6, 17]. Few studies have focused on the rationale that exists on a project level. Wistrand [9] is a notable exception; he introduced the concept of collective rationality resonance in a group. However, he did not discuss how to collect data to fill and visualise this concept. Karlsson [10] proposed a data collection and analysis technique for collective rationality resonance based on self-reports coming from project members. But, this approach still departures in an individual approach towards method rationale whilst focusing on resonance.

3 Conceptual Framework

Given the aim of this paper and the state-of-the-art in existing research there is a need for additional conceptual work in order to measure the collective method rationale of a project. Figure 1 presents the main concepts of the existing research together with our additional concepts for addressing rationale as a project group phenomenon. The figure is illustrated using a UML Class diagram.

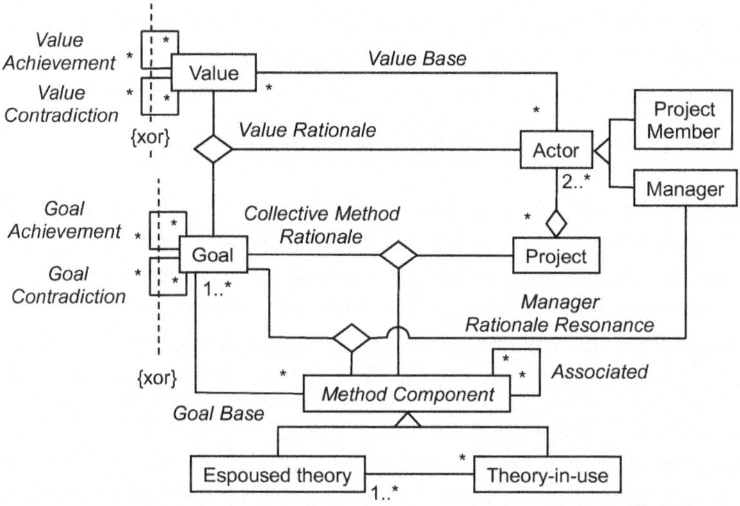

Fig. 1. Modified method rationale theory

The conceptual framework builds on the method component concept, which is in line with Wistrand [9] and Karlsson [10]. Method components as espoused theories offer possible achievable goals that are anchored in values. Project members have selected method components as a means to receive guidance concerning project tasks. The goals of the selected method components constitute the collective method rationale, either as a plan (espoused theory) or as executed (theory-in-use).

In order to measure collective method rationale we need to discuss the internal structure of the method component concept. A method component is a self-contained part of an engineering method, and consists of five types of method elements that all are related to goals: artefact, actions, actor role, concept, and notation [18]. *Action* expresses the activities that need to be done to transform input *artefacts* into defined output *artefact*. *Actor role* expresses who should carry out or participate in a specific action. *Concepts* guide the actor towards certain aspects of the engineering task. Finally, the method element *notation* expresses how the results should be represented when documented.

When examining the method elements, actions are of particular interest. Project members propel projects forward through actions that consume time. Time is often considered one of the most important volume metrics of a project, and shows the emphasis put on specific parts of a project. Time is also part of official project artefacts such as project plans and time report sheets. Hence, we have added time as a characteristic to the action method element. Considering that an engineering method contains a number of selected method components we can define the *relative collective method rationale* towards a specific goal, X, as follows.

$$\frac{\sum_{k=0}^{\substack{\text{Number of method}\\ \text{components targeting}\\ \text{overall goal } X}} \text{Time units for method component } k}{\sum_{n=1}^{\substack{\text{Number of method}\\ \text{components in the}\\ \text{engineering method}}} \text{Time units for method component } n} \tag{1}$$

and

$$1 = \sum_{m=1}^{\substack{\text{Number of}\\ \text{overall goals}}} \begin{matrix}\text{Relative collective method}\\ \text{rationale for overall goal } m\end{matrix} \tag{2}$$

This definition of measuring relative collective method rationale introduces a restriction on the method component's conceptual model. In the original concept [18], actions can be performed with multiple goals in mind. However, in these metrics a method component only have one overall goal.

4 Research Method

The research approach applied in this study is characterised as action research [19], carried out as a collaboration project between academia and industry. The parties involved are companies from defence and motorsport industry. The approach follows the traditional "canonical" action research process-model with iterations through the five stages of diagnosing, action planning, action taking, evaluating and specifying learning [20]. The paper covers the second of four planned iterations to develop a method and a computerized tool for benchmarking project and organisations with regard to the rationale behind chosen engineering methods. The first iteration has been reported on in Karlsson et al. [21]. Below we discuss each of the five stages of the second iteration.

4.1 Diagnosing

During the diagnosing stage, we analysed a subset of the overall industry and research problem. In addition, the identified state-of-the-art research was analysed together with our industrial partners during a series of workshops. Based on the results we formulated an aim for the second iteration: to develop a concept, a metric and a computerized tool to capture and visualize the collective method rationale employed in a product development project.

4.2 Action Planning

During the action planning stage, we focused on conceptual work and elicitation of the requirements for the second version of the computerized tool. We introduced the concept of collective method rationale into the existing conceptual framework of method rationale. In addition, we operationalized this concept as a metric to be implemented in the computerized tool. The operationalization resulted in a number of requirements (user stories) concerning modifications and extensions of the tool. In parallel with implementing the computerized tool we searched for a suitable goal nomenclature to use during process modelling. Given the industry problem of comparing projects and organisations with regard to the rationale behind chosen engineering methods, we needed a nomenclature that could be used across projects as well as organisations. We chose to use the goal structure in the Capability Maturity Model Integration for Development (CMMI-Dev) v1.2 [22]. It contains an established set of generic goals for product and service development. These goals are structured in a hierarchical fashion; goals that can be found across projects and organisations.

4.3 Action Taking

During this stage we made a first full-scale test of the modified tool and the newly developed metrics. Data from an implemented product development project at a motorsport partner were collected, modelled and analysed using the computerized tool. The project was chosen based on reasonable size and complexity, and availability of data and contact persons. The data collection took place at the premises of the motorsport partner at two separate occasions. Given the industry's overall benchmarking interest of actual practices, we chose to model the theory-in-use version of the method. This meant that we collected data about the enacted method.

We used semi-structured interviews, project reports and log books to reconstruct the project. Our interview questions focused on executed method components and their parts, including goals, deliverables, start and finishing dates, main activities, consumed time and applied outsourcing strategies. The interviews were held with the project manager. In the case a method component targeted multiple overall goals, the project manager was asked to (a), if possible, divide the method component into two or more components, or (b) pin point the main overall goal that had consumed the most work effort during the method component's execution. Notes were taken during the interviews and the project manager reviewed the documentation in order to validate the data and to authorise that it could be used as part of the research project. These notes were used for reconstructing the method in the computerized tool. Finally, each of the 23 identified method components was traced to one of the 22 top-level goals in CMMI-Dev. This analysis was carried out together with the project manager.

4.4 Evaluation

During the evaluation stage we arranged a joint workshop to discuss the initial results. First, we presented the current version of the conceptual framework and the metrics used. Second, we presented how the chosen project had been modelled. Third, we presented the analytical results (see Fig. 2) and how to interpret the way collective method rationale is visualised. Finally, we conducted a feedback session where we discussed (a) the usefulness of the analysis in relation to the industry problem, and (b) problematic aspects during data collection and modelling.

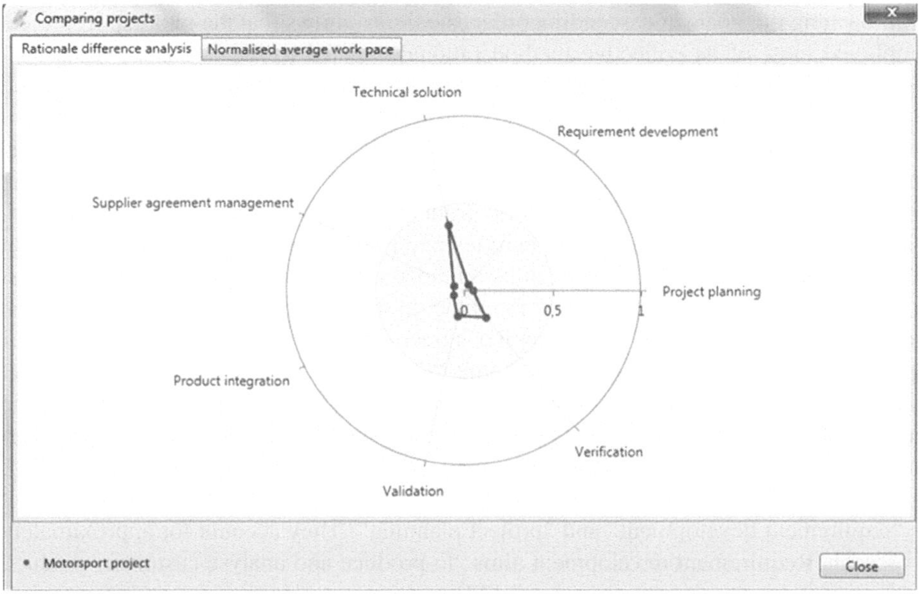

Fig. 2. The motorsport project's collective method rationality profile

4.5 Specify Learning

During the specify learning stage we structured and assessed the results into lessons learned and change requests for the next iteration. Lessons learned contained advices on how to use the conceptual framework, the metrics, and the computerized tool.

5 Results – Empirical Example

Our chosen motorsport partner develops, designs, sells and leases cars for rally cross and extreme motorsport. The company also operates its own team internationally in several rally cross championships. The analysed motorsport project was a 13-months development project of a new car. The project was executed in a fifty-fifty work share division between our motorsport partner and a business partner. Our motorsport partner had the main responsibilities for the development and the final assembly of the cars. Marketing activities of the new car were integrated into the project and executed jointly with validation activities related to driver experiences resulting in signed car contracts prior closure of the development project.

5.1 Results from Action Taking – Modelling and Analysis

Figure 2 illustrates the results of our analysis using the relative collective method rationale as a radar diagram. This enables us to create a visual profile of the project's employed rationale, where the relative collective method rationale of each analysed goal is plotted as a value between zero and one.

The radar diagram has seven axes, one for each goal we have identified. Approaching the goals in descending order, the figure shows that the motorsport project employed most of its collective method rationale related to the "technical solution"-goal. Technical solution according to CMMI-Dev means, "to design, develop, and implement solutions to requirements" [22]. Almost 43 % of the efforts have been put into this particular goal. The "verification"-goal is the second most employed rationale in the project, accounting for approximately 17 %. Verification means spending resources "to ensure that selected work products meet their specified requirements" [22]. The "validation"-goal, i.e. "to demonstrate that a product or product component fulfils its intended use when placed in its intended environment" [22], is the third most focused part of the collective method rationale. In the project it accounts for 15 %. The goals "product integration" and "supplier agreement management", each account for approximately 8 %. Product integration aims "to assemble the product from the product components, ensure that the product, as integrated, functions properly, and deliver the product" [22], and supplier agreement management means that the project has put effort into activities in order to "manage the acquisition of products from suppliers" [22]. Finally, the collective method rationale that has been employed the least in the project is "requirement development" and "project planning". They account for approximately 4 % each. Requirement development aims "to produce and analyse customer, product, and product component requirements" [22] and project planning means "to establish and maintain plans that define project activities" [22].

5.2 Results from Evaluation – Workshop with Practitioners and Researchers

The evaluation was conducted as a half-day workshop. The practitioners concluded that the concept and its operationalization were straightforward and applicable. As an example, one practitioner said: "[T]he informative and straight forward approach gives it a high potential to become widely used in practice in our organisation". However, during the workshop challenges with low data resolution were discussed. The discussion centred on how the size of the method components could affect the collective method rationale profile. Coarse-grained method components give an imprecise profile, which might be sensitive to how the components were classified with regards to the overall goal. The project's resulting profile was perceived as easy-to-grasp. The practitioners used words like "informative" and "simple to interpret". However, the participants discussed how the radar diagram would work when larger projects are modelled that include all 22 goals in CMMI-Dev. This is illustrated by one of the practitioners: "The analysed project has seven goals. A project with a lot of goals will most probably have a less interpretable profile than the analysed project".

5.3 Results from Specified Learning

Based on the workshop and the modelling activities two lessons learned were made. First, we must be able to handle a larger number of goals than only the seven identified in the pilot project, without cluttering the visual presentation. However, this is still only a potential problem, and modelling of additional projects will show if this must be addressed. We can conclude that we need to use the area in the radar diagram more efficiently, because some of the values get cluttered in the centre of the diagram. Second, there is a need for more fine-grained method components, in order to improve the analytical precision. This does not call for design changes of the computerized tool. Instead, we need to adapt the way data is collected and which kind of data we use.

6 Conclusions

The concept of method rationale has in previous research mostly focused on an individual's preferences towards engineering methods and how project members choose among different method parts based on these preferences. In order to understand how method rationale can be captured on an aggregated level, such as in project teams, we have proposed the concept of collective method rationale. In this paper we have shown how a modified version of the method rationale theory can be applied to capture collective method rationale of a project. We have presented metrics for capturing relative collective method rationale and used it to analyse a project at a motorsport company. We have shown the collective method rationale using a radar diagram in a computerised tool. Based on the feedback from practitioners this seems to be fruitful way to convey the metrics and the analysis.

References

1. Ågerfalk, P.J., Åhlgren, K.: Modelling the rationale of methods. In: Khosrowpour, M. (ed.) Managing Information Technology Resources in Organizations in the Next Millennium, pp. 184–190. IDEA Group Publishing, Hershey (1999)
2. Hirschheim, R., Klein, H.K., Lyytinen, K.: Exploring the intellectual structures of information systems development: a social action theoretic analysis. Account. Manag. Inf. Technol. **6**, 1–64 (1996)
3. Rossi, M., Tolvanen, J.-P., Ramesh, B., Lyytinen, K., Kaipala, J.: Method rationale in method engineering. In: Proceedings of 33rd Hawaii International Conference on System Sciences (HICSS-33), vol. 2, p. 2036. IEEE Computer Society Press, Maui, Hawaii (2000)
4. Ågerfalk, P.J., Wistrand, K.: Systems development method rationale: a conceptual framework for analysis. In: Camp, O., Filipe, J., Hammoudi, S., Piattini, M. (eds.) Proceedings of 5th International Conference on Enterprise Information Systems (ICEIS 2003), pp. 185–190. Escola Superior de Tecnologia do Instituto Politécnico de Setúbal, Setúbal (2003)
5. Stolterman, E., Russo, N.L.: The paradox of information systems methods – public and private rationality. In: British Computer Society 5th Annual Conference on Methodologies

6. Karlsson, F., Ågerfalk, P.J.: Towards structured flexibility in information systems development: devising a method for method configuration. J. Database Manag. **20**, 51–75 (2009)
7. Rossi, M., Ramesh, B., Lyytinen, K., Tolvanen, J.-P.: Managing evolutionary method engineering by method rationale. J. Assoc. Inf. Syst. **5**, 356–391 (2004)
8. Ralyté, J., Deneckère, R., Rolland, C.: Towards a generic model for situational method engineering. In: Eder, J., Missikoff, M. (eds.) CAiSE 2003. LNCS, vol. 2681, pp. 95–110. Springer, Heidelberg (2003)
9. Wistrand, K.: Method rationale revealed - communication of knowledge in systems development methods. Ph.D. thesis, Swedish Business School, Örebro University, Örebro (2009)
10. Karlsson, F.: Longitudinal use of method rationale in method configuration: an exploratory study. Eur. J. Inf. Syst. (2012)
11. Jayaratna, N.: Understanding and Evaluating Methodologies. McGraw-Hill, London (1994)
12. Russo, N.L., Stolterman, E.: Exploring the assumptions underlying information systems methodologies: their impact on past, present and future ISM research. Inf. Technol. People **13**, 313–327 (2000)
13. Brinkkemper, S.: Method engineering: engineering of information systems development methods and tools. Inf. Softw. Technol. **38**, 275–280 (1996)
14. Fitzgerald, B., Russo, N.L., Stolterman, E.: Information Systems Development - Methods in Action. McGraw-Hill, Berkshire (2002)
15. Argyris, C., Schön, D.A.: Organizational Learning II. Theory Method and Practice. Addison-Wesley Publishing Company, Reading (1996)
16. Ågerfalk, P.J.: Towards better understanding of agile values in global software development. In: Krogstie, J., Halpin, T.A., Proper, H.A. (eds.) 11th International Workshop on Exploring Modeling Methods in Systems Analysis and Design (EMMSAD 2006), pp. 375–382. Namur University Press, Namur (2006)
17. Karlsson, F., Ågerfalk, P.J.: Method configuration: adapting to situational characteristics while creating reusable assets. Inf. Softw. Technol. **46**, 619–633 (2004)
18. Karlsson, F., Wistrand, K.: Combining method engineering with activity theory: theoretical grounding of the method component concept. Eur. J. Inf. Syst. **15**, 82–90 (2006)
19. Baskerville, R., Wood-Harper, A.T.: Diversity in information systems action research methods. Eur. J. Inf. Syst. **7**, 90–107 (1998)
20. Susman, G.I., Evered, R.D.: An assessment of the scientific merits of action research. Adm. Sci. Q. **23**, 582–603 (1978)
21. Karlsson, F., Linander, F., Von Schéele, F.: A conceptual framework for time distortion analysis in method components. In: 19th Exploring Modelling Methods for Systems Analysis and Design (EMMSAD 2014), Thessaloniki, Greece (2014)
22. Software Engineering Institute: CMMI for Development, Version 1.2. Carnegie Mellon University (2006)

An Integrated Conceptual Model for Information System Security Risk Management and Enterprise Architecture Management Based on TOGAF

Nicolas Mayer(✉), Jocelyn Aubert, Eric Grandry, and Christophe Feltus

Luxembourg Institute of Science and Technology, 5 Avenue Des Hauts-Fourneaux, 4362 Esch-sur-Alzette, Luxembourg
{nicolas.mayer, jocelyn.aubert, eric.grandry, christophe.feltus}@list.lu

Abstract. Risk management is today a major steering tool for any organization wanting to deal with Information System (IS) security. However, IS Security Risk Management (ISSRM) remains difficult to establish and maintain, mainly in a context of multi-regulations with complex and inter-connected IS. We claim that a connection with Enterprise Architecture Management (EAM) contributes to deal with these issues. According to our research agenda, a first step towards a better integration of both domains is to define an EAM-ISSRM conceptual integrated model. To build such a model, we will improve the ISSRM domain model, a conceptual model depicting the domain of ISSRM, with the concepts of EAM. The contribution of this paper is focused on the improvement of the ISSRM domain model with the concepts of TOGAF, a well-known EAM standard.

Keywords: Information security · Risk management · Enterprise architecture · TOGAF · Compliance

1 Introduction

Nowadays, Information System (IS) security and Risk Management (RM) are required for every organization that wishes to survive in this networked world. Whether for purely compliance purposes, business development opportunities, or even governance improvement, organizations tend to implement a security strategy based on an IS Security RM (ISSRM) approach. However, organizations have to deal with pressures that increase the complexity of managing security risks: regulatory pressure involving ISSRM requirements [1–3], increasing number of threats and complexity of current IS [6, 7], lack of efficiency in the process followed [1], or difficulty to have a clear and manageable documentation of ISSRM activities [1]. Due to this complexity, new solutions are required to address security risks. Classical ISSRM methods [1, 2] are indeed not suitable to deal with the complexity of organizations and associated risks, in a context of compliance and governance.

J. Horkoff et al. (Eds.): PoEM 2016, LNBIP 267, pp. 353–361, 2016.
DOI: 10.1007/978-3-319-48393-1_27

Enterprise Architecture Management (EAM) has shown to be a valuable and engaging instrument to face enterprise complexity and the necessary enterprise transformation [3, 4]. EAM offers means to govern complex enterprises, such as, for example, an explicit representation of the enterprise facets, a sound and informed decisional framework, a continuous alignment between business and IT, and so forth [5]. By integrating EAM with ISSRM, we aim to be able to deal with the preceding listed issues related to the complexity of organizations and associated risks.

In earlier work, we have integrated the concepts of existing ISSRM standards and methods into a domain model, that we called the ISSRM domain model [6]. The goal of our research is to improve this model by extending it to a framework (modelling language, method, and tool) that incorporates results from EAM research [7] and that can be used in practice. A first step is to define an integrated EAM-ISSRM conceptual model which will be called the "EAM-ISSRM integrated model". This paper describes part of this work and its contribution is focused on analysing if and how the concepts that are part of TOGAF, a well-known standard in the domain of EAM published by The Open Group [8], can be used to improve the ISSRM domain model. Note that we do not propose a modelling language, although this task is part of our next objectives, but we define an underlying conceptual model for such a language. This model will be a key artefact towards the definition of a dedicated modelling language and of the associated ISSRM method.

In the following section, the background of our work is described: it introduces the ISSRM domain model and the TOGAF standard. Section 3 presents the conceptual alignment between the concepts of TOGAF and those of the ISSRM domain model, and then explains the key conclusions. An integrated EAM-ISSRM conceptual model based on TOGAF is proposed in Sect. 4. Section 5 is a comparison with related work. Finally, conclusions and future work are presented in Sect. 6.

2 Background

2.1 The ISSRM Domain Model

In our preceding work, the concepts of ISSRM have been represented as a domain model, i.e. a conceptual model depicting the studied domain [6]. The ISSRM domain model was designed from related literature [1]: risk management standards, security-related standards, security risk management standards and methods, and security requirements engineering frameworks. The ISSRM domain model is composed of 3 groups of concepts: *Asset-related concepts*, *Risk-related concepts*, and *Risk treatment-related concepts*. Each of the concepts of the model has been defined and linked one to the other, as represented in Fig. 1.

Asset-related concepts (light grey boxes) describe assets and the criteria which guarantee asset security. An asset is anything that has value to the organization and is necessary for achieving its objectives. A business asset describes information, processes, capabilities, and skills inherent to the business and core mission of the organization, having value for it. An IS asset is a component of the IS supporting business assets like a database where information is stored. In our context, and as described in

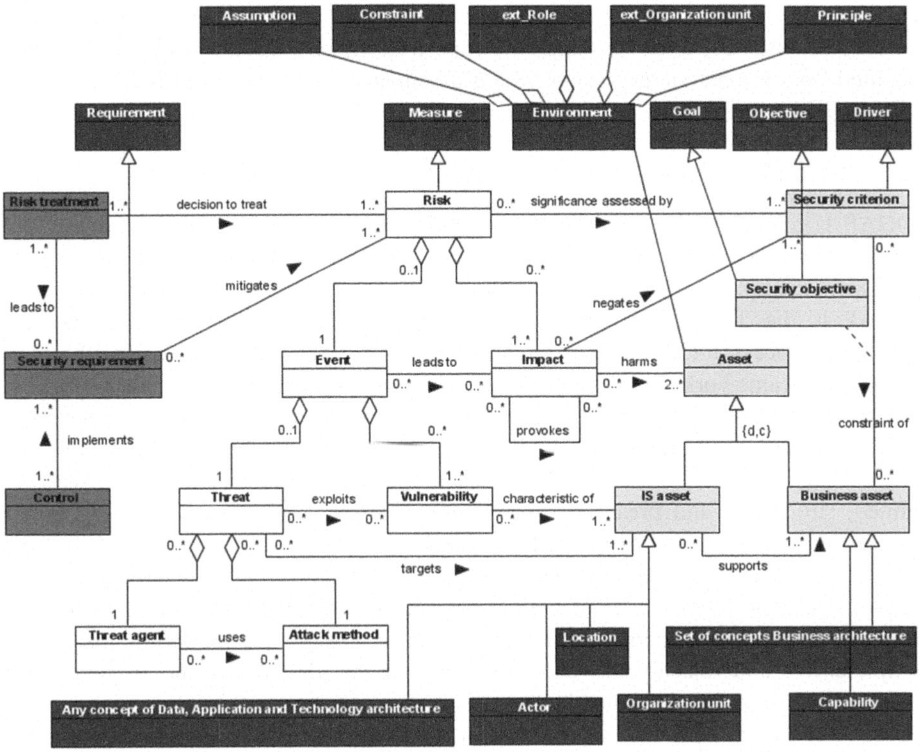

Fig. 1. EAM-ISSRM integrated model based on TOGAF

the ISSRM literature [1], an IS is a composition of hardware, software, network, people and facilities. A security criterion characterises a property or constraint on business assets describing their security needs. The most common security criteria are confidentiality, integrity and availability. A security objective is the application of a security criterion on a business asset (e.g. the confidentiality of personal information).

Risk-related concepts (white boxes) present how the risk itself is defined. A risk is the combination of an event with a negative impact harming the assets. A negative impact describes the potential negative consequence of an event that may harm assets of a system or organization, when an event causing this impact occurs. An event is the combination of a threat and one or more vulnerabilities. A vulnerability describes a characteristic of an IS asset or group of IS assets that can constitute a weakness or a flaw that can be exploited by a threat. A threat characterises a potential attack or incident, which targets one or more IS assets and may lead to the assets being harmed. A threat consists of a threat agent and an attack method. A threat agent is an agent that can potentially cause harm to IS assets. An attack method is a standard means by which a threat agent carries out a threat.

Risk treatment-related concepts (dark grey boxes) describe what decisions, requirements and controls should be defined and implemented in order to mitigate possible risks. A risk treatment is an intentional decision to treat identified risks.

A security requirement is a desired property of an IS that contributes to a risk treatment. Controls (countermeasures or safeguards) are a designed means to improve security, specified by a security requirement, and implemented to comply with it.

2.2 TOGAF

TOGAF is a framework — a detailed method and a set of supporting tools — for developing an enterprise architecture [8]. It is a standard established and maintained by The Open Group, an industry consortium focused on IT standards. A key aspect of TOGAF is the TOGAF Architecture Development Method (ADM), a tested and repeatable process for developing architectures. The ADM includes establishing an architecture framework, developing architecture content, transitioning, and governing the realization of architectures. The TOGAF Architecture Content Framework (ACF) provides a structural model for architectural content, developed all along the different steps of the ADM, which allows major work products to be consistently defined, structured, and presented. The TOGAF ACF is structured according to its Content Metamodel. This metamodel is a single view that encompasses all four of the TOGAF architecture domains (Business, Data, Application; and Technology Architecture), and that defines a set of entities that allow architectural concepts to be captured, stored, filtered, queried, and represented in a way that supports consistency, completeness, and traceability. The TOGAF Content Metamodel and its associated glossary are of particular interest for the analysis performed in this paper. More information about TOGAF can be found in the TOGAF 9.1 reference book [8].

3 Conceptual Alignment Between Concepts of TOGAF and Concepts of the ISSRM Domain Model

The conceptual alignment consists of identifying the semantic correspondence between concepts of TOGAF and concepts of the ISSRM domain model. This task has been performed by a focus group composed of five people. Three of them are ISSRM experts and two of them EAM experts. All of the members of the focus group are researchers having a good theoretical knowledge of ISSRM and/or EAM. Moreover, two ISSRM experts are also experienced ISSRM practitioners (in total during the 10 last years, they have performed more than 20 real-world applications of ISSRM in organizations, going from SMEs to European institutions). The EAM experts are practitioners in the discipline, regularly facing real challenges from enterprises, and one of them demonstrate proven experience in the application of the TOGAF framework: rolling out the ADM in large companies, setting up and customizing TOGAF repositories corporate-wide and in the scope of projects. Alignment decisions were taken only once a consensus has been found among the members of this focus group.

3.1 Alignment Approach

The approach followed is inspired by Zivkovic et al. [9]. Each relation between concepts is classified according to the following semantic mapping subtypes:

- ***Equivalence***: *concept A* is semantically equivalent to *concept B*;
- ***Generalisation***: *concept A* is a generalisation of *concept B*, i.e. *concept B* is a specific class of *concept A*;
- ***Specialisation***: *concept A* is a specialisation of *concept B*, i.e. *concept B* is a generic class of *concept A*;
- ***Aggregation***: *concept A* is composed of *concept B*, i.e. *concept B* is a part of *concept A*;
- ***Composition***: *concept A* is composed of *concept B* (with strong ownership), i.e. *concept B* is a part of *concept A* and does only exist as part of *concept A*;
- ***Association***: *concept A* is linked to *concept B*.

The output of this step is a table, highlighting the relations between the concepts of TOGAF and those of the ISSRM domain model. Such a table is presented in a technical report [10] which aims to perform similar work with other EAM references including ArchiMate, DoDAF and IAF.

3.2 Alignment Key Conclusions

Based on the definitions of the TOGAF Content Metamodel [8], and the definitions of the concepts of the ISSRM domain [1, 6], the conceptual alignment aims at finding the structural and semantic correspondences of the concepts defined in TOGAF with those of the ISSRM domain model. In other words, the alignment highlights the capabilities of the TOGAF approach to represent ISSRM concepts.

A detailed analysis of the results of the mapping is given next.

- Most of the core concepts of Business Architecture in TOGAF are specific kinds of Business Assets. *Capability* is also considered as a Business Asset, although it is not part of Business Architecture concepts.
- All of the TOGAF concepts of the Data, Application, and Technology Architectures are specialisations of the concept of IS asset. More specifically, they are representing IT assets, i.e. IS assets of hardware, software or network kind. The only exception is *Technology Component* which is an abstract entity, as well as the concept of *Business Service,* which is a specialisation of Business asset.
- Data, Application, and Technology Architectures are adapted to represent an IT system, but are lacking people and facilities class of IS assets, necessary to define an IS in an information security context. However, they can be represented with the help of the following concepts of the Business Architecture: *Organization Unit*, *Actor* and *Location.*
- *Event* has no mapping with any ISSRM concept. It is defined as an organizational state change that triggers a *Process*, and has thus no correspondence with concepts

of the ISSRM domain model. The ISSRM domain model aims indeed at identifying structural concepts at stake, and not at handling behavioural and methodological aspects of ISSRM.

- *Gap* and *Work Package* have also no mapping with any ISSRM concept. They are related to the project management aspects of architecture design and have thus no correspondence with concepts of the ISSRM domain model.
- *Driver* is a generalisation of the Security criterion concept. In our context, we have one main concern that is IS security, leading to drivers that are ISSRM security criteria (i.e., confidentiality, integrity, availability, etc.). Regarding our scope, the conditions that motivate the organization to define its (security) goals are related to the need of confidentiality, integrity or availability of information processed in the IS. In the same vain, the concepts of *Goal* and *Objectives* are a generalization of Security objective.
- *Measure* is considered as a generalisation of Risk, because a risk is a specific kind of measure. A risk is indeed an indicator or factor that can be tracked to determine success or alignment with *Objectives* and *Goals* (i.e. confidentiality, integrity and/or availability of Business Assets).
- *Requirement* is a generalization of Security requirement.
- The concepts of *Principle* (e.g., standard to be followed, regulation, etc.), *Constraint* (e.g., customer data is not harmonized within the organization) and *Assumption* (e.g., the application to be used shall be security certified) are associated with the concept of Asset, as well as *Organization Unit* and *Role*, because the latter can also be used to represent stakeholders (e.g. regulation organization, customers, shareholders, etc.). All of these concepts are indeed used in TOGAF to represent aspects considered as part of the environment of the assets and identified during the context establishment step of the ISSRM process [2]. Concepts currently composing the ISSRM domain model are the set of concepts used during risk assessment and risk treatment steps.

To summarize, we can draw two main conclusions from the alignment. First, although the mapping is complex, TOGAF brings a more fine grained representation of (business and IS) assets than the ISSRM domain model. Second, TOGAF considers the concepts that are part of the environment of the assets. This is not the case of the ISSRM domain model.

4 EAM-ISSRM Integrated Model Proposal Based on TOGAF

The preceding conceptual alignment between TOGAF and the ISSRM domain model, and more specifically the key conclusions coming from this alignment, have highlighted that a set of concepts of TOGAF, when used in an ISSRM context, are specialisations of ISSRM concepts:

- The concepts of the Business architecture are specialisation of Business asset, except *Location*, *Actor* and *Organization unit* that are specialisation of IS asset. *Capability* is also a specialisation of Business asset.

- The concepts of the Data, Application and Technology architecture are specialisation of IS assets except *Technology Component* that is an abstract entity.

Some other concepts, always when used in an ISSRM context, are generalisations of ISSRM concepts:

- Security requirements are specific instances of *Requirement.*
- Risk is a specific instance of *Measure.*
- Security criterion is a specific instance of *Driver.*
- Security objective is a specific instance of *Goal* or *Objective.*

Finally, some EAM concepts of TOGAF have been identified as related to concepts of the ISSRM domain model:

- *Assumption, Constraint, Principle,* as well as *Role* and *Organization Unit* that are external to the IS (represented as *ext_Role* and *ext_Organization unit* in Fig. 1) are part of the environment of the assets studied. A new concept entitled "Environment" has been added to the model and is composed of the preceding concepts.

The resulting EAM-ISSRM integrated model is shown in Fig. 1. It lies on the ISSRM domain model, depicting the state-of-the-art concepts of ISSRM, and is improved with EAM concepts, represented by black boxes with white names. In summary, a refinement of Business and IS assets has first been added, allowing to better model the complexity of current targets of ISSRM. Second, concepts related to the environment of the IS and thus to context establishment requirements have also been added. It helps to avoid that organizations provide insufficient ISSRM reports by bypassing some fundamental aspects of ISSRM, and allows also tackling our challenge of dealing with regulatory pressure involving ISSRM requirements.

5 Related Work

The Open Group, in a white paper published in 2015 [11], analyses different approaches to modelling enterprise risk, as well as security concepts, based on ArchiMate 2.1. However, the scope of this white paper differs from our scope because they also consider non-security related risks (strategic, financial, project, etc.) with information security risks (i.e. risks harming confidentiality, integrity and availability of information). Barateiro et al. [12] propose an alignment between Risk Management, Governance and Enterprise Architecture activities in order to provide a systematic support to map and trace identified risks to artefacts modelled within an EA. Innerhofer-Oberperfler and Breu [13] propose an approach for the systematic assessment and analysis of IT-related risks in organizations and projects. The goal of the approach is to bridge the different views of the stakeholders involved in security management. SABSA [14] is a methodology for developing risk-driven enterprise information security and information assurance architectures and for delivering security infrastructure solutions that support critical business initiatives. The methodology relies on the SABSA model, which is based on the Zachman framework [3] adapted somewhat to a security view. Goldstein and Franck have proposed a set of 23 requirements a modelling approach should satisfy to deal with IT security design and management [15]. We share the common objective to define a Domain Specific Modelling Language (DSML) enhancing an existing method for enterprise modelling. Their scope is wider as ours, but includes some basic and relevant aspects related to ISSRM. The CORAS approach is a model-driven approach in the sense that graphical models are actively used throughout the whole risk analysis process to support the various analysis tasks and activities, and to document the results [16]. However, CORAS introduces its own kinds of diagrams and does not rely on EAM models to perform ISSRM. As a conclusion, all of the preceding research works are providing some initial and promising inputs towards leveraging EAM to deal with security and/or RM issues. However, to the best of our knowledge, there is no extensive and mature research work trying to benefit from research in EAM to improve RM in the specific field of information security and proposing a complete and fully integrated conceptual model of both domains.

6 Conclusions and Future Work

In this paper, we have described how we developed an integrated EAM-ISSRM conceptual model based on the ISSRM domain model and the TOGAF standard. First, we have analysed the concepts of TOGAF with regards to the concepts of the ISSRM domain model. The result of this analysis is presented under the form of a conceptual alignment table [10], highlighting the relations between the concepts of TOGAF and those of the ISSRM domain model. After having performed this alignment, the key conclusions are summarised, and then, an integrated EAM-ISSRM conceptual model has been established.

As mentioned in the introduction, our work is part of a larger project, and is not limited to TOGAF, that is only one relevant EAM approach. Other references from the EAM literature will also be taken into account to be representative of the domain. To facilitate a high acceptance level of our extension by practitioners, we plan to focus on conceptual models that are used in practice. The EAM-ISSRM conceptual model will be iteratively improved when considering additional references. Then, after having established an integrated EAM-ISSRM conceptual model based on a representative set of references, it is necessary to validate the results obtained. To do so, we plan to get information about the utility and usability [17] of the EAM-ISSRM integrated model by means of a validation focus group.

Acknowledgments. Supported by the Luxembourg National Research Fund, and financed by the ENTRI project (C14/IS/8329158).

References

1. Mayer, N.: Model-based Management of Information System Security Risk (2009)
2. ISO/IEC 27005:2011: Information technology – Security techniques – Information security risk management. International Organization for Standardization, Geneva (2011)

3. Zachman, J.A.: A framework for information systems architecture. IBM Syst. J. **26**, 276–292 (1987)
4. Saha, P. (ed.): A Systemic Perspective to Managing Complexity with Enterprise Architecture. IGI Global, Hershey (2013)
5. Lankhorst, M.: Enterprise Architecture at Work – Modelling Communication and Analysis. Springer, Heidelberg (2013)
6. Dubois, E., Heymans, P., Mayer, N., Matulevičius, R.: A systematic approach to define the domain of information system security risk management. In: Nurcan, S., Salinesi, C., Souveyet, C., Ralyté, J. (eds.) Intentional Perspectives on Information Systems Engineering, pp. 289–306. Springer, Heidelberg (2010)
7. Mayer, N., Grandry, E., Feltus, C., Goettelmann, E.: Towards the ENTRI framework: security risk management enhanced by the use of enterprise architectures. In: Persson, A., Stirna, J. (eds.) CAiSE 2015. LNBIP, vol. 215, pp. 459–469. Springer International Publishing, Heidelberg (2015)
8. The Open Group: TOGAF Version 9.1. Van Haren Publishing, The Netherlands (2011)
9. Zivkovic, S., Kuhn, H., Karagiannis, D.: Facilitate modelling using method integration: an approach using mappings and integration rules. In: Proceedings of the 15th European Conference on Information Systems (ECIS 2007) (2007)
10. Mayer, N., Aubert, J., Grandry, E., Feltus, C., Goettelmann, E.: An integrated conceptual model for information system security risk management and enterprise architecture management based on TOGAF, ArchiMate, IAF and DoDAF. Technical report. Available on demand (2016)
11. Band, I., Engelsman, W., Feltus, C., González Paredes, S., Hietala, J., Jonkers, H., Massart, S.: Modeling Enterprise Risk Management and Security with the ArchiMate® Language. The Open Group, Midrind (2015)
12. Barateiro, J., Antunes, G., Borbinha, J.: Manage risks through the enterprise architecture. In: 45th Hawaii International Conference on System Science (HICSS), pp. 3297–3306 (2012)
13. Innerhofer-Oberperfler, F., Breu, R.: Using an enterprise architecture for IT risk management. In: Presented at the Information Security South Africa 6th Annual Conference (2006)
14. Sherwood, J., Clark, A., Lynas, D.: SABSA ® Enterprise Security Architecture (2010)
15. Goldstein, A., Frank, U.: A language for multi-perspective modelling of IT security: objectives and analysis of requirements. In: La Rosa, M., Soffer, P. (eds.) Business Process Management Workshops, pp. 636–648. Springer, Berlin Heidelberg (2013)
16. Solhaug, B., Stølen, K.: The CORAS language - why it is designed the way it is. In: Safety, Reliability, Risk and Life-Cycle Performance of Structures and Infrastructures, pp. 3155–3162. CRC Press (2014)
17. Nielsen, J.: Usability Engineering. Morgan Kaufmann, Burlington (1994)

Separation of Modeling Principles and Design Principles in Enterprise Engineering

Tetsuya Suga[1(✉)], Peter De Bruyn[2], Philip Huysmans[2], Jan Verelst[2], and Herwig Mannaert[2]

[1] Tokyo Institute of Technology, 2-12-1 Ookayama, Meguro-ku, Tokyo 152-8550, Japan
suga.t.ac@m.titech.ac.jp
[2] University of Antwerp, Prinsstraat 13, 2000 Antwerp, Belgium
{peter.debruyn,philip.huysmans,jan.verelst,herwig.mannaert}@uantwerp.be

Abstract. An agile enterprise requires evolvable information systems and organizational structures. Some design theories, e.g. Normalized Systems theory, which were originally developed for designing information systems, have been generalized and extended for the design of organizations. In addition to information systems, Normalized Systems theory has recently expanded its applicability into the organizational level, including business process. This resulted in a set of 25 design guidelines for Normalized Systems Business Processes. On the other hand, Enterprise Ontology provides advantages in understanding the essence of organizations for massive abstraction and complexity reduction. Since these two streams of research apparently have similar goals, i.e. designing enterprises, using different approaches, some early studies tried to compare or combine them. However, most of them achieved limited success. This research investigates the literature, looking for a new way to connect them. It concludes that it may be possible to sequentially utilize those two artifacts in two different phases of enterprise engineering.

Keywords: Enterprise engineering · Design principle · Modeling principle · Enterprise ontology · Normalized systems theory

1 Introduction

Enterprise engineering is an emerging sub-discipline of systems engineering that studies enterprises from an engineering perspective. Loosely summarized, enterprise engineering has attempted to view enterprises from the perspective of engineering and then (re)design and (re)implement them. Many researchers and practitioners have been working on this new challenge and have produced a variety of artifacts, such as ArchiMate [1], Enterprise Ontology (EO) [2], 4EM [3], MEMO [4], Normalized Systems theory (NS) [5], S-BPM [6], and so on. On the other

J. Horkoff et al. (Eds.): PoEM 2016, LNBIP 267, pp. 362–373, 2016.
DOI: 10.1007/978-3-319-48393-1_28

hand, some of those artifacts seem to exhibit some overlap in purpose. However, since they have been developed to achieve their own specific goals, they have their own aptitudes by nature. Instead of pursuing the ultimate and apparently arduous goal of unifying them into a single theory, it seems both feasible and valuable to explore a way to combine some of those artifacts in a beneficial manner.

Therefore, this paper tries to find a possible way to combine two artifacts that have recently raised interest, namely EO and NS, rather than unifying them. Indeed, there are several existing studies which tried to compare and potentially find a clue to the unification of the two artifacts in the past. However, most of them achieved limited success, possibly because the two artifacts were compared in the same class of artifacts. In contrast, the authors believe that they should be located in different classes: **modeling principles** and **design principles**, respectively. Therefore, this paper investigates the literature, keeping this hypothesis in mind. Stated another way, this study will answer the following research questions: (1) Is EO a modeling principle? (2) Is EO a design principle? (3) Is NS a modeling principle? (4) Is NS a design principle?

The remainder of this article is organized as follows: Sect. 2 provides brief introductions of the theories of EO and NS, related past works, and the basics of modeling and design principles in the context of model-based systems engineering. Section 3 is the main part of this paper, answering the research questions by collating descriptions of EO and NS with ones of modeling and design principles. After reflection and discussion in Sects. 4, 5 concludes this article with possible future directions for research.

2 Literature Review

2.1 Theoretical Foundation

Enterprise Ontology.[1] EO can be loosely described as a well-founded distinctive set of notions, theories, and a methodology for grasping and steering the complexity of enterprises. Here, *enterprise* is an overall term to identify an intentionally created entity of human endeavor with a certain purpose, e.g. a company, organization, business, governmental agency, and so forth [7, p. 4]. Although EO may accommodate more than one methodology in principle, there exists only one methodology available at this moment, known as "Design & Engineering Methodology for Organizations (DEMO)". The basic assumption of EO is that enterprises are highly complex, as well as highly organized, entities, and thus, a formal theory and methodology are required to achieve the purpose of an enterprise [7, p. 4]. By collating this comprehension against the definition of a system, enterprises are regarded as systems and are now a subject for systems engineering.

[1] The contents of this part are mainly based on [2], unless otherwise stated.

The Four Axioms. EO defines its ways of thinking in four *axioms*[2]. The **operation axiom** states that "[...] the operation of an enterprise is constituted by the activities of actor roles, which are elementary chunks of authority and responsibility, fulfilled by subjects" [2, p. 81]. It also classifies the activities and facts produced by the activities as either production acts/facts or coordination acts/facts (C-acts/facts). The **transaction axiom** states that C-acts are performed sequentially following the steps in the universal pattern, called a *transaction* (Fig. 1a). Some C-acts may be performed implicitly or tacitly. The **composition axiom** defines how transactions are interrelated: every transaction is enclosed in another transaction, or is triggered by actor roles in the environment, or is self-activated. This provides a well-founded definition of a business process: a collection of causally related transaction kinds. The **distinction axiom** defines another classification of human activities into *original*, *informational*, and *documental*. Indeed, this axiom asks modelers to ignore informational and documental activities for a substantialreduction of complexity.

The Organization Theorem. In mathematics, a theorem is a statement that is not self-evidently true but is proven to be true as a logical consequence of axioms. Similarly, as derived from the aforementioned four axioms, the **organization theorem** states that an organization is a heterogeneous system that is constituted as the layered integration of three homogeneous systems: the B-organization for operating *original* activities, the I-organization for operating *informational* activities, and the D-organization for *documental* activities (Fig. 1b).

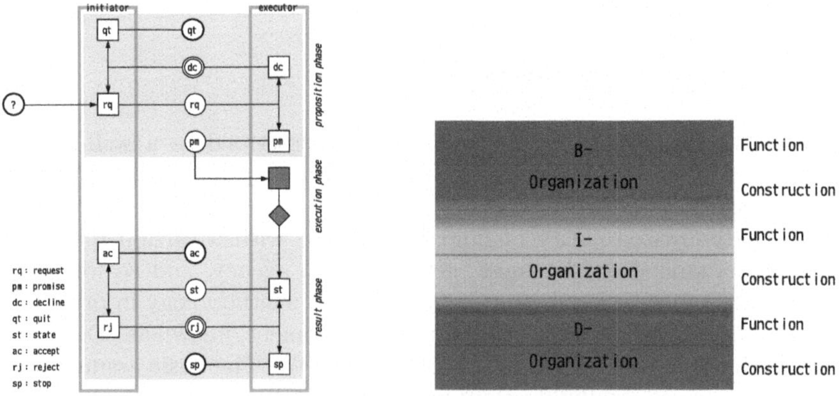

(a) The Standard Transaction Pattern [2, p. 94] (b) The Organization Theorem [2, p. 118]

Fig. 1. Concepts in enterprise ontology

[2] An axiom is *a statement or proposition which is regarded as being established, accepted, or self-evidently true* [8]. Although it is possible to discuss whether these axioms are correct or the best for managing complexity in enterprises, those arguments are somewhat beyond the scope of EO.

Normalized Systems Theory.[3] NS theory aims to design systems pursuing evolvability and observability, originally in the field of information systems development. The basic assumption is that information systems must be able to evolve over time while accommodating future changes which defy Lehman's law of increasing complexity, which is a part of his software evolution laws [9]. To accommodate future changes, information systems must exhibit stability against those changes. It means that the impact of a change should only be dependent on the nature of the change itself [5, pp. 106–107]. Otherwise, if the impact of a change —*ripple effect*— is dependent on the size of the system, thus if it requires more effort as the information system grows, the ripple effect is specifically called a *combinatorial effect.* High evolvability is achieved by removing combinatorial effects.

NS Theorems. NS gets involved in the process of transforming requirements R_i (i.e. functions) into primitives P_j (i.e. construction). In order to achieve a good F-to-C transformation that does not produce any combinatorial effects, NS has proposed a set of four NS *theorems* [10, pp. 88–96][4]:

– SoS; Separation of States	When a primitive uses another primitive as it is executed, both primitives should be separated by a state.
– SoC; Separation of Concerns	A primitive should only contain one concern.
– VT; Version Transparency	A primitive which is used by other primitives should be version transparent.
– IT; Instance Traceability	The input received to execute a particular primitive instance, as well as the output delivered by that primitive instance, should be traceable to the particular version and instance of that primitive.

If the transformation is performed along with the theorems, it should look like Fig. 2b, in contrast to a typical transformation like Fig. 2a, which may contain combinatorial effects. These theorems are independent of application domain.

$$\begin{bmatrix} P_1 \\ \vdots \\ \vdots \\ P_n \end{bmatrix} = \begin{bmatrix} x_{1,1} & \cdots & \cdots & x_{1,l} \\ \vdots & \ddots & \cdot^{\cdot^{\cdot}} & \vdots \\ \vdots & \cdot^{\cdot^{\cdot}} & \ddots & \vdots \\ x_{n,1} & \cdots & \cdots & x_{n,l} \end{bmatrix} \times \begin{bmatrix} R_1 \\ \vdots \\ \vdots \\ R_n \end{bmatrix}$$

(a) A Typical Transformation

$$\begin{bmatrix} P_1 \\ \vdots \\ \vdots \\ P_n \end{bmatrix} = \begin{bmatrix} x_{1,1} & & 0 \\ & \ddots & \\ & & \ddots \\ 0 & & x_{n,l} \end{bmatrix} \times \begin{bmatrix} R_1 \\ \vdots \\ \vdots \\ R_n \end{bmatrix}$$

(b) A Normalized Transformation

Fig. 2. Conceptual function-to-construction transformation in NS [10, p. 76]

[3] The contents of this part are mainly based on [5], unless otherwise stated.

[4] NS theorems in their early stage in software were defined in a different way (see [5, pp. 112–119]).

Guideline and Element. From the theorems, a set of *guidelines* can be derived for a specific application domain, such as information system management, business process reengineering, accounting, enterprise resource planning, etc. The guidelines can be actualized by *elements*, which are reusable sets of primitives. Guidelines and elements are often dependent on specific application domains, in contrast to theorems. In software engineering as a specific application domain, six NS guidelines are derived from the four NS theorems and are implemented by a set of five *elements* (which allow the expansion of software which adheres to these principles): data element, action element, workflow element, trigger element, and connector element. In business process engineering, the theorems are re-interpreted to derive guidelines. The theorems produce 25 specific guidelines named Normalized Systems Business Process (NSBP) guidelines. Currently, no elements implemented by NSBP are available.

2.2 Related Works

[11] studies an alignment of the construct of EO and that of NS by expressing the transaction pattern of EO in the form of NS elements, namely data elements and workflow elements. In order to implement transactions without combinatorial effects, it prescribes two guidelines: (1) additional state transitions need to be created in order to comply with the SoC and SoS theorem, and (2) the cancellation patterns should be implemented with extensions to accommodate their adherence to the NS theorems. The study mainly discusses an emergence of combinatorial effects during the implementation process from the ontological model to the real implementation. Put another way, whether combinatorial effects may occur within the ontological model and even how to remove combinatorial effects remain beyond the scope of the study.

[12] also studies an alignment and combination of EO and NS by establishing a linkage and collaboration between agile enterprises (realized with EO), and agile automated information systems (developed with NS). This research proposes mappings of concepts in EO onto elements of NS with wider coverage than [11]. It also points out that aspects such as user interfaces and non-functional requirements, which are not presented in EO, are considered as aspects in cross-cutting concerns, which should be addressed separately from the functional requirements in NS. Moreover, it reveals that NS does not yet support all concepts of EO, such as a derived fact kind and information link.

[13] is another work with an approach different from the previous two studies [11,12], in which NS elements for software are directly compared and mapped to EO. Instead of the direct approach, this study compares EO concepts and not NS elements for software but the guidelines of NS Business Processes (NSBP), which are derived from NS theorems for the business process domain. Then, it analyzes to what extent the NSBP guidelines are consistent, complementing, or conflicting with prescriptions from EO. This study concludes that 13 of 25 NSBP guidelines are consistent, 12 of them are ignored and don't appear in EO, and 4 of them are conflicting (there is some overlapping).

In these studies on the relationship between EO and NS, the two artifacts are compared in the same class of artifacts.

2.3 Model-Based Systems Engineering Methodology

This section revisits model-based engineering (MBE) to formulate distinct perspectives on modeling principles and design principles to prompt a good understanding of this article.

Modeling and Design. MBE is sequentially decomposed into two parts: *modeling* and *design*. Since these terms mean different things to different people, the following paragraphs are cited from the literature to formulate the meaning of them within the scope of this article: Quote 1 for an overview, Quotes 2 and 3 for modeling, and Quote 4 for designing.

Quote 1 [14, p. 2]. *John G. Truxul, former Dean of Engineering at Brooklyn Polytechnic Institute, says, "Systems engineering includes two parts: modeling, in which each element of the system and the criterion for measuring performance are described; and optimization, in which adjustable elements are set at values that give the best possible performance."*

Quote 2 [15, p. 107]. *A conceptual model is a mental image of a system, its components, its interactions. It lays the foundation for more elaborate models, such as physical or numerical models. A conceptual model provides a framework in which to think about the workings of a system or about problem solving in general. An ensuing operational model can be no better than its underlying conceptualization.*

Quote 3 [16, p. 1]. *The role of conceptual modelling in information systems development during all these decades is seen as an approach for capturing fuzzy, ill-defined, informal "real-world" descriptions and user requirements, and then transforming them to formal, in some sense complete, and consistent conceptual specifications.*

Quote 4 [17, p. 4]. *The engineer, and more generally the designer, is concerned with how things ought to be how they ought to be in order to attain goals.*

Principles. Let us focus on the role of principles in modeling/design as a normative notion that guides system design. A modeling/design guideline is a guideline or a set of guidelines that assist(s) us to achieve a good model/design and avoid a bad model/design. It also defines what is *good* and *bad*. It is often referred to as design guidelines, patterns, architectures, theories, et cetera.

Modeling Principle. The nature of modeling is characterized by three concepts: **mapping**, i.e. which element in the real world and which element in the model should be mapped with each other; **reduction**, i.e. which element in the real world should be selected or ignored; and **pragmatism**, i.e. models as the outcome of modeling activities should be made to be utilized [18, p. 157]. Thus, a modeling principle should provide guidelines for mapping, reduction, and pragmatism.

Design Principle. The nature of design is difficult to summarize. Nevertheless, an anatomy of design theory proposed by [19] defines the characteristics of information systems design theory (regarded as a design principle) by specifying core components: **purpose and scope**, i.e. what the system is for and what the scope of the theory is; **constructs**, i.e. what the entities in the theory are; **principle of form and function**, i.e. what the abstract description of an artifact is (describing either product or method/intervention); **artifact mutability**, i.e. how and to what degree the changes in state of the artifact are anticipated; **testable propositions**, i.e. what the true/false statements are for the design theory; **justificatory knowledge**, i.e. what the kernel theories[5] of the design theory are; **principles of implementation**, i.e. what the processes of implementing the theory (either product or method) in specific contexts are; and **expository instantiation**, i.e. what a physical prototype is. Even though this anatomy was proposed in the context of information system design, it seems able to cover other disciplines to a certain extent.

George Klir (1996) "Review of Model-Based Systems Engineering", in the International Journal of General Systems, Vol 25 (2). p. 179.

3 Separation of Modeling Principles and Design Principles

This section examines EO and NS by comparing each of them against the characteristics of modeling principles and design principles, as revisited in Sect. 2.3.

Is EO a Modeling Principle? [2, p. 10] states that "Our goal is to understand the essence of the construction and operation of complete systems; more specifically, of enterprises." This adheres to the general characteristics of modeling in the sense of Quote 3. It is also stated that "Firstly, the P[rocess]M[odel] facilitates discussions about the redesign, as well as the re-engineering of business processes [...]." in [2, p. 10], which also adheres to Quote 2. This point is also supported by the fact that the acronym of DEMO, a methodology of EO, was initially Dynamic Essential MOdelling (and later Dynamic Essential Modeling of Organizations). Therefore, EO is along the lines of modeling.

Moreover, EO seems to fully satisfy the conditions as a modeling principle as formulated in Sect. 2.3. As explained in Sect. 2.1, the operation axiom defines what and how the **mapping** should be—i.e. what the elements in enterprises are, and how to identify these elements—and the distinction axiom defines the **reduction**—i.e. which among these elements should be included in the model. The general direction of EO also adheres to the concept of **pragmatism**. Therefore, EO can be regarded as a sort of modeling principle.

[5] kernel theory: underlying knowledge or theory from the natural or social or design sciences [19].

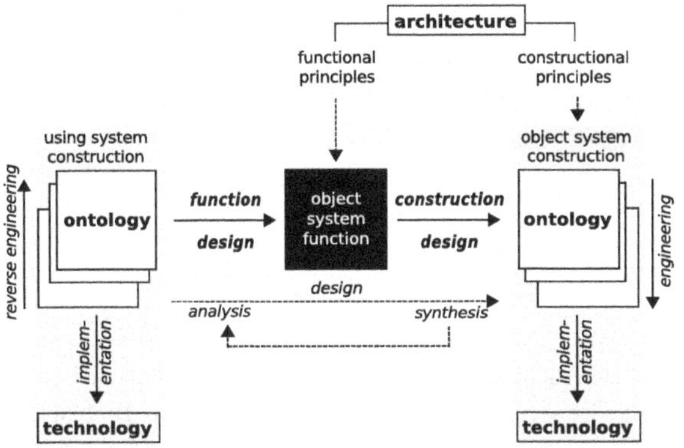

Fig. 3. General system design process (The term *principle* used in the figure refers somehow to a different notion than previously mentioned) [20]

Is EO a Design Principle? In EO, it seems that there does not exist any statement regarding design principles except the system design process [2, pp. 73–77], called the Generic System Design Process (GSDP) in [20]. GSDP defines the first step as *function design*—designing the function of the object system (OS) based on the construction of the using system (US)—and the second step as *construction design*—designing the construction of the OS based on the function of the OS (Fig. 3). However, it does not define guidelines for the substantial procedure, i.e. design principles, in the function design or construction design. Those substantial guidelines are called *architectures* in GDSP [20], but the content of the architecture is not specified there. Put differently, GDSP prescribes an ideal design process from a meta-meta-level. Therefore, EO is substantially not a design principle.

This observation is supported by comparing GSDP to the components of design principles prepared in Sect. 2.3 and finding that they are just not on the same wavelength. For instance, **purpose and scope** might mean to "understand the essence of the construction and operation of complete enterprises", but they are too abstract in contrast to the ones in NS—to be evolvable. Similarly, although **constructs** might be actor roles and transaction kinds, these are as primitive as attributes and methods, or at the most classes; it seems unknown how to aggregate those primitives into reusable elements, for achieving the purpose (which is also as yet unspecified by EO). The **justificatory knowledge** of EO is social science and systems engineering. However, other components, except the ones mentioned so far, are misted. Therefore, it is hard to assert that EO is a design principle.

Is NS a Modeling Principle? It seems that NS does not define anything about **mapping** in either of information systems or business processes. Indeed, research in NSBP employs an external artifact, namely Business Process Model and Notation (BPMN), for mapping the real world to the models. The transformation matrix may look like a mapping, but this is not the one specified in Sect. 2.3, where mappings between objects in the real world and elements in the model are defined, because the transformation matrix represents another kind of mapping from the function (requirements R_i) in the model to the construction (primitives P_j) in the model: $R_i \rightarrow \{P_j\}$. This is also the case for **reduction**. Therefore, it is asserted that NS is far from a modeling principle.

Is NS a Design Principle? It is almost an established understanding that NS is a design principle. NS was originally a design principle in the domain of information system development, but has been generalized and extended to be a design principle in the domain of business processes. In both the domains, the purpose is the same, i.e. to enhance evolvability and observability. The components of design principles are fully specified in [21]. Therefore, NS is regarded as a design principle.

4 Discussion

Reflection on EO. A question then arises: what is the rationale behind the absence of design principles in EO? The answer might be given if we see the motivation of EO: starting from the point that enterprises as a phenomenon existed in the real world, but no models were available, due to the lack of modeling artifacts, to explicitly identify the components and capture interactions and mechanisms. Although EO with DEMO is occasionally considered as a design theory for organizations, the result of this present research implies that EO has accomplished the hard and important work of making enterprises design*able* and engineer*able*, rather than continuing to propose guidelines for better designs of enterprises on the layer of models. This achievement has definitely had an impact, as supported by the fact that EO and DEMO have been used on many occasions.

Strictly speaking, EO includes GSDP, as seen in Sect. 3. However, GSDP can be positioned in the meta-meta-level and still allow room for design principles at the meta-level to get involved. In other words, EO is noncommittal and neutral regarding design principles. Thus, as long as the model is made to adhere to the standards of EO, EO does not provide any decision criterion to evaluate the model— i.e. whether a model is better or worse than another model for the same requirement.

Another interpretation is that EO as a modeling principle may work with more than one design guideline. The design principles might be brought by NS and/or other design principles (e.g. Service-Orientation systems [22]). Unless the design principles are ones analogically transplanted from other disciplines, they can be directly built on EO, as seen in [23], in which guidelines for splitting and allying enterprises are proposed based on organizational science. "Neither modeling principles nor design guidelines are superior, nor does one include the other. Modeling principles and design guidelines are at work in different layers. In other words, if either modeling principle or design principle is ignored, the whole process of engineering cannot be completed.

Reflection on NS. Another question arises: what is the rationale behind the absence of modeling principles in NS? In part, it is because that computers have been developed with the real world and conceptual models together. Here, models may refer to models represented by modeling languages such as Unified Modeling Language, or even refer to source code written in a programming language. Since the behavior of computers or CPUs is fully understood, we are knowledgeable about the components of software and their internal working mechanisms. That knowledge guarantees the solid and fine-grained alignment between these models and actual behavior including electronic phenomena in semiconductor circuits. Therefore, it requires almost no concern, and we take it for granted. This seems to be a clue which leads to answering why modeling principles are not often discussed in the field of software engineering. Instead, many discussions are diverted to the next step, i.e. how to develop a good design. Put differently, this idea is supported by the fact that when NS was extended into the business process domain, a modeling principle was required, and indeed BPMN was adopted.

5 Conclusion

The primary conclusion is that there is an orthogonality or complementarity between modeling principles and design guidelines. In other words, modeling principles and design principles are at least two different independent variables in enterprise engineering. This implies that EO as a modeling principle may work with design principles such as NS. In general, more than one design guideline can be employed at the same time. For example, the service-orientation design principles can be another design principle for designing enterprises. It may happen that some design guidelines conflict with each other.

The results also show that substantial design guidelines may swing and miss in a certain modeling principle, at least in EO. On the other hand, a substantial number of NSBP guidelines do not emerge in EO models because what the NSBP guidelines state are observed in the informational layer, and thus, are ignored in DEMO models. Moreover, the possibility should not be dismissed that a modeling principle itself might conflict with a design principle. Indeed, [13] pointed out that a very few components of EO conflict with the design guidelines of NS.

The direction of future research is to explore other principles that might be helpful in designing and instantiating enterprises. One approach is to fix a selection of the modeling principles and use design principles as a free variable. For instance, an as-is EO model (DEMO model, not EO or DEMO itself, but a model) can be redesigned for evolvability and observability by deriving a design principle from NS by analogy. The same original as-is DEMO model can also be redesigned differently for a service-oriented structure by deriving a design principle from service-oriented systems by analogy. The other approach is to fix a selection of the design principles and use modeling principles as a free variable. For example, NS may be able to provide a design principle for DEMO models.

It may also furnish one for ArchiMate models, for instance. Since the existence of congeniality or uncongeniality between modeling principles and design principles are implied in the previous paragraph, this direction also awaits further investigation.

Acknowledgment. We thank Professor Junichi Iijima at Tokyo Institute of Technology, for assistance and comments that greatly improved the manuscript and presentation.

References

1. The Open Group, Archimate 3.0 Specification, Van Haren Publishing, Ed. Van Haren Pub (2016)
2. Dietz, J.L.G.: Enterprise Ontology: Theory and Methodology. Springer, Heidelberg (2006)
3. Sandkuhl, K., Stirna, J., Persson, A., Wißotzki, M.: Enterprise Modeling: Tackling Business Challenges with the 4EM Method. Springer, Berlin Heidelberg (2014)
4. Frank, U.: Multi-perspective enterprise modeling (MEMO) conceptual framework and modeling languages. In: Proceedings of the 35th Annual Hawaii International Conference on System Sciences, pp. 1258–1267 (2002)
5. Mannaert, H., Verelst, J.: Normalized Systems: Re-creating Information Technology Based on Laws for Software Evolvability (2009). http://www.koppa.be/?page_id=454
6. Fleischmann, A., Schmidt, W., Stary, C., Obermeier, S., Börger, E.: Subject-Oriented Business Process Management. Springer, Heidelberg (2012)
7. Hoogervorst, J.A.P.: Enterprise Governance and Enterprise Engineering. The Enterprise Engineering Series. Springer, Heidelberg (2009)
8. Oxford University Press. (n.d.) "axiom". Oxford Dictionaries. Accessed 15 Apr 2016. http://www.oxforddictionaries.com/definition/english/axiom
9. Lehman, M.M.: Programs, life cycles, and laws of software evolution. In: Proceedings of the IEEE, vol. 68, no. 9, pp. 1060–1076. IEEE (1980)
10. De Bruyn, P.: Generalizing normalized systems theory: towards a foundational theory for enterprise engineering. Ph.D. thesis, University of Antwerpp (2014)
11. Huysmans, P., Bellens, D., Van Nuffel, D., Ven, K.: Aligning the constructs of enterprise ontology and normalized systems. In: Albani, A., Dietz, J.L.G. (eds.) CIAO! 2010. LNBIP, vol. 49, pp. 1–15. Springer, Heidelberg (2010)
12. Krouwel, M.R., Op 't Land, M.: Combining DEMO and normalized systems for developing agile enterprise information systems. In: Albani, A., Dietz, J.L.G., Verelst, J. (eds.) EEWC 2011. LNBIP, vol. 79, pp. 31–45. Springer, Heidelberg (2011)
13. Van Nuffel, D., Huysmans, P., De Bruyn, P.: Engineering business processes: comparing prescriptive guidelines from EO and NSBP. In: Shishkov, B. (ed.) BMSD 2013. LNBIP, vol. 173, pp. 84–105. Springer, Heidelberg (2014)
14. Chapman, W.L., Bahill, A.T., Wymore, A.W.: Engineering Modeling and Design. Systems Engineering (Book 2). CRC Press, Boca Raton (1992)
15. Pollack, H.N.: Uncertain Science.. Uncertain World. Cambridge University Press, Cambridge (2005)

16. Bubenko Jr., J.A.: From information algebra to enterprise modelling and ontologies - a historical perspective on modelling for information systems. In: Krogstie, J., Opdahl, A.L., Brinkkemper, S. (eds.) Conceptual Modelling in Information Systems Engineering, pp. 1–18. Springer, Heidelberg (2007)
17. Simon, H.A.: The Sciences of the Artificial. MIT Press, Cambridge (1969)
18. Stachowiak, H.: Allgemeine Modelltheorie. Springer, Wien (1973)
19. Gregor, S., Jones, D.: The anatomy of a design theory. J. Assoc. Inf. Syst. **8**(5), 312–335 (2007)
20. Dietz, J.L.G., Hoogervorst, J.A.P.: Enterprise ontology in enterprise engineering. In: Proceedings of the ACM symposium on Applied Computing - SAC 2008, p. 572. ACM Press (2008)
21. Huysmans, P., Oorts, G., De Bruyn, P., Mannaert, H., Verelst, J.: Positioning the normalized systems theory in a design theory framework. In: Shishkov, B. (ed.) BMSD 2012. LNBIP, vol. 142, pp. 43–63. Springer, Heidelberg (2013)
22. Lupeikiene, A., Caplinskas, A. (n.d.) From needs to requirements specification in service-oriented systems engineering. Accessed 15 Apr 2016. http://www.mii.lt/paslaugu_internetas/rodikliai/1veikla/1.2p.pdf
23. Op 't Land, M.: Applying architecture and ontology to the splitting and allying of enterprises: problem definition and research approach. In: Meersman, R., Tari, Z., Herrero, P. (eds.) OTM 2006 Workshops. LNCS, vol. 4278, pp. 1419–1428. Springer, Heidelberg (2006)

Author Index

The manufacturer's authorised representative in the EU is Springer Nature Customer Service Centre GmbH, Europaplatz 3, 69115 Heidelberg, Germany. If you have any concerns regarding our products, please contact ProductSafety@springernature.com

Printed and bound by CPI Group (UK) Ltd, Croydon, CR0 4YY
01/10/2026
02225952-0014